Writing Reconstruction

GENDER AND AMERICAN CULTURE

Coeditors
Thadious M. Davis
Mary Kelley

Editorial Advisory Board
Nancy Cott
Jane Sherron De Hart
John D'Emilio
Linda K. Kerber
Annelise Orleck
Nell Irvin Painter
Janice Radway
Robert Reid-Pharr
Noliwe Rooks
Barbara Sicherman
Cheryl Wall

Emerita Board Members
Cathy N. Davidson
Sara Evans
Annette Kolodny
Wendy Martin

Guided by feminist and antiracist perspectives, this series examines the construction and influence of gender and sexuality within the full range of America's cultures. Investigating in deep context the ways in which gender works with and against such markers as race, class, and region, the series presents outstanding interdisciplinary scholarship, including works in history, literary studies, religion, folklore, and the visual arts. In so doing, Gender and American Culture seeks to reveal how identity and community are shaped by gender and sexuality.

A complete list of books published in Gender and American Culture is available at www.uncpress.unc.edu.

Writing Reconstruction

RACE, GENDER, AND CITIZENSHIP IN THE POSTWAR SOUTH

Sharon D. Kennedy-Nolle

The University of North Carolina Press

Chapel Hill

*This book was published with the assistance of the
Authors Fund of the University of North Carolina Press.*

© 2015 The University of North Carolina Press
All rights reserved

Designed by Michelle C. Wallen
Set in Miller by codeMantra, Inc.
Manufactured in the United States of America

The paper in this book meets the guidelines for permanence
and durability of the Committee on Production Guidelines for
Book Longevity of the Council on Library Resources.

The University of North Carolina Press has been a member of the
Green Press Initiative since 2003.

Cover illustration: Octave Thanet, "The Great Southern Problem," from
An Adventure in Photography (New York: Charles Scribner's Sons, 1893), 155.

Library of Congress Cataloging-in-Publication Data
Kennedy-Nolle, Sharon D., author.
Writing reconstruction : race, gender, and citizenship in the postwar south /
Sharon D. Kennedy-Nolle.
   pages cm. — (Gender and American culture)
Includes bibliographical references and index.
ISBN 978-1-4696-2107-4 (pbk : alk. paper)
ISBN 978-1-4696-2108-1 (ebook)
1. American literature—Southern States—History and criticism.
2. Reconstruction (U.S. history, 1865–1877) in literature. 3. Race awareness in
literature. 4. Gender identity in literature. 5. Southern States—In literature. I. Title.
PS261.K38 2015
810.9'975—dc23
2014032687

For My Family

CONTENTS

Acknowledgments xi

INTRODUCTION. Owning Up to Citizenship 1

CHAPTER 1. Constance Fenimore Woolson and the Tourist Outback of Florida 25

CHAPTER 2. Sewing on the Badges of Servitude: Albion Tourgée v. North Carolina 76

CHAPTER 3. African American Literary Activism in a Divided District: Storer College and the *Pioneer Press* of West Virginia 123

CHAPTER 4. George Washington Cable and the Wages of Ventriloquized Performance in New Orleans, Louisiana 178

CHAPTER 5. Iowa's American Gothic in Arkansas: The Plantation Fiction of Octave Thanet 230

CONCLUSION. The Strange Career of Reconstruction Writing 281

Notes 303

Bibliography 343

Index 377

ILLUSTRATIONS

FIGURE 1. William Gilmore Simms, title page,
War Poetry of the South (1867)   6

FIGURE 2. Map of Military Reconstruction: 1865–77   8

FIGURE 3. "What Are You Going to Do About It?," Oliver Marvin Crosby,
Florida Facts Both Bright and Blue (1887)   26

FIGURE 4. "Confederate Monument," *Harper's New Monthly*,
December 1874   40

FIGURE 5. "Uncle Jack," *Harper's New Monthly*, January 1875   42

FIGURE 6. "A Split among the Truly Loyal Radicals!,"
Greensboro Patriot, 24 September 1868   91

FIGURE 7. "The Brand," *A Royal Gentleman* (1881; 1967)   119

FIGURE 8. "Storer College, Harper's Ferry, West Virginia"   140

FIGURE 9. "Group Portrait of the 46 Members of the Niagara Movement [Second Meeting] Held at Storer College, August 15–19, 1906"   154

FIGURE 10. Joseph Pennell, "A Crevasse,"
Creoles of Louisiana (1884)   188

FIGURE 11. "'Mark Twain'–Cable Readings," programme,
Brooklyn Academy of Music, 21 February 1885   212

FIGURE 12. Octave Thanet, "The Great Southern Problem,"
An Adventure in Photography (1893)   261

FIGURE 13. A. B. Frost, "Fairfax Rutherford, Esq.,"
in Octave Thanet, *Expiation* (1890)   271

FIGURE 14. "A New England Society Dinner at Delmonico's," cover of
Frank Leslie's Illustrated Newspaper, 5 January 1878   283

FIGURE 15. "His Great Work Unfinished," January 1890,
Judge magazine   300

ACKNOWLEDGMENTS

A labor of seemingly endless reconstruction itself, this book began at the University of Iowa many years ago. My gratitude commences with Kathleen Diffley, Linda Kerber, Leslie Schwalm, Ed Folsom, and Rich Adams for their smart counsel, concerted interest, and good cheer. I also owe thanks to the wonderfully provocative Walter Benn Michaels, who once casually asked me, "Do you happen to know of any Reconstruction novels?" Leslie Schwalm introduced me to the scholarly treasure trove of Freedmen's Bureau records. Leslie's scholarship has always inspired my own work, and her passion to unearth and understand African American women's roles in Reconstruction is undeniably contagious. Early conversations with Lea Vandervelde were instrumental in clarifying my thinking about the complex legal world of property relations. I also benefited from a Carl Seashore Fellowship from the University of Iowa, which launched my research. The University of Iowa College of Law Library has also been an invaluable resource, not the least of which was rendered by Don Ford, FOIL librarian at Iowa Law. Don's incredible research assistance, reading of the manuscript, and elucidation of many points of law regarding married women's property rights have all informed this book for the better, and I am most grateful.

Anyone who has had the privilege to work with Kathleen Diffley knows well her incredible graciousness and warm spirit. She has read countless drafts of every chapter, answered endless e-mail queries, and offered innumerable suggestions, always rendered with a saintly patience and unsurpassed encouragement. With her incisive comments and signature talent for the well-turned phrase, she has taught me much about the craft of writing. The gifts of her sage advice and abiding friendship have meant so much.

This book would not have happened without Linda Kerber. She championed my cause from its beginning as she spurred me to always aim high, imagining a valued place for my book on the scholar's shelf. Compassionate, wise, and incomparably nurturing, she inspires the highest standards of feminist scholarship and "the best and brightest" ideal of community, as her loyal legions of former students will attest. For me, she read many drafts of every chapter, always asking the tough questions with unerring instinct, enthusiasm, and gentle humor. Her adamant faith sustained my determination to see this project through.

Kathleen's and Linda's relationship with me has evolved over the years from mentors to colleagues and valued friends, and it would not be an exaggeration to say this experience has transformed my life in many ways.

I owe a major debt of gratitude to Sylvia Frank Rodrigue, copy editor extraordinaire and the best sort of friend. With great patience and kindness, Sylvia steadfastly brought not only a sharp eye but a historian's expertise and wordsmith's care to my manuscript. Many, many times has her editorial vigilance saved me from myself. A special thanks to Steven Miller, coeditor of the Freedmen and Southern Society Project at the University of Maryland, for his willingness to lend his expertise on the Freedmen's Bureau and carefully comment on all that I sent his way.

Thanks are also due Director Marlin Thomas and my colleagues in the Samuel Rudin Center at Iona College for providing the time and support to complete manuscript revisions. Satisfying relentless calls for assistance, Ed Helmrich transformed himself from Ryan Library's manager of interlibrary loans into a dedicated research assistant and overall man Friday for me. In the process, he became a dear friend. His constant belief in this book kept me going more times than I can say. I am also grateful to reference librarians Cynthia Denesevich and Adrienne Franco for all their research assistance. Iona's graphic designer, Jason Katterhorn, offered many insightful suggestions for my map.

I am delighted to thank at last the archivists, librarians, and curators of manuscripts at the many repositories I have visited. At Harpers Ferry National Historical Park, Nancy Hatcher was ever an effervescent source of help; Judith Mueller initiated me into the archival mysteries of Storer College; historian Pat Chickering and Park Ranger Guinevere Roper arranged further contacts and enthusiastically shared their own research. I also must thank Rosemary Clifford McDaniel for opening her home to me for an interview and sharing her valuable genealogical research on her illustrious cousin. Connie Park Rice of West Virginia University interrupted her own research to kindly answer questions regarding J. R. Clifford. I am grateful to Michael Dougan for providing helpful information about Octave Thanet when I began this project and to Bailey Romaine of the Newberry Library for her diligence in locating obscure Thanet materials so promptly. My thanks extend to Paul Harrison, National Archives;

Sara Logue, Manuscript, Archives, and Rare Book Library, Emory University; Lisa Farrar, Archival Assistant, Oberlin College Archives; Kathleen Reich, Professor Emerita, Archives and Special Collections, Rollins College; Patti Philippon, the Mark Twain House and Museum; and Steven Case and Cynthia Etheridge at the Government and Heritage Library at the State Library of North Carolina. Kevin Fredette and Christelle Venham at the West Virginia History Center deserve special mention for their many prompt retrievals of archival material, often on short notice. I am also pleased to acknowledge the assistance extended by the staffs at the Howard-Tilton Memorial Library, Manuscripts Department, Tulane University Archives; the Storer College Archives, West Virginia University; the Greensboro Historical Museum; the Chautauqua County Historical Society Museum; the New York Public Library; Yale University Library; the Rare Book Room, Duke University; and the Moorland-Spingarn Research Center, Howard University.

I've benefited from the camaraderie and professional support of the Constance Fenimore Woolson Society. Better colleagues cannot be found. This remarkable group of scholars has provided unstinting encouragement of my work on Woolson. Thanks are due particularly to Vicky Brehm, under whose editorship a version of some of the material in Chapter 1 appeared, and to Cheryl Torsney, Anne Boyd Rioux, Katie McKee, Sharon Dean, and Caroline Gebhard for their helpful suggestions at so many points along the way. I have also been the ongoing beneficiary of the collective wisdom of the Midwest Modern Language Association's Civil War Caucus Group, whose members have provided opportune feedback and helped refine my ideas.

I would like to thank the dedicated staff at the University of North Carolina Press, particularly Mark Simpson-Vos, Ron Maner, Jay Mazzocchi, Lucas Church, and Nancy Raynor—with whom it has been a pleasure to bring this project to fruition—and to the Gender and American Culture Series editors, Mary Kelley and Thad Davis, for their support. I also owe much gratitude to the anonymous readers the press secured; their critiques improved this work immeasurably. A special thanks to cartographer Bill Nelson for tackling my map assignment on short notice. All errors of commission or omission are my own.

My parents, Ann Linden Guida and Don Guida, always believed. My mother has especially been my most devoted advocate, and that has meant all the difference. This book belongs to my children, Patrick, Warren, and Sinclair, who spent the formative years of their childhood growing up with it. Inevitable academics themselves, they look next to a book that features the children of Reconstruction. I am grateful for their love, patience, and enthusiasm. My husband, Chris, selflessly took time from his own work to support mine. His keen editorial eye improved these pages inestimably. He has faithfully served in all branches of the spousal arts, from managing all the minutiae of manuscript-making to homemaking, and much more. This book must then also be for Chris, who makes everything possible.

Writing Reconstruction

Introduction

OWNING UP TO CITIZENSHIP

The unending tragedy of Reconstruction is the utter inability of the American mind to grasp its real significance, its national and worldwide implications.
—W. E. B. Du Bois

With this statement, W. E. B. Du Bois concluded *Black Reconstruction in America*, his brilliant reexamination of the post–Civil War era. He sought to reconstruct the common, pernicious perceptions most Americans held about the era. Lamenting their apparent inability to grasp that Reconstruction was a problem pertinent to "the very foundations of American democracy," Du Bois wistfully added that if this understanding had been achieved, "we should be living today in a different world." Writing during the depths of the Depression and influenced by the rise of fascist dictatorships across Europe, Du Bois was appropriately pessimistic, but his conclusion was not entirely correct. A remarkable and diverse group of American writers had sensed the promise of Reconstruction for African Americans and thought it worth celebration and commemoration. The literature they created deservedly occupies a unique place in literary history.[1]

Witnesses to the drama of Reconstruction, these writers crafted their observations into an idealistic literature as they explored the new constitutional guarantee of citizenship for the freedpeople (as former slaves were then designated). Writers of the post–Civil War era helped initiate what Du Bois characterized as "the beginning of Negro Development" by celebrating a truly new birth of freedom for this country. They envisioned new ways for former slaves to participate fully in the nation's cultural, political, and economic life as citizens. However, the creation of this body of writing, its publication, and its reception also contributed to the "unending tragedy" Du Bois poignantly described. This story's trajectory points to what went awry as Reconstruction unfolded and explains why the period is often marked as much by misunderstanding and misplaced faith as by inspired reform and genuine hope.[2]

Finding themselves on southern soil in diverse locales and at various times from 1865 to 1890, Reconstruction writers produced an astonishing body of work. Reconstruction literature, as I define it, constitutes not only novels, short stories, travel sketches, and poetry but also letters to the editor, newspaper columns, and essays, all of which advocated political and social change. While no canonical masterpiece emerged, the popular texts that appeared challenge literary scholar Daniel Aaron's dismissal of Reconstruction as a time in which "literary genius did not vanish, but the War cannot be said to have inspired much of it."[3] From article to novel, the literature under consideration here played an important role in affecting the course of Reconstruction by influencing public opinion and by giving voice to the aspirations of millions who were newly free. This book chronicles the progression over time and space of northern writers who came to the American South as tourists, some of whom decided to stay, as well as native southerners, some of whom felt they had to leave.

In 1867 the federal government divided the former Confederacy into five military districts, and representatives from each district are featured herein. The writers—northern traveler Constance Fenimore Woolson, controversial carpetbagger Albion Tourgée, activist students at the historically black Storer College, southern reformer George Washington Cable, and part-time plantation mistress Octave Thanet—created distinctive visions from the bitterness and hope of the districts in which they lived. I chose these writers because they provide particularly illuminating examples of the provocative ways in which literature dovetailed with geography during this period. This sampling serves as an introduction to the ways in which this literature influenced and was influenced by military districting and its aftermath.

Woolson's Reconstructive vision emphasized other Americans—immigrants, ex-slaves, and Native Americans—who had rightful claims as citizens. She used the open-ended travel sketch to dramatize their multiple voices and to relocate national origin myths from New England to the ancient cities of Florida. Stressing the rise of a consumer culture in eastern Florida, Woolson carved out a role for nonwhite Floridians as key players transforming Military District Three into a tourist paradise. She focused on reconstructing the meaning of work to privilege the independence, dignity, and freedom of laborers in making their work arrangements, yet her positive portrayals were often qualified by her capitulation to market pressures and editorial demands.

Eminent jurist Tourgée's first novel, *Toinette* (1874), and its revision, *A Royal Gentleman* (1882), boldly focus on the attempts of a freedwoman to claim her citizenship, to own property, and to achieve an identity apart from her status as owned property. Written in North Carolina, which was located in Military District Two, the novel was Tourgée's most ambitious and creative effort to realize the promise of the postwar years for African Americans. In these two novels, Tourgée had already rehearsed the arguments that he would set forth before the Supreme Court as defense counsel for Homer Plessy in 1896: Americans wrongfully understood race to be a badge of servitude. Both his fiction and his legal defense tried to change that perception. His vision of Reconstruction was informed by the free love movement, the woman's suffrage campaign, revised inheritance laws, increasingly severe antimiscegenation statutes, and the emergence of trademarks and reputation as protected forms of property. Tourgée relied on local strong Unionist sentiment to suggest the mutual benefit of cross-race and cross-class alliance between Toinette and a yeoman woman. For all his serpentine maneuvers to empower freedwomen, however, Tourgée could not escape a traditional preference for property ownership as the primary component governing all transactions and relations, especially intensified by an increasingly commodified culture.

A freedpeople's college founded in 1867 in Harpers Ferry, West Virginia, is the site of fascinating gendered and racial dynamics in an area that became a new state during the Civil War. Storer College faculty inculcated the contrary virtues of self-sufficiency and indebtedness, initiative and patience, economic self-interest and sacrificial duty that reflected their abolitionist agendas while also paradoxically enabling Jim Crow docility. Black women were particularly targeted for lessons in citizenship that included self-effacing civility, restricted movement, and mannerly service. Drawing on the industrial base and political upheaval characterizing their corner bordering Military District One, students John Clifford and Coralie Franklin resolved the contradictions of a Storer education in highly gendered and class-conscious journalism that aimed at building up a black economic and social infrastructure in Harpers Ferry. Both writers manipulated the rhetoric of reputation to urge African Americans to agitate for civil rights. Complementing Clifford's demands that black veterans foster intraracial economic cooperation through building small businesses were Franklin's appeals to black women to make common cause with white women over a host of progressivist reforms. A casualty of the civil rights movement, Storer was closed in 1955 as West Virginia implemented the 1954 landmark Supreme Court decision of *Brown v. Board of Education* that finally overturned *Plessy v. Ferguson*.

Cable's 1880 novel, *The Grandissimes*, spotlighted black New Orleans Creoles. Inspired by the ever-shifting ethnic boundaries of the commercially developing New Orleans, Cable emphasized the malleable virtues of Creole identity as his characters stood in for various southerners, from fire-eating conservatives to the free *gens de couleur*. Cable argued that successful postwar development of Military District Five depended on commercial, intercultural, and interregional diversity. In his joint stage appearances with Mark Twain during 1884 and 1885, Cable suggested that alternative, homosocial tropes of national reunion outstripped sectional romance. His performances, which humorously conflated African Americans with caricatured Creoles, contradicted his activist claims against broad social equality and for judging individuals, not races. Taken together, Cable's literary work and stage performances ultimately demonstrate that, in the 1880s, local color and national taste conspired to effect a reconciliation that was built on slavery.

Octave Thanet's 1890 novel, *Expiation*, is a transitional tale from the fading promises of Reconstruction to the coming reality of Jim Crow and the Lost Cause. Thanet's distinctive vision of Reconstruction was informed by her part-time residence in both Iowa and Arkansas for more than twenty years. Acknowledging the relatively high degree of political activity among black middle-class women in moderate Arkansas, Thanet created assertive black female characters who talked back to their masters and criticized the false pretensions of southern white manhood. Like Tourgée, Thanet crafted empowering cross-class and cross-race alliances among women. But her endorsement of black participation in emergent consumer culture was checked on her property and in her fiction by her confinement of African American influence to the plantation store and its invidious credit system. In an unexpected twist on the conventions of postwar plantation fiction, Thanet ultimately replaced disgruntled black sharecroppers with happy white tenants. Her vision of a New South peopled by a white labor force with a familiar Midwestern labor ethic was historically accurate in Military District Four, where the majority of Arkansas boosters were transplanted northerners and midwesterners.

Together, these writers' efforts constitute a literary activism on behalf of freedpeople and all Americans seeking to realize the ideals of citizenship set forth in the three Reconstruction Amendments to the Constitution. As it turned out, the military districts that incensed southerners became a template on which northerners could impose new regional identities that would transcend state allegiances to the Confederacy. It is primarily for its role in reconstructing the American South and its citizenry in a postwar nation that Reconstruction literature is important.

Writing Reconstruction aims to revise the standard periodization of the literary canon by making a place for Reconstruction literature as a diverse, dynamic body of work. It spans the era from 1865, the year William Gilmore Simms began editing *War Poetry of the South*, to 1890, the year Henry Grady appealed for a "New South" that had decisive negative ramifications for freedpeople's civil rights. But in 1865 that New South was hardly discernible in the smoke rising from the ruins of Simms's native Charleston. As author of over eighty-two novels, Simms saw his own work as "really, though indirectly, revising history." Appreciating the role of literature in crafting collective memory, this eminent literary statesman argued that *War Poetry of the South* was "essentially as much the property of the whole [nation] as are the captured cannon" of the late war. Nevertheless, the selections from *War Poetry*, which first appeared in local wartime newspapers and were often composed by the southern women to whom the volume is dedicated, express patriotic sentiments at odds with Simms's bold assertion of their national appeal. Its verse, elegiac for the Lost Cause, and its frontispiece illustration of a lyre before a wreathed broken column place the collection squarely within the Romantic tradition (Fig. 1). Simms's hope for a southern literature based on vindicating the Confederate cause was dashed, but his anthology would help forge a southern-rooted national literature dedicated to circumventing defeat.[4]

Nearly twenty-five years later, Henry Grady's last speech, "The Race Problem of the South," refashioned the Charlestonian's enthusiasm for a largely plantation South by substituting industrial development built on northern investment, white supremacy, and recognition of the Lost Cause. Grady's reassuring paternalism, like many Reconstruction texts, hastened the breaking of postwar federal commitments to African Americans by helping to defeat the 1890 Lodge election bill, which would have mandated the federal supervision of elections. Similarly invoking a militant memory of the region's defiance of the federal "cannon" that "thundered in every voting district of the South," Grady called for his Boston audience to endorse white home rule. Despite differences in vision, both men deeply believed, as Simms put it, that words shape "the progress of a nation" as much as events themselves do. Shortly after the war ended, Simms died a disappointed man, asking "for my epitaph—Here lies one, who after a reasonably long life, distinguished chiefly by unceasing labor, has left all his better works undone." It was an epitaph that could equally apply to Grady, whose premature death foreclosed the realization of his ambitions. It was left to Reconstruction literature, by its creative vitality, to fulfill these men's aspirations for a southern contribution to reconstituting the

FIGURE 1. William Gilmore Simms, title page, *War Poetry of the South* (New York, 1867).

postwar nation. Although sharing the enthusiasm of Grady and Simms to celebrate a distinctive American South, Reconstruction writers corrected the nostalgic visions of these men by according African Americans different roles to play in the postwar drama. As both echoes and countervoices to Simms and Grady, Reconstruction writers sought to make something new rise from the ashes of Appomattox.[5]

Reconstruction of the American South started in 1863 with President Abraham Lincoln's issuing of the Emancipation Proclamation, which abolished slavery in the states that were still in rebellion, thus requiring all Americans to rethink the meaning of citizenship. However, it was not until the war's end that Reconstruction began in earnest. Deeply engaged with the free-labor and civil rights issues resulting from slavery's abolition, writers of the era envisioned a postwar America that embraced the promise of the new constitutional amendments and recognized the former bondspeople as a property-owning, productive citizenry. Many Reconstruction writers sought to construct districts of cultural influence that would finally achieve full citizenship for *all* Americans. Acknowledging the inherent framing of citizenship as a matter of gendered rights, they proved they were aware that domestic obligations were often used to justify limiting a woman's obligation to the state. Reconstruction writers challenged that rationale by creating influential roles for female heroines to play that expanded their domestic authority. But the authors' radical scenarios, which also were responsive to the intensified pressures of the changing literary marketplace, prompted conservative backlash. Analyzing the interplay of the writers' specific ambitions and missed opportunities makes it possible to understand why the bright visions of Reconstruction opportunity darkened into the realities of Jim Crow segregation. Their body of literature attests to spectacular ambition and ultimate failure.[6]

Studying this period's literature helps illuminate a time most often approached primarily through its political and legal discourse; however, an appreciation of Reconstruction's significance relies on an understanding of the impact of military districting. In response to widespread racial violence, the Military Reconstruction Act, passed on 2 March 1867, divided the eleven states of the former Confederacy into five military districts under the supervision of the army, as the map "Military Reconstruction: 1865–77" reveals (Fig. 2). Although the states retained their boundaries and political divisions, federal partitioning created Military District One from Virginia; Military District Two from the Carolinas; Military District Three from Alabama, Georgia, and Florida; Military District Four from Arkansas and Mississippi; and Military District Five from Louisiana and Texas. The placement of Union armies still in the field determined the actual district borders, and the provisional redrawing of boundaries as occupied zones threatened traditional conceptions of sectional unity and familiar state loyalties. As a check on the Black Codes and the swift return of ex-Confederates to office under President Andrew Johnson's feeble Reconstruction plan, each district was supervised by a brigadier general, whose duty was "to protect all persons in their rights of person and property, to suppress insurrection, disorder, and violence, and to punish or cause to be punished, all disturbers of the public peace and criminals." All civil government authority was rendered provisional and subject to the full control of national military power.[7]

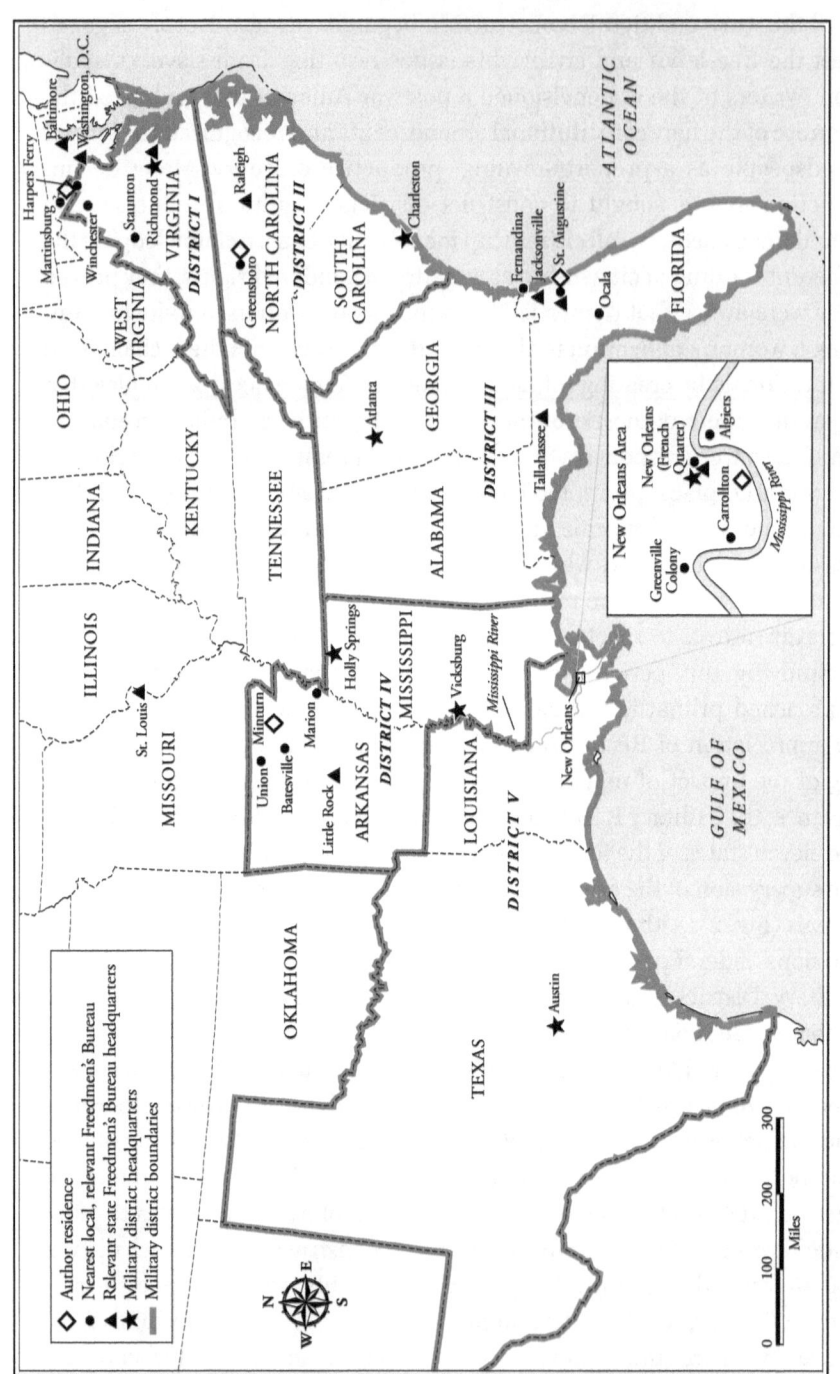

FIGURE 2. Map of Military Reconstruction: 1865–77.

Military Districts were established on 11 March 1867.

DISTRICT ONE: *Virginia*

Military District One headquarters was located in Richmond, Va.: 11 March 1867–29 January 1870.

Until May 1866, the two West Virginia counties, Berkeley and Jefferson, were under the subassistant commissioner for the 6th District of Virginia; in the first half of 1866 they were placed under various bureau jurisdictions. In June 1866, they were made part of the Shenandoah Division of the Freedmen's Bureau, which also included six Virginia counties. These counties were overseen by the following Freedmen's Bureau subassistant commissioners (until the September 1868 closing of the Harpers Ferry office and the bureau's removal in October 1868):
Baltimore, Md.: June 1866–September 1866
Richmond, Va.: September 1866–March 1867
Washington, D.C.: March 1867–December 1868

Active troop presence in Virginia ended in January 1870.

DISTRICT TWO: *North Carolina, South Carolina*

Military District headquarters was located in Charleston, S.C.: 11 March 1867–28 July 1868.

Freedmen's Bureau headquarters: Raleigh, N.C., June 1865–May 1869.

Active troop presence in North Carolina ended July 1868.

DISTRICT THREE: *Georgia, Alabama, Florida*

Military District headquarters was located in Atlanta, Ga.: 11 March 1867–28 July 1868.

The Florida Freedmen's Bureau headquarters changed location several times:
Tallahassee: September 1865–May 1867
Jacksonville: May 1867–August 1868
St. Augustine: August 1868–November 1868
Jacksonville: November 1868–July 1870

Active troop presence ended in Florida in December 1876.

DISTRICT FOUR: *Mississippi, Arkansas*

Military District headquarters:
Established in Vicksburg, Miss.: 26 March 1867
Relocated to Holly Springs, Miss.: 15 October 1867–January 1868
Reestablished at Vicksburg, Miss.: 9 January 1868–26 February 1870.

The Arkansas Freedmen's Bureau headquarters:
Established in St. Louis, Mo.: June 1865–October 1865
Relocated to Little Rock, Ark.: October 1865–April 1869

On 28 July 1868, Arkansas was removed from District Four and put into the U.S. Army's "Department of Louisiana," which was not part of Reconstruction's system of military districts.

Active troop presence ended in Arkansas in June 1868.

DISTRICT FIVE: *Louisiana, Texas*

Military District headquarters:
Established in New Orleans, La.: 19 March 1867
Relocated to Austin, Tex.: 18 August 1868–31 March 1870.

The relocation of the military headquarters to Texas occurred after Louisiana was transferred on 28 July 1868 from District Five and put into the U.S. Army's "Department of Louisiana."

The Freedmen's Bureau headquarters: New Orleans, La., June 1865–January 1869

The Freedmen's Bureau had four offices clustered in the greater New Orleans area:
New Orleans (French Quarter)
Algiers
Carrollton
Greenville Colony (Camp Parapet, Jefferson, Jefferson Parish, La.)

Active troop presence ended in Louisiana in April 1877.

Its most contested form was the Bureau of Refugees, Freedmen, and Abandoned Lands, which, from its 3 March 1865 inception until its 30 June 1872 closure, primarily oversaw the transformation of ex-slaves into laboring citizens. Under the aegis of the War Department and headquartered in Washington, D.C., the bureau provided multifarious forms of assistance to freedpeople and white refugees, including issuing rations and clothing, furnishing transportation, helping organize schools, operating hospitals and refugee camps, settling apprenticeship and other local disputes and managing labor contracts. Appointed as commissioner of the bureau, Major General O. O. Howard oversaw the operation of its many field offices, staffed by both military and civilian personnel, scattered unevenly throughout the South as well as the former border states and the District of Columbia. Implementing the dictates of bureau policy to accord with the particular circumstances of local exigency was the job of the nearest bureau agent assigned to the area. This officer thus became a critical force in effecting postwar change, as Reconstruction writers recognized.

Indeed, the course and outcome of Reconstruction were shaped by the training, tactics, strategies, and personalities of military officers, many of whom found themselves in uncomfortable positions of political authority. In the face of urgent problems, they had to find pragmatic, expedient solutions to avert famine, restore civil order, and try to spur economic recovery, all of which set the tone and established the substance for the presidential Reconstruction policy that continued to influence later congressional policy. The Military Reconstruction Act set the terms by which each state could rejoin the Union, including writing a new constitution that included adult male suffrage and the ratification of the Fourteenth Amendment. As states were readmitted to the Union, boundaries of the five districts were collapsed, and duties of the army were truncated. Nevertheless, this reconfiguration added further confusion as conflicts between the army's responsibilities and the demands of changing civil authorities increased.[8]

Until the notorious Compromise of 1877 saw federal troops retired to their barracks in return for the election of a Republican president, defeated Confederates would endure the presence of the federal army. An unwelcome challenge to the cultural identity of the "South," occupation and partitioning prompted defiant backlash. Nevertheless, occupation also created opportunities for self-redefinition that some writers were quick to seize. Each Reconstruction writer helped refashion the meaning of regionalism to reclaim the territory below the Mason-Dixon line from defeat and military occupation. Reconstruction writers viewed their districts as representative of a political, social, and cultural entity that transcended local, even sectional, borders.

The years after the Civil War, despite the setbacks of the Compromise of 1877, were a time "of experiment, testing, and uncertainty" when "alternatives were still open and real choices had to be made," as historian C. Vann Woodward put it. Recently, scholars have argued that it was only with the 1891 collapse of the Republican Party's commitment to the Lodge Bill that Reconstructionist agendas were finally set aside. Through the early 1890s, authors' popular stories, poems, columns, letters to editors, and essays kept some of these "alternatives" for genuine change before the public eye. Their literature reveals the many ways in which far-flung readers were sent a moral imperative to embrace change that went well beyond the realm of political rhetoric and legal decisions. Much Reconstruction writing was initially dominated by educated, white, largely middle-class writers already influential in the popular press. Local events prompted their calling to literary activism. George Washington Cable, for example, first made his voice known by reporting for a Crescent City newspaper in 1869. Similarly, Albion Tourgée founded a radical local newspaper, the *Union Register*, in 1866 when he formed a Loyal Reconstruction League in Greensboro, North Carolina. Constance Woolson, Octave Thanet, and other writers found their way into the "mainstream" press fairly quickly in the early 1870s in such new journals as Philadelphia's *Lippincott's* and New York's *Galaxy* as well as in other widely circulating northern periodicals, for example, Boston's *Atlantic Monthly* and New York's well-established *Harper's Monthly*.[9]

Alternatively, African American writers John Clifford and Coralie Franklin rose to national prominence because of their political involvement, which sprouted from literary activism that began during their student years at Storer College in Harpers Ferry, West Virginia. Other African American authors shared many of the themes and interests in civil rights. Popular white Reconstruction writers were joined by black men and women, writing despite considerable white resistance to allowing African Americans to publish their works in the national press. These black writers intersected, often anticipating trends, with more popular white voices that have since achieved some degree of recognition. In fact, an undeniable literary and intellectual tradition forged by African American women writers dates from the colonial period and extends well beyond the genre of slave narratives.[10]

Reconstruction writing is found at the crossroads of the periodical press and "mainstream" book publications. However, there is generally not evidence for a strong African American presence in nineteenth-century mainstream book publishing, especially during the first two postwar decades. It was the emergent black periodical press that constituted, in Eric Gardner's words, "*the* central publication outlet for many black writers—and especially for texts that were *not* slave narratives"—during the nineteenth century. While reliable statistics on African American literacy are notoriously difficult to locate and interpret, broad gains in postwar literacy and the establishment of black colleges—there were 85 founded between 1865 and 1885—contributed greatly to the strengthening and vibrancy of African American print culture. The students of Storer College, for example, built a strong literary and political community through their publications. In 1882, one graduate, John Clifford, launched the *Pioneer Press*, which became the longest running African American weekly publication of its era. Scholars must repair to these forgotten periodicals, rich in diverse topics, to recover the multitude of African American voices among Reconstruction writers.[11]

Many African American writers published during the 1860s and 1870s, notably Frances Ellen Watkins Harper, Charlotte Forten, and Elizabeth Keckley, but their work falls outside the scope of this book. Keckley and Forten focused more on wartime than postwar events, and even though Forten spent 1871 teaching in postwar South Carolina, she evidently did not keep a journal for that year. Harper, who had traveled widely throughout the South during the immediate postwar years, wrote poems and novels; however, she did not experience Reconstruction by residing in one military district, and that lack of specific locale is reflected in her generic settings and broad treatments of the period. Harper, Forten, and Keckley had, by 1871, moved to permanent homes in northern cities. The Reconstruction writers I consider wrote about events they had witnessed while living in one setting. Their work possesses certain distinctive literary contours that resulted from military districting.

However delineated by their locales, Reconstruction writers nevertheless demonstrate the centrality of gender to the postwar era. From the literary activism of columnist Coralie Franklin to the political conservatism of novelist Octave Thanet, *Writing Reconstruction* captures a range of literary production by neglected women writers across the political spectrum. Their literary visions entail a shared commitment to revising contemporary understandings of gender relations and women's roles within civic culture as a core component of achieving genuine postbellum change. Because African American men had achieved the vote with the passage of the Fifteenth Amendment, Reconstruction writers concentrated primarily on ways in which African American women could meaningfully participate in shaping the polis. Cable, Tourgée, Woolson, and Thanet helped model postwar political reform by the varied cast of female characters—black, white, Minorcan, Creole—they created. By focusing on the gendered lens of Reconstruction writing, this book helps overturn the insistent masculinist focus of traditional southern studies, which persists in the work of some New Southern critics.[12]

Reconstruction writers proposed a radical repositioning of women's place in the home, workforce, and marketplace. Exploring the differences among these writers, each residing in a different military district, permits a more nuanced understanding of the important cultural work of representing women as property owners, workers, and consumers. Each writer's literary output reflects a gendered reconception of postwar citizenship, informed by the tangle of local politics with federal intervention as much as by creative temperament. Their distinctive strategies particularly influenced the next generation of African American women's writing that helped distinguish the period known as "the Woman's Era" of activism. Reconstruction writers helped pave the way for the more prolific output of writing about the interconnectedness of gender to race and racial relations during this time, notably that by Octavia Albert, Pauline Hopkins, Anna Julia Cooper, Ida B. Wells, and Lucy Delaney. Like their aforementioned counterparts of the 1860s and 1870s, these writers have also been the subjects of substantial scholarship and are not a major part of this study.

Reconstruction writers' strategies for reimagining gender relations and expanding the postwar roles of women in various public spheres provide useful models for a revised performance of gender. They celebrated freedwomen as critical agents of resistance to the ever-hardening ground of Jim Crow segregation. In this regard, they are the forebearers of the writing produced during the 1880s and 1890s by African American women whose heroines continued to resist the severe social prohibitions, violence, and legal racial sanctions then imposed. As the voting rights of African American men eroded in the 1880s and 1890s, the attention of Reconstruction writers would shift to highlighting women's consumption habits as a political tactic. Citizenship was often staged by black women as an identity to be performed in stores and on sidewalks through attention to dress, gesture, and demeanor. Whether acting in roles that range from consumers and writers to students and servants, freedwomen were central to the implementation of postwar change, and Reconstruction writers celebrated their prominence.

Indeed, most Reconstruction writing—whether fictional or factual—suggests that southern black women, far more than Yankee troops, were the ultimate occupying "enemies within" the southern plantation household, poised to battle against defiant former Confederates within each military district. Reconstruction writers demonstrated that bourgeois black women's exclusion from formal political spheres was empowering as it allowed them to infiltrate and gain knowledge of the power structure without arousing suspicion; the blossoming of their 1890s political activity derived from their participation in what Elsa Barkley Brown first identified as the "internal political arena" of the immediate postwar era.[13]

A key factor of the success of these Reconstruction heroines was their use of disguise, dissemblance, and secret places from which they operated to overwrite their oppression. Indeed, secret places and disguise were key to postwar claims to citizenship because they enabled subversive strategies to be formulated and rehearsed against the gendered and racially coded power structures behind southern relations. The writers' black heroines undermined the plantation household from clandestine sites, where alternative histories were imagined and identities were rehearsed for performance on a large communal stage. Their stories enrich and complicate present understandings of the wants of postwar black women as well as the perception of those wants.

Moreover, in venturing these innovative, often daring, representations of African American women as agents of social change, Reconstruction writers anticipate the important models of racial progress Booker T. Washington and W. E. B. Du Bois offered at the close of the century. Storer College students and their fictional counterparts in Reconstruction novels offer activist stances that blend the divergent philosophies of the two leaders. Reconstruction writing is keenly grounded by a pragmatic sense of the need to maintain economic self-sufficiency and viable political survival, reflecting a sensibility akin to Washington's. However, prompted by their education, Storer students aspired to achieve higher ideals for themselves, and they wrote about the evolving cause of racial uplift in many, often conflicting, voices. As testimony to the black intelligentsia's dynamism and scope, which exceeded the Du Bois–Washington divide, Reconstruction literature deservedly occupies a unique niche in literary history.[14]

Sharing a passion for civil rights with their black activist colleagues and friends, Reconstruction writers were also affected by local circumstance. The social, economic, and political impact of federal occupation registered differently in each military district because each was informed by a host of varying historical relations and haphazardly arising situations. They were also influenced by the interaction of cultural forces with troop allocation, the commitment of often isolated, local Freedmen's Bureau agents, the attitudes of commanders, and the influx of refugee populations. Further crystallizing each district-bound vision were the preoccupations of writers with other fermenting legal and economic issues of the period, such as women's rights, socialist labor agitation, and the creation of a consumer culture.

Taken together, the writers featured herein—Woolson, who toured the exotic enclaves of Florida; Tourgée, who battled his small piedmont town of Greensboro, North Carolina; Storer students, who pursued knowledge at the historical industrial and railroad juncture of Harpers Ferry; Cable, who charmingly riled his metropolitan neighbors in New Orleans; and Thanet, who farmed Ozark outposts—continued to speak for a "South" that was never a unified cultural entity except as a defeated Confederate nation. Even Simms, an ardent advocate of southern nationalism, had encountered intraregional outcry against his "palmetto partiality" in favoring selections from South Carolina for his *War Poetry*. Contrary to his ideal of a distinctive, monolithic southern identity, outside influences, found, for example, among his northern literary contacts, contributed to building a more composite, assimilationist culture than he would have conceded. For Reconstruction writers endeavoring to build a rejuvenated national literature, the harsh reality of military occupation became a primary resource from which to draw new, even more manifold notions of an American South than Simms had entertained.[15]

Compounding the distinctive historical vicissitudes each writer faced were the pressures of the intensely competitive literary marketplace. Writers were necessarily attentive to the professionalization of publishing, which was characterized by a dramatic increase in the variety and number of periodicals that enjoyed ever-widening circulation. Moreover, their agitation for copyright reform helped secure the 1891 passage of the International Copyright Act, which heralded nothing short of "the creation of a *new* marketplace" for American book publishing, as Christopher Wilson has shown. The Act, which assured the recognition of written work as legally protected literary property, resulted in a sea change for the industry, with ramifications on many fronts, including "an increase in competition for authors, the growth of modern book advertising systems, the emphasis on best-sellers, and the enlargement of publisher book planning." Writers publishing into the last two decades of the nineteenth century and beyond, such as George Washington Cable and Octave Thanet, would find their control over their artistic production ironically eroded by the increased editorial intervention of publishers keen to profit from the greater markets created by the Act's passage. How they chose to respond made all the difference in their careers and in their contributions to the legacy of Reconstruction in history and memory.[16]

For many Reconstruction writers, one unforeseen consequence of trying to satisfy market demand was that the printed articulation of their progressive visions actually paved the way for their doom. The publication of these novels, stories, and articles envisioning a radical change spurred conservative reaction, inadvertently helping to hasten the return of southern Democrats to office. Often this irony was due to the timing of their appearance in the marketplace at critical moments of waning reader interest in the difficult implementation of Reconstruction. In other cases, it was the result of editorial insistence that rhetoric be curbed. Sometimes writers toned down their radical views to capture a broader readership or the favorable attention of a critic. Reaffirming an inherent commitment to the core Republican ideal of property ownership, Reconstruction authors fashioned plot twists that ultimately checked the reformist impulses of their African American characters. The endings of their stories ultimately crept toward conservatism. Whether due to selective editing, limited vision, or unfortunate timing, the literary success of Reconstruction narratives invited their historical failure.

These influential narratives not only reveal the fine-grained complexity of Reconstruction but also widen the compass of historical inquiry. For decades the popular view of Reconstruction as a tragic mistake that undermined white southerners' authority while victimizing black southerners unprepared for the responsibilities of citizenship held sway until it was challenged by Howard Beale's groundbreaking 1940 essay, "On Rewriting Reconstruction History." Since then the scholarship on this period has been invigorating, rich, and extensive, particularly the recent focus on the agency of the former bondspeople in making the postwar nation. Steven Hahn's pioneering *A Nation under Our Feet*, followed up by regional studies such as Susan O'Donovan's *Becoming Free in the Cotton South*, for example, have been instrumental in showcasing freedpeople as political agents who built an infrastructure of communication for activism and mobilization long before suffrage and advent of the Freedmen's Bureau. The rich and varied work of historians such as Leslie Schwalm, Hannah Rosen, Elizabeth Regosin, Mary Farmer-Kaiser, and Noralee Frankel have particularly foregrounded the key roles freedwomen played in reshaping their postwar lives and reorganizing their communities on the political, economic, social, and cultural fronts of freedom. For the past seventy years, some historians have debated whether the era was one of continuity or change. Reconstruction literature shows that the era was complexly both, and it changes a fundamental understanding of the Reconstruction period itself.

Reconstruction was, in part, a drama of intertextual collision. The interplay of spectacle with popular reaction, character with performance, and plot with the historical event on record demonstrates Reconstruction literature's importance. The work published during the 1870s and the 1880s reveals that the battles of Reconstruction were fought as much on the literary terrain of the editor's desk, the novelist's page, and the journalist's column as in the courthouse, the Freedmen's Bureau office, the state legislature, and the streets themselves. As stories of compromise and ambivalence, Reconstruction narratives went well beyond representing a regionally diverse drama of northern will against southern recalcitrance. For these postwar writers, history was more than background context; rather, history was partly made in the textual representation of events. It is precisely in the interaction between local events, ordinary people, and the textual representations of them that alternative political identities were reconstructed for ex-slaves.

This book was inspired by the historicist literary scholarship of the past twenty years, which has focused renewed interest on popular literature read within its own cultural and political moment. Beginning with the pioneering work of Jane Tompkins on the abolitionist epic *Uncle Tom's Cabin*, scholars have rediscovered the merit of popular literature in performing various kinds of "cultural work" and have made a place for it within the canon. This book is situated at the nexus of Civil War history and popular literature made more familiar by scholars including Alice Fahs, Kathleen Diffley, Lyde Cullen Sizer, and Elizabeth Young. Analyzing popular literature's significant political engagement has also secured greater scholarly recognition of a broadened female authorship and its importance. Brook Thomas has done pioneering work by exploring the many interconnections between nineteenth- and twentieth-century legal and literary history. More recently, literary scholars Deak Nabers, Stephen M. Best, Gregg D. Crane, and George S. Jackson have begun to read the formal, aesthetic conventions of postwar literature as creative models for staging some of the legal issues of Reconstruction. My engagement with the intricate history that partitioning provoked builds on the work of these talented scholars.

Writing Reconstruction takes an initial step toward recalibrating the literary canon's traditional periodization. It is the first systematic study of Reconstruction fiction since Robert Lively's 1957 book, *Fiction Fights the Civil War*, which broadly categorized sectional novels on the Civil War from 1866 to well into the twentieth century. Recognizing the aesthetic, historical, and cultural value of Reconstruction writing helps to revamp literary periods and the prevailing assumptions about them. These narratives correct the critical tendency to pluck Mark Twain as the quintessential regionalist writer out of an otherwise crowded literary assembly. The writing produced during the 1870s and 1880s actually retains enough power to counter the course of literary scholars who routinely veer to Henry James and European models for America's postwar cultural authority. Indeed, as Frances Smith Foster has persuasively argued, it is particularly the neglected contributions of African American writers that have critically informed the "new American literature" as manifested in regionalism and realism on both sides of the Mason-Dixon divide. By making the prevailing constructs of race and gender and their implications for citizenship critical to the literature of this period, I seek to add to the scholarship on the development of American popular writing and thereby help close the gap from romance to realism. Reconstruction narratives matter not only for their activist spark but also for their enduring contribution to literary studies as both enterprises of artistic invention and acts of commemoration.[17]

In my remapping of the historian's military district into the literary critic's region, I seek to call attention to postwar cultural geography. Applying the template of military districting to postwar literature allows a new understanding of the networks and affinities among authors, texts, and the evolving experience of occupation. Reconstruction writing made regionalism a literary force that salvaged southern identity and self-possession from sectional defeat and northern imposition. This was especially true when regionalist writing began cresting the literary horizon as a Gilded Age staple of popular magazines. Although sometimes overlapping in focus with local color travel sketches and short stories that capture the dialect, setting, and other particulars of a region, Reconstruction writing is generally free of that postwar genre's often condescending tone to its subjects. Reconstruction writing's engagement with national political and economic developments challenges regional literature's critical categorization as a mere wistful detour from the literature of realism. Some literary critics, notably Amy Kaplan and her fellow contributors to the *Columbia Literary History of the United States*, have dismissed regionalist writing as "a kind of literary tourism," designed to satisfy the longings of the "modern urban outsider." As a response to federal occupation, the writing under consideration here redefined the concept of the "South" to be greater than James Cox's formulation of the region as a coalescing "negative identity." Literary regions are profoundly vital to national identity, not marginalized, "nostalgic" alternatives to realism's preoccupation with manifestations of centralized power that Eric Sundquist has suggested. In fact, Reconstruction literature supports Marjorie Pryse's early call for rethinking regionalism as a vigorous "critique of hierarchy based on geographical and ideological differences," one which Pryse and Judith Fetterley have offered in conceiving of regionalist writing as the protofeminist site of an intensely gendered conversation. Some literary scholars such as Tom Lutz value the genre for its open-ended dramatization of contemporary debates about cultural difference from multiple points of view. More recently, other literary scholars such as Paul Giles, Philip Joseph, and Jennifer Greeson have welcomed regionalist literature for its articulation of a contradictory and uneven relationship between literature and a greater global space which questions assumptions about literary history, territorial boundaries, and national identity.[18]

Reconstruction narratives in all their complexities occupy this disputed terrain, appearing during a postwar moment when the impetus toward a coalesced national identity vied with resistant regionalist celebrations of locale. Writers of occupation narratives performed "acts of reconstruction" designed to render the threat of social change into palatable form for an emergent national readership. In their competing bids to restructure the nation, Reconstruction writers suggest that later local literature needs to be contextualized in this historically fraught moment when the claims of kin were real and insistent, particularly in the defeated American South. Inaugurated by the demands of war, new and diverse notions of southern identity were borne across state lines.

The imposition of military districts laid the groundwork for an even more radical rethinking of regionality. The celebration of immigrant life within authors' respective districts challenges traditional conceptions of a coherent southern identity. Their shifting, multisectional perspectives also affirm recent scholarly suspicions about supposedly tidy sectional differences and their effect in crafting narratives of national history as historians look, for example, at the role of black activists outside the South in influencing national Reconstruction policy. Each writer's focus on a district's particular cultural heritage, colonial origins, and changing local population during this turbulent time situates that work within the context of a greater global network. Reconstruction narratives particularly enrich the field of "New" Southern Studies as it has been recently and more comprehensively revisioned.[19]

During the 1870s, Reconstruction writers crafted plots driven by freedwomen's exercise of their rights as the Supreme Court began interpreting the meaning of the Fourteenth Amendment. Through their heroines, the writers portrayed citizenship via the acquisition of political agency as a legitimate identity for African American women otherwise denied the franchise. Still later, when African American men were disfranchised, Reconstruction narratives continued to focus on strategies by which African American women could expand the influence of their political voice. Reconstruction writers celebrated their initiative by crafting plots about positive, dynamic heroines who performed as citizens successfully engaged in political and economic fields, not in sharecropping.[20]

Diverse texts of disparate regions, these narratives were nevertheless unified by several shared terms that anchored political jargon and helped configure historical memory. Responding to the popular discourse surrounding citizenship, Reconstruction writing revolved around four key ideals—labor, duty, reputation, and property—that predominated in contemporary economic, legal, and political debates. Upon these critical concepts, the identity of citizenship as a gendered and racialized construct was being reconsidered and ultimately redeployed. All four terms, like citizenship itself, changed meaning after 1865 under the pressures of historical contingency.

Of the four terms, "property" has had the most historical import for citizenship. Although the term was removed from the final draft of the Declaration of Independence, the link of independence to ownership in real or landed property, inherited from William Blackstone, Thomas Hobbes, and particularly John Locke, has remained vital to an understanding of American citizenship predicated on a right to "life, liberty, and property." Even a cursory glance at the number of articles exploring the theoretical bases and applications of property rights that inform American law shows its influence to be astounding. The concept of property underwent the most extensive postwar change in meaning. Furthered by a series of challenges to the Fourteenth Amendment, the meaning of property was radically reconceptualized from mere ownership of physical things to an expanded set of rights and interests in intangible things. While the majority opinion in the *Slaughterhouse Cases* sharply curtailed the scope of the Fourteenth Amendment in articulating an expanded definition of citizenship, the Supreme Court's dissenting opinions in those cases were vital in renegotiating an expanded meaning of property.[21]

Situated in tension with the radical changes in property definitions, the importance of persons as property has had continued significance for social and political thought. Slavery has remained central to this country's racialized notions of legal jurisprudence, demonstrated by contorted efforts to codify the positions of slaves within a democratic society. As a categorization of property, slavery has had ongoing implications for all Americans. The issues of bodily ownership and rights in property informed the work of Reconstruction writers in provocative, gendered ways. The former slaves understood the traditional importance of property ownership for citizenship, and they, too, became active agents in helping contour its postwar redefinition. They inherited a substantial tradition of property ownership, even while they themselves were classified as property, and they continued to understand property as inevitably tied to extensive kinship claims, defined in both extralegal and, in the postwar years, increasingly legal contexts. Encouraged by the 1866 passage of the Southern Homestead Act, the freedpeople showed impressive ingenuity in their attempts to obtain land. Their grassroots political activism across the South illustrates their experiential knowledge that the acquisition of landed property was central to the electoral process, beginning with voter registration. Whenever their efforts were thwarted, freedpeople devised other means to claim the rights and privileges of citizenship, including acquiring other forms of property. In their focus on freedwomen's enterprise, some Reconstruction writers explored the value of these alternative acquisitions, while others posited strategies by which freedwomen could assert their citizenship in ways that obviated property ownership.[22]

Not only would "reputation," "duty," and "labor" be eventually reconfigured as alternative forms of property or harnessed to support all kinds of property ownership for the former slaves, but these terms would also be co-opted to serve the interests of white conservatives. With emancipation came the outrage of defeated Confederates, who had forfeited much property without compensation. They demanded restitution for their losses in money, homesteads, slaves, and honor, and that demand helped provoke debate about the meaning of these essential terms to Americans. Confederate claims, coupled with the aspirations of ex-slaves, made it impossible to think of citizens without considering the status of ownership in a body, a name, a deed, a piece of workmanship. Defeated Confederates, modifying Reconstruction solutions that endorsed property ownership for the former slaves, began to redeem the property of their reputations through a sense of patriotic duty anchored in the Lost Cause. However deployed in newspaper columns, magazine articles, or legal briefs, "reputation," "duty," and "labor" were creatively deployed in postwar print culture to reaffirm property ownership as the hallmark of an honorable citizen.

Reputation, for instance, was critically tied to the success of freedpeople in acquiring property. Capable of being earned through hard work, reputation was considered by northern jurists of the time to be a property intimately bound up with a market society and therefore entitled to protection under defamation law. For southerners, by contrast, reputation was an ascribed status of fundamental *inequality*, one tied to filling the requirements of social position and therefore best protected by a code of honor. In his preface to *War Poetry of the South*, Simms categorizes his collection as an "honorable" work, part of a literature "essential to the reputation of the Southern people." Writers within each military district discovered, in their bid for regional authority, that southern conceptions of reputation as honor clashed with northern definitions of reputation as a form of property that particularly grounded freedpeople's exertions to obtain their civil rights. With their own reputations tied to their latest sales and buffeted in the literary marketplace, many Reconstruction writers sought to reconcile these differing regional meanings of the term, thereby capturing a broad readership.[23]

Indeed, "reputation" historically carried a highly gendered, racialized, and regionalized charge. For example, the demands of Confederate veterans for property restitution were fueled by an ongoing sense of entitlement to access the bodily "property" of their former female slaves, whose assertion as "women" and "citizens" deserving of protection and respect particularly outraged these veterans. Vicious dramas of sexual violence perpetrated by white southern men against freedwomen played out in courtrooms and congressional hearings throughout the South until the military's withdrawal from the region foreclosed such opportunities for redress. These women staked their credibility on establishing "virtuous" reputations as "honorable women" to hostile interrogators who tried to refute their testimony. Moreover, the treatment they were accorded by Freedmen's Bureau agents, for example, was determined in part by an assessment of their perceived "worthiness" informed in part by their reputation. In their attempts to revise this discourse, Reconstruction writers created heroines who entered public spaces confident of their ability to speak out against injustice and defend their newfound status as citizens. These writers also portrayed successful black women for whom reputation was both earned by hard work and inherited through families of moral distinction.[24]

Caught up in the regional discord over the meaning of reputation were "labor" and "duty," ideally suited as concepts to be harnessed by freedpeople, ex-Confederates, and congressmen contending over the right of landless ex-slaves to be citizens. The lineaments of the postwar struggle over the meaning of free labor were shaped by the historical understanding of the wage-labor relationship as unfree, made evident, for example, in the congressional debates over the Thirteenth Amendment, which abolished slavery in 1865. Eight years later when Justice Stephen J. Field wrote his germinal dissent in the *Slaughterhouse Cases*, organized labor found that the courts made the collective interests of workers subordinate to the legal claims of property owners in a market economy. Slavery's abolition helped replace the personal subordination of slaves to owners and gave workers voting rights. However, preoccupation with supporting free market principles severely restricted the use working people could make of their political rights, while also circumscribing their behavior through various institutionalized forms of discipline. Reconstruction writers probed the increasingly knotty tie of work to citizenship by exploring nearly every aspect of the labor question, including the duty of American workers to labor.[25]

In their focus on the meaning of "labor" for freedpeople, Reconstruction writers also contributed to this ongoing dispute by highlighting its gendered contours. From redefining the meaning of work and the relationship of workers and employers to recasting issues of production and distribution, Reconstruction writers imagined empowering freedwomen as both workers and consumers. They reassured readers of the ability of freed laborers to transform into dutiful, entrepreneurial agents who succeeded in a variety of occupations that contributed to the national economy. Yet they also portrayed African American women as entitled to exercise the choice of not laboring outside the home by highlighting images of freedwomen invested in caring for their families and improving domestic life with a degree of interest that anticipated the Progressive Era. This study traces the paradoxical deployment of labor in its relation to duty, property, and reputation by both conservatives and radicals.

In the hands of Woolson, Tourgée, Clifford, Franklin, Cable, and Thanet, Reconstruction writing exemplifies how fictional maneuvers could recast historical developments. By fashioning their stories into fictional test cases of the Reconstruction Amendments, these writers helped limn the nation's future while reconstructing its past. Their creation of a collective memory for their northern readership helped satisfy Simms's ambitions for a Southern-inflected national literature while realizing Grady's dreams for a New South anchored to northern capitalist interests. But these writers' ambitions went much further. Some Reconstruction writers may have helped co-opt Radical Reconstruction, but their imaginative vistas often foregrounded the former bondspeople as agential figures of positive change, thereby furthering reform impulses among postwar readers.

In focusing on their respective regions, Reconstruction writers also look backward as they help reorient the founding of an American literature from regional repositories beyond New England. They nudge readers toward a broader understanding of American literature that recognizes the impact of other ethnic minorities at different moments of acculturation other than when the *Mayflower* dropped anchor. These narratives demonstrate that the efforts made by Herman Melville and Walt Whitman to found a uniquely American literature were never just theirs and never just resolved by the Civil War. Future work on forgotten texts of this period will continue to show that such an ambitious enterprise, in fact, gathered even greater urgency in the troubled peace of these decades following the Civil War. Constance Woolson was among the first of Reconstruction writers to embark on an exotic journey toward obscured national origins. Sharing many South Carolinian sympathies with Simms, she went further South in search of better health and encountered a district still swamped by war. In recovering a lost American paradise, hers was a trip at a Reconstructive moment that Simms could not yet imagine and Grady could no longer remember.

Chapter 1
CONSTANCE FENIMORE WOOLSON AND THE TOURIST OUTBACK OF FLORIDA

In another twenty years, I think the war of 1861 will be more a thing of the past than that of 1776; because we shall not want to remember it.
—Constance Fenimore Woolson

Northern white writer Constance Fenimore Woolson's travel sketches and stories about Florida, written from 1873 to 1879, showed readers different possibilities for reconstructing the South. A decade earlier, many white southerners worried that freedpeople would not work hard for their former white masters, now employers. This vexing concern, as well as anxiety over freedpeople's place in American society more generally, permeated the genre of tourist literature, which grew after the Civil War. One such publication was Oliver Martin Crosby's *Florida Facts Both Bright and Blue*. The guidebook's appendix of essays by "Resident Experts" specifically addressed "The Productive Capacity of Florida for the Sustenance of Population, Based upon its Climatic Conditions." Introducing this appendix was an illustration featuring a sitting freedman with a cane—or is it a hoe?—in hand whose gaze directly confronts the reader. The caption reads, "What Are You Going to Do About It?" (Fig. 3). While making gender central to her vision of Reconstruction, Woolson was one writer who did "something about it."[1]

More than any other Reconstruction writer, Woolson imagined freedpeople, particularly freedwomen, as successful citizens in an ethnically diverse country. While others viewed the freedpeople as exclusively a labor force, Woolson saw a cultured community in which women played agential roles in advancing political reform. Despite Woolson's prediction that the Civil War would be soon forgotten, the issues for which the war was fought certainly were not. Her writing contributed to ongoing debates over the definition of citizenship, the meaning of freedom, and the fate of free-labor ideology. Her magazine articles helped foster the rise

FIGURE 3. "What Are You Going to Do About It?," Oliver Marvin Crosby, *Florida Facts Both Bright and Blue* (New York, 1887), n.p.

WHAT ARE YOU GOING TO DO ABOUT IT?

of a consumer culture, transforming eastern Florida (part of the Third Military District, which also included Georgia and Alabama) into a tourist paradise for northerners. Woolson is unique, however, because her work both lured readers to Florida and drew their attention to those already established there.

Woolson achieved this end using three key strategies. First, her travel sketches relocated national origin myths from New England to the ancient cities of Florida, taking advantage of the state's varied colonial history. Most broadly, her reportage of the Floridian landscape helped piece together a southern identity that attracted northern consumers, thus helping reformulate divided national identities along a gendered axis. Woolson offered an alternative to the prevailing North-South reconciliation formulas by rejecting both carpetbag reclamations of the South and resurrections of a cavalier ideal. Instead, her emphasis on Florida as a place of endless acculturation paved the way for a reception of the newly emancipated slaves.

Woolson's second strategy used the open-ended travel sketch to focus northerners on the freedpeople and recognize their rightful place in

Florida's cultural, political, and economic life. Having caught the prospective sojourner's eye, her travel pieces gave voice to the aspirations of Florida's freed men and women and their treasured sense of freedom. She reassured anxious northerners that freedpeople could transition to citizenship productively by describing the state's other ethnic residents, notably the Minorcans, immigrants from one of Spain's Balearic Islands, who transitioned from indentured servants to independent citizens. The Minorcans, particularly Minorcan women, served as a role model for freedpeople as they engaged in various profitable cross-cultural economic and social exchanges.

In her third strategy, Woolson substituted a work ethic suitable to Florida's challenging climate and landscape for the northern, gendered work ethic. In doing so, she was sensitive to contemporary tensions between the rights of laborers and fears of vagrancy and dependency on poor relief. Woolson tackled freedpeople's transition to free labor by highlighting the economic relationships already forged among all kinds of Floridians, and not simply on sectional cooperation; hers was a Reconstructive voice that helped rehabilitate the region. She highlighted Minorcan women, in particular, who challenged gender and ethnic subordination in becoming enterprising workers. In their casual approach to earning a living, Woolson's Minorcan characters collapsed the distinctions between labor and leisure, being debated in publications such as the *Florida Facts* illustration.

As a corollary to her free-labor vision, Woolson presented a few select black characters who succeeded admirably as professionals and artists. These characters were inspired by her free-labor vision, the trend toward developing professions, and the recognition of workers' rights. She emphasized the right of the ex-slaves to choose the terms of their labor, arguing for their independence, dignity, and freedom in making work arrangements.

At the same time, Woolson was keenly responsive to the rapidly changing literary marketplace, which was driven by reader interests and editorial demands. Woolson's travel writings reflected northern ambivalence over acknowledging freedpeople as American citizens, a tactic that registered with conservative readers. Inherent within each of her strategies for reconstructing a place for freedpeople as citizens are moments of hesitation, contradiction, and even reactionism. These moments are characterized by a range of literary devices Woolson deployed, including fateful plot turns and some stereotypical portraits of freedpeople, Minorcans, and other migrants to Florida. The timing of her work in the marketplace, compounded by her literary choices, also helped diminish the opportunities for the ex-slaves and migrants to assimilate.

Specifically, Woolson's portraits of freedpeople sometimes dismiss their rights and desires. While her travel sketches promoted tourism, her short stories and some of her poems positively discouraged readers from residency by highlighting the plight of migrants who end up consumed by the state. This consistently negative portrayal of residency had decisive ramifications, particularly for freedpeople eager to become property holders. Stressing the dangers of the ubiquitous swamp, Woolson showed Florida's land not to be a worthwhile investment for freedpeople seeking to acquire property, a traditional means of citizenship. She further resisted portraying freedpeople as influential consumers whose newfound purchasing power could assert their citizenship rights against disfranchisement, a strategy popular with other Reconstruction writers. Her unflattering, occasional portrayals of lazy Minorcan men, of inevitably disappearing Native Americans, and uneducated freedpeople also undermined her endorsement of Reconstruction's ideals by catering to fears about intermarriage. Finally, the most damaging consequence to her vision of Reconstruction was that her reassuring portrayals of independent freedpeople misled readers into believing that federal occupation was no longer necessary. The appearance of her magazine articles during the late 1870s may have inadvertently damaged the hopes of freedpeople, whose interests were already compromised by the lawless violence of this frontier district.

Woolson, Magazines, and Florida's Postwar Travel Boom

Woolson made her first visit to Florida in 1873, along with her recently widowed sister, hoping the climate would help their ailing mother. The state had become a mecca for such convalescents. Woolson believed that a landscape's recuperative power could also reconstruct its beholders' identities; she was drawn to Florida's balmy prospects and considered retiring to its remote, wild backwaters. Before quitting the United States for Europe, she wintered in Florida until her mother's death in 1879. Fantasizing that she would like "to turn into a peak" when she died, Woolson believed then that people were, finally, what they saw, and she offered ailing readers a chance at recovery through her writing, particularly her travel sketches. Woolson, an admitted northerner and Republican, greatly preferred Florida to other southern states because she enjoyed its cosmopolitan flavor that brought together people from all "points of the compass," which she highlighted in all her work.[2]

Woolson was neither the first nor the only one to transform Florida into a healing tourist paradise. An eclectic group of reformers came together in Fernandina and Jacksonville at the war's close, keen to both develop Florida for northern tourists and help freedpeople realize their citizenship through mission work, education, and agricultural reforms. Tourism, as John Sears argues, had "played a powerful role in America's invention of itself as a culture" since the 1820s, when there were monied citizens with enough leisure to take advantage of an improved transportation system.[3]

While the circumstances of Woolson's time in Florida may make her seem part of the stampede of "sick Yankees in paradise," as Nina Silber puts it, her work did not help "to soften and sentimentalize the 'negro problem,'" as Silber claims travel writing did. Silber believes such writing tended to portray freedpeople as little more than picturesque appendages to a feminized, ruined landscape. She conjectures that the South was an escape from northern ills, rendering it, in her words, "devoid of political content." However, Woolson's writing, in trying to solve the "problem" to everyone's satisfaction, recharged Florida's scenery with meaning and made it crackle with political intent.[4]

Indeed, the Reconstruction of Florida began with words, since the state largely lacked the agricultural and export revenues that other states soon reestablished after the war. In guidebooks and magazines, this region was deliberately repackaged from being a military district of sectional and interracial conflict to an inviting resort. As one Florida guidebook writer put it, "the press is a great power to build up the 'waste places,' and the people cannot afford to hinder its growth among them." Florida promoters advocated transplanting Yankee capital and labor to Florida to jumpstart the state's postwar economy. Travel writers made economic development of the state's resources increasingly dovetail with the tourist industry by, for example, making steamboats on the Ocklawaha River part of "the packaging of nature."[5]

Magazines were an integral part of the tourism boosting Florida's development and helped promote sectional reconciliation. Beginning with the newly launched *Appletons' Journal*, Florida became a key literary property over which magazines waged battles. Drawing on extant tourist interests, the magazine featured a tour up the St. Johns River in a travel sketch that inaugurated its successful *Picturesque America* series on 12 November 1870. Woolson soon contributed to this enormously popular series, which helped transform war-torn southern landscapes into prized subjects for national art and best-selling periodical literature.[6]

Although Woolson began publishing her Florida work in *Appletons' Journal*, her southern material was primarily published in *Harper's New Monthly Magazine*, whose long-standing editor and distinguished man of letters, Henry Mills Alden, was particularly close to her. A little over a decade after its 1850 founding, the magazine had a circulation of around 200,000 in the United States and could boast of the widest readership of any magazine of its kind, largely because of its serious focus on travel. While the magazine's editors did not especially boost southern writers until the late 1880s, they did adopt a postwar stance of reconciliation and neutrality toward the South to meet the intensified competition from the postwar debut of *Scribner's Monthly*, *Galaxy*, and *Appletons'* as well as New York's *Putnam's* and Philadelphia's *Lippincott's*. All five, but especially *Lippincott's*, became more cordial to southerners as publishers quickly came to see in southern travel pieces a lucrative educational tool. Within this competitive context, Woolson's publishing record with *Harper's New Monthly* attests to her success in providing images of Florida to mollify and acculturate, rather than antagonize, her northern readers.[7]

Woolson's writing about Florida began with poetry. "Dolores" appeared in the 11 July 1874 issue of *Appletons' Journal* and was soon followed by "At the Smithy," appearing in the 5 September 1874 issue. Next, "The Florida Beach" was featured in the *Galaxy* in October 1874. *Harper's New Monthly Magazine* ran both "Pine Barrens" and "Matanzas River" in December 1874 and "The Legend of Maria Sanchez Creek" in January 1875. In addition to "Black Point," which appeared in *Harper's* in June 1879, Woolson published four stories set in Florida at the tail end of Reconstruction: "Miss Elisabetha," in *Appletons' Journal* on 13 March 1875; "Felipa" in *Lippincott's* in June 1876; "Sister St. Luke" in the *Galaxy* in April 1877; and "The South Devil" in the *Atlantic Monthly* in February 1880. These latter stories soften the otherwise grim picture of bankrupt southern cavalier ideals found in her 1880 collection *Rodman the Keeper: Southern Sketches*. This collection also boasted a title which confounded the distinction between fiction and reportage, one which critics weighed in evaluating Woolson's literary achievements as a balance between artistry and actuality.

Although consistent with other women travel writers who celebrated Florida's inviting atmosphere of "gendered freedom," Woolson departed from conventional formulas that prevailed in travel writing about Florida. Historian Susan Eacker identified three motifs that characterize postbellum travel writing on Florida: the "edenic, the exotic, and the exaggerated," which Woolson tended to resist, especially the "exaggerated." While some reviewers of the 1870s, notably those writing for the *Nation*, criticized women writers' input on Reconstruction politics, an area in which they were told they had no rightful place, the frequent appearance of Woolson's Floridian work in magazines suggested otherwise. The record of Woolson's views about Reconstruction outside of her magazine work is slight; therefore, it is from her published work that one deduces an explanation.[8]

Many critics were consistently impressed with her southern stories as a perceptive contribution toward Reconstruction. A reviewer for the *Atlantic Monthly* marveled at the "strangeness" of her characters, concluding that Woolson had "at least pointed out a region where much can be done, and where she can herself do good work." A *Scribner's* critic carped that Woolson's northern tourist "appears as a *deus ex machina*" amid "forlorn and broken lives" whose suffering has been "needlessly prolonged by the thievish rule of the carpetbaggers." Nevertheless, he enthused, "It is impossible, after having read her book, to doubt that the South is just as she pictures it." In coupling an admiration for her exotic setting with her characters, William Dean Howells singled out "The South Devil"; sensing Woolson's reunionst sentiments underneath her sympathy for southern suffering, he concluded her work is "necessary" to those who "would understand the whole meaning of Americanism."[9]

Woolson's travel sketches cluster around the years 1874 to 1876, between the poems and the stories about Florida she wrote over her six years in the state. Her work found a ready audience as northerners began to flock to Florida after the war, despite the often violent resentment of some white residents. Her first sketch, "A Voyage to the Unknown River," appeared in *Appletons' Journal* on 16 May 1874. This was soon followed by her most substantially developed sketch, "The Ancient City," which was published in *Harper's New Monthly* in two parts in December 1874 and January 1875. *Harper's* published her final Florida sketch, "The Oklawaha," in January 1876.

Florida and the Freedpeople: Survival on a Lawless Frontier

During the years Woolson resided in St. Augustine, the state gained a public image of extremes. That Union-occupied city was already noted for its pitched sectional sympathies during wartime, combining the "bitterness of Confederate zeal with the warmth of Unionist welcome." Like other defeated southerners, Floridians resisted Reconstruction, beginning with the 1865 suicide of its Confederate governor John Milton and his successor's theatrical inauguration to the tune of "Dixie." The state, with a population of only 3.4 inhabitants per square mile in 1877, was known to be a lawless frontier that harbored vigilantes. Unlike other southern states, Florida also was without a statewide system of political patronage to help provide order. Plagued since 1868 by factionalism and leadership dispersed over isolated areas, the state's Republican Party was not equipped to protect freedpeople's interests. In fact, the majority of Radical Republicans holding office during Reconstruction were black and white carpetbaggers, many of whom had flocked to Florida to speculate in railroads and the state's natural resources. Testifying before the Joint Committee on Reconstruction in 1865, customs collector John Recks maintained that "the only way for this government to make these people its friends is just to keep them down."[10]

Constituting a sizable minority of the state's population (48.8 percent) were the freedpeople, grappling with the possibilities of citizenship in this unbridled territory. Their efforts, despite the return of Democrats to office in 1877, were part of a long-standing, continuous history of statewide struggle. During the Civil War, black regiments constituted a significant, valiant presence in Florida, possibly the largest concentration of troops proportional to the total number of Union troops in the state. From the early 1862 enlistment of "contraband" in the East Gulf Blockading Squadron, which helped suppress the illicit African slave trade, to the engagements of the self-described "dusky warriors" of the 2nd United States Colored Troops in Florida, black soldiers made the struggle, in the words of one Confederate, "a war for . . . possession of this country."[11]

In the postwar years, black Floridians had to contend with extralegal violence on many fronts. There were marauding bands of night riders known as the Young Men's Democratic Clubs, particularly in the largely black counties of the northeast, five of which were put under martial law in June 1866. The Klan first made its ongoing presence known in the town of Palatka after the May 1868 elections; the organization helped usher in "Redemption," the term conservative southern Democrats preferred to describe their return to power. Even staunchly Democratic historians of the period such as William Watson Davis conceded that "in this contest for a very necessary supremacy many a foul crime was committed by white against black. Innocent people suffered." In response, black Floridian strategies of survival revolved around "mutual aid, labor struggle, historical memory, armed self-defense, and independent voting as cultural and political acts of survival and resistance," as Paul Ortiz has noted.[12]

Entering into this chaotic situation was the Bureau of Refugees, Freedmen, and Abandoned Lands, which aided southern freedpeople in complex, often contradictory ways. Organized during the war but established in Florida in September 1865, the agency maintained fairly cordial relations with white Floridians, a feat made possible because the state had suffered relatively less in war and occupation than had other southern states. Freedmen's Bureau agents, throughout their tenure in Florida, were overall cautious, skeptical, and often discouraging regarding the ex-slaves' political involvement. Nevertheless, black Floridians, led by dynamic, educated Republicans such as Josiah Walls, Charles Pearce, and John Wallace, pressed for their political and civil rights as more African Americans migrated to Florida than left it between 1860 and 1880. Despite its considerable drawbacks, the bureau's presence was crucial in curtailing lawlessness, which skyrocketed after the military was withdrawn; thus, to the freedpeople's benefit, Florida was the last state to request troop removal and the reinstatement of civil government, which was established in July 1868.[13]

Implicated in the antagonism black Floridians faced were overriding demands for their constant labor by both the Freedmen's Bureau and planters anxious to cheat the freedpeople. A chief duty of the bureau, however unfair, was to negotiate labor disputes and enforce labor contracts. Contemporary discussion of the rights of freedpeople revolved around free-labor ideology. In his directive to subassistant commissioners, Assistant Commissioner John Sprague provided seven criteria to be covered in their monthly reports, five of which revolved around freedpeople's labor: a focus that typified bureau communications. Although its agents comment fairly consistently on the ex-slaves as hardworking, the bureau had free rein to round up and transport the unemployed under guard to plantations. Woolson's travel sketches, with their distinctive appeal to tourists, were an entering wedge into the discussion of free-labor ideology by helping to expand the roles freedpeople could play in the Sunshine State.[14]

Woolson's Travel Sketches and the Training of the Touristic Eye on Florida's Freedpeople

In an area where little was owned, cultivated, or traditionalized, Woolson dramatized the virtues of the ephemeral: romance, health, and distraction. She utilized the loose form of the travel sketch, free of the structural conventions of other genres, to craft open-ended scenes of speculation and serendipity that highlighted Reconstruction's positive changes. A premier example is her travel sketch "The Ancient City," where a disparate group of tourists set out to tour St. Augustine, a city of ruins upon ruins. Prominent among the group is Sara St. John, whose name recalls the popular Florida tourist excursion along the St. Johns River, which these tourists navigate. Sara also happens to "write for the magazines" and is therefore prone to find "the inevitable descriptive article behind every bush." While giving women journalists agential voices in the Reconstruction South, Woolson gently mocked herself through the careerist ambitions that lie behind Sara's touring. Sara finds a "banner of proof sheets" from "every sunshiny hill" as she constantly converts the landscape into good copy. Sara and the other tourists view Florida with what sociologist John Urry has described as a bourgeois "romantic gaze." Through Sara, the gendered "imperial eye," as titularly captured by Mary Louise Pratt, commanding a landscape can be turned inward by parody. Woolson was not alone in recognizing how scratched the ideological lens was through which the landscape was glimpsed and then reconstructed.[15]

Woolson shrewdly manipulates gendered stereotypes to reveal the transparent role of tourist writing in constructing regional reputation. Her tourists' offshore glimpses of a passing Floridian or a scenic view float tantalizing possibilities before the reader. Without the constraints of conventional fiction, the travel sketch permitted Woolson to wander metaphorically and required fewer of the tidying resolutions of plot closure. Unifying this work was Woolson's gendered pattern of characterization. Utilizing the same narrator, Martha Miles, in several of her sketches, Woolson yokes together a disparate group of northerners, describing Florida chiefly through their exchanges that dim the masculinist, imperial gaze.

With nicknames such as "the Kaiser," "the Duke," "the General," and "the Generalizer," Woolson's male tourists mock northern imperial pretensions toward Florida and its inhabitants. Possessing "large atmosphere," they convey much of Florida's history. Yet they supplant local preoccupations by their smug pronouncements and factual intrusions, provoking local resentment. Apart from commenting on the "pathos" found in Native American refugee camps, the General of the travel piece "The Oklawaha," for example, is rarely sympathetic to Native American suffering. Regarding the circumstances leading up to the Second Seminole War, he speaks in cold telegraphic summations: "Time up; not a red-skin ready; troops sent; war." Set against these mildly lampooned, authoritative male tourists are the female tourists, who react with barbed humor and intelligence. Ermine's launch into nonsensical ditties, for example, helps silence the General, while leaving the Naturalist "utterly bewildered," as he "retreated hastily" to collect specimens alone.[16]

Woolson's work, straddling sectional readerships, documented with some ambivalence the dramatic increase of affluent northerners in Florida. Travel writers came to recognize a third category of consumers existing between tourist and resident. As represented in travel literature, these northern "sojourners" had such proprietary airs that they could almost pass for Floridians. Constant touring gave them an aura of residency. Guidebook writer George Barbour declared, "Florida is rapidly becoming a Northern colony." Indeed, antebellum Florida had already evolved into two regions so different in "racial demographics and the mechanics of race relations" that historians Irvin Solomon and Grace Erhart have argued, "Two Floridas shared one state in 1860." Prior to the war, the state's northern plantation cotton belt more closely resembled that of the elite Deep South, but south Florida, as they show, was characterized by undeveloped frontier populated by a few slaves and hardscrabble farmers, many of pro-Union sentiment. Living on the coast more than a decade later, where northern desires for tourism and development prevailed and yet were influenced by northern Florida's ideology of slavery, Woolson registered the contradictions in her work.[17]

By representing her tourists' quirks as gendered northern consumer demands, Woolson showed how rumor, memory, and curiosity made Florida's reputation for leisure itself a commodity. In "The Oklawaha," Woolson echoes Barbour's comment only to immediately question it: "O lovely, lazy Florida! Can it be that Northern men have at last forced you into the ranks of prosaic progress?" Maintaining that only "the sterner sex thought it could," Woolson challenged the wisdom of applying a northern masculinist template of development onto Florida. While Woolson's female characters are not exempt from shopping sprees, they are far more willing to browse, passing up temptations to acquire, than are her male characters.[18]

In "The Ancient City," Woolson notes the negative impact of this consumption on the locals who "regret the incursion of rich winter residents, who buy up the land for their grand mansion, raise the prices of everything, and eventually will crowd all the poorer homes beyond the gates." In her letters, Woolson contrasted their income, appearance, and manner with hers, noting "the grandees are arriving and we are beginning to breathe that tiresome atmosphere of gold dust and ancestors which has oppressed us for two long winters." Sympathizing with local resentment over this civilian occupation, Woolson gently chided these northerners to expand their scope, if not their largesse, and to acknowledge that the pasts of the locals were not for sale. Woolson aligns her tourists' gendered sympathies with those of Florida's residents to resist wholesale cultural buyouts. Male tourists such as the Duke of "The Oklawaha" dismiss Florida's distinctive vegetation ("If you had asked him what he saw, he would have promptly replied 'Trees.' . . . Why should a man bother himself about what kinds?"). Female tourists from the "The Ancient City," such as the poised narrator Martha Miles, Iris Carew, her exacting governess, Miss Sharp, and even the ambitious reporter Sara St. John, respectfully observe, inquire, and record indigenous experience.[19]

Through the more sensitized questioning of these female tourists, Woolson asked readers to reinterpret the myths of the founding of American identity: "It is all natural enough, if one stops to remember that fifty years before the first settlement was made in Virginia, and sixty-three before the Mayflower touched the shores of the New World, there were flourishing Spanish plantations on this Southern coast." "The Ancient City, Part I," makes the same point when the tourists insist that "all Northerners" make "the common mistake" of misreading the land as something new because of its sparse population. While some of Woolson's tourists, like Sara, grow impatient with the professor's ongoing history lesson, others, such as the ever-inquisitive Miss Sharp, demand to hear more, recognizing they cannot escape encountering the ancientness of the Ancient City. Woolson's stories are an attempt to retrieve this forgotten memory and to reorient her readers from looking only to the northeastern United States to recall the country's past. Moreover, her stories also jar readers from identifying Florida as the exclusive representative of "The South." Instead, Woolson repositions the state within the greater context of the Global South by celebrating the Floridian proclivity to diversify and hybridize.[20]

A cornerstone of Woolson's Reconstruction vision for Florida thus became her emphasis on the state's varied cultural origins, which rendered any white northern or southern proprietary claims on it void. Since the Paris Treaty of 1763, when Spain ceded Florida to Great Britain, Florida's political instability had legitimated the residents' tendency to change cultural identities and to amalgamate. Those identities have been almost ceaselessly creolized by Florida's exchange among Great Britain, France, Spain, and the United States. Woolson, acknowledging the repercussions of this fluctuating identity, reminded her readers that the identities of southern cities were built from complex histories of their denizens' savage acculturation. Floridian cities in Woolson's work are built around the presumed mortality of monuments. While tourist John Hoffman mockingly laments "Poor Florida! nobody wanted her" in recounting the state's history, Woolson made it clear that this was the source of the state's appeal:

as the title to the territory was bandied about, the swamplands kept this promise of constant cultural regeneration and recycling. Woolson shared the assessment of fellow writer-in-residence Harriet Beecher Stowe, who found the swamps of St. Augustine to really be "one vast reservoir of infinite suggestions and rich material, that have come down from all the prominent nations of the earth as a legacy." Woolson captured this international aspect of the Florida swamp in ways that established it as a virtue for those readers narrowed by sectional prejudice.[21]

Woolson's portrayal of the swamp was in keeping with her presentation of St. Augustine, a city with a compelling European past. Woolson established St. Augustine as her "literary capital," rather than that other ancient haunt, Charleston, South Carolina, a city that appears "finished" by its "colonial traditions." It was St. Augustine that Woolson saw beckoning different immigrants, including freedpeople, who respond to the city: "Be then our mother—take us for thy children." Woolson's settings recast presumably backwater cities of convalescents like St. Augustine as sites of debate among freedpeople, visiting northerners, and southern planters. Her portrayal was accurate, since St. Augustine and other nearby towns experienced explosive postwar population and economic growth, which provided African Americans with the best opportunities for work and political office through the 1870s.[22]

Moreover, Woolson recognized that the city was a historically significant sanctuary for runaway slaves who increasingly capitalized on the Spanish Crown's offer of religious refuge in St. Augustine, made official in 1693. In return, black laborers and artisans not only helped found the Ancient City but also defended it with a militia formed as early as 1683. In Spanish Florida, particularly St. Augustine, both male and female slaves acquired a legal personality and social opportunities significantly better than their Anglo settlement counterparts. The Spanish established Gracia Real de Santa Teresa de Mose as a military redoubt against the British just two miles from the Ancient City, in response to the many fugitive slaves who started to pour into Florida from South Carolina and Georgia in the 1730s. This redoubt, under the jurisdiction of a freed black soldier, prospered as a settlement for fugitive slaves, who were granted freedom by the Spanish. Before the end of the first Spanish regime in 1763, hundreds of runaways had received land and arms to defend the Crown, augmented further by refugees of the American and French Revolutions. Woolson had to reckon with a black property-holding class nurtured by Spanish law and custom and the Crown's geopolitical need to hold the frontier threatened by the Anglos. She did so by using both travel sketches and short stories to dwell on the import of these earlier Spanish and African ruins for problematizing any fixed Anglo notions of a "nativist" southern identity.[23]

However, while her short fiction tends to emphasize the fatigue and futility of conquest, her travel sketches reinject mystery into discovery. This point is forcefully made in "The French Broad." Published in *Harper's New Monthly Magazine* in April 1875, this time her northern tourists arrive at Pete's Rock in North Carolina and debate Pete's identity. Was he an "Injun," with his arrow "aimed at the destroyers of his race," as the rock's shape suggests? Was he a British officer under Cornwallis who retreated there? Or was he a black man warning slaves of approaching Confederates? Woolson explains that his mysterious identity "remains unfinished to this day," which creates a narrative and cultural space for diverse people to claim citizenship by laying claim to the rock. The debate about this southern rock prompts familiar cultural resonances of the founding of America signaled by the events at that *other* rock in Plymouth.[24]

Woolson's presentation of the debate over the origins of Pete's Rock was in keeping with the tourist industry's promotion of Florida as a region that possessed an alternative American history. Many guidebooks were quick to point out, for example, that St. Augustine was the oldest city in the country, founded fifty-five years before the Pilgrims landed, in contradiction to traditional assumptions about the country's origins. The open-ended speculation surrounding Pete's Rock implies that northerners must acknowledge this history; this southern "New World" of theirs is not so new and not just for them, after all.

For Woolson, the charm of the Floridian landscape was that it legitimated particular ways of seeing the freedpeople's claims on citizenship in the South. Woolson made the Maria Sanchez Creek, which was filled in 1888, even more enigmatically symbolic of Florida's gendered exoticism than Pete's Rock is to North Carolina. The freedpeople's "Africa" of "The Ancient City" is reached by crossing the Creek. Yet Martha's narrative attempt to unravel who Sanchez was and what her connection might be to the freedpeople remains frustrated. Her perplexity over Sanchez's identity further appears in two other scenes in "The Ancient City," until Martha confesses that the identity of this "mysterious watery heroine ... perfectly haunts" her. The creek becomes a strange "old friend of the dismal swamp" to Iris Carew, while Martha Miles finds it a gripping and "muddy sort of a ghost." Whereas the swamp becomes a fatal lure for Carl of the insistently jungle-obliterating Deal Brothers in "The South Devil," the Sanchez Creek remains part of an invitingly feminized landscape, like the "silver draperies" of that riparian "witch," the French Broad. By navigating, as opposed to damming or draining, these fluid byways, the female tourists can connect to an inherently gendered geographic history. In any event, the clear right to title, crucial to claiming the traditional privileges of ownership, cannot be deciphered from the elusive, feminized landscape.[25]

The tourists' competing explanations for the origins of Pete's Rock and Maria Sanchez Creek suggest that the southern landscape contained nothing inherently coded as cavalier privilege. The tourists eventually vote on the best story about Pete's Rock, and their speculations dramatize the self-reflexivity of the travel sketch, which resists delimiting the southern landscape to a single perspective or owner. Indeed, Woolson uses the travel sketch to dispossess the most conventionally expected owner of southern land—the ex-Confederate soldier. In "The French Broad" the tourist party encounters Captain Phil Romer, C.S.A., an emasculated, disabled recluse overcome by his losses in the war. Having retreated to the mountains, the half-blind, one-legged Romer depends on "my man Pomp" for help and knits to make a living. He confesses to the compassionate tourists that "we are most of us dead down here," checking their boasts of righteous Union victory. Now bereft of family and having grown "prematurely old," Phil settles into "a comfortable backseat," briefly accompanying the tourists. At the state line, he rides off as "the solitary figure" soon "lost in the pine trees" and the "dark canon" of the French Broad.[26]

Conceding himself to be "a useless hulk," Phil embodies one feared postwar outcome for white male southerners—the extinction of race and gender. In defeat, the proud, masculinized "Southron" suffered a loss of idealized status. Woolson recognized this embittered casualty of war by foregrounding his postwar absence or disabilities in her work. Woolson boldly demonstrated in this and other travel sketches that this former southern icon did not dominate the postwar southern landscape—politically, culturally, or financially. "Confederate Monument," an illustration accompanying "The Ancient City, Part I," reinforces Woolson's assessment (Fig. 4); the illustration's one-legged veteran could very well be Phil Romer, his forlorn stance before the broken monument a far cry from the elaborate Lost Cause productions surrounding monument unveilings. The monument's sheared-off column recalls the Romantic frontispiece of *War Poetry of the South*. Unlike the casual placement of the lyre and book before the column to signal recent human activity for Simms's collection, "Confederate Monument" foregrounds the fence, fence post, and curb to underscore the forsaken, off-limits Confederate past. Moreover, the engraving's dark diagonals emphasize the starkness

FIGURE 4.
"Confederate Monument,"
Harper's New Monthly,
December 1874, 12.

CONFEDERATE MONUMENT.

of the unadorned column to enhance the sense of permanent "Southron" impotence. Although Woolson's effacement of the Confederate veteran was idealistic and naive, she cleared a path for others to follow in staking claims on the nation's attention.[27]

In particular, Woolson's travel writing put freedpeople, especially women, and their aspirations on the touristic map. Her portrayals show a community of actively engaged citizens, intent on claiming their rights and freedom, particularly through the church. This picture was largely accurate, despite considerable Klan harassment. A vibrant part of an ethnically rich, multicultural postwar world, Woolson's former slaves stand out as successes against fading white planters, disabled veterans, and sickly tourists. Indeed, the vote of freedmen was perceived as a threat to white Democratic rule until 1884, particularly in the northern Black Belt and port city counties, where Woolson had visited. That year, black Floridian leaders formed, in alliance with white, Anti-Bourbon voters, the Independent Party to tackle the "emergency" of their rapidly eroding influence in Floridian politics. Although defeated in the 1884 elections, the coalition mounted enough of a serious political threat that conservative Bourbons responded by devising even more effective means to ensure disfranchisement. In her portrayals of African Americans cutting across genres, Woolson brought them further to the foreground as she celebrated their successes. But in her travel sketches, with the lens of the tourist gaze, she particularly addressed the issue of emancipation and what freedom actually meant to the ex-slaves.[28]

Through the perspective of her female tourists, Woolson accurately captured postwar interracial, gendered differences over the legacy of slavery, and even the meaning of American citizenship itself. A "lady" boarding with the tourists remarks that the former slaves were "well-cared for" and "led easy lives" in bondage. But now, she complains of the freedpeople, "They do not quite know how to take their freedom yet. . . . They don't know what to do with it yet." This observation was characteristic of many white Floridians, as Woolson was acutely aware. Addressing the Florida General Assembly, Governor-elect D. S. Walker condescendingly commented about the freedpeople: "It is not their fault that they are free; they had nothing to do with it. But they are free. They are no longer our contented and happy slaves. . . . They are now a discontented and unhappy people, many of them houseless and homeless, roaming about in gangs over the land." Woolson's travel sketches persistently exposed this as wishful thinking.[29]

Woolson's freedpeople, especially those women represented in travel pieces such as "The Ancient City," articulated in word and deed exactly what freedom meant. The northern tourists encounter freedpeople who assert a right to move about in the South, building churches, attending schools, and running businesses. Some ex-slaves have the "oddest" ideas of freedom, demanding their own cabins and insisting on always "going and coming through the front door; . . . no matter who is present." One

FIGURE 5.
"Uncle Jack," *Harper's New Monthly*, January 1875, 170.

UNCLE JACK.

freedman maintains that with emancipation, "I breave anoder breff ebber sense, dat I do." Similarly, "Uncle Jack," although offered a new home and job, chooses to remain in his slave cabin, claiming his freedom precisely by asserting his immobility. A relatively atypical illustration, "Uncle Jack" conveys a portrait of a proud, thoughtful, elderly man whose gaze directly meets and challenges the reader's eye (Fig. 5). A visual counterpoint to the *Florida Facts* freedman, "Uncle Jack" resists the nostalgic attempts of tourists to frame him for display. At the same time, he will not leave Sara's field of vision. Rather than become an object for visual consumption, Jack paves the way for the next generation of black consumers, like those who would graduate from Storer College.[30]

Even more compellingly, the tourists further encounter the stereotypical "old auntie" full of "long digressions" about "ole massa" and "ole miss" who nevertheless surprises them by asserting that freedom means enjoying a class-based gentility. Unlike Uncle Jack, this freedwoman talks back to the tourists, clearly defending her rights to citizenship. Of her twins, she proudly, if somewhat absurdly in such derelict circumstances, proclaims: "De great ting is dis yer: Lou-ee-zy's free, and Low-ii-zy is free! Bot' ob dem! Bot ob dem, ladies!" The twins' mother disdainfully answers Martha's question about whether she was more "comfortable" in slavery by exclaiming, "What's dat to do wid de acquisition ob freedom?" Throughout Woolson's sketches, it is predominantly freedwomen, such characters as the twins' mother, who challenge Martha's classed, romanticized notions of bondage and assert a claim to their citizenship. Reacting to these changes, narrator Martha asks every freedperson she meets whether he or she were happier in bondage, sentimentalized into the "old times." She discovers that "no matter how poor and desolate they may be," they rejoice in their freedom.[31]

These were also the findings of Freedmen's Bureau agents. Reporting on the freedpeople's first freedom celebration in Ocala City, Agent Jacob Remley describes an "orderly" and "well-conducted" meeting with a procession of some 600 participants with 10,000 freedpeople of all ages in attendance. Often ignored or subsumed in the categorization of "freedmen" in postwar discourse, Woolson's freedwomen educated bureau agents, tourists, and speculators as well as her readers that freedom was a fundamental political right of self-ownership; their answers to Martha's questions comport with freedchildren's compelling assertion that "to be free was to be their own."[32]

"The Ancient City" put freedpeople's, particularly freedwomen's, emancipation and their labor on the touristic agenda. The tourists' encounter with freedwomen prompts their exploration of the nearby district of Africa, which Woolson described as "a long struggling suburb . . . not unlike the real Africa, between the Maria Sanchez Creek and the Sebastian River." Easily accessible by bridge, Africa's well-cared-for cabins and church becomes the focus of the tourists' conversation. Woolson saw a vital community, where other travel pieces dismissed such "Nigger-towns" as a "collection of shabby, more or less tumble-down and ramshackle shanties," in the words of one English traveler. Likewise, Oliver Crosby opens his guidebook by noting that the "squalid negro cabin and its poverty-stricken inhabitants" would produce "keen disgust." But Woolson saw nothing for which to apologize. Woolson uses the flourishing presence of Africa and Minorca Town, a nearby ethnic enclave in the heart of St. Augustine with which it is compared, to disorient readers and tourists keen to locate a quintessentially southern locale.[33]

Martha is so intrigued that she hires the young black guide Victoria Linkum. With a name that signifies contemporary tensions between colonial enterprise and emancipation, Linkum, "jest borned when Linkum died," represents those African Americans raised entirely in freedom and poised for leadership. The names of this generation of citizens proclaim the centrality of national issues to their identity. Linkum and her mother, Aunt Viny, reflect those defiant black Floridian women who seized wartime opportunities for acts of rebellion, retaliation, and freedom, an eventuality over which they rejoiced. Characters such as Linkum cast "a shadow" over the names of the dead on the Confederate Monument, like the "old negro Uncle" who happens to pass by. When Martha asks him if he knew any of the commemorated soldiers, he admits, "My ole woman took car' ob some ob dem when dey was babies." His answer reminds readers that the freedpeople's community never stood in isolation; instead, it was inextricably connected to the state's white colonial past. These interracial, gendered relationships of great interdependency were not easily dissolved and continued in postwar caste formation, emancipation notwithstanding. The stories of Victoria Linkum, Uncle Jack, and other freedpeople contribute foundationally to what one historian has called a "testimonial culture" built on the stories of Jim Crow survivors of their history.[34]

But not every reader wanted to hear those stories, an uneasiness Woolson's travel sketches also capture and try to resolve. Sara, contrary to the adventurous Martha, elides the St. Augustinian suburb of Africa with continental Africa. Any kinship she might feel ("Did you enjoy the afternoon, Sara?" . . . "I can not tell you how much.") paradoxically depends on distancing herself from the freedpeople as she focuses on the "thousands of miles of heaving water, with no land between us and Africa." Sara's insistence on unmediated distance qualifies her ability to empathize: "If I thought there was so much as one Canary Island, the sense of vastness would be lost. I stood on that beach and drew in a long breath that came straight from the Nile." Ironically, Sara can only share the air of the freedman's "breff" if he is exiled from the peninsular Africa to continental Africa. Her colonizing tendency is to always interpose continental Africa into her field of vision as she asserts to her suitor John Hoffman that North Beach is not between "us and the ocean" but between "us and Africa." Her insistence on this point causes another tourist to ask in front of Hoffman, "What is it that attracts you toward Africa?" She replies "promptly" that it is "Antony" in his dying love for Cleopatra. Sara's sentimentalizing figurative colonization helped equip some northern white readers to consider the freedpeople's future while reconsidering their place in it. Woolson recalls Sara's colonial sentiments of longing in an untitled poem featured in the short story, "Black Point": "We call across to Africa— / The waves from mile to mile / Bear on the hail from Florida / And the answering sigh of the Nile." Woolson herself seemed to waver between Martha's adventurous curiosity about Florida's enclaves and Sara's distanced reverie about Africa.[35]

Woolson's ambivalent identifications may have been a ploy to avoid any sectional bias that would alienate potential readers. Her qualified endorsement of the freedpeople was similar to her structuring of sectional impartiality into her 1876 short story "Crowder's Cove: A Story of the War." Featuring two more strong female characters who vie for the reader's sectional sympathy, its plot would seem to argue against the moral corruption and impracticality of neutrality, yet the narrator actually endorses its merits throughout by refraining from judgment. The jarring tension between the story's plot and narration forces a reconsideration of the economic interests served by neutrality, despite Woolson's own competitive stake in remaining neutral in the literary marketplace. Likening the freedpeople's suburb to a distant continent was part of Woolson's attempt to situate Florida's potential for reconstructing the nation within her readers' imaginations. Several of Woolson's other travel pieces and poems imagine the state itself to be remote and dreamily alien. In "The Florida Beach," which appeared in the *Galaxy* in October 1874, the beach on which the tourists sit is distanced from the mainland "like a fringe to the dark green winter land." It leaves them desirably marooned and therefore free to entertain ideas of hemispheric breadth; their thoughts travel like the commercial ships that "pass far out at sea" coursing "along the warm Gulf Stream / from Cuba to tropic Caribee." Like Sara, these tourists too "call across to Africa," listening for "a murmur of 'Antony! Antony!'" in the waves' "refrain." And the refrain of that undertow is textually real: "The Ancient City, Part II," opens with the final stanza of "The Florida Beach," foregrounding the question of why they must ever leave the beach, while "The Ancient City, Part I," opens with a poem reminding readers that this "world is far away." This line is so often murmured by Woolson's tourists that they convince themselves, citing more poetry, that Florida's "old attraction" of "'over the hills and far away' is the dream of all imaginative souls." In much of Woolson's work, the tourists' meandering becomes a metaphor for the psychological roaming required to imagine Reconstruction.[36]

Florida's inspiring isolation became an item in popular culture. Woolson's characters admit that the popularity of Foster's "'Swannee Ribber'" owes its "dominion to the fact that it is 'far, far away.'" In "The Oklawaha," Woolson's tourists also agree that "it is always beautiful beyond," for "human nature journeys hopefully in that." Besides allowing for the recuperation of sick northerners, tired of being part of an "enterprising population," the distancing of the land also invites "Rip Van Winkle," Washington Irving's character whom Woolson appropriates. Woolson's "Rip" calmly gazes up at the tourists, recalling the moment he "awoke" in Irving's forest. The presence of Rip Van Winkle suggests that radical change occurs in Florida by the simple passage of time, just as it did in his native New York. The constant references to distance in Woolson's work imply the necessary space for Reconstructive developments. Woolson created a telescopic opportunity for readers, acclimated to such alienation in her work, to encounter other Americans without having them placed on their doorsteps.[37]

With their allowance for varying points of view, narrative disjunctures, and open endings, Woolson's travel sketches capture the shifting complexity of her political allegiances. With each daring portrayal of freedmen and their vision of freedom came retrenchment. The dead-ended foreclosures on her characters' development rendered homesickness for the South—a feeling the expatriate Woolson confessed to a reviewer of her *Rodman the Keeper: Southern Sketches*—a prerequisite for northern visitors. Woolson's Florida beckoned especially those northern visitors, like her mother, vulnerable to sickness. They could come to Florida only when so impeded by illness, weakness, or age that they could not reconstruct the state with Yankee zeal.[38]

Woolson, following traditional European and North American writing about the tropics, represented the Floridian landscape as both pestilential and paradisiacal, thereby sustaining a dualistic vision of experience for residents and tourists. Woolson's distinction between these two types of visitors, though sharp, was on a continuum with other travel writers who cautioned eager readers not to pack too quickly. Woolson's work helped construct an "imaginary geography." Drawing on a tradition of Western imperialist imagery, Woolson invoked a range of discourses drawn from the social and medical sciences, government, tourism and business about the tropical American South. Yet her construction was distinctive. Rather than encouraging the view that the region was "in need of colonial uplift" like latter American enterprises, her stories discouraged contemporary white northerners from reconstructing the South.[39]

Woolson's Short Stories and the Disillusionment of Residency

The lighthearted play of visual and romantic prospects in Woolson's travel narratives differs from the grounded reality of Woolson's short stories, in which residents, usually disenchanted, property-owning men, try to survive in places where the land adamantly refuses cultivation. By emphasizing the unsure footing of residents in the untamable Florida wilds, Woolson critiques the notion that land-ownership should be the primary criteria of citizenship. Woolson's disassociation of the status of property ownership from participation in the polis is unusual among Reconstruction writers as is her rejection of plantation hierarchy, a nostalgia upon which contemporary plantation fiction capitalized. Each of Woolson's Florida stories, so concerned with choked passion, ends tragically, with the main character exiled, homesick, dying, or entrapped.

Nowhere is this more evident than in "The South Devil." With its opening quotation from Joaquin Miller about the swamp snake's "great black love" for the white-limbed trees, "The South Devil" draws immediate attention to Florida's fatally sensual, racialized temptations. Woolson's treatment of the swamp in her short stories as well as in her travel writing was part of a broader postwar literary trend that David C. Miller has called a "flourishing of genteel exoticism" that nonetheless contained "more than a trace of consumerism." Postwar writers, according to Miller, repositioned the southern swamp to both resist and express the dominant industrial-capitalist order that so many northern tourists sought to escape. Far from finding the "mystery and repose" that were, Miller argues, "the two qualities most prized in swamp landscapes," however, Woolson's characters agitatedly consume to the point of self-destruction. Whether in a swamp or on a New England farm, consumerism, Woolson suggests, was a deadly consequence of a capitalist economy.[40]

The story focuses on the fortunes of two northern half brothers—one enterprising, one slothful—who come to Florida to escape heartache and consumption. The story illustrates how a swamp literally "haunts" Carl to his death by luring him into it, despite his weakened condition. While lovelorn Mark loses himself in hard work, sickly Carl loses himself to the music of the "South Devil," a local swamp at whose heart is "a riot of intoxicating, steaming, swarming, fragrant, beautiful, tropical life." After Carl's Gothicized death, the story ends with Mark, "his face" resolutely turned "northward" like a "giant full armed." Mark fears that if he remains, "his brain would be affected" by the swamp's "intoxicating perfume," causing him to also "wander within and die." He flees Florida because he knows "there would be no one to rescue *him*." Carl and Mark share the obsessive tendencies of such other Woolson characters as "Felipa's" titular protagonist or "Miss Elisabetha's" Doro, swamped by unfulfilled desires. Carl is literally consumed by his passion for Florida, while Mark, with the "old New England spirit rising within him again at last," realizes his preferred passion for a "certain blue-eyed woman" lies northward. While other travel stories coached readers to experience the swamp as an antidote to Yankee acquisitiveness, Woolson's story of the Deal brothers' entanglements teaches the unnavigability of postwar desire. Their story corrects contemporary perceptions of Florida as escapist retreat; whether it ends in death or a train ticket north, Florida was but a conduit to some form of consumption.[41]

In nearly every sketch and story, cultivated plantations succumb to the wild overgrowth that eventually conquers all colonial enterprise. Woolson emphasized that Floridian plantations, unlike those in other southern regions, changed hands quickly. The tourist John Hoffman bemoans, "Poor Florida! she is full of deserted plantations!" Moreover, Woolson accurately represented Florida's poor settlement. In 1871 Floridians protested Republican efforts to raise property taxes as "impracticable" because of the state's relatively sparsely settled territory. Rowland Rerick recalls their outrage over the governor's persistence in collecting the taxes, and they soon impeached him.[42]

In "The South Devil," Mark Deal's fruitless endeavors deter any carpetbaggers keen to apply northern, gendered schemes of enterprise to Florida for quick profit. For all his laboring at land cultivation, he finds only unremitting work and little reward. Precedents of failure emerge: he discovers "traces of former cultivation" that confront him with evidence of "old tracks, furrows, and drains in what we thought primeval forest; rose bushes run wild, and distorted old fig trees meet us in a jungle where we supposed no white man's foot had ever before penetrated; the ruins of a chimney gleam whitely through a waste of thorny *chaparral*." Spurning with "sudden repugnance" this land of "never-ending rest," Deal kicks aside his orange crop, "over-ripe with rich pulpy decay," and dreams of New England's "firm apples" instead.[43]

As carpetbaggers poured into Florida, Woolson's short stories encouraged them to keep going by highlighting the evils that befell lingering tourists. She refused to extend an invitation to settle the region with industrious workers, as Octave Thanet would later propose for her military district. Woolson's short stories oddly reconcile disabled southerners, like veteran Phil, with ill, lingering northerners by having both succumb. Woolson links actual illness and homesickness by having characters arrive literally sickened by northern conditions while simultaneously pining for them. "So many of them die" in the "sunny land," like the young wife the lighthouse keeper had nursed in the short story "Sister St. Luke." She was unable to recover from former hardships in the North: "the sun, with all his good will and with all his shining, not being able to undo in three months the work of long years of the snows and bleak east winds of New England." Despite the sun and the sea, the nun has an "intense yearning" to return to her convent because "here so lost, so strange am I, so wild is everything." Under the care of two sailor rogues, Keith and Carrington, she overcomes her fears of this wilderness in order to rescue the sailors when their boat capsizes in a tornado. Yet the lush terrain induces such a fatal longing that the sailors conclude "she will die of pure homesickness if she stays here much longer." The story ends with her return to the pent-up convent, where she seeks a less sensuous, more "heavenly" life.[44]

Woolson's other exiled northerners fare worse in Florida, never to find even an earthly reward. Transplanted New York spinster Miss Elisabetha has lived a brutally frugal life so that she can provide for her talented, but unappreciative, warbling ward, Doro. "Miss Elisabetha" begins with a poem describing a woman so witheringly lonely that, with "haggard cheeks" and "desolate eyes," she has become little more than a ghost. The lines anticipate the story's profiling of premature aging. The title character's advance into becoming an "old woman with foolish fancies" is considerably hastened when Doro tries to escape Florida with an exotic vacationing chanteuse. The arrival of the seductive Cécile Kernadi portends a consumer flood, that "great tide which now sweeps annually down the Atlantic coast to Florida." Denied Kernadi, Doro rejects Elisabetha's gifts of getaway money, gives up music, and marries commonly, sealing his fate to die unsung in Florida. Elisabetha outlives Doro to be "an old, old woman, but working still," however futilely. Her struggling becomes a willful disability. Foreshadowing the state's future reputation as a retirement home, Miss Elisabetha represents the human corollary to Florida's ruins. She personifies Woolson's claim that the state is "the only gray-haired corner our country holds."[45]

Woolson also represented the land as either untamable or a ruin to justify effacing Native Americans from the Florida scene, casting further shadows over her support for African American citizenship. From the region's colonial beginnings until the conclusion of the Second Seminole War, Native Americans had sustained social and cultural alliances with African Americans, yet Woolson dismissed them, contradicting her celebration of other ethnic Floridians. "The Ancient City" offers a lesson in cultural erasure. The tourists discover that a cemetery was built upon a former Native American village obliterated by the Spanish, who had erected a chapel there, which was destroyed by the Native Americans during a later massacre. Both the cemetery and the chapel retain the name of the village. Unlike the ruins left from other civilizations, all that is left of Woolson's Floridian Native Americans, then, are their names. Woolson's preference for preserving "Indian" names over actual Native Americans fits within a broader travel discourse that classified Native Americans as a national eyesore, best removed to reservations "where," as Oliver Crosby puts it, "they will be less in the public eye."[46]

In both sketches and stories Woolson allows Native Americans to be located only in the lexicon of the landscape. Her travel sketches always feature an academic authority keen to explain Native American etymology and history. In "The Oklawaha," for example, the General, upon arrival at Payne's landing, feels compelled to discuss King Payne, a Seminole chief. Payne's tribal origins lead the General to explain that the Oklawaha River took its name from Native Americans, a "darker-skinned race descended from the Yemasees." In a possible allusion to William Gilmore Simms's wildly popular 1835 novel *The Yemasee*, a stirring prototype for dramatizing the Native American's extinction from the southern landscape, these explanations disqualify their claims to citizenship. Coupling Native Americans with "ownership" of land seems almost oxymoronic to the tourists. King Payne and his Seminoles never owned but merely "occupied," like the passing tourist, a "vast extent" of Florida. Woolson links their dismissed "occupation" to the unpopular federal occupation of the 1870s, thus disqualifying any Native American hopes for citizenship as well as any military schemes of Reconstruction.[47]

As with her burlesquing of journalistic ambitions through Sara St. John, Woolson mocked Native American pretensions to naming land by parodying their language. In a humorous aside, the "Ancient City" tourists literalize Chief Coacoochee's name, which means "Wildcat," suggesting that he was actually a cat who had once escaped from Fort Marion. This semantic confusion grows into linguistic slapstick as the tourists play off the pronunciation of this name given to the son of King Philip. Iris calls him "Caloochy," while Sara chimes in that he must be like Pontiac, "always turning up when least expected," with "something about the Caloosahatchee too." Another deadpan tourist qualifies: "Are you not thinking of the distinguished chieftains Holatoochee and Taholoochee?" Finally, the scene degenerates into vaudeville as the Captain confesses, "For my part, I can't think of any thing but the chorus of that classical song *The Ham-fat Man*, 'with a hoochee-koochee-koochee.'" His name made nonsensical, the chief, as a subject of history, is made irrelevant.[48]

Woolson's erasure of Native Americans also rationalized freedpeople's failure to secure land-ownership. Other Reconstruction writers tried to stretch definitions of property in order to include freedpeople as capable owners and citizens, but Woolson circumvented the legal and social tangles that would ultimately trip these writers up. Woolson adhered to a traditional understanding of citizenship found in real property ownership; however, by portraying Florida real estate as worthless, she made ownership lose its appeal. While potentially accurate, Woolson's dismissal of land opportunities for freedpeople ignored their hopes for a homestead, which, owing to Florida's vastly unsettled territory, were long-standing and passionate.[49]

Nevertheless, their hopes were often frustrated. Owing to Freedmen's Bureau efforts, Florida provided more homesteads for its freedpeople than did any other state; however, most homesteaders did not prosper because of the land's poor quality, the lack of basic provisions, and the determined opposition of white southerners who feared a labor shortage. Writing in 1870, Ledyard Bill, for example, movingly described the typical "touching" plight of an aged ex-slave, a "worthy, industrious, hard-working, and native citizen," who was cheated by whites and "half denied the right" to own a homestead on even "worn-out and unimproved land." Woolson would have referred him to "The Ancient City's" Uncle Jack. Despite the entreaties of the plantation's new owner that Jack move to a new "picturesque porter's lodge," he will not budge, preferring his old home. Uncle Jack's "dislike to any elevation" and preference "to be right on the ground" literalized freedpeople's ties to the land. One bureau agent commented, "The disposition amongst the freedmen is to settle on the land, where they were raised. They call it their home and wish to make it their resting place." In Woolson's travel sketches and poems, few cultivated land, and therefore no one needed to possess it. In reality, land-ownership became a spectator sport for the freedpeople.[50]

With so many languishing, Woolson's readers may then fairly ask, does anyone prosper in Florida? If so, how? The answers lie in a visit to cemeteries. In "The Ancient City" the tourists remark upon the "ugliness" of the Protestant cemetery. Its numerous headstones tell "the same sad story of strangers in a strange land—persons brought here in quest of health from all parts of the country, only to die far away from home." In contrast to the dead-ended fate of these "strangers," about whom "there is nothing to speak," the dead in Tolomato Cemetery stimulate conversation. Here the tourists discover a hidden, colorful history of Florida made evident by "the names on the low crosses, nearly all Spanish, Minorcan, Corsican and Greek, [all of which] bore witness to the foreign ancestry of the majority of the population." At the expense of the Native Americans who previously claimed the site, the visit gestures to Woolson's celebration of the ethnic immigrant population of Florida as a means to address the needs and prospects of former slaves transitioning to freedom.[51]

While Woolson's portrayals of Native Americans and northern white immigrants told a cautionary tale to those eager to relocate, they did not cancel her optimistic vision for freedpeople. Woolson demanded the recognition of black contributions to Florida by diverting attention from the traditional to the neglected. In her first strategy, Woolson told a different story about Florida, emphasizing the importance of its diverse cultural history to the nation's founding. The otherwise overlooked presence of freedpeople was essential to her descriptions of postwar Florida. Woolson's emphasis on Yankee failures to settle Florida paved the way for focusing on the assimilative success of another group.

The Minorcan Experience: Template for Freedpeople's Success

To keep northern readers interested in the freedpeople, Woolson next focused on the Minorcans, who functioned as a viable cultural authority in Florida. She was careful to recount their history. The Minorcans descended from 300 families that the Scottish Dr. Andrew Turnbull brought from Minorca, one of the Balearic Islands owned by Spain, to Florida in 1768. They worked, along with Greeks and Italians, as indentured servants on Turnbull's indigo plantation south of St. Augustine. Much like the African slaves who labored alongside them, these immigrants experienced "almost unrelieved misery" in "sickness, death, protests and punishments." Turnbull's cargo of Minorcans, French, Corsicans, Greeks, and Italians was the first mass ethnic migration to the New World, but more than half would be dead when his New Smyrna plantation collapsed just nine years later.[52]

Woolson's focus on ethnicity was perhaps the only practicable way to frame the problems of freedpeople as legitimate *national* concerns because of the increasing national indifference and sectional hostility focused on them during the mid-1870s. The Minorcans were useful for Woolson not only because of the similarity of their suffering to that of slaves but also because of their recovery from servitude and subsequent transformation into successful citizens. Like the freedpeople, the indentured Minorcans sought and won their emancipation; they appealed to the governor for freedom and had it granted in 1777. Weathering the second Spanish occupation of Florida, they, too, experienced the confusion of successively imposed foreign governments. The Minorcans survived and transitioned to freedom by retaining their cultural traditions and dialect, expressed through their staunch devotion to family and to the Catholic faith. From the time of their arrival until the Civil War, the Minorcans favored the local over the federal and were openly hostile to first British and then Union vandals. Some who worked hard as sharecroppers, fishermen, and traders were eventually able to accrue land and ships. Woolson spotlighted the self-determination and self-sufficiency of Minorcan women, while downplaying their tenacious "American" entrepreneurship. Woolson relies on flattering gendered stereotypes to present the Minorcans more favorably to those who balked at the influx of immigrants. This detouring of race through ethnicity and gender reflected Florida's changing demographics, particularly in the eastern counties along the St. Johns River.[53]

To introduce the Minorcans, Woolson created seductive cultural interpreters such as Eugenio, a romantic poet who joins the tourist group of "The Ancient City" a week after their arrival in Florida. Using characters like Eugenio as foils, Woolson sifted Minorcan interracial exoticism through a sensual, cultural sieve to present these immigrants more acceptably as once-removed. From "another literary world entirely," Eugenio, with his "bon European" repartee, links the foreign Minorcans to classical European culture to interpret the landscape exotica for the tourists. He suavely paves the way for the foreign to become intimately familiar to northern readers. John Hoffman shuffles Minorcan origins to include the "Greek Islands" and Corsica, telling the tourists what they want to hear. "The Greek Islands did you say? Is it possible I may see before me any of the relatives of Sappho?" exclaims Sara. Hoffman answers with a "Maybe," tantalizing her that she might meet young girls "with roses in their glossy hair, and as their dark eyes meet yours, you are reminded of Italy." In "The Oklawaha," Eugenio's enticing counterpart is Ermine Treshington, whose stylized stances prompt such questions as, "What is romance?" among the other tourists. Her dramatic posing in her "Greek draperies" causes Martha to note, "Miss Treshington's profile, hair, and draperies were such that, give her a background, and irresistibly your thoughts turned at once to the Palmer Marbles." Woolson makes mysterious Minorcan residents, and, by extension, the freedpeople, not only familiar but desirable to readers.[54]

Deploying gendered language, Woolson freed tropical features from stereotype and made them attractively interracial. Woolson depicts the Minorcans, "these dark-eyed, olive-skinned people" who live "in tranquil content," as a cultural prototype of assimilation for other dark-skinned Americans. Rather than recasting Minorcan women as versions of mulattos, she emphasizes the white regularity of their features while stressing the darkness of their eyes and complexions. John Hoffman assures the other tourists who seek classical European exotics in "The Ancient City" that "you will see some dark, almond shaped eyes, now and then a classical nose, often a mass of Oriental black hair." In her 1874 travel sketch "A Voyage to the Unknown River," Woolson explored inland Florida, describing a Minorcan woman as having "no color in her face; the heavy black hair, brows, and lashes, seem to cast a shadow over the clear olive skin; but she lifts her eyes again, and all the color and the warmth of all the tropics lies hidden within." To allay white fears of miscegenation, Woolson portrayed Minorcan women as passive sensualists rather than demonizing them as sexual predators. The "fair" young woman of diminutive features is rendered attractive by conventionally coded white standards of femininity, with her "*trainante* voice," "slender foot," and "fanciful" hairdo capped by "a spray of yellow jasmine." Like other travel writers, such as William Cullen Bryant, Woolson thus complimented the physical appearance of Minorcan women.[55]

At the same time, she, like Bryant, conflated her description with those of freedwomen, suggesting the possibility of compatible fates. Bryant's Minorcans, with their "foreign physiognomy" and "strange language," occupied the liminal space of the exotic. Yet Bryant also admired them because of the bold temperament, or "spirit," they shared with white settlers. Nested within Bryant's description of the Minorcans was his complementary description of the "St. Augustine Negroes," whose "gentle physiognomy" made them a "good-looking specimen of the race." Woolson, following Bryant, suggests that the Minorcans assimilated both the black and white races, while emphasizing the distinctive, local nature of Minorcan customs.[56]

Often identified only by the tinge of their complexions, the "dark lady" and her "brown baby" became, for the northern tourist, virtually interchangeable with the freedpeople. In her 1874 poem "Dolores," Woolson describes the Minorcans as "A simple folk came from the Spanish / isles / Now, tinged with the blood of the creole / quadroon." Woolson's verse recalls Bryant's description of the Minorcan as melded with the African, similarly acknowledging miscegenation: "The Spanish race blends more kindly with the African, than does the English, and produces handsomer men and women." Woolson's Minorcans have both a composite phenotype and a history that incorporates the racialized experiences of both black and white Americans; like the ex-slaves, they have struggled for freedom, and like the white settlers, they now bask in their security. With cross-cultural references interlaced with conventional descriptors for African American as well as white women, Woolson's gendered prose was even more ambiguous than Bryant's as to which race the Minorcans belong. Such determinations were, in fact, problematic, given the mixture of ethnically diverse inhabitants that informed social caste in cities such as St. Augustine by the late eighteenth century.[57]

Woolson's subdued handling of ethnic sexuality across relaxed racial lines extended beyond the confines of St. Augustine's Minorca Town to encompass Florida's wilds. Drawing on this greater variegated landscape, she reconstructed the stereotypical image of Americans built along a stable racial binary. The freedpeople's "Africa," for example, can only be reached by crossing a creek suggestive of ethnic and racial murkiness. According to "The Legend of Maria Sanchez Creek," a poem about a thwarted interracial romance that tourist John Hoffman presumably found in the town archives, Maria "*is* rather brown," yet she "blanches" after a "norther" arrives. Denied rescue by the "norther," the "senorita" Sanchez is literally absorbed into her environment, consumed by alligators. With the creek as her namesake, the legendary Maria Sanchez, a "Spanish maiden," naturalizes racial and ethnic hybridity.[58]

Like the lush entangling layers of swamp vegetation, Floridian bloodlines could not possibly be kept distinct. Other Reconstruction writers such as Tourgée and Cable labored at naturalizing mixed racial and ethnic identity in their plots, but Woolson relied on the natural order of chaos inherent in the Floridian vegetation of "The South Devil": "The sweet orange-trees, crape-myrtles, oleanders, guavas, and limes planted by the Spaniards had been, during the fifty years, conquered and partially enslaved by a wilder growth . . . the whole bound together by the tangled vines of the jessamine and armed smilax." In this entangling environment, it seems natural that Deal's gamekeeper had "probably Spanish, African, and Seminole blood in his veins." This botanical and social Darwinism was not entirely haphazard, however. Spanish law provided for European-African unions, which were "common and accepted," and for the inheritance rights of the offspring of such alliances.[59]

Serving as regional ambassadors to Woolson's tourists, her Minorcan women emerge as the cultural backbone of a diversified Florida. Woolson believed that at least some aspects of cultural identity were a matter of proud choice and that not every woman would choose to be perceived as part of the majority. In "Black Point," the innkeeper admits to having been born in Pennsylvania and christened with the name Amelia Jane, but "having married a Florida sailor of Spanish descent, she had become a Valdez" and so now answers to the name Donna Teresa, as rechristened by her guests. In "A Voyage to the Unknown River," a Minorcan woman is asked by a northerner whether she is a Minorcan in the invitingly negative form ("You are Minorcans, are you not?"). "Throwing back her head, with a quaint little air of *hauteur*," she takes advantage of the phrasing to answer, "We are Spanish." Her proud disposition resembles that of Victoria Linkum and other freedpeople of "The Ancient City." Woolson reshapes the clash between black and white southerners through the cultural complementarity of the Minorcan, epitomized by the layout of Minorca Town with its side streets of "odd names" like "St. Hypolita, Cuna, Spanish, and Tolomato." Intermarriage allowed the Minorcans to preserve their cultural heritage—while becoming interracial. Their experience suggests one method of becoming an American citizen. Woolson shows that the question for most Floridian women, as for Amelia Jane, was simply which cultural road they would choose as they provide the leadership for cultural assimilation.[60]

Despite her mostly positive portrayals of many Minorcan women, Woolson frequently represented the Minorcans in conventionally racist ways. These stereotypical portrayals occur more in her short stories than travel sketches; they may be a function of gender as much as genre and visitor expectations of Florida. Woolson's disabled tourist identified with the leisured pace of the Minorcans, while the frustrated resident saw the Minorcans as an obstacle, further impeding ambitions gone awry. Woolson also acknowledged, with some ambivalence, the views of Floridian white supremacists who opposed intermarriage.

Woolson recognized that for those northerners who chose to stay in Florida, being neighborly to so much ethnic exoticism resulted in fence building. In "Miss Elisabetha," the title character's gate, so often left unlatched by the freedpeople, become a "standing bone of contention" between Elisabetha, "the mistress," and "the entire colored population of the small village," who resent the imposed boundary. Yet she soon learns that she has no control over these boundaries. Her ward, Doro, rejects her plans to have him live a life abroad, "suited" to his "descent." He chooses, instead, to stay in Florida, marry the Minorcan Catalina, and have her live with him and Miss Elisabetha. His decision fills the "speechless" Miss Elisabetha with horror: "To live with them always—with *them*!" Like Amelia Jane Valdez, characters such as Doro suggest Woolson's faith in each individual's reconstruction as the first step in postwar healing. Yet Doro's triumph over Elisabetha ends uneasily, as Catalina "queened it right royally" over Elisabetha's house in which her "careless, idle, ignorant happy brood" of "brown brothers and sisters ran riot." No longer a protégé of his aunt, Doro now sounds his own "improvised melodies" of Minorcan songs over her piano's broken keys. Doro's marriage and bountiful crop of offspring imply that acculturation inevitably will continue, despite Miss Elisabetha's efforts to educate Doro to maintain boundaries.[61]

Woolson's ambivalence over the powers of cultural assimilation is most vividly dramatized in her short story "Felipa," which focuses on an orphan Minorcan girl's extreme manipulation of her identity in order to win acceptance from Christine, a visiting tourist with whom she becomes infatuated. Christine, however, sees only "an ugly little girl" and likens Felipa to her mutt, Drollo. Felipa's Minorcan grandparents, who speak a patois of Greek, Italian, and Spanish, are equally dismissed as "slow-witted" with minds that "rarely rose above the level of their orange trees and their fish-nets." Despite her passion and intelligence, Felipa, like Uncle Jack, is abandoned by the tourists, who "leave her to her kind." The tourists' hasty exit suggests how easily the Minorcans, like the Native American and ex-slave, were classified as a distinct, inferior species, in accord with the prevailing scientific racism.[62]

The girl's desperation to be both like and liked by the blanched Christine crosses established racial and gender boundaries. Edward, Christina's suitor, hopelessly tries to reinforce these boundaries by reminding the "little monkey" that her desire must be thwarted "because you are so dark, you know." Felipa's repeatedly emphasized darkness is aligned with the natural wild landscape; she is a "dark-skinned yellow-eyed child" who is "the offspring of the ocean and the heats." As with the Deal brothers of "The South Devil," a study in contrasts is immediately set up when Felipa covets the overly cultivated "pre-Raphaelite lady," Christine. With her nearly albino appearance, Christine is the polar opposite of Felipa's tropical darkness. These extremes structure a scenario contrived to test the limits of a chosen gender identification. Attired in boy's clothes, Felipa cultivates a "different look," causing Edward to mistake her for a "little fellow" called "Phillip." Felipa's cross-dressed identity extends to her perceptions of Christine and Edward, whose identities she had "a curious habit of confounding." The narrator, a "poor and painstaking" artist, can only explain Felipa's habit in racialized terms as "a case of color-blindness." Woolson toyed with staging the changeability of racial identity when her "Ancient City" tourists visit a Methodist church, where "singularly enough," they hear the repeated refrain of the freedpeople's "favorite hymn": "Shall wash me white as snow / White as snow," in a literal performance of the ex-slaves' desire.[63]

If the short story can be read as an allegory of acculturation, then Felipa stands as a vivid example of the performative nature of identity.

Her fate illustrates the failure of such performance: although she persists to the point of assaulting Edward and attempting suicide, her outrageous behavior only succeeds in postponing Christine's departure and marriage to Edward. Woolson shows performed identity as double-edged, unlike Thanet, who endorsed it as a relatively easy way for planters to regain authority. While the narrator admires Felipa's strong individualism as part of her "latent beauty, courage," the other tourists treat her as "a rubber toy or a little trapeze performer." However, like "The Ancient City" tourists who try to frame Uncle Jack and other misfits, the narrator attempts a painterly solution: she tries to "fix" her "likeness" by sketching her. When that fails, she applies her paint directly to Felipa, making her up for tableaux vivants. Felipa ultimately retaliates by eating the paints, a self-destructive protest against this imposition of identity. With changing "quicksilver reality," Felipa defies being pigeonholed into traditional gender and racial roles, which were often imposed to domesticate the postwar world. Her character highlights the constructedness and inherent flexibility of identity as a source of promise for reimagining postwar southern relations, yet its dynamism is ultimately only reactive and self-destructive.[64]

Through "Felipa," Woolson entertained the extremes of freedom from restraint and categorization in ways that resonated with readers worried about its southern expression. Indeed, Woolson sometimes hesitates about the ability of the ex-slaves to navigate through the opportunities created by emancipation. In "Dolores," Woolson dramatized lingering Floridian questions about what knowledge, if any, beyond laboring was suitable for freedpeople. To explore this issue, Woolson again showcases the heroism of a Minorcan woman in helping reconstruct the military district. Through the postwar plight of the title character, this poem assesses the worth of education for the dispossessed. Dolores, a young Minorcan, tries to make a desperate living selling oranges to the northern soldiers, but they ignore her, busy with the military duties of occupation. Finally, a northern army surgeon intervenes. He cures her husband and buys oranges for his patients, and in an echo of advice many northerners offered to the freedpeople, this "Northern saint" urges Dolores, "See, build me no shrines, but take this / small book / And teach the brown baby to read." Dolores's encounter with the northern surgeon could be read as an ironic comment on the ex-slaves' transition to freedom at Reconstruction's close: "The sad war is over. . . . The blue-coated soldiers depart / The brown baby reads the small book. . . . But all his new English words never can / change / the faith of Dolores' fond heart." "Dolores" suggests that the freedpeople will successfully assimilate through education while maintaining their cultural uniqueness, just as the Minorcans have. Yet the poem shies away from outright assurance.[65]

Reflective of Woolson's faith in Florida's distinctive capacity to sustain interregional and interracial cooperation, both Dolores and the sick soldiers benefit from the army's extended "occupation" of the local church as a hospital. But when occupation ends, Dolores is left vulnerably alone, and the last lines find Dolores, having built a shrine to the surgeon, "Dead, with the book in her hand," foreshadowing the fate of many freedpeople whose essays at self-improvement met violence. The boat adrift with the Minorcan's corpse at the shrine suggests a fatal uncertainty about the freedpeople's ability to pilot their own transition to freedom. When the soldiers ignore Dolores's plight, despite her naive adoration of them, Woolson foreshadows the country's own turn away from the needs of freedpeople. Although agential in bringing reform to the military district by persistently seeking contact with the northern soldiers, Dolores's attempt to achieve literacy has little meaning for her, though it does hold some promise for her child.[66]

In this parable of Reconstruction, military occupation benefited Floridians by fostering education and recovery, although its imposition also brought bewilderment and crippling dependency to Floridians like Dolores. While recognizing freedpeople's ambitions, particularly for education, Woolson acknowledged the cautionary control of local authorities. Considering legislative changes that accorded with the Reconstruction Amendments, appointed state commissioners unequivocally stated that freedmen must first learn that "their new-found liberty is not license" but rather "ordained by God and a necessity of their condition." Once restraint was "properly inculcated," there "will be time enough to attend to the culture of the intellect."[67]

Nevertheless, Woolson's travel sketches often highlight just that cultivation. After a visit to a freedpeople's community whose residents share a common desire to learn, rather than common burden to labor, Woolson's "Ancient City" tourists depart "strongly impressed." Sara relates a stop at a Methodist Sunday school, describing the curriculum in detail. She appreciates the diligence of the variously aged students, particularly admiring the elderly who read with such "intense eagerness." These reactions were shared by Freedmen's Bureau officials. Although teachers' monthly reports complain that freedpeople could contribute little, if anything, for their children's education, bureau agents were consistently moved by their interest. Joe M. Richardson, citing the bureau's allotment of funds for school construction, book supplies, and, eventually, teachers' salaries, concludes that "perhaps the most important contribution of the Freedmen's Bureau in Florida was in Negro education." The success of the bureau's schools convinced previously apathetic white Floridians of the merits of public education and helped spearhead a broader push for a tax-based, statewide system in the 1868 Constitution. Woolson's highlighting of freedwomen like Victoria Linkum, Minorcan women like Dolores, and the many students learning to read helped further Florida's educational reform. Efforts by Dolores to establish contact with Union soldiers who could foster learning place the initiative for an education with freedpeople themselves, where it correctly belonged.[68]

Woolson's Laboring Floridians: Redefining Work and Play

The fear registered in "Dolores" of encouraging freedpeople's dependency on the government had been evident since the inception of the Freedmen's Bureau. The bureau's enforcement of labor contracts reflected a national sentiment, especially strong in the depression years of the 1870s, that sought to insure the involuntary labor of the poor. Moreover, this sentiment was informed by an Anglo-American legal system that was based upon a paradigm of unfree labor. The renewed emphasis on compulsory labor was also a result of increasing uncertainty over the meanings of labor itself. In the congressional debate that abolished slavery, legislators were grappling with what "free labor" meant. Beginning in the 1870s, the rapid changes in the social definitions of basic categories of work, ownership, and labor produced "confusion and anger, a loss of bearings, and a gathering of forces" that would continue to be expressed in the following decades.[69]

For many northern lawmakers who advocated vagrancy legislation, a system of compulsory labor for all free dependents was not at all at odds with a condemnation of the South's infamous Black Codes; viewing the wage laborer as the marketplace standard of independence, they argued that the bureau's rules were applied indiscriminately, while the Black Codes targeted black southerners. The rationale for compulsory contracts and for vagrancy laws exposed the pivotal role of compulsion in a free-labor economy—a role that labor leaders, like southern proslavery agitators before them, were quick to acknowledge. As soon as the Civil War ceased, journalists coupled reportage of the ex-slaves' reaction to emancipation with discussion of their labor arrangements and vagrancy concerns, while their editors reprinted bureau circulars focused on labor. Questions posed by the Joint Committee on Reconstruction, such as "What is the prevailing opinion in regard to the rights that should be extended to freedmen?," were routinely answered by assessing how hard the freedmen were working to raise white planters' cotton. Adrift in a more northerly river, Dolores would probably starve.[70]

These discussions not only took place in newspapers and congressional hearings about Reconstruction but also were a feature of guidebooks and travel writing in magazines, to which Woolson contributed. Florida guidebooks routinely assessed freedpeople's labor derisively as "the Negro Problem." George Barbour, for example, dismissed "colored laborers" as "always uncertain, indolent, and negligent, unless closely and incessantly watched." Describing his experience as commissary over black railroad workers, he dwelled on the "antics," concluding that "the negro will not play a permanent or prominent part in Florida"—a position Woolson disputes. Pitted against the interests of northern corporate developers and white Floridian boosters were the persistent aspirations of both freedmen and -women like Dolores; they fought for the rights of labor and land-ownership in an all-out struggle in which development was prioritized over democracy.[71]

Nor did Woolson rebuke her choice to sell oranges only when necessity demanded, nor did she rebuke Dolores's refusal to plan and save, having given "no thought of the morrow, no laying in store." Instead, the poem critiques the northern work ethic and its often unaccommodating imposition on other cultures and climates. It was a criticism that freedpeople themselves expressed to the bureau agents who were on hand to enforce it through labor contracts. Other Floridian writers, such as Harriet Beecher Stowe, saw the state's climate as particularly antidotal for the ills of beggary, and Stowe, in fact, devoted a "Letter from Florida" to persuade her readers of this cure's merit. Stowe's letter explicitly engaged the contemporary discourse about beggary to sell Florida's kind climate as a solution to the "true question of these times." By sustaining the destitute with plenty of year-round work opportunities, she maintained Florida amply fulfilled charity's demand to "*give work*, not alms." Woolson's portrayal of frustrated, transplanted northern men transformed Stowe's prescription into a misdiagnosis.[72]

Woolson did not see a problem with the productive capacity of Florida. She consistently elided the question, making it inapplicable, even inappropriate, to ask. Instead, she explored what "work" meant in Florida. Consistent with the ambivalent symbolism David Arnold has found characteristic of tropical discourse, Woolson found both fecundity and disease coexistent in Florida.[73] However, Woolson focused on the successful indigenous efforts by the dark-skinned Floridians to thrive, offering their lifestyle as an alternative to other American patterned distinctions between labor and leisure. "Black Point" opens as a tourist sketch and for a page gives a straightforward presentation of Woolson's views of Florida's necessary languor:

> The most subtle charm of Florida . . . is found in the absence of the atmosphere of labor, either in the present or the past. . . . Through the South at the present day . . . there is . . . often a torpor of regretful memories, which as effectually as the presence of toil prevents the formation of that atmosphere of indolence—indolence unpursued by disapproving conscience—which is Florida's deepest charm. It is not rest for rest follows labor. Here is no labor and never was.[74]

From the romanticized perspective of the tourist, Woolson replaced an understanding of labor as work done upon the land with an understanding of the land as nearly self-producing. Writing as legislators attempted to insure workers' rights to the "fruits of their labor"—a popular phrase used to signify the laborer's right to attain property beyond his mere wages—Woolson disrupts the meaning of the fruition of work. By having the fruits literally drop into Minorcan laps, as with Dolores, Woolson downplayed the roles of Minorcans as laborers, despite the historical record of their enterprise and Dolores's sincerity. Human labor as the supreme organizing force of life is marginalized, as a line from "Pine Barrens" suggests: "O happy pools! no duty do ye know save simple beauty / Ye care not for the harvest-time, ye neither toil nor spin." Repulsed by this kind of "child's play," Iza Hardy castigated his readers that "there is no room for dreaming or idling for the *bona fide* settler" in Florida. What Hardy and other writers warned against as a sinful temptation, Woolson celebrated as a gift of providence. Woolson's Florida provided the chance to exchange the drudgery of work for more meaningful occupations.[75]

Other northerners saw endemic laziness that needed ousting, but Woolson found charm. Using Florida as the premier example, Ledyard Bill simply accepted that the "South is full a hundred years behind the North" and chalked up the "universal indolence of southern populations" as due to the "enervating climate." Woolson agreed but saw this as admirable adaptation. In observing why so few Floridians perambulate, "The Ancient City" tourist John Hoffman murmurs that "climate here has something to do with it." In her portrayals of the Minorcans' improvised communities, Woolson assimilated regional approaches to work and leisure, redefining these notions rather than redefining property, as Tourgée and Thanet would later do. Woolson alone tackled the reconstruction of work, offering Florida as an example for postwar healing nationally. She tapped into an emergent redefinition of labor relations. Grounded in the philosophy of possessive individualism, it was a paradigm of modern free labor in which workers could no longer be compelled to labor. Woolson's respect for the elevated status of workers reflected her century's development of this model, evidenced in the passage of the federal Anti-Peonage Act of 1867, which outlawed both voluntary and involuntary servitude.[76]

Woolson restructured the meaning of work by recasting moral judgments characterizing low worker productivity from laziness into neutral observations about the nature of indolence. In her portrayals Woolson capitalized on the earlier etymology of "indolent" as a state of freedom from pain, in this case the pain of drudgery, to categorize Minorcan activity. Whereas "lazy" implied slothful, the claim of "indolence" allowed her Floridians to assert a casual living (as opposed to ardently earning a living). Relying on the state's natural productivity, Woolson refashioned a northern understanding of labor as sweated work into a meaning connotative of greater ease and leisurely pace. She expressed her own desire to "buy a wee cottage down there; set up a crane and three orange-trees; and never stir again." For Woolson, the poor could be free to be the "most indolent of all," because the landscape often relieved them of the necessity to produce: "With wood in the forest for their small fires, with fish in the brown rivers, why should they strive or save? Here at last is a country where there is no 'must.'" Her images assert that all Floridians—rich and poor, men and women—were entitled to free time as well as greater lassitude in their labors.[77]

Woolson's substitution of indolence for laziness had political implications. If Florida were naturally productive, the issue of how to compel freedpeople to labor (through enforced contracts, apprenticeship laws, or vagrancy statutes) was tacitly resolved. In constructing her fantasy of a place not only free of production but also free from the desire to produce, Woolson uplifted Floridian workers above northern complaints of laziness while also offering an alternative to those troubled by the "Gilded Age's" deleterious economic conditions. In particular, Minorcan disengagement from a northern drudged work ethic saves them from the "consumption" that afflicts her overly enterprising northern characters like the Deal brothers. By naturalizing native indifference to hard labor, Woolson circumvents northern opinion that the freedpeople were incapable of labor.

Writing at a time punctuated by anxiety over renegotiated understandings of the marketplace after the 1873 panic, Woolson spotlighted the Minorcans as alternative, grassroots exemplars of economic collaboration in Florida. Their example could be applied elsewhere to successfully integrate freedpeople, particularly women, into the national economy. Woolson, here as elsewhere, recognized the fluid Floridian economic relationships between Minorcans and free black persons, often former runaways, which dated back to the Spanish rule. A few guidebook writers like Oliver Crosby recognized the wisdom, if not inevitability, of Yankee accession to indigenous farming methods. Crosby gently ridiculed the "northern settler" who, like Woolson's Mark Deal, is initially "hampered by his conceit" in thinking he "'will show the slow-going natives a thing or two'"; eventually, he must admit that "these natives can teach him." Foregrounding more than just the economic advantages that accrue, Woolson's work shows the social and cultural gains to be reaped. Her Minorcans, though poor, remain independent and not "compelled" either to beg or to labor hard. By situating labor differently within their lives, they triangulate the tense, bifurcated racial stereotyping at times evident in the stories. The labeling of Minorcans as "servants" dovetailed well with contemporary references to bondspeople found in Civil War stories and plantation narratives as "servants," never slaves.[78]

Woolson's emphasis on the Minorcans was especially shrewd, since their initial status as "indentured servants" typified the experience of most newcomers to this country. A key tenet in gradual abolition legislation, indentures were used as a means to phase out black bondage. Yet while paradoxically intended to push African Americans toward legal freedom, indentures were also misused to keep them in unending bondage. The vaguely Europeanized Minorcan servants negotiated the muddied waters between voluntary servitude and slavery while assuaging those northerners who doubted the transition's success. Their successful transition from servitude to free labor paralleled the changing national perception of indentured servitude itself from a form of voluntary to involuntary labor—a paradigmatic shift toward conceptualizing the modern notion of free labor.[79]

Focusing on the national implications of Reconstruction, Woolson, like Cable, dramatized the economic benefits of acculturation that result from interregional and interracial cooperation. In "Sister St. Luke," industrious Vermonter Melvyna's successful marriage to Pedro, the "acquiescent and admiring" Minorcan lighthouse keeper, reflects Woolson's larger vision of "this vast, many-raced motley country of ours." Unlike the Deal brothers,

Melvyna has adapted to Florida and its ethnic inhabitants explicitly by intermarriage with the natives; instead of making pies out of pumpkin, she substitutes "such outlandish things as figs, dried oranges and pomegranates" which Pedro obligingly eats. In their mutual care, Melvyna's "quick enterprising step" has fallen into march with the "loitering" Pedro, with whom "you could not argue." Typifying successful adaptation to Florida, these helpful "Pedros" proliferate. These Pedros highlight the cultural and commercial advantages of mixed ethnic and racial ties for Floridians, as well as the Minorcans' capacity to assimilate. A fisherman/lighthouse keeper called Pedro also appears in "Felipa" and "Miss Elisabetha," providing an alternative unifying link for the various southerners and transplanted northerners.[80]

Minorcan acclimation to Florida reinforced freedpeople's, especially women's, insistence on making their own choices—a central component of free labor. Upon being asked what her "brown baby" will do without an education, an "Arcadian" mother answers in black dialect, "Why live here or somewhars, jes as we're doing. That's all *he* wants." Woolson forcefully staged freedpeople's, particularly women's, demand to control their own time and work. What initially may have appeared to readers as insolence, if not indolence, was recast as independence. In "The Ancient City," one tourist comments on the seemingly quixotic willfulness of elderly ex-slaves: "Rules kill them, and they cannot change. We had best leave them alone and educate the younger generation." Woolson's tourists find that they must accept the freedpeople's behavior as a normative condition of freedom: "The negroes, especially the elderly, like to cook when they are hungry, and sleep when they are tired, and enjoy their pipes in peace." Freedpeople's resistance to "the rules" dramatized the contemporary ideal that all laborers—not only ex-slaves—enjoy autonomy, dignity, and stature equal to that of their employers. These simple assertions of the right to structure their own leisure were but part of a range of rights and prerogatives freedwomen, in particular, sought to claim after the war at great cost.[81]

As postwar national debate over free-labor ideology often crystallized around gender roles, Woolson made women agential to presenting her revision of the meaning of labor. Her strategy reflects postwar realities in which freedwomen, as historian Leslie Schwalm has shown in her focus on low-country South Carolinian rice plantations, "were still embattled, deeply, entangled in the contested supply, organization, and control of labor." Directly countering contemporary fears about "female loaferism," Minorcan women such as "Dolores," keen to sell her oranges, showcase freedwomen's initiative to earn a living and to structure the terms of their labor. Such discretionary but considerable contribution to their household economies not only helped women stave off debt and even accumulate some wealth but also provided necessary resources for community development. Indeed, historian Sharon Ann Holt describes the freedpeople's household production as "the heart of their rural entrepreneurship."[82]

In spotlighting Minorcan women's enterprising labors, Woolson allays fears that freedwomen will no longer labor while situating their initiative in a broader exploration of a revised meaning of work for women of all races and classes. In "A Voyage to the Unknown River," a Minorcan woman calmly sits "braiding palmetto," as she speaks to the tourists. Challenging stereotypical expectations about Anglo-American women's domestic duties, the Minorcan woman does not cease from her labors to wait upon the intruding tourists asking for a drink; instead, she directs them to a cup and well while she continues to braid palmetto as naturally as her hair, which is "braided fancifully" with jasmine. Her actions reflect that of many freedwomen in domestic service who refused to subordinate themselves to white people, as they had in slavery, or to embrace conventional gender roles that support a northern free-labor society.[83]

While affirming gender's centrality to a free-labor social order, Woolson does not repudiate it entirely. Instead, her female characters suggest an alternative understanding of its terms, so as to restructure it. Like Sara, the journalist who always is working even while sightseeing, the Minorcan woman's labors blend with leisure. The fluidity of the palmetto braider's movement, despite a late-hour interruption, disrupts the connotation of work as toil distinct from socializing. There is no discernible difference between labor and leisure, because labor is disassociated from the tedious physical exertion traditionally implied by the word. Woolson's presentation of a different, gendered image of work from that often found in capitalist societies allowed northern readers to identify with these female Floridian laborers: like the tourist whose only work is to consume sights while on the move, Woolson's laborers work for and with pleasure to satisfy their basic needs. Both the palmetto weaver and the tourist enrich the Floridian economy while laying claim to their rights to decide and define the use of their time.

Woolson relies on gender differences to qualify her valuation of Minorcan labor. She modified her touristic appreciation of languor by condescendingly describing the acclimation of Minorcan men. For example, "Sister St. Luke's" Pedro gives himself over to a "very mild dissipation," provoking the narrator's curt dismissal that the Minorcans hardly "do anything more than smoke, lie in the sun, and eat salads heavily dressed in oil." Woolson's emphasis on indolence reflects projected northern desire, especially that of invalids who came South, discovering that even travel, as Ledyard Bill noted, was "a burthen and labor." This distinctive type of tourist, unlike the investor, the immigrant, or gadabout, would necessarily pause more and perhaps appreciate Woolson's focus on the freedpeople and Minorcans. No longer framed by the gaze of the tourist searching for the sweating worker, Uncle Jack is free to share the view.[84]

Again Woolson spotlights the enterprising efforts of a woman to make cross-cultural contact prosper. Elisabetha buys daily fish from the Minorcan Pedro at the same time as she "has drilled" him "in his own art by sheer force of will" to sell his remaining catch at profit to those too "lazy" to fish. Likewise, she learns palmetto braiding from Minorcan women but has profitably improved on it "with original ideas" so that "all down the coast, and inland . . . there was a demand for her work." The Minorcans, in turn, had learned braiding from the Spanish, who had learned it from the Native Americans. Elisabetha ekes out her living by giving music lessons to the coastal Spanish demoiselles. Like most of her Minorcan neighbors, she is not a northern-styled entrepreneur and her higher prices are "little enough to northern ideas," but Woolson carefully points out that "her wares found ready sale." While Elisabetha fails to impose her ideals on Doro, she succeeds, like Dolores, when she engages in a more egalitarian social and economic barter with her exotic neighbors. Woolson dramatizes the bright prospects for these small, culturally cross-bred and beneficially interdependent communities, eschewing any prospector's "get rich quick" schemes for Florida. Whether through the palmetto braider, Dolores, or Miss Elisabetha, Woolson emphasizes the key roles women play and the distinctive cross-cultural strategies they use in successfully initiating and developing interwoven economic and social relationships.[85]

Woolson embraced the demands of ex-slaves as part of an emergent, worthwhile discourse about the rights of workers to self-government. This right was a hallmark of the possessive individualism informing the development of free labor, as abolitionist discourse informed the postwar public debate over the meaning of self-ownership in "the labor question." Southern workers' strategies of self-empowerment included sharecropping and paramilitary clubs, whereas northern workers increasingly focused on collective action applied to municipal reform. Woolson's imagining of entitled workers accorded with an Anglo-American pattern of various work practices transformed into the elite status of professions marked by independent, self-regulating organization. Increasingly during the nineteenth century, but particularly in the 1870s, this transformation was accomplished through the rise of formalized course study, standardization, the accreditation of college courses, licensing requirements, and the formation of national professional societies such as the American Medical Association and the American Bar Association. An important shift in rhetoric—the replacement of the adjective "professed" by "professional" to denote "occupational" or "vocational"—also occurred. This rhetorical replacement signaled postwar Americans' increasing awareness of "profession" as a secular entity apart from its theological roots and subject to the vicissitudes of the marketplace. The professionalization of work in accounting, engineering, law, and the liberal arts was aided by private and public institutional affiliation, and the creation of professions was greatly enabled by the rise of corporations and by federal intervention in the form of research funding. The result was an enhancement of these fields with greater wealth, status, and prestige. Despite its tensions within democratic traditions, professional status was destined to replace "land, family, or social status as the primary indicator of achievement." The enhancement of some kinds of work created a middle-class niche between the laborer and the proprietor or capitalist. Woolson opened this niche to freedpeople, whose success showed how the professional attributes of autonomy and career development benefited the entire community.[86]

Woolson used the category of "profession" to address concerns about freedpeople's labor because of its persistent associations with self-regulation, as opposed to marketplace and government control, and with service to others, as opposed to self-interest. Portraying freedpeople as competent professionals capable of exerting self-command challenged the popular stereotype of African Americans as children, transferring their perpetual dependence from their masters onto the federal government. The notion of service to others as a worthwhile occupation rather than as a slavish requirement cast freedpeople's aspirations as dignifying and less threatening to whites.

Woolson's black professionals demonstrate social position, incorporating all the prerogatives of esteemed citizens. Because the professional sold his labor, but not the right to be commanded, the achievement of professional status was especially attractive for circumventing the contentious debate over worker entitlement to more than the property of their labors. The proprietary honor and authority invested in professional status lingered, especially in the South. To have a profession was to secure the title of gentleman, a property of reputation, as Albion Tourgée would soon discover, that was valued highly. Acquiring this property would appease those freedpeople frustrated in their attempts to buy land, offering another route toward recognition of their civil rights. Crucial to professionals' achievement of cultural authority was their manipulation of language, from monopolizing an esoteric knowledge through jargon to relying on metaphor and analogy to gain credibility—techniques Woolson used to advantage.[87]

Woolson defied convention by representing freedmen as professionals worthy of esteem, who bask in the status of their expertise rather than collapse from their labors. Their dedication augurs what Storer College students would achieve, pursuing a course of self-interested duty. Judges and esteemed artists, Woolson's characters have attained a status, marked by training and self-sufficiency, conveyed by their titles and shingles. These freedpeople are recognized for their talent, skill, and individual creativity, not by their output for someone else. In "The Ancient City, Part II," the northern tourists purchase carvings from an African American coquina sculptor referred to only as "the native artist." His distinctive shingle, replete with his design insignia and written in his own awkward hand, "Cokena Work Done to Order," is one of the illustrations for "The Ancient City." This recognition of his sign, however spelled, as a subject worthy of illustration helps ensure a more widespread stamp of freedpeople's talent on the postwar South. Not only the superb craftsmanship of this "artist's" work but also the attributes of international high culture on display in his studio, filled with "rare antique vases, Egyptian crocodiles, Grecian caskets, and other remarkable works," impress the northerners. To the tourists, his "cheerful shining countenance" represents "another witness for the capability for education." With his "evident pride in the specimens of his skill," the freedman revises the nostalgic stereotype of the fading artisan with that of the apprentice-trained master. This artist, a "cripple," could evoke particular empathy from invalids as he transforms his "crumbling rock," creating beauty from disability. Like the Minorcan women, the artist reveals his work to be a labor of love, thereby eliding distinctions between work and leisure.[88]

With his carved statue of Henry Clay on his roof, this craftsman's eclectic sculptures masterfully anticipate northern tourist preoccupation with collecting various specimens of southern life. Indeed, the artist's display of the "Great Pacificator" is a smart bid to satisfy the tastes of local residents who crave his likeness. Having deemed Clay as the "beau ideal of the South," the locals, according to Woolson's tourists, have insured that all northern visitors encounter his likeness "everywhere on the way down" by placing statues of him all over the South. Specializing in figurines of Clay, the author of the Compromise of 1850, Woolson's "dusky artist" is himself positioned as a gentlemanly figure of national and racial reconciliation, pursuing high cultural ideals. Like Woolson, he achieves some measure of success in meeting both local and touristic demand with his eye-catching roof designs. Although the tourists' visit to the "Cokena" artist is but one brief episode in their day, his character, built around his talent, makes a lingering impression. He shows the favorable place freedmen had in the postwar economy. The purchases of the northern tourists confirm that his labors yield real profits, an outcome denied another disabled character, the Confederate veteran Phil Romer. Woolson's portrayals of freedmen as cultured professionals in fields other than cotton cultivation allowed northern readers to appreciate not only the contribution they could make but also the power they could wield in society.[89]

In contrast to the prosperous artist, Woolson's struggling, aged white blacksmith of another poem, "At the Smithy (Pickens County, South Carolina, 1874)," starves. In this dramatic monologue, which appeared in *Appletons' Journal*, Woolson meditates on the tragedy of the war's decimation of the body and spirit of white southerners. She suggests that it is less the old-time artisan that is vanishing than a race beginning to exchange occupational statuses with the freedpeople. The smithy signifies an occupation, and by extension, a racialized hierarchy, in decline. As one of "The Ancient City" tourists observes, "the *ancien régime* has passed away." Like Phil Romer, the blacksmith, a Confederate veteran who lost four sons in battle, has had his fortunes turned by the war. As opposed to the upbeat "Cokena" artist's sign, a full-length illustration of a bent-back, "old and tired out" white man, hunched over his labors, accompanies this poem. Confronting readers with a different vision of a New South, this image appeared on the cover of *Appletons' Journal* for 5 September 1874.[90]

The poem's final stanza offers a solution to the smithy's preoccupation on his painful loss by distracting him; he now must tend to the business of freedpeople. The unexpected arrival of a well-to-do black client interrupts the smithy's monologue, compelling him to activity. The poem concludes with an affirmation of the role of African Americans to the New South's economy as more than common laborers: "There's a horse wants a shoe— yes, they're / turning this way; / It's Judge Brown, of this district. (Eh, what's / that you say? / He's colored? Of course we're used to that / here)." Judge Brown is identified by his occupation, not race; the fact that he is "colored" is parenthetically incidental to the smithy. When he arrives at the smithy, Judge Brown is treated with deference that suits his status: "Let me hold your horse, judge. Run Joe, / bring a chair." It is now the white laborer, no longer the black servant, who is waiting on a different, new master.[91]

These Reconstruction changes were not always welcomed by white Floridians, such as the thirty-seven white men who petitioned the Freedmen's Bureau against black Floridian participation in a town meeting and in the legislature as "a disgrace against civilization." Yet the final stanza of "At the Smithy" makes clear that some Reconstructive agendas had nevertheless been accomplished. By giving business to the struggling blacksmith, Judge Brown, as a well-heeled consumer, plays a vital role in resuscitating the South's postwar economy, just as the "Cokena" artist or the palmetto-selling woman satisfies consumer demand. Woolson's portrayals of Judge Brown and the artist exemplify the freedpeople's successful accomplishments, earning a professional status that entitles them to a chair. She imagines that a different kind of southern occupation, premised on the freedpeople's intellectual and artistic merit, might replace that of the military.[92]

While these representations do not abound in Woolson's work, when they appear they stand out as reflective of the benefits as well as the controversy postwar change provoked. For example, in Woolson's 1889 novel, *Jupiter Lights*, an African American drayman refuses to move over when confronted by the oncoming traffic of a proud white judge. Like Judge Brown, the drayman demands respect with a defiance that nearly prompts retaliation by her frightened white characters, a reaction Woolson knew some of her white readers would undoubtedly share. Similarly, a black, federally appointed postmaster, aided by his tenacious wife, hangs on to his job and his "dignified manner," despite being illiterate. Finally, an African American blues singer performing aboard a passenger ship transfixes his interracial audience. Possessing "one of the sweetest voices in the world," the singer, like the "Cokena" artist, affirms the cultural contribution African Americans could make to an integrated postwar American society. Such portrayals insist on the reality of African American ascendency to professional and artistic status and on their corresponding right to respectful treatment as citizens.[93]

By the 1880s, such white southerners as Woolson's smithy had acquiesced to this emerging class of prosperous freedpeople. A new politics of consumption began to emerge and to become the battleground for asserting claims to citizenship, as Octave Thanet's work would showcase. In his analysis of tourism's impact on contemporary global society, sociologist John Urry describes a new, expansive kind of citizenship, one which he characterizes as progressively "more a matter of consumption than of political rights and duties." This "consumer citizenship" includes an understanding that people increasingly consider themselves to be citizens on the basis of their ability to purchase goods and services in a global market. It is tempting to apply Urry's "consumer citizenship" to the postwar years, when the concepts of nation and the citizen were renegotiated on several fronts. Embattled legislatures, African American consumers, and Reconstruction writers like Woolson and Thanet sought to redefine these concepts along Urry's axes of mobility and purchasing power, often contradictorily, as represented in travel literature.[94]

Although endorsing the consumption habits of white seasonal tourists, contemporary guidebook presentations of the former slaves as consumers showed anxiety and contempt. Iza Hardy devoted a chapter section, "Our Colored Brethren," to addressing the advent of freedpeople as pushy consumers. He noted that the black hotel workers had such "a great interest in and admiration for the 'white folks' dress, especially if it came from far off—Paris or London," that some insistently tried to buy clothes off the tourists' backs. Hardy's contemptuous comments were part of a popular discourse hostile toward prosperous freedpeople, since they were positioned to be aggressive consumers and, by implication, proactive citizens. Interracial tensions were heightened by smuggling between Florida and Cuba, a concern that evidently "received as much attention as any other single problem." Florida was distinguished among southern states by this illicit, profitable trade in material goods.[95]

For other travel writers, the people Woolson portrayed as "ladies," artisans, and jurists were relegated to menial jobs; their class pretensions would have to be nurtured privately. Hardy mocked black Floridians for their gentrified ambitions and investment acumen while working subordinate jobs. He wrote in amazement of freedpeople such as his chambermaid, "an old woman with a good-natured black monkey face," who actually turned out to be the proprietress of three cottages and a big bankbook holder. "Looking at her," wrote Hardy, "one would not have imagined her the possessor of a bank account at all, still less of savings counted by the thousand!" Hardy seemed especially affronted by freedpeople's attempts to appear professional, such as those of "the negro who officiated as groom, coachman, gardener, and general outdoor *factotum*," as well as a preacher, appearing as "quite a clerical *beau* in his ministerial array." George Barbour sneered at the consumer-oriented habits of some black workers: "*They* put on airs, joked, smoked cigars, ate melons . . . and went on a trip down the river to Jacksonville, bought watches, canes etc. *They* were the winning gamblers." In such salvos against black consumers, these travel writers, unlike Woolson, could not avoid racist stereotyping.[96]

Consistent with her disdain for the consumption habits of affluent northern tourists, Woolson participated temperately in this discourse. While St. Augustine invalids engaged in their "daily occupations" of counting new visitors to the Ancient City, Woolson highlighted black residents as the visible beneficiaries of tourist spending. In this respect she was unique among travel writers of this period. By making the "blazing fire" of the "contrabands" a symbol for "the hilarious joy" of the Ancient City "over the coming of its annual victim, the gold-bearing northern tourist," Woolson's ex-slaves were poised for the windfall. Yet Woolson stopped short of portraying the ex-slaves positively as consumers, just as she warned northerners of the fatal allure of Florida's swamps. In "The South Devil," Woolson played up the seamier aspects of this stereotype in describing the "Northern mulatto attendant" of the Esmeralda Parlors, an unsavory gambling house. Dressed "more faultlessly than any one else in San Miguel," the attendant represents freedpeople's pretensions. Woolson reduces him to a "piece of bronze insolence" because he has evidently profited from the ill-gotten gains of the casino. While Woolson's timely tourist images for northern consumers may have contributed to a new kind of "consumer citizenship," they also suggested that it was one which not all African Americans apparently were entitled to buy. Coming when it did, it was a suggestion that many of her readers would find apropos.[97]

Woolson's travel sketches and poems appeared as northerners wearied of the difficulties of implementing congressional Reconstruction. As President Ulysses S. Grant himself noted in response to the 1875 terrorism in Mississippi, "The whole public are tired out with these annual autumnal outbreaks in the South, and the great majority are now ready to condemn any interference on the part of the government." Navigating the cross-currents of public opinion, Woolson portrayed the ex-slaves to skeptics as something other than failures in freedom. Nonetheless, her portrayals of successful freedpeople, especially women, as consumers and producers could miscarry: they reassured those northerners desirous to believe the Redeemers' arguments that the Freedmen's Bureau was no longer necessary.[98]

Appearing on the eve of the restoration of southern Democratic governments and the ousting of carpetbaggers, when northern intervention remained critical to freedpeople, Woolson's message helped rationalize northern indifference. The official end of Reconstruction came in 1876, hastened by early bitter divisions within the Republican Party itself. Culminating in the state's pivotal role in the Compromise of 1877, Reconstruction died as violently as it had lived in Florida. Beginning in the early 1870s with the Black Belt county of Jackson, vigilante violence eroded Republican control: "Law and order became a forgotten issue as the blacks retaliated. But they were not able to maintain their cause against the onslaught of militant Klan-like elements." As one aging black man, witnessing the inauguration of Conservative governor George Drew, declared, "Well, we niggers is done."[99]

Woolson's message at this time suggested that northerners were in firm cultural and political control of the South without actually having to remain there. This rationalized reassurance is most evident in the final lines of the poem "Matanzas River." Composed as "light comedy" by one of the northern tourists in St. Augustine, the poem romanticizes the pressing need of black Floridians for ongoing northern intervention; by speaking for them, the river ultimately speaks against their plight: "Voices of the river, calling 'Stay! Stay! Stay! / Children of the Northland, why flee away so soon away?'" The northerners reply, "Though we go, dear river, / Thou art ours forever." By staking for northerners a sentimental and politically false claim to the South, these lines exonerate northerners of any postwar responsibilities to the region. Marketed to appeal to a broad swath of readers, Woolson's portrayal of a reconstructed Florida misled as much as it soothed readers into complacency.[100]

Constance Fenimore Woolson's work crafted a complex ideal, national in scope and ironic in outcome, of a reconstructed America. Indicative of the cultural power of travel narratives to create magazine fictions, her vision challenged the conventional touristic frame of reference by presenting the ex-slaves as a vibrant part of an acculturated community. In particular, she featured freedwomen as outspoken, self-assured citizens who advocated for educational and labor reform as well as their right to leisure. With their initiative and tenacity poised against defeated, subdued white southern men, Woolson complicated the definition of a "southerner" by tapping into other sources of human potential in Florida. In emphasizing its distinctive history, varied inhabitants, and enticing situation, Woolson argued that the appeal of the region lay in its constant flux and opportunities for creative cultural and economic mixing. In her sketches, stories, and poems, Woolson's freedpeople, particularly women, confidently assert themselves as citizens and as free workers entitled to set the conditions of their labor in fields other than agriculture. With uncommon foresight, Woolson envisioned freedpeople as worthy contributors to American life, active in emergent professions, ranging from law to the arts.

Woolson's vision was greatly enabled by her focus on Florida as a paradigm for southern Reconstruction and national healing. The state's colorful history and culturally diverse citizenry provided a viable alternative to popular sectional reunion tropes and conventional understandings of labor, especially the northern work ethic. In particular, Woolson focused on the diligent labors of proud Minorcan women to showcase the valued labors of freedwomen as spearheading the transition to free-labor ideology and educational reform. Woolson's Florida offered a different postwar beginning for the nation, shifting the spotlight from the usual actors, ex-Confederates and white carpetbaggers, to Minorcans, immigrants, and freedwomen. Achieving results that reflected her own ambivalence, Woolson capitalized on the virtues of the open-ended tourist sketch for voicing multiple views and manipulating perspectives from which readers could identify.

Ironically, the popularity of Woolson's sketches pointed toward a reduction, rather than an increase, in opportunities for black Floridians because they implied that the military support for Reconstruction was no longer necessary. This was a message newly elected white southern Democrats wanted northerners to embrace, and Woolson's writing, as part of touristic literature, played into their hands. The further ridicule of freedpeople in Florida guidebooks was part of a broader discourse that recognized the emergent power of consumerism to thwart disfranchisement. While other Reconstruction writers, notably Thanet, would embrace consumer politics as an empowering strategy for freedpeople, Woolson, consistent with her disdain for northern consumerism, seemed to spurn it, even while highlighting African American economic success.

Further undermining the freedpeople's cause was Woolson's occasional pitch to conservative, skeptical readers, which relied on racist tourists, negatively stereotyped Minorcan men, and a misplaced attention to the symbol of the "Indian" rather than the plight of Native Americans themselves. Despite these qualifications, Woolson's vision, predicated on the cultural choices of individual Americans, remains compelling. She succeeded precisely because readers *did* remember the war that Woolson was certain would be forgotten, especially the national promises made from its toll that her work kept recalling.

It would take a Reconstruction writer of another military district to shift the terrain of this postwar debate from the imperial touristic eye found in Woolson's lighthearted travel sketches to the seasoned vision gained from long-term residency. Experiencing fourteen years in the Second Military District, Albion Tourgée would press for Reconstruction to be taken in more radical directions than Woolson could have ventured.

Chapter 2

SEWING ON THE BADGES OF SERVITUDE

Albion Tourgée v. North Carolina

Excuse for being it has, . . . in the fact that I looked, and saw, and a voice said 'Write!'
—Albion Winegar Tourgée, Toinette

While it may be argued that Constance Woolson, indeed all Reconstruction writers, were as summoned to the pen as was Albion Winegar Tourgée in writing his first novel, *Toinette*, his postwar experience remains unique. Bringing to bear his formidable legal and journalistic expertise on the tumultuous events unfolding around him, Tourgée was hardly a touristic bystander. A combat veteran, carpetbag jurist and politician, he was a leading actor in Reconstruction's violent drama as it played out "in the very theater of its enactment." His passionate commitment to social justice helped shape the course of Reconstruction in the Second Military District. Though he did not remain in the postwar South as long as plantation mistress Octave Thanet did, his years in the Tar Heel State overlapped neatly with military occupation.[1]

Residing in Greensboro, North Carolina, from 1865 to 1879, Tourgée confessed that he felt compelled to record the political and social upheaval—what he euphemistically called the "incidents" of Tar Heel Reconstruction—because they "had passed before my eyes with such vividness that I could not but write." It was near Greensboro that the largest force of Civil War troops surrendered under Joseph E. Johnson some two weeks after Appomattox. And it was there that Tourgée wrote *Toinette*, the first of his many novels to explore "the miracle of Emancipation" when "it was fresh to the minds and hearts of us all." Although he modestly characterized his efforts "as a recreation, merely," Tourgée's 1874 novel quickly went into a second edition. He revised it as *A Royal Gentleman* in 1881.[2]

A controversial, yet nationally acclaimed novel, *Toinette* set forth the Reconstruction themes that would become the basis for his later best sellers and would help launch Tourgée's literary celebrity in the early 1880s. Written under a nom de plume, the novel provoked speculation about the author's heritage because of its even-handed regional treatment. Most reviewers, both North and South, praised the novel for its realistic, fair-minded, and dramatic narrative. Tourgée understood literature's preeminent role in shaping perceptions of the American South, and he portrayed Reconstruction's "incidents" in a way that would show the promise of citizenship for African Americans. Taken together, his creative work enabled many Americans to imagine a truly new birth of freedom.[3]

Tourgée's writings, both fiction and nonfiction, would have a lasting impact not only on the course of American literature but also on the future of American law. Twenty-one years after he wrote *Toinette*, Tourgée would present his brief on behalf of Homer Plessy to the Supreme Court, challenging segregation's separate-but-equal logic as it was enforced on railroad cars. The arguments about citizenship, property, and social equality that he marshaled in 1895 had been rehearsed in *Toinette* and *A Royal Gentleman*, which are both saturated in legal discourse. Although Plessy lost his case and Jim Crow segregation remained in force for fifty-nine years, the reasons for that defeat can also be glimpsed from the historical tensions shaping Tourgée's literary work.[4]

Of all Tourgée's novels, *Toinette* is of most interest here because it dramatizes Reconstruction's issues by focusing on a freed*woman* who struggles to achieve her citizenship, gaining property and some independence from her former master in the process. Reconstruction's promise and frustrations remained a perennial topic in Tourgée's six novels on the Civil War and its aftermath, notably in his best-selling *A Fool's Errand* (1879) and *Bricks Without Straw* (1880). However, this first novel shows his unbounded optimism about Reconstruction and arguably constitutes the most ambitious and daring creative expression of his ideals. The novel commands attention because it challenges what legal scholar Robin West has described as the U.S. legal culture's trivialization of "women's suffering." Building upon West's observation, literary scholar Thadious Davis has recognized that even today "there remains little conception that ... slave law pertaining to black women, could have any bearing on the world of 'white' legal jurisprudence and its consequences for women as a class." Perhaps symptomatic of this disregard, *Toinette* and its revision, *A Royal Gentleman*, have been largely ignored by literary scholars. Yet the two novels constitute Tourgée's most thorough exploration of the legal treatment of property rights and the ongoing issue of bodily ownership.[5]

Tourgée exposed black women's centrality to this country's racialized legal system by creating a heroine and other female characters who function as agential figures of transgression and hybridity in their quest to live as citizens. Their struggles embody the ongoing dilemmas inherent in property ownership, particularly property in persons, for all Americans. As a willful black female subject, resistant to subjugation by her master, Toinette is intent on exercising agency by claiming ownership of her body and her rights. The bold actions of Toinette and other female characters dramatize gender and caste oppression, as the novel questions whether the Thirteenth Amendment had effectively abolished slavery. Tourgée's vibrant yet thorough exploration of the legal ramifications of the Reconstruction Amendments distinguishes him from other writers of this period. Advertised as a "companion piece" to *Uncle Tom's Cabin* and favorably compared by critics with that novel, *Toinette* testified to gender's impact in shaping slavery's legacy for both master and ex-slave.[6]

Wanting to do more to help freedwomen secure their rights, Tourgée republished the novel as *A Royal Gentleman* in 1881, after he had left Greensboro and settled in Chautauqua, New York. He added telling illustrations and made significant changes to the ending that reflected freedwomen's more straitened prospects. Neither novel reflected the prevailing national drift toward conservatism. Rather, just as Tar Heel politics would vacillate into the 1880s, the novels zigzag, drawing upon contemporary women's rights thinking and legal developments. Central to both novels is Tourgée's insistence that Reconstruction begins with a restructuring of gender, class, and race relations within the plantation household. He offered three primary strategies for ensuring the civil and political rights of African Americans.

First, both novels set up the heroine's claim to the plantation's title through inheritance, but the plots demonstrate the unreliability of that legal mechanism to convey property to African American women. They also explore the value of various gendered and racial shake-ups in household ownership, including cross-racial alliances between women. In *Toinette*, Tourgée offered intermarriage as the bold solution, relying on the marriage contract as a means to secure his heroine's rights and interests. Even though that solution significantly qualified the terms of the marriage to conform to segregation's culture, the novel's daring ending helped provoke backlash, such as a surge of newer, more punitive antimiscegenation statutes throughout the American South.

Tourgée next utilized the postwar expanded definition of property to include two intangible interests that could empower freedwomen. In *Toinette*, Tourgée focused on a worker's rights to the fruits of one's labor, a property that ex-bondswomen might acquire more easily than land and could use as a basis to assert citizenship. In *A Royal Gentleman*, Tourgée replaced that solution with an emphasis on reputation as a form of property.

His third strategy proposed that freedwomen might claim this northern form of reputation as property, even though it clashed with southern notions of reputation as honor. Demonstrating that literacy was crucial in his heroine's bid for the property of reputation, Tourgée capitalized on changes in the publishing industry, the development of public libraries, and the postwar emphasis on public education. Tourgée's successful publicization of his own literary persona informed this strategy, as he pitted varying regional definitions of reputation against one another to enhance his own celebrity.

Neither novel, however, could escape the association of citizenship with land-ownership. Although he explores the benefits of owning alternative forms of property, Tourgée eventually endorses property as a core component of American identity itself. In both novels, recategorizing all relations as obligatory, enslaving, and driven by the marketplace would cancel out ancillary appeals to the women's rights discourses of self-ownership and free love. Beginning with the "gift" of the slave Toinette to Geoffrey Hunter, the plot of both novels is built around the complications resulting from the changing status of freedpeople from chattel into persons.

The interplay between these statuses anticipated Tourgée's *Plessy* defense, in which he argued that his client, a man who could easily pass as white, was being denied the property of a white man's reputation by being assigned a seat in the "colored" car. Like Plessy's forced assumption of a racial identity inextricably informed by slavery's legacy, the characters in Tourgée's two novels wear permanently affixed "badges of servitude," to borrow his *Plessy* brief's memorable phrase. Tourgée thus expounds on capitalism's underlying dictates, which impose a psychological branding on Americans that signifies their bondage to work and home. Compelled to display their emotional badges of love and obligation, his characters affirm possession as the fundamental premise of relations. By showing all relations as propertied transactions, the two novels inadvertently ensured that these badges became more visible while remaining fixed, with American women held particularly fast by their bonds.

Tourgée and Tar Heel Reform

Tourgée took up his pen almost as soon as he laid down his gun. Initially the twenty-seven-year-old Union lieutenant was interested in moving South for health reasons, like Woolson, as well as for speculative business prospects. Tourgée was the product of pioneering parents whose Jeffersonian sensibilities caused them to renounce manufacturing in favor of homesteading on Ohio's Western Reserve. While a student at the University of Rochester, Tourgée developed interests in literature, politics, and law, the last two blossoming into a career after he resigned from the army following a serious back injury. All three interests were shared by Emma Kilbourne, whose reformist impulses included a strong commitment to women's rights and racial equality that went back to her abolitionist upbringing on the Reserve. The two were married in 1863 and together faced the challenges of Reconstruction at some great personal cost.[7]

The Tourgées were part of the initial postwar wave of carpetbaggers who would help transform North Carolina into a New South destination. Tourgée chose Greensboro, the seat of prosperous Guilford County, noted for sharing with neighboring counties in the Piedmont a Unionist and antislavery tradition among a distinctive literate yeomanry, a tradition Tourgée would re-create in his fiction. In Greensboro he leased a nursery and more than 700 acres of plantation land on which freedpeople labored.[8]

Soon Tourgée's paramount business in North Carolina became its politics. From the time he arrived in Greensboro in fall 1865 until his departure fourteen years later, Tourgée worked zealously for the Republican Party's radical platform of equal rights for freedmen, who comprised one-third of the state's eligible voters. He became more politically active with each passing year. In 1866, he founded a Loyal Reconstruction League and established a radical paper, the *Union Register*. The next year, Tourgée devised and lobbied for an extensive federal program to help freedpeople become landowners. In addition to his duties as an elected state Superior Court judge in 1868, he revised North Carolina's civil procedure code and was a prominent delegate to the state's constitutional convention that year. Tourgée also involved himself in many other local civic reforms, from organizing a fire department to working pro bono for the Methodist Episcopal Church to helping found a "normal school" for freedpeople that became Bennett College. Tourgée's multifarious interests testify to his boundless energy, enabling him to remain in the Tar Heel State until 1879, despite the overwhelming political difficulties he encountered.[9]

North Carolina Reconstruction:
A Story of Marked Men

Within the Second Military District, which consisted of the Carolinas, there was great promise for recognizing freedpeople's entitlement to all the rights and duties of citizenship. North Carolina, a comparatively liberal state, had a relatively small black population. Most of its farms were modest and slave free, presumably assuring a smoother transition to free labor than in large plantation areas. As early as June 1865, Tourgée corresponded with Provisional Governor William W. Holden, who apprised him of the depreciated prices of land and the high demand for skilled labor in the state. Holden assured Tourgée that North Carolina was hospitable to enterprising Yankees: "There is nothing in the feeling of the loyal people of this state which would make it unpleasant for northern labor to come into our midsts."[10]

Holden, however, spoke prematurely in assuring Tourgée of North Carolina's safety. Far from enjoying a return to law and order, postwar North Carolinians experienced ongoing extralegal violence as common, stemming from guerrilla warfare, Regulator attacks on tax collectors, harassment of the freedpeople and their allies, and the rise of white terrorist organizations. Considered a "marked man" because of his Unionist sentiment, Holden would soon declare two nearby Piedmont counties to be in insurrection. His state militia proved inadequate to combat escalating violence by the Greensboro-based Klan, whose state membership peaked at an estimated 40,000. Holden employed two dozen detectives during his tenure and suppressed habeas corpus, resulting in his impeachment on 22 March 1871 when the Democratic State Legislature returned to power.[11]

Tourgée quickly became acquainted with the problems afflicting black North Carolinians, who found justice hard to obtain either in a courtroom or on a dark country road. The state's postwar era was marked by interracial violence as African Americans resisted the steady erosion of their rights. Even in Unionist strongholds like Appalachia, the Freedmen's Bureau struggled to protect freedmen's rights and to build a coalition with white Republicans. The bureau met with resistance because the mountaineers' long-standing economic and social ties to the South prevailed. No doubt Tourgée had witnessed enough interracial "rows" to concur with one vulnerable freedman who feared that without bureau support, "we might just as well be in the open field, and the hail beating down as big as hen's eggs on our heads."[12]

The local Democratic press interpreted every Republican reform, from establishment of public schools to passage of the Fifteenth Amendment, as an attack on the "crime" of owning property. The *Raleigh Daily Sentinel* suspected the Republican Party to be a cabal of Unionists and Radicals united "in order to vent their spleen upon some one for the loss of their property." Arguing for the organization of a "White man's party" to counter the "Black Vomito," the *North Carolina Progress* accused Republicans of having "thrown down the gauntlet in exhibiting readiness to rob the Southern landholder of his property by arbitrary, unconstitutional, savage legislation." Decrying the 1868 convention's proposal for free public schools, the *Greensboro Patriot* saw in the plan a scheme to "grind property-holders to powder."[13]

Tourgée was personally targeted in these newspaper attacks as an outspoken Radical Republican sensitive to African American desires for land-ownership. Moreover, he fueled their assaults by leniently excusing freedpeople's thievery, a habit, he claimed, they had been taught by their masters. Publishing his comment, the *Patriot* countered that "the judge was probably speaking from experience—as he claims to have been for years in the Federal corps of one of the most noted pillagers that ever robbed a henroost or made war upon the smokehouses and pantrys of defenseless women." In this context of heated public debate, Tourgée's novels, in their bid to make freedwomen citizens by acknowledging their grievances as legitimate, would inflame his fellow North Carolinians.[14]

From *Toinette* to *A Royal Gentleman*: A Reconstruction Revised

In addition to his political involvement, Tourgée was busy writing *Toinette*. The novel begins in antebellum days, focusing on Toinette's quadroon mother, Belle Lovett, once a mistress and slave on Lovett Lodge, a plantation owned by Arthur Lovett. Belle's seduction by Arthur and subsequent revenge upon him take place in two key, adjacent settings: the library and the secret room, which was built for Arthur and Belle's trysts. Although Arthur frees Belle and gives her a share of his vast estate, her manumission is later challenged in the state courts, and she is resold into slavery along with the three children she bore Arthur, including Toinette. Still later, Belle, along with Toinette, is bought by lawyer and nearby plantation owner Manuel Hunter and his son, Geoffrey, who do not know her real identity. An embittered Belle assumes a false identity as "Mabel" and works as their cook. Outraged by Arthur's intended marriage to his "pore [*sic*] white" neighbor Betty Certain, Belle prevents the marriage by killing Arthur for what she perceives to be his betrayal of her freedom and love, and then runs away. Actually Arthur had planned to marry Certain in order to ensure that his legacy to Belle and their children would be guaranteed if he should suddenly die. Unaware that Belle is the murderer, Certain agrees to carry out his will, if Belle can ever be located.

The Hunters acquire the depreciated Lovett plantation cheaply because of the murder. Knowing Arthur's intentions in his mysteriously lost will, the Hunter family is ever uncertain of their right of title. After Manuel Hunter sells Toinette to Geoffrey, Belle begins to stalk the plantation, disguised as a ghost. Outraged by seeing the pattern of servitude repeat with Toinette, Belle tries to kill both Geoffrey and Toinette, using the secret room as her base of operations. When Certain apprehends her, a repentant Belle learns the truth behind Arthur's intentions, realizes her error in murdering Arthur, and kills herself.

The novel's focus then shifts to Toinette, who becomes a wealthy woman by inheriting Lovett Lodge, upon her mother's death, although that legal claim is unrecognized by Geoffrey and other southerners. After Geoffrey Hunter abandons home to fight for the Confederacy, Toinette goes to Oberlin, Ohio, and delivers his child. Returning to Virginia to work in a Union hospital at City Point, Toinette hopes to reunite with Geoffrey. There, Toinette is reminded of her servitude when a blinded Geoffrey exposes her as his former slave. She nevertheless secures an operation to restore Geoffrey's sight. After the war, Geoffrey presses Toinette to resume their affair, but she refuses. He pursues Toinette, who flees north again, where she achieves a different kind of emancipation. Although Toinette is more than adequately supported by Lovett Lodge's profits, remitted to her by Certain, she becomes a successful chanteuse. Eventually, in abolitionist Boston, she and Geoffrey reunite. The shock of seeing Toinette perform onstage causes Geoffrey to again lose his sight. At this, Toinette marries him and happily tends him as his nurse.

In his revision Tourgée replicates *Toinette*'s story nearly word for word, making significant changes only at the end. He eliminated the last four chapters, which included, besides the nuptials, important scenes describing Toinette's successful postwar years as a celebrity chanteuse. The revised novel ends with Toinette's ringing personal declaration of independence from her former master in a closing letter to Geoffrey. The revision's letter emphasizes a greater egalitarian relationship imagined between Toinette and Geoffrey in the secret room. Still, Toinette leaves Geoffrey for a future life of very uncertain prospects and leaves the reader in the dark as to the future civic status of freedwomen.

America Declared:
Life, Liberty, and the Pursuit of Property

As jurist and attorney, Tourgée recognized the pivotal and long-standing importance of duty and property ownership to definitions of American citizenship. He made the issue of property ownership central to his novels, reflecting his Guilford neighbors' sentiments. The founders privileged property protection as a defining right of American citizens in a range of texts, from the Fifth Amendment in the Bill of Rights to James Madison's *Federalist No. 10*. Borrowing from the liberal political theorist John Locke, the founders understood property broadly as "that which men have in person as well as goods." As the "property" of God, men had a duty to unite with others to preserve "their lives, liberties, and estates."[15]

The contrary impulses to reform and to retrench operating within Tourgée's novels can be understood in light of the postwar crisis in the status of property and the consequent reaffirmations of its significance to American citizenship. The two novels were literary test cases for the politically divisive issue of whether the postwar understanding of citizenship continued to emphasize the importance of property ownership, with which it was traditionally associated. As part of a long string of legislation beginning in the 1790s which first opened the franchise to northern propertyless white men, the Reconstruction Amendments further deemphasized this association. As Eva Saks has summarized, in the immediate postwar period, white property was undermined by several key developments: the threat of land distribution, the fall in the value of land, the rendering of Confederate money as worthless, and the loss of slaves as property. With the last development, Saks points out, the "value of white skin dropped when black skin ceased to signify slave status." Clinging to what property they still possessed in land, the former Confederate masters were hostile to any Jeffersonian-inspired legislation that attempted to decouple the franchise from the requirement of landed property ownership. Nor were they tolerant of any attempt to expand the definition of national citizenship to include the former slaves or white women.[16]

The issue of property ownership especially helped shape the contours of Reconstruction in the Second Military District. Despite their Unionist leanings, white North Carolinians whose property was threatened bristled against the general feeling of angry entitlement, especially for land, expressed by freedpeople. North Carolinian ex-slaves had more than a simple interest in owning land; they felt, according to the Freedmen's Bureau assistant commissioner, that they had "a certain right to the property of their former masters, that they have earned it." Indeed, historians have shown the importance of land acquisition and ownership for black North Carolinians, particularly antebellum free people, to achieve wealth, education, and social status and to satisfy their political and entrepreneurial ambitions. Yet land-ownership eluded many black North Carolinians. Other North Carolinians, including President Andrew Johnson, opposed their dreams of a federal land redistribution policy.[17]

Against this backdrop of great real estate ferment, Tourgée's novels complemented the judicial trend toward expanding legal definitions of property beyond tangible objects to encompass and protect valuable interests. By the nineteenth century's end, the number of exceptions made to a Blackstonian definition of property as an "absolute dominion over things" necessitated a rethinking of property as a "set of legal relations among persons." This capacious understanding of property would soon evolve to encompass anything that had determinable value in the marketplace, including a person's right to the fruits of his or her labor and, in its final form, a person's right to labor. The Fourteenth Amendment's 1868 ratification and changes in equity jurisprudence furthered this trend toward the creation of nonphysical forms of property. In particular, the amendment's due process clause, protecting citizens against deprivation of life, liberty, or property by the state, was quickly taken up by litigants seeking to protect both new and old forms of wealth. Several significant court cases arose and treatises were written in the 1870s which helped reconceptualize property to include goodwill, rights of accession, trade secrets, and trademarks.[18]

In this context, the *Plessy* jurists would set a precedent by trying to contain the meaning of white selfhood by fixing it as an object of property that could be measured by lineage, blood, and appearance. For decades after *Plessy*, southern courts strove to make whiteness an object of property in cases involving defamation, miscegenation, and writs of mandamus to enforce school segregation. Yet the changing meaning of property as a set of relations undermined their endeavors, and they had to recognize racial identity as a form of new property, subject to community prejudice, and therefore alienable. The courts ironically helped destabilize white selfhood. Their efforts to establish an inherent identity for whiteness led them to be "the conduit through which entitlement of whiteness emerged as the impertinent possession of an imagined community." The process of their deliberations inevitably demanded proof of white identity that required the community's consideration and thus paradoxically produced the means for misrecognition and passing. In his novels Tourgée would highlight reputation as well as several other new properties for his heroines to own, but first he built his plots around more conventional means of accessing land.[19]

I Bequeath, I Buy, and I Do:
Traditional Routes to Land-Ownership

The foundation of Tourgée's Reconstruction vision in both novels was land-ownership for freedwomen, necessitating a restructuring of gender and class relations within the patriarchal household. The radicalism of this vision was its emphasis on women claiming economic, political, and social powers over their former masters, many of whom were temporarily disfranchised for having earlier held Confederate offices. Both novels set up scenarios in which Belle and her daughter Toinette should inherit Lovett Lodge. Yet plot machinations also foil their attempt to reveal just how fragile legal mechanisms were to inherit property for slaves and women. While Belle is manumitted and leaves Lovett Lodge under Arthur Lovett's will, her manumission is challenged and the will is later lost, driving her to desperate acts. Toinette fares better. Her claim to the plantation is upheld by virtue of inheritance from her mother and from her father's recently found will, but pressing circumstances force her to flee. Although she reaps the benefits of the plantation's profits, Toinette never actually sets up residence; in both novels, she remains an absentee owner.

Tourgée strengthens Toinette's inheritance claims to Lovett Lodge through three methods: he reconstructs her class position, making her an educated lady worthy of the claim, while forging an alliance between her and Certain, who is made executor of the estate after Arthur's death; he reconstructs the postwar gender roles of black veterans to further topple the white master as traditional owner from the household hierarchy; finally, from the alliance between Certain and Toinette, he advocates "joint tenancy" reforms in property ownership, which correspond to his work toward building a class-based interracial coalition among North Carolina Republicans. While running for election to the state's 1868 constitutional convention, for example, Tourgée tried to strengthen democracy by advocating reforms in areas including apprenticeship laws, debt collection, the poll tax, women's rights, criminal proceedings, and homesteading for black residents, all of which appealed to a broadened constituency. His novel's bold maneuvers radically reconceptualize freedwomen's role as profitable landowners, and they constitute one of Tourgée's most compelling claims to greatness as a visionary reformer.[20]

Critical to Tourgée's elevation of Toinette from slave mistress to an educated and refined independent citizen—married or not—was a radical reconstruction of southern class positions for black and white women and of race relations. Her mother, Belle, was raised to have "all the accomplishments of a lady" by her master, Arthur, who becomes *her* "servant of servants." Likewise, Toinette's claims to respect are founded upon her own elevated status as a lady. Her declaration to Geoffrey of independence from him was an inherently class-based appeal, nurtured by her upbringing as his "protégée." While a slave on the Hunter plantation, Toinette is "pet chattel," indulged and educated. Not obligated to labor physically, she is given "next to nothing to do, and every possible liberty." Once Toinette inherits Lovett Lodge from Belle (whose own name suggests the southern debutante), Certain insists that Toinette live "as a lady ought to live," with all of life's fineries, derived from the plantation's profits. Toinette can pass in white face so well that Certain declares, "you orter have been my daughter." Toinette's enhanced class status allows readers to see Geoffrey's pursuit as trespassing upon a lady's right to privacy. Toinette rebukes Geoffrey: "You would never dream of intruding upon one who you would term 'a lady' after she had declined an interview, but you cannot regard your freedwoman as having even the paltry right of refusing her presence, when you choose to demand it." Typical of white southerners' hostility to freedwomen's assertions, Geoffrey underscores race boundaries in his perception of class pretensions: "Freedom does not make you white any more than Lee's surrender made me black. You are not a lady and need not try to act the part of one." Yet Toinette persists in envisioning relationships with white men based upon cooperation and equal opportunity for aspiring freedwomen.[21]

Toinette's ambitions reflect ideals found within the historical record of black female activism. This reconstruction of Toinette's class position made black female Americans visible. Toinette's class status, literacy level, and expectation of full civil rights resembled North Carolinians born in freedom. One real-life counterpart near Greensboro was Hillsborough's Blanche V. Harris, an Oberlin graduate, prominent educator, and reformer. Employed by the American Missionary Association (AMA) and, later, the Society of Friends, Harris was on her way from Ohio to teach North Carolina freedpeople when she was forcibly ejected from the ladies' car. Harris then initiated a complaint to the Greensboro agent of the Freedmen's Bureau, an action preceding Tourgée's publication of *Toinette* by seven years. By demanding her civil rights under Reconstruction, Harris was, like many other black women, a catalyst for the initial wave of Jim Crow legislation.[22]

These black women, representing the emergent, reform-minded middle class, brought the bulk of suits challenging racial discrimination in public transit in the years before Jim Crow. While Tourgée contrives the first version of his story to permit Toinette to ride first class, he also has her utilize her class position to challenge the violation of her civil rights, much as Plessy would later do. Moreover, as a light-skinned African American like Plessy, Toinette would more plausibly be in a position to own the plantation. Black Tar Heel landowners were characterized by four attributes: they were mulatto, they lived in urban areas, they had known antebellum freedom, and they had occupations other than farming. In fact, in 1870 roughly 4,000 black North Carolinians owned real estate; among heads of households, mulatto men were about four times more likely to be landowners than were the state's darker-skinned African Americans.[23]

Tourgée declared in his preface to *A Royal Gentleman* that he had written *Toinette* partly to prevent upcountry yeoman farmers from being "unfairly massed" with those designated as "poor white" and "white trash," when "in fact they ranged from this type up through the better class of 'croppers'—the *metayers* of the South." Indeed, to help Toinette make the transition from owned property to property owner, Tourgée relied on the white, nonslaveholding Betty Certain, an example of individuals who have also been traditionally overlooked by historians as agents of Reconstruction. Although the narrator classifies her as a "poor white," the local doctor reminds the Hunters that Certain, like Toinette, possesses "a very *un*-certain position in society," which soon gains her "*entrée*" to Lovett Lodge, making her "a sort of privileged character here ever afterwards." Like Toinette and Belle, Certain enjoys a flexible class position in society, to live "out of her sphere," made evident by her sudden ability to change dialects, revealing a "diction" which "showed something of the culture her words implied." Certain used the Lovett library extensively, again like Toinette and Belle, yet her name reaches back to her grandfather, who began life as an indentured servant, soon rising to social and financial success like Woolson's once-indentured Minorcans.[24]

Certain has a depth and vitality that goes beyond Thanet's celebrations of Arkansan yeowomen's independence because of her cross-gendered as well as cross-classed position. Categorized as "a strange compound," she is described emphatically in terms that override her gender to accord with her position as plantation overseer: of "a lean, muscular build," Certain, in her cumbersome boots, "walked on with a heavy, deliberate stride, like a man" about the plantation. Recalling the same strong capability as her great-grandfather, the "right-hand of the Earl," she evokes awe as "the neighboring planters looked on in amazement."[25]

As her name implies, Certain operates with a sure-handedness that enables her to rescue Lovett Lodge from wartime destruction while never surrendering her own family's small tract of adjacent land. She is one of the few owners who, during the war, had the foresight to realize that "slave property was a dead loss" but that the real estate market would soon recover when the fighting stopped. Employing only "hired hands," this advocate of free-labor ideology soon doubles Toinette's acreage with the best land in the country. Certain's abilities surpass Geoffrey's and Arthur's capacities as economic managers, making Toinette the "equal of Geoffrey Hunter in everything else, and more than equal in wealth." Her shrewd management of Toinette's income strengthened Toinette's assertions of her rights to citizenship. Like many freedwomen, Toinette sought to redefine the nature of her labors and her relationship with a former master. Tourgée's novelistic experiment in land redistribution resulted in women property owners with a solid claim of equality to back them up.[26]

The two novels stage Toinette's protracted negotiations with Certain, which underwrite her freedom. Certain reminds Toinette that "you must have money to live on, and I must stay here and make it," and, through her factors, assures her that she may "draw on me through them for whatever funds you may require." Certain's accomplishments as confidante and estate manager for both Arthur and Toinette match her success as plantation "overseer." The property never is rightfully or legally Geoffrey Hunter's when it passes from Arthur Lovett to Belle and then to Certain to manage as executor. To compensate the Hunters for their faulty title, she asserts her power by insisting, "I will repay you out of such portion of the estate as falls to my share." Her earnings and right to title outstrip the white master and nearly make him into an object of charity: "The poor white woman was determined that it should be as she decided, or she would not move in the matter at all. So the young aristocrat became the object of her magnanimity." Certain's yeoman business acumen and gumption, evidenced by her occasional lapses into upcountry dialect, coupled with her education, make the farm successful, allowing her to stand up to Geoffrey. Moreover, Tourgée makes it clear that this strength of character was as independent of her class as it is of gender: "She would have been strong-minded enough had her station in life been different."[27]

Certain's spectacular successes as master are but one instance of how Tourgée capitalized on postwar gender relations turned upside down. Her actions are patterned on the many women who, since the war's onset, had had to run plantations in place of their warring husbands. Yet, as Thavolia Glymph has shown, with emancipation, the plantation home, as workplace, was restructured, and relationships between former slaves and former mistresses necessarily changed; one startling example was that white (usually elite) women often depended on black women to be their employers as they sought to eke out a living. Certain's persistent cross-class devotion to a freed black woman at the expense of the former white master shows how far Tourgée was willing to press the boundaries of postwar change.[28]

Certain's gender transgressions invest her character with a strength and integrity that defy stereotypes of Tar Heel women as "slatternly" and indecent, propagated by contemporary observers, though her actions draw on the North Carolina yeomanry's frontier traditions of rough justice. Possessing a "certain masculinity of appearance," she is fiercely protective in her love for Arthur and Toinette. Armed with an ax, she wounds a vigilante whose band threatens Arthur because of his relationship with Belle, and this rescue of Arthur wins his admiration and an offer of marriage. Later, she wrestles Toinette's attacker to the ground. Her severely masculinized words and deeds make her appear as a caricature of a white man, so that the "astounded" Geoffrey must conclude, "There was no chance of patronizing this woman. . . . She was evidently the master of the situation." Much like Thanet's cross-class, gender-inverted women who show up weak white masters, Certain's unnatural masculinization bolsters Geoffrey's unnatural emasculinization.[29]

Certain's seemingly topsy-turvy character reflects that of many poor women whose gendered behaviors were intertwined with their attitudes about race. In fact, the Freedmen's Bureau records from Greensboro contain cases of violent conduct by poor white women. For example, Lyda Thompson and Letta Eckel were each fined five dollars for disorderly conduct after a physical altercation. Thompson told an intervening freedman that "no damnd upper country nigger should run over her." Thompson's comments recall Certain's own ambivalent racial consciousness, defined by competition with freedpeople; Certain, for example, defensively asserts to Geoffrey, "You think a 'poor white' has little right to know more than a nigger." Certain's gender inversion complements her racialized role in the Lovett household, and her masculinity highlights Toinette's genteel femininity, an attribute typically denied in representations of black women.[30]

Certain's aggressive character is visible in Tourgée's bid to reconstruct gender roles in the southern piedmont. Other local newspaper writers risked incendiary portrayals of forward southern women and dangerous sexuality itself for partisan political purposes. Embattled meanings of masculinity were at the heart of midcentury codes of honor, and they came under renewed scrutiny after Appomattox. Local conservative newsmen had long attempted to turn Tourgée into a Republican symbol who

FIGURE 6. "A Split among the Truly Loyal Radicals!," *Greensboro Patriot*, 24 September 1868.

conspires with an emasculated Negro population. The *Greensboro Patriot* had ridiculed Tourgée's unsuccessful congressional bids against the uneducated William Henderson, who had recently been falsely indicted for stealing a mule. A *Patriot* cartoon featured Tourgée atop a pig with a caricatured freedman, proclaiming, "Hold on, little 'manhood,' we'll beat the mu-el man!" (Fig. 6). The mule, a traditional symbol of miscegenation, was depicted as an object of desire for both candidates.[31]

Tourgée also scrutinized postwar meanings of masculinity, contrasting Reconstruction's challenge with the regression toward conservatism. In his fiction and speeches, Tourgée deployed a gendered and racialized discourse to discredit Confederate veterans like Geoffrey Hunter. Tourgée's efforts joined those of such freedmen as Frederick Douglass and John Clifford, who championed black veterans' war service as the dues of citizenship. In his notorious series of "C" letters to the *Greensboro North State*, he attacked Democratic candidates for a state superior judgeship, Daniel G. Fowle and David Schenck, by blasting the wartime careers of these "thirteenth hour" Confederates. His scathing portrayal apparently provoked Fowle to assault him physically, an attack which editors then used to portray Tourgée as a cowed, bloody victim. In contrast, Tourgée began an 1868 speech by recalling the "dusky martyrs" of Fort Pillow who taught the "noble lesson of manhood." He saw the Fifteenth Amendment as "the recognition of the rights of manhood," which was to be "the crowning glory of civilization."[32]

To underscore the valor of black soldiers, Tourgée created characters like Toinette's brother, the intrepid color-bearer Fred Lovett, who "proved himself worthy of a knighthood" when he wrapped the flag around his body rather than surrender at Fort Pillow. Tellingly, Fred's body is found on the field with his deed of manumission, a photograph of Lincoln, and a copy of the Emancipation Proclamation stained with his own blood. Although Tourgée demurred, "there may have been no Fort Pillow at all, in fact," he inserted a newspaper account of the outrage directly in the text, further proving his reliance on journalists to authoritatively reconstruct "manhood" to include the valor of both races. In Sergeant Lovett, the colonel's "dead favorite," the ideals of high moral fiber and physical bravery reach an apogee. Tourgée compares Fred's supreme sacrifice with Geoffrey's bravery at Fort Stedman to emphasize the latter's lack of moral courage: Geoffrey would "rather have faced Fort Hell at its hottest" than marry Toinette and risk nuptial scandal. He imagines he can rely on his war record, as "the man who was first over the walls of Fort Steadman [*sic*]," but ultimately "he lacked nerve." Toinette's definition of manhood, the hero who would defy the gossips and marry her, is set against Geoffrey's definition as the hero who leads the charging crowd. Lamenting Geoffrey's cowardice regarding marriage to her, Toinette asks with "something like contempt": "Where was his manhood, that he should sit down like a child and say, 'I would, but I dare not?'" Her critique reflects a postwar reassessment of southern honor and masculinity, measured against the defeated Confederate veteran.[33]

Tourgée crafted the alliance between Toinette and Certain to show the common interests in property ownership of the yeoman class and the freedpeople. In accord with Reconstruction's reality, Tourgée's novels demonstrated a successful cooperative venture in which white women also gained by freedpeople's emancipation. The Republican Party's appeal during Reconstruction was based on an alignment of the lower classes of both races, and subsequent Democratic exertions to restore a hierarchy of elite North Carolinians to power were as much class based as racist. Western white yeomen were justifiably wary of the labors of eastern Democratic elites to build a coalition centered on white supremacy and a qualified suffrage that would exclude unpropertied white men. It was this commonality of interests that Tourgée the politician found so appealing in building a local constituency. Tourgée, the 1868 Constitutional Convention's candidate, borrowed the rhetoric of slavery to ally freedpeople and yeomen against the aristocracy's interests: "Do you choose to governed [sic] yourselves or be ruled by those who still crave the name of 'master!' . . . Will the 'new people' have a 'new state,' or the old one, patched up, with its whips and stocks, its oppressive system of taxation and its tyrannic landed aristocracy!"[34]

In the context of Toinette and Certain's relationship, Tourgée first imagined the benefits of joint property ownership, an option women's rights advocates wanted for married people and a cheaper alternative to individual home ownership for freedpeople. At first "exhilarated by the air of liberty," freed North Carolinians saw "the property accumulated by their labor as in part their own, and demanded a share of it" as they looked to form cooperative ventures. Belle shares this conviction, as evidenced by her determination to keep the deed to Lovett Lodge. Upon Arthur's death, Certain is made the estate's executor, with the understanding that she and the displaced Belle each own half. After Belle's death, Toinette becomes heir, to whom Certain explains, "The lawyers tell me that we are what they call joint-tenants of it all, with equal rights and powers over it." Together, Certain, a yeoman farmer, and Toinette, a freedwoman, realize what women's rights advocates had been demanding without success for four decades.[35]

In both novels, Belle and Toinette's bonds to Certain supersede their business partnership. Even when Certain discovers that Belle murdered her fiancé, Arthur, she overcomes her vengeful rage. Feeling nothing but pity and kindness upon learning of Belle's misguided motive, she earnestly goes beyond "my duty to act towards you" as executor by protecting her and trying to prevent her suicide. Certain intends to join Toinette in the North once the Lovett plantation can be sold at great profit for "in any event I meant to keep with you." Of their status as women, she avers, "Thank God we are—so we can trust each other." When Certain reminds Toinette that "the 'poor-white' and the slave are too nigh of kin to marry," she hints that an almost incestuous familial tie, indicative of a long line of miscegenation, bonds the women. Moreover, the success of this bond signals the reconstruction of property relations. While Toinette never resides in Lovett Lodge as its recognized owner, *Toinette*'s ending offers a Reconstruction vision with the planter class toppled through equitable distribution of land for other freed North Carolinians. The "princely domains" of Lovett Lodge and the Hunter home are carved up into the "homesteads of thrifty Carpet-baggers and the truck-patches of aspiring Freedmen." The South, with the recognized presence of carpetbaggers, appeared truly poised for resettlement.[36]

Toinette's "post nubila" ending highlighted Tourgée's even more radical proposition for securing the rights of African Americans: intermarriage. In sanctioning the former master's marriage to the ex-slave, Tourgée suggested that Toinette has the right to possess Geoffrey Hunter and make a wifely claim for his love. Tourgée's reliance on the ties between familial relations and property ownership was not fortuitous, however, for the marriage contract had long been the chief legal mechanism for transmitting property. Moreover, the period in which Tourgée was writing was known as the Age of Contract and, not coincidentally, as the Age of Realism. As an attorney and writer who offered a realistic vision of postwar life, Tourgée turned easily to the revised possibilities to be found in contract law, from the fields of marriage to wage earning, as a means of improving the freedwomen's lives on economic, social, and political fronts.[37]

Many North Carolinian women recognized that marriage provided a means to increase their authority within the state, and Tourgée grasped its distinctive potential to restructure postwar southern households. Precisely because of its capacity to fix legal statuses and create a property relation, marriage came under renewed scrutiny at this time by white southerners. For freedwomen keen on destabilizing slavery's traditions, marriage became critical as both a civil right and as a means to access various social privileges. Yet the benefits of marriage clashed with the postwar emphasis on marriage as a means to prevent freedwomen from threatening civil society. Bureau agents routinely considered freedwomen's marital status, a relation they actively promoted, in deciding their appeals. The gains afforded by marriage were also offset by the state-enforced subordination and dispossession all women encountered as wives. Often victims of sexual abuse by their former masters, many North Carolinian freedwomen shared Toinette's plight, if not her material advantages. Appealing to the Freedmen's Bureau, these women suffered in their domestic relations with both white and black men. Their complaints in Greensboro ranged from abandonment to demands for child support, and they also went to the courts, pressing charges against men for physical assault.[38]

Recognizing women's disempowered position, Tourgée tried to help married North Carolinian women who resembled Toinette in their dependent status as *femme coverts*. Common law required a husband to represent and support his wife in return for the use of her real property and absolute rights in her "personality" and broadly defined "services." As a *femme covert*, she was entitled to only dower rights, that is, one-third of her husband's estate was available for her use during her lifetime. North Carolina's 1872 legislation, later tightened by an 1876 State Supreme Court ruling in *Pippen v. Wesson*, curtailed the extent of married women's property rights. *Pippin* reaffirmed the common law practice of restricting a married woman's power to contract.[39]

With his usual reformist zeal, Tourgée drew on judicial interpretations of civil rights legislation to work for women's rights because he was, as he put it to a friend in New York, "in favor of enlarging the sphere of woman's capacity, to the utmost limit of her preparation and capacity." In particular, Tourgée helped draft the 1868 Reconstruction Constitution, which included a provision for joint property reform. This provision also protected women from their husbands' debts while granting them full inheritance rights, providing there were no children. Tourgée drew on the reform he helped create in proposing marriage as a means for Toinette to inherit Lovett Lodge. Yet the capaciousness of Tourgée's vision within *Toinette* is constrained by social and legal boundaries that sought to curtail the power of marriage.[40]

Many white North Carolinians used prohibitions on interracial marriage to repair damaged, racialized ideals of manhood and to resist Reconstruction's legal rights claims. Emily Van Tassel shows how white southerners attempted to restore the antebellum "moral economy of dependency" that suffused patriarchal households and formed a model for the slaveholding South by dramatizing their tautological reasoning: "interracial marriage and the social equality it was made to represent was used to forestall access by blacks to a whole range of public rights and privileges because such access, according to its opponents' beliefs, must ultimately lead to intermarriage." Although statutes against interracial marriage had existed since 1661, debate and legislation intensified during the postwar crisis in the status of property. White North Carolinians used a gendered discourse to dramatize what they saw as the dangerous manifestations of social equality resulting from integrated public schools and universal manhood suffrage. Invoking the Fourteenth Amendment, Freedmen's Bureau agents overrode local resistance to enforce the issuing of marriage licenses to interracial couples. However, in 1868, following the end of the federal presence in North Carolina, legislators acted with impunity to strengthen laws against miscegenation throughout the postwar South.[41]

Beginning in the 1870s, white southern legislatures and courts added to this anxious atmosphere by regulating the status of the marriage contract. Miscegenation law, according to Eva Saks, governed the marriage contract (and, by extension, inheritance and legitimacy) and "upheld the purity of the body politic through its constitution of a symbolic prohibition against the dangerous mixing of 'white blood' and 'black blood,' casting social practices as biological essences." By representing Toinette as nearly white skinned yet fractionally black in blood, Tourgée invoked the "anxiety about representation, the body, ownership and reproduction" that Saks claims is inherent in miscegenation discourse.[42]

Tourgée highlighted Toinette's dilemma in the novel's first footnote:

Nothing else appearing, the fact of slavery within three generations made the fairest Saxon, in the eye of the law, a "colored person." ... the law ... prevails in nearly all of the States, both Northern and Southern, prohibiting the marriage of persons of colored blood with whites, and presuming all to be colored who have more than one-sixteenth of negro or Indian blood. It would seem that Toinette did not fall within this category, in strictness, but the fact that she had been a slave fixed her status in his mind as clearly as if she had borne the features of the despised race.[43]

Toinette's ability to pass successfully as the white widow, "Mrs. Lovett," and then to become Mrs. Geoffrey Hunter proves the limits of miscegenation law to stabilize property in race. Physically, she possessed the "property" of whiteness, but the law's genealogical search to determine whether a "crime of blood" had been committed was the equivalent of a title search used to deny her ownership.

Toinette's problematic racial status points to the difficulty of relying on legal solutions such as antimiscegenation statutes or segregated schools to stabilize racial identity as a fixed category of meaning. Their inadequacy was made clear early through the press's rising hysteria that perceived any Reconstruction attempts to amend laws as potentially miscegenistic. Hostile Democratic editors in North Carolina recast political issues swirling around the proposed Reconstruction Constitution, such as the establishment of public education, as having calculated miscegenistic repercussions. The *Raleigh Daily Sentinel* published an 1868 series of tracts, "Thoughts for the People," which culminated in an appeal to white mothers to resist, or otherwise "you surrender your little daughter ... *into the embraces of a barbarous negro!*" Such shrill rhetoric forced some members of the constitution's drafting committee, of which Tourgée was a member, to issue their own tract assuring voters that neither integrated schools nor the militia, and certainly not intermarriage, were "encouraged," despite Radical Republican influence: "All these matters are left now, as they always have been . . . to be regulated by the representatives of the people in the General Assembly." In July 1874, the *Patriot* reported that a "colored" Republican, John H. Williamson, introduced a resolution that urged his fellow congressmen to vote for "such a bill as will secure equal civil and political rights AND AGAINST ALL BILLS TENDING TO AN ENFORCEMENT OF SOCIAL EQUALITY," which was hailed as thankful proof that not all Republicans favored social equality. The following year the *Daily Sentinel*, again targeting North Carolinian white women, used miscegenation fears to defeat the Reconstruction Constitution. The editors revived the fear of social equality by reprinting an 1868 overwrought appeal from the *North Carolina Statesville American* that addressed the "Ladies," who "more than any others have a deep interest in *voting down the Constitution.*" Urging readers to choose between the "white or the black man's party," the *Sentinel* editors then warned, "There is no middle ground. You must fight with us, or go over to the enemy or *run.*"[44]

Tourgée and other Reconstruction era writers, however, showed that there was a middle ground and that it was very accommodating to the work of resisting segregation. Booker T. Washington, ever pressed by the demands of fund-raising for Tuskegee, found himself in transit most of the time. He unwittingly revealed in his preface to *Up from Slavery* that "much of what I have said has been written on board trains, or at hotels, or railroad stations while I have been waiting for trains," demonstrating that even from the humiliating circumstances of segregation, an African American could articulate the cause against Jim Crow. While disavowing social equality, Washington and others were persuasive regarding the mutual benefits from continued interracial cooperation. Following Tourgée, Washington offered several examples of racial identity's social, alien, and arbitrary nature that he experienced when he traveled.[45]

As the political divide was increasingly drawn along racial and gendered lines, the press used miscegenation discourse to slander Tourgée for his interest in freedwomen. When the Tourgées legally adopted a young freed girl, Adaline Patillo, the *Daily Sentinel* sneered, "This is generous in the Judge—very generous! Is Tourgée a married man?" Yet Tourgée was not above publicly accusing a critic, such as Gus Atkinson, "sometime mayor of Milton," of being a "practical miscegenationist" in order to defame him. When it was revealed that Tourgée wrote *Toinette*, the *Baltimore Sun* sniffed, "When we say that . . . the Southern press and people, according to his own account, denounce the book as 'pestiferous and incendiary' because it leans to miscegenation, we think we have said all that is necessary to indicate its character." The *Charlotte Observer* was less tactful when it shrieked: "The real purpose of Tourgée was to POPULARIZE INTERMARRIAGE BETWEEN THE RACES IN NORTH CAROLINA."[46]

Other reviewers, including those writing for southern newspapers, shared that conclusion but did not condemn it. They either lightly passed over—or even singled out for praise—the novel's interracial marriage. The *Nation* felt that the novel's happy ending "impaired" only the "literary unity of the book." The *Nashville Christian Advocate* mildly noted that *Toinette* ends "as every orthodox novel must wind up, with matrimony— only the peculiarity in this case is that the mulatto women gets wedded to her old master." The *Atlanta Methodist Advocate* opined more boldly, "We have nothing to say about amalgamation, only this, that marriage is more honorable than adultery. . . . If white men prefer colored women to those of their own race, they ought to be compelled by law to marry them." For these writers, evidently, the marriage institution redeemed any purported disgrace between the races.[47]

If not as intentionally as the *Charlotte Observer* suggested, Tourgée's novels did problematize the logic behind antimiscegenation statutes by dramatizing the gap between social and legal definitions of race. Tourgée imposed certain qualifications on Geoffrey and Toinette's union that blunt the ending's daring. These conditions confuse distinctions between love and slavery, a persistent connection made by those who opposed the subordination of wives. Although women's rights advocates had long drawn a parallel between the wife's servitude and the slave's, congressional Republicans limited the scope of emancipation to a question of race. Despite "earnings" legislation that sought to give women ownership over their wages outside marriage, judicial opinions interpreted these statutes to strictly limit wives' liberty to contract to within the bonds of marriage. Read almost as Tourgée's own capitulation to local antimiscegenation law, a measure of servitude is upheld in the first novel as the precondition for Geoffrey's marriage to Toinette.[48]

In the novel, servitude's obligations both create and conceal Toinette's marriage, revealing the gendered, racialized meaning of freedom. When Geoffrey finds Toinette again, she is on stage, performing under a new "master," and when he hears her sing, he jumps up and shouts her name. Amazingly, amid the applause Toinette can distinguish his voice. This moment of aural recognition shocks him back into sudden blindness. Geoffrey's convenient disability fulfills the ideal of political equality that Tourgée would argue for Plessy: "Justice is pictured blind and her daughter, the Law, ought at least to be color-blind." Geoffrey's impairment requires Toinette to nurse him again, which she instinctively does, as his lover and former slave, abandoning her newfound successful career: "Meantime, the *artiste* was transformed into the nurse, and now the training of the camp hospital came more into play. . . . How she thanked God for the training he had given her!" The problems of social equality are circumvented in accord with the trend in segregationist thinking, which customarily allowed African American nurses to accompany white children when working as their servants. Although Toinette could ride with their son in the white car, she would still not be permitted to ride with the adult Geoffrey in the same railway car; nevertheless, his nearly infantilizing impairment legitimates her required presence in a service capacity.[49]

Tourgée's radical vision of a blissful interracial marriage is compromised by Toinette's and Geoffrey's roles. On the one hand, Toinette assumes a masterly authority in that she insists on taking Geoffrey to *her* home. Situated in a Bostonian "leafy suburb with springy turf and cool breezes," the "cosy" home was purchased with the income from Toinette's singing career. The bucolic setting confirms her success in achieving ownership of property and herself. Ensconced in her authoritative domain, the helpless Geoffrey must wait "with a look of wondering worship" for *her* return. On the other hand, Toinette can only be imagined as a wife to Geoffrey if she is a full-time nurse. The duty and labor due her husband define the terms of her domesticated position. The love that redeems the inequality of gender relations ultimately reasserts the authority—albeit now crippled—of southern white men. Tourgée's vision thus harbors southern Democratic sentiments in its hierarchical subordination of women to white masters. Through women's devotion, the reconstructed fate of the blinded Geoffrey extends the life of veterans like Woolson's half-blind Phil Romer, literally swamped by defeat and disability. Ironically, the master's disability enables his empowerment. Accommodating the scores of disabled veterans of postbellum days, the white man as literal patient could legally be served by the black mistress.[50]

Toinette's relation to her master as first his slave and then his wife also blurred long-standing legal distinctions between a wage contract and marriage. Indeed, the nineteenth-century bourgeois ideology of separate spheres originated in liberal political economy, whose theorists had established that the wage contract necessarily enabled household dependencies. By the time Tourgée's novel appeared, labor reformers and many Republicans were using an implicitly racialized logic to maintain these distinctions. As Yankee wives increasingly became hirelings, their commodified labor conflicted with their husbands' property right to their services, a situation the courts' narrow interpretations of postwar earnings laws had hardly remedied. Their newfound contract rights left these women doubly burdened: bound to the marketplace under a system of wage slavery, they also remained bound to their husbands without clear ownership of their labor or themselves. This was a dilemma Toinette, even as a Bostonian, wage-earning *artiste*, confronted when she married. North Carolina freedwomen, however, were not permitted a choice between housework and wage work. Alarmed at the growing presence of camp refugees, Freedmen's Bureau agents demanded that their children be bound out to "relieve the women of their burden so that they may work for themselves." *Toinette*'s ending revitalizes the antebellum hierarchy of dutiful subordination between the genders as well as between the races to fit Reconstruction realities and reflects the extent to which the gendered roots of Reconstructionist thinking were "Redemptionist."[51]

In *A Royal Gentleman*, Tourgée jettisoned intermarriage as a solution for property acquisition. A year later the U.S. Supreme Court would hold in *Pace v. Alabama* that the state's punishment of interracial fornication more harshly than intraracial fornication was constitutional under the Fourteenth Amendment because it punished black and white violators equally. The court's logic set up an important precedent for the rhetoric of Jim Crow segregation. With antimiscegenation laws and rulings in place firmly enough that North Carolinians relied upon their precedence to enforce segregation statutes, Tourgée could no longer offer interracial marriage as a solution for freedwomen seeking to obtain their rights, including property ownership. *A Royal Gentleman*'s outcome questions the ability for freedwomen to claim a reputation based on the contemporary tenets of "honorable womanhood," that is, that they were women deserving of respect and entitled to marry white men.

Working for a Song:
Claiming the Fruits of Her Labor

Drawing on the core tenets of Republican ideology, the ending of Tourgée's first novel featured Toinette as a successful citizen and worker. The penultimate chapters linger over her profitable rise to stardom as a chanteuse, as she claims the right to the fruits of her labor, one of the new forms of property. Property's redefinition as something more abstract than land began with Justice Stephen J. Field's famous dissent in the 1873

Slaughterhouse Cases, which Tourgée drew upon in his *Plessy* brief. After the *Slaughterhouse* decision, jurists increasingly argued that the notion of a worker's capacity to labor or a capitalist's entitlement to profit was the core of a citizen's personal rights and freedom. Crucial to this accommodation was the belief that wage laborers, through their labor, would become the petty entrepreneurs of the Republican ideal. Foregrounded in the congressional debates surrounding the Thirteenth Amendment was a discourse not only about the amendment's abolition of slavery, but also about what constituted fair and just labor relations, including respect for the laborer's "right to the fruits of his labor"—a right that was linked to the right to acquire property. Provisional Governor Holden defined freedom in his first address to North Carolina's freedpeople: "Freedom does not mean that one may do as he pleases, but that everyone may, by industry, frugality, and temperance, improve his condition and enjoy the fruits of his own labors, so long as he obeys the laws."[52]

Tourgée shared the belief that laborers' rights to the products of their work was a property right worth protecting. He framed his political rhetoric around the rights of laborers pitted against those of property holders: "Shall the poor man's labor be taxed four or five percent, and the rich man's property but one-third of one percent? . . . Shall the honest and capable, though landless voter, be allowed to hold offices of trust and emolument, or shall that privilege be granted only to the lord of the barren acres?" In his 1868 Constitutional Convention speech, Tourgée declared that the war had been "not simply between slavery and the non-enslavement of that race, but between the principles of free labor, free speech and free truth." In both addresses, Tourgée drew on the core tenets of Republican ideology, even as the labor movement's agitation revised it into a reactionary defense of liberalism.[53]

Tourgée remained true to his faith in free labor by championing the place of freedwomen in the labor force. Married to an independent-minded woman who managed his finances and much else, Tourgée, in 1878, argued easily for women's rights to labor outside the home. He successfully defended Tabitha Holton's right to practice law by arguing that as courts held the term "free white" to include "free black" after emancipation, they should also include women, for whom a similar emancipation was taking place that needed to be recognized. Invoking Toinette's experience using the same racially enslaving language that he would repeat in his *Plessy* brief, Tourgée condemned the severity of public reaction against the idea of a businesswoman to be equivalent to putting "a brand like a spot of leprosy" upon her. Tourgée met "chivalric" objections by arguing that by "debarring a woman from any honorable means of self-support" adds "ten-fold to the power of temptation." Tourgée's ideal was not entirely fictional. Within North Carolina black women did achieve a measure of success as entrepreneurial business owners, even while black men were losing their businesses.[54]

Similarly, Toinette never actually faces poverty. Her ability to work and her mother's inheritance of the Lovett plantation provide the means for her to leave Geoffrey and support her four-year-old son, the fruit of another kind of labor. Passing as a white widow in the North, Toinette is reborn; the "menial nature" had "died in her soul," replaced by "the free woman, pure and noble, self-reliant and brave." When Toinette looks for work, her "unintended heritage" of "scholarly ancestors" makes it "instinctively" plain that she was not meant for "any of the thousand and one ordinary 'Wants-Female' that grace our daily papers." Yet she casts about for employment "in the way of doing, achieving, something for herself" which lies at the heart of Republican ideology.[55]

In the Republican tradition of the artisan-entrepreneur who owns the products of her labor, Toinette possesses the "true spirit of the artist," recalling the independence and craftsmanship of Woolson's African American "Cokena" artist. Hardly the typical wage laborer selling her right to work, Toinette becomes a "musical celebrity," performing with "all the perfection and finish which high art could give to native genius," which assures her of further financial independence. Although her racial identity is understandably masked to some northerners, it is not to Tourgée's readers, allowing Toinette to join a nineteenth-century national tradition of skilled, entrepreneurial African American women—a tradition unlike the usual categorization of black women's work as exclusively abolitionist and reform oriented. Through their writing about their self-supporting work as honorable and respectable, these women left a discursive legacy revealing their cultural authority, which helped adjudicate class, racial and gender norms. Toinette pursues an honorable profession, which enhances her reputation and allows her to remain self-supporting. Because Toinette's debut takes place in an international forum, the Peace Jubilee concert, she also becomes an agent of sectional reconciliation and national rehabilitation. Glorying in her self-reliance and secure in her fortune as an heiress, Toinette, a forerunner of Du Bois's Talented Tenth, achieves a celebrated independence while serving as a model for black female readers, in much the same way Woolson's Minorcan women do.[56]

Not all North Carolinians agreed with Tourgée's appeal for women's rights as an extension of freedmen's rights. Instead, conservatives pitted the two against each other, as did the newly formed National Woman Suffrage Association after the Republican Party made the drive for the Fifteenth Amendment, in Wendell Phillips's words, "the Negro's hour." Reacting against the Fifteenth Amendment's enfranchisement of freedmen, the conservative *Sentinel* urged that "we need the conservative influence of women's solid virtue, devotion, patriotism, and quick perception to leaven the corrupt mass of universal male franchise." They concluded that if the amendment passed, "we want the women to go along too." In its coverage of the Holton case, the *Greensboro North State* concluded with the exasperated comment, "What next?" *A Royal Gentleman* answered boldly by emphasizing another new, abstract form of property: the gendered, racialized property of reputation.[57]

Reading, Writing, and Real Estate: Using Literacy to Claim the Property of Reputation

By 1876 Reconstruction policy had been defeated in North Carolina and Charles Sumner's civil rights bill was in trouble. White southerners voted the Democratic ticket—no longer fearful of land distribution, the possibility of military presence, or federal interference—and congratulated themselves on an almost royalist restoration of power. As hopes of reconstructing the nation faded, Tourgée's "re-creation" of race relations had to be reconstructed to conform to stark realities. During the mid- to late 1870s, Tourgée was preoccupied with financial problems: his business had failed, *Toinette* was a commercial flop, and his judgeship was terminated. Local political hostility contributed to his law partnership's failure to flourish, forcing him to obtain a post as a federal pension agent and move to Raleigh.

Tourgée responded to the adverse political changes with calculated caution designed to try to prevent the region's further political backsliding from black civil and political rights. In 1876, fearing the Republican Party would collapse, Tourgée repositioned himself as a shrewd gradualist on the issue of social equality and denounced the 1875 civil rights bill as "a blisterplaster put on a dozing man whom it is desirable to sooth [*sic*] to sleep." Opposing this "pure folly," Tourgée advised fellow Tar Heel Republicans to "forget the Negro a bit" and trust the freedpeople to "acquire property, stability, and self-respect" on their own. Further, Tourgée repudiated the revival of the Union Leagues and advised James E. O'Hara, a black candidate for presidential elector, to withdraw. Through fraudulent voting practices, the 1876 elections saw North

Carolina Conservatives return to power, and the state constitution was quickly revised.[58]

Five years later, the property and position of southern whites like Geoffrey Hunter were again secure as reflected in Tourgée's new title, *A Royal Gentleman*, which "its main character naturally demands." Although the political situation for black Americans was darkening, they retained some opportunity in North Carolina through the 1880s, unlike in other southern states. Consequently, Tourgée did not abandon his work on behalf of black people; instead, he opted to "sacrifice principles to political expediency," and he continued to revise his strategies and modulate the tone of his rhetoric at times.[59]

Tourgée shared Crèvecoeur's belief that the definition of an American citizen began with propertied personhood. With "the foundation of a good name," he claimed, using the example of a male immigrant, a person was freed from servitude and "possessed of the deed." In the nineteenth century the concept of reputation as property, achieved by an individual's exertion and valued by the marketplace, had also deeply informed defamation law. Tourgée's *Plessy* defense would further this understanding of reputation by claiming that a man of seven-eighths white blood was denied his *reputation* of being white by the conductor. Others called the right for women to control their own bodies "self-ownership," invoking Locke's claim that "every man has a *property* in his own *person*."[60]

Tourgée's unorthodox reasoning upset the traditional "formalisms" of late nineteenth-century legal discourse that "sought to separate the political from the social and to distinguish between legally recognized rights and legally created rights." In *Plessy* Tourgée spun two significant strands of argument: he demonstrated that racial identity was arbitrary, social, and alienable, not the immutable, coherent construct that it was traditionally considered to be. Second, he showed that the property interest of identity had to be located through associational evidence like witness testimony, custom, and the community's valuation of reputation. The right of self-possession suggested that identity was an inalienable property that even light-skinned freedwomen could claim.[61]

However, this claim ran against slavery's enduring legacy in which bondspeople were denied ownership of their bodies, labor, and anything produced by their labor. As Stephen M. Best has argued, slavery, in conjunction with the development of intellectual property law, has been part of "an ongoing crisis involving the subjection of personhood to property." The legal system of slavery underwrote an entire culture that legitimated property in persons, which proved to be hard to change. This legitimation pertained particularly to freedwomen, who were still targets of sexual violence. Although reputation has historically carried an overdetermined meaning, this was reinforced during the postwar years when the gendered and racialized meaning of citizenship was in flux. Throughout the Second Military District and elsewhere in the South, freedwomen's assertion of themselves as "women" and "citizens" entitled to respect and protection inflamed their former owners, who continued to see them only as property to which they should have unrestricted access.[62]

Moreover, their claims to "womanhood" continued to be contested, as Hannah Rosen has shown, by interrogators in congressional hearings and courtrooms who questioned their claims to this identity. Compelled to establish a "virtuous" character before they would be seen as creditable witnesses, these women staked their testimony on the gendering of their reputations. Functioning as discursive acts of Reconstruction, their testimony thus entered a national political discourse informed by racialized and gendered notions of "honorable womanhood," which their experience sought to revise. Toinette undergoes a similar questioning by Geoffrey and other white men about her right to a reputation as both a plantation mistress and respectable lady suitable for marriage to a white man. Through the plot of both novels Toinette constantly struggles to defend her rights to claim this reputation in order to live a life as a propertied female citizen deserving of respect. To do so requires access to real estate and education for freedwomen; both Toinette and her mother, Belle, rely on the usage of secret rooms and the exercise of a fundamental literacy.[63]

As he would in his *Plessy* brief, Tourgée highlighted the tensions and ambiguity of self-ownership discourse by cleaving the legal recognition of racial identity, an entity subject to the variability of community judgment, from property claims for the self. Tourgée argued that "in any mixed community, the reputation of belonging to the dominant race, in this instance, the white race, is *property*." Tourgée claimed that the conductor, in his refusal to allow Plessy a seat in the white car, had deprived his passenger of his property, just as Toinette is deprived of the property of her reputation, without the "due process" that was protected under the Fourteenth Amendment. In the novel, however, holding real property is still a condition of Toinette's filing a claim for herself. Tourgée links the ownership of the gendered property of reputation to possession of real estate: he makes the Lovett home's secret room and its annex, the library, key sites for claiming that ownership. Tourgée recognized the entwined nature of property (both real estate and reputation) and citizenship implicit in Crèvecoeur's definition. Whoever claims ownership of the locales of tryst and rebellion is empowered: Toinette and her mother rehearse and execute scenes of seduction and revenge there. Each woman claims the secret room from her master. They attempt to reconstruct the white master and convert the scene of their seduction into a scene of revenge and liberation. In this quintessentially reconstructive space, freedwomen are not consigned to attics and madness, but they are free to convert words into actions.[64]

Literacy played a critical role in advancing Belle's and Toinette's strategies to realize their citizenship through acquiring the property of reputation. Tourgée recognized literacy's long-standing association with achieving the ideals of citizenry in a republic. As patriotic duty, the ability to read and write determines whether Toinette and especially Belle were empowered free agents or reenslaved mistresses. The library, with its false windows and wardrobe leading to the secret room, becomes the battleground for determining the political consequences of the act of reading. The library was thus a literal and symbolic counterpart to the secret room for staging citizenship claims. Arthur's reading of "a collection of works on the institution of slavery" encourages him to stop supporting it. The presence of these works on his library shelves, in turn, helps ruin his reputation, as his neighbors begin to speculate that he is "not sound on the slavery question." Tourgée dramatizes how books become potent agents informing readers' destinies and libraries create an expanded American literacy that includes slaves.[65]

The library, as antechamber to the secret room, is an open secret, an architectural prelude to the redemptive powers of love and dispossession found there. Arthur first encounters Belle reading in the library's armchair, mistaking her by her dress and demeanor to be "a young lady." Belle reveals to her disbelieving master her status: To his question, "What! You a-a-a-slave?" she replies, "Yes, sir," and realizes that "for the first time in my life I felt the degradation of my position." Now acting the master, Arthur orders "my girl" to read Byron, inducing her to feel "what it was to be a *slave*." Arthur punishes Belle for "trespassing" on his "dominions" of the library through words, rather than the lash. Her clandestine efforts to gain an education capture the typical, usually surreptitious manner in which slaves obtained learning. She gains the keys to the library but also the fate of becoming Arthur's mistress. In keeping with the propertied nature of relationships, Belle finds that now Arthur becomes her "servant of servants." She confesses, "From that moment I loved Arthur Lovett with all the intensity of a wild, ungoverned nature." Belle's experience shows how seduction could enslave readers and how readers can be complicit in their enslavement.[66]

The act of reading also prompts flights of freedom. Belle chooses to read Byron's *Mazeppa*, a Ukrainian officer's account of his punishment for seducing a count's wife, which she finds liberating; he is lashed upon a wild horse, which gallops to its death and his release. The scene dramatizes a long tradition within African American print culture in which the act of reading was transformational. Belle becomes so caught up in the liberating escapism of Byron's story that she reads it to herself, altogether forgetting Arthur. Belle's performance blurs the "racial legibility" that the moral ethics of melodrama tend to underline. After finishing, Belle finds that she can no longer say "Marse Arthur" to him. Belle's reading is so transforming that Arthur must again ask, "And you say you are my sister's maid?" His question shows that her status as property has been challenged.[67]

When the library changes function from the scene of seduction to that of revenge, reading again becomes an accomplice. Belle relates her final meeting in the library with Arthur immediately after describing their first meeting, suggesting a parallel between the two scenes. When she learns of Arthur's intentions to marry Certain, she feels "mad—raging mad" and justified in murdering him. On the night before he is to marry Certain, Arthur retires to the library to smoke and read. He is in the armchair when Belle sneaks up and stabs him for disowning her love. He was found with the book "pressed between his leg and the chair arm." Belle feels justified: "Considering Arthur to be guilty of all the wrong and treachery which I supposed to have been practiced toward me, I easily convinced myself that I had only meted out to him the justice he deserved." This act of reading induces a deadly sleep, earns Belle a "reputation as a girl of desperate temper," and insures that the secret room be sealed up.[68]

Next Belle tries to utilize the property of reputation to secure Lovett Lodge by pretending to haunt it. Using the secret room as a base of operations, Belle dons Certain's wedding dress and, with hair "as white as snow," becomes the estranged "white" woman. Belle literally makes white femininity hypervisible, not to seek protection from white patriarchal chivalry but to threaten it. As the racialized dramatization of the "woman in white," Belle, much like Stowe's Cassy who torments Legree, gains a mastery over the house occupants by terrorizing them. In reversing racial visibility, Belle also disrupts gender hierarchies. As a mulatta, she already represents a "terrifying figure of monstrosity" for late nineteenth-century readers. Belle's gothicized white femininity, highlighted by her ghostly robes, augments this threat to upset racial categories of identity. Her visitations also embody a haunted truth that Tourgée would return to in the *Plessy* case: the "reputation of being white" was indeed "the master key which unlocks the golden door of opportunity."[69]

Arthur's murder, followed by Belle's ghostly stalking of Lovett Lodge, has practical consequences on the real estate market. Armed with the house keys, "a sort of badge of the ownership which I had in the premises," Belle takes the first step to remove the badges of servitude, hinting at her eventual restoration of the plantation under Arthur's will. Sightings of "spectral figures" give the place a "bad name," devaluing the property and eventually helping return it to Toinette. Geoffrey himself speculates that the haunting figure is "trying to give the premises an unenviable reputation," which would "depreciate its value," especially among the "superstitious" slaves, who refuse to work there. Tourgée showed again that reputation as property has worth in that it affects the value of real property.[70]

Belle's acts of resistance were not unusual for freedwomen in North Carolina and elsewhere. Before "haunting" the Hunter plantation, she ran away from it when she learned that Toinette had been sold. She returned to the neighborhood in disguise. Truancy, as historian Stephanie Camp has demonstrated, was a common strategy of resistance among freedwomen who could not flee to the North precisely because of the familial responsibilities that bind Belle. Belle exemplifies what historian Joanne Braxton has described in her analysis of the genre of African American female autobiography as the archetypal "outraged mother," one who pursues desperate, heroic actions to protect her children. As Mary Farmer-Kaiser and others have shown, freedwomen made nearly "superhuman efforts" to secure their children and obtain enforcement of their parental rights. The records of bureau court cases in Greensboro evidence other "outrages" perpetrated by freedwomen against their former owners. Their "misbehavior" extended to defying bureau authority when necessary. As freedmen failed to secure the degree of independence and authority over their families that white men had long enjoyed, "free women" challenged their gendered and racial status as dependents of white and black men, claiming the privileges of citizenship and autonomy.[71]

It was education that made possible Toinette's and Belle's self-advocacy. Freedwomen particularly prized education: one bureau agent marveled at the sight of four generations of a family of North Carolina freedwomen, from "a child six years old" to her "great-grandmother, the latter over 73 years of age," learning to read. Literacy was essential for their security, freedom, and independence, as freedwomen applied their education from writing complaints to securing rations to signing petitions. Overwhelmed by the freedpeople's sixty-seven complaints made in one week, the Greensboro subassistant commissioner complained that many were "frivolous," lodged only from a "notion that it is a fine thing to have a quarrel with their old owners." Bureau records show, however, that literacy gave freedwomen as well as men greater political involvement. Their signatures appear in letters of complaint as well as petitions such as that signed by some 115 North Carolinian ex-slaves who eloquently detailed their hardships and requested assistance from the Freedmen's Bureau three years after the war. By dramatizing the necessity of literacy for his heroines' freedom, Tourgée emphasized the importance of education and educated freedpeople in realizing the promise of American citizenship. He had already publicly gone on record over this, notably in influencing President James A. Garfield to endorse federal aid for black education in order to change both the South's party politics and the section's deep-rooted, feudalistic ideology.[72]

By foregrounding the importance of reading, Tourgée recognized the importance of interpretation over authorial intentions. His heroines' cultural literacy makes them adept at reading circumstances with enough social acuity to challenge them effectively. They were thus aligned with an emergent tradition of black women's writing that relied on the racially indeterminate trope of the mulatta character for a variety of functions, including staging the importance of social literacy, that is, the ability to "read" different communities. The dramatization of reading is both an admission of the power of regional readers and an acknowledgment of the author's limitations to change political realities. This was especially true for *A Royal Gentleman*, Tourgée's more circumspect revision, which he completed after leaving North Carolina.[73]

The complexity of the reading process in affecting realities is urged again when Tourgée focuses on Toinette's expressive powers. Toinette accomplishes with a pen what Belle accomplishes with a knife. She writes her final letter to Geoffrey, in which she claims the property of reputation by an argument of self-ownership, in the secret room. Moreover, Toinette's declaration of independence from Geoffrey is supported by her insistence that he read her farewell letter in that room. Together, her declaration and stipulation of where Geoffrey should read it constitute a claim to title. Toinette "the lady" recognizes her personal status as one of her most precious rights, a recognition many black women shared in advocating the self-conscious presentation of respectable public behavior as a tool of racial advancement.[74]

In both endings Toinette makes a supremely personal yet intensely political claim as she protects herself "from temptation and shame." While this letter is also featured in *Toinette*, the revised novel showcases Toinette's radical sentiments and ends on a resounding note with her demands for a woman's rights, especially a wife's, to her labor, her share of assets, her wages, and to her own person. Although their relationship appears consensual or, rather, codependent, the elements of sexual coercion underwriting master-slave relations follow Toinette into freedom. In her refusal to give Geoffrey the right to sexual access to her, Toinette's letter thus takes its place in a tradition of African American women writing emancipatory narratives that were key to reasserting control over their bodies and redefining their sexual relations with masters.[75]

Disdaining the "moral bondage" of concubinage in favor of "being true to herself," Toinette joined a host of women's rights advocates who desired a relationship with men not based upon obligation. In refusing to be "the willing instrument" of Geoffrey's passion, Toinette asserts: "I must, I will, respect myself." Toinette echoes Francis Dana Gage, who declared, "Let us own ourselves, our earnings, our genius." Avowing that her love for Geoffrey is a "gift," Toinette imagines that in the secret room, which was first built for her mother's dalliances with Arthur Lovett, they were "peers and partners in heart." Although both novels show Toinette understands that her former relationship with Geoffrey was free of the masterly appropriations of women's bodies, the revision's word choice suggests Tourgée utilized more rhetoric from the free love movement. Also deleted was a paragraph in which her freely given love is contrasted with his "shackled" spirit to convention. Geoffrey no longer appears as "my king, my conqueror," but as "my friend, my companion," and her "devotion" replaces "bondage."[76]

Though Toinette loses the title of Geoffrey's wife in *A Royal Gentleman*, she gains the novel's last word: her strident refusal to resume her relationship with Geoffrey. With this change Tourgée recognized the unfortunate reality that white southerners like Geoffrey refused to budge on their understanding of reputation. Tourgée changed regional tactics; by exercising her right to claim the property of reputation, Toinette revises a more northerly notion of reputation to encompass women. In the revision's last chapter, "The Seal of the Sepulcher," the equitable transference of property to the former slaves does not occur as it does in *Toinette*. Geoffrey reads the letter and he abandons the house, "casting a sad and regretful look back at the room which had so many and such strange memories connected with it." After he leaves, Certain promptly seals up the secret room permanently. At last the master is dethroned.[77]

Or so it would seem. In making Toinette's appeal based on her right to the property of reputation, Tourgée tried to discount other, gendered understandings of reputation that informed defamation law as practiced in the American South. In particular, Tourgée underestimated an even older meaning of reputation as honor, which dates back to ancient deference societies. This concept of reputation as a fixed, given identity presumes male citizens are inherently unequal because they are born into and occupy different social positions. Consequently, any loss of reputation cannot be repaired by damages, only by vindication or the restoration of honor. Such a remedy recalls the code of honor resonant in the American South, where, not coincidentally, most defamation cases arose to protect the social inequality Tourgée was trying to dismantle.[78]

The incompatible understandings of reputation as property and as honor play out in Geoffrey and Toinette's relationship in ways that capitulate to the inherent racial and gendered bias of defamation law. This understanding of reputation as honor is exactly what Geoffrey posits in his refusal to marry Toinette and in his outrage at her refusing him. As Certain reminds Toinette, Geoffrey will never violate the "custom" that permits interracial concubinage while criminalizing marriage, because he is afraid of "dishonor; the loss of reputation." Moreover, Toinette's refusal to commit fornication, to protect her reputation, furthers the legal separation of the races and sexes, a position to which Tourgée was increasingly drawn. Tourgée reconciled both meanings of reputation to serve the privileged interests of white men like Geoffrey. In claiming her right to an honorable reputation, Toinette closes her letter by vowing to make *Geoffrey's* "reputation, honor and prosperity" paramount. This was one change to her letter that Tourgée did *not* make. In this final turn of the screw, reputation as property, an understanding which benefits Toinette's claim to be her own mistress of the estate, nevertheless also upholds the prevailing regional conception of a white man's reputation as honor. This outcome accords with that of late nineteenth-century southern courts, which increasingly construed these two meanings of reputation to be compatible in defamation law. J. Allen Douglas explains: "Southern courts wove the dual concerns for personality and property together, forming a legal idiom in which reputation appeared as honor that could be protected as a property interest in the self. In the southern legal cosmos, in short the law of defamation protected white identity as property; thus, honor and property flexed the same legal muscle to define the meaning of white subjectivity." Geoffrey's entitlement to protect the property of his reputation as an honorable, white gentleman prevailed, as it would not for Homer Plessy.[79]

Selling Carpetbagger Tourgée: Cultivating Regional Rifts in Reputation

In his attempt to cash in on the postwar reading boom that had revitalized the publishing industry, Tourgée saw that Reconstruction could be a best-selling literary theme. Book publishing had profited enormously during the war, as soldiers necessarily found themselves with more leisure time for reading. Indeed, the war fundamentally expanded the ranks of American readers and produced lasting effects on reading habits and tastes. The efforts of the military, charitable organizations, and individual entrepreneurs paved the way for the postwar growth of public libraries, which found a legitimate place in American lives along with reading itself. Between the publication of Tourgée's two novels, the American Library Association was founded and the Dewey Classification System was created, helping standardize cataloguing for immense collections. Stimulated by advances in cheap paper manufacturing, the publishing industry stepped up its marketing to meet the burgeoning demand. The postwar proliferation of firms with budgets to support advertising and marketing increased industry competition, lowering prices and making more books available. The era of pressurized publishing, in which satisfying the tastes of an expanding readership was imperative, had begun. Recognizing the boom in the publishing industry, a *New York Tribune* editorial concluded that "whoever starts in the book trade . . . with a low opinion of what is demanded by the public makes a great mistake."[80]

Tourgée's sales records show that he did not err. Between 1882 and 1887 he ranked ninth among such popular authors as Henry James, George Cable, and William Dean Howells. John B. Ford and Co. published *A Royal Gentleman* at a moment when the market had turned bullish on Reconstruction policy. Publishing the entire run of Tourgée's Reconstruction novels, Ford worked by subscription, which left Tourgée's novels vulnerable to changing readership tastes given that a market for the books had to be created by soliciting individual orders. Moreover, like many subscription publishers, Ford employed Civil War veterans as book agents, scripting moving stories of their injuries to tell to their prospects. Thus, the drummed-up market for Tourgée contributed to the kind of stories he would write profitably. With the market already glutted with war books by 1870, subscription publishers like Ford, which had made a serious dent in the market, found Tourgée's preoccupation with the drama of Reconstruction lucrative.⁸¹

Soon after the Civil War ended, Tourgée's vitriolic pen tried to renew the conflict in North Carolina by engaging the public in a gendered discourse about reputation that parodied southern notions of reputation as honor in an attempt to undermine their fixity. Southerners measured a person's worth by calculating the years spent in a region, cultivating its land and its people—a measurement Tourgée would mock. In his zeal to initiate change and incite uproar, he routinely antagonized editors, often suspiciously disclaiming his desire to descend to the level of the sensational.

Local editors, like Josiah Turner of the conservative *Raleigh Daily Sentinel*, provoked in kind with typical fulmination against the entire Republican Party: "Profanity, obscenity, licentiousness, and vulgarity, and their plottings to secure ill-gotten gain, are the rule with this class of men. . . . Their very breath is contaminating. . . . *The whole party is ROTTEN, ROTTEN TO THE CORE*." In a review of Tourgée's work, the *Greensboro Patriot* suggested snidely that his "only aim" was to "excite contention and promote discord" among southerners. Later reprinting one of his letters to the *Republican*, the paper noted his vain "weakness for getting into print."⁸²

Tourgée responded by refuting their charges, and then he proceeded to attack the "unwhipped, loudmouthed, bitter, stay-at-home-rebels" who were "squatting on their little forms and snarling at every stranger who shows his face." Borrowing the protocol of a duel, he closed one letter, like Toinette's, with an affirmation of southern chivalric codes to debase his adversary's stature on its own ideological terrain. He gave the paper twenty-four hours to reply before he would take the controversy over whether his name was more "honorable" than the editor's to another periodical. The paper responded by labeling him a "rotten mackerel" that "stinks," an "emissary of Northern obstructionists" keen on "the complete subjugation of the South" but who ultimately will "*prove nothing on us*!" This notorious bickering over reputation strengthened regionalist loyalties and increased newspaper sales, as North Carolinians united against Tourgée in their defense of reputation as honor.⁸³

Born out of his conviction that "a public man is public property," Tourgée's novelistic flirtation with reputation as property could be attributed to his love of his own literary reputation. He was intensely sensitive to criticism and collected all his reviews, underlining praise and crossing out disdain. Actively embracing mysterious identities and contriving scenarios that fanned his notoriety, Tourgée walked a tightrope of identity between the differing regional poles of reputation in order to boost book and pamphlet sales. He had originally published *Toinette* under the pseudonym Henry Churton, the prior owner of Tourgée's home, signaling his identification of landed property with personhood. Analogous to the exposure of Toinette's identity in the hospital, Tourgée was exposed as an impostor when reviewers suspected Churton was a pen name. Once Tourgée's identity was revealed, the reviews became inflammatory, helping to sell more copies.[84]

Similarly, in a series of letters to the *National Anti-Slavery Standard*, Tourgée adopted the pseudonym "Wenckar" to argue that "the Radicals of North Carolina must be taught to stand up to the right bravely, and do battle for themselves." As he taught the radicals how to battle, Tourgée also lured state Democrats into the fray by lampooning them in his infamous "C" letters. Tourgée created such a storm of excitement that, as readers clamored to know who "C" really was, the paper could not meet the demand for copies. Amused by the flurry of interest, "C" speculated on possible candidates, dismissing that "bad radical Tourgée" because the letters had "too much truth in them." Confounding regional ties of identity while blurring the traditional lines of the partisan press, Tourgée manipulated pseudonyms, encouraging his readers, like his characters, to challenge their fates.[85]

Whether as "C," Henry Churton, Jedu Lagby, Wenckar or another pen name, Tourgée was a literary carpetbagger, changing authorial vestments to blend with the region in which he was speculating. His multiple identities ultimately befuddled his opponents. One editor exclaimed of the "venal and vicious" Tourgée, "Who is he, what was his birthplace and what his antecedents, nobody seems to know"—precisely the exasperated recognition with which Tourgée was most at home. Some editors routinely impugned Tourgée's reputation by suggesting he had a questionable, even criminal, past. Although Tourgée felt, upon leaving North Carolina in 1879, that he "almost" had "knit my heart into the land," he also proudly proclaimed his Greensboro homestead "Carpet-Bag Lodge."[86]

Tourgée's use of pseudonyms to "pass" in North Carolina resembled Toinette's attempt to "pass under false colors" up North. He also met her fate in his inability to resist displaying his own badge of servitude: Tourgée remained enslaved to promoting interregional controversy, even to the point of inventing explanations for his somewhat marred physiognomy. Responding to a letter in the *Standard* that labeled him as "Cain-marked," Tourgée falsely claimed that he had acquired his glass eye stopping a Confederate bullet that had left him with a "mark of fiendish hate upon my visage." Thus "marked for life by fratricidal rebels," Tourgée further disfigured himself by transforming the mark into his own brand of regional enmity. Just as George Cable furthered his credentials as spokesperson for the Creoles by falsely suggesting that he was a Creole, Tourgée remade his false eye into the property of a trademark to speak for both North and South.[87]

Keeping his glass eye turned on reputation as honor and his good eye on reputation as property, Tourgée perfected a bifocal Reconstructionist vision shaped by the regional tastes of readers, the flourishing postwar marketplace, and the feuding local press. Whereas *Toinette* was conceived out of the hope that a literary text could be a prime agent of political change, *A Royal Gentleman* showed a sobering acknowledgment that novels were written to appeal to readers' preferences, both political and aesthetic. For all his clever courting of regional controversy, Tourgée's vision of Reconstruction was ultimately accommodating, since the defiant carpetbagger straddled regional readerships. *Toinette* and *A Royal Gentleman* engaged the interests of freedpeople trying to make the transition to citizens, but they also restored the shaken chivalric self-images of other readers. Accommodating both former masters and former slaves, former Yankees and former Confederates, the novels helped unite postwar Americans with a common commitment to property ownership.

A Return to the Brand and the Badge: Affirming the Propertied Nature of American Identity

In his preface to *A Royal Gentleman*, Tourgée opined that the "*unconscious* evils" of slavery had left indelible "marks" on both former master and slave, "beyond the power of Military Proclamation, Constitutional Amendment, or legal enactment" to remove. This understanding of identity as permanently marked property foreshadowed Tourgée's defense of Plessy, a man who wore a "badge of servitude" imposed by Jim Crow segregation. Because of the degree to which the classification of persons as property was psychologically and socially ingrained, Tourgée looked to literature rather than law to change hearts and minds. Yet, rather than eradicating badges of servitude in his critique of capitalism, Tourgée extends them until his story was itself a branding.[88]

In Tourgée's novels, *all* the characters—black and white—speak of immovable badges or brands that signify a property relation to others. Early in both books, Tourgée has Geoffrey, a product of the market economy, speculate on Toinette as a mistress when he "began to estimate the market value of this piece of humanity." Certain reminds Geoffrey that whenever she lapses into dialect, she is like his branded horse: "I show the 'pore white' brand. It's on my tongue and in my heart." Geoffrey soon concludes, after having "confounded... the chattel with the child," that "very plain distinctions are sometimes difficult to maintain." Similarly, in "The Travesty of Peace," *Toinette*'s penultimate chapter, Tourgée analyzes the capitalist brand of ownership that distinguishes all Americans. He scorns how European aesthetic ideals of art and the social values of peace are necessarily coopted in America, the world's greatest marketplace, where "Art follows Commerce from necessity." The narrator describes New Yorkers: "Men are priced and reported like the droves at Communipaw; for a small fee, you can learn of their worth—in goods and morals—at current market prices." Tourgée concluded that "everything bears a trademark, and is bought and sold." Tourgée recognized that the supposedly distinct spheres of the market and home were actually folded into one; because the wage contract priced a free man's labor so low as to replicate servitude conditions, his entire family become hirelings forced into market relations. His novels testify to the ubiquity of trademarks, another badge signifying people's greater servitude to the market-driven notion of ownership's supremacy.[89]

Although Tourgée deleted this chapter in his revision, the characters and plot of both novels make clear his belief that Americans were known by what price they fetched. Tourgée's emphasis on trademarks reflected the nineteenth-century legal trend toward recognizing them as still another form of property deserving protection. His rhetoric was especially relevant, for it was precisely during the 1870s that this legal protection was extended to those objects with a "distinctive" and "readily identified" mark such as a brand. Accompanying these dramatically expanded meanings of property was a sense that American life had become little more than a commodified existence, a sentiment which Tourgée shared. His writing anticipated the criticism of Du Bois some thirty years later that Americans live only by the "Gospel of Pay."[90]

For Tourgée, justice was always achieved by determining who had the greater creditor's claim. In a speech on voting rights, he prefaced his list of all the postwar wrongs the ex-Confederates had done to the former slaves by declaring that the rebels "owed a debt [to the freedpeople] which eternity is hardly long enough to liquidate." His rhetorical bias reflects an emergent midcentury jurisprudence, which was evidently "willing to recast political relations between citizen and state as economic relations between creditors and debtors." As moral and financial responsibilities become intertwined in *Toinette*'s plot, Tourgée imagines a world of unlimited liability, emblematizing the Age of Contract.[91]

Ownership is so imbedded in Tourgée's work that it is grammatically staged as a transaction governing relations. Certain confesses to Geoffrey Hunter, "I will own to you that I had not thought of leaving until a few days ago." Hunter replies that she need not think of it at all, for she is "inseparable" from the real estate like "the ivy on the chimney or the ghost which is said to cling to its bounds." He later concedes that he too owes "an incalculable debt, which he could never discharge," to those who have helped him, and now they "seemed to hold a lien upon his life." Toinette's embrace of self-ownership to achieve her civil rights is dismissed by the narrator, who declares that "nothing was hers, not even herself. She doubted if her soul was." Toinette differs from the other characters by the degree, not the kind, of ownership she is allotted.[92]

Tourgée's punning chapter titles, such as "Bond Given and Costs Paid" and "Not in the Bond," make clear the entangled nature of property ownership and emotion in a "bond," even in the seemingly egalitarian one Certain forges with Toinette. Certain insists that "a pore white woman couldn't always be bought" and that she stays only because she has grown to love Toinette. Certain's "faithful stewardship" over Toinette is defined by her possessive demands, recalling Geoffrey's obsessive ownership. Certain declares: "I am almost glad there is a bar to your marriage with Geoffrey Hunter; I shall have you all to myself now, and there is nothing to prevent *my* loving you." She rationalizes her devotion in terms of ownership, explaining to Toinette: "I have a double claim on you: your father's memory and injunction [to care for the children that he had with Belle], and the love that grew up between us before I knew who you were." By invoking Geoffrey's paternalistic claims, Certain in some ways replicates the masterly relation. In setting up "a kingdom" over which Toinette's son is "the undisputed autocrat," Certain creates an interracial family complete with typical nineteenth-century debts of obligation and servitude. When she hears the "prattling" of her child, "the iron of slavery entered deeper into her soul than ever before." Children are the nexus of slavery and love, reminding black and white women alike of their common bondage to men. Tourgée implies that, for women, only relationships predicated on servitude are tenable.[93]

In both novels Tourgée argues that in a gendered market economy, romantic love and slavery are nearly synonymous property relations. Avoiding the criticism leveled at Harriet Beecher Stowe that *Uncle Tom's Cabin* demonized all master-slave relations, Tourgée claimed that his intention was to showcase "the whole system of the Southern civilization— the Master and the Slave, separated by the whole diameter of the social sphere, and yet united in a common destiny by that universal passion, love." Yet by establishing love to be both the inherent problem and solution in master-slave relations, Tourgée locked himself into a gendered tautology he could not escape.[94]

The market of romantic love reveals personhood itself to be a form of property. Belle protests its generational pattern by first *disowning* her love for Toinette and then throwing off her turban, that "cursed badge" she was forced to wear. Her own experiences as mistress and slave taught her the bitter verisimilitude between love and slavery. The radical power of Toinette's love for Geoffrey, in which "all the shackles of the world were cast aside," dispossesses her. Tourgée explicitly equates the willing devotion of Toinette's love with the enforced obligations of slavery in describing "Love's private mark," which is "plainly inscribed on her face." Toinette realizes that with her increasing love for Geoffrey, her claims on him will likewise increase: "She felt a sense of ownership in him. He was *her* Mass' Geoffrey!" Indeed, Geoffrey later confesses that his obsessive love has let "the chains of the slave" be "transferred to the master." Although Toinette likes to believe that their love has freed her from being a "chattel-real," the narrator knows otherwise: "Now were they double master and slave—once by the bill of sale, among his valuable papers and effects, and once by acquisition in the market-overt, where Love is auctioneer."[95]

One scene in the chapter "In His Mark" shows vividly the indelible harm caused by the badge of servitude. The scene dramatizes the damaging psychological consequences that result from southern statutes designed to keep people unequal and apart. Geoffrey is recuperating in spring 1865 from a blinding war wound in a Richmond hospital, while his former mistress has been passing as "Mrs. Antoinette Hunter," a white, widowed northern nurse. On a bet made with his hospital inmates that Mrs. Hunter is indeed his "free nigger," Geoffrey "imperiously" calls to her: "I say you, girl, Toinette! Toinette!" His command obliterates five years of Toinette's freedom, self-esteem, and pride. As Tourgée put it, "The old life o'erwhelmed and possessed her, like the evil spirits, which entered into Magdalen. She was instantly the slave Toinette and heard the master's voice." Suddenly recast as a "guilty loiterer," she capitulates immediately to Hunter's call, answering "Sir?" with "the inimitable, indescribable intonation of the slave." Indeed, Toinette's capitulation to Geoffrey's command destroyed her reputation when "the mark which slavery had put upon her head" was revealed. Toinette thus bears the mark of a woman's—and a slave's—degraded subjection.[96]

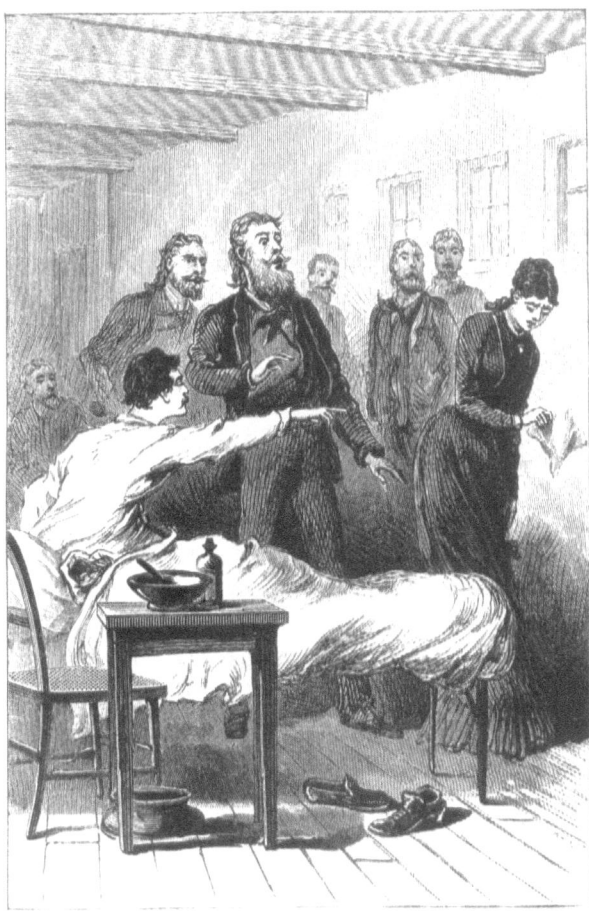

FIGURE 7.
"The Brand,"
A Royal Gentleman
(1881; Boston: Gregg
Press, 1967), 378.

THE BRAND.
"*He cried out imperiously:* '*I say, you girl, Toinette!*' . . . *The free white, intelligent, interesting, beautiful Mrs. Hunter was lost for a moment. . . . She started, and answered instantly with the inimitable and indescribable intonation of the slave—*' *Sir!*'"—p. 378.

The illustration "The Brand" depicts Toinette's cruel exposure. Hunter and the other patients point to her as if seeing an actual "brand" on her cringing body (Fig. 7). Her knee-jerk acquiescence to this old bond of ownership suggests that neither passing, education, nor a career can overcome the fundamental brand of servitude. Toinette faces an uphill battle against the terms imposed by American law and politics. Despite all her endeavors to "*be* what she seemed—a lady," Toinette's unmasking suggests the limitations toward overcoming the caste legacy of slavery. Her badge of servitude was again stretched to "cover up" their interracial marriage when she must serve as his nurse in order to be his wife.[97]

The futility of women's escaping servitude is reflected in Toinette's struggle to find a name without servile associations. Initially, she had followed the "custom" of assuming her former master's name. Then, in her desire to "cut" her son "off from his own past and hers," she changed her name to Antoinette Lovett. She assumes her father's name because "slavery and the past should drop out of her life at once." Yet this choice further binds her to the past and deepens her sense of being chattel property tied to a plantation: "When she went away from Lovett Lodge forever she would take with her its name." Her father remains always her master, and her name becomes her final brand, signifying her gendered, racialized status as traded from Arthur Lovett to Manuel Hunter and then to Geoffrey.[98]

Through their engagement with the problematic nature of property, Tourgée's novels show that the desire of lovers is linked with their roles as owners. His conclusions make clear that this desire extends beyond lovers to include readers. The allegorical differences between the final paragraphs of the two novels reveal his last grasp for readership and his own share of the literary market. While *Toinette* closes with the "eager hands" of the present reaching for the "grim" future, *A Royal Gentleman* has those hands visibly bound with "fetters of brass," which the past had "forged." Both novels affirm that only the future can possess a secret "no man knoweth," an absolute title of possession conveniently left anonymous. For Tourgée the future's secret was the increasing gendered bonds—both political and literary—he felt constraining him to publish a Reconstruction vision readers would continue to buy.[99]

Tourgée began paying his dues with the return of the southern Democrats to power. In his preface to *A Royal Gentleman* Tourgée complained, "The trouble is that the Northern man has made up a South for himself." His idealistic and imaginative search for ways to empower freedwomen ultimately affirmed a conservative vision of citizenship, making him an ironic part of that "trouble." Turning to legal remedies, Tourgée's faith in artistic power to reconstruct the viewer's political vision dimmed. On the eve of the Plessy case in 1893, Tourgée received a letter from a Little Rock, Arkansas, black artist asking how to publicize the southern injustice of lynching through his paintings. He replied, "I do not see how I could give you any advice upon the subject of which you write. I have no interest in any such work and know of no one who has." Tourgée, the creative writer and master publicist, was speechless.[100]

With each passing year, it seemed that the lucrative interregional angle of controversy that Tourgée had exploited was becoming blunted. As historian C. Vann Woodward observed, the Supreme Court decision against Homer Plessy, handed down three years later, was paradoxically promulgated by two judges from Massachusetts; their involvement "bridged the gap between the radical equalitarian commitment of 1868 and the reactionary repudiation of that commitment in 1896" in helping to make "separate but equal" the law of the land. Although he remained ever the reformer, Tourgée's zeal was tempered by declining health and burdened by heavy debt, particularly after the bankruptcy of *Our Continent*, his nationally circulated magazine. This impoverishment, although eased at times by erratic earnings and a pension, plagued him for the rest of his life.[101]

Rewarded for his years of service to the Grand Old Party, Tourgée was appointed United States consul to Bordeaux, France, in 1897. After the Wilmington race riot of the following year, it was perhaps only from the safety of that distant vantage point that Tourgée could maintain an active interest in American civil rights. Writing to President McKinley in response to the riot, Tourgée despaired, "Every day I have grown less and less hopeful with regard to the outcome," yet he continued to urge both the president and black leaders to support the struggle. As an alienated expatriate, Tourgée saw his country reconciled over the denial of citizenship for African Americans. How far away his "Carpet-Bag Lodge" must have seemed from his Bordeaux consulate desk. For their part, his former Greensboro neighbors could not put Tourgée far enough away.[102]

Nevertheless, in their nearly torturous attempts to empower freedpeople, Tourgée's two novels represent valiant efforts to reconstruct the postwar meanings of property to benefit the country's new citizens. Even though his stories contain circular arguments that uphold the cherished value of landed property for citizenship, his clever contriving of the expanded meanings of property was prescient, particularly his suggestion of the laborer's rights and reputation as powerful possessions for freedwomen to acquire. What worked so spectacularly at building his own career—his strategic machinations with the regional meanings of reputation as both property and honor—faltered for freedwomen when the opportunities of Reconstruction began to dwindle by the end of the 1870s. Yet the envisioning and articulating of these opportunities offered bold hope. Moreover, Tourgée's innovative thinking about the utility of property ownership to secure the rights of citizenship informed his legal arguments against segregation, registered in American law for decades.

More than any other Reconstruction writer, Tourgée's flamboyant, well-publicized quarrels with the press both illuminated and blinded his vision for reconstructing the meaning of property, particularly the property of reputation. Tourgée's flirtation with outrageous celebrity informed his core contribution to literary Reconstruction: he made freedwomen the visible agents of freedom, as, in reality, they were, attempting radical solutions to empower themselves. Drawing upon reforms in married women's property laws, joint tenancy, self-ownership, and the flourishing of the free love movement that occurred during the Age of Contract, Tourgée engaged contemporary women's rights discourse to further empower women as citizens through renegotiated contractual relations. Tourgée recognized the need to restructure the plantation household along gender as well as racial and class lines, which he believed inextricably linked.

Yet for all his ambitious idealism, his novels inadvertently affirm the significance of property as an inescapable part of American identity. They particularly reinscribed the duty and labor of slaves for their master onto all postwar women as a defining precondition of their relations with men. His reaffirmation of propertied personhood anchored by a capitalist economy ultimately helped reunite the postwar nation toward paradoxically conservative conclusions about Reconstruction. Within the context of rising postwar interests in literacy, libraries, and publishing, his dramatization of reading as a politicized act is ingenious and daring. Finally, Tourgée reminded his readers of literacy's importance in shaping one's fate as he tried to shape fiction within the literary marketplace.

Carved from Virginia—later to become the First Military District—was a region that would showcase literacy as a potent tool of social change wielded by African Americans in both public and personal domains. The new citizens of West Virginia took advantage of the distinct opportunities afforded by their state's postwar establishment in ways that furthered the civil rights all freedpeople demanded.

Chapter 3

AFRICAN AMERICAN LITERARY ACTIVISM IN A DIVIDED DISTRICT

Storer College and the *Pioneer Press* of West Virginia

Our people must learn to allow a man to say what he thinks without wanting to kill him for it. God gave us minds with which to think. We should be conscious that we are thinking right, and then boldly advocate, and defend our thoughts.
—John Robert Clifford, Pioneer Press

On 3 January 1867 prominent northern journalist Mary Clemmer Ames heralded a new year and a new era for black and white West Virginian women. Her controversial column welcomed the arrival of "Yankee Teachers in the Valley of Virginia." These women of "elegance, beauty, and wit" had arrived with "jaunty hats and natty jackets" to "brighten the lot of the lowly, to deliver from ignorance and vice the victim race." They came to teach at Storer College, the new freedmen's school in the mountain pass that John Brown had made famous. Yet the narrative of the Yankee teachers, upon whose womanly shoulders, Ames optimistically concluded, "another South, regenerated and redeemed," would rest, was only one part of the story. With each passing decade, Storer College students became increasingly instrumental in shaping their education and attaining some realization of their civil rights.[1]

This chapter examines the extant writing of former slaves and their children, who were among the first to achieve literacy and find a political voice in the newly created state of West Virginia. Their long-forgotten letters, articles, and poems published in yearbooks, the *Storer Record*, and one graduate's local newspaper, the *Pioneer Press*, support the growing recognition that to speak of an African American literature necessarily requires embracing a broader sense of form and genre. These newspapers and their readership attest to the viable presence of a black community that coalesced in print culture. Contributing the literature of an otherwise overlooked locale to the new regionalist scholarship informing nineteenth-century black studies, these West Virginia publications also affirm the importance of the periodical press for black writers.

What emerges from the various written records is a highly gendered, racialized, and class-inflected conversation among the new graduates, their mentoring "benefactors," and the local community of Harpers Ferry. Although not technically within the First Military District, which comprised Virginia, Harpers Ferry, home to the federal arsenal, was situated on the border, and the town played a strategic role in the war. Postwar federal presence remained strong in this region, particularly in the form of the Freedmen's Bureau, as soldiers encountered intense local resistance, including a legal challenge, to incorporation into West Virginia that lasted throughout Reconstruction. The history of Storer College's embattled relation to the white residents of Harpers Ferry and its black student body reveals how gender, class, race, and region knotted with the postwar issues of labor, property, reputation, and duty to inform the meaning of citizenship. Tracing the rhetorical fate of these four terms in the writing of Storer College officials, teachers, local newspaper editors, and Storer graduates brings greater understanding of Reconstruction's haphazard course.

Storer College, beset by contrary regional and racial impulses, formulated a mission that yielded contradictions. The college faculty prepared students to assume the rights and obligations of citizenship by inculcating in them the lifelong habits of hard work and duty to others and by building trustworthy character. Yet the students learned corollary lessons at Storer: their labor was to be largely manual, they would be serving the property interests of white employers, and building a good reputation would be an exercise in the necessary art of self-effacement. These contradictions played out along highly gendered lines; female Storer students and faculty were expected to comport to not only a racialized but also a gendered hierarchical structure, which doubly subordinated them.

College officials were at cross-purposes in trying to secure northern funding while placating hostile local southerners; they urged students to embrace the tenets of bourgeois individualism while encouraging them to adhere to the hierarchy of plantation paternalism. An examination of the school's papers reveals an unofficial "secret history," as school officials later termed it, that expresses the white administration's divided thinking. It was a secondary and shadowy chronicle of racist attitudes that eventually soured the faculty's progressive ideals.[2]

Storer students had to negotiate the contradictory advice they received from the faculty, who demanded self-interest and selflessness, as well as autonomy and perpetual indebtedness. Eager to please but also anxious to achieve their own dreams of success, students, particularly women, had to reconcile their education with their ambitions. Their writings, as well as those of teachers, administrators, and journalists, dramatize that the burgeoning market for the printed word was the new terrain upon which the property of reputation was staked. The paths of labor, land-ownership and duty proved to be serpentine for leading freed West Virginians to empowerment. For some who endured many legal disabilities under conservative state laws, particularly West Virginia women, reputation became a kind of property beneficial toward creating intraracial community and performing racial uplift. Others experienced scandal when the local press and Storer administration attacked the reputations of students and teachers who did not conform to their expectations. A case in point is that of Sarah Jane Foster, one of the first "jaunty hats" to arrive in this troubled region. Foster, a white Free Will Baptist teacher, underestimated local prejudice and misread regional attitudes. Her story reveals the disastrous consequences that ensue from blind idealism.

Counterpointing Foster's harrowing tale, the journalistic writing of two of Storer's most prominent graduates, John Robert Clifford and Coralie Franklin Cook, reveals the shrewd ways students resolved their conflicting education. For both Clifford and Franklin, duty, labor, reputation, and property ownership translated into gendered tools used for the work of "lifting as we climb." This was the motto of the National Association of Colored Women's Clubs (NACWC), an organization which Franklin helped found in 1896. Franklin adopted gendered rhetoric focused on black women as the builders of an interracial coalition centered on progressive reform, which made their needs and contributions visible. Clifford targeted fellow black Civil War veterans as the primary engineers of intraracial economic infrastructure. His incendiary local newspaper, the *Pioneer Press*, challenged the college's mission and editors of the local conservative press. Clifford's and Franklin's differing rhetorical tactics show that the freedpeople's vision of Reconstruction was riven with internal contradictions.[3]

The various Reconstruction proposals afloat in West Virginia evidence that postwar restructuring of race relations cannot be understood without assessing changes to gender, regional, and class relations. As played out in the popular press, college administrative correspondence, and student writing, the rhetoric surrounding this controversial Harpers Ferry college was in keeping with both Thomas Jefferson's sense of revelatory confluence and John Brown's insurrectionary challenge that defined this riparian community. Within two decades the male and female graduates of Storer would help chart the troubled course of Reconstruction. As teachers and journalists superseding Ames and her much-admired Yankee teachers, these former students would wear the jaunty hats, which they bought at the high price of ostracism, harassment, and scandal.

A New Birth of Old Dominion Social Dynamics

Although slavery was never the primary reason for the 20 June 1863 "dismemberment" of West Virginia from the Old Dominion, its amplified presence provoked bitter sectional conflict. The state's wartime "partition" from Virginia was not simply the result of conflict between "mountain democrats" and "plantation oligarchs"; rather, it was due more to the efforts of a western Virginia political and social elite who vied with easterners to control the valuable resources of the wilderness and the Baltimore and Ohio Railroad.[4]

When the western part of the state considered secession during the famous Wheeling Conventions of May and June 1861, delegates tried to remain silent on the issue of emancipation. Nevertheless, the interest in annexing the two richest slaveholding counties—Berkeley and Jefferson, the respective homes of John Clifford's newspaper, the *Pioneer Press*, and Storer College—meant that slavery had to be addressed. In the end, the abolition clause of the new state's 1863 constitution specified gradual emancipation. Within seven years Democrats, committed to white supremacy and labor control, had "redeemed" the state, and West Virginia retained some of the South's most prejudicial attitudes and barbaric practices—particularly lynching—toward African Americans.[5]

The Gordian Knot of black suffrage, white disfranchisement, and the new state's incorporation was vividly dramatized by the local press. Particularly outspoken were two staunchly Democratic, long-standing Charles Town weekly newspapers: the *Virginia Free Press* and the *Spirit of Jefferson*. H. N. Gallaher, the prewar editor of the *Virginia Free Press*, fought for the Confederacy while the federal army demolished his paper's office. Embittered and vengeful, he renewed publication on 24 August 1865 with a vow to remember the "melancholy record" of the war dead. Gallaher's sentiments were shared by the newspaper's friendly rival. The *Spirit of Jefferson*'s various owners and editors kept it fiercely Democratic. George Haines, who had defended Harpers Ferry and had been a prisoner of war, assumed the editorship of the paper in 1875. An active Lost Cause veteran and secretary of the Lee Memorial Association, Haines ran the *Spirit* for the next thirty-nine years.[6]

These newspapers suggest that the regional incorporation of Berkeley and Jefferson Counties into West Virginia was indissolubly connected with the granting of civil rights to African Americans. The editors stubbornly refused to include "West" into their mastheads until 1871, when the Supreme Court ruled against Virginia's attempt to recover Berkeley and Jefferson Counties. Haines framed the regional transfer as an illegitimate racial amalgamation, while the *Virginia Free Press* bemoaned that Jefferson County had been "given the 'hind teat' of the bastard progeny of a Black Republican conception." Both steadfastly opposed black suffrage.[7]

White residents of Berkeley and Jefferson Counties remained more hostile to abolition without property compensation than they were to incorporation into West Virginia. The two counties contained 30 percent of the slaves in the region that would become West Virginia. However, the ire of white residents was mitigated by a different economic dynamic, characterized by smaller, more diversified farms, than that found in plantation strongholds. Towns such as Martinsburg and Harpers Ferry were not genteel, quintessentially plantation communities; rather, they were enclaves of industrialism with large immigrant populations, including free African Americans. The 1799 construction of the U.S. Armory and Arsenal helped make Harpers Ferry a transportation hub, and Martinsburg expanded in 1824 when the Baltimore and Ohio Railroad arrived, allowing the creation of a manufacturing center for flour and woolens. Slaves and free black people were integral to this industrial area, providing skilled and unskilled labor in quarries, mills, forges, canal construction, and the government gun factory. By 1840 the presence of free black people in Harpers Ferry, Bolivar and Virginius Island equaled that of the slave population.[8]

Because of its well-established industrial opportunities for free African Americans, Harpers Ferry became a postwar terminus for black refugees seeking Freedmen's Bureau protection and employment. In 1869 freedpeople comprised some 25 percent of the town's population. Along with the industrialism of the area, the continued intrastate migration of African Americans heading farther west into the state had a significant effect on the lives of black Harpers Ferry residents. After West Virginia was incorporated, some politicians took advantage of the growing black vote. The black population of West Virginia grew 44 percent between 1870 and 1880 and continued to increase through the 1890s.[9]

Former Confederates found intolerable the idea that the state had more than 2,000 black voters while more than 25,000 white men were disfranchised. In addition to the legacies of slavery and regional annexation, the historically vexed issue of representation had an ongoing effect. These factors, combined with the wartime destruction and federal occupation of the area, made the majority of Democratic white residents particularly hostile to granting suffrage to the freedmen. Struggling ex-Confederates were agitated to desperate measures by the wholesale destruction of all the newly reconstructed factories and homes on Virginius Island and much of Harpers Ferry by the devastating 1870 autumn flood. That fall, West Virginia Democrats, running as "a white man's party," regained power, and de facto segregation took hold. In 1871 an amendment was proposed as a compromise that would "let up" some restrictions on ex-Confederate voting while also removing the word "white" from the state constitution. The new 1872 constitution barely was passed by a vote of 36 to 30, making it nominally possible for African Americans to vote and hold office.[10]

Education Incorporated among the Ruins

The history of Storer College's precarious place in this eminently southern yet comparatively industrialized county whose denizens had given 16 percent of the white population to the Confederate Army explains a great deal about the outcome of Reconstruction here. Distinguishing this region was the long and turbulent nature of the federal occupation. United States troops were active in Harpers Ferry beginning with John Brown's raid in October 1859. During the war the town changed hands fourteen times, and there were periods of months when no force—military or civil—controlled the town. Residents often found themselves fending off marauding raiders and reconnaissance parties. By the war's close, returning civilians found their homes in a state of semiconfiscation, rented out by the federal government to officers and workers or destroyed by the armies.[11]

The desolation extended to the "campus" that would become Storer College, which was originally a "normal school," or a teacher training institute, in the abandoned home of the U.S. Arsenal paymaster on Camp Hill. On 1 October 1867 nineteen freedpeople started their first lessons in reading and writing directly below a sick Union veteran and his family who were squatting upstairs in the badly shelled building. Teacher Anne Dudley recalled, "Only war-riddled buildings and ruins everywhere. Not a tree or fence left. . . . near by were 300 rude soldiers' graves." The town's postwar material decay corresponded to a perceived moral decay among its residents. A Freedmen's Bureau agent, who followed after the federal army, prophesied for Harpers Ferry: "The future of this place is dismal in the extreme and I can only compare it to a nest of paupers. If, the whites are shiftless, caring nothing for law, decency, or order, how can it be expected that the colored people will be better?"[12]

Frustrated in their work to redraw boundaries that the war and its aftermath had erased, white residents' irritation was underscored by the loss of property, the six-year-long occupation, and the influx of loitering black refugees. Alongside the eviction of squatters and the restoration of property was a corresponding desire to impose racial segregation on public facilities. Bureau agents noted with disgust that in the mixed economy of Harpers Ferry, it was the poor white people whose "repugnance to the black race is greater than their betters." They were opposed to granting the ex-slaves education, suffrage, and any of the prerogatives of citizenship. Throughout the state, Freedmen's Bureau agents encountered hostile white West Virginians of all classes poised against freed West Virginians, who were politically assertive.[13]

Storer's establishment anticipated general trends in northern philanthropy that were increasingly shaped by local white hostility to funding black education. In contrast to the reluctance of West Virginia officials to provide African Americans with an education, the founders of Storer College, the Free Will Baptists, had been deeply committed to improving the status of African Americans since their formation in 1778. In 1864, at the suggestion of the War Department, the Free Will Baptists entered an alliance with the Congregationalist-based American Missionary Association (AMA), the leading religious group assisting the freedpeople, and began establishing missions in the Carolinas and Virginia. In conjunction with the Freedmen's Bureau, they appointed Reverend Nathan Brackett, a Free Will Baptist clergyman and U.S. Christian Commission veteran, to superintend freedpeople's education in the Shenandoah Valley. Under his guidance, the Free Will Baptists set out to match the $10,000 founding gift of Maine businessman John Storer to charter the school as a college in 1868.[14]

Beginning with their 1867 petition to Congress to found a school at Harpers Ferry, freedpeople continued the traditionally aggressive Free Will style by making Storer theirs—an ambition that fit well with John Storer's initial goals. In Storer's bequest he demanded that "colored persons of suitable character" be on the Board of Trustees, and indeed, Frederick Douglass was one of the earliest and most outstanding examples of the fulfillment of that bequest. Details of his contribution as trustee are not well known, and Douglass himself later minimized his degree of involvement because of his obligations to other boards. However, he delivered a stirring commencement address eulogizing John Brown to the fourteenth graduating class on 30 May 1881. John Storer also insisted that all students contribute at least one dollar to their education annually, although indigent students could attend for free or be given work opportunities. Although these ambitions were initially unrealized, attendance grew dramatically.[15]

Even before the Freedmen's Bureau had arrived, freed West Virginians of all ages made plans to secure schooling. From petitions and fund-raising to buying land, erecting schoolhouses, and teaching, freedpeople across the south exercised tenacity and creativity in pursuit of education. Moving anecdotes of their extraordinary exertions abound. Mary Brackett Robertson, a Storer teacher and daughter of Nathan Brackett, recalled how one prospective student walked a long distance to Storer in order to conserve his resources. Unfortunately, he put his hard-earned savings in his shoe, and when he arrived the money was ground to a powder. Like the well-meaning student's funds, the students' future as productive citizens in this town could be pulverized.[16]

The local press fueled ongoing hostility, which "intensified to fever heat," to Storer's establishment. Residents advocated having the school's March 1868 charter revoked, creating such an uproar that a federal agent was sent to investigate requests for the reclamation of government property that had been donated to the school. That effort failed, but the editors ridiculed the school's ambitions. When covering the school's December 1869 dedication, for example, the *Virginia Free Press* commented that "on Thursday 23 ultimo, the colored element of the county had quite a jollification at Harpers Ferry," in which "the speaking was well spoken of by those who heard it." Fully two years after the AMA teachers had arrived, the *Virginia Free Press* editor defiantly maintained, "we did not and will not open our arms and our houses to any Yankees from Maine . . . who come down to affiliate with the negroes and go arm in arm with them." Whatever the topic, the editors hardly concealed their hostility and persistent snideness. For example, the *Spirit of Jefferson* scorned a "radical convention" of black and white people held on campus in October 1871. Deriding it as a "black and tan" convention of the "15th amendment class," the *Press* added, "If the secretary of the convention will furnish us with names and color of members composing this 'sweet-scented' conclave, we will publish the proceedings without money and without *price*." Still angered by the federal army's use of black soldiers to recruit local African Americans for war service, the Democratic papers kept close watch on any upstart political activities on campus.[17]

It was upon this foundation of resentment and rubble that Storer College was erected. Noting the fierce local opposition to black education, Louise Wood Brackett, Nathan Brackett's wife, argued that "but for the aid of the Freedmen's Bureau and the military in places, some of these schools could not have been started at that time." Scholars have since agreed, arguing that the bureau's most important service was the establishment and support of schools for black West Virginians. Storer College tried to offer an "education without distinction of race or color," and it initially attracted a few white students, but community prejudice followed by legislative decree made biracial education unsustainable. Brackett and his teachers were ostracized as "moral lepers" and distrusted by white people, who felt "we had all come to help colored people from some base or at best sordid motive." Brackett, whose life was threatened in nearby Charles Town, faced petty harassment by "blood hounds" who threatened arson. Kate Anthony, daughter of a Storer trustee, recalled that escorts proved necessary and that both teachers and pupils went armed during the first years. Through the years 1866 and 1867, students were harassed by visiting furloughed cadets from the Virginia Military Institute, culminating in a confrontation between a female teacher and the cadets that supposedly resulted in an apology from Robert E. Lee. Perhaps unsurprisingly, Storer remained the *only* school for black West Virginians seeking teaching or academic degrees until 1892, when the state established the West Virginia Colored Institute.[18]

Straddling Both Sides:
Storer's Project of Regional Reclamation

By recasting local racial antipathies as regional differences, Storer officials devised a public relations policy that took into account the town's political climate. President Brackett, proud to have been the first Yankee to ride unarmed up the Shenandoah Valley after the war, was pleased to have been chosen a common agent, "perfectly trusted" by both sides, to renew North-South ties. While routinely peppering the local press with college catalogs and announcements, he told an interviewer from Lewiston's *Daily Evening Journal* that northerners failed to "understand fully the feeling of the South" and were generally "not fair in their judgment." Brackett appeared apologetic for the freedpeople's behavior. He conceded to the *Journal*'s largely white Maine readers that the ex-slave perhaps had suffered more from his friends, who "have persisted in clothing him with virtues he does not possess, in asking for him privileges that he does not appreciate, and imposing upon him obligations that he is not prepared to meet."[19]

The faculty-supervised *Storer Record*, which began in 1883, also mediated the school's image among the local community, alumni, and northern benefactors. College officials were mollifying in their solicitations from local sources. For example, Brackett declared that the college would "welcome" state supervision of an industrial school, in order to "insure the friendship and cooperation of the great mass of the good citizens of the county and State." While courting local favor, Brackett and the college's trustees also solicited funds ardently from northern Free Will Baptists. Trustee Silas Curtis instructed teachers to record "any incident, anecdote, or circumstance" regarding the students that "might be interesting to friends of the cause," for publication in the Free Will *Morning Star*, to keep up "the interest among the givers." Storer trustees minimized local prejudice: they noted "with great reluctance" that "while the better class of citizens of Harpers Ferry are friendly to the school, some still retain the old-time prejudice against whatever tends to elevate the Negro," made evident in the state's cutting of funds for industrial education.[20]

Storer officials made their overall mission in Harpers Ferry one of regional reclamation. They sought to impose northern, gendered ideals of bourgeois individualism—hard work, self-reliance, and enterprise—upon their students. However, they lacked both Cable's spirit of compromise and Woolson's tact. Recognizing that they were "to teach many things that are done in the New England home and churches," Lura Brackett Lightner, sister of Nathan Brackett, affectionately known as "Lue," intoned a militant moral imperative: "A part of our work now is to strike down the numberless weeds that have taken vantage of the loosened soil to choke out the good seed." Proud of their regional heritage, the faculty assumed a northern superiority. President Henry McDonald recalled of Lightner: "In her centered the fine traditions and ideals of New England. Though she lived her life in the south, she never became transformed by what she called the subtleties and insincerities." A newspaper editor fired back that these "nigger teachers" had the "permission of the South to remain in their own land. But the meddlesome disposition of New England Yankeeism, will not permit them to do this." Recognized for what it was, Storer's project of regional reclamation met with equally vigorous resistance.[21]

The self-righteous piety of Free Will Baptist teachers reflected part of a northern domestic culture that valued women's activism outside the home and scorned privileged white southerners' refrain from toil. Women in the Free Will Baptist Women's Missionary Society played a prominent role in

Storer's development as they "listened patiently to each new project and it was to them that the leaders still turned for financial and spiritual aid." This particularly feminine contribution dovetailed nicely with New England praise for the value of elbow grease to oust the southern habits of leisured womanhood that Mary Clemmer Ames had attacked. Two pioneer Storer female teachers, Anne S. Dudley (later a trustee) and E. H. Oliver, received credit for the first Free Will Baptist church that was organized in the Shenandoah Valley at Martinsburg. Similarly, Brackett was eulogized as "a son of toil" who "chose labor as a part of his education, a part of his virile manhood," as opposed to "the little man," who "shirked" work in order to live "the soft, easy life of the voluptuary." The eulogist's recasting of Brackett as masculine fieldworker expressly challenges southern patrician notions about the master's indolence. Storer College was caught up in postwar changes for southern families, a domestic restructuring based on northern-styled individualism and contractual relations.[22]

Like their fictional counterpart, Albion Tourgée's Betty Certain, female teachers openly identified with a strident masculinity to promote New England ideals of labor. Proclaiming "I had the honor of marching into town with the Brothers in Blue," Anne Dudley, like Ames, reveled in the antagonizing of the Harpers Ferry community by the occupying army. Inspired by the federal presence, she flagrantly embraced a militant style. Dudley had students perform "Song of the Try Company" at an 1867 local exhibition. The song had the refrain, "They never say can't, they never say die / Who march in the ranks of Corporal Try." In 1873 Dudley organized and toured in New York with her own student choral army, the Union Chorus (later renamed the Harpers Ferry Singers), to raise money for building Myrtle Hall, a girls' dormitory. Reminiscent of Stowe's Miss Ophelia, the martial educational methods of Dudley and Lightner posed enough of an implicit challenge to both the racial and gendered conventions for white women's behavior that they, like the outspoken Ames, were rebuked by the male editors of the local press.[23]

Outraged by Dudley's accusations that Harpers Ferry slaves "ploughed all day in yokes made of three iron bars one and a half inches thick, and were whipped with chains," the *Spirit of Jefferson* condemned her "monstrous falsehood," labeling her a "reckless calumniator." In further riposte, they reprinted rejoinders from other southern newspapers to recast her zeal for regional reclamation as part of a plot for inciting regional rift: the *Baltimore Methodist Protestant* found the northern "system of lying" to be "causing the South to look upon the North as a race of Shylocks and liars and the North to look upon the South as a race of barbarous loafers," and the *Lynchburg Virginian*, ridiculing the Free Will baptismal practices, chortled: "Would it not be well to give Miss Dudley ... another dip and hold her under the water a little while longer this time?" Provoked by Dudley's unconventional behavior, local editors scrutinized Storer students even more closely. Undeterred, she condemned this journalism as further evidence of Southern degeneracy.[24]

Despite the challenge to conventional gender roles made by the teachers, the college's familial, hierarchical model of citizenship echoed the antebellum ideology of republicanism, upheld through the subordination of household dependents. The Brackett family's nepotistic involvement in the school over several generations reinforced this paternalism. The infusion of bourgeois market practices into postwar industrial towns like Harpers Ferry, along with the concurrent rise of plantation fiction, conspired to repopularize this ideology. It is within this context that the Free Will Baptist mission of Storer College was planted. As a northern institution imbued with bourgeois ideals of self-sacrifice and duty, Storer College used the plantation household as a model for organizing social relations. Students idolized President Brackett as being Christlike, with his "radiant life spent itself in perpetual endeavor for the uplift of the colored people.... LEADER! TEACHER! FATHER!" Preceptress Lue Brackett Lightner served under her brother in a school that she saw as "a large and well-organized, self-dependent, self-sufficient, and happy family." Unfortunately, black students were encouraged to continue to play the sentimentalized role of servants in this family. One writer characterized the relation of Miss Lightner and her students as one in which "it would have been much easier in some cases to permit the relation of maid to mistress. The girls actually quarreled over the privilege of waiting upon her." Anne Dudley had her troupe, the Harpers Ferry Singers, perform only "plantation melodies with a few exceptions," because "the real heart cry of their souls was in slavery." The story of Storer College's straddling of regions through appeals to antebellum nostalgia and commitments to bourgeois individualism challenges those historians who draw sharp lines between southern paternalism and northern capitalism. Storer College exemplified their mutuality in this aggressively industrial New South territory.[25]

A Contradictory Curriculum and Its Consequences: The Duty of *Labor Omnia Vincit*

Storer's aims, at once entrepreneurial and pious, engineered contradictions in grafting northern labor ideals onto southern labor systems. The resulting curriculum, infused with a northern work ethic, Christian values, and pragmatic negotiation with southern racial attitudes, was commonplace among the freedmen's schools. While Storer officials certainly disagreed with white residents who saw the ex-slaves as an uneducable lot who "live[d] alone upon pillage" by defining freedom as a refusal to work, they shared their paternalism. In praising the pursuit of scholarly accomplishments, faculty also insisted upon the value of manual labor. "The Negro's ability as a scholar" and "his faithfulness as a laborer" were yoked together in the *Storer Record*'s rhetoric to blunt a student's ambition so that "we need not despair concerning his future." While the AMA at Atlanta, Fisk, and Dillard Universities had been able to avoid such conflict by organizing either an academic or an industrial program from their inception, Storer's ambivalent agenda reflected conflicting racial, gendered, classist, and regional attitudes toward free labor. The resultant clash of opposing educational philosophies was not unique to West Virginia; it was echoed, for example, in Woolson's postwar Florida.[26]

Storer faculty enacted the college's motto, *Labor Omnia Vincit* (Work Overcomes All), by using students to construct school buildings. Following Booker T. Washington's call for self-sufficiency, students were inculcated with a labor ethic that also reflected the Free Will Baptist determination to avoid financial obligation. Storer officials boasted that the college was "saving" students from "the humiliation of becoming the recipients of charity," while "giving them the discipline of labor." In contrast to Woolson's fine-toothed distinction between laziness and indolence, the college's coupling of studying with toiling made student "free time" unthinkable. Reflecting the success of Storer's indoctrination of constant industry, one student reflected, "How can a person be satisfied doing nothing? . . . Languor is a cause of idleness." Unlike Tourgée's gentlemen masters, black students were never free to engage in any speculation, be it in the financial markets or in leisurely asides. Recast as an educational tool of self-help, student labor saved Storer from "the *dragging weight of debt*," which the school boasted was "one familiar cry [that] has never been heard from Harpers Ferry." Yet the school was nearly always in the red for its first thirty years. Rather than borrow, the college would simply cease construction; rather than hire laborers, the school required that the students do all the work, with cheerful mien. Like all the buildings at Tuskegee, Storer's Anthony Memorial Hall, dedicated on 30 May 1882, was built entirely by students. By 1889, the Women's Missionary Society had raised funds for an Industrial Department, housed in a building that the students also constructed.[27]

Although the school discouraged financial liabilities, it promoted a sense of perpetual moral indebtedness among its students that was coupled with their injunction to labor. This association reinforced antebellum legal precedence in which slaves figured as debtors. Stephen Best explores how indebtedness served as "a ruse of consent" designed to cover nothing less than "the Constitution's sanction of the expropriation of labor." Storer officials' treatment of their students as laborers perpetually indebted to their pedagogic benefactors continued this ruse at a time when many white Americans wanted freedpeople's labor to continue to be extracted under a capitalist economy. One student ended his address to the class of 1893 by stating, "And let us all remember that what we achieve depends largely upon our own efforts: 'In the struggle for gold and the scramble for pelf / Let this be your motto, rely on yourself.'" As a recent graduate, Hamilton Hatter represented the successful embodiment of both manual skills and scholarly accomplishment. Newly appointed principal of a nearby school, Hatter donned overalls to finish a plumbing job that, left undone, would have delayed the school's opening. Always "ready for business," Hatter's actions exemplified the racially resonant moral that "the man who isn't afraid to use his hands is the coming man." This hands-on training included employing students as domestic servants to wait on summer guests who boarded in the school dormitories. The college evidently had plans to have the business be run by a student "company" in the future so that students could obtain "business training" and share in the profits.[28]

College officials rationalized their vocational requirements by highlighting deficiencies in the changing class composition of the student body, a rationale that would increasingly be adopted by black colleges in competition for funds with vocational schools. As opposed to conventional arguments that as students progressed "up from slavery" they would be more capable of pursuing academic work, Storer faculty felt that the postwar creation of middle-class black families produced a renewed need for training a genteel servant class. In her condescending assumptions about the required role of black women as laborers, Mary Brackett Robertson was deferential:

> At first the pupils represented a superior class . . . brought up in homes of refinement and wealth . . . travelled quite extensively, some had been abroad. Dignified, courteous, earnest, and self-respecting . . . but gradually these adult students whose hands had been trained in slavery for valuable service began to be replaced by a younger group

brought up in homes where mothers . . . had little opportunity to teach or train.[29]

According to Robertson, African Americans had attained more culture and gentility as slaves trained to serve wealthy families than in the presumed leisure of freedom. Robertson added that Storer officials had acknowledged the increasing discrimination against African Americans, which made "only a small proportion of those seeking an education" likely to find professional employment. Nevertheless, by the end of its first thirty years in operation, Storer had graduated more than 600 teachers and 400 ministers. Despite this impressive achievement, the 1890s Jim Crow racial retrenchment led the faculty to steer students toward industrial education within a state that was rapidly industrializing. Storer faculty attempts to remedy this labor deficiency point to yet another way the college's paternalist curricula would continue to subordinate African Americans, particularly women, to an inferior economic and social position. Although Storer had offered sewing courses since 1870, the domestic sciences curriculum was continually expanded, culminating in a formal three-year program in 1898. Moreover, domestic science courses became mandatory for women in 1893. Graduating from the "plantation household" of Storer ensured that African Americans, whatever their personal ambitions in this distinctly non-Tidewater region, would know how to please white employers. Opportunities for black women in West Virginia remained largely confined to domestic and personal service as a pattern of racially segregating work opportunities emerged.[30]

Not all students acquiesced to Storer's mandatory "service" courses. The earliest extant records of student writing reveal begrudging complaints, however softened by humor, against the ever-increasing surveillance, discipline, and restrictions. The inevitable conflicts that erupted between freedwomen and their northern educators were hardly unique to Storer, but by the 1890s, the college's foundation in the plantation household had begun to crack. When student Louisa Hartgrove boycotted sewing class, she was expelled. Her mother defended her daughter's protest and chastised President Henry McDonald: "I suppose you was hire [*sic*] to instruct and not to obstruct. And I told her not to go into that sewing class because if she wanted to waste her time on making those foolish dollies, she could put that period into something that will benefit and also other and herself. I shall wait for a answer." This incident suggests that Storer women valued labor differently from white male educators. Recognizing that labor was not synonymous with an education, Mrs. Hartgrove clearly hoped her daughter would aspire to become something more than a seamstress. Women such as Louisa Hartgrove represented a new postwar generation that caused Mary Brackett Robertson to lament the passing of genteel servants trained by obedient mothers. Storer's emphasis on homemaking classes corresponded with prevailing attitudes regarding the purpose of women's education in both public and private schools in the Eastern Panhandle, even while a broader curricula was increasingly being offered postwar women in West Virginia. The key difference was that Storer women, unlike their white female counterparts, were being trained primarily to serve in households other than their own. McDonald reinstated Louisa, "provided she would do what she had been told to do." Storer faculty fell back upon a religious paternalism to reassert authority.[31]

Students like Hartgrove were asked to subordinate their independent desires to the greater good of the school. Always at hand were such examples as Lue Brackett Lightner, who, in becoming a freedpeople's teacher, knew that "she was choosing a life of complete ostracism from people of her own race." However, Lightner and her white colleagues were free to pursue their own agendas in their teaching. In a gesture characteristic of her paternalism, Dudley wrote the 1867 valedictory address to be given by a Martinsburg student graduating from the freedpeople's school; focusing on student gratitude, the address emphasized their "appreciation of the debt we owe to you." Similarly, Nathan Brackett was eulogized as a man "happy in the absolute giving of his life to serve," as opposed to the "mere money-gatherer." He was endorsed as a role model for students who were asked to reflect, "Does that sacrificing and suffering friendship put you under any obligation to do your best, to carry on the cause to which he dedicated his life?" In this regard Storer officials differed from the AMA, the largest and most successful benevolent society, which stressed rather the debt *due African Americans* because of the legacy of slavery. Storer students were instead reminded of their great moral debt to their southern-styled benefactors while being counseled in northern fashion to avoid all financial debt. This had profound implications for their efforts to realize their citizenship, particularly through the conventional venues of land-ownership.[32]

A Contradictory Curriculum of Entitlements:
Land, Reputation, and Loss of Movement

Storer officials recognized the importance of land-ownership as a traditional route to citizenship. The *Record*'s pages are filled with appeals echoing Crèvecoeur's ideals, linking farming to the virtues of moral industry in order to keep freedpeople from vagrancy, idleness, and squander. The *Record*'s editors identified the northern dream of small farm proprietorship as key, for "no people ever become self-reliant and independent, until a generation has grown up nourished by the fruit of its 'own vine and fig tree.'" Nathan Brackett was particularly involved in helping the students secure land. He had "during the past thirty years, deeded property, ranging from one fourth of an acre to eight or nine acres," to some forty students. The roll call of owners and the accompanying complimentary comments on their mortgage status created a public debt of gratitude due Storer from what is normally a private transaction. Celeste Brackett Newcomer recalled the "common practice" of black townspeople bringing her father their weekly wages "until the lot was paid for." Although college administrators were sincerely involved in helping the students and townspeople acquire land, their advice belied the reality that few black West Virginians could become homeowners easily.[33]

While land-ownership often proved elusive, farming was not. Both male and female students were obliged to work the college's 152 acres, known as Smallwood Farm. Free Will Baptist chroniclers euphemistically referred to this laboring as "gardening." As subsistence farming, which necessitated women's labor, predominated in rural West Virginia well into the twentieth century, agricultural training had its uses. Despite this regional reality, college officials' attitudes toward local prejudice, coupled with their philosophy of financial debt avoidance, labor, and moral indebtedness, hampered student efforts to become proprietors.[34]

Land-ownership and ties to a stable community were endorsed for their potential to avoid interracial conflict. Brackett helped African Americans obtain homes, but he may have inadvertently helped create segregated neighborhoods. The *Record*'s routine admonitions to stay put, be patient, and keep busy facilitated a Jim Crow sense of place, while stemming the ongoing black exodus to western parts of the state for attractive jobs in industry. Migration to cities was discouraged because students would have to compete with other workers. The 1892 winter issue of the *Record* featured a census of black homeowners, including those with the "most nicely kept yards" in town, revealing that all the owners lived within one mile of campus. After unwittingly delineating, in effect, the boundaries of the black sections of Boliver Heights and Harpers Ferry, the anonymous writer concluded, "When the time comes that the colored people of the South, live in their own homes, cultivate their own farms, and read their own ballots, there will no longer be a race

FIGURE 8. "Storer College, Harper's Ferry, West Virginia." Postcard images adopted from W. E. Dittmeyer, n.d., Storer College Documents, Harpers Ferry National Historical Park, Harpers Ferry, West Virginia.

problem." For the author, the race problem could be solved by black ownership characterized by creating distinctly separate spaces from whites, that is, by segregation.[35]

This protective distancing increasingly outstripped geographic boundary markers in delimiting shared social and economic spaces. Storer's campus setting, squarely in the white residential area of Harpers Ferry, demanded additional sequestering—a situation unlike that of most historically black colleges and universities. As Kendrick Grandison has shown, building placement was a critical factor in the establishment and flourishing of a black college during this time. Commanding Camp Hill, the college materially and psychologically confronted its white neighbors, necessitating a delicate negotiation of space for survival in Harpers Ferry (Fig. 8). Storer College claimed valuable real estate, and its buildings, once used by the loathed federal government as commanding headquarters, had charged historical significance.[36]

When the occasional rowdy behavior of Storer students posed a risk to those buildings, the backlash was immediate. During the 1867 Christmas holidays, the students had had an "exhibition of some kind" which resulted in "a disgraceful general fight, and on which occasion firecrackers were freely used in the house which greatly endangered the property by fire." Their behavior also sparked a letter of concern from the Harpers Ferry ordnance officer to the chief of ordnance in Washington, D.C. He urged that the transfer of the property from the War Department to the Freedmen's Bureau be made contingent upon the buildings' use designated "for Educational and Religious purposes only"; without "some restraint placed upon the parties now occupying" the property, the officer explained, it would "soon be so changed that it would be valueless to the U. States."[37]

Perhaps in response to such incidents, the number of rules proscribing undesirable student behaviors dramatically increased in the 1880s and 1890s, as a black middle class took root and white sentiment in favor of segregation increased. The 1869 catalog specified that any on-campus activity that might draw undue attention to students, including to "jump, dance, or scuffle," was not permitted; neither was drinking, smoking, or carrying weapons. Students were prohibited from attending town parties and from taking any excursion off campus "in mixed company," except by permission. A little over a decade later, the 1882–84 catalog pointedly made a virtue of Camp Hill's "isolation from the little town and all outside society" which "renders it especially favorable to study," and the 1869 "Prohibitions" list was nearly doubled. Routinely warned against the "growing evil" of pleasure trips, "which have almost without an exception terminated in wrangling and disorder," students were increasingly confined to campus. New rules forbade loitering and leaving town without permission, while others controlled more tightly student boarding arrangements. By the late 1890s, the rules expanded to forbid student socializing in resident homes. The faculty found subtle ways to limit student visits to town, such as the published note that "Pela Penick keeps school books" and sundry supplies, to save them from "the trouble of going to town." By 1897 a "marching" rule was in place, requiring "students to march in military columns to and from their recitations." By 1898 the loitering rule was expanded to forbid students from visiting campus buildings "during study hours or on Sundays," and they were forbidden to "give literary and musical entertainments out of town during the school session without special permission." The cumulative effect of the rules was to make students docile and invisible to the surrounding community.[38]

Coupled with movement curtailment was social monitoring, a function Coralie Franklin, along with many other black women, would soon assume as an intraracial classed duty necessary for racial uplift. School officials endorsed a code of conduct, labeled "A Better Way," in which students turned from "direct struggle" to "the gradual removal" of prejudice; they were encouraged to cultivate benevolent exemplary lives, which "lift up the wronged to a high and nobler plane." This became a patterned response among other middle-class black West Virginians as segregation took greater hold. On and off campus, students were encouraged to develop a practice of self-scrutiny and self-effacement that would minimize attention from white residents. Such *Storer Record* articles as "The Make-You-Rich-Quick Association," which appeared in February 1895, admonished students from joining freedpeople's cooperative ventures outside Storer. All students were always to be kept busy. The *Record* published letters from graduates who proudly reproduce their laborious schedules as proof of their "success." Student rooms were to be kept "at all times open" for inspections by "a committee of men and women," who gave "spicy" weekly reports, while student time was filled with daily prayer meetings, chapel, classes, and chores. In short, the college's incessant sermonizing to save money, work hard, avoid cities, and keep busy conspired with local prejudice to discourage freedpeople from organizing and pursuing any off-campus enterprise.[39]

Storer faculty members were charged with a moral responsibility from the outset. The 1869 catalog emphasized that "the Teachers will spare no pains, both by precept and example, to inculcate good morals, habits of industry and self-dependence." Students were encouraged to internalize this scrutiny, as student editor W. H. Gordon reminded classmates: "Remember that the future prosperity of the race to which you belong is in your hands; therefore you cannot afford to indorse [*sic*] a single measure that tends to impede its progress." Exhorted to self-reliance while compelled to serve as the college's domestics and carpenters, the students were learning to be both independent and obliged.[40]

Female students were especially targeted for the "careful protection" of maternal surveillance. By the 1880s, additional movement restrictions were placed upon them, as outlined in a separate "prohibitions" catalog section directed to "Young ladies." Wayward young women were monitored with letters and prayers by preceptresses such as Lue Brackett Lightner, who functioned more like "a social worker" in her dedicated "follow-up." Lightner's behavior was indicative of the gendered infrastructure of peer surveillance and moralizing intervention that produced "heart-searching results" and "changed lives." According to Franklin, Lightner would not let a "promising girl" drift and "slip from her." Likened to Bismarck by students, Lightner also had, according to her niece, "an almost unerring scent for the guilty when wrong doing had to be hunted down." "Good" behavior was elicited by leaving students afraid and at the mercy of Lightner, who perpetuated an atmosphere of white vigilance in which "the guilty feared her uncanny skill in detection." As matron of Myrtle Hall, she functioned as "leader, mother confessor, and final arbiter in all their difficulties."[41]

Storer faculty made the cultivation of appearance and manners a core component of citizenship for all students. Nathan Brackett gave daily talks on citizenship that loosely knit civic responsibilities with manners to help students survive in the less-than-welcoming white community. Brackett's daughter recalls:

> There were so many things to talk about: citizenship, like marriage, was not a state to be entered into lightly, but reverently, discreetly, and in the fear of God. The ballot is a sacred trust. Public questions and men were discussed. . . . Acts of Congress were explained. Humbler subjects included personal hygiene, cleanliness, care of the teeth, necessity for frequent bathing, how to make a bed, social relations; the courtesies of daily conduct, honesty, truthfulness, good manners at table, consideration of others, the dignity of labor![42]

Interlacing lectures about the ballot and civil rights was instruction in local visibility: the importance of deportment, manners, and a neat, modest appearance. Mixing personal hygiene with civics suggests that Brackett made these issues interdependent for freedpeople, particularly women. College officials targeted female students and monitored their dress in disguised sensitivity to class, not racial issues. The 1882–84 catalog devoted an entire section to "school dress," enumerating acceptable fabrics for girls while endorsing the value of "'simple' dress." Not allowed to "appear at public or other exercises of the school expensively or showily dressed," girls were admonished not to wear jewelry and trimmings. The 1889–91 biennial catalog went further: "We wish our students to be neatly and comfortably clad, but we are not willing to have even the wealthy dress in a manner to make the prudent and indigent uncomfortable." By 1905, they were required to make their graduation dresses. Amid a long list of "do nots" that presupposed student imprudence, the *Storer Record* editors cautioned students not "to buy or lend luxuries." Beginning with her newspaper columns in the late 1880s, graduate Coralie Franklin reclaimed this discourse of appearance to make black women visible, authoritative practitioners of what historian Evelyn Higginbotham has characterized as the "politics of respectability."[43]

Storer's linkage of appearance to citizenship situates the college in a greater postwar racialized discourse about freedpeople's entitlement, particularly women's, to display their status. While African American women saw their appearance as a cultural and individual expression, white people saw this as an intolerable assumption of privilege. Since the close of the war when the *Spirit of Jefferson* editors felt "compelled" on 5 December 1865 to assess the town's "colored population" for their readers with "candor," the local press rewarded those African Americans who turned the other cheek. Praising African Americans for being properly "polite and submissive to their superiors," while noting that their "status" had been "fixed" as citizens, editors expected that they would continue to be "respectful as to all proper submission." They had little confidence in freedpeople to organize their lives without masters.

Like Storer faculty and students, reporters conflated self-presentation with the attainment of citizenship but with different effect. The local press focused on appearance to derogate student activism. The *Virginia Free Press* described Storer's 1872 commencement: "We understand the assemblage of colored people . . . was simply 'tremenjus.' Boquets were much in demand by the *fairer* portion of them . . . to 'shower upon the stujents.'" With a condescending rhetoric borrowed from minstrelsy, the *Press* editor had this malicious last word to demean the assembly's propriety, implying that the former slaves had not achieved an education as much as airs. When Storer students protested the addition of a segregated car to the rear of a train for their families to attend graduation, the local press promptly chastised them for both their seeming ignorance and pretentiousness. "Being educated to a very fine point," these "Ebo-shin gents and brown-skin ladies" assumed privileges, with which they had no business meddling, and confused them with rights. The reporter concluded: "No wonder they clamor continually for 'equal rights' as many don't know it when they've got 'em—in truth, don't know whether they come tied up in a paper or are kept in a jug." This contemptuous dismissal of African Americans as citizens suggests that Storer students had far more at stake than carpetbaggers like Tourgée in the making of their reputations.[44]

Misplaced emphasis on outward image had the effect of undermining students, leaving them with only the appearance of citizenship. While reputation was relevant for claiming political agency, Storer officials distracted students from the fight against injustice. Achieving respectability and self-responsibility misdirected students from challenging discrimination.

Attempts to mold student moral life within the confines of the campus indirectly helped foster student docility, even apathy, regarding the diminution of their civil rights. Student outrage against prejudice was not tolerated, and the faculty often rationalized it as idiosyncratic oversensitivity. Mary Brackett Robertson recalled: "These ambitious freedmen were very jealous of their new found dignity and readily resented any real or fancied reflection upon themselves or their race. Sometimes hours of explaining were required to smooth the ruffled feelings of those who thought they detected an insult in the words of some well-meaning visitor. For this reason, perhaps, 'Pettyness,' 'Jealousy,' 'Imagining a Slight' were so forcibly and successfully held up by the Principal as childish." Robertson reduced civil rights issues into a question of maturity and lack of cultivation that required personal counseling. Reconfiguring racism as the result of personal shortcoming had implications for student activism. While student acquiescence to a southern definition of reputation based on honor rather than on northern self-interest enabled them to survive in Harpers Ferry, it also paralyzed them from effectively challenging community injustice.[45]

When Reputation, Race, and Gender Collide: The Regional Sexualization of Sarah Jane Foster's Teaching

Female teachers also felt the political force of differing regional understandings of reputation, which compromised their Reconstruction work. The story of white Free Will Baptist teacher Sarah Jane Foster is nearly an allegory of the fate of this region's Reconstruction: the very behaviors that made her professionally successful as a teacher also brought about her removal. Local white citizens attacked Foster's relationships with her black male students to divert them from their real fear: the propriety of white women pursuing professional careers.

Though not a member of the Storer College faculty, Foster was hired by the Reverend Silas Curtis, a Storer trustee, and supervised by Nathan Brackett under the auspices of the Shenandoah Mission of the Free Will Baptist Home Missionary Society, the AMA, and the Freedmen's Bureau. She was thus directly in the orbit of the school's educational philosophy and Reconstruction practices. Hers was an "uncommonly bad," poorly equipped, "small basement" elementary school classroom in Martinsburg. With roughly eighty day students and another forty-five attending at night, Foster taught basic literacy and math skills to freedpeople of all ages. Her short-lived career points up the gendered and racialized importance of reputation to citizenship and to American notions of personhood in the body politic. The scandal involving her dramatizes the local translation of racial injustice into sexual oppression and of questionable professional behavior into sexual impropriety. Her story forcefully demonstrates how gender, race, and reputation became the levers determining the local outcome of Reconstruction.[46]

But in the winter of 1865 when Foster arrived in West Virginia, she entertained high hopes and deep convictions about her undertaking. Nathan Brackett found nearby Martinsburg congenial to the cause of black education, and Foster initially reported the town to be so "intensely Union" that "a rebel is worse off here than farther North." Yet the educators' perceptions did not accord with those of the experienced Freedmen's Bureau agent Captain J. H. McKenzie. The month after Foster's arrival, McKenzie reported that "the late rebels here manifest a purpose to oppress the colored people all they can . . . and rent all their spite upon the heads of the poor Blacks." He then described the repeated attempts of "rowdy" elements to disrupt Foster's school. Teenage boys had thrown a boulder against the school door, which was "clean carried off its hinges." The intruders were fired upon by the freedpeople, who chased and caught two of them. Upon arrival, McKenzie arrested the boys and kept them in jail overnight. McKenzie noted that some months prior to Foster's arrival, another local teacher's efforts to start a night school for freedchildren were met by "a mob of from thirty to forty men" who attacked her school at least three times, "for the purpose of entimidating her." McKenzie thus depicted the prevailing "spirit of Mobism that exists here" to show the need for stationing troops there. The degree, if not kind, of terrorism directed against Foster was fairly commonplace throughout the South.[47]

Nearly as soon as she arrived, Foster ired local whites by allowing herself to be chaperoned by various freedmen who were her students, including her assistant, the notoriously named John Brown. These escorts felt, not unrealistically, that she needed protection from the hostile white townspeople. But after just three weeks at Martinsburg, Foster confided in her diary that both she and her chaperones had been threatened because of this escort. Tensions so escalated that on 22 January 1866, class was canceled, yet Foster defiantly paraded down the full length of a Martinsburg street with one of her black male students, "just to show that I did not mean to be driven off by the roughs." Her landlord, Joseph Hoke, a Storer board member and the county prosecutor, "seriously advised" that she not go to teach a class the next night. When she insisted, Captain McKenzie, fearing an imminent mob assault, escorted her home with pistol in hand. Ostracized, she was forced to change boarding arrangements. Brackett, accompanied by the superintendent of the Shenandoah Valley schools, responded the next week by placing "a veto on my long days' works." Foster's adamancy made her a target of gendered surveillance.[48]

Foster responded to the growing local threats and school reproach with redoubled recalcitrance and naive earnestness. Outraged, she wrote in her diary: "I heard tonight that I was going to marry John Brown. What next? Well let the fools talk. Can't they have wit enough to let me alone?" Rumors escalated of Foster being promiscuous, a "half-nigger" or married to a black man. Her duties included visiting student families and this furthered more gossip. Local backlash only fueled Foster's defiance: "People may talk. The scholars know that I am clear of blame." She disregarded the whisperings: "Pooh. They haven't wit enough to lie straightly and sensibly out here." Even in her letters to the *Zion's Advocate*, Foster dismissed the harassment: "I don't mind such things at all. . . . Mrs. Vosburgh [a friend] was actually asked by a neighbor . . . 'if I were not part nigger.' I hope they will believe it, for then surely they could not complain of my teaching the people of my own race." At times, she seemed almost habituated to the provocation; after hearing "several pistol shots," she encountered a group of white men, one of whom grabbed her arm. She wrote to her Zion readers, "I paid no attention to his rudeness, slipped away from his grasp, and soon placed several groups of my pupils between us, coming home without further annoyance." She told Brackett about the rumors, and he supposedly laughed it off. Less than a week later, however, Brackett transferred her to Harpers Ferry. Her replacement was the no-nonsense Anne Dudley.[49]

During her four-month tenure in Martinsburg, Foster directed much attention to her students, whom she grew to love. She particularly nurtured her relationship with John Brown, whom she regarded as the "firmest support in the school." Part of her devotion revolved around effecting his conversion, as she exhibited the missionary spirit required by the AMA. Throughout her diaries, Foster comments on his spiritual struggles, while admiring the "fine, intelligent face" of this twenty-one-year-old local carpenter whose speeches she found "so grand and noble." Brackett shared her esteem for Brown, encouraging him to study at Bates College in Lewiston, Maine. After she was transferred to Harpers Ferry, Foster confided to her diary: "I would not like Mr. Brackett to know that I have written three times to him [Brown]. I fear he might half blame me though he thinks the world of John. I believe that I am right though [in corresponding with Brown]."[50]

Whatever the nature of her relationship with Brown, Foster was undoubtedly dedicated to her students' well-being and to her work. On 14

March 1866, she declared in her diary that "I am in love with my work," and that was the cause of her problem: Foster's love and her work were conflated not only by her but also by residents who made Brown the nexus of her devotion. From innuendo and gossip the reactionary townspeople transformed Foster's relationship with Brown, perhaps only platonic, into one exclusively sexual. The behavior of this dedicated carpetbag teacher so outraged white citizens that it resulted in her dismissal, presumably to save her life. After she finished the spring 1866 term at Harpers Ferry, Foster was terminated. She was subsequently hired by the AMA to work under noted African American educator Francis L. Cardozo of Howard University, but she was later dispatched to an isolated, malarial plantation district in South Carolina. She died from yellow fever in 1868.[51]

Foster's experience, while dramatic, was hardly unique. Foster and Brown's predicament was part of a larger postwar phenomenon that entangled politics with sex as ex-Confederates connected black men's attainment of citizenship rights with sexual access to white women. This presumptuous sexuality enabled outraged, disfranchised West Virginian ex-Confederates to oppose the freedmen and reassert their traditional privileges of masculinity, including authority over black men, black women, and white women. This fear of unruly black passions, made evident in the intensified postwar policing against miscegenation, went hand in hand with dread of black suffrage. West Virginia passed a harsh anti-miscegenation law in 1882.[52]

It was also in West Virginia that a notable murder case arose involving an extramarital alliance between a white man and a black woman. *Strauder v. West Virginia* became the occasion for a test of the violation of the Fourteenth Amendment against a black man. Found guilty of murdering his adulterous wife by an all-white jury, defendant Taylor Strauder successfully appealed to the Supreme Court in 1879 to reverse the lower court's decision on the grounds that his rights had been violated under the equal protection clause of the Fourteenth Amendment. Justice William Strong found that the West Virginia statute was "practically a brand upon them, [black citizens] affixed by the law, an assertion of their inferiority, and a stimulant to that race prejudice which is an impediment to securing to individuals of the race that equal justice which the law aims to secure to all others." Writing the majority opinion, Strong used language that eerily foreshadowed Tourgée's brief for Homer Plessy. This overturning of the West Virginia statute that categorically excluded African Americans from jury service was a landmark victory in an otherwise bleak legal landscape of suits unsuccessfully invoking the new amendment to obtain redress. Strauder's outcome later inspired Storer graduate John Clifford to argue against segregated schools based on the Fourteenth Amendment, another West Virginia case which set an important precedent for future cases challenging school segregation.[53]

The elevated level of community interest in the purported crime of Annie Strauder in pursuing an illicit, mixed-race relationship and in Taylor Strauder's defense of his brutal response to her infidelity echoed the interest that had surrounded the teaching of Sarah Jane Foster and other northern women: both demonstrate how violations of gender conventions easily knotted with violations of racial and regional boundaries. Drawing swords with Foster's friend Mary Clemmer Ames, Democratic editors quickly sexualized the suspect presence of these northern teachers in order to contain their professional activities. Of particular threat was that these women were now perceived to assert another kind of jurisdiction over the former property of white males. Ames used the northern teachers, those "useful, self-reliant independent creatures," to criticize a "Virginia belle," whose "idea of ladyhood is a life of helpless, aimless idleness." Storer officials found this Ames article pleasing, but the *Spirit of Jefferson* found her "venomous effusions" to be an example of "puritanical hate" and "hypocritical cant" from the North. The determinedly Democratic newspaper justified the "Virginia belle's" dislike of the northern "amazons," like Foster and Ames, because their motivation was dismissed as merely for the "almighty dollar." Forcing themselves where "their presence is neither agreeable or useful," these Yankees, the newspaper warned, might nevertheless "excite in the bosoms of the male portion of the downtrodden race feelings of a different character to those of gratitude," which "may assuage the grief of those 'red-lipped school girls.'" The furious reactions provoked by the article and by the teachers' threatening presence itself help explain why Foster became an easy target for violence; she violated not only presumptions about the capabilities of former slaves but also those about women's roles.[54]

The hostility of the local press toward northern teachers as manifested in sexual slurs reflected a postwar gendered and racialized focus on reputation that nearly all the Reconstruction writers of this study encountered. Foster's case pointedly illustrates the postwar fragility of reputation, dependent upon ties to the land, family, and community. Contemporaries were well aware of the southern political tactic of besmirching offending carpetbaggers' reputations, as Tourgée painfully discovered. One Republican committee member queried a witness for a congressional report on Klan violence: "Do you know a single northern person, male or female, who has come down into this country and taken an interest in your political affairs, who has not suffered in character; who has not been maligned?" The denial, given the hundreds of pages of other overwhelming testimony to the contrary, was hardly convincing.[55]

The community's handling of Foster's unnamed crime attested to the potency of silence in transforming racial into sexual oppression. Storer faculty contributed to this conspiratorial silence in their preoccupation with the *appearance* of her alleged crime. Much like the redemptive performance of reputation that Thanet would soon stage for her novel's protagonist, Fairfax Rutherford, Foster's behavior became a kind of allegorical performance that would be "read" in true Hawthornian fashion by the community. The Reverend Silas Curtis advised Brackett on the affair:

> I hope you will take occasion from this to give every one of your teachers a good *sound, thorough, lecture* on their *deportment* and charge them to take an effectual warning from the affair at Martinsburg. I shun the *very appearance of evil*. . . . But I would not be too severe on Miss Foster, if she has not intentionally committed any crime. Still the cause and we much suffer on account of her indiscretions. I hope others will learn to be more cautious and careful. They should remember that rebel eyes are constantly upon them seeking some occasion to injure them and retard or prevent our work of mercy among the Freedmen. What can you do with Miss Foster, poor girl! I pity her and shall pray for her.[56]

Storer officials were aware that the real culprit was not Brown but the "rebel eyes" of the white voyeur-editors reading Foster's actions. No doubt these same eyes kept Storer students under surveillance and teachers on guard for their appearance. These eyes were "constantly upon" the teachers, "seeking some occasion to injure them," in order to assure white male supremacy against women and black Americans.

Foster contributed to the ensuing conspiratorial silence and inadvertently encouraged her loss of reputation by refusing to name publicly the "crime" of which she was accused. When the scandal broke out, she forthrightly informed her *Zion's Advocate* readers of the harassment. After her transfer and dismissal, Foster resorted to euphemism, referring to the affair only as a "disturbance." While Foster retaliated by publicly protesting her dismissal, she also respected the conventions that demanded linguistic discretion to protect readers' sensibilities. This reliance on euphemism and silence came at a high cost; in her discussion of the human body as the nexus for abolitionist and feminist discursive practices in sentimental fiction, Karen Sanchez-Eppler has shown that such conformity to the "dictates of a linguistic delicacy" functioned as an "essential prop both for the subordination and demoralization of women and for the exploitation of slaves." Foster represented herself as a hardworking teacher who disagreed with her boss about a move she felt to be "not wise," but "of course I submit quietly." Her circumlocution, although understandable, weakened her attempts to vindicate herself in print and expose the accusations for what they were: malicious rumor. Later Foster told her readers that it was she who *chose* not to return to West Virginia to resume her work. Foster's observance of propriety sanctioned "appearance" as reality and implicitly acknowledged the threat of white male desire for sexual assault and violence that always lurked in "rebel eyes."[57]

Foster's need to feel professionally accountable and vindicate herself alternated tensely with her desire to appease and assure her readers that she was a virtuous Christian woman. As she painfully discovered, the two were conflated because contemporary notions of reputation for women relied upon the gendered markers of self-image. In his later recommendation of Foster to the AMA, Brackett could not resist mentioning that Foster's strength as a "zealous, enthusiastic missionary" made her "a little rough in manners," which "exposed" her to "scandal." Brackett's comments prompt consideration of what the price would have been had Foster been more explicit.[58]

Foster's rhetorical balancing act underscores the importance of readers in deciding her reputation. What made Foster a superb teacher—diligence, disregard of prejudice, and respect for human potential that translated into teaching long hours within the black community—were the Reconstruction values that brought about her defeat and deprived Martinsburg African Americans of her services. Her story suggests that the ideals of teachers like Foster were challenged by the very processes of implementation. This paradox was also felt by Storer students as they left the relatively safe confines of the campus to pursue careers. Their contradictory educations had to be reconciled to accommodate their social ambitions, political activism, and professional success. By 1880 the college had begun to fulfill John Storer's dream that freedpeople take authoritative roles in shaping their own education. Records from 1884 show that Storer had provided at least some training to 400 teachers serving in five states, and 112 had graduated with teaching degrees. Jefferson County alone had twenty active "free schools," which were taught by former Storer students. Students began campaigning for an endowed chair to be filled by a black person, and in 1880, two graduates, Coralie Franklin and William Henry

Bell, were the first to receive full-time faculty appointments. It was not until 1944, however, that Dr. Richard McKinney became Storer's first African American president. While the contradictions behind Storer's ambivalent curriculum were eventually resolved, further ironies arose as graduates reconstructed the regional meaning of labor, duty, property, and reputation to suit themselves. This negotiation is best reflected in the divergent careers of two of its most stellar successes, Coralie Franklin and John Clifford.[59]

Student John Clifford, the *Pioneer Press*, and the Manly Wagers of Reputation

In its enmeshment of sexuality, race, and reputation, Foster's experience resembles that of Storer graduate John Robert Clifford, an educator and lawyer who founded the *Pioneer Press* newspaper. However, the far more savvy Clifford deployed a defiant strategy for empowerment, one that hinged upon a hard-won postwar construction of manhood for other enterprising black veterans. The details of Clifford's life say much about postwar opportunities in the Mountain State, particularly the roles black West Virginians saw for themselves in crafting an ongoing Reconstruction. He was born in 1848 in Williamsport, (West) Virginia, to free black parents, who sent him to Chicago at around age twelve to receive an education because there were no black schools in his home county of Grant. He joined the army in March 1865 and fought in the 13th U.S. Heavy Artillery under Grant in Kentucky, Tennessee, and eastern Virginia. After the war Corporal Clifford finished high school in Chicago and returned home in 1870. He taught in the greater Wheeling area for a few years before entering Storer. He graduated from Storer in 1876 and then taught in Martinsburg at the all-black Sumner School, where he later served as principal until 1885.[60]

Clifford's accomplishments in journalism are equally notable. While teaching, he founded the *Pioneer Press* in 1882, the first black newspaper in West Virginia. Published in Martinsburg, it continued under his editorship until 1917, making it the longest running black newspaper in the United States at that time. A forerunner of the explosive proliferation of African American newspapers between 1890 and 1910, the *Pioneer Press* critically sustained political community regardless of disfranchisement.[61]

Despite these considerable achievements, Clifford's accomplishments in law are his most outstanding, rivaling those of Tourgée. Ambitious and energetic, he passed the bar exam in 1887 to become West Virginia's first practicing black attorney. In February 1892 Clifford became the first black attorney to practice before the Allegheny County Bar in western Maryland. Clifford waged his fiercest battles against Jim Crow at the same time Tourgée was helping Homer Plessy challenge segregated travel in Louisiana. His commitment to pursue legal remedies against discrimination was itself an accomplishment. The daunting challenges faced by Clifford and other nineteenth-century black lawyers made him, in legal historian Paul Finkelman's words, part of an elite group of "social engineers" whose trailblazing efforts "changed the social landscape of America."[62]

In his fight for the legal and civil rights of African Americans, Clifford won renown for challenging school segregation under West Virginia's 1872 constitution. In *Martin v. Board of Education*, he argued that the state's law that prohibited the attendance of children of both races in the same school denied black children "equal protection of the laws," as stipulated in the Fourteenth Amendment, when it failed to provide separate schools or permit the five children of Thomas Martin to attend white schools in Morgan County. Clifford lost, but his September 1896 appeal made him the first African American attorney to appear before the West Virginia State Supreme Court. In upholding the lower court's 1893 decision that the state constitution held predominance over the Fourteenth Amendment, the justices applied a logic similar to that of the U.S. Supreme Court in deciding the *Plessy* case four months earlier. Judge Marmaduke Dent famously opined that "social equality can not be enforced by law," a pronouncement succinctly summarizing current judicial thinking from the *Slaughterhouse Cases* to *Plessy*. Although he lost the appeal, Clifford's constitutional challenge to the doctrine of "separate but equal" would be affirmed in *Brown v. Board of Education* some fifty-eight years later.[63]

Clifford was more successful in representing West Virginian Carrie M. Williams, an African American teacher who protested her school board's curtailment of the school term to five months only for the district's black children. Clifford advised Williams to refuse to sign a contract for the shorter term and, instead, simply continue teaching the full term of eight months that white students enjoyed. When the school year ended, the school board refused to pay her full salary, allowing Clifford to successfully bring suit on the teacher's behalf on charges of illegal discrimination. *Williams v. Board of Education of Fairfax District* affirmed the right of African Americans to an equal, if separate, education under state law. According to Paul Finkelman, this 1898 landmark decision was "one of the few civil rights victories in a southern state's highest court before the turn of the century."[64]

FIGURE 9. "Group Portrait of the 46 Members of the Niagara Movement [Second Meeting] Held at Storer College, August 15–19, 1906." *Seated 7th left to right*, John Robert Clifford; *8th left to right*, William Du Bois. Storer College Documents, Harpers Ferry National Historical Park, Harpers Ferry, West Virginia.

Attorney Clifford's considerable professional attainments propelled him to champion civil rights on a national level. Well-known in party politics and a regular at the state's conventions, Clifford was described as "progressive, independent and ambitious." He belonged to many civic organizations, including the American Negro Academy, the Knights of Wise Men, the Masons, and Carter G. Woodson's Association for the Study of Negro Life and History. In 1905 Clifford helped found the Niagara Movement for Civil Rights, which soon came to Storer's campus (Fig. 9). Prompted by frustration with Booker T. Washington's accommodationist policies and organized by W. E. B. Du Bois among others, the Niagara Movement was the first collective effort by African Americans to insist on full citizenship rights. From 1911 to 1913 Clifford served as president of the National Negro American Political League, and in 1915 he helped form the West Virginia Civic League, the precursor of the National Association for the Advancement of Colored People (NAACP).[65]

Clifford's achievements and civic activism would seem to exemplify all the aspirations Storer faculty had for its students, particularly the Free Will admonishments to perform community service, work hard, and seek self-improvement. After his graduation Clifford appeared to maintain active if not especially cordial relations with his alma mater. In December 1876 Nathan Brackett officiated at Clifford's marriage to Mary Franklin, Coralie Franklin's sister. Although few issues from the 1890s exist, his paper regularly carried ads for Storer, and Clifford participated in Storer's vacation teaching institutes. The college newspaper applauded him for "winning laurels in the circuit courts of Berkeley County." Yet Clifford sharply rejected Storer's inculcation of the value of menial labor, slavish manners, and sense of obligation to white people. Clifford's achievement turned out to be a nightmare for the college.[66]

Clifford positioned his newspaper to move beyond the servile identity for citizenship that Storer faculty had encouraged in the 1860s and 1870s. He utilized the contradictory language of solvency and duty that he had learned at Storer to advocate black civil rights. With articles by Storer graduates and nationally known African Americans, the *Press* transformed the application of Storer ideals such as duty and indebtedness. Clifford repudiated any debt, moral or political, that Storer faculty had pressed on its students: "We cannot admit that we are debtors to the [Republican] party. . . . we are tired of being told before each recurring election that the Negro is a republican because he *owes* that much to the party. We want *all parties* to understand that principles with us are sacred things, and not objects of merchandize. . . . Are we understood?" Similarly, African American *Press* contributor James H. Jones, principal of the Wheeling schools, argued that "the duty of the hour" was protest against disfranchisement, because "the Negro's condition is chargeable to the whole nation, and justice demands that the whole nation pay the bill." Clifford's newspaper recast the moral duty of freedpeople as an obligation to collect a debt now owed *them*.[67]

Like Mary Clemmer Ames and Tourgée, Clifford contended with the local Democratic press, but he also battled with local Republicans. Although he endorsed Radical Republican policy, Clifford had a long-standing antagonistic relationship with prominent local Republicans who resented what they saw as his upstart manner. Undoubtedly bolstering his antagonism to Republicans was his witnessing of the August 1874 lynching of John Tallifero in Martinsburg, a murder in which at least one local Republican, George Evans, was involved. When Evans was later appointed Martinsburg postmaster, Clifford spearheaded a protest and supported the Democratic candidate, J. Nelson Wisner. Understood as a response to the 1880s rise of the lily-white movement—an anti–civil rights movement within the Republican Party devoted to winning back white voters from the Democratic Party by purging black leaders—Clifford's tactics were not unique. Many African Americans felt compelled to adopt what historian John M. Giggie has called a "philosophy of pragmatic calculation," courting whatever party in power might be responsive.[68]

Clifford's swing allegiances to the Democratic Party might also be understood as yet another ironic result of Storer's inculcation of Free Will faith. After roughly 1884, Clifford evidently endorsed "independent" voting. Clifford insisted that racial interests must supersede party loyalty, as did ethnic interests, until "every citizen black or white" is given "his alienable rights." In recognizing the advantages of whiteness, Clifford chafed: "To the Irishman, the German, and the Jew courtesies are shown and to the Negro *demands* are made." Freedom for Clifford came to be defined as a politically iconoclastic free will.[69]

Clifford called on black West Virginians to act as members of a greater cohesive community by printing articles and letters by nationally known African American activists and educators writing from around the country. This variety showed readers the common interests and diverse Reconstruction approaches of other black literary communities. Assistant editor George T. Jones joined in the debate against Eastern European immigration and tried to divert national attention from black citizens as scapegoats to unassimilable foreigners, thereby making a place for black citizens in the polity. As Clifford saw the erosion of black civil rights on a national scale, he tried to make his paper the leading editorial arbiter of justice challenging a corrupt judicial system. His "labor of love" was to build "an independent union of colored men" that "will be the downfall of any political party that refuses them justice and protection." The *Pioneer Press* valued unity in numbers as it tried to unite scattered ex-slave families and to celebrate black protest.[70]

The newspaper also advocated uplift through property. Himself a landlord, Clifford championed deeds to land, not tools to farm; confrontational action, not acquiescence; entrepreneurial ventures, not idle passbooks. Rejecting Storer's entreaties to farm land, the *Pioneer Press* advocated land-ownership—regardless of what one did with it. The paper praised attainment of landlord status in a way that recalls Woolson's poetic celebration of professional status. Noted Baptist minister and dean of Shaw

University professor Albert W. Pegues commented on the prosperity of black North Carolinians: "In recent years their attention has been given more to the accumulation of property than to becoming skilled in politics. To my mind this is quite a step in advance. . . . In every town many own their town lots upon which are varied buildings from the fine house down to almost no house; *but they are theirs*." In "Private Property in Land," George T. Jones offered a short world history on land-ownership to illustrate the merits of proprietorship. In "Stay on the Farm," farming was portrayed as an "honorable way" to earn a living that offered opportunities to be both "independent" and at "leisure" for other pursuits. Clifford would find nothing amiss in a black youth's poring over a "French Grammar" in a squalid cabin, a scene that Booker Washington had famously condemned.[71]

Clifford's rallying political vision was market oriented. Capitalizing on the long-standing industrial base of Harpers Ferry, his paper thrived because he targeted the interests of an emergent community of profitable black businesses struggling against discrimination. Increasingly replacing postwar domestic servants were African American hotel keepers, who owned four-fifths of the business in Harpers Ferry from 1880 to 1900. Instead of laundresses there were owners of laundries like the Harrises of Shepherdstown. Rather than Storer's plan of saving funds, Clifford's *Pioneer Press* advocated petty entrepreneurship to fight bigotry. He wrote, "The Negro must embark in all the business enterprises. Ah! That same old complaint in Martinsburg as elsewhere[:] 'Can't get the patronage of the race.' No matter if you cannot at the start, you will finally break down the wall of prejudice. Let us try it anyway." Probing for reasons behind the evident lack of racial unity, the *Pioneer Press* foregrounded a series of questions, such as, "Why is it that the colored man who is always talking about building each other up in business passes by the colored man's grocery to trade with a white grocer?" Not only the grocer but his (affluent) customer would be the foundation for a racially autonomous and economically united community. In trying to reach potential readers, Clifford pleaded for strengthening the black consumer base of Harpers Ferry through education.[72]

Embracing a range of black economic classes was a complex Reconstruction vision Storer College never achieved in the 1860s and 1870s. By the 1880s, however, the graduates of freedpeople's schools such as Storer had made this vision attainable for African Americans born in freedom. *Pioneer Press* articles written by the "Talented Tenth" of Harpers Ferry urged industrial education coupled with academic training, a policy known as "dovetailing," which Booker T. Washington endorsed at Tuskegee. The *Pioneer Press* celebrated African American cultural contributions from patent development to painting. Drawing the likeness between an educated and an uneducated man to "churned and unchurned milk," one writer urged a school for the "higher training" of African Americans. West Virginia educator J. L. Champ put it more concretely: "Duties to self imply that 'he not use his liberty as an occasion to the flesh, but by love serving one another.' What we mean to impress, is the necessity of cultivating race pride, of fostering the acquisition of property, accumulation of wealth, and these by encouraging men of small capital to form associations, and to enter into the various fields of trade, —in union there is strength." Such comments show that the newspaper would search far afield, even amid the controversial terrain of labor trade unionism, for racial empowerment. For example, the paper reported on developments within the Knights of Labor, arguing "wherever and into whatever organization we can go, where manhood, blind to color or past condition, is the badge of admission, we should take up our bed and walk." Despite Clifford's allegiance to a Du Boisian program of political activism, his paper's endorsement of economic solutions for black advancement also nodded to Booker T. Washington's materialist strategy of building a petite bourgeoisie from the ground up. Whereas Washington urged economic development to promote interracial harmony, Clifford advocated the strategy in order to sustain an independent black community supported by its own economic infrastructure.[73]

Early in his newspaper's publication history, Clifford foresaw success achieved by a classed and racial solidarity. He confidently claimed in August 1885 that "the *Pioneer Press* is read and appreciated by the best people of the State, and is destined to be one of the best papers in the country." The "best people" were increasingly defined as educated petty entrepreneurs, like Clifford himself. Recognizing the economic benefits of racial and economic solidarity, Francis Cardozo likened social structure to the floors of a building, with the lower classes providing a necessary foundation that was outstripped in importance by the independent middle stories of the "farmer, merchant, and mechanic." Such thinking thwarted the Storer emphasis on training a servant class, which was in any case increasingly rendered obsolete in the wake of black advancement.[74]

In a move that reflected Storer's emphasis on the importance of appearance to achieving civil rights, Clifford acknowledged that the complement of solid economic achievement was the social success profiled by the "best people." Alongside etiquette articles, such as "How to Act at the

Table" (July 1887) or "A Phonic Lesson" on proper elocution (March 1887), were society columns like "Social Life in Parkersburg" and the popular "Parkersburg Pickings" that profiled successful individuals. Those leaders working politically for racial uplift were acknowledged in the regularly featured column "Some Race Doings." These were the prospective authors of the great "Race Literature" of their people, for "no race can, or will write another people's history." As contributor "E. E. U." declared, "If forth from the fiery ordeal of slavery ... there has come a Still, a Douglas, a Frances Harper ... what brilliant stars ought the race to now produce?" This enthusiasm for stellar black talent implicitly acknowledged that little was being done for the race by whites.[75]

Clifford imagined his paper as striking out on a new postwar frontier of racial advancement to resist legal segregation. Yet this path had its downside. It took paradoxical and tragic turns for many working-class African Americans. Begrudged or denied goods and services by whites, they became dependent on entrepreneurial black business communities, who inadvertently profited from their constrained choices. While Clifford may not have been one of a calculating elite who capitalized on racial subordination, he nevertheless derived unintended benefit from segregation. Echoing an old Storer theme, many *Pioneer Press* contributors endorsed the evolutionary logic of survival of the fittest, an inevitable result of slavery, to help rationalize changing class and caste distinctions. A shift from an earlier egalitarian tradition of emancipation, such thinking, as historian Kevin Gaines has demonstrated, reveals the many ways in which racial uplift internalized dominant white modes of hierarchical power relations structured by racism.[76]

Clifford's favored deployment of gender to dislodge any racialist or class presumptions of his readers reveals, as in the Foster case, the particular ways in which these variables were mutually constitutive. With his paper's original masthead, "Bullets in Time of War, Ballots in Time of Peace," Clifford utilized a popular, gendered rhetoric that championed the valor, manliness, and entitlement of the black male veteran. The *Pioneer Press* exemplifies the close, important postwar connections forged between black veterans and newspaper editors to empower the new citizens. A veteran himself, Clifford made the black soldier into the prototypical patriotic figure, the eleventh-hour rescuer of an ungrateful Union which had enslaved him: "Show to the world that we are men. Had it not been for you, it [the Union] would have been shattered and the shackles still on your hands. Your bayonets and bullets brought about your freedom, and for it, you are obligated to no party as much as you are to yourselves. Then let us with as much manliness protect it with the ballot."[77]

Repeatedly invoking a long-standing gendered rhetoric of political rights, Clifford and many of his contributors, much like Tourgée, refashioned citizenship bids into a contest of manly valor. This tendency was evident even in a small item in the 30 May 1888 issue on the public collection of funds to send black delegates to the Fairmont Convention, which was meeting to select delegates to the Republican National Convention. Clifford saw the fund-raising as demeaning vote buying, and he argued that "there is as much glory of being *men* in politics as there is in anything else," for "it is the only true and proper way to beget respect." In a strategy similar to Dudley's Try Company song, Clifford's articles such as "Don't Whine" from October 1886 and "Hard Heads" from February 1887 used militant rhetoric to resist accommodation. The nation's inevitable savior, the black man should logically be the natural inheritor of citizenship. Clifford's attempt to monumentalize the black veteran as the worthy, virile inheritor of citizenship was at odds with the nation's calculus of his value. Because of the black soldier's identification with slavery and his tenuous hold on the social prerogatives of citizenship and moral agency, he was perceived as a threat to the ideals of white, self-disciplined masculinity then under construction. Clifford's insistence that black residents were entitled to a black policeman, whose appointment was a "manly act" by the city council, was risky in a town that had loathed the black Union soldiers garrisoned there. When white Jefferson County Republicans failed to nominate any black delegates to attend the Second Congressional Convention to be held in Keyser, West Virginia, Clifford praised black protestors "manly enough to upbraid them." In response, thirty-two readers canceled their subscriptions the following month, a reaction Clifford rebuked "because we had the manhood to assert our rights." Insisting his *Press* has "never backed down one inch," Clifford rejoined, "if there is not enough manly men of color to support such a paper, why let it die." Indeed, Clifford's brash "right is might" tactics alienated many black West Virginians across party lines.[78]

Clifford's challenge to racist presumptions relied paradoxically on reinforcing delimiting gender stereotypes. His paper's steadfast focus on black veterans invited the subordination of black women to them. With the significant exception of Coralie Franklin's "Woman's Column," the paper relied primarily on male contributors who nominally accorded black women a right to industrial education. For example, contributor Albert W. Pegues argued that "the redemption and uplifting of the race depend upon the young people of both sexes"; however, he devoted only one sentence regarding women's industrial education: "Let the girls learn dressmaking, housekeeping, the various forms of needlework as well as fitting themselves for the higher callings." While boys could be trained for the professions, it remained unclear as to which fields those "higher callings" translated into for women.[79]

Fellow contributor Francis Cardozo clarified black women's options. Matter of factly noting "there are female lawyers, doctors, ministers and teachers" as if it were commonplace, Cardozo argued that "with regard to women doing anything else that men do, I presume no one but an ultra Bourbon objects." However, Cardozo used women's professional success to undermine their demand for the ballot as unnecessary: unlike suffragists, these women were "applying themselves in a more practical manner to the accomplishment of the rights of women to practice the professions by actually engaging in these vocations successfully." While occasionally printing items noting black women's professional success, Clifford favored those educational "improvements" to women's colleges made by adding a "wholesome department of domestic economy." He elaborated: "household occupations are in themselves an intellectual and moral exercise of no mean importance, after which any lady has enough surplus time for books and the arts." The paper reinforced as much as it reflected a gendered reality in which its editor advocated domestic training for black women to meet the needs of their husbands, much as Storer did for them to satisfy upper-class white employers. Clifford's gendered appeal to black youth echoed Washington's command to "cast down your bucket where you are." Clifford's exhortations, however, enabled only ambitious black men to rise beyond the shadow of the bucket.[80]

Making a Man of Mark:
Clifford Wields the Bloody Shirt of Reputation

Like Tourgée, Clifford acquired the property of a reputation through ownership of the printed word. More than the market for real estate, the market for the printed word helped forge a postwar culture in which competing views of Reconstruction could be aired. A camaraderie of cross-reference built up among editors. To attest to his own reputation for doing the "noble work" of journalism, Clifford, for example, reprinted the *Central Methodist*'s good wishes for his success on 30 April 1888 when he upped the newspaper's publication frequency that year. Clifford also sparred with editors at rival papers. For example, in quoting another editor who had claimed that "Clifford is the father of [hostile Republican leader] Flick's defeat," Clifford rejoined: "Then call me daddy." Yet the sparring often went beyond play. Clifford always positioned his maverick *Pioneer Press* to incite controversy and to seek redress of injustice.[81]

Whereas Tourgée, as a white judge with some clout, could playfully use editorial pseudonyms to create the illusion of consensus and authority, Clifford often required the backing of local white civic leaders in order to achieve the same effect. When *Martinsburg Herald* editor John Reilly accused Clifford in the 9 July 1887 issue of bribing the State Supreme Court to grant his law license, Clifford responded by launching a war on reputation. That same month he collected and published in the *Press* testimonials of fifty prominent citizens addressed to the Martinsburg Board of Education attesting to his character. He courted endorsements by influential white men such as J. Nelson Wisner, editor of the local Republican newspaper, the *Martinsburg Independent*. He had studied law under Wisner, and they shared editorial offices. The collective testimonial also appeared on 25 July 1887 in the *Martinsburg Independent* and *Men of Mark*, which concluded: "They have indeed cause to fear such a man, who not only has power and influence to back him, but who will stand up for his rights and accept nothing which reflects upon his race." Clifford successfully capitalized on his competitor's attacks, using them as pretext to print the testimonials, sure proof of the widespread support he could garner.[82]

Yet the support of local white men—Democrat or Republican—was not always assured. Even Wisner was not entirely above racial slurs. Once he ran this troubling item, a note of appreciation for Clifford's gift of fruit, promptly rephrased in derogatory terms: "Prof. J. R. Clifford has our thanks for a basket of very fine peaches—a donation to 'Master' from 'Cuffy's' [*sic*] own tree." He nevertheless printed his paper in the *Independent*'s office until 1888, at which time he even shared the *Independent*'s masthead, "Here shall the Press the People's Rights Maintain Unawed by Influence and Unbribed by Gain."[83]

Again recalling Tourgée, Clifford thrived on scandal and waved the printed page like a bloody shirt to provoke reaction. His vituperative attacks on the reputation of others helped shore up his own reputation as an idealistic and determined civic leader. His clever tenacity is best evident in his dealings with long-standing rival white prosecuting attorney U. S. G. Pitzer, against whom he had squared off in numerous legal battles. Shortly after his arguments against segregation in the *Martin* case, in September 1895, Clifford found himself arguing in the Berkeley County Courtroom that African Americans be allowed to serve on juries, as the 1881 *Strauder* ruling had affirmed. Even though black West Virginians were supposed to be impaneled to serve, most counties refused to permit it. His insistence that African Americans be allowed to serve enraged prosecuting attorney Pitzer, who brutally assaulted him. Pitzer struck Clifford three times with bench weights "causing the blood to run down into his shoes." The men then wrestled to the ground until Clifford was pulled off Pitzer. Although he did not evidently pursue assault charges against Pitzer, his pension file indicates that the head trauma produced "permanent nerve damage from the blows to his head." Clifford successfully argued for an integrated jury but lost the case "due to an arbitrary ruling of the court." He adroitly used this assault to bring about Pitzer's defeat in fall of 1898, when Pitzer was running as the Republican candidate for Congress. During the campaign Clifford exacted some political revenge by engaging in mudslinging theatrics. In a move designed to insure Pitzer's defeat, he ran against him as an Independent. While campaigning, Clifford took to literally waving in public the "bloody shirt" he had worn that day Pitzer had beat him in court as he campaigned throughout the county. Although Clifford did not win the election, his exposé helped defeat Pitzer.[84]

Of most dramatic consequence, on 2 December 1899 Clifford's *Pioneer Press* attempted to expose Storer's "secret history," as Lue Brackett Lightner termed it, by publishing six allegations against Nathan Brackett and the college. In publicizing the "secret history" to correct an institution he saw as overly controlling, Clifford used print culture in the same way that Tourgée's Toinette does to gain access to the secret room and check Geoffrey's overreaching authority. Clifford targeted Brackett with being "a sad failure" as a teacher, and his charges ranged from moral infractions to improperly ordaining ministers to poor business integrity. Clifford's allegation of discriminatory boardinghouse practices may have had some merit.

Since 1876 local black West Virginians, with the strong support of college officials, had tried to make Storer "a popular resort" by renting out campus buildings to both black and white families, vacationing often from nearby Washington, D.C., in order to raise needed revenue, support local families, and provide necessary summer jobs for students. When renting to black families proved no longer profitable, the Board of Trustees eliminated it, while continuing to provide lodging for white families at other locations, even though students charged that these rentals were also unprofitable. Yet Kate Anthony, daughter of a trustee, described boarding as a "matter of no inconsiderable financial interest to the school," while providing students jobs as "intelligent, honest, and faithful attendants." Having "begun and carried on under the auspices of the school," the boarding business had also been "the principal agency in bringing into the market certain portions of the school farm." With several hundred annual guests, the boarding business grew so successful that Camp Hill had become "the center of life in the town."[85]

The origins are unclear, but Clifford's vitriolic attitude toward Brackett seems to have been long standing. In 1886 Clifford had reprinted Brackett's accusation that Clifford was a "traitor to his own race" for supporting a Democratic candidate. Clifford sarcastically defended his choice as a right whites enjoy: "But pardon me, my lord, they are white men whose political freedom of action is an unquestionable right." His 1899 formal charges against the college regarding the boarding business began to percolate in print at least two years earlier; in April 1897 the college's Board of Trustees, sufficiently alarmed by his *Pioneer Press* accusations, passed a resolution condemning the charges proffered by "a discharged teacher, an excommunicated preacher and one or two other parties" as "false and slanderous." Nor did Clifford's animosity toward Brackett and the wake of bitterness it generated apparently ever die down. Some sixty years later, daughter Mary Brackett Robertson complained to a relative, "I presume you *do* know that John Clifford, editor of the *Pioneer Press* in Martinsburg, a very nasty, hostile and unprincipled sheet was a thorn in the flesh for Storer College for many years."[86]

While some students agreed with Clifford that the college policy was discriminatory in favoring white boarders, others defended the practice by noting the college had "let" its six buildings to black families who managed the boarding for both black and white families during summers. According to African American James Robinson, the first summer landlord (along with his wife) of Lincoln Hall, this had been the only available lodging for African Americans since the war; he maintained that its termination was a bottom-line decision not based on discrimination. In the *Record*, students flatly denied the college's involvement beyond charitable purposes: "We say again Storer College is not in the boarding business. She does not even board students but turns the business over to colored families"—a technicality that Brackett also used to defend himself. In a separate item, students defended the impartiality of the Board of Trustees, condescendingly adding, "The men who raise the color cry are usually those who have been disappointed or have made failures." Robinson vindicated Brackett and characterized the scandal as "the malice of disappointed men," with Clifford out only to increase circulation figures: "Advertise in my paper, lend me a few hundred dollars or I will destroy your reputation through the press is the spirit of the whole crusade [*sic*]."[87]

Brackett answered Clifford's charges, which were printed in the *New York Age*, by questioning the integrity of his paper. Dismissing Clifford as a man "hissed out of the alumni meeting," Brackett nevertheless felt compelled to answer to his handling of the "Hartgrove case," regarding the student whose mother did not want her to take sewing, which developed into a legal dispute; Brackett notes that Clifford "made frantic efforts for several years to maintain his claims in court, but both the Justice and Circuit Courts have sustained Storer College . . . and Clifford, or his friends, have had both judgment and costs to pay."[88]

Clifford's relentless assault on the reputation of Brackett and the college inflicted serious damage as the publicity widened. Anguished over the toll the scandal had taken on her parents' health, daughter Mary Brackett Robertson despaired that Clifford's muckraking had succeeded in prompting a lawsuit against her father on the same charges that Clifford had made. Decrying the "the filthy by-ways" of Clifford's insistent coverage in prompting the suit and fearing what else may follow, Robertson wondered: "Have not the wretched vultures been left with a feeling that possibly they have won a mixed victory?" She pleaded with the investigating committee to publish their vindication of her father as soon as possible.[89]

But the committee delayed publication in order to obtain an endorsement by the Board of Trustees and to prepare for Clifford's next onslaught. According to committee member Laura A. DeMeritte, Clifford had threatened further that he had "reserve charges" against Brackett waiting in the wings. He then issued an ultimatum in the *Pioneer Press*: "If they [the committee] send him kith and kin away, none of the damaging facts in our possession shall go in print, otherwise . . . they will settle it forever to his eternal shame." A full six months later, the committee entirely vindicated Brackett in its report, adopted unanimously by the Board of Trustees. On 26 May 1900, the Board published a resolution condemning Clifford and his supporters and chiding them for their betrayal when they should be the college's "most loyal and devoted supporters." Storer officials considered Clifford's 1899 allegations against them to be a "circus," and they branded him a promoter of interracial discord. College officials reduced Clifford's motivations into a mere bid for wealth and fame. Yet preceptress Lue Brackett Lightner also wondered what the white Storer boarders "would think if they knew our secret history." Her comments, suggesting that Clifford's allegations may not have been unfounded, are strong evidence for the double-edged nature of the school's Reconstruction agenda.[90]

At the time the Storer allegations were materializing, the larger white community moved in to check Clifford's zeal. In the 3 June 1899 issue of the *Pioneer Press* Clifford attacked Reverend Newman, a black Hagerstown Free Will Baptist pastor, and deemed immoral the minister's alleged misconduct with a married woman. The following month Clifford was arrested on charges that he violated the Comstock Law, which prohibited the "mailing of indecent and obscene matter." Brackett used Clifford's arrest to clear his own name: "Thirty-four years of my life I have devoted to work among the colored people . . . and yet on the mere charge, without proof, of a man who publishes a paper so indecent that the post office authorities have arrested him . . . you would have me condemned." Clifford was found guilty and fined $100. However, as late as 1906, he was awaiting imprisonment, for he had evidently yet to pay the fine.[91]

Clifford attempted to recast his arrest by claiming to be a victim of local harassment, and he declared he would "write . . . anything else that would save his race." He contended his prosecution was a "factional persecution" by politicians antagonistic to his independent political stance. He vaingloriously vowed "to God and man": "I am done with the Republican party and it shall never be recalled this side of eternity. . . . This is the third time they have tried to imprison me because they could not use me." Nor would this be the last time Clifford and his writing ran afoul of public opinion. The federal government ultimately closed the *Pioneer Press* in response to Clifford's editorial opposition of U.S. entry into World War I.[92]

Clifford's embattled career is instructive about the paradoxical nature of Storer's mission and of Reconstruction's legacy. His example shows that the college's contradictory messages to students did not always produce docile citizens. Storer planted the seeds of hope, pride, and ambition in Clifford to achieve professional and national recognition as a civil rights leader. Storer could also inspire his vision of an intraracial coalition dependent upon graduates in industrial education as the foundation for racial solidarity and economic autonomy. Yet Clifford's considerable accomplishments signaled Storer's failures as well as its successes when his allegations came back to haunt them.

The same Storer forces that made possible Clifford's renown also tempered his political success. His daring contribution to West Virginia's Reconstruction ignored the region's distinctive political proclivities and invited backlash. Southerners had long-established racialized and gendered practices of enforcing obedience and proper conduct beginning in childhood and revolving around public approval. The outcome of his strident struggles suggests that he might have been more successful if he had been more attentive to Storer's lessons in the art of compromise and diplomatic negotiation. Clifford, like Storer, tried to pursue two ultimately divergent strategies: he lashed out against segregation, yet he also shunned interracial cooperation. Moreover, his success signaled his own downfall, since he leaned too much on the property of reputation. Despite Clifford's assaults on the reputation of others in the community, his paper survived as long as it did partly because of another voice found within its pages.[93]

Engaging the "Personal Touch": Student Coralie Franklin's Use of Domestic Rhetoric, Progressive Reform, and Interracial Appeal

In addition to his wife, Mary Franklin, Clifford relied on his sister-in-law and fellow Storer graduate, Coralie Franklin, who deployed an entirely different strategy of gendered rhetoric to empower African American women. Indeed, Clifford's inclusion of Franklin's monthly "Woman's Column" distinguished his newspaper, qualifying the claim of Jonathan Daniel Wells that, unlike white newspapers that had long carried such columns, "postwar black newspapers remained almost entirely male bastions until after the turn of the century." Complementing Clifford's embattled demands for civil rights were her quieter, equally classed, unyielding feminine appeals for racial uplift. Franklin's education, interests, and social position served her well. Born in Lexington, Virginia, in 1861, Franklin attended Storer College and graduated in 1880, five years after Clifford. She also attended Emerson College, Martha's Vineyard Summer Institute, and the Shoemaker School of Oratory. From 1882 to 1893 Franklin taught oratory at Storer, and in 1894 she became a trustee. Upon her death in 1942 she established a scholarship for Storer students.[94]

Franklin's marriage to prominent Washington, D.C., educator George William Cook (1855–1931), a member of what one historian has called "the most distinguished family in the District," ensured her place among the black elite and propelled her civic and education work. Cook served Howard University for fifty-eight years in many important teaching and administrative capacities. As representatives of the "Black Four Hundred," the Cooks associated socially with civil rights leaders and outstanding politicians such as Frederick Douglass, Blanche K. Bruce, John R. Lynch, and Archibald Grimké. To fulfill her aspirations for black women, Franklin refitted the ideals of her Storer education to work with, not against, the influence of these urbane social ties until her death.[95]

Like Clifford, Franklin was active in a variety of civic and reform organizations, including the Mount Hope Woman's Christian Temperance Union, the Free Baptist Women's Missionary Society, the Delta Sigma Theta Sorority, the Board of Public Welfare, the National District Social Hygiene Association, the Juvenile Protection Association, and the Red Cross. She taught English and elocution at Howard University from 1891 to 1900, when she became chair of oratory. She founded the Washington School of Expression. She also became superintendent of the National Home for Destitute Colored Women and Children, located in Washington, D.C., in 1893 and later served on the district's Board of Education from 1914 to 1926. In celebrating Franklin's civic work, the NAACP's *Crisis* described her as "a quiet, tactful, high-minded woman of culture and public spirit." Through her journalism, educational outreach, and political work on behalf of black women, Franklin was a center-stage participant in what historian Martha Jones has described as African American "public culture." Franklin engaged in building an ideological, gendered, and often interracial community, an effort that places her in a long line of nineteenth-century black women activists from Fannie Wright to her D.C. colleague Anna Julia Cooper.[96]

To reach the widest possible audience, Franklin, like many other postwar black women writers, relied on journalism to tackle the most pressing political and social issues relevant to African American women. Beginning with her "Woman's Column" in February 1887, Franklin wrote for Clifford's *Pioneer Press* for at least a year. While Franklin shared many of Clifford's ambitions to shape postwar race relations, she employed very different, gendered rhetoric. She emphasized a politics of respectability designated primarily for women. Unlike Clifford, Franklin saw that Storer's moral agenda could be positioned to better serve students. In an article written for the Free Baptist Women's Missionary Society, Franklin praised the education she had received from these "miracle-workers," especially their "'personal touch,' which is now, as it was then, the mightiest leverage for social uplift." Storer officials reciprocated her affection, describing Franklin as "a woman of great charm and personality whose life compasses the whole Storer road." Franklin's publicized nods of gratitude to Storer helped her win the school's cooperation as she transferred the burdens of teaching to herself and other African American women eager to shape their own education. For her efforts, she certainly would qualify as a member of what Evelyn Brooks Higginbotham has distinguished as "the Female Talented Tenth."[97]

Franklin tailored the racially imposed ideals of Storer to suit her own benevolent purposes. She reconciled the college's often conflicting emphases on self-interest, solvency, and obligation by yoking them to the classed goal of racial uplift. Franklin adopted the college's moral agenda of duty, self-sacrifice, appearance, and industry to keep black *women* visible; she was particularly skillful in encouraging women's reform work outside the home. A devout Baha'i since 1913, Franklin deployed Storer's rhetoric of Christian and patriotic duty to summon African Americans to help themselves: "Every graduate became a missionary and felt in duty bound to do unto others *as had been done unto him.*" She insisted that black graduates, not white teachers, must assume power for Storer to "fulfill its mission." Addressing a largely white northern readership, Franklin argued that "it is *their* home environment, *their* aspirations and ambitions, their future usefulness that must decide the courses of study and the broadening and developing of the work of the school." Her emphasis was no doubt also shaped by her years at Howard and in the Washington, D.C., public schools, both of which struggled to maintain independence from white interference. Borrowing Clifford's rhetoric of ownership, Franklin welcomed the opportunity for elite black women to lead in building community.[98]

Franklin's compliance with Storer's demands that black women carry Christian burdens of self-sacrifice and self-effacement may make her appear as a kind of "Jane Crow," although she would have disparaged the term. Instead, she transformed "separate but equal" scenarios into occasions for both intraracial leadership and interracial teamwork that benefited women by taking them outside the home. While Clifford sought to ally with Civil War veterans, Franklin identified with white progressive women, whom she beckoned to "join gladly in this movement for mutual understanding and helpfulness between the races." Her writing situates her within a greater tradition of nineteenth-century African American female orators and journalists who participated in reform politics using a variety of discursive strategies.[99]

Nowhere is this variety more evident than in her writing for Clifford's *Pioneer Press*. From columns on cleanliness and sanitary reform, like the May 1887 issue's "Cleanliness is Next to Godliness," to those such as "The Domestic Circle," in the 29 February 1888 issue, which equated home building to nation building, Franklin embraced progressive reforms. She revived the rhetoric of "Republican Motherhood" to include black women as authoritative participants in the greater public sphere. Directed toward improving the lives of former slaves, this rhetoric can also be located within a tradition developed by African-American women preachers, writers, and educators. Once Franklin quoted educator Friedrich Froebel to infuse the Storer ideals of labor, piety, busyness, and duty with a gendered, racial mission: "'Labor is the price which the gods have set upon all that is excellent.' Above all things, *do something*!" With a tone at once aspiring and genteel, Franklin was adept at manipulating the sentiments of white, domestic, middle-class culture to promote racial uplift as a woman's civic duty. Her columns softened Clifford's demands for confrontations with whites into gendered appeals for cooperation among black and white leaders of equal ranking.[100]

In this regard, Franklin targeted Storer's black female graduates, especially given the increasing disfranchisement and marginalization of black men from politics. Her debut *Pioneer Press* column, "The True End of Female Education," appeared in February 1887 and reprinted an article by Anna E. Brown, who stressed, in line with Storer precepts, that it was a woman's "duty" to "continually be self-improving." Brown argued that the goal of female education was to "exalt the moral character" and to learn that "active disinterested virtue is the true source of happiness." Franklin capitalized on Storer's domestic rhetoric to legitimate the necessary labor of black women outside the home to challenge gender proscriptions. In a letter to the *Storer Record*, Franklin proudly cited Storer women who, as "representatives of a superior womanhood," were doing work at the National Home for Destitute Colored Women and Children in Washington, D.C., that had made "the salvation of the race largely dependent" upon them. Franklin, who served as matron there, singled out a night nurse who administered to white and black patients alike, noting that she would not "be regarded as inferior to any other in our national citizenship." Her nurse would walk the floors of Professor Cardozo's house of black class hierarchies and open the windows to white help.[101]

Franklin's journalistic call for women's "heart work" anticipated the opportunity for women to fill the ever-widening gap between the "head work" of Du Boisian higher education and the "hand work" of a Washingtonian industrial education. In "The Girl Graduate," Franklin celebrated the common "mission" of all women to labor for "the right, the pure, and the true." Six months later, she praised a whole roster of working women from a railway president to cotton pickers in "Here and There in Woman's World." In "Moral Education," Franklin's use of domestic rhetoric echoed Cable's criticism of wealthy and reclusive black Creoles as she used the image of a sumptuously furnished but windowless home as a metaphor for the need for woman's "heart work." Franklin shared a progressivist ethos with other educated middle-class and elite black women, embracing the difficult work of interracial civic reform.[102]

While reform work earned black women their good reputations, Franklin made clear that it was their standing in the community that really mattered, as she invoked a southerly sense of reputation. Implicitly acknowledging a black woman as a rightful judge of femininity, Franklin relied upon the heft of her outstanding reputation within the National Woman Suffrage Association (NWSA). At a reception held in her honor by Susan B. Anthony, "Rochester's 400" peppered Franklin with questions about "her work among the colored people." As a "highly cultured" woman "possessing many admirable qualities," she "quite won the hearts of her new acquaintances." So skillful was Franklin in maneuvering her reputation to advantage that she, along with Mary Church Terrell, was considered to be the "conscience of the conservative woman suffrage movement." Whatever her cause, Franklin consistently refrained from Clifford's tactic of using reputation as a weapon. "Mortified but not surprised," she refused to endorse his boarding school allegations; when those "chestnuts were in the fire" and "they needed to be pulled out," Franklin aligned herself instead with the faculty and became "somewhat blistered in pulling them out." Nurtured by Storer's moralizing education, Franklin understood that reputation was a political asset to be protected at all costs.[103]

Franklin saw that all West Virginian women were encumbered by the conservative attitudes of lawmakers and judges that served to disempower them. Residents of a state geographically isolated and characterized by a rural culture with strong roots in Protestant fundamentalism that emphasized female subordination, these women did not achieve real reforms in property, divorce, and alimony until well into the twentieth century. Nevertheless, factors such as the state's industrial leanings and its desire to distinguish itself from Virginia helped further the adoption of some legal reforms beneficial to women. The state's complex mix of backwardness and progressive impetus in recognizing women's legal rights gave Franklin an area on which she could find common ground with white women.[104]

Franklin's conciliatory approach resembled that of Booker T. Washington, who, according to biographer Robert Norrell, "made racial interdependence a fundamental principle of his materialist strategy for African Americans." Like many women of her generation, Franklin's active involvement in the Woman's Christian Temperance Union (WCTU) helped her endorse suffrage, racial uplift, and interracial cooperation. Her routine publishing of WCTU chapter notes reminded readers of the commitment to industry, decency, and family that black women shared with white women. Elected president of the local Storer chapter, Franklin described one interesting exchange among the male and female members to underscore the need for women's suffrage: "One [brother] said, 'Can we vote if we stay?' and when asked to join as honorary members, said, 'Do you think that taxation without representation, is right?' We answered sweetly, 'No gentlemen, this is an object lesson for you to think about.'" Quite unlike Clifford's chest pounding, she occasionally inserted exchanges like these to register her point.[105]

At a time when race relations were straining in the violent South, Franklin chose to stress the ties that bound abolitionists to suffragists. Playing off racial and gendered agendas to advantage, she saw the vote as a self-help strategy for racial uplift. As a delegate to the Woman's League at the Atlanta Exposition of 1895, Franklin shrewdly used the clamor for suffrage to stress the accomplishments of black women activists and, in a "spirit of gratefulness," to ask for greater interracial cooperation. Yet she did not hesitate to fault white suffragists for their racism in her column. She condemned some delegates to the NWSA-sponsored International Council of Women for their "scorning even the presence of the old man eloquent," Frederick Douglass. "Sullied of heart and dwarfed of conscience" they had violated "the first great lesson of human rights." Still later, Franklin knew when to cut interracial ties; she declined the NAACP's invitation to attend the Woman's Party Convention because she did not support "its methods." She further admitted: "The old Nat'l W.S.A. of which I was once an ardent supporter and member, turned its back on the woman of color ... so I have not been 'active' although I was born a suffragist."[106]

Franklin's literary contribution to the *Pioneer Press* and other periodicals can be situated in a broader, nineteenth-century tradition that linked the acquisition of literacy to citizenship and political participation. This tradition was distinguished by black women's increasing activism in both the secular and sacred realms of public life. African American literary societies, church groups and, later, women's clubs, with which Franklin was so involved, became the venues for middle and upper-class black women to disseminate the importance of this linkage for all black Americans.[107]

A supporter of both Washington and Du Bois, Franklin especially admired the latter's writing. In an undated book review of *Dusk of Dawn*, Franklin praised him as a "prophet and guide of Dark America," whose poetic prose reflects the "power of poise." Franklin nevertheless nurtured literary ambitions that came to fruition later in life. While dismissing her work as a "scribbling hobby," she professed an interest in writing antebellum southern stories. Her writing was informed by her activism as surely as it was for Ida B. Wells, Pauline Hopkins, Katherine Davis Chapman Tillman, and other contemporaries. Under their auspices, black women crafted what historian Darlene Clark Hine has called a "culture of dissemblance," which fashioned race leadership around replacing degrading stereotypes of black women's sexuality with positive ones.[108]

Like Clifford and Tourgée, Franklin stressed opportunities for African American women to be consumers of the printed word. Her entreaty for the "profitability" of reading engendered an appreciation of the political power of consumerism. In a time of increasing emphasis on genteel contemplation, Franklin drew from child development theory the importance of nurturing and of literacy, which she coupled with strategies for economic agency. Buying books and other consumer goods bespoke status and influence, as Franklin, an active member of the Book Lovers Club, knew firsthand. Yet Franklin advocated more than a subscription to the *Youth's Companion*: she endorsed the fashioning of a lifestyle that privileged the *leisure* of reading as she stipulated the need for a home library, family discussions about books, and family time to read aloud. Like Tourgée's Toinette and Belle in their secret pursuit of education, Franklin's class-inflected proposals implied that the family who made room for literacy made political participation possible. Franklin's own formidable powers as a lecturer and reader were praised in the *Pioneer Press*: "There is not one in fifty who would step upon the stage and read the same piece to the same audience. She puts pathos and perceptible inspiration into the word of God when reading it." Franklin transformed Storer's call to duty into a politically expedient demand for genteel leisure best satisfied by black women. She departed from Woolson's strategy of highlighting the merit of leisure in freeing people from the desire to produce. Instead, Franklin's endorsement of family literacy was productive in prompting the desires of politically astute readers to buy (into) certain images of African Americans as cultured and refined.[109]

Beyond promoting literacy, Franklin supported black women's right to claim domestic refinement within their homes. Cultivating a proper home life was seen as a crucial part of racial uplift. In light of Jim Crow's encroachment into public arenas, the home remained one of the few areas within the control of black women. As Franklin's writing demonstrates, the home could be shaped to counter denigrating stereotypes of black women. Her insistent focus on home life represents what Valerie Sweeney Prince has described as a literary "passion" for "this sacred place," which "ran like lifeblood through the African American psyche." Franklin's celebration of bourgeois domesticity for African Americans anticipated a trend in sentimental fiction by late nineteenth- and early twentieth-century African American women writers. Eager for her readers to take advantage of low-cost literature, Franklin advised that providing periodicals at home ensured moral character development and was a "safeguard against many an evil."[110]

Keeping literature accessible was also a calculated strategy of appearances. Franklin argued that reading store-bought books not only improved the experience of childhood but also offered a way to make the race appear more respectable, a labor for which black women were seen as especially fitted by organizations such as the NACWC. Amid pleas for women to keep busy with an ever-widening agenda of racially progressive reforms, Franklin converted Storer's teaching on the necessity for self-effacement into an asset for public activism. By counseling the importance of appearance in crafting a public persona apart from her private life, Franklin gave credibility to the importance of building a southern-defined sense of reputation for black women to be influential in their community.

Situated within the pages of Clifford's vitriolic rhetoric, Franklin's quietly dignified columns underscored the sharply gendered and classed nature of the Reconstruction vision of African Americans. Female *Pioneer Press* readers had to sort out their priorities along gendered lines. Like Storer students caught between contrary faculty advice, they needed to reconcile Clifford's calls for militant resistance with Franklin's subtle appeals for calculated compliance on a range of issues, including suffrage. For example, in the 30 April 1888 issue, Franklin's endorsement of the "grand success" of NWSA's International Congress was juxtaposed with the tempered enthusiasm of influential educator Francis Cardozo for suffrage. In "Women's Rights," Cardozo wryly demurred that women endowed with "finer emotional and moral powers" should defer the ballot to men until they can "show the same intellectual power" and thereby "justly claim equality." Further rhetorical challenge to Franklin's praise for "the silvery white pioneers" of suffrage ("What pluck, what perseverance, what untiring zeal and above all, what conviction they have shown!") was Mrs. Fountain's "Leap Year Advice," which burlesqued women's appeals to equality. Caught in the ideological cross fire, female readers had to develop a kind of bifurcated vision that would allow them to reconcile the *Pioneer Press*'s conflicting sentiments. Reading Clifford's paper trained black women to exercise their political free will.

The Niagara Movement: Storer's Legacy

For Storer students, exercising political free will would increasingly mean rejecting Storer's founding paternalistic vision in favor of their own. Indeed, it was Storer students who would deliver the uprising that John

Brown had anticipated forty years earlier. The meaning of Brown's actions continued to haunt Harpers Ferry as an ever-widening drama of conflict pitting Storer students, the national black press, and the NAACP against college officials, the town and the United Daughters of the Confederacy. In the 1890s the college worked to bring back John Brown's fort to Harpers Ferry and later, in 1909, had it installed on the campus as a museum. Nevertheless, in 1914 Storer College president Henry McDonald noted with perplexed dismay: "It seems strange that the colored people should not look upon Brown as their great liberator, but they seem to pay but little attention to what he did and suffered for them."[111]

Claiming the legacy of a Baptist Free Will education, Storer graduates had set themselves free. Strengthened by Clifford's friendship with Du Bois and other black intellectuals, Storer students launched the second meeting of the annual Niagara Movement from their campus in 1906, bringing their ambitions onto a national stage where they would assume the agenda for racial progress. The conference was a culminating rejection of the college's conflicting and paternalistic mission. It would be a high-water mark for Storer in many ways, as student stridency elicited baffled and hurt faculty reaction.

Student participation in the Niagara Conference produced much of the embarrassingly hostile confidential correspondence that comprised Storer's "secret history." Confessing that she "missed the courtly deference of the old days," Lue Brackett Lightner was especially perturbed that these "fine looking, fine appearing, gifted prosperous" student activists were motivated only for "office and advancement themselves." She felt threatened that they would "dare not be affable to a white person especially in the presence of each other for fear of being servile." Noting that Franklin "wept all through the John Brown meeting," Lightner was "alarmed over the state of her nerves." Lightner then declared unequivocally that "it is an awful thing to be colored." She fumed about the lack of gratitude the participants showed to their presumed white benefactors: "Not a word of appreciation for any past favors or consideration. What can be done for people who are contemptuous of their friends, envious of their enemies, and suspicious of each other?" Faculty disillusionment with the Niagara Movement can be read as a triumph for the students, who would make their own mark on their education.[112]

The story of Storer College teaches that Reconstruction was as much about revising race, gender, and class constructions as about reworking local relations. Increasingly prosperous students took the founding ideals of hard work, self-help, and duty to craft an alternative reconstruction of Harpers Ferry, a town that most certainly would have had a different postwar life without the college's influence. In an environment keenly unsupportive of black education, let alone black civil rights, the faculty promoted survival against local ostracism, harassment, and violence. Their surveillance of students and imposition of a regimented code of conduct subordinated student ambitions to the debilitating legacy of slavery.

The contradictory mission of the college was partly the result of the clash among regional and gendered ideologies as it sought to impose a northern ethos of bourgeois values on an area defined by paternalistic ties. The hierarchies of the plantation household complemented Free Will adherence to self-sacrifice and humility, even while they provided opportunities for change. The cases of Foster and Clifford confirm the ease with which issues of racial equality were transformed into issues of gender and sexuality whenever these hierarchical racial boundaries were threatened. Nevertheless, with the advent of a more prosperous second generation of African Americans raised in freedom, many students resolved these contradictions so as to realize their ambitions. In their embrace of racial uplift, students reconciled Storer's inculcation of duty and indebtedness with self-interest by assuming their teachers' moral responsibilities.

Whereas some students like Coralie Franklin worked within the system to successfully empower black women, others like John Clifford openly defied any sense of regional compromise to their eventual detriment. Neither Clifford's clamor for intraracial "union" nor Franklin's cautious courting of interracial coalition building were free of the strong class biases that limited their vision. The very success of a student like Clifford also proved Storer College's shortcomings by the ways in which college officials responded to his attacks on their reputation. Evident in the writings of graduates Clifford and Franklin, as well as the bitter lessons of Sarah Jane Foster's experience, the property of reputation—in all its regional, racial, gendered, and sexualized facets—became critical to reconstructing the region. Foster's defense, Clifford's assaults, and Franklin's appeals—all show how the rhetorical crafting of reputation in print culture could help decide Reconstruction's local battles. Ultimately, a more southern notion of reputation acknowledging the force of community obloquy prevailed. The stories of all Storer students illuminate the importance of attaining literacy to citizenship and of print culture, in general, to political engagement.

The double-edged nature of the college's mission, which would both disable and empower African Americans like Franklin and Clifford, fostered a healthy questioning of authority and obligation. The legacy of this college community exemplifies the ways in which Reconstruction visions were riven from the beginning. As a final historical irony, Storer College was closed in 1955, as the state legislature used the *Brown v. Board of Education* decision to cut off school funding while opening other West Virginia schools to African Americans.

Reconstruction's ironies would soar to dramatic heights in New Orleans as performed in George Washington Cable's Military District Five.[113]

Chapter 4
GEORGE WASHINGTON CABLE AND THE WAGES OF VENTRILOQUIZED PERFORMANCE IN NEW ORLEANS, LOUISIANA

Writers will write about their own state, their own town, possibly their own little neighbors, but they will never conceive of their audience as less than their entire nation.
—George Washington Cable, commencement address, 15 June 1883

In the opening chapter of George Washington Cable's novel *The Grandissimes* (1880), one of the characters taunts "Cityoen" Agricola Fusilier, the novel's fire-eating Creole. "Ah! mo piti fils," he cries, "to pas connais to zancestres? Don't you know your ancestors, my little son!" Ventured at a quadroon ball at which everyone is disguised so well that they have difficulty recognizing each other, this jab resonates on several levels of representation. Cable intended to make *The Grandissimes* "as truly a political novel as it has ever been called." Its plot is propelled by the life-and-death consequences of representation, especially for slaves and freedpeople, who assume disguises for survival, crossing racial, ethnic, and gender boundaries. Cable's quadroon ball sets the stage for the critical roles that performance and performed identities would play in reconstructing southerners and northerners.[1]

Cable, a New Orleanian, deploys three key strategies to suggest a healing reconciliation and durable change. First, he highlights the endless malleability of Creole identity to question traditional valuations of heritage; his emphasis on New Orleans naturalizes the hybridized nature of American identity, rendering it prototypically Creole. Next, he offers four characters whose intertwined stories emphasize the needed reconstruction of all sections of the country toward compromise. Finally, Cable dramatized his Creole characters onstage, taking the performative nature of identity to new heights of benefit and risk, as his shows were timed with the publication of his controversial essays.

The characters' opening disguises foreshadow the shape-shifting reality of political and social life in postwar New Orleans. Cable relied on masks and innuendo to set the stage for his Reconstruction drama. By situating the novel's action during the Louisiana Purchase of 1803, Cable highlighted issues of cession, insurrection, and changing national allegiances. He drew parallels to the Pelican State's experience of a protracted federal occupation as part of Military District Five from 1865 to 1877. Cable focused on the city's Creole population to empower freedpeople. To refashion identity from a fixed trait into a performed construct, he looked to their multiraced, mixed ethnic heritage to solve the country's postwar problems. The composite nature of Creole identity, with its confused, contested meanings, provided a unique opportunity for this district's Reconstruction, which Cable used as a model for incorporating the nation's newest "cityoens," the freedpeople. The opening ball at the Théatre St. Philipe provided the first opportunity for disparaged residents of New Orleans—quadroons, free black Creoles, impoverished white women, and the enslaved—to take center stage.

Yet Cable's broad deployment of Creole identity illustrated the inherent difficulties of mixing different local colors to please national palettes. As a strategy to empower freedwomen, the malleability of Creole identity proved to be a double-edged sword. Set against the flourishing capacity of most of the white Grandissimes to reinvent themselves is the gradual enervation of the novel's black characters, particularly women, who meet exile and untimely death. Although giving voice to dispossessed women who achieve vengeance, Cable's Creoles also express the resentment of the defeated white "Southron," who retaliates in vigilante violence. While slashing at prejudice, Cable's dramatic manipulations helped eliminate the possibility of a sustained change in that district. In scene after scene, *The Grandissimes* doubles back on itself in a plot of regional and gendered checks and balances. The novel yields a series of thematic and structural compromises indicative of the city's postwar political duality.

The story follows the fortunes of protagonist Joseph Frowenfeld, a young northern American who has immigrated with his family to French colonial New Orleans in 1803. Through his connections with the city's elite Creole family, the Grandissimes, Frowenfeld enters into a profitable business partnership with Clotilde Nancanou, a white Creole woman, which blossoms into a satisfying marriage. Frowenfeld cultivates a friendship with Honoré Grandissime, the white patriarch who presides over his family's muddled commercial investments and real estate holdings. Honoré's troubles involve his alienated, miserable black half brother of the same name who has grown wealthy enough through vast rental incomes to become a rentier, a person of independent means. While Honoré f.m.c. (free man of color) has prospered financially, the fortunes of the white members of his estranged family are less secure.

On the eve of the Louisiana Purchase, the family's land titles become questionable and they must enlist the f.m.c.'s help or declare bankruptcy. This prospective alliance arouses the ire of many of the white supremacist Grandissimes, especially fire-eating cousin Agricola Fusilier. Honoré's woes are compounded by his love for Clotilde's mother, Aurora Nancanou, a charming Creole widow who dooms herself to poverty because she will not retract her husband's accusation that Agricola had cheated him at cards. At stake was the Nancanou plantation, which the old planter won. Agricola, however, was willing to forfeit his winnings if the Nancanou family would clear his honorable reputation.

Questions of honor surround not only the Grandissime family but also Agricola's earlier treatment of Bras Coupé, a proud slave who refused to labor and incited a revolt, behavior for which he is martyred. Coupé had his defenders, including the beautiful quadroon Palmyre, who vows to avenge his death by killing the old planter, whom she loathes. Palmyre succeeds with the help of Clemence, a vendor and slave, who is murdered by a white vigilante band of Grandissimes as punishment. Spurned Palmyre and Honoré f.m.c. exile themselves to France, where he commits suicide. Caught up amid these intrigues, the interloper Frowenfeld tries to help everyone, achieving mixed results.

Cable's best novel thus defies easy categorization into pro-Reconstruction or proreconciliation agendas. He tried to promote national reunion by reconstructing sectional differences. Like his contemporaries, Cable engaged a Reconstruction discourse that centered on landed property, reputation, duty, and labor as he confronted local circumstance with national imperatives. Cable argued that political and social progress in New Orleans was as necessary and natural as the city's trade expansion, blurring traditional boundaries to make way for new, egalitarian marital and business partnerships among those of different races and sectional persuasions. His use of doubling characterizations and reliance on an indeterminate narrator, however, converted this duality into an asset for Reconstruction but only compromised results for freedwomen. Cable called for a Reconstruction that entailed a commitment to self-scrutiny and to active moral duty for all Americans. For Cable, a healed nation depended as much upon the reconstruction of the censuring northerner as upon that of the recalcitrant southerner. Pressured by his editors, Cable never could afford *not* to conceive of his audience as nationally defined, and he made creative choices that sometimes compromised his fiction's radical political vision.

Four years after the novel's publication, Cable took the issues of national conciliation and the performance of cross-racial and gendered, ethnic identity in an unusual direction by burlesquing scenes from *The Grandissimes* and his other works on national stages with Mark Twain. The duo, engaged in what Twain called "the highway robbery business," helped shape distant perceptions of interracial relations during this crucial postwar period. The combined stage presence of Twain and Cable represents a final twist on the doubling dualities at play in *The Grandissimes*. Playing against Twain's broad buffoonery, Cable reanimated his novel's primary strategy for empowering freedpeople by legitimizing the voice of local minorities and founding a new kind of "whiteface" for the stage. By speaking both for and about black Americans, these joint performances mediated a range of responses.

The performances were inflected by Cable's public addresses protesting the violence against African Americans denied their civil rights. His dramatic pitch to amusement seekers would also, in effect, caricature the Creoles and, by extension, the freedpeople. The stereotyped nature of Cable's onstage Creoles and his popular descriptions of African songs and dances contradicted Cable's appeal at the lectern for recognizing individuality over race and for respecting the difference between social and political equality. The timing of his essays, novel, and stage performances helped negate his most radical endorsements for the political and economic equality of black Americans. Examining the drama of his conflicted political vision as it unfolded provides insight into the performative complexities of Reconstruction policy itself.

A Confederate Yankee in a Bourbon Court

In May 1865 twenty-one-year-old Cable returned from the war to his native city. Sensing creative possibilities within its cosmopolitan diversity, he scribbled poems and prose in his free time. The former Confederate cavalryman wore many hats in New Orleans. His work as a surveyor, reporter, census taker, and counting house agent ensured his familiarity with the city's inhabitants and problems. Like Hawthorne, Cable kept the lucrative latter job until 1881, when he was able to support his family from his writing. During the 1870s, Cable also developed a lifelong commitment to activism; his civic work included prison reform, asylums, and record preservation for the state historical society. But it was his early journalistic experience, along with his interest in literature, local history, and reform, that influenced his novels. Cable passed some of his first short stories on to Edward King, the renowned author and journalist, who was in town during early 1873 to research his "Great South" series for *Scribner's Monthly*. King helped place Cable's first story, "'Sieur George," with Richard Watson Gilder, *Scribner's* associate editor, who became the publisher for nearly all of Cable's books. As Cable's "unofficial agent" for many years, King also provided Cable entrée to the editorial offices of other major eastern magazine publishers, including *Harper's Magazine, Appletons' Journal*, and *Galaxy*. Encouraged by Gilder and Assistant Editor Robert Underwood Johnson and bolstered by *Scribner's* publication of his first short story collection, *Old Creole Days* (1879), and *The Grandissimes*, Cable set out to write full-time.²

During Reconstruction Cable resided in a city described by one contemporary as "a halfway house between California and civilization." Twenty-three years before it was the staging ground for Homer Plessy's suit, New Orleans provided the setting for the 1873 *Slaughterhouse Cases*, which became the occasion for the Supreme Court to first interpret the Fourteenth Amendment. Focused on the legality of a sanitation statute, the case nevertheless had enormous repercussions for the meaning of citizenship, labor disputes, and the significant redefinition of property in American law. Of most relevance to Cable's Reconstruction vision, the decision curbed federal power, leaving the protection of black civil rights up to individual states. Although Cable did not address the particulars of that case while he lived there, he did protest publicly against segregation. Cable called the Crescent City home until 1885 when his controversial writing prompted him to pull up stakes for a more congenial Northampton, Massachusetts, where he remained a much-loved civic activist until his death in 1925.³

The Big Easy and Military District Five

Characterized as "a unique epicenter of violent politics," Louisiana distinguished itself in Military District Five, which included Texas, and earned a reputation for large-scale political corruption during Reconstruction. The Pelican State's military occupation lasted until 1877, longer than anywhere else in the former Confederacy. Federal presence was justified in light of such atrocities as the brutal Colfax Massacre of Easter 1873, in which more than sixty freedmen were murdered. That bloodbath unleashed further vigilante violence, including the notorious Coushatta Massacre of August 1874, helped bring about the end of Republican rule in Louisiana, and set in motion *United States v. Cruikshank*, an important Supreme Court test case of the Enforcement Acts of 1870-72, passed to enforce the Fourteenth and Fifteenth Amendments.[4]

The temporary capital and largest city in a state that contributed more black soldiers to the Union army than any other southern state, New Orleans was wracked by discord as contending political factions sought municipal power. Beginning with an explosive all-day street battle in July 1866, events in the Crescent City helped decide the trajectory of Reconstruction for the entire South. Chronic postwar tumult in New Orleans was characterized by Democrats' repeated challenges to incumbent Republicans. In the 1870s the city had two state governments in operation. Federal military presence varied in the city, reaching its peak before the November 1874 elections, when the city had the largest stationing of troops since initial occupation in 1862. This was President Ulysses S. Grant's response to the attempt by the White Leagues to overthrow the overwhelmed Republican governor William Pitt Kellogg. The Republicans kept power until the 1876 elections only because of federal intervention, as Democrats used organized intimidation and violence, from initial, covert vigilante action to the advent of paramilitary organizations, including the Knights of the White Camellia, the White Leagues, and ex-Confederate militias.[5]

Cable's writing for the right-wing *New Orleans Daily Picayune* during 1870-71 had already brought him into direct conflict with its white supremacist staff, making it clear that he would inevitably have to turn to fiction to present his views. After Cable resigned as a reporter in 1871, he wrote occasionally for the *Daily Picayune* while working in the counting house of cotton factor William C. Black and Company. His articles included attacks on the city's corrupt lottery system and historical sketches celebrating the city's churches and charities.[6]

But the 1866 riot had already inaugurated a long conflict with national repercussions. According to one historian, its effect was equivalent to that of Fort Sumter for the Civil War. Northern public opinion, convinced that the South was unrepentant, abruptly shifted support to the Radicals in Congress, helping to oust administration Democrats and secure passage of the Reconstruction Acts of 1867. Because of its strategic geographic position and distinctive demographic composition, New Orleans was an object of scrutiny for four presidents—Abraham Lincoln, Andrew Johnson, Ulysses Grant, and Rutherford Hayes—who each saw the city as a staging ground for their plans for Reconstruction. Nevertheless, within the Crescent City and much of Louisiana, a state of practical anarchy existed from 1871 until 1877, when the "Redemption" government under Conservative Democratic governor Francis T. Nicholls retook power.[7]

Beginning with its opening chapter, "Masked Batteries," which suggests both artillery unit and dancing array, *The Grandissimes* was born from New Orleans's penchant for doubling as a compromise to Reconstruction mandates. As a structural model for the novel, the municipal government's dramatic dualities provided both opportunity for Cable and his downfall as he focused on the city's black and white Creoles.

The Contested Meaning of "Creole" in the Crescent City: A Short History

While the exact meaning of "Creole" has long been disputed, historical usage has suggested that the term originally referred to natives of Louisiana between 1720 and 1861 and included both black and white residents. "Creole," as Gwendolyn Midlo Hall has pointed out, has "been redefined over time in response to changes in the social and racial climate." After the Civil War, white Europeans claimed the term exclusively by promulgating "myths," in Joseph Tregle's terms, about Creole origin, history, and culture. But black Creoles also promulgated their own self-serving myths. For both white and black Creoles, ethnicity—grounded in Francophile, Catholic, and literate forms—became a means to distinguish themselves from Americans during the Louisiana Purchase and from freedmen and Radical Republicans eager to integrate the city after the Civil War. These Creoles also stood apart from the *français de dehors*, "the foreign French" immigrant population whose first language was French. More recent scholarship has embraced the fluidity of Creole identity as a marker for understanding the constructedness of identity itself. Nowhere is that construction better showcased than in New Orleans, where racial, social, and class distinctions were always dynamic, despite the desires of white Creoles for distinctiveness.[8]

From the city's eighteenth-century colonial beginnings, racial identity was flexible, ambiguous, and subjective in New Orleans. During Spanish rule, free people of color or *libres* forged an identity, due primarily to improved material conditions in the capital city. Through the gendered channels of marriage, fictive kinship, and participation in militias, these free people of color advanced "in terms of demographics, privileges, responsibilities and social standing." *Libre* women fared better in shaping their lives than either white or slave women, although they lacked the "paternal protection" afforded white women, as historian Kim Hanger has shown. While subordinated as women, they were not assumed to marry, and so, they could exercise "greater control over business enterprises, property, and their daily lives." Because they were considered to possess impure bloodlines and thus lack honor and virtue, society was less invested in policing their behavior, so they "had more flexibility to maneuver within the system." On this fluid frontier, New Orleans developed as a rich, multicultural entrepôt in which *libres* could identify with other *libres*, whites, and slaves depending on their generation and societal position.[9]

After the 1803 Louisiana Purchase, New Orleans was a transit point between the western territories and the northeastern states. Soon it had the fourth largest population and the second largest port for trading and immigration in the country. Adding to the city's racial and linguistic diversity were refugees from Cuba and Saint-Domingue. These refugees continued the city's legacy of Spanish influence to make it a *Caribbean* city by midcentury; from the founding of the first Spanish newspaper in the United States to supporting at least twenty-three other periodicals in Spanish, the city held rank as the "undisputed capital of Hispanophone print culture." German immigrants, from which Cable's Frowenfelds were drawn, also comprised a significant part of the city's population. The political divisiveness of New Orleans began around 1836, when the city was partitioned into three municipalities, reflective of the growing ethnic and economic rivalry between the French Creoles and Anglo-Americans. Adding to the mix was discord between the Know-Nothing Party and the city police force, which was largely composed of immigrants until 1855. Mobilized as a political force, the immigrants also provided the rank and file of a burgeoning Unionist movement, hoping to throw off yet another New Orleans duality: the twinned oppression of Know-Nothing government and slavery.[10]

On the eve of the Civil War, New Orleans had the largest population of African Americans and black Creoles in the South, many of whom enjoyed the benefits of shared city life despite statutes enforcing segregation. For example, Louisiana was the only state that allowed slaves to use the courts to sue for their freedom. Slave women took advantage of this legal opportunity: of the twenty-seven freedom suits filed in the New Orleans district, twenty-six were filed by women. Black Creoles were among the most prosperous, wealthier than any other black group in the South, twice as wealthy as foreign-born Americans, and slightly better off than the country's northwestern and northeastern whites. Most had family members like Cable's Honoré f.m.c., who had long enjoyed freedom, wealth, and education, if not the full rights of citizenship. Such advantages would position them to effect ongoing political reform. The history and presence of so many free people of color should have helped transform New Orleans into a major site of black progress during the postwar years.[11]

However, New Orleans had also been home to the continent's largest slave market, which, as Walter Johnson has powerfully shown, left a lasting ideological mark on the city. Black Creoles were caught in the persistent shadow of what one fugitive called the "chattel principle," which kept a market-determined value hovering over slave heads. After 1803 black Creoles began to experience a decline in status as tightening manumission laws and other exclusionary measures restricted their mobility while inaugurating one of the city's most prevailing postwar dualities: a binary racial order. Black Creoles, increasingly conflated with slaves by white Americans, reacted with protest. Drawing on French republican thought, they established a rich antebellum literary tradition of social and political dissent. In 1861, black Creoles raised three regiments to defend New Orleans. This action recalled their organization of militias against servile revolt during the colonial period. Despite these ongoing efforts to win acceptance into the white slaveholding community, black Creoles found themselves harassed, segregated, and arrested. With federal occupation in the spring of 1862, they offered their services to the Union.[12]

During the occupation, black Creoles nonetheless experienced a further decline in status as authorities abridged civil rights they had enjoyed before the war. Ironically, this decline was precipitated by Union troops, who intimidated and abused them, forced their conscription, and excluded them from public transportation. The city furthered hostility against all black Americans by ignoring their complaints in civil courts, failing to provide aid to the indigent, and enforcing the Black Codes. Black Creoles and ex-slaves had to battle not only local white hostility but also contend with the Freedmen's Bureau. For example, black Creoles had attended schools since 1822, and many felt, like Cable, that education was the best means to assimilate. Under General Banks, however, the bureau began levying a tax that decimated school attendance. On many fronts, black Creoles experienced the deleterious effects of a two-caste racial system imposed by the occupying army and later Jim Crow laws that lumped them with the ex-slave population. In response, some black Creoles stressed their "third caste" status as a distinctive ethnic group, one distinguished by the "Latin-culture Negro" as opposed to the "Anglo-Saxon-culture Negro."[13]

Cable, who once considered "The Peculiar People" as an alternative title to his first book, *Old Creole Days*, was amused by these attempts to establish caste distinctions. Nevertheless, his fiction unflinchingly registered the force of their plight. Cable studied their history and that of the Crescent City itself, while not at work in the counting house. His findings would influence his creative work and his nonfiction *The Creoles of Louisiana*, which he published in 1884.[14]

Mapping the Geography of Creole Identity: The "Peculiar People" in Cable's *The Grandissimes* and *The Creoles of Louisiana*

Cable envisioned a Reconstruction that was far more egalitarian in recognizing and respecting disparate elements than what finally emerged. Of most significance to the freedpeople, Cable's fictional characters foregrounded citizenship's potential as a performed identity. Cable's Creoles, unlike Constance Woolson's Minorcans, stood in for a variety of southern types, including the vengeful ex-bondswoman, the unrepentant fire-eater, and the New South commercial hero, which allowed for various points of view, including the freedpeople's, to be aired.

Following publication of *The Grandissimes*, Cable grappled with Creole identity more thoroughly in *The Creoles of Louisiana*. Like his first novel's opening chapter, which confounded the certainties of identity through disguise, Cable's history bluntly opened with the titular question, "Who are the Creoles?" Cable asks this question again in Chapter 6, which begins with the beguiling "What is a Creole?" His dramatization of the question demonstrated the difficulty of procuring a definite answer. Cable stressed that this term was "adopted by—not conceded to—the natives of mixed blood," emphasizing the very creativity inherent in the term's definition. Replying to a reporter's inquiry, Cable acknowledged the multiple meanings of "Creole" but defined the term as a valued character trait, stressing that it carried a "qualification of peculiar excellence . . . of which the possessor is very proud."[15]

With a malleable definition, Cable transformed the prickly question of Creole identity ("Who are they?") into a geography problem ("Where are they?"). In *Creoles of Louisiana*, a detour through the Crescent City's swampy terrain demonstrates that regional character is derived from local landscape. Cable's foregrounding of geographic boundaries as markers for shifting Creole identity was enhanced by Joseph Pennell's appealing sketches of New Orleans when the book was serialized in *Century*

A Crevasse. (Story's Plantation, 1882.)

FIGURE 10. Joseph Pennell, "A Crevasse," *Creoles of Louisiana* (New York: Charles Scribner's Sons, 1884), 270.

Magazine from January to July 1883. Combined with Pennell's lavish landscapes, Cable's descriptions emphasized a broader vista, where the inhabitants, emergent from the "forlorn confusion" of the swamp, bayou, and freshet, found themselves "conforming to the mold of their nearest surroundings."[16]

In the novel, too, the swamp, quite unlike its fixed meaning in Thanet or Woolson, hovers in the background as a place of independence, refuge, solace, and murder. As suggested by Pennell's "A Crevasse," the city defined itself by its proclivity for all kinds of maelstroms (Fig. 10). The changing environs of Cable's New Orleans were nearly imprinted on its denizens. Just as Canal Street emerged from a drained swamp, so Cable showed that the Creole emerged from a background that was part Choctaw, part pirate, part slave, part convict, part European nobility, and part *filles-de-cassette*, young French girls imported as intended brides to the colony. Agricola's pretensions to pure blood are part of familial myth.

Cable used the city's naturally dynamic commercial development as catalyst for his Reconstruction vision. When Canal Street's "slimy old moat" was transformed into a shopping mecca, Portuguese, French, Creoles, and Americans intermixed to form a mass of buyers and sellers who eschewed ethnic distinctions in favor of a sale. The 1871 establishment of the city's Cotton Exchange spawned six other powerful exchanges by 1890, ensuring that New Orleans remained, at least for a time, the South's premier commercial center. With a strategy reminiscent of Tourgée's literary investment in market-driven proprietary relations, Cable argued that the capacious meaning of the term "Creole" was inevitably compounded to include commodities: "At length the spirit of commerce saw the money value of so honored a title, and broadened its meaning to take in any creature or thing of variety or manufacture that might become an object of sale." Through his celebration of Creole acculturation, Cable presents Reconstruction as another natural episode in the city's cultural evolution.[17]

Despite the opaque and elastic nature of Creole identity, the fate of the Creoles converged with that of the freedpeople even before the Civil War. In his history Cable showed that as early as 1803 the position of Creoles was analogous to that of the postbellum freedpeople. Their education was similar to what O. O. Howard would later recommend to the freedmen, exhorting them to learn civic duty and the tradition of liberal republicanism. Cable cited Poydras, a "wealthy and benevolent" Creole, who conceded, "We must be initiated into the sacred duties of freemen and the practices of liberty." Cable stresses that this educational phenomenon was on no small scale. "Between 1804 and 1810," the population of New Orleans "doubled," not with Anglo-Americans who were "numerically feeble" but with the refugees of the French West Indies: "whites, free mulattoes, and black slaves in almost equal numbers." Both Cable's history and his novel document the inevitable entanglements of Europeans with their slaves, creating caste-bound, gendered relations that continued to define the region.[18]

In *The Grandissimes* Cable conflates the experience of black Creoles and former slaves as their linked misfortunes make them fall under "the Shadow of the Ethiopian" that blights New Orleans, and he suggests the shadow is that of Bras Coupé's retaliation. Originally entitled "Bibi," the story focuses on the efforts of Bras Coupé, a Jaloff prince, to resist the degradation of slavery by refusing to work, running away to the swamp, and placing a voodoo curse on his master—actions that recall the earlier slave insurgencies in Saint-Domingue and nearby Pointe Coupee. Coupé's curse blasts the entire plantation, leaving pestilence and starvation. His action suggests that perhaps this prince needs to be recognized by white Louisianians as much as an Indian princess (Agricola's esteemed ancestor) does. Captured and tortured, Coupé lifts the curse on his deathbed, in an act of forgiveness for his besieged mistress. Magazine editors had rejected the story of this black slave for "its unmitigatedly distressful effect," in the words of the *Atlantic Monthly's* George Parsons Lathrop, and it languished for several years until incorporated into *The Grandissimes*. His *Scribner's* editors did not agree with the political overtones of the Bras Coupé episode and scorned his presentation of such intelligent black characters as Clemence. For Cable, however, this tale was the centerpiece "around which the whole larger work [of the novel] is built."[19]

Fitting the story into the novel—both thematically and textually— encouraged Cable to imagine how freedpeople would fit into postwar southern society. He shows the centrality of freedpeople to the South by demonstrating the story's profound effect on the novel's other characters. Bras Coupé's tale becomes a recurring reference point. The characters are compelled to tell "the same dark story" in a kind of Thanet-styled strategy of expiation. On one day alone the Jaloff prince's story is told by Raoul, Honoré, and Honoré f.m.c., and the reader learns the whole tale through Aurora Nancanou. So potent is Bras Coupé's suffering in showing the maiming effect of slavery that characters grapple with representing its impact on their lives: Raoul aspires to paint a "pigshoe" of Bras Coupé, and Palmyre makes a model of his severed arm to practice voodoo and kill Agricola. Cable himself felt compelled to perform the scene of Bras Coupé's death during his debut reading at Johns Hopkins in March 1883, which he later developed into a solo reading program entirely devoted to dramatizing his story. The tantalizing ambiguity in his characters' differing versions raises doubt and hope for the ex-bondspeople's prospects.[20]

Confounding the revisionist import of the story of the Jaloff prince is the "dead stock" of the past that informs Creole character. The Grandissime home, that "great mother-mansion," where all these "Knickerbockers of New Orleans" once gathered for their *fête de grandpère*, gave way to "invaders" and was later torn down as the city expanded. Gendered strategies become key to reverse the marginalization of this once "masterly" house. The Grandissimes' necessary social and economic diversification depends upon incorporating new blood in marriages and other partnerships with outsiders. Amid this proliferation of hybridized Creoles, the galvanizing question of Cable's *Creoles*, "Who are the Creoles?," became rephrased in his novel by its main protagonist, Joseph Frowenfeld, as "Who are my neighbors?" What begins as a "mental diversion" for the convalescing Frowenfeld becomes the major problem of the novel: understanding a social web of gendered relations based on genealogy and spun with a southern ideal of "cherishing the unity of our family." Cable recognized that for some Creoles the past, as important as geography, does more than haunt the present—it structures it. Because the past lives in the present, Frowenfeld learns much about the city's origins from watching the Founders' Day parade in the Place D'Armes. Frowenfeld's position as a spectator is analogous to that of the reader who, with him, seeks answers to the mysterious question of Creole identity.[21]

Indeed, *The Grandissimes* so masterminds the art of ambivalence that no easy conclusions are reached about Cable's vision of Reconstruction. The novel reaches the same conclusion that Cable's *Creoles* does in answering the slippery question of Creole identity: it keeps the question paramount in the reader's mind, but as a question unanswered. Frowenfeld's initial bafflement over the identity of Honoré Grandissime (until he realized that two men share the same name) is continued more disturbingly by closer kin Hippolyte Grandissime, who later asks exasperatingly, "*Who is* Monsieur Honoré Grandissime?" The writer provides no easy answers.[22]

The Compromised Road to Reunion:
Four Characters and Four Axes of Reconstruction Intersect

Cable's gendered vision of Reconstruction as a compromised negotiation involving all Americans is crystallized by four male characters in *The Grandissimes*, three of whom are Creole and one a northern émigré. Cable tests the transformative capacities of each to change identity, compromise demands, and negotiate his interests. Each character's response to Reconstruction is articulated along the four axes of its discourse: property, duty, reputation, and labor. The two subsidiary characters, Agricola and Frowenfeld, investigate the meaning of landed property and duty, respectively. They also represent the South and the North, whose sectional polarities are both in need of reconstruction. The white patriarch Honoré and his black half brother, Honoré f.m.c., demonstrate the centrality of reputation, race, and labor to Reconstruction as Cable probes the limits of this ethnic group to participate in postwar change. The fates of all four characters limn Cable's vision of a reconstructed nation.

With a name connotative of plantation agriculture, Agricola Fusilier, that "high priest of a doomed civilization," is the unreconstructed southerner who craves the maintenance of a patriarchal caste system based on land-ownership, slavery, and violence. He warns Frowenfeld: "Beware, my son, of the doctrine of equal rights—a bottomless iniquity. Society has pyramids to build which make menials a necessity and Nature furnishes the menials all in dark uniform." His racist and gendered beliefs, reinforced through dueling and gambling, all turn on his need to "vindicate his honor" through the violent subordination of black women. His masterly instigation results in Palmyre's wrath, the loss of the Nancanou estate, and the deaths of slaves Bras Coupé and Clemence. Admonishing Frowenfeld that "tradition is much more authentic than history," Agricola mocks the Creole virtue of adaptability by calling the liberal Frowenfeld "son" and by labeling himself "Citizen" Fusilier.[23]

Cable exposes Agricola's pretensions to white male supremacy as hypocritical and false. The "Citizen's" admiration for the "old cast-iron tyrannies" of Europe is fed by uncertainty about his New World genealogy. A descendant of a Native American, Agricola is defined by his casuist insistence on the illusion of a pure white genealogy. While Agricola is proud of his Indian ancestor, it is only because she was a princess. Although "less responsible entanglements" are winked at, in marriage the old planter is of the "royal house of the Fusiliers." They always prefer to marry into the Grandissime stock, which has "kept itself lily-white ever since France has loved lilies." And while worshiping French, Citizen Fusilier reminds Frowenfeld, though with contempt, that he can also speak Choctaw as well as English. Because "our circle must be protected"—that is, the reputation of white, propertied men—Agricola relies on words to incite and deceive. When the wounded Frowenfeld flees Palmyre's house and is exposed to public censure, the old planter offers to use his own reputation as moral collateral as a means to restore Frowenfeld's besmirched one; with "benevolent mendacity" he offers to say that Frowenfeld's wound resulted from a fall, when in reality Frowenfeld had received a blow by Palmyre's servant who misunderstood his attempts to minister to her wound, a wound she received after she tried to kill the "Citizen."[24]

To counter the emergent threat of empowered black women keen on redressing their grievances, the old planter invokes traditional southern belief in white male supremacy to rally support. Later in the novel, when Agricola learns of Palmyre's renewed conspiring with Clemence to voodoo him, he appeals to his mob of "kinsmen" with a rhetoric similar to that of secessionists and Klansmen: "The time has come when Louisiana must protect herself! If there is one here who will not strike for his lands, his rights, and the purity of his race, let him speak!" Calling for "a few feet of stout rope" by which to teach black Louisianians to "know their places," the old planter incites a crowd of Creoles, whose first target coincidentally becomes the American Frowenfeld's store. Agricola's gender and racially targeted actions resemble tactics used by the neighboring planter elite to rouse support for violence from common folk. "Gone over to the enemy" is how Agricola casts any contact with the Yankees, the progenitors of the New South carpetbaggers, that "race of upstarts." Claiming to having "lost his glasses" so that he can no longer read his own white supremacist diatribe, *Philippique Géneralé*, he is the epitome of a people who, in Honoré's words, "are too *close* to see distinctly," blinded by their incestuous desire for exclusiveness. Insisting that "the old Louisiana will rise again. She will get back her trampled rights," a dying Agricola refuses to imagine the territory's incorporation into America any more than many fire-eating southerners could fathom the Confederacy's reincorporation.[25]

Yet the old planter's death at the hands of Palmyre permits the union of Honoré and Aurora Nancanou. His elimination signifies Cable's desire for a new "dawn" that holds no place for unreconstructed southern men. Although other white characters in *The Grandissimes* share some of Agricola's prejudices, they survive because they can change and incorporate difference. For example, Raoul asserts, "I don't care if a man are good like a h-angel, if 'e had not pu'e w'ite, *'ow can 'e* be a gen'leman?" Later in the story, however, he defies his vigilante cousins and strives to save Clemence. Similarly, Aurora, in refusing to sign Agricola's statement that he gambled without cheating, is a "perfect specimen of Creole pride," although pride dooms her to poverty. By the novel's close, she too relents and marries into the feuding Grandissime clan, a move which considerably enlarges her estate.[26]

The character Joseph Frowenfeld allows Cable to explore the regional and political antipode of Citizen Fusilier. Frowenfeld's investigation into Creole identity shows that northern conscientious duty is insufficient for reconstructing southern hearts and minds. Frowenfeld exemplifies northern readers whose Radical Reconstruction agendas fueled southern resentment and stifled their initiative to change. Despite his unfamiliarity with New Orleans, this "sermonizer" pontificates about injustice, but the effect is deadening. On the question of cession, his "merciless" and "unattainable" arguments tend to "give out more heat than light," provoking only "resentment" and "hostility." Honoré dismisses his offer to be peacemaker among the Grandissimes: "'Oh!' said the Creole, with a little shrug, 'you may do anything you can—which will be nothing.'" Instead of walking around the "prickly bush" of southern slavery, Frowenfeld, like Bras Coupé, mistakenly wants "to lay hold of it with his naked hands and pull it up by the roots"—a strategy with deadly consequences. Despite Frowenfeld's centrality as a cultural bridge to the mysterious Creoles, he is often the most underrated and criticized character in the book. Cable's editor Robert Underwood Johnson faulted him for creating a character who was weighted down with too much "goodness" and "not mixed with enough humanity," while present-day critic Louis Rubin also sees him as "high-minded but wooden and lifeless."[27]

Frowenfeld's saintliness and strident idealism are qualities that Cable targeted for Reconstruction because they inhibit any real progress in a society that "*is* sore to the touch." He must learn to conform his idealism to the context, as Honoré advises: "Mr. Frowenfeld, you never make pills with eight corners, eh? . . . No, you make them round; cannot you make your doctrines the same way?" The wounds of New Orleans must be healed by less heroic cures than his, and eventually the immigrant's moralistic rigidity is filed away enough to allow him to fit. Frowenfeld adopts the prevailing gender-coded strategy of women reformers, using tact and patience to influence the Creoles. Mastering "the art of courteous debate," he prevails in an informal exchange on the Grandissime verandah where "truth and justice made some unacknowledged headway." No longer driving home his criticism or demands, he learns how to parley and concede in order to effect change.[28]

His reconstruction commences with his study of the Creoles, likened to reading as a tool of postwar change, which Tourgée had endorsed: Frowenfeld begins "at once the perusal of this newly found book, the Community of New Orleans." Reconstructive reading of this community "volume" entails that its "displaced leaves would have to be lifted tenderly, blown free of much dust, re-arranged, some torn fragments laid together again." Although the aged physician and sharp-eyed observer, Dr. Keene, advises Frowenfeld to "take" the Grandissimes "in the mass—as you would shrimps," Frowenfeld learns through his community-text that they are distinguishable. "Shifting like the fragments of colored glass in the kaleidoscope," they prove Cable's insistence that no race can be judged, only its individual members on their own merits. At the same time Frowenfeld learns firsthand the degree to which southern family matters, like those of the Grandissimes, shape the greater community culture.[29]

Although Frowenfeld sets up his makeshift library in the apothecary's back room, his plein air study is his front shop. Free of the gendered and racial constraints that hid Toinette's reading room, Frowenfeld's shop reflects Creole culture. It is a "place of art exposition" and a fishnet catching a variety of Creole artifacts: "A pair of statuettes, a golden tobacco-box, a costly jewel-casket, or a pair of richly gemmed horse pistols—the property of some ancient gentleman or dame of emaciated fortune, and which must be sold to keep up the bravery of good clothes and pomade that hid slow starvation." All of these items tell stories, reveal elusive histories, and proclaim opinions that the reader and Frowenfeld must fathom. By selling them, Frowenfeld participates in the upholding of Creole appearances and reputation. It is through this medium that Frowenfeld sees Creole culture, for it is "natural that these things should come to 'Frowenfeld's corner,' for there oftener than elsewhere, the critics were gathered together." As an eclectic and public space, Frowenfeld's shop offers a window into reconstructing the city.[30]

Frowenfeld's assistant, Creole Raoul Innerarity, that "treasure" of a Grandissime cousin, acts as cultural interpreter. He explains the complexities of Creole behavior while often smoothing the way for Frowenfeld to engineer his plans for social reform: "To a student of the community he was a key, a lamp, a lexicon, a microscope, a tabulated statement, a book of heraldry, a city directory, a glass of wine, a Book of Days, a pair of wings, a comic almanac . . . a Creole *veritas*." The definition of Raoul constitutes a list, like the items in Frowenfeld's window, which are endless and varied. Within hours, "his words had done more to elucidate the mysteries in which his employer had begun to be befogged than half a year of the apothecary's slow and scrupulous guessing."[31]

Cable deploys a gendered strategy to complete the reconstruction of Frowenfeld's character. He transitions from student to participant in Creole New Orleans by his financial partnership and marriage with Clotilde, the daughter of Aurora Nancanou, who continues Frowenfeld's education where Raoul left off, while providing needed funding to replenish his stock. Frowenfeld's apothecary shop prospers when he shares rental and finally personal space with the Nancanous. Cable stresses that they first conceived a financial arrangement by "signed regular articles of copartnership," a "purely business" arrangement, however scoffed at by a cynical Dr. Keene, which was followed by marriage nearly fifty pages later. These new familial and property ties offer an egalitarian alternative to the outmoded gendered schema of subordinated relationships that Agricola demands.[32]

In this revised culture, home and work inform each other differently. Cable's model marital partnership between an Anglo-American and a French Creole was the same cross-ethnic tie pursued profitably by many white Louisianians after the purchase. Unlike Thanet's or Tourgée's radical revisioning of property ownership, Cable advocated the stabilizing acquisition of property by differently partnered owners, a solution possible because colonial New Orleans recognized provisions in Spanish law that counted marital property as communal, allowed mixed heirs to inherit and women to retain control over their property regardless of marital status. Frowenfeld's "compromise" mimics Cable's own truce with an increasingly recalcitrant South, which by the 1880s would no longer abide by the radical reconstruction once possible in the 1870s.[33]

Cable's boldest experiments in Reconstruction were through the dynamic Creole patriarch, Honoré Grandissime. In his attempted suturing of northern profit and ideals to southern chivalry, Cable uses this central character to probe the malleability of regional meanings of reputation. The man whose name epitomizes the importance of keeping up moral appearances seems to be the quintessential southern gentleman committed to preserving his reputation. He seconds Agricola's endorsement of caste as he rationalizes his political apathy: "I am afraid to go deeply into anything, lest it should make ruin my name, my family, my property." He further admits that his whole life has been governed by the dictum "peace first and justice afterwards," a philosophy shared by many postwar white southerners hostile to freedpeople's claims for civil rights and by many northerners tired of ongoing southern resistance and soothed by President Grant's "Let Us Have Peace" campaign. Honoré struggles with his conscience to surmount local criticism and arrive at a new, if commercial, understanding of his reputation.[34]

Cable personifies the Grandissime mansion to show how closely identified Honoré and his clan are with the landed interests of patriarchy. Bearing Honoré's "erring ways" with "a look of patient sadness," the mansion speaks for the family in desiring Honoré to be haughty, "an inflexible of the inflexibles." Honoré is the heir to the family's burden of tradition as well as its financial supervisor in land dealings. He "incited" a Grandissime-De Grapion reconciliation and violated protocol by becoming a businessman: "shop-keeping, *parbleu*!" "For years" he maintained "a kind of custody of all my kinsmen's property interests, Agricola's among them." Weary and burdened with his family's past, Honoré reminds Frowenfeld that he has eaten much of the fruit from the tree reverently called "our dead father's mistakes" and concludes that "a man who has to do that must expect to have now and then a little fever."[35]

Being a merchant provides Honoré with his identity, informing his ability to assume risks and leverage his credit in social contexts. He tries to see sensitive social issues in terms of profit and loss: "Mr. Frowenfeld, my habit is to buy cheap and sell at a profit. My condemnation?

My-de'-seh, there is no sa-a-ale for it! It spoils the sale of other goods, my-de'-seh. It is not to condemn that you want; you want to suc-*ceed*." He exudes a confident prosperity that makes his reassurances to his kin creditable. He daringly uses annual Grandissime reunions to advocate moral reforms, although the family had hoped "he would outgrow such heresies." Sensing the impending financial loss to his family as their land titles become worthless under American control, Honoré commits "apostasy" by courting the "arch-usurper," the new American governor William C. C. Claiborne. He gains influence with the northerner and not only helps to avert a riot but also satisfies the Grandissime family's clutch at power: "When this interview finally drew to a close the governor had made a memorandum of some fifteen or twenty Grandissimes, scattered through different cantons of Louisiana who . . . would not decline appointments." Much like Frowenfeld's cross-ethnic marriage, Honoré's efforts to cement ties with the Anglo-American governor echo practices adopted by white French Creole and Anglo-American planters, who, in recognition of their shared interests, developed close social, economic, and political ties in rural Louisiana soon after the purchase.[36]

As a white southern gentleman, Honoré's need to keep his honorable reputation intact lags behind his talent for turning a dollar. The merchant's fiscally guided morality hinders him from restoring the Nancanou titles; he delays, recognizing that it will result in the Grandissimes' poverty and ostracism, leaving him the object of the "community's obloquy." Unlike Storer College students who applied their obligations to serve toward racial uplift, this merchant cannot hear the call of duty. Unlike Frowenfeld, he does not see moral obligations, only their prices: "I do not say the duty, my-de'-seh, a merchant talks of values." Herein lies a major preoccupation of the novel: How can Honoré's commitment to keeping the community's high regard be reconstructed to support more northern, postwar notions of justice for the dispossessed?[37]

Honoré walks this interregional tightrope between scoring Yankee profits and placating his southern community. With his light "touch here to-day and word there to-morrow," Honoré was "ever lifting the name, and all who bore it . . . a little higher," unlike Frowenfeld's wrongheaded bluntness. If Agricola mocks American pretensions to citizenship by being Citizen Fusilier, Honoré mocks his family's pretensions to caste privilege by invoking those pretensions with exaggeration. Warding off any charges of radicalism, Honoré self-reflexively counters: "Do not mistake me for one of your new-fashioned Philadelphia *'negrophiles'*; I am a merchant, my-de-seh." Honoré's criticism of "negrophiles" follows just after his sincere admission that Bras Coupé's death "changed the whole channel of my convictions." Often torn between his conscience and his family burdens, his desire for Aurora and his fear of repercussions, Honoré, a bit like Tourgée, poses behind his good Creole name as he manipulates the kind of Creole character he wishes his family and friends to see.[38]

In trying to be a good merchant and a good man, Honoré must reconstruct his sense of reputation by mixing southern "honor" with northern "commerce." Through his friendship with Frowenfeld, Honoré's reconstruction consists of learning to narrow the gap between theory and practice. In theory, Honoré admires Bras Coupé's audacity, for "*there* was a bold man's chance to denounce wrong and oppression!" Yet, when Honoré acts on his admiration and says "some indignant things in the African's favor," the consequence is that Bras Coupé's Spanish owner resolves to punish the slave. Honoré must find a middle way, overcome his propensity to "condemn—too cautiously—by a kind of elevated cowardice," and behave more conscientiously.[39]

Upon this moral scaffold, however, Honoré is no Reverend Dimmesdale, that Hawthornian martyr, and no John Clifford. Against a wincing Frowenfeld, who argues for restitution "at any cost," Honoré remains cautious, unwilling to act on "impulse" even under the persuasive influence of the Nancanous. He recognizes that restoring the title of the Nancanous would sell out his family, for "to commence selling must be to go on selling," when parting with the family's questionable titles to raise revenue. Finally acting out his conscience, Honoré provides some measure of restitution to his half brother, Honoré f.m.c., and to the Nancanous, despite family censure. Honoré is so reconstructed by this one honorable act that to some Grandissimes he no longer seems to be the reassuring family patriarch. As with Frowenfeld, it is Honoré's involvement with a white Creole woman, Aurora Nancanou, that completes his reconstruction.[40]

Part of Honoré's restitution is a willingness, almost corporeal, to incorporate the suffering of others into himself. He offers to be maimed like Bras Coupé, if "the value of peace" could only be taught to his family: "I would give you, if that was your price—he ran the edge of his left hand knife-wise around the wrist of his right—'that.'" Cable suggests that Reconstruction implies a revisioning of the South's honor code to permit an evenhanded empathy with its victims. Risking community condemnation of his reputation, Honoré leads his family away from the dead financial and generational stock of Agricola toward greater prosperity by imagining new titles, new occupations, and new kinds of partnerships for Creoles. His old allegiance to "my name, my family, my property" is revamped to accord with realizing a profit in alliances forged with black Creoles. By incorporating Honoré f.m.c. into the family business, Honoré profits. Those who could not accept the incorporation of black wealth into the family become bankrupt, left with their "pathetic pride," until it "bled them to penury." Rather than seeing good business and high ideals at odds, as did Tourgée, Cable complements them in a New South commercial vision.[41]

A certain tidy reciprocity characterizes the reconstruction of Frowenfeld and Honoré; learning to be a little more like each other, their marriages and other newfound partnerships symbolize what was perhaps the only road to national reunion still open in the 1880s. The two men's reconstruction resulted in the exile of Honoré f.m.c., which could be interpreted as a reconstruction of the mutually corrupt rival factions of New Orleans politics that tried to eliminate the "swing vote" of African Americans. The Reformers, representing the business elite, would have been sympathetic to Honoré's interests, while the powerful and established Regular Democratic Organization (also known as the "Ring," or the "Old Regulars") representing ward-based, working-class immigrants, would have pursued Frowenfeld's vote. The Freedmen's Bureau advocated a mutual reconciliation between the former master and slave, a relationship that was reconstructed only by the added factor of the wage. The compromised reconstruction of Frowenfeld and Honoré endorses Cable's assertion that "this is a world that allows nothing without its obverse and reverse." As the novel's ending suggests, Aurora's declared "No!" to Honoré's marriage proposal really signifies "Yes" when she embraces him.[42]

Using the gendered strategy of marital alliances to satisfy the plot's moral compunction, Cable lets the market arbitrate Reconstruction's compromises, making them both rewarding and honorable. Decisions exclusively based on Agricolan notions of noblesse oblige become outmoded, whereas those based entirely on Frowenfeldian conscience become impracticable, and Honoré, already a consummate businessman, learns the art of risk management. The novel's denouement rests on a brokering between southern honor and northern ideals of Reconstruction and a mediation between kinds of Yankee investment with New South capitalism.

All of Frowenfeld's assistants are recruited through the Grandissime clan's recommendations, while Honoré f.m.c. forms a lucrative partnership with his half brother. Honoré f.m.c. joins the mercantile house, saving the Nancanous from eviction and the family from bankruptcy. His only condition is that the name be changed to *Grandissime Brothers*, which Honoré "reverently" acknowledges is "easy" as "my very right to exist comes after yours." Local businesses run by both black and white

Creoles are, in Raoul's words, "better dis way." In fact, local Louisiana merchants who operated general stores like Frowenfeld's relied on kinship ties, confirming Raoul's opinion that businesses profited when conducted as "family affairs." Good business in the South still meant good knowledge of your neighbors and good use of your relatives. This was long understood by African Americans, who recognized the important mutual relations of property and kinship ties, particularly in the postwar world.[43]

While this arrangement allows Honoré f.m.c., the latest partner to join the Grandissime firm, to profit financially, it cannot forestall his personal ruin because Honoré f.m.c. suffers under "the shadow of the Ethiopian," which, like Tourgée's "brand," renders him and his class "free in form but slaves in spirit." The shadow turns his fraternal partnership into something gothic, contentious and unproductive. Honoré gives it palpable form when he expostulates, "Ah! my-de-seh, . . . I am *ama-aze* at the length, the blackness of that shadow! It is the *Némésis* w'ich . . . glides along by the side of this morhal, political, commercial, social mistake!" The shadow distinguishes between the two Honorés: "He was like the sun's warmth wherever he went; and the other Honoré was like his shadow." The distinction implies a complementarity which the proposed partnership would flesh out. Contrary to the experience of African Americans who benefited from kinship ties, Cable makes the biracial gain one-sided. When Honoré calculates how he has "come out," he concludes that he has been the "beneficiary," while his black brother has received "only a public recognition of kinship which had always been his due. Bitter cup of humiliation!" The elevation of Honoré f.m.c. to equal footing in the partnership causes some Grandissimes to seethe; in fact, it becomes the excuse used by Hippolyte Grandissime, an otherwise minor character, to pull the trigger on Clemence.[44]

The novel's shadow symbolizes a people so oppressed that their very corporeality is erased, yet made unforgettable. In the chapter "Paralysis," Cable describes Honoré f.m.c.'s unrequited love for the quadroon Palmyre and his hatred for Agricola, the combination of which leaves him incapacitated, reinforcing his servile nature. Frowenfeld characterizes this Honoré and his class as the "saddest slaves of all" for their luxuriant indifference to injustice. For a "paltry bait of sham freedom" they have agreed "to be shorn even of the virtue of discontent" and "endure a tyrannous contumely which flattens them into the dirt like grass under a slab." Unlike the ex-slaves, for whom freedom was too often defined by white southerners as a duty to labor, Honoré f.m.c. is denounced as a "warning to philanthropists."[45]

Reflective of his psychological stasis, Honoré f.m.c. retreats into a dark, indulgent interior. His home contrasts sharply with Frowenfeld's commercial corner and the Grandissimes' breezy social verandah: "The rooms were so sumptuously furnished; immovable largeness and heaviness, lofty sobriety, abundance of finely brass mounting, motionless richness of upholstery, much silent twinkle of pendulous crystal, a soft semi-obscurity." The opulent extravagance of his bedroom feeds its enervating atmosphere, suggesting a kind of slothful sensuality, causing the discerning Dr. Keene to remark, "You don't call this a hiding-place, do you—in his own bedchamber?" Unlike Honoré's cultivated leisure, Honoré f.m.c.'s environs are lethal, reflecting his "feeble" and "motionless" state of "extreme languor."[46]

Similarly, the bedridden Palmyre's apartment is organized around her bedroom, reflecting both wealth's torpor and the dark surplus of her frustrated energy channeled into voodoo. A shelter from white society, her black Creole apartment is a kind of interior swamp, predatory to all who enter, indicated by "a small table of dark mahogany supported on the upward-writhing images of three scaly serpents." Frowenfeld realizes this firsthand, reeling from the blow to his head struck by Palmyre's slave after he visits. No longer the refuge from which Bras Coupé could strike out for his rights, the swamp, as incarnated in these rooms, corresponds to an equally parasitic interiorized state in its occupant. Worse, Palmyre's and the f.m.c's privileged retreats have alienated them from what Booker T. Washington extolled as the dignity and glory of labor. Washington's cure for these black Creoles would be to "plant them upon the soil, . . . where all nations that have ever succeeded have gotten their start."[47]

Roused by Honoré f.m.c.'s reclusive apathy, Frowenfeld tries to goad him into becoming a leader of "the down-trodden race, with which this community's scorn unjustly compels you to rank yourself." Honoré f.m.c.'s refusal, because the slaves' "cause" was "lost" in Africa, leaving them "prisoners of war," opposes the foregrounded masculine activism of a Bras Coupé or a John Clifford. The f.m.c. can barely articulate what he perceives as the uselessness of "the force of their own arm" to resist oppression, and he therefore maims himself psychologically in a manner oddly like that of Bras Coupé. When Honoré f.m.c. demurs, saying that "Ah cannod be one Toussaint l'Ouverture," Frowenfeld instead counsels a feminized tactic, "the work of patient and sustained self-sacrifice." Rather than inspire insurrection, Frowenfeld tries to stir up "a noble discontent" so that "you give yourself to your people," much like Coralie Franklin and other members of Du Bois's Talented Tenth successfully did. But the f.m.c. also refuses to consider this. Rendered "palsied and withered," Honoré f.m.c., in refusing to advance the cause of black Louisianians, claims that if he tried, "I h-only s'all sooggceed to be one Bras-Coupé." (Ironically, his one intervention—killing Agricola—promotes more tragedy, helping to prompt Clemence's death to avenge the murder.) Frowenfeld's attempts to help him, however resisted, represent another path-breaking approach by Cable to envision the Crescent City's immigrants and *gens de couleur* working cooperatively—a refreshing alternative to the long-standing rivalry between these two outsider groups.[48]

In reality, many free men of color, like Homer Plessy, sought an active role in postwar politics. Drawing on their French political heritage of *liberté, égalité* and *fraternité*, black Creole activists made a determined effort, culminating in the *Plessy* case, to realize Reconstruction ideals and resist Jim Crow. Their ward clubs thrived in New Orleans, a situation enhanced by the commitment of former slaves to political involvement. While indicting slavery and the general economic exploitation of black people such as Bras Coupé, Cable, unlike Tourgée, did not seem interested in reflecting postwar accounts of *les gens de couleur*'s ambition to leadership, only their frustrations and failures.[49]

Events conspire in the novel to force Honoré f.m.c. and Palmyre into exile in France, a challenging path for many black Creoles seeking to escape prejudice. Palmyre, left "high-strung, resolute," and Honoré f.m.c., rendered "haggard, woe-begone, nervous," each suffer "under a great strain." With no hope of securing Palmyre's love, the free man of color leaves her all his wealth and commits suicide, leaving little hope for black New Orleanians. Consistent with these characters' marginalization, the failures of the black Creoles to stop the abridgment of their rights led to their withdrawal, causing observers such as Charles Dudley Warner to note, not long after he had helped launch Cable's stage career: "It is quite evident that the peculiar prestige of the quadroon and octoroon is a thing of the past. Indeed, the result of the war has greatly changed the relations of the two races in New Orleans. The colored people withdraw more and more to themselves." On the question of whether former slaves could become productive citizens in this indolent city, Cable, the most progressive essayist of his time, was the most pessimistic novelist.[50]

The Darker Side of Cable's Reconstruction Strategy: The Shadow of the Ethiopian Lengthens over New Orleans

Cable's dismal portrayal of the free people of color accurately reflected their fate. Their postwar position worsened as other Americans collapsed their interests into those of the freedpeople because both were black. They found themselves increasingly competing in the postwar labor market with freedpeople, as the city's population swelled with refugees. By 1870 the black population of New Orleans exceeded 50,000, twice what it had been in 1860. Many of their landholdings were lost during the first fifteen years after the war. While owners of urban real estate, like Honoré f.m.c., were somewhat able to weather the postwar economic turmoil, Creole planters faced a loss of property in slaves, difficulties in securing farm help, and the flooding and crop failures of 1866 and 1867, all of which resulted in bankruptcies and foreclosures. Black Creoles found the 1870s to be a time, as the *Weekly Louisianian* put it, of "retrograde movement with our rights invaded, our privileges abridged, and the terms of our 'continuance in the land' dictated."[51]

Spurned by white conservatives and betrayed by white Republicans, some black Creoles sought to make common cause with the freedpeople in advocating political equality and suffrage. Black presence registered within the state Militia and the Metropolitan Police Force until the end of military occupation. Efforts to build a racial, cross-class, and later biracial coalition played out in the press, particularly on the pages of *La Tribune*, the first black daily newspaper in the United States. The newspaper began to publish less in French and to feature more articles on the freedpeople's condition, criticizing their neglect by the federal government, the bureau, and the Union army. Cable's Palmyre and the slave Clemence reflect the qualified success of this coalition, as their avenging alliance achieves some measure of retaliation in Agricola's death but costs Clemence her life. Ultimately, class and ethnic distinctions, buttressed by differences in religion, made black Creoles and freedpeople distrust each other, and the opportunity to pursue a coalition distinctive to this military district was lost.[52]

Nevertheless, the novel fails to imagine *any* black characters—free or enslaved—as productive contributors to the community. Bras Coupé, a martyr to the refusal to work, likely played on readers' fears of insurrection and planters' fears of losing a labor force. Bras Coupé's problems begin because he sees work, that "loathed word," as far beneath his princely status. When the overseer asks him to hoe, he responds violently, reading labor as a penal "sentence" to "WORK." As Palmyre wasted her energy in obsessional voodoo, Bras Coupé allowed his ferocity to be siphoned off in alcohol and dancing in Congo Square. While Coupé's independent stand is noble, his story, read as a potential response to postwar conditions, boded ill for freedpeople. His excesses, demands for privileges, and defiance in the swamp bolstered accusations of laziness and arrogance made by white southerners and Yankees against the freedpeople. No doubt, Louisiana planter harassment and cheating, coupled with crop failures and floods, dimmed the enthusiasm of some ex-slaves to sharecrop; nevertheless, Coupé's refuge in the swamp to avoid labor affirms white dismissal of black workers, despite their mistreatment of them.[53]

Through his portrayals of black Creoles, Cable intensifies the bleak prospects for the freedpeople's transition to free-labor ideology. Cable's black Creoles are far from the productive citizenry Woolson imagined in her African American "Cokena" artists or judges. Somber and immobilized, Honoré and others of his class live on their rent checks instead of their own labors, and they cast aspersion on Cable's vision of prosperity for African Americans in a postwar South constructed on commercial interests and manual labor. Like many other wealthy black New Orleanians, Honoré f.m.c. and Palmyre employ slaves. Living in urban seclusion, his Creole characters eschew manual labor, as Frowenfeld learns when he offers to dig ditches only to be reproached as a "*dos brilée*" ("a [sun] burnt-back") by Honoré. Agricola's death signifies the obsolescence of the plantation economy, while Clemence's death represents the eclipse of a black workforce.[54]

On one side of the Gulf of Mexico, Woolson capitalized on Florida's fertility to redefine work and extend a nativist conception of leisure for *everyone*. On this side, Cable suggested that Louisiana's fertility and industry remains unexploited, and a racialized leisure time prevails, spent in deadly pursuits directed against the freedpeople. In his history, Cable pointed out how Louisiana's "soil of unlimited fertility, became through slavery, not an incentive to industry, but a promise of unearned plenty." His portrayal is at odds with that of the Freedmen's Bureau, whose head, O. O. Howard, rejected the racialized notion of southern white leisure as "not a true, substantial freedom."[55]

Cable's version is also at odds with freedpeople's understanding of freedom as located in autonomy and economic prosperity, made evident by their extensive efforts to participate in politics, impact labor arrangements, and acquire land. Their earnest hopes to obtain a farm, sparked by the June 1866 passage of the Southern Homestead Act, were thwarted because of the poor quality of available Louisiana land. Other factors included President Johnson's closing of land offices, slow bureaucracy fed by prejudice, and the early postwar political climate, which offered freedpeople false hope that they would receive already cleared confiscated lands and prevented them from filing claims for new lands. Contrary to the historical record of black Louisianan activism, Cable's account reinforced readers' biases that freedpeople would not, indeed could not, transition to citizens.[56]

Whereas Thanet turned to a white midwestern workforce to achieve postwar prosperity, most of Cable's white Creole Louisianians languish, dooming the New South. It remains unclear how his vision of a New South economy girded by purely commercial interests could be sustained. The city's commercial prosperity distracts readers from postwar concerns about field labor, but the new image of white-collar labor is not comforting. The only office spotlighted is the Grandissime counting house, with its "cemetery-like silence" maintained by aged clerks who have acquired "sore eyes," or a "jaded look," from too much "night revelry" rather than hard work. Just as "water must expect to take the shape of the bucket," so will Cable's Creoles "import cargoes of Africans," "bribe the officials," "smuggle goods" and hire "colored housekeepers" rather than work themselves. When Frowenfeld preaches the value of hard work, his words fall on deaf ears: "Nothing on earth can take the place of hard and patient labor. But that, in this community, is not esteemed; most sorts of it are contemned." Despite his reconstruction, part of Honoré Grandissime's "nature" and "art" as a merchant is to "wear a look of serene leisure." Other white Creoles in the novel, such as Hippolyte, Sylvestre, and Agamemnon, have little to do other than fish, drink at Maspero's, and stroll. The plight of the starving and unemployed Nancanous, in arrears with their landlord, raises the question of what tenants do to eke out a living.[57]

Just as the two Honorés pursue different paths of reconstruction, so too do Cable's overt activist pitches to his readers diverge. A compromised reconciliation registers in the narrator's fierce, if wavering, addresses. Set ironically against clichés like the slaves are "the happiest people under the sun" (a phrase which the narrator invokes twice) are the quiet pleas of "We ought to stop saying that" which assert Cable's commitment to correcting the misperceptions of plantation fiction that writers like Thanet would revive. Initially, the omniscient narrator is precise: "It was in the Théatre St. Philippe, in the city we now call New Orleans, in the month of September, and in the year 1803." Yet, by page three, the narrator becomes doubtful and self-reflexively withdraws: "But all this is an outside view." Like the Creole "we," the narratorial "we" often becomes "a word that does much damage" because of its potential for racial exclusiveness. The reader wonders whether Agricola's comment applies to the narrator and to Creoles: "H-my young friend, when we say 'we people' we *always* mean we white people. . . . What else could I mean?" Put in the mouth of the novel's fire-eater, this rhetorical question gestures toward the possibility of greater racial inclusiveness and greater interregional cooperation at the expense of black people. Like the lingering question over Creole identity that Cable keeps raising, this question forces the reader to ponder the possibilities of both scenarios for the New South.[58]

Cable based national reconciliation upon a shared resignation to injustice for African Americans perpetrated by white Americans on both sides of the Mason-Dixon line at the same time he questioned that resignation. Asides such as "Ah! What atrocities are we unconsciously perpetuating North and South now, in the name of mercy or defence, which the advocating light of progressive thought will presently show out in their enormity?" could be interpreted as Cable's self-reproach for participating in the increasing trend toward national reconciliation formulas. When addressing both northern and southern sympathies, the narrator advocates a national reconciliation based in part upon Lincoln's "new birth of freedom" and in part upon shared crimes toward African Americans.[59]

"Shoo! Shoo! Dis yeh country gittin' too free!": The Price and Punishment of Freedom for Black Women

While issues of free-labor ideology percolate in the treatment of Honoré f.m.c. and Bras Coupé, such matters become moot when applied to women. After raising awareness of women's limited opportunities, *The Grandissimes* works against widening their roles beyond the domestic sphere. Colonial gender conventions, compounded by class restrictions, demand an enforced leisure for white Creole women. Their labors are worthless, although the Nancanous, for example, are willing workers. While Aurora shows much pride and determination to remain independent, declaring, "See what a woman can do," she can actually do little. Her daughter Clotilde protests this devaluation of upper-class women's work: "Look at me: I can cook, but I must not cook; I am skillful with the needle, but I must not take in sewing; I could keep accounts; I could nurse the sick; but I must not." Like Toinette, Clotilde is cheated of her right to achieve economic autonomy.[60]

The Nancanous ultimately prosper, but only through complying with the restrictive conventions of the marriage contract. Similar to Geoffrey's subordination of Toinette and the Storer College faculty's treatment of its students, Aurora's rights are granted only at the behest of a white man. As the progressive Honoré tells Aurora just before he returns her property to her, "You ought to want your rights. You ought to have them." Clotilde replies eagerly, "Then why do you not give them to us?" Aurora cynically observes that rights are denied women in order to force them to marry: "Ha! Women talk about marrying for love; but society is too sharp to trust them, yet! It makes it *necessary* to marry." Both Aurora's and Clotilde's profitable marriages also engender a new set of obligations and dependencies, dimming their pretense to equality.[61]

In this critique of women's subordination in conventional marriages, Cable attempted, as did Tourgée, to broaden the venues of citizenship rights and privileges denied to women. Aurora reminds Honoré bitterly that there is much social injustice hiding behind Creole pretensions of honor, which have deprived black Louisianians and women of their civil liberties: "There are many people who ought to have their rights. There was Bras-Coupé; indeed, he got them—found them in the swamp." Despite the parallel, white Creoles such as Aurora and Clotilde are more successful than any black characters in dramatizing their plight; they receive sympathetic hearings and redress of their situation by Honoré despite the family's obloquy. He nobly acts "in the name of justice and fear of God" to restore their inheritance—motivations that never benefit Palmyre or Bras Coupé.[62]

Although Cable tried to diffuse the explosive subject of slavery for his postwar readers by recasting it as a "double bondage," which all Creole women endured, his dilution of the term subordinated freedwomen. Black Louisianian women, both Creole and free, suffered doubly on account of their gender and racial positions, making them a "special target" for postwar violence. Unlike white Creole women like the Nancanous, however, both Clemence and Palmyre are denied the option to marry whom they choose to escape their plight; they had to earn their own way out of slavery, only to encounter further exploitation.[63]

The experience of Palmyre and Clemence as slaves highlights the twining of gender and race in oppression. Palmyre "stood all her life with dagger drawn, on the defensive." Denied the chance of realizing her own miscegenistic desires, she is reduced to being a sexualized pawn whose marital fate is bartered among the Grandissime men, Agricola, and Bras Coupé. Palmyre's plight is that of many quadroons in a situation made worse by American antimiscegenation statutes. Louisiana law tried to restrict white men from providing for their mistresses too generously. By 1816, women were required to show both proof of paternity and acknowledgment of it in order to receive the maximum quarter of an estate. Palmyre's mistress, Aurora, like Tourgée's Belle, unsuccessfully tries to protect her right to choose a partner. She can only pine to marry the white Honoré or be forced to marry the slave Bras Coupé. Enumerating their lack of civil rights and exploitation, Cable sympathized with these free women of color whose prostitution yielded, despite opulence, "a poor freedom . . . indeed." Cable concedes that having "heard of San Domingo . . . the lesson she would have taught" Bras Coupé was "Insurrection." Even the otherwise sensitive Frowenfeld, blind to Palmyre's desire to exert her own volition, urges her to consider Honoré f.m.c.'s marriage proposal; he sees the union's value as only a vehicle for racial uplift. It is "with ill-concealed scorn" that she replies, "What is all that? What I want is vengeance!" Consumed by a single-minded motive to avenge her abuse, she sometimes appears unsexed to the point where she is mistaken for "a little man" or a "fellow" notably "small." Debased by men, she is often likened to an animal, embodying a "femininity without humanity . . . a creature that one would want to find chained."[64]

Similarly, the slave Clemence, like the "feline" Palmyre, has inherited her feelings "through ages of African savagery." While Palmyre's outrage burns like "fire in the wall," Clemence copes with "fires that do not refine, but that blunt and blast and blacken and char," leaving her choking "on the cinders of human feelings." Clemence, too, has suffered, knowing her family only through its loss on the auction block, including her many children of "assorted colors." Such experiences have rendered her an outlaw of sorts, to whom "the order of society was nothing. No upheaval could reach to the depth to which she was sunk." Like Palmyre, she has been denied that "profound respect which is woman's first, foundation claim on man."[65] Exploited by men against whom they devise strategies of survival, Palmyre and Clemence form a partnership in crime and grief, and more broadly, they take their place in a continuum of black heroines from Jacobs's Linda Brent to Albert's Charlotte Brooks.

Indeed, polarized gender alliances and divisions help drive the novel's racialized tragedy. Palmyre's hatred, centering on Agricola and the white, male authority that he represents, forges her bond with Clemence, while Agricola's loathing for Palmyre constitutes a gendered feud running throughout the book. Unlike the more successful gendered alliance of Betty Certain and Toinette, Palmyre and Clemence achieve empowerment with high cost. Like their real-life counterpart, Marie Laveau, they use voodoo as both a legitimizing cover and source of authority for their activism. In choosing to "smash" rather than "crack" (the more prudent course advocated by Honoré Grandissime) the gendered egg of Creole prejudice with voodoo, as illustrated by the smashed egg on Agricola's door, they wind up with much of the egg on themselves.[66]

Their adroit deployment of language both advances and impedes their subversion. Rumors circulate about them that terrify white men like Agricola into states of disability. However permitting Palmyre some freedom of movement, the terror she generates closes in on her like the bear trap laid for Clemence, who is caught executing her voodoo commands. Just as the masked Palmyre taunts Agricola in the opening chapter, so does Clemence hide her darker motivations behind her songs and "professional merry laugh." Her peddling, a traditional occupation for the Crescent City's free women of color, required a savvy cheer. Clemence's mask of submission to her white customers allows her to disguise her ridicule of them. Her double vocality is evident in her wily encounter with Dr. Keene, who insists, "You niggers don't know when you're happy." Clemence indignantly corrects him, winning her point by adding quickly, "We donno no mo'n white folks!" She insists that it is white people who "*wants to b'lieb* we is . . . fo' dey own cyumfut." She denies further that she charges white people with lying; rather, it is the devil that makes them lie. Clemence's songs, and Cable's later performance of them, were ethnographic and insightful as they uncovered African-Creole protest, satire, and lament in the seeming nonsense of the lyrics while highlighting the inevitable enmeshment of Europeans with their slaves. Meanwhile, the Grandissimes, targets of her songs' sarcasm, were darkly "charging their memories with her knowing speeches."[67]

The abusive experiences of Palmyre and Clemence and the deaths of Bras Coupé and Honoré f.m.c. suggest that while collective resistance of black Louisianians, expressed through voodoo or violence, might accomplish retaliation, it also unleashes self-destruction. Compelled by the clan to perform on the Grandissime verandah, Clemence's duet with Raoul fatally incriminates her in Palmyre's plot against Agricola. The Grandissimes link her performance with the voodoo visitations connected to Agricola's death. Her fatal song and dance, like that of Bras Coupé in Congo Square, marks a racialized boundary within the uses of performed identity as a strategy of subversion. Other Reconstruction texts, notably Woolson's "Felipa," only flirted with this possibility. Clemence's desperate declaration, "W'at we want to be insurrectionin' faw? We de happies' people in de God's worl!," further ensnares her.[68]

The uselessness of words in effecting real change is evident as they mount up on the page when Clemence pleads for her life. Her begging for "clemency" underscores the tactic's inefficacy for African Americans against white vigilantism. Before her murder, the narrator criticizes the tautological rationale for southern vigilantism: "It is barely now, that our South is casting off a certain apprehensive tremor, generally latent, but at the slightest provocation active, and now and then violent concerning her 'blacks.' This fear has always been met by the same one antidote—terrific cruelty to the tyrant's victim." The offsetting quotation and third-person pronoun reassert the South's custodial repossession of African Americans from northern troops at the same moment the text's punctuation and word choice question that repossession of a destabilized racial category. While Cable may have been ambivalent about women's subversive agentiality, his willingness to address extralegal violence directed against them was unique. He boldly helped pave the way for later exposés on terrorism, notably the writing of Ida B. Wells-Barnett.[69]

Gender continued to shape unevenly Cable's creative development as it informed his racialized assumptions about the prospects for African Americans after Reconstruction. Evident in a series of letters exchanged during 1882, gender also structured his personal and professional relationship with Twain, helping to usher in their onstage collaboration two years later. Upon seeing a portrait of "an old Mammie" Cable's sister had painted, Twain was so enraptured he asked for a copy. Cable obliged and presented "Madame Maptiste" as a gift, although Twain offered to "pay for his Mammy." Hanging the portrait in his library for inspiration, Twain prized this rendering of the black Creole nurse so much that he declared it was one "I could not manage to get along without at a pinch." This exchange helped build their fraught partnership on the shaken foundations of slavery. Like Cable's fictional creations, Palmyre and Clemence, in the hands of white male supremacists, Madame Maptiste's portrait became the nexus of negotiation between men, a transacted object by which Cable's contrary views about the roles of free women of color can be limned. Just as this black Creole woman's ethnic identity was reconstructed by this correspondence, so were the Creoles changed into African Americans by the joint performances of Twain and Cable. Their provocative collaboration helped reframe their audience's understanding of race, gender, and ethnicity, as well as the postwar role of the ex-slaves, into one uncomfortably complex.[70]

Strategy Onstage:
Those "Twins of Genius" Performing Identity

On 5 November 1884 Cable and Twain began a four-month tour with eighty stops that brought them as far north as Canada and as far south as Kentucky, with midwestern stops as far west as Iowa. After more than 100 performances, the two disbanded on 2 March 1885, and Cable continued the lecture circuit alone. Together, the men devised an extensive repertoire. Twain promoted his new novel, *Huckleberry Finn*, while Cable offered songs and renditions of predominately Creole characters from his work, including his latest, *Dr. Sevier*. For two hours they alternated onstage, beginning typically with Cable reading "Richling's Visit to Kate Riley" followed by Twain dramatizing "King Sollermun." As the tour continued, the men's repertoire evolved. Cable substituted scenes from *The Grandissimes* and added more Creole songs, while Twain added such pieces as "Why I Lost the Editorship," "The Jumping Frog," and "The Stammerer." Sometimes Twain also read selections from Joel Chandler Harris, Robert Browning, or Shakespeare.[71]

Although later Twain scoffed that "Cable wouldn't read in Heaven for nothing," a particular cultural negotiation was enacted by the tensions—the same gendered and racialized tensions that informed their portrait exchange—in their stage performances. As Stephen Railton has suggested, Twain aimed to entertain the audience, while Cable leaned toward reforming it. At one point Twain complained that "there has been a thundering sight too much of him," so he had Cable begin while the audience was still being seated. A gleeful Twain reported the result that "only half the house hear C's first piece—so there isn't too much of C anymore." Nevertheless, Twain's humor and Cable's daring gendered interracial portraits checked and balanced their mutual reconstruction of postwar race relations.[72]

The tour embodied the national tendency for political doubling that resulted from the recent federal occupation. Though billed by their manager, James Burton Pond, as the "Twins of Genius," Cable and Twain were fraternal twins at best. Reviewers elaborated on their antithetical appearances, performative styles, stage mannerisms, brands of humor, and reading selections. A typical reviewer declared, "The men are as different in the appearance as in their readings, and the contrast but enhances the character of the entertainment." Another critic made even their gender oppositional by describing Cable as "a small, weak, affected, effeminate-looking man," compared with Twain, "a manly spoken fellow, a man cut out after the pattern of a man." Cable's slight appearance enhanced his convincing impersonation of his dainty Creole and immigrant female characters. The disparity between the gag-loving, tall Twain and the deadpan, diminutive Cable was not coincidental; the authors devised ways to play off each other, such as entering the stage from opposite sides, counting on their sheer physical differences to provoke laughs.[73]

The uneven pairing of the two performers carried over into their representational clout, with Cable viewed as an also-ran, a regional mannequin to Twain's all-American persona. They were sometimes titled "'Mark Twain'–Cable Readings," emphasizing the off-kilter pairing. Twain was

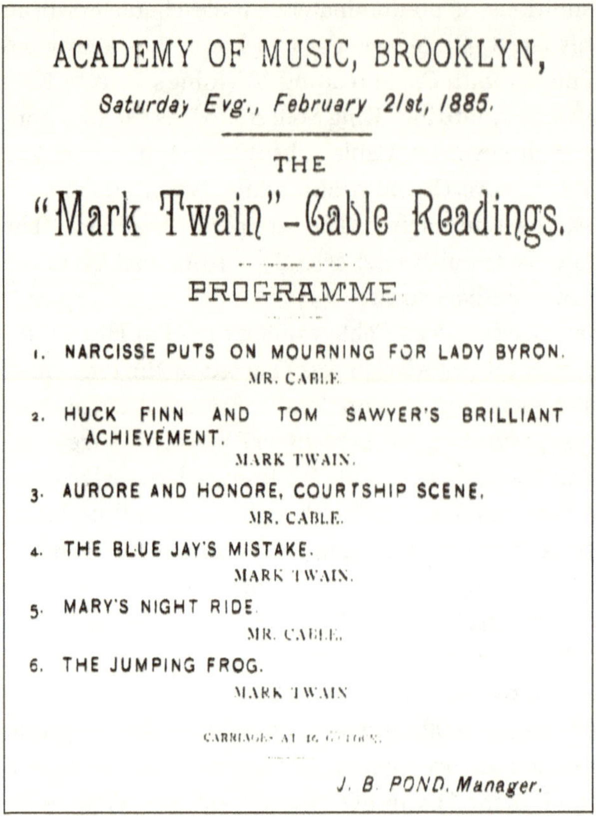

FIGURE 11. Illustration from: "'Mark Twain'—Cable Readings." Programme. [Brooklyn, N.Y.]: Brooklyn Academy of Music, 21 February 1885; with Charles L. Webster's advertisement of S. L. Clemens's *The Adventures of Huckleberry Finn* on the verso. Courtesy of The Henry W. and Albert A. Berg Collection of English and American Literature, The New York Public Library, Astor, Lenox, and Tilden Foundations, New York, N.Y.

> ACADEMY OF MUSIC, BROOKLYN,
> Saturday Evg., February 21st, 1885.
>
> THE
> "Mark Twain"-Cable Readings.
>
> PROGRAMME
>
> 1. NARCISSE PUTS ON MOURNING FOR LADY BYRON.
>   MR. CABLE.
> 2. HUCK FINN AND TOM SAWYER'S BRILLIANT ACHIEVEMENT.
>   MARK TWAIN.
> 3. AURORE AND HONORE, COURTSHIP SCENE.
>   MR. CABLE.
> 4. THE BLUE JAY'S MISTAKE.
>   MARK TWAIN.
> 5. MARY'S NIGHT RIDE.
>   MR. CABLE.
> 6. THE JUMPING FROG.
>   MARK TWAIN
>
> CARRIAGES AT 10 O'CLOCK.
>
> J. B POND, Manager.

already famous, and a common perception of him as an accessible, fictional creation enacted by Samuel Clemens sharpened the regional lens with which audiences viewed Cable's performances. With his Creole characters sandwiched between Twain's all-American folk culled from *Huckleberry Finn* and selections that pitted Americans against Europeans, Cable's portraits were set up to be exoticized for audiences (Fig. 11). Unhampered by fame, Cable acted in a way that produced the illusion of being a Creole. The two men's contrasting performances situated them both within contemporary debates about the nature of "absorbed acting," representation, and authenticity. Together, they helped introduce a legitimate place for the enactment of local color humor.[74]

Although Cable pinned the success of Reconstruction on the mutual interests of northern and southern men like Frowenfeld and Honoré, the lopsided stage pairing of Cable and Twain capitalized differently on the country's developing culture of reconciliation. Beginning after Grover

Cleveland's election in 1884, the tour succeeded partly because Twain and Cable played up their transsectional homosocial fraternization with audiences. Their uneven stage pairing suggests that alternative tropes of reunion circulated during the later postwar years beyond those Nina Silber has identified. Throughout, Cable shrewdly maintained a profile of regional accord as he asserted to a Boston reporter: "Do you know, though, that I heartily dislike those sectional terms 'North' and 'South'? . . . I have wiped the word 'South' out of my vocabulary, and have publicly exhorted people to do the same. Our boundaries are state boundaries, not sectional. I like the grand and comprehensive term 'Our country.'" His meeting with the venerable John Greenleaf Whittier was acclaimed as both regional embrace and literary repair to the fabric of *national* culture rent by war: "It was the singer of New England . . . welcoming his younger brother from the low shores of the Mexican gulf. . . . It was one of the fathers of our literature hailing one of her youngest sons." Complementing this paternalism, Twain and Cable's unequal, fraternal coupling was the "literary bridging of the bloody chasm" and a "rostrum rapprochement of Louisiana and Connecticut." Composed of diverse ethnic, gendered, and racial materials, their joint appearances became a bridge that spanned more than sectionality as they tried to straddle hybrid cultures. Their twinned performances helped make the troubles of local politics into national entertainment.[75]

Uniting audiences beyond the laughter was a sentimental interest in exotic cultures. Relying on comic skits, song, and dance, Cable's performances were structured in a mode akin to blackface minstrelsy, a performance style familiar to northern audiences. Cable gratified the "contradictory racial impulses" that Eric Lott argues are inherent to antebellum audiences of minstrelsy. Cable's postwar "love and theft" of Creole culture provided a local color bridge to reunion built on the material relations of slavery. Twain, like Cable, played upon southern resonances in his background and delivery to further both ticket and book sales. The most popular selections from *Huckleberry Finn* were "King Sollermun" and "How Come a Frenchman Doan' Talk like a Man," humorous treatments of master-slave interactions. Both passages spoof Jim's lack of education and Huck's pretensions to semiliteracy and situate these characters well within the minstrel tradition. Through it, Cable and Twain were presenting regionalist perspectives on the South that were "twinned" after all. Yet Cable's ambiguous Creole portraits, like the one of Madame Maptiste that he gave to Twain, also frustrated his audience's pretensions to ethnic and racial purity; his onstage portraits helped reconstruct the foundations of the bridge to reunion.[76]

Cable as Ethnic Interpreter

At the heart of Cable's contributions were his multifariously classed, gendered, and raced representations of Creoles. He manipulated the concept of identity from a stable self-image into a series of dramatic gestures to be performed. In an age of increasing anxiety about authenticity and the penetrability of racial boundaries, Cable's dramatic Creole play participated in minstrelsy's jocular celebration of ambiguity and distortion. Using stagecraft to expose the constructedness of identity, Cable's kaleidoscopic performances anticipate some of Twain's later fiction, in which, Henry Wonham has argued, "mediation without end is the message." Initialized by Cable, a chain reaction of ethnic empathy was created through which his audiences could proximate a theatricalized different identity.[77]

Cable, a founding member of the Louisiana Historical Society, scrupulously researched his portrayals, plots, and dialect to fend off southern criticism aimed at his Reconstruction politics. Indeed, many southern critics enthused as much as their northern counterparts over the Creole dialect he used in his writings. No less a personage than William Dean Howells, upon hearing his wife read parts of *The Grandissimes* aloud, became "intoxicated with their [Creole women's] delightfulness" and gushed, "We speak nothing else now but that dialect." Similarly, the *New Orleans Daily Picayune* commented that his "careful rendering of dialect reveals patient study of living models . . . its truth to nature is striking," while the *New Orleans Times-Democrat* noted: "He gives us the Creole, not perhaps as the upper crust thinks Creoles to be . . . but just as they are. . . . [He] treads upon the Creole toe only accidentally."[78]

Enthusiasm for Cable's onstage Creole impersonations was widespread. Likened to Dickens, Shakespearean actors, and Hawthorne, he was hailed as a regional interpreter of ethnicity to northern audiences, just as his oft-impersonated character from *The Grandissimes*, Raoul Innerarity, was a Creole cultural interpreter to Frowenfeld. Johns Hopkins University president Daniel Coit Gilman insisted that even "the most sensitive Creole could not take offense at his photographic pictures. Indeed the charm of the entertainment was the tone of verity which pervaded it." Cable's reputation as a masterful Creole impersonator was enhanced by Twain's act, since Twain's selections like "Tragic Tale of a Fishwife" comically highlighted the difficulty of learning another language or understanding a foreign dialect.[79]

Capitalizing on the "cult of the vernacular," as Hamlin Garland characterized it, Cable's dialect, with its admixture of French patois, Gallicized English, and Negro slang, was itself performative amalgamation. Critics such as a *Tacoma Ledger* reporter praised this aspect of his performance, with appreciation for how his "voice and personality change with kaleidoscopic rapidity" so that "he becomes the soft spoken negro or the excitable French Acadian." Audiences readily responded to the mixed blend of character, race, and ethnicity. One London reviewer had to reassure his readers that Cable was "perfectly white in color," because "they seem to think that a creole is a sort of half-breed negro who speaks with a french accent." Cable's performances, improvised and endlessly revised, thus "package," in W. T. Lhamon's words, a "politics of fluid identity" that resists racial stereotyping.[80]

In trying to dramatize the easy assimilation of the Creole and the former slave to his rapt listeners, Cable was pleased that northern audiences "*forgot* themselves" and enjoyed a momentary identification with the Creoles of a lighthearted South. Distinct from other Reconstruction writers, Cable induced a temporary identity amnesia in his audiences, enabling them to identify with Creoles and, by extension, with freedpeople, in performances that championed them as citizens worthy of center stage. Charles Dudley Warner praised Cable, "a master of the Creole dialect," for his ability to introduce to his audiences a "life and society unfamiliar to them" while "entrancing them with pictures the reality of which none doubted and the spell of which none cared to escape." Warner saw in Cable's Creole portrayals a solution to the recent "pother" over realism precisely for his talent to both present and recast even sordid realities with an appealing "idealizing grace" for audiences. Sensitive to political ramifications, Cable advised Twain to alter the title of his selection involving Huckleberry Finn and Jim from "Can't Learn a Nigger to Argue," to "How Come a Frenchman Doan' Talk like a Man?" Cable thus transformed a racial judgment into a gendered question of misunderstood nationality and dialect difficulty. Relying on humor, song, and play under Creole guise, Cable's overall performative strategy anticipated later black performers, who used "hokum" as "their modus operandi," as Karen Sotiropoulos puts it, to both sell black culture and challenge Jim Crow.[81]

In true minstrel tradition, Cable introduced his Creole portraits for laughs. Tellingly, he chose only droll scenes from *The Grandissimes* like "Raoul Innerarity Exhibits His Paintings" and "Raoul Innerarity Announces His Marriage," that avoided Raoul's more serious efforts to save Clemence's life. Moreover, it was the comic Creole excerpts from his works that were chosen for promotion. One advertisement quotes the *Waterbury American* stressing that all but two selections from *Dr. Sevier* "dealt with the humorous phases of the tale," relying on the "soft loquacity" of the novel's comical accountant, Narcisse. The exaggerated humor of these selections reinforced the illusion of Cable's ethnic authenticity while encouraging the audience's inclination to identify with his charming characters. Cable was pleased when "some little boys paid us the highest compliment" in declaring that they "would rather hear us anytime than go to any circus" or even to "see Buffalo Bill."[82]

Cable's waggish showmanship of identity could be shortsighted in shifting Reconstruction visions away from his audience's recalling the grave tolls of the war. His highlighting of these amusing, racially inflected Creole characters of the novel had the inadvertent consequence of trivializing recent political crises. Scenes such as Raoul's comical insistence on the merit of his painting, revealingly titled "Louisiana rif-using to hanter de h-Union," recalled to audiences the long-standing refusal of the Democratic twin of Louisiana's government to cooperate with the intervention of General Grant and Congress in the reconstruction of their affairs. Similarly, Cable's inclusion of "Aurora and Clotilde Discuss the Civilization and Climate with Frowenfeld" renders Frowenfeld's passionate protests against slavery into a weather complication. Cable was more pleased by the audience's laughter than bothered by their missing any point underneath the jest. He winked at his dramatization's suggestion that the Creoles, and, by extension, African Americans, were flighty and unprepared for the responsibilities of citizenship. After reading at Johns Hopkins, he wrote tongue in cheek to Twain: "It's touchingly gratifying to hear them laugh & applaud where nothing funny is intended."[83]

Gender intersected with racial inversion and ethnic caricature to both entertain and reorient audiences about the performative nature of identity, particularly suited to changing gendered roles. His impersonations of women became the primary vehicle by which Cable won audiences over to Creole culture. On 5 April 1883 the *Hartford Daily Courant* enthused: "Talking a little, reading a passage, moving about the stage, and occasionally indulging in dramatic strokes of gesture and attitude, he made appear, little by little the charm and grace of the women he wished us to know ... so delicately ... did he bring out the real character and the life of the people." Yet these charming portrayals of ethnic women like the Nancanous or *Dr. Sevier*'s Irish maverick, Kate Riley, tended toward caricature that ignored women's cultural clout beyond the domestic sphere. Even his occasional inclusion of the novel's final scene between Aurora and Honoré Grandissime, while romantic, played up Aurora's winningly cute humor and trivialized her plight. Similarly, Riley's brave willingness to join her husband on the front line was sidestepped in favor of her more humorous wrangling over tamer domestic crises.

In contrast, Cable's dramatic scenes that empower women, such as his popular "Mary's Night Ride Home," were reserved for his white female characters. Cable often closed performances with this frequently requested drama featuring a young Union-sympathizing wife bravely crossing Confederate lines to reach her dying husband. Like the qualified ending of *The Grandissimes*, this thrilling climax to both *Dr. Sevier* and Cable's stage performance relied on both toppling and reinforcing gendered conventions. Through this female character, Cable at once revises and ennobles the Lost Cause, carefully balancing his sectional sympathies. Although Mary, at once brave and yet dependent on men like her crafty yokel guide, is an Ohioan, she "passes" as a Southerner. By giving this soon-to-be widow the last word in his performances as she chooses to remain in the South, Cable used gender and racial conventions to remind his audiences of those who purportedly needed the protection of Dr. Sevier and other white southern men to maintain the status quo.

Yet Mary's postwar fate signals a strategy by which white southern women could somewhat escape that status quo. Unlike her Creole and immigrant counterparts who refocus their energy on domestic concerns, she "pursued her calling" by assisting Dr. Sevier as a protosocial worker. Somewhat muting her professionalism, Mary sought to appear to her hesitant clients as less a "benevolent itinerary" and more "a personal friend" mediating between the rich and poor, accommodating Dr. Sevier's ideals and her husband's dying wishes. Like the Frowenfeld-Nancanou partnership of *The Grandissimes*, this novel offers a model for white women to profitably join the duties of home and work.[84]

Stage appeal, however, dictated that Cable dramatize Mary's ride, not her more quotidian postwar career. Such gendered dramatizations helped reclaim the production of racial representation for "new" southerners keen to restore white male supremacy. The value of the performances was underscored both by their demand and their increasing length ("from six minutes to *fifteen* minutes!" a jealous Twain complained). Unwittingly counteracting the "redemptive" effect of what he called "that infernal Night Ride," Twain agitated to have Cable's stage time shortened. In this context, gender became key in making the Twain-Cable tour both liability and asset for reconstructing southern heads and northern hearts.[85]

"Nigger from the Ground Up": Cable's Minstrel "Occupation" of Creole Songs

Cable's rendering of Creole songs underscored the cultural benefits of racial amalgamation. As Gavin Jones has shown, Cable's clever linguistic mixing of French and African songs in *The Grandissimes* celebrated cultural hybridity while foregrounding the influence of African American vernacular in his satirizing white Creole pretensions to ethnic purity. Louisiana Creole is already hybridized, with a vocabulary rooted in French and an African grammatical structure. Cable's transliteration of songs and scoring of music with a double meaning constitutes a careful interpretation in which he is the necessary liaison between largely white audiences and his provocative material. With every show, the easy elision between Cable's performance of popular Creole songs and African dances and songs began to suggest that his interpretation of "Creole" could increasingly mean *only* African. His Creole songs, some of which were also included in *The Grandissimes*, were the most popular part of his program, which also featured the songs of Place Congo, famed New Orleans site of slave congregation. "Pov' Piti Momzel Zizi," for example, which laments the status of free women of color, was requested in advance twelve times by Washingtonians on 24 November 1884. A *Boston Evening Transcript* reviewer characterized his "Creole Songs" as a "curiously-mingled medley of French troubadour grace and wild African fervor, illusion-producing, haunting, evanescent, yet unforgettable." By praising the songs' ethnic hybridity, critics found a cultural backdoor through which to enthuse about African music and dance.[86]

The racialized rambunctiousness of the songs delighted northern audiences. For example, New Yorker H. C. Bunner, mildly taken with the "utterly amateurish" reading, raved: "But the singing—that caught everybody. It was absolutely artless. . . . But the *go* and the lilt, and the solid, keen enjoyment he took in it! And the strong pulsing wild melodies! Nigger from the ground up, and full of life. The huge house woke up as if you had turned a dynamo on it." Bunner's offensive categorization of the music places Cable's performance within the minstrel tradition, and however jocularly, he recognized the Creole amalgamated dramas could be interpreted as threatening. Despite their immense popularity, Cable remained ambivalent about performing the songs. While he appreciated that the songs were "always encored," and he responded by including more, he found performing them to be burdensome for unclear reasons; waiting to go on to sing, he averred: "I always shrink from this, the only thing I do shrink from."[87]

Cable's interest, however, in recovering the cultural history of the songs was genuine. He wrote musicological essays and published them in tandem with his performances. These pieces nevertheless reflect a contemporary sentimental stance toward his subject that assumed hierarchical, inherent differences between races. In "Dance in Place Congo," for example, Cable pities the slave dancers' deformed bodies, clothed in rags and coarsened by their hard labors, but he uses the contemporary racial clichés of "sprightly 'boys'" and "thick-lipped 'gals'" to describe them. Cable exoticizes them into primitive animals dancing until "with foam on their lips" they "are dragged out by arms and legs" in a "frightful triumph of body over mind" to songs of nevertheless "fantastical comicality." Likewise in "Creole Slave Songs," Cable sees the slave as "a nearly naked-serpent worshipper" and trivializes the Creole lure of voodoo into childish superstition: "But fear naught; . . . If you have on your premises a frizzly chicken, you can lie down and laugh—it is a checkmate!" Cable's writing echoes the "sensationalism, embellishment, and conjecture" found in contemporary New Orleans voodoo narratives. This discourse, as Michelle Gordon has shown, upheld the need for white supremacy by staging a fantasy of degenerate and hypersexual black Americans unfit for citizenship. Like his performances, Cable's musicological essays were at cross-purposes with his endorsement of black civil rights.[88]

Delivered when the nation still felt the sectionally polarizing effects of military occupation, Cable dramatized an "occupation" of black Creole identity that was caught up in social conflict. His minstrelsy valorized the crossing of racial and ethnic lines into entanglement, an effect southern critics interpreted as proof of his lurking liberalism. Cable put the mutually constitutive categories of blackness and whiteness in tension by performing a black Creole identity that is, by definition, ethnically amalgamated. His displacement of racialized identity through ethnicity created a dual counterfeit for audiences to access pleasure and to repair sectional rifts through a privileged southern exoticism. As Daphne Brooks has argued, the heterogeneous figure of blackface, while performing "blackness," also produces a version of whiteness that would "reaffirm the superior skill of white performers to invade, occupy, and ventriloquize alien 'blackness.'" At the same time, Cable's theatrical figure emphasized the Creole as both a third category of subjectivity and a symbol of hybrid identities and surplus. Appropriating contemporary elements from the symbolic language of minstrelsy, carnival, and his native city's Mardi Gras, Cable's infatuation with exoticism thus helped reaffirm a fortified white male southern identity even while he undercut it. Cable's performances thus reinforced as much as they defied conservative racial hierarchies. They also invited spectatorial revision, as evident by the reaction of African Americans.[89]

The Joke's on Whom?: A Black Spectator's Response and the Play of Ventriloquism

Even while engaged in a nostalgia that traded in derisive representations of African Americans, Cable's portraits attempted an investiture in the postwar figuration of *emancipated* blackness. As much as minstrelsy could denigrate African Americans, it also could highlight "a toughened version of blackness" while forging interracial connections, as W. T. Lhamon has demonstrated. Cable's portrayals of characters with whom his audience could identify provided a way for them to appropriate a complex version of black culture that could be accessed apart from its association with slavery. Cable's representations acknowledged transgression of the color line and encouraged freedpeople to "act up" as a strategic first step in claiming the rights and privileges of citizenship.[90]

This is evident in the reaction of Cable's interracial audiences and his ability to play off their pleasure for the sake of a better joke. At a performance in Oberlin, Ohio, for example, Cable recalled that "a most comical thing occurred" while he was performing "Mary's Night Ride." Acknowledging Cable's "mimicked African enunciation and the old southern title of respect," a black audience member "let go a suppressed but loud titter of the purest Ethiopian character" at Cable's impersonation of a black guide. The laugh, according to Cable, "brought down the house," a disruption that subverted the selection's reinforcement of the gender and racialized subordination to white southern men. Cable attributed the laughter's "character" and "irrelevancy" to helping produce "the best bit of reading I had ever done in my life."[91]

This added-on bit of what Joseph Roach would call "whiteface minstrelsy" mockingly exposed the contrived nature of Cable's surrogacy, while transforming the performance into something else. The black spectator's placement, sitting "behind me in a sort of choir loft all alone and in sight of everyone," raises questions about the assumed racial dynamics in the spectacular character of identification. His segregated seat placed him onstage, yet also in a judgmental position. The intermixed positions of audience member and performer disrupt white control of black culture while unsettling white notions of authenticity. The impromptu exchange draws on minstrelsy's greater complex currents of representation intertwined within satire, parody, and burlesque. Capitalizing on minstrelsy's traditional valuation of audience participation, its extemporaneous nature captures minstrelsy's signature play of confusion over who imitates whom. In this improvised dueling of racial masquerades, the black spectator's laughing participated in a tradition of African American humor that ridicules the self-importance and pretense of white people in authoritarian roles.[92]

To other listeners, Cable's songs and comic scenes, aided by Twain's racialized buffoonery, spotlighted Cable's willingness to cross the color line. Cable's racialized ventriloquism had so succeeded that, by 1890, the *San Antonio Express* declared: "The Caucasian can not change his skin any more than the Ethiopian, but in his moral being Cable is no longer a white man." Cable proved what Tourgée would soon argue on behalf of Homer Plessy: there was an elasticity to racial identity, and this racial subjectivity had a property value, which was located in a social self delineated by community valuation. As the *Express*'s condemnation made evident, the combination of Cable's performances and activism had damaged his reputation as a white man, alienating him from the property of his racial identity. It was just one spark in the critical firestorm following Cable's publication of "The Freedman's Case in Equity," an essay that forever changed public reception of his Creole performances.[93]

"The Most Cordially Hated Little Man in New Orleans"

In January 1885 Cable published an appeal for black civil rights, "The Freedman's Case in Equity," in *Century Magazine*, which led to a confrontation with the resiliency of binary racial categories within American culture. In the same issue the magazine included excerpts of *Huckleberry Finn* that had particular minstrel emphasis: "Jim's Investments" and "King Sollermun." Twain's hilarious pieces that make sport of Jim, each illustrated with his caricature, counteracted Cable's earnest claims. The resulting counterpoint further heightened the tensions between Twain and Cable. Against this textual interference, Cable made his case for black civil rights by drawing a sharp racial divide: in order to persuade readers of the merit of civil equality, he had to assure them their fears of social equality would never be realized. "The Freedman's Case" distinguishes between civil rights, to which freedpeople were entitled, and social relations, which neither race purportedly wanted. Cable followed a practice in use since antebellum times when politicians across the political and sectional divide differentiated political, legal, and social equalities. During Reconstruction both Republicans and moderate Democrats manipulated such distinctions to both advance black rights and uphold racial difference. Basing his case for the freedpeople's entitlement on individual merit, Cable posited a class-based meritocracy to replace a race-based system of caste, a scheme not too different from Clifford's. But Cable's stance in the essay was directly challenged by his performances, and his attempt to appeal to individual merit rather than broad racial categories was insulting to Creoles, whom his performances trivialized into humorous stereotype. The conflict between the logic of his essay and the drama of his entertainment helped intensify the feeling that Cable was "the most cordially hated little man in New Orleans."[94]

So many letters deluged the *Century*'s offices that the editors invited Henry W. Grady, famed editor of the *Atlanta Constitution*, to write a response to "The Freedman's Case." Grady argued that black and white people were guided by an unerring "race instinct" to shun social mingling. He claimed southern African Americans desired segregation and refused many rights of citizenship, preferring the "clear and unmistakable domination" of the more capable southern white race. In "The Silent South," a rebuttal to Grady's essay, Cable wrote: "Having made it plain that the question has nothing to do with social relations, we see that it is, and is only, a question of *indiscriminate civil rights*." Cable drew upon specific examples provided by Booker T. Washington, who privately averred, "If a few more Southern people would come out as boldly as Mr. Cable has, it would help matters much."[95]

Indeed, Cable's speaking on behalf of African Americans was a ventriloquist gesture that many African Americans appreciated, largely because they felt silenced themselves. Shortly after "The Freedman's Case" appeared, a Madison newspaper featured an exchange of letters between Cable and Arthur Lee, an African American. Lee endorsed Cable's ventriloquism as a needed Reconstructive tool: "You, sir, have raised a hope in our bosoms that our old neighbors and friends are at last allowing their own hearts to speak for us. . . . Sir, if you are not inundated with grateful letters from colored people, it is not because of any lack of a keen sense of appreciation, but alas! So few of us *can* let you know how we feel toward you." Cable responded, encouraging Lee and other eloquent "men of color" to voice the plight of all Americans; he urged him to write "for the public" for "nothing will work more powerfully for the *special* interests of the colored people than for black men to make themselves felt." Cable insisted on rhetoric that rose above the pitch of special interest groups, who would benefit anyway: "Let colored men show such sagacious, active interest in the rights and interests of all men, that all men, shall gradually be won to regard them as valuable accessions to the community." Just as his performances prompted spectators like the "Ethiopian" to speak up and be heard, so Cable's writing invited African Americans onto the stage of public activism.[96]

Letters from African Americans throughout the country praised Cable's political activism; his was a voice of encouragement that reverberated nationally within African American print culture. In his urging of black West Virginians to support the Independent Party, West Virginian newspaper editor J. R. Clifford, for example, relied on Cable as an influential authority within the local community. In September 1888 Clifford devoted an entire paragraph to reprinting Cable's admonition to black Americans to vote irrespective of party loyalty, which concluded: "You will never get your rights until the white man does not know how you are going to vote." Clifford endorsed Cable's sentiments: "The world knows that Mr. Cable is the Negro's best friend and that no man is doing more to solve the Negro problem with the pen than he is doing." But rather than letting Cable have the last word, Clifford asserted his own plea to readers to "stand by the race and its interests first" and align with any party that "actually accords to every citizen black and white his inalienable rights." Cable's appeal also reverberated with southern white writers. Catching wind of the Lee-Cable exchange, the editor of the *New Orleans Daily Picayune* chastised Cable for his reply to Lee in an editorial patronizingly titled, "Fie! Fie! George."[97]

Before Cable's fame spread as a Creole interpreter, some white southern newspaper editors had endorsed his first pleas for black civil rights, but such praise vanished under the accumulated effect of his performances and his essay. A regional controversy ensued over Cable's purported indulgence in ethnic stereotype, which made his political views subject to attack as being hypocritical. The attention to Cable's caricaturist portrayals reflects the Jim Crow beginnings of the so-called "coon" era, which was characterized by an increased intolerance for ambiguous racial categories. "The exaggerated ethnic image" soon became, as Henry Wonham has argued in regard to Twain's fondness for ethnic comedy, "a testing ground for assumptions about the nature of individuality in the context of late nineteenth-century anxieties over a changing social and economic landscape."[98]

By the eve of the Cable-Twain tour, local critics, still praising Cable's portrayals, were warning Cable that he "should not play too much to the galleries," while cautioning readers that Cable's "mimicry" was "dangerous and misleading" because it could result in "caricature" of the Creoles. Creole poet Adrien Rouquette had already parodied Cable as the "High-Priest of Negro-Voudouism," whose use of black Creole dialect in *The Grandissimes* bastardized white Creole culture by encouraging that "all diverse colors intermarry and blend into one sole mongrel color." Attending one of Cable's 1884 readings, a Creole complained that his characters were of "the lowest grades," conflating Creoles with "'Cadiens,' 'Chacas,' 'Choupics,' 'Patassas,' Mulattoes, Negroes." Another outraged "Old Creole" offered Cable a duel. Tracking the hullabaloo, the "Lounger" columnist for the *Critic* concluded, "The Creoles are buzzing about his [Cable's] ears and stinging him with redoubled fury since his recent reading."[99]

Cable's use of dialect became truly controversial after "The Freedman's Case" widely appeared and he gave literal voice to his writing onstage with Twain. His performances made his sympathies for the two hybrid cultures all too clear, despite the essayist's claims to the contrary. It was this conflation of racial and ethnic types that inflamed southerners. Local historian Charles Gayarré attacked Cable's Creole portrayals in print and in lectures. Charging Cable with creating "effete and imbecile" characters of "amiable idiocy," Gayarré insisted that an educated Creole never addressed "any one of his equals in the jargon of the negro." Gayarré further contended that Cable's diabolical ambition was to demean the reputation of all white Louisianians by placing them below black Louisianians, who are "destined to africanize the entire South." Cable's lifelong friend Marion Baker kept Cable apprised of local hostility, adding, in one letter, "Gayarré is making a pretty good living attacking you." When "The Freedman's Case" had first appeared, Baker had confided to Cable, "You can form no idea of how bitter the feeling is against you."[100]

Cable came under intense personal attack as a sectional traitor. The *New Orleans Daily Picayune* described Cable as "a Southern writer of ability" who uses "rabid malignity" to "attack the people and institutions of the country where he was born." Similarly deriding Cable as "not a true son of the South" for his "negromania," the *New Orleans Times-Democrat* questioned Cable's purposes and integrity. In one issue, the paper carried the denunciations of nine other southern papers for his purported desire for social equality. Southerners attributed Cable's motives to Yankee greed. Across the South, other white southern newspapers, such as the *Selma Times*, countered Cable's activist appeal to black Americans with their own brand of ventriloquism, printing letters supposedly written by black readers accusing Cable of writing the essay for "the purpose of pleasing a certain class of *Northern* people and filling his pockets with gold." The Reverend R. L. Dabney agreed, accusing "the blunderer" of the base motive for writing the essay, resulting in a "hallucination" of distorted reasoning that alienated him from his people. The *Nashville Daily American* pronounced Cable a "slanderous renegade who crooks the knee to Yankee malevolence 'that thrift may follow fawning.'"[101]

The controversy took on national proportion as prominent northern magazine critics debated the justification of the increasing southern animus. Some saw the cumulative damage as being done to the South's standing, not to Cable's. Declaring that the purported charges were "far more damaging to the reputation of the section than anything the offending author could say," the *New York Tribune* took southerners to task: "A people who cannot stand criticism or mild caricature . . . is necessarily in a callow state, so to say, unfledged." The *New York Star* countered that southerners saw Cable's tabloid victimization as calculated self-promotion: "These stories of the southern people's hatred and vindictiveness toward Mr. Cable generally circulate about the time he starts on a lecturing tour or launches a new book and as advertising material they may be valuable."[102]

These critics had a point about Cable's self-promotional tendencies. His manager, James Pond, advertised the solo performer's transcendent national reputation as both Creole impersonator and activist: "Wherever he is heard, either as a delineator of his own characters or speaking on the topics of the times, there is but one verdict—*success*." Billing Cable as a "man with an earnest purpose and profound convictions," Pond mentioned Cable's "success" five times in one paragraph, as if to convince potential ticket buyers that Cable had prevailed over the controversy swirling around his reputation. Likewise, advertisements featured Cable as an agent of reunion, introduced rave reviews from California to New York, and thereby dispelled any negative headlines that might linger in the mind of the potential ticket buyer. Pond's profitable strategy recalled Tourgée's attempts to manipulate controversy into celebrity. While not motivated exclusively by profit, Cable was nevertheless manipulated by market forces attuned to sectional malice.[103]

The Wages of Ventriloquism in the Marketplace

Cable's entire career was defined by trying to meet the exacting tastes of his editors. It is hard not to read his creative work today without recalling Edmund Wilson's morbid characterization of his literary career as a "slow strangulation," indeed, as "one of the most gruesome episodes in American literary history." Cable and his editors, who worked both at *Scribner's Monthly Magazine* and at Charles Scribner's Sons publishing company up to 1881, so scrutinized his writing for controversial elements that his talent was compromised. Although he consistently battled their editing, Cable's deference to genteel conventions diminished his stature for some present-day critics. Long after he published *The Grandissimes*,

Cable admitted that "the primary impulse toward my first sustained novel was an ambition kindled by the unexpected invitation of a magazine's editors." The invitation, however, developed into a forced dependency as his Scribner's editors, sensitive to the conservative tastes of their largely white, educated, northern readers, censured any potentially inflammatory material. Nearly every manuscript page of *The Grandissimes* bears the extensive penciling of three consultant readers, constituting a record of warring pens that lasted almost two years. Editor Robert Underwood Johnson went so far as to caution Cable on 11 February 1880: "You must remember that my reputation as an editor is involved as well as yours as a writer." Cable's concession for fitting Bras Coupé into the novel was to turn himself into a raconteur of the lighter, more entertaining side of Creole life, trivializing the very concerns raised by the episode.[104]

By the time he considered a stage career, Cable felt indebted to the magazine editors who had given him a platform in print. He gave great consideration to the role of the literary marketplace in his performances. Financially insecure, Cable valued the guidance of Scribner's editors Roswell Smith and Richard Watson Gilder, who urged him to the stage, sponsored lucrative engagements, arranged publicity, and planted favorable reviews. Cable felt not only obligations of gratitude to these increasingly interventionist literary benefactors but also a keen need to win their approval through entertainment. Characterizing Gilder's reaction and that of other literati to his Creole dialect as "the wittiest uproar that *ever* I heard in my life," Cable judged this performance as his "greatest success," confirming the decisive role of not just humor but also editorship in his shows.[105]

In earning the wages of ventriloquism, Cable became both puppet and puppeteer. His love of approval and desire to entertain transcended any qualms he might have had about preserving dramatic integrity. Defending the accuracy of his dialect, Cable once falsely claimed to a northern editor that "though it does not absolutely prove anything I will add that I am a creole myself." His initial success with Twain prompted Cable to boast: "O no. We don't like attention, do we? . . . And when we're waltzed out to the long supper table at the head of the column & when men stand around in groups and stretch their ears to hear what we say, of course it's very unpleasant, and all that sort o' thing." Twain complained that Cable had become "one of the most spoiled men, by success in life, you ever saw." Cable's aspirations for winning national attention through his Creole characters impeded his ability to express an unambiguous vision of Reconstruction. If Cable was in fact "strangled" by his endeavors to placate the demands of northern literary editors, he wove some of the skeins himself.[106]

Cable cultivated his ambivalence as he sought to appease northern editors who frowned on "unpleasantness" and southern critics who cringed at Cable's "negrophilic" Creole representations. The resulting complications are evident in his performances. Sensitive to editorial criticism about his delivery, Cable took professional voice lessons, but his efforts resulted in another "slow strangulation." In his attempt to project his voice farther in order to reach a larger national audience, his voice became flat and lost its regional flavor. A fade into bland generality also characterized Cable's later novels, notably *John March, Southerner* (1890). For the duration of his increasingly "managed" career, Cable sought to placate publishers who were intent on expanding sales and readers who were by then saturated with local dialect.[107]

Like William Gilmore Simms, Cable always aimed for a national audience, but his ambition proved impossible to fulfill. Cable differed from Simms in what he thought should be the rightful subjects of southern literature. His concern with the status and quality of southern literature was intertwined with his interest in redressing the provincial prosecession and proslavery attitudes that hamstrung the South. Cable managed to speak on behalf of many struggling to be heard in public culture, particularly African Americans, although his dramatizations were often interpreted against them. His performances captivated audiences who began to identify with his mixed-race Creole portraits, even as the portraits confused his admirers. In his attempt to please very mixed audiences, Cable's voice became entangled with the dynamics of the changing literary marketplace, itself caught up in tempestuous postwar politics. A savvy Cable showed early a jaded awareness of how easily outmoded sectional literary products were repackaged to satisfy emergent imperial tastes. Cable urged young southerners: "Go you to New Mexico. That is the New South. And make haste friend, or they will push you on into South America, where we have reshipped the separate sort of books printed for the Southern market." He saw that a profitable elision of the local-color literature of the American South, burdened by slavery, defeat, and occupation, could be reconstructed to fit a hemispheric consciousness. The vicissitudes of Cable's reputation cannot be understood without accounting for the shifting reputation of the South in postwar print culture. The tour and Cable's political activism revived the performative contradictions of Reconstruction itself as they were revised over time and "sold" to audiences of differing political persuasions.[108]

The persistent and vehement criticism of Cable the novelist and performer as a retort to Cable the essayist affirms fiction's power to influence politics. Operating like his native city's dual governments, Cable used character doubling and counterpoint on both page and stage. The articulate rancor inherent in the print culture enveloping him—from editorials to fan mail—increasingly shaped his work and its reception for decades. In 1932, seven years after his death, Grace King explained that "Cable proclaimed his preference for colored people over white and assumed the inevitable superiority . . . of the quadroons over the Creoles. He was a native of New Orleans and had been well treated by its people, and yet he stabbed the city in the back, as we felt, in a dastardly way to please the Northern press." The actions of this native son who sought literary fame beyond the Mason-Dixon line were similar to his character Honoré Grandissime, as Cable broke with a regionally extended family, yet the price he paid in ostracism and exile resembled the fate of Honoré f.m.c.[109]

Cable's genius was staked on New Orleans's swampy boundaries, the shifting alliances, as he transformed them from a political liability to a literary asset. In dramatizing American identity as a performed construct, Cable trained his vision on the Creoles as a model for freedpeople because they had successfully adapted during an earlier time of geographic and social flux. It was a strategy reminiscent of Woolson's successful deployment of Minorcans in her work. Having had editors' words put into his work for so long, Cable perhaps found it easier than did other Reconstruction writers to ventriloquize marginalized Americans. Yet as audience reaction and critical reviews demonstrate, this flexibility of Creole character proved dangerously two-sided. In foregrounding Creole identity as a perpetual question natural to native soil, Cable called into play a controversial question: for whom was he speaking?

As he explored the limits of Reconstruction discourse, Cable, like the great House of Grandissime itself, was beset by its dualities, necessitating compromise along the lines of property, duty, labor and reputation. The novel's plot resolution and ambivalent narrator raised doubts about its author's aspirations for the former slaves and for the postwar economic and social regeneration of a "new" South. The tragic failures of his black characters to flourish, despite their cross-racial and gendered partnerships, qualifies Cable's Reconstruction vision.

Although caught in an editorial crucible, Cable displayed a deft ability to maneuver. *The Grandissimes* urged all Americans to examine the attitudes on which they were raised. The novel demanded nothing less than the mutual reconstructions of character across sectional, racial, and gendered lines. This creative strategy distinguishes his contribution to Reconstruction literature. His literary activist engagement with the ideological legacy of slavery places his writings on a continuum of work by African American women writers. He joins authors from Harriet Wilson to Pauline Hopkins in condemning injustice against African American women and inspiring their reform work. Pitched into the quagmire of local repudiation and national applause, his work always retained a foothold on the radical promise of a Bras Coupé to both inflame and enlighten. As such promise dimmed in disfranchisement, segregation, and extralegal violence, Reconstruction writers looked even more to black women as critical agents of reform and resistance. Living in a military district renowned for its guerrilla warfare, Octave Thanet, in her exploration of new forms of property, dramatized the agentiality of her black heroines even as she feared its unleashing.

Chapter 5
IOWA'S AMERICAN GOTHIC IN ARKANSAS
The Plantation Fiction of Octave Thanet

Nor has anyone done the post-bellum life of the South better than Octave Thanet, tho not to the manner born.
—Thomas Wentworth Higginson

Alice French's 1890 novel, *Expiation*, written under the pen name Octave Thanet, opens in Arkansas in the Civil War's final year. However, the novel dwells on the blighted landscape to comment on postwar conditions, just as the 1803 setting of Cable's *The Grandissimes* was a foil to comment on Reconstruction. Within Military District Four, confused identities and displaced property predominate, and neighbors are hard to distinguish from robbers on the prowl. Dead bodies in the mist add to the landscape's violent harshness. Fairfax "Fair" Rutherford, the craven protagonist, travels on a road that is flooded, gnarled, and rarely straight, yet navigation is but one part of Fair's challenge to "expiate" for the guilt of defeat felt by white southerners. His success will pivot on a radical reconstruction of gendered roles performed in the plantation household and the untamed wilds of Arkansas.[1]

The novel's opening gambit, which sets the scene for Fair's expiation of his own cowardice, is the attempt to deliver money to the Confederate-sympathizing Rutherfords by a trusted yeoman, who is found murdered. Plot twists allow the Rutherford money to change hands several times, keeping it from a band of swamp-dwelling guerrillas. Through this convoluted tale, Thanet shows that in Arkansas country the premium was on easily transferable property rather than the destroyed land and defunct slaves. With a story line built around the constant exchange of goods, Thanet, distinctive among Reconstruction writers, explores the value of acquiring money and portable property as a consumer strategy for freedpeople to realize the ideals of citizenship.

Even before Fair and a host of other Arkansans fall into the gang's hands, Fair, who is returning home after living abroad, remarks, "What a country to live in!" His comment reflects Thanet's gloomy view of the postwar nation's prospects. Yet, by the close of *Expiation*, Thanet converted Fair's initial exasperation into "rapturous exclamation" as he begins to realize the kind of opportunities New South advocate Henry Grady had first pitched to New Yorkers in his "New South" speech given four years before the novel appeared. Thanet reconstructed the Arkansas landscape into a place of possibility where the dispossessed could hope to gain property without resorting to robbery. At the same time, *Expiation* is the most nostalgic for bygone days even while it eagerly anticipates the New South.[2]

Thanet's writing, inflected by her New England origins, her midwestern upbringing, and her southern sojourning, fashioned a vision of postwar national unity, one that was complex and wrought with gendered and racial contradictions. A central component of her vision focused on the former slaves' place in the postwar nation. When the prospects for African American political involvement began to wane in the late 1880s, Thanet, more than any other Reconstruction writer, turned to the New South promise of full participation in the market economy as a ticket to citizenship. As elsewhere, the transition to freedom of Arkansas ex-slaves was embroiled in the broader issue of free-labor ideology, particularly after the 1873 depression. Suspicious of unions yet concerned about the plight of the poor, Thanet crafted a vision that simultaneously addressed these issues of transitioning and labor unrest. Reform-minded yet politically conservative, the ambivalent Thanet wrangled with these issues in all her fiction as she witnessed labor struggles in both Iowa and Arkansas.

In discussing the empowerment of former slave women in *Expiation*, Thanet relied on a restructuring and expansion of gendered roles behind three principal strategies. First, like other Reconstruction writers, she attempted to invert the gendered power dynamics of the plantation household to benefit women, particularly black women—an approach that drew on her own distinctive tomboy childhood and later role as a planter. She focused on two settings, the library and the swamp, to stage the wartime crisis in white male authority. Second, she crafted numerous scenarios in which black women challenge authority through verbal assault. Their "back talk," gossip, and critical judgments interrupt the household chain of command and reorder plantation lives and routines. Third, recognizing the difficulty ex-slaves faced in buying land, Thanet celebrated opportunities for them to own other assets. In a bid to further their assertion of citizenship rights, she endowed them with significant clout as consumers.

Behind Thanet's reformist concern, however, lurked an ambivalence that checked her investment in freedwomen's prospects. In some stories her black female characters are caricatured or silenced, whereas in others their threatening judgments and frightening stories meld into a broader twangy Arkansas dialect, rendering their voices indistinguishable from those of other sharecroppers. Inspired by a state with a proclivity to blend cavalier charm with frontier justice, Thanet ventured daring representations of black and white women citizens who challenged convention in both public and private arenas only to follow them with a quick foreclosure of these radical possibilities.

To check the loose tongues of allied black and white women, Thanet imposed tightened, nearly incestuous, familial bonds and cross-class alliances spearheaded by white men. While imagining empowering roles for white southern women, Thanet used her female characters to help reestablish patriarchal authority. In the entangled plot, gender becomes the novel's ironic linchpin to redeem Fair, "correct" the Reconstruction's racial inversions, and restore white men's privileged place in the home and greater polity.

Finally, in a vision reflective of her midwestern disdain of immigrant labor and New England admiration of homegrown industry as much as her Arkansan racism, Thanet had the native white male laborer replace the dissatisfied black worker. Rather than making freedpeople's claims to citizenship paramount, her fiction focused on the reconstruction of veteran planters into farmers and handymen, able to tackle all the demands of running a plantation. Dramatizing their struggle to rehabilitate the damaged ideals of honor, reputation, and duty, she revamped plantation fiction. Thanet allied herself with the Lost Cause movement as her male protagonists reclaim their jeopardized property and authority. In this effort, portable property, in the forms of props and disguise, served planter interests.

Because she sensed a genuine change in heart and head might be too difficult for the defeated, Thanet, echoing Cable, endorsed a strategy that promoted the performance of identity. She valorized the posturing of midwestern laboring attitudes by southern planters as an integral component to the reconstruction of the region and the reunification of the nation. The expatriate, befuddled bumbler Fair would soon become a respected American hero by virtue of his ability to act the part. Through costume, a Fair of refurbished masculinity helps reverse the defeat of "Southron" virility occasioned by the ignominious capture of Jeff Davis in supposed feminine disguise.

By championing the performance of labor and chivalry over earnest conviction as a means to repair damaged postwar reputations, Thanet anticipated the Rough Rider flourish of brash masculinity that would characterize the 1890s. In a disturbing home-front expression of this imperialist model, *Expiation*'s story affirms the legitimacy of white southern males to restore their fallen authority by pursuing vigilantism. Woolson's writing may have dulled a reader's perception for the need for Reconstruction, but Thanet's writing stymied the need for it, by putting white supremacist violence in the context of Arkansan folk tradition.

Thanet capitulated to the current political climate and to her own ambitions to be a successful writer of national import. She refashioned the southern "Negro question" into a solution to the "Labor question," as nineteenth-century pundits phrased the issues percolating around free labor ideology and the labor-reform movement. Thanet suggested the applicability of expiation to the overbearing victor as well as the defeated rebel as she tapped into the emergent national mood to reassess the harsh excesses of an imposed Reconstruction. Her work symbolizes the legacy of regionalism, which itself can be understood as a nativist response to the imposition of military districts. It also shows how regional cooperation could replace sectional reunion as a trope for resolving sectional strife. Thanet's vision of regional interdependence served less as literary test case than as blueprint for the intricate national negotiation behind the Plessy decision, which institutionalized segregation, just six years later. Thanet's local color sketches helped realize a national paradigm that prized the contribution of southern literary voices to shaping the nation, a recognition for which William Gilmore Simms, that antebellum advocate of southern letters, had long campaigned. Of all Reconstruction writers, Thanet brought to bear the broadest regional perspective on postwar challenges in her Arkansas fiction.

Living the Dream as Planter and Writer: Thanet's Place in Plantation Fiction

Thanet's geographically diverse upbringing made her a distinct voice among Reconstruction writers. She was born in 1850 in Andover, Massachusetts, a town where Harriet Beecher Stowe, Elizabeth Stuart Phelps, and Anne Bradstreet once lived. When she was six, Thanet's family moved to Davenport, Iowa, a Protestant, staunchly Republican, cosmopolitan, immigrant river town. Her father, an opinionated and entrepreneurial railroad president, entered local politics and at one point was mayor of Davenport. Thanet entered Vassar College in 1866, but feeling socially outcast after presenting herself as a "carpenter's daughter," she transferred to Andover's Abbott Academy. Her 1868 graduation was followed by a European tour and a father's gifts of a writing desk, inkwell, and letter basket.[3]

Thanet launched her career by writing scholarly essays and fiction to articulate her labor theories. She was the first to tap into the violent strikes rocking the Midwest and reposition them as a dramatic foil to discuss older Reconstruction issues of free-labor ideology and the need for vigilante community reaction. Witnessing the hardship caused by crop failures and market panics in the 1870s prompted Thanet's interest when strikes in Chicago and Moline threatened her father's speculative interests. In 1877 she was horrified to watch how a 10 percent wage cut by four railroads sparked a series of strikes by farmers, mill hands, and miners and subsequent riots that spread from Baltimore to Chicago.

In response, Thanet crafted her first story about labor issues, "Communists and Capitalists," which focused on the July 1877 strike. "Communists and Capitalists" dramatized Thanet's strong commitment to Spencerian philosophy, which espoused the inherent superiority of the middle class over the poor, who suffered on account of their own shiftlessness. Appearing in *Lippincott's* in October 1878, it was the first of many writings that crystallized her labor philosophy, which was shaped in part by her close friendship with Andrew Carnegie.[4] Thanet soon created a body of work built around labor strife, which she pitched to prospective editors, such as *Appletons'* Ripley Hancock, who acknowledged: "Your outline of the story ["We All"] interested me greatly and I quite agree with you that the Labor Question has an importance."[5]

In "Communists and Capitalists" and the 1893 short story "The Strike at Glascock's," Thanet attacks unions as not only hostile to productive labor but also to the American family, while "Otto the Knight" (1888) recast unions as a criminal cabal of dynamiting anarchists. She was particularly antagonistic to the influential Knights of Labor, whose republican ideals translated into a program of radical political and social reform that improved economic conditions. After the Pullman Strike in Chicago had closed her father's manufacturing business in 1894, Thanet covered the strike that same year in "The Contented Masses," which evinced a hostility to unions that only intensified with age. In this thinking she resembled Anna Julia Cooper. However, whereas Cooper strategically invoked nativist anxieties and excoriated organized labor in order to boost the value of black laborers, Thanet eschewed both black and immigrant workers in favor of a white nativist labor force.[6]

In the winter of 1883, Thanet left Iowa and turned South. With her companion, Jane Crawford, she visited the resorts of Aiken, South Carolina, much in the tourist spirit of Woolson. Although Thanet was disappointed in her first glimpses of the region, Crawford had just inherited property on the Black River near Minturn, Arkansas, that Thanet found delightful. Located in the northeastern corner of the state in Lawrence County, the second-oldest county in Arkansas, Clover Bend was a five-thousand-acre plantation, complete with seventy-five workers, a cotton gin, grist, and windmills, one of the few still intact after the war. Though sandwiched between the important federal post of Batesville and the strategic town of Pocahontas, Lawrence County seems to have been buffered from radical political reconstruction. This may be because plantations in this upland county were not characterized by the intensive and exclusive cotton production found in the delta. Nevertheless, the area was not immune from the postwar violence that characterized Reconstruction in Arkansas.

Thanet and Crawford soon set up housekeeping together in an arrangement that lasted their remaining lives. Although Thanet was only a lifelong tenant, she was deeply involved in running "what was once the largest tract under single management" in Arkansas, supervising the plantation's many improvements while her largely silent partner, Crawford, oversaw gardens. The only other shareholder besides Crawford was the plantation manager, Colonel Frank W. Tucker, a veteran of the 50th Massachusetts who settled in Arkansas in 1870. Until 1909, Thanet and Crawford wintered at Clover Bend, which they renamed "Thanford" after an 1896 fire. Neither tourist nor resident, Thanet was the only Reconstruction writer considered here who sojourned both above and below the Mason-Dixon line for nearly three decades.[7]

Dividing her seasons between playing Arkansas plantation mistress and Iowa labor watchdog, Thanet brought to her work the stereooptic vision of national reconciliation that her dual residences afforded. Thanet's attempt to realize her fantasy of the privileged planter's life inspired her writing with new subjects and newfound intensity, and she began to write for ten to twelve hours daily. Beginning in January 1884 with "The Bishop's Vagabond," a short story placed in the *Atlantic*, her work appeared regularly in other top-notch publications such as *Harper's New Monthly*, *Century*, and *Lippincott's*. In 1887 Houghton Mifflin published her first collection of short stories, *Knitters in the Sun*, just three years after Thanet and Crawford had arrived in Arkansas.[8]

Declaring that a "story is built like a house," Thanet extended her carpentry metaphor to writing by carefully crafting stories for different markets. To capture a broad regional interest, in 1891 she titled her second collection of stories set in Arkansas and Iowa, *Otto the Knight and Other Trans-Mississippi Tales*. A reporter likened all her hard work in hammering out stories of different regional woods ("Hard western timber on one side for a certain market, tender pine and fragrant balsam for another class of periodicals") to a house builder laboring "as a man might work, with the sweat on his brow and the ache in his back from dawn until night." Her labors as planter and writer, however mediated by Thanford's ever-growing cadre of black and white employees, had earned her the right to speak for and about laborers.[9]

Thanet's experiences in Arkansas enabled her to join Thomas Nelson Page, Joel Chandler Harris, and Joseph Eggleston in the 1880s revival of plantation fiction. These writers defended antebellum institutions and resisted the imposition of military districts. They reworked the national paradigm of the 1830s "Old South" fiction with regional nuance that reflected the repercussions of federal intrusion. Ranking Thanet's work on a par with that of Cable, Woolson, and Harte, contemporary critic Thomas Wentworth Higginson argued that regional fiction would help redefine American literature, and, as the epigraph to this chapter shows, he correctly identified Thanet's emulation of an antebellum plantation ideal. As Paul Buck noted, regional plantation fiction thrived in part because the death of slavery allowed sectional points of contention to give way to reconciling Lost Cause idealizations and white supremacy.[10]

Thanet's celebration of Arkansas was within and yet against the conventions of plantation fiction. Into a yearning for a romantic, pastoral landscape, Thanet injected her Iowan mythic ideal of agricultural white labor, Protestantism, and republicanism. Testimony as much to her multiregional positioning as to her ambivalent stance on Reconstruction, she could name Cable and Page in one breath as two of her favorite writers to journalist Mary Reid in August 1894. Her own labor problems led Thanet to revise plantation fiction in distinctive ways by replacing the former slave and sharecropper with the white male farmer. Appearing just three years after Page's best-selling *In Ole Virginia*, Thanet's *Expiation* features main characters originally from Virginia, allowing the novel to critique and transform two of the three "staples" of Page's fiction, which Lucinda Mackethan has identified: the high moral quality of the southern gentleman and the dedicated labor of the beloved, essential slave.[11]

Some of her contemporaries found her writing overly romantic. Fellow Iowan writer Hamlin Garland criticized Thanet for lacking the laboring experience of farm life that would have given her a less naive perspective: "What do you know of the farm realities I describe? You are the daughter of a banker." A critic for the *Atlantic Monthly* faulted her for relying on "melodrama," while the *Dial*'s William Morton Payne, though praising Thanet's work for its "earnest thought" and "faithful realism," found her "study of the labor question" to have a "considerable element of romantic adulation."[12]

Nevertheless, Thanet's appreciation of a regionally nuanced New South was factually grounded. Unlike other southern states, the self-proclaimed "Land of Opportunity" became home to transplanted northern and midwestern business leaders who flocked to Little Rock in the 1870s. Despite a lack of planter alliances, the new settlers helped produce a boom in manufacturing, especially in the cotton seed, timber, and oil industries. Southern planters, empowered by northern capital and white supremacist ideology, sought midwestern workers as a migrant work force, just as African Americans were leaving the region for the Midwest. Contributing to the postwar western-edged realignment were many of Thanet's fellow Iowans, who moved south as teachers and plantation lessees. In reality, much of postwar southern agriculture was more accurately characterized, to borrow Moon-Ho Jung's description of southern Louisiana's sugar region, as a "complex proletarianization that tied nearly everyone to the fluctuations of global capitalism." Yet Thanet's writing helped keep Henry Grady's dream of small, independent producers and New South boosters alive.[13]

Differentiating herself from her fellow writers, Thanet moved against contemporary nostalgia for the Old South by conflating the planter's concerns about sharecroppers with those of the capitalist about striking factory workers and, more generally, by highlighting the increasingly consumerist culture shared by both rural and urban workers. Drawing parallels between the difficulties of the transition to free labor by former slaves and the unrest of striking workers, Thanet applied her solution broadly to what she termed as a problem of unrestrained or "emancipated" laborers. Thanet could speak of sharecroppers and factory strikers together because she, like other southerners and such black reformers as W. E. B. Du Bois, saw them as different facets of the same labor question. Du Bois, writing from the other end of the political spectrum, declared that the New South labor system was being dominated by "the sons of poor whites . . . thrifty and avaricious Yankees, and unscrupulous immigrants" to create a new slavery ruled by "the cold question of dollars and dividends" under which "all labor is bound to suffer."[14]

Refusing to polarize rural life from urban existence, neither Thanet nor Du Bois was wrong. Beginning with the formation of the Colored National Labor Union in 1869, the increasingly organized demands of black workers from the factory to the field, representing local communities throughout the country, had to be acknowledged. Their demands were nurtured partly by their common interests in markets, one which Thanet shared. Thanford depended on imports from distant metropolises. Rustic and isolated, the plantation was accessible only by steamboat coming up the Black River from its junction with the Mississippi River, which, along with a new railroad six miles away, brought in lavish supplies from all over the country. Visitor Evelyn Schuyler Schaeffer noted: "A certain Frank Wahl of St. Louis, sends semi-weekly, baskets of beef. . . . A man in Texas sends them the earliest strawberries; another in New Orleans shrimps and Gulf fish; and Pierce of Boston supplies the tinned goods and wines." From these weekly deliveries of delicacies, elaborate gourmet meals were prepared and dished out by servants in livery, making life at Thanford much like that at an English country estate. Thanet's vision of Reconstruction thus recognized the practical need for interdependence among rural and metropolitan inhabitants, with cities such as Chicago providing a nexus, especially as railroads flourished.[15]

Thanet's distinctive triregional perspective was articulated not only in her writing but also in her courting of publicity, and critics responded enthusiastically. Her success can partly be understood by her positioning of both herself and Arkansas as hybrids. When asked from where the great American novel would arise, she cleverly answered: "It will be a toss up between the West and the South. I suppose, though, I'm prejudiced, for I am both Western and Southern. However, I have two generations of New England blood to back me, and ought not unduly to favor any locality." Thanet came from Pilgrim stock on both sides of her family, an ancestry of which she was deeply proud, evident by her active involvement in the elite National Society of Colonial Dames and several other heritage organizations. Her celebrity was grounded in her adroitly balanced position as a writer attuned to three distinct regional cultures, making her work an embodiment of reconciliation sentiments that ranged beyond easy sectional dichotomies. Even Clara Barton confessed in a fan letter that "to know you were my country-woman, a Massachusetts girl! . . . While reading of Octave Thanet, I had always placed her in my mind away down South somewhere, or even in the West." A writer for the Arkansas

Historical Association celebrated her roots, which helped make her reputation as "the best short story writer in the world." Her multiple regional affiliations were evident even in her physiognomy: "Her fair complexion, blue eyes, light brown hair, tender conscience and love of learning ally her to New England; her charming manner, splendid speech and magnificent physique are Southern; while a humorous mouth and vigorous practical mind bespeak her a daughter of the West."[16]

True to her endorsement of a Protestant work ethic that prized sustained toil, Thanet's career as a writer reveals her extensive labors to court readers, placate editors, and fetch a high price in the changing publishing industry of the 1880s. Her magazine writing came of age during a period in which the industry stabilized as a business, replacing the ideal of the paternalistic "gentleman publisher" with a more impersonal, profit-conscious mode of operation. Unlike George Washington Cable, whose literary acclaim peaked with his novels of the 1880s, Thanet's novelistic output crested after the successful agitation for copyright reform in 1891, a result that dramatically ushered in a changed publishing landscape. Accordingly, she thought of her authorial persona and her subject matter with a promotional savvy that Cable would not dare imagine. By 1905, she would be publishing her novels with the recently revamped, profitable midwestern firm of Bobbs-Merrill. In yet another instance of Thanet's personal spin on southern charm and western push to make a sale, she stirred up paternalistic impulses within her editors while forthrightly negotiating her price. Equipped with a good sense for public relations, when asked in a questionnaire who her "favorite heroes in real life" were, she responded, "Magazine editors." Her strategies show how deftly women could court social convention and professional ambition for gain. The masculinized connotations of her pen name aligned Thanet with her male editors, who she was sure were biased against women writers. Thanet's assertive sales tactics reconfigured a mode of professional relations where much more parity existed between author and publisher in the common interests of profit than the midcentury paternalistic decorum of "gentlemen publishing" would reveal.[17]

Yet, in his biography tellingly titled *Journey to Obscurity*, George McMichael documents the fading of Thanet's reputation due to her capitulation to market demands. Her implicit "sell-out" to "the commercial principles of decency prevailing in the New England and the Middle West" created "her greatest failing": "an inability to rise above the lure of American success and to establish a firm and independent vision of her own." It was, however, Thanet's very attentiveness to the political and social climate of her time—particularly her keen pulse-taking on issues of labor and race relations—that made her work so distinctive and popular, especially among male readers, many of whom were veterans. Thanet answered and filed letters from readers who sent her story ideas, manuscripts, requests for personal advice, and general praise, including at least one request that she write a history of Arkansas. Indeed, she was dubbed the "Prophet of Arkansas" by the *Nation*, whose editors found her popular work took "high rank among the color sketches of our country."[18]

By summering in Iowa and wintering in Arkansas, Thanet drew upon the concerns and culture of the two regions to create a fiction of unique political and economic import. Her accomplishment exemplifies the complexity of the geographic counterpoint inherent in regionalist writing that many critics have recently rediscovered. Thanet's ambivalence regarding freedwomen's roles as postwar citizens reflects not only the various locales of her upbringing but also her residency in a state that championed hardscrabble individualism as much as cavalier paternalism. Imposing her regional biases on a state with a history of complex interracial relations proved to be as ill fitting a venture as the cobbling of Arkansas into Military District Four.

Guerrillas in Their Midst:
The Ongoing Civil War in Military District Four

By opening *Expiation* with Fair's disorientation in the swamp, Thanet captured Arkansans' wartime and postwar ongoing isolation, disruption, and tangled loyalties with shrewd historical accuracy. The state was not unified in its response to secession, and over the course of the Civil War residents raised both Confederate and Federal regiments. In March 1862, after the Confederates lost the battle of Pea Ridge and their departing forces scattered, the state was left so defenseless that Governor Henry M. Rector threatened to secede from the Confederacy. In response, the Confederate government authorized the raising of independent guerrilla companies, and Federal counterinsurgents attacked both the Confederates and civilian property in reprisal. The wartime chaos in Arkansas included Federals fighting guerrillas, white residents fighting black residents, and Unionists fighting Confederates. It was from this disturbing, confused regional mood that Thanet first pitched "this Expiation idea" to a publisher as an "epic of the guerrillas," which was "honest and drawn from life," warning that it might be "too sensational" but "it isn't quite so bad as it sounds." In reality, constant danger overwhelmed the state's residents; as one Arkansan put it, "The citizen is regarded as lawful prey."[19]

While Arkansans had difficulty distinguishing friend from foe, emancipation threw the meaning of citizenship itself into a state of confusion. The Unionist government of 1864 adopted a constitution that granted basic civil rights to black Arkansans, but few white Arkansans could accept extending the vote to freedpeople. After the war's official end in 1865, and despite the best efforts of twenty-five Freedmen's Bureau agents, violence continued in Military District Four (which also included Mississippi), and by 1867 it was constant. Bureau reports document, often in harrowing detail, the continual harassment and murder of Arkansas agents.[20]

Although reports vary, the Freedmen's Bureau generally supported the use of some 5,526 black Arkansan troops to further black socioeconomic and political advancement while quelling white threats. One bureau official argued vociferously that the "one complete remedy" for Arkansan unrest was maintaining "negro troops in their midst." Another agent, however, described conditions of understaffing, sickness, and purportedly poor discipline among black troops to argue for their mustering out. In the Trans-Mississippi West, black Arkansans were among the first to serve the U.S. Army, and they had distinguished themselves in many expeditions and engagements. Their bravery ignited the rage of the slave owners who faced them in battle. After the Battle of Poison Spring on 18 April 1864, for example, victorious Confederates killed many of the black troops who had surrendered. White rage did not stop after Appomattox. In fact, as one historian concluded, "No Arkansan in 1867 or 1868 would have believed the Civil War was really over." By the gubernatorial election of 1868, reportedly more than 200 citizens, mostly black and white Unionists, had been murdered in Arkansas.[21]

The following day, November 4, newly elected Republican governor Powell Clayton declared martial law. Dividing Arkansas into four military districts patrolled by a state militia, he intoned: "A reign of terror was being inaugurated in our state which threatened to obliterate all the old landmarks of justice and freedom, and to bear us onward to anarchy and destruction." In the northeastern district, Thanet's terrain, violent controversy surrounding the use of the state militia was fiercest. The antagonism was fed by demanding black Arkansans and resistant white Arkansans, who, as one bureau agent put it, simply "could not realize that the colored man was free." When the bureau departed Arkansas in 1869, guerrilla warfare entered politics. A fusion party composed of Republicans and Democrats willing to compromise and opposing Clayton retook legislative seats, and partisan violence ruled the state for years. When Thanet arrived, she found herself in a cauldron of local racial hostility.[22]

Despite the violence, key demographic changes enabled some black Arkansans to carve opportunity out of the state's political turmoil for a few years. Arkansas had a comparatively tiny antebellum population of free black people because Arkansas officials, operating within a tightly controlled system of slavery, discouraged African Americans from settling in the state. Their antipathy increased following the 1857 Dred Scott decision; Arkansas legislators voted to expel the state's 144 free black residents by January 1860 and to reenslave any who remained. Although this law was never enforced, its passage caused many black Arkansans to leave.[23]

Nevertheless, after the war Arkansas experienced a boom in postwar black migration. In fact, more African Americans came to Arkansas than to any other southern state, almost tripling the black population between 1870 and 1890. Sensing the initial tolerance and moderation there, freedpeople were inspired by influential African Methodist Episcopal bishop Henry McNeal Turner, who prophesized that "Arkansas is destined to be the great Negro state of the country." With this increased electorate, black Arkansans capitalized on their political strength. In postemancipation Arkansas, they formed an emergent political culture of solidarity, through participating in marches and attending conventions. The 1865 Little Rock Colored Citizens Convention, for example, met to explore how best to "elevate" the race to the 1868 convention that redrafted the state constitution. Eighty-four black legislators served the state between 1868 and 1893, largely due to Fusionist cooperation. Black political influence was sustained by the frontier aspects of Arkansas, which formed the groundswell of the agrarian movement's challenge to southern Democratic power. Historian Richard Niswonger claims that "no state illustrated more graphically the struggles and upheaval within the one-party system as the agrarian tide swept the Democratic dyke."[24]

An alliance of poor black and white farmers with Republicans, known as the Agricultural Wheel, threatened to undermine Democratic control. Founded in 1882, the Agricultural Wheel and another farmers' organization, the Brothers of Freedom, formed the beginnings of the state's vital third-party movement. They were soon augmented by close contact with Thanet's nemesis, the Knights of Labor, which had at least one local assembly in Lawrence County and in each of the surrounding counties of Greene, Craighead, Jackson, and Independence. Arkansas was distinguished among southern states by this successful political coalition of industrial and farm workers—both black and white—to form a viable independent party. Thanet observed that they shared a common distrust of "money power." They erected a platform of demands, including government ownership of communication and transportation networks, free coinage of silver, a graduated income tax, and the abolition of the convict lease system. The trajectory of this third-party movement reveals the complexity of class and political differences within the state's black community. Further reflecting the state's long-standing agrarian temperament wedded to emergent industrial interests, the influence of Booker T. Washington remained strong in the Land of Opportunity long after Reconstruction.[25]

The combination of labor and farm interests with freedpeople's rights was just the sort of coalition that Thanet feared, and it prompted an immediate, violent backlash. Both the Democratic Party's accession to some agrarian demands and its use of election fraud, violence, and disfranchisement caused the 1892 demise of this astounding third-party movement. One consequence was the emigration of many black Arkansans to Liberia in the 1890s. Their determination to leave was a measure of how disfranchisement and violence had felled their hopes for prosperity in Arkansas. For those who stayed, a class-stratified African American community coalesced in racial solidarity and self-help against Jim Crow, structured around education, social, and religious institutions.[26]

Expiation: How Fiction Fights Southern Defeat

Thanet's *Expiation* picks up where Woolson's tourist sketches left off. The novel's young protagonist, Fairfax Rutherford, could be taken for one of the "dead down here" in Woolson's "The French Broad." Woolson pitied her humiliated white men, but Thanet focused on the rehabilitation or "redemption" of this Lost Cause son so that he might regain the honor, reputation, and property the white southern elite deemed worthy of a planter heir from one of the state's first families. Fair, who had spent the Civil War years in Europe, was spared the battlefield glory of his now-dead brothers, and when he returns home in the novel's beginning, he is oblivious to the guerrilla warfare ravaging Arkansas.

Fair soon stumbles upon a mysteriously dead local yeoman, Jim Fowler, who had been on a mission to collect and deliver considerable funds to the Rutherfords for their illicitly sold cotton crop before he was intercepted by marauding guerrillas led by Dick Barnabas. Aware of dangers on the road, Fowler had concealed the money and misled the robbers into thinking his mission had failed, but they killed him anyway. Taking the well-hid money from Fowler's boots, Fair continues the journey toward Montaigne, the

Rutherford family plantation. After being mildly wounded, he escapes his pursuers and passes the money on to Parson Collins, whom he encounters next when the Barnabas gang waylays them in the swamps. They threaten to torture Fair into revealing his family's hidden money. Terrified and unable to lie on his honor as a Rutherford gentleman, Fair "passes the buck" by betraying the parson. When the parson refuses to reveal the money's location, Barnabas forces Fair to shoot the parson or to die himself. Overwhelmed, Fair faints with the cocked gun in his hand, and in the actual moment of shooting, one of the gang pulls the trigger for him, but Fair later learns that the parson was only wounded.

The second half of the novel shifts to exploring how Fair can "expiate" for his cowardice. Questioning his role as a southern man of honor and courage, Fair becomes convinced by his cousin Adèle that he must atone for his cowardly behavior by capturing and killing Barnabas and his gang. In effect, he needs to become another Barnabas in pursuit of vigilante violence. His efforts both reaffirm and refuse the South's code of honor for white men, since he performs his expiation only in a nominal way, all the while doubting himself. By the novel's close, Fair has helped suppress the Barnabas gang, shoring up planter authority to maintain order and protect property. Fair, however, remains a troubled and admitted coward. His dependence on Adèle, a local woman of unusual influence and manly valor, further destabilizes notions of white southern male superiority. Behaving in unconventionally gendered ways, Adèle plays a critical role in Fair's "redemption."

Of Upside-Down Castles:
Gender Trouble in the Library and the Swamp

Historian LeeAnn Whites has categorized Confederate defeat as the catalyst for a "crisis in gender," which led to a "domestic reconstruction of white southern manhood" that began with women at home and radiated outward to more public spheres. As defeat and occupation curtailed their public authority, veterans were forced to redefine their antebellum identities from defenders of slavery to defenders of their families. While supporting this interpretation, Thanet's novel also suggests an ongoing gendered interdependency between public and domestic spheres, as well as antebellum and postwar motivations more complex than the unilateral process Whites identified.[27]

With judicious references to the Chesapeake culture throughout the novel, Thanet upholds the Rutherfords' tidewater ties to the land and community, staging them best in the library and swamp. As in Tourgée's novel, the planter's library in *Expiation* offers white men a refuge in which to repair damaged codes of honor and to reconcile yeomen and women to the old planter order. But in wartime Arkansas, that experience is under siege for all who enter, proving the difficult transfer of regionally cultivated predilections and gendered habits. Library reading in *Expiation* becomes both conduit to freedom and relay to enslaving tradition. The political efficacy of literacy for either shoring up or revising tradition is under question in the story.

A wobbly cornerstone of the Rutherford library is the writings of Michel de Montaigne, after whom the novel's plantation, modeled after Clover Bend, was named. Inherited "like the family prejudices, his tradition of honor and his father's sword," the French essayist remains a crucial ballast for the Colonel, Fair's father, against the wilds of Arkansas. Montaigne's words form a transatlantic bridge for the European-educated Fair to his father and his proud patrician heirs. Whenever "he was in trouble," the Colonel always resorted to Montaigne's essays "until he was sure of his composure." At the moment of Fair's greatest disgrace, which smears the reputation of the entire family, Montaigne's words *"Ecraser l'infame,"* or "Crush the reviled," return to haunt him with connotations of justifiable violence. Fair's father suffers as though "struck" with "a mortal blow" as his own "stainless honor" is imperiled; he understands that a gentleman "is the Southern title of nobility; and the Rutherfords had been gentlemen for centuries." Yet now they fail him, as he reads the great essayist "upside down," so great is his distraction. If the Colonel had been paying attention to the skeptic's wise thoughts on cowardice, expiation, and honor, he would not have so misread him and instead would have found an ironic understanding of human nature much more capacious than his own brittle dreams.[28]

In a surprising gender inversion, Adèle also reads Montaigne. Like Tourgée's Toinette, she repairs to the library to pursue an education designed to transform her "from a madcap into a proper, young lady," a role bathed in domestic subservience to the master. Yet her reading also inspires her courage to resist that role. Following every demure appeal to Fair ("I'm only a girl and I don't understand much about politics") is a strong assertion of her activism. Adèle also reads Fair's letters penned from abroad, which cause her to mistakenly idolize him. Each letter "wove a fresh charm about her hero," creating plantation fiction and encouraging Adèle to imagine Fair as a gallant "Southron." Adèle's tutelage in this "miserable room" shows the active role literate white women played in supporting the cavalier ideal as well as subverting it.[29]

Structural elements ripe for remodeling were built into the library's crucial role in upholding patriarchal control. While there is no secret room, Thanet lampoons the Rutherfords' pretensions to cavalier authority through the library's mockery of chivalry. The walls are decorated in "what in antebellum days was known as a 'landscape paper,' representing innumerable castles on the Rhine." Due to a mistake by their paper hanger, the "castles were made to stand on their heads," much like the Colonel's volumes of Montaigne. The family leaves the castles upside down as a visual revocation of the antebellum plantation as "medieval idyl" and its attendant cavalier ideal turned on its head.[30]

Further revising that gendered ideal are the library's paintings. The current Mrs. Rutherford's landscapes are hung on the library's badly papered walls, asserting an overriding feminine presence. They transfix the Colonel whose "custom" is to "sit and smoke before them, and contemplate them with innocent pride." Most prominent are the portraits of the "three former mistresses of Montaigne" (including Fair's mother). Their likenesses are so frequently commented upon and addressed by the family that they seem minor characters. Their gazes function as a reference point in moments of moral qualm, as on the eve of Fair's departure to help snare the Barnabas gang, causing the Colonel and Adèle to reflect on Fair's mother, who would have judged his behavior. Thanet suggests a more compassionate than scornful valuation of Fair's behavior, and by the novel's close, Fair's "redemption" is recognized not only by his father but also by his mother's portrait. It matters much that a weeping Colonel says to Fair, "She—she's proud of you, too." It is also in the library that an emboldened Adèle speaks up to help resolve the impasse between a humiliated Fair and his chagrined father.[31]

The Arkansas swamps, however, stage even more radical revisions of masculine and feminine behavior. The library's outdoor counterpoint offers gritty obscurity, a quality that made the swamps ideal grounds for guerrilla warfare. Lacking the consuming allure of Woolson's Floridian swamp, Thanet's isolating wildernesses are an apt metaphor for Arkansas's dark history of conflicting allegiances and internal discord. Unionist and Confederate families, politically divided from their neighbors, used the circumstances of war to transform themselves into guerrillas. They regrouped into state militias, Klan chapters, and other vigilante bands well into Reconstruction and beyond. Indeed, the deserved nickname of Arkansan desperado Cullen Baker, "Swamp Fox of the Sulphur," attests to the terrain's value.[32]

Thanet's work repeatedly invokes the tenacity of the savage landscape embattled against civilization. In her essay "Plantation Life in Arkansas,"

Thanet structured the narrative of her swamp-laden plantation, Thanford, around its history of violence, referencing an "endless store" of "blood-stained legends" and ghost stories so that they seem a natural feature of Arkansas home life. Violence is so endemic to the swamp, a place, as in "Ma Bowlin," where "Peril hid underfoot, and beauty was plain above," that Thanet maps it into all her fiction. In "The Loaf of Peace" (1888), the meeting place for a duel is the swamp's "blasted cypress," found on the brink of a "slash," the local lingo for a ravine. Similarly, in "Whitsun Harp, Regulator" (1887), a "bare spot dented by cypress trees" signifies where "Old Man Bryce's cabin stood until the guerillas murdered him and his wife and burned their bones under their home," a true story recounted in "Plantation Life." Thanet takes advantage of the fact that Arkansan domestic and feral borders blur in brutality. In *Expiation*, for example, Fair learns the armed boundaries of the area, for "rarely did a rider venture across the 'creek,'" and "when visitors did come, they rode armed to the teeth, the very women had revolvers stowed somewhere about their rusty cotton riding-skirts."[33]

A profoundly gendered place, Thanet's swamp tests the viability of masculinity when built from violence. In exposing the upper moral limits of the refined gentleman planter under siege, the swamp also reveals his primitive lower registers. The only other character besides Barnabas who thrives in the swamp is Slick Mose, a dangerous "creature" in "gibberish" communion with the swamp's animals. Mose, embodying what D. H. Lawrence called America's malignant capacity for "dark suspense," suggests that white men who are lured into swampy territory emerge primitivized, an outcome quite unlike that of Cable's Bras Coupé, who appears ennobled by it. With his "slim figure," "oval of one smooth cheek," and "delicate beauty," Fair, consistently compared to his mother and whose very name suggests femininity, is doomed from the start.[34]

Thanet positioned the Arkansas swamp as the site for testing Fair's mettle and then reconstructing his identity to conform with chivalry's code of honor. Trapped at Barnabas's hideout, Fair finds his cowardice exposed: "The old dread met me as soon as I touched the old swamp." When Barnabas invokes the reputation of the Rutherfords as "high-toned gentlemen" who would never lie, he offers Fair an impossible way out: if Fair can swear on his "honor's a gentlemen" that he does not know where the money is, Barnabas will free him. Of course Fair fails the grayback's testing of his honor because he, as a gentleman, cannot lie and soon, in fact, betrays the parson to save himself. It is in the swamp that Barnabas, leader of a notorious gang of Confederate guerrillas commonly called "graybacks," judges Fair: "You' the onlies' cyoward I ever knowed er you' name."[35]

During his tribulation in the swamp, Fair suggestively faints with his pistol cocked, which is then fired by a gang member. The phallic imagery used to represent Fair's humiliation and cowardice hints at the entanglement of sexuality, violence, and shaming within postwar vigilante terrorism's design to reinvigorate white male supremacy. It is in the swamp that Fair will later try to "prove" his worthiness as a planter's son by being capable of performing vigilante reprisals. Yet when the graybacks are finally cornered, Fair rides away from the shooting, admitting, "I hadn't the nerve to look at them being killed." Still later, when Fair traps Barnabas in the swamp, he cannot kill him. Instead, he feels a womanly compassion, concluding "with an inexpressible sinking of the soul" that "I am a coward again."[36]

The swamp exposes the vacuity of Fair's masculinity, but it affirms the genuinely heroic, masculinized behavior of Adèle. Adèle's actions there showcase her unusual but vitally masculine role in ensuring Fair's expiation. She found the swamps around Montaigne a place of consolation when Fair departs for Europe. Thanet portrays the "singularly fearless" white Adèle, who enters and exits the swamps with heart and mind intact, in marked distinction to the white men who find themselves depraved or vulnerable in the swamp. Indeed, "no one but Adèle would have leaped unhesitatingly from log to log, to follow Mose into the brake" to rescue the wounded Parson and the fainted Fair and retrieve the Rutherford money. Thanet suggests that murky, unstable places like the Arkansan swamps offer the best opportunities for women to assume authority. Her male characters are compelled to duel or murder in the swamp, but her female characters are compelled to acts of brave rescue.[37]

Thanet creates white Arkansan heroines who, inspired by the swamps, play inverse gender roles, much like Tourgée's Betty Certain. "Whitsun Harp, Regulator," for example, opens with the "po'ful handy" and "handsome" Polly Ann Shinault, with hatchet in hand, mending a boat just as naturally as her husband, Lum, who "had the habit of helping his wife about the house," next "deftly wiped the dishes and brushed out the room." Even the titular child of her 1887 short story, "Ma Bowlin'," already characterized admiringly by her father as "powerful spry" who "hopped like a 'coon,'" emerges from the swamps cured of her mental infirmity.[38]

The equally masculinized manner of *Expiation*'s Adèle surmounts even the confines of class privilege. Thanet characterizes Adèle as a strong, "awfully brave" tomboy in counterpoint to Fair as "the prettiest, sweetest, and cleanest little boy that she knew." It is Adèle who leads Fair on "jaunts" and "into breakneck sports." After she was "thrown into a thorn bush," Fair "wept over the piteous sight" of her injured arm, but she just "laughed merrily, and vowed that it didn't hurt her." Similarly, she endures a tooth extraction without a sound while Fair, in hiding, "howled at the top of his lungs." Still later, she draws from this childhood history to elicit his confession of cowardice, that "before he ended he was sobbing as uncontrollably as, when a terrified child, he used to be comforted back to courage in her arms."[39]

This pattern of inverse gender roles broadens to include Adèle's assumption of economic and physical mastery. Whereas the Colonel was willing to let Confederate soldiers destroy their cotton crop as a war measure, Adèle, acting in his stead while he is away fighting, refuses. Hiding the cotton in the swamp, she sells it "off slick." When the Colonel sets off to help entrap the graybacks, he naturally tells Adèle, "*You* look ayfter Fair." Exposed as a coward, Fair reclaims public authority by first surrendering domestic authority to the militant Adèle. When Fair finally begins to atone for his cowardice by joining in to fight the graybacks, Adèle is left on a roof to watch through a spyglass. Her desire to see the battle, if not actually participate in it, is frustrated by a wounded Confederate veteran who hogs the spyglass and demands that she literally support *him* while he stands on a chimney. Though resentful of her subservient position, Adèle begrudgingly props him up, literalizing what she does for Fair.[40]

Thanet's other female characters challenge gendered conventions while driving *Expiation*'s plot. Mrs. Crowder serves as spy, "tampering with the mails" without "any compunction," and it is "owing to her information" that the graybacks are intercepted. Mrs. Fowler, having lost her husband to the graybacks, screams for an oath to avenge her husband's murder: "I want 'em *killed*! . . . I want t' see it, myself!" Her bloodthirsty reaction causes Fair to quake: "Dear me, what a Rob Roy MacGregor's wife sort of woman she seems to be!" Women in *Expiation* claim the swamp as a source and a symbol for their unconventional empowerment, just as they reclaim the library. Showing their capacity to appreciate the swamp's weird beauty, Thanet's female characters place it on display. For example, Mrs. Rutherford keeps "bunches of swamp hackberries and holly twigs in showy vases." The swamp's symbolic presence indoors reflects Arkansas women's increasingly agile presence within its wilds.[41]

Thanet's river town experiences informed her female characters' defiance of convention. Her unorthodox Davenport girlhood had saved Thanet from the boredom of rural western life and the domestic conventionalities imposed on New England women. Life on the Mississippi River brought her into contact with a variety of people: avante-garde eastern gentility, like family visitor Bronson Alcott; rough westerners, including Native American prisoners; and unseemly southern hemispheric travelers, such as Cuban prostitutes. With tongue-in-cheek humor Thanet enumerated a typical week's activity for a lively young girl: "I feel rather knocked up, having killed a snake, shot a bird, fired a revolver . . . walked incalculable distances, waded in the Mississippi and finally gone to a party to end up the week." This curious mix of wayward play and genteel pretensions equipped Thanet with unusual verve to imagine liberal, outspoken roles for women.[42]

Thanet's experiences at Clover Bend confirmed the swamp's potential for her own gendered reinvention. Despite Thanet's efforts to remake the plantation with tidewater manorial pretensions, Thanford was still located in the "worst swamp in Arkansas," smack between the Ozark family farmers of Powhaten (the county seat) and the planters of Walnut Ridge (the future county seat). Their location forced Thanet and Crawford to transform from "helpless women, accustomed to have men open doors for us," to "accomplished paper hangers and house painters," white washers, machinists, and carpenters, as well as "our own best glaziers." Moreover, Thanet delineates the acquisition of these stereotypically "male" skills from a cadre of female employees.[43]

Despite her own transformation, in *Expiation* Thanet stages a series of countermoves that compromise challenges to planters' authority and show how straining allegiances in Civil War Arkansas required the vigilance of such planters as Colonel Rutherford to remain intact. Beginning with Confederate general Kirby Smith's 1862 authorization of partisan William Quantrill to impress locals, Confederates used tactics similar to Colonel Rutherford's to suppress dissenters. From vigilante activity to domestic abuse, in District Four violence became a nearly normative response for defeated Confederates desperate to regain their lost authority and forfeited property. The postwar survival of white men necessitated a strong appearance of cohesion, and Thanet uses the swamp and library to stage their resurgence. After all, it is in his library that the Colonel convinces some of Barnabas's guerrillas to join his band. By attempting to shore up the library's shaky foundations while providing reassurance to the anxious parson, Thanet's white male characters close ranks, forming a xenophobic community that held onto their plantations and took back the swamps.[44]

Whereas Woolson and Tourgée welcomed interracial and other hybrid social alliances as postwar solutions, Thanet rejected them. Instead, she highlighted the inbred pattern she saw in white Arkansan marriages to counter any cross-racial or ethnic familial hodgepodge. The library portraits remind Fair that he has witnessed several stepmothers in his own time, some of whom his uncle had vied for. Colonel Rutherford's taking of a fourth wife seems "almost indecent" and remains a "sore point" for Fair. He sees the tendency toward inbred families ("everybody seems to be marrying his or her third or fourth") as peculiar to Arkansas, muttering, "I daresay it's the country." Yet, by the close of the novel, he, too, helps maintain southern elite white control: he marries his cousin Adèle.[45]

Bolstered by intrafamilial alliances and cross-class allegiances, local white men took concerted action at those moments when coherence was most threatened by outsiders. One reason such fidelity was possible was the long-standing resentment many poor white Arkansans felt against black Arkansans—slave and free—with whom they competed for work. Living in a county where black Arkansans comprised less than 10 percent of the population, Thanet sidestepped this issue by limiting the representation of black men in her work and replacing them with white male servants. Nevertheless, Thanet admitted, "more than half" of their tenants and servants were black, and she had more to say about them than her white workers, for whom she felt affection and occasional annoyance. Although she claimed that "the Negro usually make a very decent tenant," she often patronizingly faulted them until she left Thanford.[46]

In *Expiation* Thanet highlights the white, reformed grayback Lige, whose name connotes the duty of a servant to his lord and who switches sides and joins the Colonel's vigilante band. In a gesture of repentance Lige deliberately intercepts a shot meant for Fair and gets "a bullet for his pains." This supreme act of loyalty, reminiscent of soldier substitutes bought by the wealthy, resonates with the devotion characteristic of subordinate classes to the planter class. In a reciprocal gesture of class conciliation, Lige is taken to the Rutherford plantation to die in comfort, atoning for having joined the Barnabas gang. The scene's poetic justice is another attempt to restore a very shaky hierarchy of caste in which Fair's class triumphs, for "the poor fellow's got to die."[47]

Thanet also restores hierarchy by using the library setting to foreclose opportunity for married women. Thanet felt that these genteel women, however empowered, should remain subordinate in a male-privileged world. Comfortably nested within a conservative status quo, Thanet was a brash and outspoken antisuffragist. Nevertheless, shortly before settling in at Clover Bend with Jane Crawford, in an essay entitled "A Neglected Career for Unmarried Women," she publicly endorsed the controversial position of single women as property owners, presenting them under the sentimental guise of pursuing the career of "householder." Beginning with the 1835 passage of the nation's first property law concerning married women, Arkansas provided some protection of their property, of which women availed themselves for decades. However, their rights were sharply curtailed because of unfavorable court decisions and the law's loose construction. Thanet's attitude was hardly unique. As Nancy Bercaw has shown in her study of Delta households, many planter women who lived in District Four challenged patriarchal conventions by taking charge of the plantations and by assuming other public roles during the war. Unlike Thanet, however, after the war many women reinscribed their identities as subordinate wives and mothers, like Adèle, within the confines of the plantation household.[48]

Thanet's ambivalence about women's place in the postwar South is evident in her conflicting treatment of Adèle's character. Adèle's authority is ultimately applied to the regressive purpose of compelling Fair to return to an antebellum code of chivalry. She not only convinces Fair that he must perform some expiation but also decides its appropriate form: ridding Arkansas of graybacks. Nothing short of the reclamation of the South and his reputation from "everlasting reproach" is at stake: "We are beaten in Arkansas; but now, if we are beaten, we have got to live. There is the land and the poor people, and it's our own country . . . you haven't any right to desert it." Adèle's entreaty epitomizes the key question in postwar Arkansas: who would own the land and make it profitable again?[49]

This question is dramatized in Fair's confrontation with Barnabas in the swamp. Fair's tribulations there really test who will inherit the New South. Thanet allowed Barnabas, the racially inferior "Jew-Injun," to dictate the terms and pronounce judgment on the hapless planter's son: "Their eyes met; the cruel old-race black ones, the frank brown-eyes of the Anglo-American; the glitter in each crossed under the torch rays like sword-blades, but it was the brown flash that wavered." These moments question the viability of white supremacy, as framed by Adèle's appeal traditionally linking white men's honor and duty with patriotic leadership. The reader has already learned about his expatriate education so that "to all intents and purposes, he had ceased to be an American." Fair's wavering at so many critical junctures in the novel becomes another opportunity for the dispossessed, such as Barnabas and freedwomen, to step in and stake a claim to citizenship.[50]

Freedwomen and the Force of Back Talk

More than any of her other fictional characters, Thanet's black female servants are poised to reconstruct the plantation household. Their vitality and enterprise make them essential to the topsy-turvy postwar world, as shown by the white characters' extreme dependence on them. While stereotypes of black servants have trivialized the import of their resistance to their masters, the "serviceability of the Africanist presence" itself is, as Toni Morrison has asserted, "central to any understanding of our national literature." Thanet's portrayals of dangerous servants affirm Morrison's claim that "Africanism becomes not only a means of displaying authority but in fact constitutes its source." Her work shares an affinity with the writings of African American women who provided testimony and protest, from precursors such as Jarena Lee and Maria Stewart to such contemporaries as Ida B. Wells and Anna Julia Cooper.[51]

Thanet deployed incisive black servants as agents of reform in much of her work. In her short story "Half a Curse" (1887), the ex-slave Venus exerts enormous authority on behalf of her former mistress to help her reclaim her confiscated property. Venus's efforts range from conjuring to initiating a lawsuit to using physical violence. Because her powers exceed those usually accorded freedwomen in southern society, the story ends with her martyrdom for her mistress, an act that results in the property's restoration. *Expiation*'s Aunt Tennie Marlow, a minor character on "the edge of the plantation," fills similar multiple roles; as midwife, nurse to Parson Collins, and "conjure woman," she had "enjoyed a great name" in the community.[52]

Thanet weaves more respectful awe around Aunt Hizzie, the Rutherfords' chief cook, who dispenses her homemade life-or-death-inducing concoctions or "mixteries" that reside on a shelf of "dark mystery." Having commandeered part of the great hall for her provisions, which compete for space with the master's cache of weapons and "all the finery of a southern rider," Aunt Hizzie refuses to budge into the background. Instead, she commands attention: "Her habit was to stand still, wherever she might happen to be, and cry aloud for whomsoever she desired to see, equally regardless of the whereabout of the person addressed." Drawn from Thanet's New England roots, Aunt Hizzie's sharp, domestic efficiency recalls Stowe's Miss Ophelia. Both her size and speech make Aunt Hizzie, "always a figure in the gallery," a contending force which reviewers recognized. A critic for the *Nation* described her type as "an indispensable scourge and blessing of Southern families."[53]

Aunt Hizzie's power resides in language. The first time she speaks, she declares her language's potency: "My word, dat er ben de mos' powerfullis mixtery dat ebber done pass my lips." Embodying the novel's gendered and racialized reversals of authority, she is especially adept at ordering other servants, whom she "cuffed and scolded," and intimidating her husband Uncle Nels, with whom she "bickered . . . whenever they met." Even after the graybacks have been vanquished, Hizzie's words retain force: "Aunt Hizzie had grewsome tales of a ghost capering on the shore, and a ghost cursing and sinking in the mire." All the locals are daunted by Aunt Hizzie, who interprets smoke and buzzards as portents to the community until Barnabas dies.[54]

Expiation highlights the efficacy of black women's language when targeted against white men. Beginning with Fair's victimization by his mammy, Thanet shows that it was not so much the female slave's fate that depended upon the master as his fate that was in the grip of *her* words. This pattern of dependency was acknowledged in former slave-master relations. In trying to persuade activist freedpeople to "make no noisy demonstrations of their political opinions" and to labor for their ex-masters, Arkansas bureau agents argued that "the planter is just as much dependent on the Black man for a living as the Black man is to the planter and his work is worth just as much to the planter as he receives for it." Thanet goes so far as to attribute Fair's cowardly character to mammy and other female slaves. His fears began "back, far back in his childhood," in "dark rooms, in negro cabins," where slave women told him "hobgoblin yarns of conjured victims." When captured by Dick and his gang, Fair can only recall "how they terrified him!," causing the narrator to exclaim: "What a ghastly fancy! Why must he remember it now?" These "horrible stories" stalk the "always right delicate" Fair, inaugurating a lifelong string of cowardly acts that serve to disable white supremacy.[55]

Female servants witness Fair's agony over his inability to play the role of master. Fair acknowledges Aunt Hizzie's presence as a frame of reference for his failure: "Poor Aunt Hizzie, she takes such pride in her 'burryin' dinners' and mine wi'l be but a poor affair. I am a disgrace all around." Aunt Mollie, another servant, is the key witness to blab about Fair's apparent display of cowardice. After just one conversation with her, even Colonel Rutherford "had shrunk into a strange silence." Thanet shows how black women's words, often discounted by plantation mistresses as incompetence and by historians as minor insubordination, were potent weapons in their arsenal of resistance, particularly in wider circulation through gossip.[56]

Creating what historian Tera Hunter calls a "war of nerves," the bondswomen's words not only terrorize Fair into cowardliness but also comment with devastating effect on his actions to the larger community. The Rutherfords first learn of Fair's cowardly plight by their habitual eavesdropping on Aunt Hizzie's arguments with Uncle Nels. The words of Aunt Hizzie and other female slaves lie at the heart of the fallen opinion of Fair and render the master speechless. Uncle Nels, with unwitting humor, raises the rhetorical questioning of the master's authority to new heights by voicing what everyone is thinking: "Cayn't *my* young marse ben a cyoward jes' much iz are torrer cullud pusson's young marse? *Somebuddy's* young marse got tuh be cyowards!" Overhearing this, the Colonel's "head fell," and he groans, "Even my niggers know it. I have lived a day too long." The Colonel now found that he "never so much as looked a negro in the face, if he could help it; the routine of the plantation seemed hateful to him."[57]

In emphasizing the effects of rumor, Thanet recognized the key role black women played in building what historian Steven Hahn has characterized as a "rural political infrastructure" of social connection that enabled grassroots political activism. Thanet's outspoken fictional servants resembled actual black Arkansan women who talked back to masters, pursued Freedmen's Bureau agents for redress, and generally exposed their masters' exploitative behaviors. In postbellum Arkansas, black women's sauciness inflamed their employers into acts of rage, and within Lawrence and other counties, freedwomen aggressively sought bureau help for a range of grievances. As one irate letter to the superintendent of education revealed, Arkansas freedwomen were much like their West Virginian counterparts such as Mrs. Hartgrove, who had protested against Storer's mandatory sewing class. Black Arkansan women could just as effectively ply their tongues in slur campaigns against offensive teachers as they did against former masters. After expelling several girls who he said had the character of "common prostitutes," irritated teacher David Casey found that "in order to be revenged, they conceived and put in circulation a slanderous report and . . . they succeeded for a time in defaming the school and everything connected with it." Like her real-life equivalents, Thanet's Aunt Hizzie refuses to fade away. Up to the penultimate page, she stays put and stays talking, causing Mrs. Rutherford to remark: "Dear me, there goes Aunt Hizzie. That woman is right trying. Never *will* move, stands right where she happens to be, and *hollers*." Her defiance is echoed in novels by African American women, ranging from Aunt Charlotte Brooks in Octavia Albert's *The House of Bondage* (1890) to Pauline Hopkins's Aunt Henny in *Hagar's Daughter* (1901–2) and Aunt Vinnie in *Winona* (1902).[58]

Thanet's dramatization shows how the impertinence of black women became one of the most subversive aspects of emancipation. A challenge to the master's absolute authority, Aunt Hizzie intimidates Fair and judges his actions. When Fair rounds up the graybacks, she sings the praises of this hollow retributive justice: "Jestice done plumb de line! Cries hypocrite, hypocrite, I despise." Like the double vocality in the utterances of Cable's *marchande des calas* (cake merchant), Clemence, Aunt Hizzie sings out a daring truth of double meaning. Indulging in dark humor when the posse ride out to confront the graybacks, all Aunt Hizzie can think of is "tuh make ready a big supper" for whomever survives, even Dick Barnabas, for he's "got a stoomick like de restis er men persons." When a dying Lige is brought to the house, Hizzie launches into a dirge that comforts Lige but annoys the Colonel, who declares: "Confound her, *I'll* go! I'll shut her up." The role of black female servants as gossipmongers helps rend the strained social fabric between white men: "Why, the very poor whites, the renters on his father's plantation, the ragged farmers in the hills . . . were *men* at least, brave and loyal, and had the right to despise him [Fair]" as the recriminations reverberate. In the long shadow cast on Fair's masculinity and honor, lengthened by the unusual influence of manly black and white women upon him, the novel rejects a postwar South fed by antebellum fantasies of an empowered Ole Marse, reared by a mammy like Cable's Madame Maptiste. Instead, Thanet exposed the frayed ties underpinning the region's social hierarchy.[59]

Aunt Hizzie's words are important not only to the Colonel and his wife but also to Adèle. Her attempts to adopt Aunt Hizzie's speech suggest even more subversive potential for freedwomen. In the unusual authority accorded her black female characters, Thanet engendered what literary scholar Elizabeth Young has described as a "counternarrative of inversion," which expresses the frustration of white women such as Adèle with the limiting proprieties of femininity. Thanet ventures more than Harriet Beecher Stowe, whose character Topsy both expresses and displaces white women's fantasies of incivility, as Young reads *Uncle Tom's Cabin*. Thanet allows her black female characters to serve as models of rebellion for her white heroine. Although thwarted, a potential alliance between black and white Arkansan women is suggested by Adèle's attempts to speak in black dialect, with similar effect to Cable performing Creole. As black dialect melds into white Ozark yeoman dialect, a verbal miscegenation is enacted, in which class commonality eclipses racial difference. With "plenty of burrs in her skirts and her hands none too clean," a handspringing Adèle asks why Fair does not speak like her, a question for which she is reprimanded for talking "nigger talk." A chastised Adèle humorously responds, "Say, I ain't gwine to talk nigger talk no mo'." This kind of talk became a marker for both racial and gender topsy-turviness, further threatening the plantation hierarchies that Thanet was ambivalently trying to shore up.[60]

Adèle's embrace of black dialect and her rejection by others for it illustrate Thanet's contradictory stance. Set against her sense of duty to maintain purebred, hierarchically subordinated families was her blithe linguistic crossing of racial, class, and gender lines, freely mixing white and black, mistress and servant, rich and poor voices in her fiction. In "Folk-Lore in Arkansas," for example, Thanet begins by admitting her "fascination" with Arkansas dialect, but she easily shifts to discussing Br'er Rabbit stories, conjuring, and black superstitions, demonstrating how Thanet, like Cable, could collapse racial differences into observations about regional dialect. Thanet could cross such lines because they were less rigidly drawn in Arkansas than in most other states, though by the time she wrote *Expiation*, the resumption of office by southern Democrats was well under way.[61]

Indicative of the changing political atmosphere in Arkansas, Thanet's imperceptible melding of black dialect with Ozark twang cut both ways. In her short stories the occasional comment of a black sharecropper is wedged between exchanges rendered in rough Arkansas dialect, effectively diminishing the freedpeople by making their plight hard to distinguish from that of white sharecroppers. In *Expiation* the culturally hybridized setting impacted the Rutherford family's speech in haphazard ways: "The Colonel's diction, become slipshod during years of careless living in the wilderness, had fits of stiffening into that dignity which pertained to a Virginia gentleman's speech when he was young." This verbal indistinguishability helps Thanet replace the laboring ex-slave with the white midwestern worker just as she mixed the speech of Virginia gentility with Ozark twang. Thanet, unlike Cable, was never a serious student of dialect, yet she declared to *Century Magazine* editor Richard Gilder that she was "prepared to wade through any amount of—ink, in defense of my dialect," because "the most interesting feature of the Arkansas dialect to me is its composite character."[62]

When servants' talk goes too far, Thanet checks their verbal verve by caricaturing them. In stories such as "The Conjured Kitchen" (1891), she ensured there was little chance of her characters becoming a Coralie Franklin. By turning joking black women into a joke, Thanet satirizes their Reconstruction ambitions as inappropriate. Aunt Callie of "The Conjured Kitchen" wishes for an "eddicated, settled-down studdy pusson" to marry her daughter, but her hopes are mocked. She settles for the comic Jerry's "mewls an' ten dolla," though she maintains she is a woman who "trabels en de kyars" or can afford a train ticket. Through caricature, the energy of an Aunt Hizzie is dissipated ("All soun' an' fury signifyin' nary!"), while her husband is simply emasculated through burlesqued speech. Even their gender reversals are mocked, as a comically abused Nels wonders "what we were all coming to when wives berated and ra'red on their husbands, so scandilus like." By curbing black servants' back talk, Thanet joined the plantation tradition that humored readers, even while it imagined a New South. Her white readers enjoyed, as Tennessee-bred New Yorker Martha M. Williams wrote to Thanet, "the dear delicious darkeys—the quaint pathetic personages that make you love while you laugh at them."[63]

Thanet made her black characters actors of Reconstruction only to discard them as background props when they became too demanding. While Woolson's black characters answer the labor question close-up, Thanet's drop it. In bondage, they had been visible at least in their labors to "make haste wid de dinner"; however, in freedom they soon become silent spectators—no longer players—on the novel's economic and political fields of Reconstruction. By the close of *Expiation* the narrator suggestively observes that the "one black spot on the plantation is out of sight of the house." The solution was inspired by Thanford. From the plantation's windows Thanet saw "away in the distance negroes and mules plowing" as scenery. Her novel offers a midwesterner's view of the reconstruction of the region's troubled economy—a view that had refreshing, seemingly unbiased appeal to readers weary of the region's problematic postwar transition to free-labor ideology.[64]

Thanet and Crawford, like other Lawrence County farmers, employed black and white workers who sharecropped more corn than cotton, earning "from seventy to eighty cents a day." Before the war, county yeomen had rented slaves from upcountry planters, which made the freedpeople's position as "free laborers" vulnerable to their former masters. As elsewhere, abuse in Lawrence County ranged from cheating, thievery, and harassment to violence. The assistant commissioner of the Arkansas and Missouri District confirmed this assessment that in areas like Lawrence County that lacked military presence, "the Negroes are still held and treated as slaves." The withdrawal of Thanet's workers to distant fields may have been part of a strategic reorganization of their homes and garden plots to remote locations so as to deny their white employers "oversight."[65]

Thanet responded to ongoing racial unrest by denying the legitimacy of its cause. Instead, she created her own plantation fantasy. Evelyn Schuyler Schaeffer describes arriving at Thanford to witness the conspicuously obedient role of black servants in meeting Thanet's many needs: "Here a very tall and handsome young black man in immaculate waiter's costume appears with tea, . . . and almost immediately a sweet-faced and daintily dressed maid comes to help the lady unpack." Similarly, distinguished Kansan editor William Allen White found that at Thanford, "There survived the civilization of the old South. The freed men were only nominally free. They lived with the land and on it, virtually serfs, and because she was passing rich, Octave Thanet lived in feudal splendor." Despite her attempts and outward appearances, Thanet encountered resistance as she tried to control her workers through paternalistic appeals, much like those used by Storer College officials.[66]

To manage Thanford's labor problems, Thanet attempted to organize the plantation workers into a racially hierarchized family, a sentimental counter to the rhetoric of union "brotherhood." Her implicit faith in racial subordination, in which the white "Arkansan rustic" was "every black man's superior," informed her and Crawford's paternalist organization of Thanford just as it girded her stance against the democratic ideals of the labor unions she attacked in her fiction. She stretched the meaning of *family* to include cooperative servants and of *plantation* to signify "a farm without its loneliness." Thanford's co-owner, Colonel Tucker, offering a blend of Confederate rank and paternal discipline, seemed the ideal overseer, for "it is he who works the hardest," according to visitor Madame Blanc. Blanc gave Thanford's black sharecropping children parting advice befitting Thanet's ideal of the adoring plantation family: "*Soyez reconnaissans à vos maîtres qui font tant pour-vous. Aimez-les. Que Dieu vous benisse!*" ("Be grateful to your masters who do so much for you. Appreciate them. May God bless you!") While Storer students were learning the contradictory merits of altruistic duty and self-interest in the name of racial uplift, Thanet's workers were learning the simpler course of blessing their masters in perpetual gratitude.[67]

Thanet's proposed model of labor organization jibed with Freedmen's Bureau practices. Local agents categorized the freed families as discrete work units, and they encouraged marriage and settlement to stabilize black Arkansans as a mobilized workforce. Thanet and Crawford founded segregated schools, in accordance with bureau philosophy that without schools freedpeople would be "a fearfully disturbing element in your population," but with schools they would become "contented and cheerful and thus promote the material interest of the employer." Similarly, Thanet argued that planters should "be friends with the poor"; participating in the workers' celebrations and mourning rituals would encourage mutual regard and quell any "unconscious inspirer of anarchists!" Quite the opposite of Tourgée's reconstructed plantation under Toinette and Betty Certain, Thanford keened for nostalgia.[68]

Thanet imposed this antebellum fantasy upon her creative enterprises, staging what she wanted to see. In the 1893 "how-to-use-a-camera" book, *An Adventure in Photography*, Thanet and Crawford photographed Thanford's racialized life. Declaring that photographs of those "primitive enough to wear working clothes" would "repay the photographer," Thanet distinguished between her "negro and renter" subjects as she and Crawford trained their camera lens on Thanford's denizens. With the exception of one photograph of male "black citizens" at a boat landing, their black subjects unsmilingly pause from their work in kitchens, laundries, and cotton fields. These studies differ substantively from their better-dressed white sharecroppers, who pose leisurely strolling, hunting, or, in the case of children, game playing or tree climbing. While mentioning a photograph of "negro boys shooting craps near the mill," Thanet quickly adds that the parked wagons "waiting for the Saturday grist explain the boys' right to be there," as if their leisure is unimaginable. While their white workers often request self-portraits, Thanet admits that capturing her black inhabitants in their "appropriate mise en scene" of work is challenging; as such, they form visual analogues to her fiction's portrayals of distanced help. Nevertheless, the photographs succeed at fixing black Arkansans in laboring roles for white surveillance.[69]

Thanet wielded her camera with an eye toward framing the power relations on the plantation. One of her photographs, "The Great Southern Problem," for example, interrupts a young black child at work at Thanford (Fig. 12). Whether intended to be ironic or serious, such captions both reinforce and refute Thanet's paternalistic opinion that "the southern planter is still the natural protector of his tenants, expected to supply all their wants from brandy in sickness to photographs in health." Although Thanet fancied herself to be a handyman as well as a benevolent planter, she could not escape dependency on her workers to sustain this fantasy of self-sufficiency.[70]

Arkansan Consumerism in Circulation: The Value of Portable Property

Despite her plantation fantasy, Thanet showed in her creative work that she heard insolent freedwomen's desires to order their lives rather than just take orders, and she shared freedpeople's recognition that the surest

FIGURE 12. Octave Thanet, "The Great Southern Problem," *An Adventure in Photography* (New York: Charles Scribner's Sons, 1893), 155.

way to claim citizenship was to acquire landed property. Yet, in Arkansas, as elsewhere, the postwar value of real estate and the meaning of property itself was in flux. As neighbor raided neighbor during wartime, many white residents fled the state, leaving their farms open to confiscation and vandalism. County tax assessments suggest staggering losses in personal and material property, with a decline of almost $34 million in the value of all land. Further, postwar vigilantes made dispossession part of their program of terror, adding to the refugee population and the further fall of property values in areas of appreciable Klan activity. As a young yeoman reminds Adèle in *Expiation*, "They says we all is fightin' fur our homes an' property, but looks like when we get done fightin' we wunt have no property leff."[71]

The departure of white Arkansans provided immediate, if temporary, opportunity to the ex-slaves. By 1864 some freedpeople rented farms; some worked at Home Farms, which were farms overseen by the federal army, while the majority labored on over 100 leased plantations confiscated or abandoned by their white owners who feared guerrilla warfare. However, the Freedmen's Bureau had concluded in 1866 that of the 9 million acres comprising the Land of Opportunity, about three-fourths of them were useless for farming. Only 1,000 of the original 26,395 claims for land made under the 1866 Southern Homestead Act were filed by black Arkansans. Only 250 of these entries were completed, because of land disputes, corruption, and fraud. As one freedman complained to General Sanborn, "You set me free but you left me there.... I cannot help myself unless I get some land."[72]

Against freedpeople's claims to the land stood white Arkansan planters and small farmers who sought to keep what remained of their landed property. In upcountry counties like Lawrence, property ownership became the key for poor white people, more than "bloodline or background," to "high social status." Competition was heightened during the 1880s and 1890s as farmers faced a series of crises, including an onslaught of natural disasters and declining production due to the credit system's inequalities. Tenant farming consequently continued to rise; by 1900, 74 percent of black farmers and 35 percent of white farmers were tenants. Expanded understandings of property as an interest favored planters like Fair, who owned the crop the sharecroppers grew, regardless of prior liens on it.[73]

Because of its association with unions, the term "property" held special currency for Thanet. She linked socialist movements with the confiscation of all private property, and so she sought to protect property's value as a basis of American economic and political institutions. Nested within her conservative labor vision was her most progressive gesture in *Expiation*: a reconstruction of property to include freedpeople as potential owners and prosperous consumers. Thanet's solution conformed to a Lockean liberal political tradition. Rather than tinkering with the terms of ownership as did Tourgée, Thanet capitalized on the recently expanded legal meaning of property in goods. Moreover, this was a form of property many freedpeople already understood. As slaves they had laid particular claim to movable, often perishable, property such as crops and livestock, and owning this property would take on even greater importance for them after emancipation.[74]

In the postwar climate of ownership anxiety, portable property drives the plot of *Expiation* and motivates all the characters. As the opening escapade shows, the easy exchangeability of cash made it dangerous and enticing because such portable property could easily fall into the "wrong" hands. Thanet makes clear that the gang's motivation is stealing from citizens whatever "dregs of property war had left them." Fair believes that the graybacks "only shot at me for my clothes or my boots or my horse." In turn, his expiation depends on displaying enough desired goods "to tempt any graybacks." Cornered in the swamp, Barnabas, like Fair, uses portable property to bargain for his life, and a grayback's wearing of stolen goods becomes the rationale for his execution by Colonel Rutherford's vigilantes.[75]

In much of Thanet's work, portable property functions as a source of pleasure and accomplishment for those unable to own land. Thanet foregrounded black and white sharecroppers as new portable property owners experiencing an enhanced status. Thanet thus reclaimed Arkansas as the Land of Opportunity, particularly its southwestern frontier with its down-to-earth "medley of magnificence and shabbiness," by emphasizing it as an ideal setting to stage successful reunion and New South rebuilding. Through the Rutherford family example of transplanted Virginians, Thanet contributed to a southern tradition that sent second sons, denied the benefits of primogeniture, to the west to prosper.[76]

Using the portable property of fabric, dress, and books, Thanet shows that it was this region's ability to meld, compromise, and reinvent that made it an appropriate site for national reconciliation. The Rutherford library's furnishings celebrate these homemade virtues. Its odd mix of the "faded pomp of old Virginia days," these "relics" among the "primitive furniture of a new country," reminded the narrator of "gold-embroidery (a thought tarnished) on a linsey-woolsey gown." To demonstrate the homespun endurance of Arkansan women over the heroines of Dickens,

Trollope, and Thackeray, Thanet uses the portable property of dresses. Adèle pores "helplessly" over imported fashion plates, bemoaning that "we never *can* make a dress like this" as she compares these "strange furbelows" to "Madame Rutherford's one cherished threadbare silk." On the shelves of Fair Rutherford's library are not only Shakespeare, Milton, and Macaulay—all volumes transported when his family moved from Virginia—but also local favorites such as "Youatt on the Horse." This literary combination of genteel culture and hardscrabble common sense typified Thanet's appreciation of the hybridity of Mississippi River culture, making Arkansas particularly well suited for portable property owners.[77]

Arkansans' talent for making "a fashion of our own" registered in the confusing wartime mélange of soldierly garb, and in the novel Thanet acknowledged that Arkansas guerrillas had strategically worn both blue and gray uniforms. Barnabas wears both a "blue Federal blouse" and "two veteran pairs of trousers of Confederate gray." Arkansans' tendency to refashion northern discards continued after the war years. With her New England admiration for thrifty consumption, Thanet noted how "'the job lot' of striped cotton that had failed to impress the Northern fancy" yearly reappeared "blossomed out like a tulip-bed," since cast-off northern goods "sold well and cheap down South." Like the midwestern retail firms that spread south in search of new customers, Thanet capitalized on this market of castoffs refashioned into "startling experiments" to highlight freedpeople as new consumers, integral to the postwar consumer culture that developed in the United States.[78]

This currency of goods took on added value because Thanet was writing fifteen years after the war. By this time, American consumer culture had intensified, and as historian Grace Elizabeth Hale has argued, consumption was beginning to become a "politicized right" for black Americans. In fact, 1880s labor activists routinely used boycotts in order to dodge the ever-tightening noose of judicial prohibition against other forms of labor protest, such as strikes. Nevertheless, equity courts ruled that the expanded meaning of property included the "pecuniary interests" of employers, and they outlawed boycotts through injunction. Meanwhile, individual household shoppers, functioning as "agents in the marketplace," circumvented the limitations of stores by purchasing goods from itinerant peddlers, "rolling stores," and mail-order catalogs. Their investment in portable property goods testifies to the increasingly long reach of the postwar commercial market economy into debt-ridden rural communities. In her writings Thanet dramatized the struggles of black women to buy goods and to identify as entitled consumers rather than as simply docile workers for demanding white employers.[79]

In the small details of status-marked material goods Thanet acknowledged the value of portable property to sharecroppers while genially masking their dependence on it. *Expiation* and Thanet's other stories showcase examples of black and white sharecroppers who, denied land, rejoice in owning plantation store-bought goods as a worthwhile payoff for their labors. Much as the store's trinkets could paper over real poverty and suffering, Thanet's stories smoothed over the injustices of the planter-owned general store, the ruinous credit system, the resulting debt peonage, and the landlords' desired control over workers. This exploitation doomed freedpeople, and on behalf of African Americans Booker T. Washington took pains to explain it to George Cable for use in his political essays. Similarly, W. E. B. Du Bois addressed the mistreatment extensively in *The Souls of Black Folk*, concluding, "America is not another word for Opportunity to *all* her sons."[80]

But Thanet's fiction targeted a different audience than the readers likely to encounter the work of Cable, Washington, or Du Bois. Originally published in the November 1888 issue of *St. Nicholas*, a children's magazine, "The Loaf of Peace" highlights the psychological payoff of portable property. A wretched sharecropper looks around, especially at "the bright tin spoons which shone in the blue glass jug bought by Mizzie's cotton-money, and the lamp filled with real coal oil," and his poverty is transformed; he feels as though he possesses "a truly luxurious and beautiful apartment." In "The Conjured Kitchen" an ex-slave is described as "a woman of property," which gains her much respect, because she has money in her store account and owns "two marble-top bureaus and a sewing machine." This was precisely the kind of misguided consumption that Washington decried. He described visiting sharecropper cabins where the families lacked essential goods but had costly sewing machines, "showy" clocks, and parlor organs: "In most cases the sewing machine was not used, the clocks were so worthless, they did not keep correct time—and if they had, in nine cases out of ten there would have been no one in the family who could have told the time of day." Outraged that the family had "one fork and a sixty dollar organ!," Washington would have scoffed at Thanet's solution of portable property that served to keep African Americans dependent, duped, and in debt.[81]

The gendered nature of Thanet's consumer appeals targeted women as the beneficiaries of portable property. Thanet singled out Arkansas boomtowns such as Hot Springs—the state's third largest city—with its bootstrapping commercial prosperity and cosmopolitan citizenry, for its potential to rival Grady's Atlanta as a New South mecca. Originally published in *Harper's Bazaar* in 1889, "Sist' Chaney's Black Silk" is set in this resort town where development had brought a "kaleidoscope of shifting figures, all tints of skin, all social ranks." The "black silk" refers to a rich dress the invalid Chaney so desires that her sister, in her all-consuming care for her, endeavors to buy for her. Much like the Florida hotel servants and "Africa" residents Woolson encountered, Chaney's demand dramatizes the postwar struggles of many black women to affirm their right to citizenship through the ownership and display of material wealth. Thavolia Glymph has shown that their purchasing power to buy even trinkets formed a "small but not insignificant part of the economic and social transformations of the southern countryside"; moreover, it granted freedwomen, like Chaney, the exercise of what Glymph calls "small rights," which crucially supported the self-determination of freedom.[82]

Chaney's longing reflected that of many Arkansas freedwomen who, refusing to make do with a "threadbare silk" like Mrs. Rutherford, wished to fashion a politicized identity through clothing. Conspicuous consumption was an important part of black Arkansans' energetic and visible involvement in politics, from Union Leagues to religious organizations, with activities ranging from political rallies to signed petitions and voting. Freedwomen used adornment to claim the public space of the streets as they marched in parades such as the one they held in Hot Springs on 4 July 1867. Led by their teacher, young women marched in patriotic dresses of white decorated with blue ribbons—outfits that drew notice—while carrying banners that proclaimed "We Trust in God" and "The Best Government the World Ever Saw." The women then solicited speeches from politicians, including the former governor of Indiana, Oliver P. Morton. As historians Shane White and Graham White have observed, the costumes and self-adornment of parade participants helped fashion "a story of self-assertiveness, of the collective use of the black body for parodic play, for contesting social space, for public expressions of unity and pride."[83]

Nevertheless, other Arkansans still saw the parade participants as property. "Pondering on this singular celebration," one bystander, visiting to partake of the healing springs, described the skin tones of their complexions as consumer goods, ranging in color "from a new saddle to a pair of boots." This witness, a self-declared "cripple," sets himself, like Woolson's Phil Romer, in disadvantaged counterpoint to the freedwomen's celebratory mobility. Offsetting his handicap is his thinking that retains the ideological residue of a slaveholding mentality. This conceptual framework permits easy comparisons of goods to freedpeople, arranged along an axis of ownership. Indeed, slaves had been the premier movable property, valued by antebellum businessmen precisely because of their portability and because traders paid for them in cash. Within postwar Arkansas parlance people remained interchangeable with portable property. Some scholars have argued that the resultant mobility, what Carole Boyce Davies has called "migratory subjectivity," translated into opportunities for African American women to develop their identities and consciousness. Regardless, Thadious Davis has observed, the "ideological and juridical residue of persons as property" inherited from slavery persists to our present century, manifesting itself in a variety of issues involving ownership and bodily rights.[84]

Thanet's short stories help perpetuate the notion of persons as property. In "Ma Bowlin'," Mrs. Brand's ex-slaves are characterized as "a decrepit old pair thrown in as 'boot' to a horse trade." Yet Brand is "much respected" because of this "vanished ownership," and she still speaks of her former slaves possessively, "as a ruined noble might feel about his patent of nobility." Similarly, her story "The Mortgage on Jeffy" (1887) dramatizes a sharecropper's agreement to mortgage her child. Drawn up to resolve a custody battle, the arrangement pays homage to the feudal tradition of owning an interest in a person as property. When baby Jeffy, or "trick," as Thanet referred to him, was abandoned under a store counter, Thanet provided a footnote for those not in the know: "Trick in Arkansas speech, means a number of things: a child, an article, a stratagem, a machine; in fact, it is as hard-worked a word as 'thing.'" Thanet made clear that in this region outward attributes signified property relations. Her black characters were identified by the "mellow intonations" of their voices, which were "as much the property of a black throat as the color of its skin." With far different significance, Thanet resembled Tourgée in recognizing that racial identity, known by appearance and community consensus, constituted a form of property; however, she and many other white Arkansans saw that particular property as inalienable.[85]

As much as Thanet's fiction endorsed freedpeople's conspicuous consumption, it also placed them under renewed obligations to whites. Visitors to Hot Springs enthused that the hospitality and entitlement to consume was extended primarily to white tourists, a situation Thanet's fiction endorses. Chaney's sister, the "indefatigably industrious" Dosier, greeted by everyone in Hot Springs with a "degree of respect," represents the idealized, efficient, black worker serving new northern clients as well as southern mistresses. Chaney, who needs her sister's care, competes against these consumers who desire Dosier's services as a bathhouse attendant. In a clever solution, developed from a white southern customer's hint, Chaney finally obtains a black silk dress on the condition that she agrees to succumb to her illness and wear it as her funeral shroud. The story's closing irony reflects Thanet's own ambivalence in staging African Americans as New South consumers.[86]

The fate of Chaney and other outspoken black characters in Thanet's fiction points to her intolerance for freedwomen's bid for political equality and economic agency. Indeed, the visibility of the freedpeople as politicized consumers, rather than producers, often infuriated local white people. In reaction to freedpeople who were showing "a disposition for and aptitude in engaging in political discussions," one Freedmen's Bureau agent advised them to "abstain from attending any political meetings, to refrain from discussing any political questions, to apply themselves to the labor of their crops." Reporting on the reluctance of freedwomen to do fieldwork, one agent complained of an employer enticing his workers to buy "large amounts of goods and useless articles" in lieu of monetary payment, a practice the agent discouraged. African American self-adornment further threatened to erase the markers of segregation and challenged southern beliefs in white supremacy. Just as Tourgée's attempt to reconceptualize property ultimately affirmed the traditional propertied nature of American identity, Thanet's reliance on consumerism as a detour to citizenship turned out to be an alternative couched *within* the traditional system of land-ownership.[87]

Both in her fiction and at Thanford, Thanet ensured that the gateway and repository for all portable property remained in the hands of the planter through the plantation store, "the centre of everything on a plantation." Thanet valued the store because it allowed her to help her employees while maintaining mastery. Since Crawford's father had prospered through providing "general plantation supplies," she and Crawford brought a good deal of business acumen to their Thanford store. The crucial point of a plantation store, of course, was the gross differential in power between the indebted patrons and the plantation owner. Many historians have documented the undermining effects of the stores: merchants urged farmers to abandon subsistence farming to grow cotton, a change which necessitated heavy food purchasing on credit and subjected them to routine overcharging. Others have taken a more salutary view of the stores, akin to Thanet's, as providing freedpeople with a sense of identity as consumers who now had purchasing choices.[88]

Whether enabling or crippling to the assertions of ex-slaves for their civil rights, the plantation store remained a central arena for freedpeople to test where, in Grace Hale's words, "segregation remained vulnerable." Unlike the increasingly off-limits polling places and courthouses, stores allowed black laborers to resist racial exclusion, since the white storekeepers' desire for the dollar often overcame their allegiance to white superiority. Thanet nodded to the corruption of the "much-abused truck system," or loan of credit by the plantation store, yet amazingly, she thought all the potential for abuse was on the side of the black sharecroppers, whose perceived character flaws and immorality the prim New Englander then greatly expanded upon.[89]

The store at Thanford provided inspiration for Thanet's writing. Rebecca Sewell reported: "It is said that Miss French had a secret cubbyhole in the commissary [of the store] where she could overhear conversations without being seen. This might account for her exceptionally skillful handling of all the shades of dialect used in this part of the South." Like the window display of Frowenfeld's pharmacy, the store's goods lured integrated, socializing crowds, and it became a focal point for the sharecroppers' pursuit of immediate material gratification, as well as for community, justice, and controlled contact with the larger world. Thanet approved the planter's omnipotence "to direct all undertakings of pleasure or profit," including "postmaster, justice of the peace, free doctor, and matrimonial adviser." Like her segregated schools, Thanet's fictional plantation stores ultimately redrew class and racial lines around the value of portable property. Sister Chaney must die for a dress, but Fair Rutherford prospers; he salvages his reputation by cleverly manipulating his appearance with the portable property of accessories.[90]

Keeping Up Appearances: Performing "Redemption"

By reconstellating the meanings of duty, reputation, labor, and property around a question of performance, Thanet put forth a vision of a reconstructed South that differed substantially from that of other Reconstruction writers. What began as a sideshow for George Cable became mainstream reality for Octave Thanet, who exposed the fallen standards of Reconstruction as the real plantation fiction. She celebrates the appearance of authority, and her novel endorses the merits of acting over sincerity, with dark consequences: *Expiation* provides dramatic rationale to justify the performance of vigilante violence against freedpeople.

Thanet established the performance of duty—both in the posse and at the plow—to be the catalyst for Fair's expiation. As Fair's disgrace reflects the South's defeat, so Adèle sees his call to duty as key to its "Redemption": "You think there isn't any more happiness left in life for you; ... But if there isn't, there's *duty*." Adèle makes clear this obligation involves not only men but all patriots of their country, to which "everyone, man or woman, owes something." It was a motto whose spirited appeal might have been inculcated into Storer College students. While Thanet, like Tourgée, valorized reputation as a form of property, she goes much further than he did in his pseudonymic romp through the press.[91]

Fair's story teaches that the restoration of a planter's duty and honor is unlikely and, indeed, irrelevant: Arkansan ownership of portable property began to substitute for land-ownership as acting began to substitute for sincerity. When Fair was young and confessed his cowardice to his father, the Colonel "caught the boy to his breast . . . as he said, 'Boy, remember it ain't how you f-feel, it's what you do-o that counts.' "*Expiation* demonstrates, as Stephen Crane would later show through Henry Fleming, that white men could achieve the appearance of honor by an almost mechanical performance of duty, an option unavailable to white women and former slaves. In privileging acted appearance over core conviction, Thanet reconstructs identity as something akin to a disguise. Adèle relies on Fair's humiliation as a spur, and the vigor of her "sermon" provokes a "long pause," after which Fair replies, "I don't suppose you have such things as clothes left in the store." For white planters, the road to "Redemption" begins with using portable property to stage a convincing performance of authority.[92]

The appearance of Fair's reconstruction as an Arkansas farmer begins with a change of clothes and speech. Reminiscent of how victors systematically stripped the battlefield dead, Dick Barnabas and his gang ransack Fair's portmanteau and strip him of his "right smart" clothes. During his period of repentance, Fair is seen "skulking about the plantation with his toes out of his boots, patches on his knees, and a battered old hat so large that he must needs tie it under his chin." Reared "delicately and luxuriously," Fair initially feels he is wearing a "convict's suit," though he soon learns to play his homespun part. A. B. Frost's illustration, "Fairfax Rutherford, Esq.," shows a thoroughly rusticated and impoverished Fair, blurring the differences between assumed status and feigned appearance (Fig. 13). In order to fit in, Fair next begins "learning the dialect of the local yeomen with tremendous zeal." Thanet thus extends the force of Cable's ventriloquist argument by providing props.[93]

FIGURE 13.
A. B. Frost, "Fairfax Rutherford, Esq.," in Octave Thanet, *Expiation* (New York: Charles Scribner's Sons, 1890), 136.

With the portable property of ragged clothes, Fair is well equipped to "redeem" the last gendered ideal of Reconstruction in a performance of labor. Indeed, his menial labors were not unusual for defeated Confederates returning to ruined homes and forfeited livelihoods. Modeled after his midwestern compatriots, Fair must convincingly appear as an earnest worker to his neighbors and family, a move hardly innocent of racialized repercussions; his disguise literalizes the Confederate appeal to yeomen that they were really of one ilk. Thanet makes central to Fair's expiation his cheerful, token willingness to do a black servant's work as "he should try in every humble way to be useful." *Expiation*'s narrator admits that there "was nothing glorious in tuning the piano, or mending chairs, or painting the ceiling of Mrs. Rutherford's sitting-room, or riding about the plantation to report the condition of fences." The real glory lay in its rehearsal of courage; the commitment to such "trivial tasks" required "more resolution . . . than has carried many a man into battle." Fair's work pays off, making Montaigne look "marvelously prosperous." Moreover, the ex-slaves are eased out by Fair's endearing performance of "domestic ingenuities." Once an important source of diversionary humor as well as labor, they are replaced by the versatile Fair: "Being a capital mimic, he could tell a story in a way to captivate his father; while his "handy ways about a house" redeemed him with his stepmother.[94]

Fair's experience proves that appearing as an authentic Arkansas planter does not require a long-standing tie to the land, only a show of masculinity acted in requisite costume. Thanks to his "polished manners, and his clothes and the very fashion of his talk," the redeemed Fair appears "in a new *role*." He asks Adèle, "Have I shown myself enough of a man to have the right to tell you how I love you?" His performance of masculinity has indeed qualified him to establish a heterosexual relationship with Adèle. His bravery all artifice, Fair remains to Adèle "a pretty soldier," resembling his mother, "that painted lady." He confesses that despite his vigilante bravura in joining his father's posse, his performance of duty is just a performance, and a poor one at that. He finally must admit to Adèle that "I am afraid of you." He soon concedes, "Well, you know how it is. I didn't perform any prodigies. I didn't bring Dick Barnabas to bay—the mule threw him. I hadn't the resolution to shoot him." The admission of his cowardice, however, compels Adèle to proclaim, "You are the bravest man in the world to me!" Accepting Fair's innate poverty of conviction becomes a condition of their marriage. By the novel's close, Fair still lacks "even those primitive, basic virtues on which manhood depends, which knit society together—courage and fidelity"; nevertheless, the novel's happy ending proves what counts: the reputation of a planter is itself a form of property.[95]

Thanet delineated well Fair's skill in the dramatic arts because she practiced them herself. At Thanford, she kept her own store of portable property on hand for home theatricals of her stories in an attic cabinet "filled with all manner of games and a closet containing costumes of sundry kinds." She scripted parts and provided local sketches in semiweekly "Clover Bend Poke Root" newsletters she sent to her family. In providing satirical news of the weather, plantation doings, and local "gossip," Thanet reinvented herself with multiple gendered roles as "Sister A. French, the evangelist" and "Bro. O. Thanet," who, among other skits, "preached the discourse" over a dead snake. As a full-time writer who relied on the plantation routine for inspiration, Thanet became a maestro at turning Arkansas itself into a script.[96]

In her writings Thanet portrayed white Arkansas labor as a regional performance given seasonally for tourists. In an *Atlantic Monthly* article, Thanet tried to present Arkansas residents as homey, hardworking folks who "let the sun shine in on poverty!" She saw few of the southern belles Mary Clemmer Ames had encountered in Harpers Ferry and even fewer of the exotic loafers Woolson had observed in Florida. By giving readers a glimpse of the off-season, less-rehearsed side of Arkansans, Thanet made clear that this view of them depended on the time of year a traveler visited the state. Unlike Florida's tropical winter attractions, the grim winter landscape of Arkansas leaves travelers with a view of wearied laziness and disorder: "Occasionally a woman, who has not had the time to brush her hair, calls shrilly to some child who is trying to have pneumonia by sitting on the ground. No one seems to have anything to do, yet everyone looks tired, and the passenger in the Pullman wonders how people live in such a hole." Comments like these helped fuel negative reactions, first articulated by federal soldiers, to the native white population as poor, indolent, and ignorant, which helped strengthen and disseminate "Arkansas traveler" stereotypes. By summer, Thanet declared, the wasted landscape becomes a garden in which "the negro's song will float through the open car window. Then the stranger will awake to the charm of the South." Because she lived in that "hole" for half a year, Thanet grasped the part-time performance of labor at its most unfashionable. In nurturing a fragile tourist trade and by implication closer North-South ties, Thanet positioned Arkansas sharecroppers to reveal unwittingly that appearance, in close accord with the seasonal landscape, was everything.[97]

Meanwhile, Arkansas, like much of the South, was suffering a labor shortage. Seeking to establish a free-labor system, the Freedmen's Bureau was involved in the resettlement of the black laboring population across the South. Within Arkansas, as early as 1865 the state legislature had established an Immigrant Aid Society, followed by a Bureau of Immigration in 1868 which unsuccessfully sought small yeoman farmers and northern capital. Some white planters, angered by black laborers' efforts to leave, tried to thwart their departure. Others hatched a variety of schemes, such as the recruitment of black workers from North Carolina to Texas, which lasted well into the 1880s. Railroad companies encouraged settlement, targeting farmers, including European immigrants, in Iowa, Nebraska, and Kansas to spur crop diversification. Such developments made Thanet fear that "we will become a syndicate, or a corporation, or a trust," easing out the plantation family. She anguished over a modernized, profit-driven New South, where tenant farmers would "expect to make money as well as a livelihood," and railway stations would replace the plantation store as a "magnet" for "loungers." Fair's very visible working presence at Montaigne was Thanet's corrective to the reality of increasing absentee landlordism in Arkansas during the 1870s and 1880s, as out-of-state corporate interests snatched up land.[98]

The Darker Consequences of Disguise: Selling Arkansas American Gothic to Veterans, Vigilantes, and Rough Riders

Thanet's strategic use of performance and disguise was no mere fictitious ploy. Performance, ignominiously literalized by Booth's deadly theatrics at Ford's Theatre, had become a constitutive force in American politics after 1865. It was utilized by both black and white Americans, from reformers such as Booker T. Washington, whose masterful self-fashioning of public personae made him the nation's "first black media celebrity," to ex-Confederate politicians such as Ben Tillman, who waged white supremacist campaigns using a variety of guises. Costumes and props reasserted white male Democratic dominance and helped construct and protect a more resilient white male southern identity based on popular performance. Through attacks of "almost scripted posturing," acted on the "domestic stage" of the home, night riders followed what historian Hannah Rosen has described as a highly gendered performance of violence enacted to "resignify race and to undermine African American citizenship."[99]

Thanet's endorsement of performance and portable property for white planters underwrote the deadliest roles white southerners performed. Whereas Woolson's treatment of performed identity resulted primarily in Felipa's self-destructiveness, Thanet's treatment took a far greater toll. In a key scene, *Expiation*'s recovered parson curiously remarks: "Madness is in their hearts while they live, and after that they go to the dead." Muttered "under his breath," the parson's cryptic comment is sparked after he looks out the hall window and sees a slave burial gang, "the black men with spades" waiting for the mortally wounded Lige to die. The parson's somber tone raises an intriguing question: does his comment apply to the soon-to-be extinct grayback or the soon-to-be ex-slave whose freedom would help bury the Old South as the otherwise benign parson knew it?[100]

The parson's troubled reflection can be read as a fearful pretext for justifying white violence against black Arkansans. In its resolute pursuit of the dispossessed turned criminal, the plot of *Expiation* complemented the country's dangerous forgiving of the inevitable mistakes made under lynch law, which in Arkansas resulted in 244 lynchings of African Americans from 1882 to 1927. *Expiation* justifies the same methods of vigilante violence used against graybacks that were also being used on African Americans. Thanet dismissed black Arkansans' real terror of white Arkansans, revealing how out of touch her coddled vision of the plantation South actually was. As she celebrates the white planter's ability to close ranks, Thanet offers a stark vision of the New South, however inflected with midwestern labor and New England disciplined thrift, that justified terrorism against freedpeople as a necessary means of reexerting authority.[101]

Moments of tense speculation and confrontation between whites and the potentially dangerous nonwhites gave rise to the novel's patterned counterpointing of freedpeople's assertiveness and white southern resistance. In fact, some black Arkansans had joined in the postwar free-for-all of violence as some ex-slaves roamed the state in paramilitary bands formed to counter Klan and Regulator violence. Aided by Governor Clayton's call for martial law and militia groups, the black men's drills and patrols provoked fear and rage among white people. Thanet's visitor, Madame Blanc, considering the labor shortage, noted that "the trees of Clover Bend could have told tales of recent hangings." In describing the warmth of the plantation store's fire, Blanc wrote without irony that "a negro never feels sufficiently roasted." She mentioned itinerant laborers quick to "draw their knives in order to obtain more than the price agreed upon" with the planters and commented that such unruly behavior, reminiscent of a union strike, warranted the proprietor's "reply to the stab with the revolver," for "under such conditions it is well to have been a soldier before engaging in agriculture." Blanc's writings reveal how easily the rationale for vigilante violence was accepted in Arkansas, and Thanet's writing endorsed the status quo.[102]

Given the similarity in tactics and strategies among the Regulators, militia groups, lingering Federals, and guerrillas, the interchangeability of a Rutherford with a Barnabas becomes condoned. The Colonel and his vigilante band feel righteous in their resort to violence. Even the parson rationalizes their tactics by quoting the Bible: "'Ride on . . . and thy right arm shall teach thee terrible things.' Terrible, verily, sir, but we must not forget they are merciful, also, since they have delivered this poor country from the spoiler." Many Arkansans felt that even bandits had to uphold a code of honor. Historian Bertram Wyatt-Brown has argued that extralegal violence, as a replacement for dueling, became a favored postwar means to restore honor.[103]

Thanet understood the long-standing prevalence of extralegal organizations as a tool to maintain slavery and inaugurate freedom; nevertheless, she refrains from showing the active involvement of black Arkansans in them. Although a paroled soldier in *Expiation* predicts that "the niggers will fight for their own necks," Thanet does not stage their participation in the uprising against the graybacks. Instead, they smilingly hover in a bit of background caricature, like Big Jim, "a gigantic negro, armed with an ax," who, when two graybacks voluntarily surrender, "showed his teeth from ear to ear" as did "all the black faces behind him." Focusing on the activities of white vigilante groups, Thanet recognized that theatrical performance was crucial to legitimizing violence.[104]

Unlike Tourgée's ancestral houses, which creaked with the ghosts of agitated servants, Thanet's homes groaned under the weight of well-intentioned planters who could double as desperado Klansmen devoted to the gory business of expiation. Although Fair cannot kill Barnabas, the narrator praises his vigilante action: none of Fair's "fearless" ancestors "ever did a braver act or one better becoming a good citizen, than he then; choosing the worst torture to a man of sensibility, the torture of inflicting pain before the risk of calamity to the commonwealth." The suffering of the graybacks is supplanted by Thanet's focus on Fair's anguish and the greater rationale that violence was essential for the country's restoration to peace and order.[105]

"Redemption" depended on privileged members of the Arkansan planter class who garnered power from fear. In nearby Fulton County, the construction of a freedpeople's schoolhouse was deliberately slowed because the chief contractor was actually a "private in the State Guard," a paramilitary organization. In Lawrence and many other counties, Freedmen's Bureau agents despaired of conditions where gruesome violence was perpetrated by "the leading citizens," while "murders [*sic*] and assassins sit upon the juries," rendering civil law "a farce," with law enforcement "a base slander upon justice." Agents often blamed extralegal violence on the political interests of ex-slaves, yet the freedpeople remained undeterred. Thanet, while acknowledging that the state had become "a refuge for human failures of all kinds," tended to discount "outrages" as "irregular, not the customary thing." She maintained that they were usually caused by outlaws from other states and that vigilante violence was an understandable "fury of impatience" in a state too impoverished to carry out justice through the proper channels. Yet Thanet's visitor Madame Blanc saw the "profession" of vigilante violence as a commonplace career, spanning generations. A frequent visitor, the "extremely kind-hearted" white local magistrate of Lawrence County, routinely hunts "bandits of every sort" with a "zeal equal to that of the former regulators." The Arkansas Regulators were, in fact, "a terrorist organization" dedicated to persecuting any white people who helped black Arkansans in any way. Against Blanc's protest of lynch law as "barbarism," he cagily "smiles without committing himself." This peculiar admixture of kindness and brutality effectively established awe, uncertainty, and obedience in Blanc, as it likely would in Thanet's readers.[106]

Thanet, well aware of the nighttime transformation of respectable Arkansans into bloodthirsty posse leaders, actually helped rationalize this behavior through her writings. The titular character of her 1887 short story "Whitsun Harp, Regulator," was based on a "well-meaning" man who felt God's "calling" for him to "compel people to behave well." The vigilante's ghost was said to haunt Thanford's dining room. With its plot driven by the "grim traditions" of endless revenge, the story demonstrates how Arkansans expect any issues involving "notions of manly honor" to be solved by gun or a lynching. When this preacher-turned-regulator dies, it is not clear which victim of his retribution was the culprit. In defending the truth of her characters' barbarous actions, she confessed to William Dean Howells that "I know these people. (I have often dined with Whitsun's real murderer . . . and they do not yet . . . think murder is a sin)." Thanet faithfully mapped Whitsun and other Arkansans' penchant for deadly doubling onto her characters as a pretense for them to swap roles, making the use of disguise, such as Fair's, both warranted and handy.[107]

Thanet's situating of vigilante violence at the postwar core of a rejuvenated white masculinity was *bien reçu*. Critics and readers applauded *Expiation* for its toughened heartiness, despite the obvious superficiality of Fair's bravery. The *Athenaeum*'s reviewer was so taken with the "vigorous description, devoted chiefly to horrible cruelties," that he attributed authorship to a man, concluding, "His story may be recommended to those who think that bloodshed keeps fiction pure." The *Dial* concurred, commenting that the novel was "strong and virile enough to warrant the use of a masculine *nom de guerre*." Comments such as these furthered acceptance of a female writer's success on the otherwise male terrain of action stories and labor union relations. Appearing in serialized and book forms, the novel's publication profitably coincided with peak membership in the Grand Army of the Republic and the advent of a "new veteran-oriented war literature," to which Thanet's work contributed. One fan wrote from a Minnesota Soldier's Home, "I will read it with a particular interest myself first and then read it aloud to some of the 'boys.' We all like war stories and I like your stories especially well."[108]

Thanet's realism was valued by journalists like Mary Reid for propagating a needed "virility" within American literature that suited the country's expansionist moment. Reid appreciated that Thanet could, according to one cited male critic, "comprehend and interpret the underside of masculinity," anticipating the white Rough Rider imperialism of the decade. Indeed, admirer Theodore Roosevelt publicly endorsed Thanet's antimollycoddling novels as well as her labor theories. He effused: "I have felt that your stories were tracts . . . I have tried to inculcate the same doctrines in speeches made to labor men, farmers, and other citizens." Although Thanet's labor solutions may have seemed nostalgic, her novel was considered firmly realist in its prescient representation of masculinity. In a friendship that spanned sixteen years until Roosevelt's death, Thanet reciprocated many of Roosevelt's enthusiasms, including his zeal for imperialism.[109]

No small part of Thanet's success with *Expiation* was her ability to weave melodrama, romance, and action around the ideals of Lost Cause patriotism. With this novel in particular, written twenty years after the Reconstruction Debates, Thanet was particularly adept at tapping into these debates to revitalize their relevancy. In keeping with the national mood of reconciliation, Thanet sympathetically dramatized the damaged morale of returning Confederates. Her rehabilitation of the cowardly Fair resembled the contemporary tactics of Lost Cause adherents as they grappled with a period of difficult change. Resonant with the rituals of the Lost Cause, *Expiation* mourns past heroism while inspiring future generations with a viable code of chivalry. Through her novel's portrayals, Thanet joined scores of southern white women dedicated to the rehabilitation of southern white men as they shaped historical memory. Thanet participated in a broader southern postwar movement through which she assumed a Lost Cause cultural authority for reconstructing white manhood.[110]

At a time when Americans began to reassess their own part in a Reconstruction that some felt had gone too far, Thanet's novel made the question of expiation finally applicable to the entire country. According to her Reconstruction vision, participation in organized violence became the nation's atonement for the excesses of the Civil War; sectional reconciliation was founded upon a shared wink at southern terrorism. Appealing to white veterans everywhere, her work highlighted a "redemption" based upon a presumed prerogative to violence. This prerogative must be maintained, she suggested, even if founded upon the exposed bankruptcy of chivalric ideals. Her fiction suggested the terms by which a newly remasculinized South could be welcomed back into the nation as it prepared for war with Spain.

Crafting gendered strategies drawn from a consumerist North, a plantation South, and a pioneering Midwest as the principal tools of Reconstruction, Thanet offers the most regionally complex proposals for revisioning this postwar Arkansan military district. Her work exemplifies the racialized consequences for southern regionalism as it pieced together a New South performance from the fallen props that William Gilmore Simms invoked in his sectional appeal for a national literature. In her steadfast focus on economics as a cipher with which to understand and resolve the troubling period's problems, Thanet shared more common ground with both Washington and Du Bois than many other Reconstruction writers, though she could not have held more divergent political views. Thanet's conservative capitalist solutions provide exemplary support for W. E. B. Du Bois's contention that Reconstruction is best understood as fundamentally a struggle between labor and capital, framed by white supremacist ideology. However, her triangulated regional resolution to sectional differences was, like Cable's Reconstruction vision, based upon the exclusion of black Arkansans as producers. Adroitly disguised by portable property, the elitist, southern planter could be made over into the hardworking, midwestern harvester.

Thanet paradoxically offered one of the most imaginatively gendered Reconstruction visions for empowering black women. Although other writers also contrived to topple the plantation household through its subordinated members, it was a maverick Thanet who further suggested using portable property as a consumer tool to empower the dispossessed. Anticipating a consumerist strategy by some sixty years, she showcased the value of acquiring and displaying this property especially by freedwomen keen on entering the political arena, through the pageantry of emancipation celebrations or of protests. Defiantly recast as demanding consumers of portable property, Thanet's black female characters were too successful to be relegated again to the roles of docile laborers. However, Thanet's emphasis on the acquisition of portable property by former slaves as a means of achieving the rights of citizenship often conflates them with their merchandise, thus reinforcing the persistent social and legal associations of property with personhood, as articulated, however contortedly, in slave law.

Thanet recognized African American women's pivotal importance to the postwar rebuilding of the South economically, politically, and culturally. Her novel demonstrates how they could bring about a planter's downfall by engaging in varied verbal acts of subversion. Thanet's portrayal of outspoken black female servants who intimidate the household speaks to a broader tradition of literary production by African American women that showcases black women as influential voices of witness and protest. Her black servants stand alongside the more developed, heroic "Aunt" characters in the fiction of the closing decade of the nineteenth century. The ability of Thanet's characters to speak out and talk back placed them in an advantageous position to become agents of Reconstruction within their communities, so much so that the politically conservative Thanet checked their advances in her fiction and on her plantation.

Thanet offered an ultimately regressive vision for the new citizens of the postwar nation because she constantly co-opted the reformist impulses within her work. This innovative thinker harnessed her formidable talents as a writer and plantation co-owner to steer a very conservative course for women, although she certainly did not follow it. Within *Expiation* nearly all her strategies for extending both freed and white women's agency ironically reaffirmed antebellum gender and racial conventions. Thanet, like her boldest heroines, ultimately upheld the traditional authority of the white male elite to which black consumers and workers were subordinate in a market economy.

Thanet emphasized the importance of appearance over substance in refashioning white supremacist agendas. In its demonstration of the uses of disguise, props, and dialect, *Expiation* teaches the merit of acting over realizing Reconstruction's ideals of labor, duty, and reputation to postwar planters. With this portable property, a way is set out for white planters to reclaim land and authority over their former slaves. Perhaps more than any other Reconstruction writer here considered, Thanet's ambivalence made her fiction the most cross-purposed. With writing situated on the cusp of the country's turn away from black civil rights, Thanet remains the most nostalgic and conservative among Reconstruction writers even as her work gains momentum in its eager embrace of a New South future.

Conclusion

THE STRANGE CAREER OF RECONSTRUCTION WRITING

You may pass force bills, but they will not avail. You may surrender your own liberties to Federal Election law—but, never, sir, will a single state of this Union, north or south, be delivered again to the control of an ignorant and inferior race.
—Henry Grady, "The Race Problem of the South"

The reconstruction Mr. Grady wants is a crime against society.
—George Washington Cable, "The Progress of the Negro Race"

On 12 December 1889, in his "Race Problem of the South" speech, *Atlanta Constitution* editor Henry Grady asserted that the power of the "white people of the South" to prevent the "tremendous menace" of black voting helped southern Democrats resume political control and shaped the region's future. White American southerners, he told a Boston audience, could solve their political and social problems without a renewed federal intervention. The answer lay in a New South program that included crop diversification, the protective tariff, industrialization, and reconciliation, with black southerners in inferior positions. Grady's wildly popular speech was immortalized by his sudden death soon afterward, and it helped pave the way for the January 1891 legislative death of Henry Cabot Lodge's proposal to require the federal supervision of elections. The defeat of the Lodge Federal Elections Bill—which opponents derisively called the "Force Bill"—marked the end of national efforts to protect black voting and ushered in the era of Jim Crow.[1]

How could such an unapologetic assertion of white supremacy follow so quickly after the popular appeal of Reconstruction writing for African American citizenship? Why was that argument so well received in Boston by an audience that included former president Grover Cleveland, industrialist Andrew Carnegie, two governors, and several congressmen? What influence, however advantageous or detrimental, did Reconstruction writers wield in building this New South? The extensive treatment Grady accorded to southern African Americans in the last month of his life—his famous "Race Problem" speech and a six-part series in the *New York Ledger* entitled "The New South"—most compellingly answers these questions. Grady's rhetorical tactics help pinpoint where and how the renegotiation of citizenship became lost ground for the freedpeople.[2]

Grady's final work helps explain the outcome of literary Reconstruction and reaffirms its enduring, if contradictory, cultural contribution. Despite the firebrand promise of much Reconstruction work, the reactionary currents that lurked beneath the tensions of these writings surfaced to help carry the smug conservatism of Grady's New South into being. Since its debut in 1862, the concept of a "New South" has proven to be as ambiguous and malleable as the concept of "the South" itself, prompting much scholarly debate. Indeed, Grady himself famously insisted that "the New South is simply the Old South under New Conditions." Eventually, the term "New South" came to signify a racialized, classed set of expectations extending well beyond a specific military district.[3]

Grady's speech was a flowering of the "Redemptive" buds that had lain dormant in Reconstruction narratives. Indeed, more than any other figure of the New South, Grady remains the most useful for understanding the fate of these Reconstructive visions, especially once occupation ended. By the time he came to Boston, Grady was nationally celebrated as the "Spokesman of the New South" because of another famous speech that he had delivered three years earlier to the distinguished New England Society in New York City (Fig. 14). Well trained in the art of oratory, Grady was the obvious heir to William Gilmore Simms in establishing a leading southern presence in the country's political and cultural affairs. Grady demonstrated how a stance and an image could persuade a receptive audience of the merits of his vision of citizenship. While deploring Grady's sentiments, Cable saw the dangers posed by Grady's persuasive delivery before the New England Society. In response Cable closed a speech before the Hartford Sumner League with a seven-stanza poem parodying Grady's posturing:

You've probably heard of one, Grady
A speech to New Englanders made he,
They thought it delightful . . .
He was eloquent, alas, was Grady;
Patriotic! And bright as a lady.
But on MEN'S EQUAL RIGHTS
The darkest of nights
Compared with him wouldn't seem shady . . .[4]

A NEW ENGLAND SOCIETY DINNER AT DELMONICO'S

FIGURE 14. "A New England Society Dinner at Delmonico's," *Frank Leslie's Illustrated Newspaper*, 5 January 1878, cover.

Living in Military District Three, Grady had witnessed much of the drama of Reconstruction. Ambitious like Clifford, Grady had his own newspaper by the time he was twenty-two. Like Tourgée, Grady, née O'Grady, relied upon humorous aliases to further his political agenda, which included civic reform. Like Cable, he turned to northern editors for work as the *New York Herald*'s Georgia correspondent when three of his own newspapers failed. He was in Florida in 1876, touring along the St. Johns and writing about the Seminoles, at the same time as Woolson. Like Thanet,

Grady was concerned with the plight of "the planting class," whom he saw enslaved to cotton and struggling under the crop-lien system; in his advocacy of crop diversity and subsistence farming, Grady resembled that native Iowan who had looked to apply a midwestern labor ethic and agricultural model to Arkansas. His New South, based in up-and-coming Atlanta, better satisfied Thanet's demand for a reinvigorated region located on a more westerly axis than had Simms's Charleston-flavored ideal. Grady practiced the very essence of Thanet's ideal Reconstruction when he pitched portable property in the form of discounted merchandise to attract new subscribers to the *Atlanta Constitution*. Under the seemingly neutral umbrella of his genial New South boosterism, Grady, however, was an ardent southern Democrat. His praise for his home's peculiarly "loyal and gentle quality of its citizenship" differed markedly from what many Reconstruction writers witnessed and decried.[5]

The rhetorical tug-of-war over the meaning of citizenship in Reconstruction narratives and the responses they provoked help illuminate the drift toward Jim Crow segregation. Relying on the same terms Reconstruction writers used—property, labor, reputation, and duty—Grady shared their thematic and rhetorical ground but erected a noticeably different ideal of citizenship. In their revisioning of the South and its people, Reconstruction narratives were alternatives that were *not* entirely forgotten, as Grady's speech reveals. Indeed, what makes them memorable is the broad, egalitarian American polity they imagined while reaffirming the caste hierarchies of the antebellum status quo.

Reconstruction Writing: A Legacy of Challenge

Grady had been dead barely a year by the time Thanet's *Expiation* appeared in 1890, but the goal of regional self-determination he had promoted—set by Reconstruction writers themselves—persisted. Their celebration of the American South as a cultural and literary entity would endure. By imagining a more diverse American citizenry, such writers as Tourgée, Woolson, and Cable helped reconstruct prevailing myths of national identity, thereby helping to reorient American literary priorities beyond the borders of their military districts. They showed that the postwar meaning of citizenship was more than just a debate about the political rights and obligations of citizens. It was a drama over property, a concept that had been central to the definition of citizenship since the country's founding. The form of this dramatic struggle was shaped in part by the writers' locations and their experiences under military occupation. Whether a passing tourist on a river cruise, like Woolson, or a long-term planter in a cotton field, like Thanet, these writers saw firsthand the militarized struggle to reconstruct the region.

Even after federal troops had departed, Reconstruction writers continued to show the dynamics of military districting and occupation in their work. Their narratives ventured scenarios of the possible that became increasingly improbable. Indeed, the very confusion that districting wrought in remapping geographic borders and changing civil authority helped set the precedent for imagining real Reconstructive change. Seizing creative opportunity from political chaos, Reconstruction writers attempted to imagine a broader American citizenry while reincorporating the South into the Union. Just as much as Tourgée's "C" letters for the *Greensboro North State* and any Storer College *Record* column, Reconstruction fiction informed and inspired readers as they spoke for the ex-slave turned citizen as well as the ex-state turned district.

At the same time, postwar writers had to make a living in the competitive literary marketplace. Their writings, therefore, should be read in the context of the district pressures and editorial demands they negotiated. For every venturesome portrayal of a freedwoman there was a counterportrayal of a defiant "Southron." For every ex-slave's act of assertion, there was an ex-master's imagined punishment. The malleability of the past is evident in the writers' struggles to craft a dominant history informed by the postwar drift of readers' tastes, editorial imperatives, and the increasing commercialization of the publishing industry.

Furthermore, these narratives can be situated within the dialectic of oppression and activism that characterizes the broader trajectory of African American women's intellectual history. The literary productions of Reconstruction writers fill a gap in this tradition, about which analyses typically jump from the antebellum years to the 1890s. From Coralie Franklin's first "Woman's Column" to the epistolary declarations of independence by Tourgée's heroine, Toinette, this writing reflects the multifaceted nature of black protofeminist thought and commitment to political reform during this era. Such characterization is in accord with the remarkable multiplicity of activist interests and roles many African American women played long before they became prominent in the "club movement." Frances Harper, for example, had accrued a long history of literary activism that took varied forms, from her membership in the Underground Railroad to her abolitionist writing to her Reconstruction lecturing throughout the South. Reconstruction writers shrewdly deployed black women's occupational abundance in the production, content, and dissemination of their writing, touching on themes from suffrage to interracial cooperation to education that continued to reverberate in African American women's thinking.[6]

Reconstruction writers' literary legacy inspired the next generation of African American literary activists, such as Octavia Victoria Rogers Albert, Lucy Delaney, Pauline Hopkins, Anna Julia Cooper, and Ida B. Wells. In their fight against segregation, disfranchisement, and racial violence, these women continued the mandate of Reconstruction writers to realize citizenship for all Americans, helping to earn this period's characterization as "The Woman's Era." These literary activists often borrowed themes Reconstruction writers had used as they necessarily looked to the past to fashion their future as progressive citizens. They inherited the issues with which Reconstruction writers had grappled, including the persistence of white ancestral authority, whose legitimacy they continued to question and even render defunct. This was a plot development some Reconstruction writers had been unable to sustain or even entertain. They continued Reconstruction writers' challenge to plantation fiction, but often in more confrontational ways. Many writers of this period used historical romances to explore the importance of interracial unions to citizenship and national reconciliation, a plot device Albion Tourgée employed, but they often reached different conclusions. Charles Chesnutt and Pauline Hopkins, for example, sought to anchor progressive ideology in notions of racial indeterminacy, but the historical consciousness of their work increasingly led to ambivalent and disillusioned endings regarding passing and interracial marriage. In combination with African American activism, black women's fictional work particularly helped challenge the subordination of Jim Crow, using both new and adapted strategies from earlier Reconstruction writers.[7]

The changed political context of the 1890s, however, forced African American women writers to create successful, inspiring narrators who draw on more self-reliant means of establishing credibility with readers than those the Reconstruction writers had devised. Reflecting the post-Reconstruction period, many writers moved from capitalizing on regional differences to emphasizing a greater community-nurtured ideal of New Negro modernity. In different ways, they linked racial uplift with the achievement of bourgeois domesticity—a strategy earlier deployed by Coralie Franklin in her "Woman's Column." In broadening the range of her "voice from the South," Anna Julia Cooper, for example, increasingly embraced a transnational perspective to challenge the intertwined nature of gender and racial oppression. She applied the discourse of bourgeois domesticity in new ways, eventually by literally situating Frelinghuysen, a college for the working poor of Washington, D.C., in her home.[8]

Across the publishing spectrum, African American print culture flourished in the years after 1880, a phenomenon envisioned by activist Reconstruction writers. This flowering was due in part to significant changes in the publishing industry, such as the 1891 passage of the International Copyright Act, the postwar blossoming of African American print culture, the expanded role of African American women journalists, and the dramatic expansion of the magazine industry. Strengthened by the 1876 creation of the American Library Association, Reconstruction's legacy of education and literacy also played a role.[9]

By 1900 African American college graduates had formed new literary communities and strengthened preexisting activist societies of readers, writers, editors, and publishers. Print culture, however, was not only the province of the black elite. Aided by new developments in printing technology at the turn of the century, publishing became a profitable and efficient business in which skilled black workers participated. At the heart of the outpouring of printed material were African American professional women like Coralie Franklin. They earned political authority and mobilized their communities by founding venues for education, such as libraries, schools, reading rooms, and literary societies, to disseminate what they called "race literature." The movement gained momentum not only from a reaction to mounting contemporary crises but also from the efforts made by their Reconstruction predecessors in word and deed.[10]

Although their best-selling writings may have been largely forgotten, the radical vision of many Reconstruction writers left strong ideological impressions on those with whom they had forged personal and professional ties, particularly Booker T. Washington and W. E. B. Du Bois, the giants of civil rights activism. Many of the intellectual seeds for black advancement, planted in Reconstruction writing, sprouted in the work of these leaders. These strategies range from materialist solutions based on black economic gain that appeared in Woolson's and Thanet's writing to appeals for forceful political activism articulated by Tourgée and Cable. The writings of Storer College students from the 1880s straddle what would soon become the antagonistic positions of Washington and Du Bois. Situated in a southern town where they confronted racism daily, Storer students crafted a Washingtonian strategy that relied on low-profile activism, dissemblance, and a concerted public relations effort to keep local whites appeased in order to survive. The next generation of Storer students, inspired by the Du Boisian ideal of an educational elite of black leaders for the twentieth century, increasingly emulated his refined example.

While Reconstruction writing combined elements of Washington's reliance on economic gain and Du Bois's demand for political activism to empower blacks, the conflicted vision of much Reconstruction writing was also registered in the ideological differences between the men. Tourgée's death on 21 May 1905 elicited eulogies for their "friend of freedom" by well-known Du Bois supporters William Monroe Trotter, Ida B. Wells, and Charles Chesnutt. It also helped spark a new departure toward achieving political and social advancement: these literary activists gathered again a few weeks later to launch the Niagara Movement, challenging the powerful cultural hegemony of the Tuskegee Machine to speak for all African Americans and marking their break with Washington. The members of the Niagara Movement opened their second meeting on the campus of Storer College on August 15, 1906. Invited by John Clifford, they came to Washington's boyhood home state to overthrow what they perceived as the Wizard's capitulation to white supremacy. Eager to set aside the Washingtonian gradualist program for advancement they saw at Storer and elsewhere, a program that had been advocated to some degree by Thanet and Woolson, they endorsed the Du Boisian resolution calling for quality education, universal justice, jobs for all workers, and enforcement of the Fourteenth Amendment to counter disfranchisement. Initially banning women from their meetings, the Niagara Movement relied on a gendered strategy that upheld conventional roles for men and women to play in the work of racial uplift, echoing Clifford's masculinist vision for racial advancement. In his closing address at Storer, Du Bois picked up the torch held by Cable, Tourgée, and Clifford. His declaration captures the spirited commitment of Reconstruction writers: "The battle we wage for ourselves is not for ourselves alone but for all true Americans. It is a fight for ideals, lest this, our common fatherland, false to its founding, become in truth the land of the thief and the home of the Slave."[11]

The Status of Property, Labor, Duty, and Reputation: Rhetoric as Tactic in the Gilded Age

As Reconstruction narratives demonstrate, the changing meaning of property became crucial for all sides in the struggle over a reconceived idea of citizenship. During this era the connection of property ownership to citizenship was reaffirmed. After the war's end a number of cases forced treatise writers to revise the physicalist and absolutist elements of

Blackstone's theory of property. By the early twentieth century, property was defined more nebulously as "a set of legal relations among persons." As Kenneth Vandevelde has demonstrated, this "explosion" of the concept of property actually "threatened to render the term absolutely meaningless" as a category of law.[12]

Reconstruction writers exploited the expanding legal meaning of property to the fullest degree to empower the new citizens. In addition to creating black characters who were prosperous landowners, they envisioned ex-slaves as productive owners of unconventional forms of property. Tourgée and Thanet explored freedpeople's beneficial acquisition of the emergent property of reputation and of portable property, respectively. For African American women readers, Franklin endorsed the worthy reputation homemaking and child-rearing afforded, thereby authorizing an activist place for African American women in the tradition of "Republican Motherhood." Clifford was fiercely committed to furthering the reputation of black men, particularly veterans, as enterprising and responsible citizens entitled to own any property they wanted. The writers' assertions and character portrayals helped undermine the claims of white southern men to authority in both private and public arenas.

Commercial arenas also experienced changes in the meaning of property during this era. Reconstruction narratives were shaped by the market demands of print culture, especially as shown in magazines, the medium on which Reconstruction writers heavily depended for a livelihood. As advertising became a professionalized industry during the late 1880s and 1890s, courts increasingly protected advertising symbols as a form of limited property. The value of language, therefore, could be protected and measured as an absolute property right on a legal continuum from symbols to trademarks. Tourgée's creative deployment of "brands" and "trademarks" for his characters thus had a relevant commercialized connotation. Recognizing the creation of other types of nonphysical property, such as business goodwill and investments protected under the new "comparative value" rule of accession, Cable and Clifford emphasized the worth of African American investment in local enterprise. Woolson likewise dramatized successful African American professionals and artists, whose valuable services enriched the community.[13]

The legal ferment over property, however, also reconfirmed its traditional forms in land and the privileged status of the property owner. The restoration of plantations and voting rights to white landowners was an early postwar demonstration of the importance of land-ownership to citizenship. Central to that affirmation was the ongoing significance of the property in slaves. The legal practice of many southern states classified slaves as real estate, not personal property. Despite emancipation, this psychological association—with its social and cultural ramifications—persisted. The repercussions of a system that classified persons as a form of property were impossible for Reconstruction writers to transcend, however emboldened they made their black characters as owners of new property. The multifarious twists and surprise endings of their plots show that these writers could not avoid returning to the conservative idea of property ownership in land as a criterion for citizenship. Land-ownership, of course, was usually privileged only for white Americans. Despite much authorial ingenuity, Reconstruction narratives edge toward "Redemptive" endings by offering postwar portraits of African Americans enslaved by the crop-lien system, segregation, and disfranchisement.[14]

Grady's arguments paradoxically turned Reconstruction writing inside out as he pursued their conservative inclinations. His preoccupation with property ownership, however, was directed toward helping dispossessed Confederates regain lost property. Arguing that freedpeople continued the wartime destruction of white southern property after the war, Grady described Liberty County, Georgia's former "ruling center of wealth and intellect," as being dominated by corrupt freedpeople, whose pagan "rites and orgies" were "paralyzing the industry of the county." The plantation home of distinguished Georgia governor Lyman Hall, a signer of the Declaration of Independence, was "now occupied by an illiterate negro," which for Grady constituted a further desecration of the county's heritage. War and occupation demonstrated all too well the alienability of property and the fragility of patrimony.[15]

Postwar changes in the meaning of property dovetailed with changes in the understanding of free labor. During the 1880s the courts were insuring that "freedom to contract," or a worker's freedom to sell his labor, was a constitutional right, while the labor movement argued that a worker forced to sell his labor fell victim to wage slavery, which contradicted his status as a citizen. Judges invoked the freedom to contract, a central tenet of antebellum republican and antislavery ideology, to defeat the labor legislation they saw as paternalistic and coercive. The emergent legal doctrine helped redefine the productive property of workers as merely their *right* to labor. Gilded Age courts increasingly expanded the definition of property to mean anything that had "pecuniary" or "exchangeable value," and they applied this idea to a person's business or labor with devastating effect for labor reformers. Judges reasoned that "because boycotts and strikes injured employers' profit-making activities, and therefore their 'pecuniary interests,' they trenched on employers' 'property.'" They could therefore be declared illegal. Some equity courts abused this reasoning to uphold injunctions against labor, stifling nearly all forms of labor protest. Witnesses to the protracted battle over the application of property to the legal relations of workers and capitalists, some Reconstruction writers, like Octave Thanet, supported the capitalists, whereas others, like Albion Tourgée, sided with the labor movement. Yet whatever their political leaning, all advocated the new citizens to be productive owners of something beyond just a right to work.[16]

In the rural South, contextual factors, such as the political clout and cohesiveness of the local black community, outside investment, federal presence, and the crop grown, influenced the degree to which southern black workers were able to renegotiate the meaning of labor. Within the cotton- and tobacco-producing states, such as Georgia and Virginia, sharecropping appeared to be a useful compromise between ex-masters and ex-slaves. It allowed agricultural workers more autonomy than in centrally controlled wage-gang labor used in Louisiana sugar production, although gang labor survived to some political and economic advantage. Yet this transitional system of labor quickly evolved into something far different. Enforced by the odious credit system of the plantation store as well as by vagrancy and apprenticeship laws, sharecropping was little less unjust than slavery.[17]

In this legal climate some Reconstruction writers tried to renegotiate the meaning of work. They grasped that the sudden experience of freedom had been defined less as something to *feel* and more as something to *do*, namely, work so as to acquire property and consume goods. But the triumph of the doctrine of "liberty of contract" to validate the practices of wage slavery undermined their efforts and forced them to turn to the creative application of property's new meanings. Woolson, Tourgée, and Cable initially focused on expanding black workers' choices and terms of labor, but they soon deployed the more ingenious forms of new property and put them at the disposal of African American characters. Storer College students attempted to transform their alma mater's glorification of *labor omnia vincit* to mean less manual labor due others and more intellectual exertion due oneself. In an attempt to restructure the meaning of work, Woolson recognized the right of all Americans to leisure. However, after the 1877 railroad strikes that set a precedent for the violent labor agitation of the 1880s and 1890s, any emphasis on empowering the exploited worker would be eclipsed. Thanet, a relative latecomer, favored protecting the owner—of a plantation or a factory—rather than the worker. Many

Reconstruction writers ended their stories by returning African American characters to lives of subordination, diminished economic opportunity, and political invisibility. Addressing the prospects for black southern workers, Henry Grady's speeches straddled rhetorically between the hope and despair of Reconstruction narratives. He advocated occupying black southerners with menial labor while white southerners assumed entrepreneurial and proprietary roles that northern investors could finance. With unintended irony, he described the New South's goal for the laboring ex-slave: "We seek to pin him to the soil with ownership, that he may catch in the fire of his own hearthstone that sense of responsibility the shiftless can never know."[18]

Reconstruction writers sought to explore the responsibilities of duty as black and white southerners contested the question of who would be the agents of its performance. The term often held a politically gendered valence: female characters felt obligations that served patriarchal interests, whereas male characters' fulfillment of duty was self-serving or to patriotic causes greater than themselves. Tourgée's heroine Toinette felt a duty to care for her former master, while Thanet's female protagonist Adèle felt a duty to help restore the former master's authority. Woolson and Cable conceived of duty as more self-interested than Tourgée's altruistic idealization. Woolson's characters feel obliged to find happiness and to professionally advance, whereas most of Cable's characters are compelled to engage in moral self-scrutiny as a first step toward reconstructing their lives and communities. Storer students transformed their college's paternalistic admonition to perform duty for others into an appeal for self-help; Clifford issued a gendered call for black men to demand their civil rights, while Coralie Franklin urged women to pursue interracial cooperation and self-improvement to remain visible agents in the twinned causes of racial uplift and women's advancement. African Americans' political activism constituted a challenge to Henry Grady and others who, seeing New South building as their racial and gendered duty, sought to retain autonomy and an authoritative public voice on very different grounds within postwar regional communities.

Many Reconstruction writers revolved the meaning of reputation around understandings of citizenship. Regional differences in assessing the value of reputation were gradually settled legally. The conflict in trying to reconcile northern definitions of reputation as property with southern understandings of reputation as honor was resolved by shifting emphases in defamation law. This conflict was most dramatized in Tourgée's work by the tormented relationship of Toinette to her former master. The couple's union is made possible only by exacting concessions from both characters. In his revision of *Toinette*, Tourgée again pits regional definitions of reputation against each other, but these two characters remain unreconciled and alienated from the family estate, resulting in little more than a hollow triumph for both. Employing the bitter irony that would later inform his *Plessy* defense, Tourgée vividly showed the value of the reputation of a white skin while exposing how arbitrary, socially constructed, and alienable that form of property was.

Indicative of a democratic yet capitalist society, American law increasingly relied more on considerations of reputation as property than as honor, and Reconstruction writing reflected that revision. Through his main characters, Cable demonstrated the consequences of acting out of an outmoded sense of reputation as honor, and he argued for the reconstruction of reputation in accord with a revised set of terms for regional and familial reconciliation. In helping to reconstruct the reputation of a wartorn region into a tourist paradise, Woolson adopted the notion of reputation as property, an asset her black Floridian characters use to further their artisanal and professional standing. Coralie Franklin saw reputation as a tool for black women to gain authority in the politics of respectability, whereas Clifford saw it more as a weapon to wield against his political enemies. Thanet exposed the southern definition of reputation as honor to be nothing more than empty rhetoric, but she nevertheless found this ideal useful when she dramatized the benefits of assuming a disguised identity for defeated planters: her novel's hero, although sorely lacking conviction, simply acts chivalrously enough to reclaim authority. An understanding of reputation as performance was gained firsthand by many Reconstruction writers as their own literary reputations were bandied about by the local press. Tourgée, Clifford, and Cable, in particular, became adept at manipulating their celebrity to weather the vicissitudes of publicity.

Grady's manipulation of reputation was crucial to his engagement with the developing push to rehabilitate the sullied honor of the defeated Confederate veteran. He maneuvered the meaning of reputation to renegotiate citizenship not for ex-slaves but for ex-Confederates. In his *New York Ledger* articles, Grady waxes sentimental over the fact that "the sign of nobility for generations to come will be the grey cap or the stained coat, on which, in the ebb of losing battle, God laid the sword of His imperishable knighthood." Through nostalgic connections between the speaker and his audience, Grady demonstrated that the repair of reputation was at the root of creating social memory. He remade the postwar meaning of the good citizen using images of the dutiful son, the loyal soldier, and the patriotic community leader. Defeat had become, by 1890, a New South asset.[19]

As the nation looked with nostalgia on the Civil War while poising itself to embark on another conflict, conceptions of duty and reputation intertwined profitably with ideals of citizenship and patriotism in the print culture of the 1880s and 1890s. Grady drew upon renewed war interest to transcend sectional animosity while capitalizing on the growing sense of American exceptionalism and expansionist interests. The same infatuation with the Civil War that sold Tourgée's novels and grounded Clifford's appeal to manhood also underwrote Grady's bids for white supremacy. Whereas Reconstruction writers had used a gendered, patriotic rhetoric to remind readers that the black veteran's contribution to the late war made him worthy of citizenship, Grady ensured that the act of remembering the defeated Confederate was inseparably tied to that of forgetting the black veteran, an act not of incidental omission but of willful choice.

The Resurrected and Reconstructed Origins of the New South

In their attempts to imagine a regional recovery in ways that would attract the broadest readership, many Reconstruction writers unwittingly helped fuel Lost Cause nostalgia. Both reviews and fan letters show that the popularity of the plantation fiction in their work sometimes eclipsed their constructions of the war and its aftermath. Inspired by their critical success, New South writers like Grady reanimated the Confederate past with gusto to supplant the postwar activism of African Americans. Grady implicated northerners in the Lost Cause on the basis of a shared racial and gendered "heritage": throughout his "Race Problem" speech, Grady addressed his audience as his "brothers in blood, in destiny," partly because of their ongoing complicity in discriminating against black Americans. Although Grady demanded political noninterference from northerners on the "race problem," he made clear that their sustained economic involvement was key to reconstructing regional identity. Echoing some of the tensions found in Reconstruction writing, Grady's speech typified what historian David Blight has characterized as "the dialectic between race and reunion" that made white Americans, nostalgic for the Civil War's battlefield heroism, forget the ideological causes of the conflict.[20]

The era's threat and promise were the warp and woof of historical representation unfolding in Reconstruction narratives. Grady wove together disparate threads to make a similar dramatic fabric. His repair of sectional antagonism through an appeal to race and gender commonality was not so far from the parting vision of Cable's *The Grandissimes*, in which white Honoré triumphed over his exiled black Creole brother. When Grady extolled property reclamation, he was echoing Tourgée's valorizations of property ownership. Grady's paternalistic appeals to duty share the same racialist assumptions that informed the rhetoric in Storer College publications. His renegotiation of work into more attitude than action recalls Woolson, while his stage performances as a New Southerner anticipate Thanet's reconstruction of humbled planters. In their compromises with the marketplace, Reconstruction writers were just as complicit as the Confederate veterans Grady commended in demoting genuine social change. Through the crafting of historical romance, Reconstruction writing contributed in part to the misrepresentation of the period.

At the same time, their writing helped usher into being the possibility for genuine Reconstruction. Near the end of *Black Reconstruction*, W. E. B. Du Bois asserts: "For those seven mystic years between Johnson's 'swing 'round the circle' and the panic of 1873, a majority of thinking Americans in the North believed in the equal manhood of black folk. They acted accordingly with a clear-cut decisiveness and thorough logic, utterly incomprehensible to a day like ours which does not share this human faith; and to Southern whites this period can only be explained by deliberate vengeance and hate." While the exuberance of many Reconstruction writers for equal rights may have been conveniently forgotten and their readers may have lost their faith, the impact of much Reconstruction writing, in all its contradictions, endures. Therein lies the importance of understanding the complex visions offered by these writers who produced a literature founded equally on witness and dream.[21]

Beyond Reconstruction:
The Fates of Five Writers and Districts

By the close of the century, the results of disfranchisement and segregation had occurred in all the former military districts of the South, but it was a regressive process of varying degree and kind, dependent on changing demographics, economics, and political culture. The post-Reconstruction life of each district writer helps illuminate the dark subtleties and larger shadows patterned within these regional variations of "Redemption."

By the time Grady delivered his last speech, Woolson was living in Italy and had just completed her third novel, *Jupiter Lights* (1889). She would remain an expatriate until her apparent suicide in Venice in 1894. Although Woolson continued to write novels set in the South, her stories were relocated to Italian settings. She was increasingly alienated from the American scenes of the New South. Yet, if she had remained in Florida, political and economic developments within the state would have challenged her vision of Reconstruction and rendered her Minorcans as outmoded models of assimilation for black Floridians. Her image of Florida as a utopian, leisured wilderness was edged out by a boom in tourism and commercial and industrial development. Although a Democratic governor took office in 1877, black Floridians, like African American organizers elsewhere across the South, tried to preserve voting and office holding through the Independent Party, the Knights of Labor, and the Colored Farmers' National Alliance. But beset by the need to address the plight of black voters without alienating white support, the Independent Party was defeated in 1884 by Bourbon Democrats who controlled the election machinery. Thereafter, black Floridians' coalition building led to the development of the Ocala Demands in 1890, a national program of economic and political reform intended to benefit farmers and workers. From organized boycotts to armed self-defense, black Floridians resisted violence, disfranchisement, and segregation up to the defeat of the Florida movement in the 1920 election. However, the Independent Revolt from the Democrats would prove to be the last major effort to incorporate black political involvement until the New Deal.[22]

Woolson's vision had become obsolete by 1890, and Tourgée's had become redundant. With the exception of his well-received novel focused on egalitarian justice, *Murvale Eastman: Christian Socialist* (1890), he retreated into trite plots and stereotypical characters in novels that did not sell well. Tourgée fared better with his influential "A Bystander's Notes," which ran from 1888 to 1898. Written for the *Chicago Daily Inter Ocean*, the weekly column promulgated his ideas for black civil rights. At the same time, North Carolina's black Republican legislators struggled with mixed success to stave off disfranchisement and to press for reforms, culminating in the spectacular 1894 success of the Fusionists. Their reformist three-year tenure in office produced, in one historian's words, "nothing short of a political revolution." The North Carolina Democrats desperately sought to destroy this Populist-Republican coalition and disfranchise African Americans. Beginning with the terrorist Red Shirts and ending with the violent overthrow of Wilmington's Republican municipal government, they restored white supremacists to power in 1898.[23]

When Tourgée tackled Jim Crow segregation in his brief for Homer Plessy, he still favored federal intervention, however unlikely it seemed. Tourgée's argument that Homer Plessy had been deprived of the property of his reputation as a white-skinned person without due process anticipated elements of critical race theory by 100 years. Although the majority in *Plessy* ruled that social mores could not be established by law, the enduring impact of Tourgée's fiction in popular literature and in his later legal thinking suggests that fiction could help establish and change those mores.

Tourgée's emphasis on legal and journalistic remedies to "Redemption" was shared by John Clifford, who continued to battle discrimination and segregation in the courtroom and in the *Pioneer Press* until its shutdown in 1917. Clifford's sister-in-law, Coralie Franklin, remained a dedicated literary activist for women's empowerment, civil rights, and education in the Progressive movement. She interwove all three interests in her "Votes for Mothers" appeal, arguing that disfranchisement on any basis "cripples the individual . . . handicaps progress . . . [and] sets a limitation upon mental and spiritual development for all humanity." Whereas her reputation prospered by her reform work, Clifford's reputation continued to be compromised, culminating in his role in a sordid family brawl, which received sensationalized press coverage.[24] One of their legacies is the demonstration of reputation's vicissitudes. In 2002 the Harpers Ferry National Historical Park launched a five-year changing exhibit to honor graduates of Storer College, including Clifford and Franklin. In 2009 the U.S. Postal Service issued a commemorative stamp in recognition of "trailblazer" Clifford's contributions to civil rights.[25]

West Virginia offered greater political and economic opportunity than elsewhere in the South. From 1890 to 1900, thousands of black southern Americans emigrated there in pursuit of work in southern coalfields and railroad construction throughout the Mountain State. West Virginia was never a major slaveholding area and thus lacked a substantial black population, but as elsewhere black residents found many of their rights abridged under segregation and disfranchisement and suffered racial violence that ranged from verbal harassment to lynching. The easternmost town of the state, Harpers Ferry, had been in economic decline since the 1869 sale of the closed armory and rifle factory, and it fell victim to floods and false prospecting rumors. The town had remained inhospitable to African Americans; some seventy-five years later, Storer's first black president saw the degree of local white hostility against Storer College when a cross was burned on his lawn.[26]

After local furor had erupted over his "Freedman's Case" and "Silent South" essays, Cable relocated his family from New Orleans to Northampton, Massachusetts, in 1886. Exhausted from battling the defaming onslaught of the southern press and the rejection of his New Orleans neighbors, Cable concluded that only another federal intervention could remedy the South's regression. He instead focused on less contentious endeavors such as fostering the quiet, moral self-improvement goals behind his Home Culture and Garden Clubs. Apart from collecting his stories in *Strange True Stories of Louisiana* (1889), Cable remained committed to novels like *Bonaventure* (1888), which shifted in focus to the Acadians as a more self-contained and less controversial community than the Creoles.

The city Cable left was still rife with the corruption, factionalism, and poverty which were manifested in dilapidated, unsanitary, and economically stagnant conditions. Black New Orleanians, comprising one-fourth of the population, were intimidated and hampered in their voting rights, but they remained important as a swing vote until they were disfranchised through education and property qualifications in 1898. Crucial to the state's return to one-party rule was the reorganization of the terrorist White Leagues into the Louisiana National Guard, which became a mobilized, highly efficient force capable of crushing discontent anywhere in the state. It is no accident that Louisiana's federally enforced state governments were followed by "one of the longest periods of unbroken one-party dominance in American history" from 1877 to 1972.[27]

While Cable, Tourgée, Woolson, and the student editors of Storer College had moved on to other interests by the 1890s, Thanet continued wintering at Thanford, inspired to write about the laboring conditions around her. Her own black workforce, which she summarized as "amiable," left her "mildly encouraged" for the future of African Americans. Thanet's Arkansan New South embodied the agrarian backbone of Grady's vision. Apart from Little Rock's development in manufacturing, the overwhelming majority of the state remained agricultural, which turned out to be an asset for the growth of the Agricultural Wheel. Arkansas spawned the Union Labor Party, a biracial coalition that almost won the 1888 election.[28]

Planter Democrats turned to racism, fraud, and intimidation to squelch the Agricultural Wheel and break off all prior alliances with African Americans. In January 1891, one year after Thanet's *Expiation* appeared, southern Democrats passed the state's first Jim Crow segregation law, which was soon followed by disfranchisement provisions to eliminate the black vote and thus ensure the return of white Democrats to office. Once the most racially tolerant and progressive state of the former Confederacy, Arkansas, despite protest registered by a conservative black middle class, would become one of the most backward during the Gilded Age.

Although there were some exceptional years and efforts, Arkansas Democrats impoverished the state by supporting fiscally lean policies that kept the state rural and underdeveloped. Arkansan farmers stayed tethered to the waning fortunes of cotton in a single-crop economy of expanding farm tenantry, dooming the state to "a legacy of poverty." Black Arkansans were effectively immobilized from mounting Reconstruction agendas for the next fifty years.[29]

From Simms to Grady:
The Reconstruction Road Less Traveled

Reconstruction narratives measure the cultural distance traversed between the time William Gilmore Simms first articulated his vision of the Old South and the moment Henry Grady revised that vision into the New South. Both men were urbane, citified easterners who looked to the west and to the plantation past for the future. They appreciated the power of the word in a politically precarious moment. For all their similarities, however, they understood the Reconstruction of the South differently. The Old South had contracted to poignant memory for the ailing and besieged Simms. His 1866 *War Poetry of the South* proposed to celebrate a literary Confederacy of sorts, a collection of narrative remnants culled from what might have been. His firm conviction that "to be *national* in literature, one must needs be *sectional*" nevertheless lived on in Reconstruction writing and continued to preoccupy southern writers for a century after his death in 1870. Southern writers inherited Simms's struggle to craft a nationalist story on a southern stage that could reconcile many contradictions, including those of slave-based aristocracy and democracy, agrarianism and the prospects of industry, tradition and dramatic change.[30]

For Grady, the Old South signified an empire of renewed possibility. His northern speeches were a gesture unifying one anxious region with another. At the time of his death, Grady was commemorated as a dedicated, laboring figure of reconciliation. His brief life embodied the Reconstruction ideals of work, reputation, duty, and property. In a two-page color lithograph, *Judge* magazine offered a posthumous tribute to Grady, the laborer for reunion who receives a laurel wreath of honor from Columbia. Prominently displayed in the background, adjacent to the affectionate allegorical figures of North and South, is a quotation from Grady's influential "Race Problem in the South" speech that emphasizes the common ground of patriotic loyalty (Fig. 15). Reconstruction and the writing it spawned made all the difference in the outlooks and reception of the two men.

FIGURE 15. "His Great Work Unfinished," January 1890, *Judge* magazine, Henry Grady Papers, Manuscript, Archives, and Rare Book Library, Emory University.

The rhetorical gap between Simms and Grady is a gap between intention and action, between nostalgia and opportunism, that Reconstruction writing undertook to fill. Simms, an ardent defender of slavery, could not or would not make his slaves work, so that his plantation, Woodlands, was never out of debt. Grady could apologize for the mistake of slavery, but he was a proponent of the racist beliefs that rationalized the peculiar institution and would help activate the Democrats' return to power. While the love of Simms for the Old South may have been more heartfelt, it was Grady's performance attesting to its worth that was more convincing. Reconstruction narratives helped rejuvenate Simms's antebellum attachments, while their emphasis on consumerism transformed them into Grady's selling points. At the same time that such narratives gestured toward a new meaning of citizenship for the dispossessed, they helped restore the hierarchical structures girding the Lost Cause. Arising from the ashes of Sherman's March, these stories helped underwrite the spirited work of revival and rebuilding from Simms's Charleston to Grady's Atlanta.[31]

For all their connivance at American conceptions of property, Reconstruction writers demonstrated that thoughts of citizenship were governed by the market. Its valuation of wage labor relations above emancipation made the realization of citizenship dependent upon claims to duty, labor, reputation, and, most important, property ownership. This capitalist investment in property was an interest that northern readers could not surrender, and it is to that readership these Reconstruction narratives ultimately belonged. At once audacious and cautious, the writing of 1865 to 1890 dared all Americans to rethink the excluded subject as familiar fellow citizen, even while discouraging that imaginative leap. Not all could "own up" to the part demanded of them in this textual performance of reconstructed identities. Nevertheless, Reconstruction writers offered models that later writers and activists adopted. Influenced by local agitators for civil rights within their respective districts, they highlighted black citizens, particularly African American women, whose heroic words and deeds kept challenging the injustices of their communities long after the Freedmen's Bureau had departed. It would take the second civil rights movement to make good on the prize of citizenship and their persevering claims.

NOTES

Abbreviations

AMA	American Missionary Association
AWT	Albion Winegar Tourgée
CFC	Coralie Franklin Cook
CFW	Constance Fenimore Woolson
GWC	George Washington Cable
HFB	Harpers Ferry Book
HFD	Harpers Ferry Documents
HFNP	Harpers Ferry National Historical Park, Harpers Ferry, W.Va.
JRC	John Robert Clifford
NYPL	New York Public Library, New York, N.Y.
OT	Octave Thanet
PP	*Pioneer Press*, Martinsburg, W.Va.
RG 105, BRFAL	Records of the U.S. Bureau of Refugees, Freedmen, and Abandoned Lands, National Archives Building, Washington, D.C.
RG 156, OCO	Records of the Office of the Chief of Ordnance, National Archives Building, Washington, D.C.
SCA	Storer College Archives, West Virginia University, Morgantown, W.Va.
SCD	Storer College Documents, Harpers Ferry National Historical Park, Harpers Ferry, W.Va.
SOJ	*Spirit of Jefferson*, Charles Town, W.Va.
VFP	*Virginia Free Press*, Charles Town, W.Va.

Introduction

1. W. E. B. Du Bois, *Black Reconstruction*, 708.

2. Ibid., 131, 708.

3. Aaron, *Unwritten War*, 339.

4. Simms quoted in Guilds, *Simms*, 342; Simms, *War Poetry of the South*, v. For more on Simms, see Mitchell, *Disturbing and Alien Memory*, 13–53; Busick, *Sober Desire*; Nakamura, *Visions of Order*; Guilds, *Long Years of Neglect*; and Guilds and Collins, *William Gilmore Simms and the American Frontier*.

5. Grady, "Race Problem in the South," in *New South*, 101; Simms, *War Poetry of the South*, v; Simms quoted in Guilds, *Simms*, 331.

6. To understand citizenship as a history of gendered obligation, see Kerber, *No Constitutional Right to Be Ladies*.

7. *Congressional Globe*, 39th Cong., 2nd sess., 1037, cited in Sefton, *United States Army and Reconstruction*, 109.

8. Study of the impact of the military dimension of Reconstruction has been neglected, in part because it has been overshadowed by the drama of the Civil War itself. The following historians' studies, however, are important exceptions: Sefton, *United States Army and Reconstruction*; Hogue, *Uncivil War*; and Majeske, "Virginia after Appomattox." On wartime occupation, see Whites and Long, *Occupied Women*; on occupation at the war's end and its immediate aftermath, see Ash, *When the Yankees Came*, and Golay, *Ruined Land*. Recent scholarship has also focused on the Freedmen's Bureau in increasingly nuanced ways; see Cimbala, *Freedmen's Bureau*; Cimbala and Miller, *Freedmen's Bureau and Reconstruction*; Farmer-Kaiser, *Freedwomen and the Freedmen's Bureau*; and Faulkner, *Women's Radical Reconstruction*.

9. C. Vann Woodward, *Strange Career of Jim Crow*, 33; for a more recent example, see Vorenberg, *Final Freedom*. For scholars who have extended Reconstruction into the 1890s based on legal and political efforts to protect black voting rights, see Wang, *Trial of Democracy*, and Goldman, *"Free Ballot and a Fair Count"*; see also Dailey, *Before Jim Crow*, a postemancipation study which ends in 1902.

10. See Waters and Conaway, *Black Women's Intellectual Traditions*; Zackodnik, *Press, Platform, Pulpit*; Foster, *Written by Herself*; and Maffly-Kipp and Lofton, *Women's Work*.

11. Gardner, *Unexpected Places*, 10; statistics in Danky, "Reading, Writing, and Resisting," 342. See also the outstanding work of Foreman, *Activist Sentiments*; McHenry, *Forgotten Readers*; and Vogel, *Black Press*, whose scholarship has helped make this writing and the communities for whom it was written more visible, complicated, and complete. Their pioneering work has helped redefine the subject and scope of African American literature.

12. The controversial work of Houston Baker comes to mind.

13. Elsa Barkley Brown, "Negotiating and Transforming the Public Sphere," 48.

14. Gaines, *Uplifting the Race*, xvii.

15. *Crescent Monthly* (New Orleans), January 1867, 77–78.

16. Christopher Wilson, *Labor of Words*, 74, 63–91. See also Spoo, *Without Copyrights*, 13–64, and Homestead, *American Women Authors and Literary Property*, 239–63. For an overview, see the classic work of Tebbel, *History of Book Publishing*, 17–130, 150–76, and Mott, *History of American Magazines*, 2:4–26, 3:3–62, 4:2–34.

17. Foster, *Written by Herself*, 132–33.

18. Kaplan, "Nation, Region, and Empire," 252; James Cox, "Regionalism," 778; Sundquist, "Realism and Regionalism," 502–3; Pryse, "'Distilling Essences,'" 12.

19. On postwar black activism outside the South, see Hugh Davis, *"We Will Be Satisfied with Nothing Less"*; Schwalm, *Emancipation's Diaspora*; Glass, *Courting Communities*; and Quigley, *Second Founding*. For outstanding examples of New Southern Studies, see the essays in Jones and Monteith, *South to a New Place*, and Smith and Cohn, *Look Away!*, as well as scholarly journals' special issues toward reinventing the field: "Souths: Global and Local," *Southern Quarterly* 42, no. 1 (Fall 2003); "Postcolonial Theory,

the U.S. South, and New World Studies," *Mississippi Quarterly* 56, no. 4 (Fall 2003); "'Southern Literature'/Southern Cultures: Rethinking Southern Literary Studies," *South Central Review* 22, no. 1 (Spring 2005); and "Global Contexts, Local Literatures: The New Southern Studies," *American Literature* 78, no. 4 (December 2006).

20. Testing the new amendment and the Thirteenth Amendment's vision of free labor were the pivotal 1873 *Slaughterhouse Cases*, litigation brought by independent Louisiana butchers that challenged a state-created monopoly as a violation of their rights under the Thirteenth and Fourteenth Amendments. On the *Slaughterhouse Cases*, see Labbé and Lurie, *Slaughterhouse Cases*, and Brandwein, *Reconstructing Reconstruction*, 61–95. On the constitutional significance of Reconstruction, see Kelly, Harbison, and Belz, *American Constitution*, 319–60, and Smith, *Civic Ideals*, 286–409.

21. On philosophers' use of "property," see Becker, *Property Rights—Philosophic Foundations*, 120–22. See also Vandevelde, "New Property of the Nineteenth Century"; Philbrick, "Changing Conceptions of Property in Law"; Reich, "New Property"; Radin, "Property and Personhood"; and Macpherson, "Meaning of Property."

22. Thadious Davis, *Games of Property*, 1–41; Best, *Fugitive's Properties*, 1–25; Penningroth, *Claims of Kinfolk*, 45–111. The Southern Homestead Act, which offered freedpeople the same opportunity to own forty acres and a mule that whites already enjoyed under the Homestead Act of 1862, was a bitter failure. The monopoly of plantations was left intact, and the public land made available was of poor quality. These factors, coupled with the ex-slaves' lack of capital to purchase land and the corruption of the federal land offices, resulted in most of the acreage being claimed by whites, who often acted as agents for railroad and lumber companies. See Oubre, *Forty Acres and a Mule*, whose work remains definitive.

23. Simms, *War Poetry of the South*, vi, v.

24. On reputation, see Post, "Social Foundations of Defamation Law"; Wyatt-Brown, *Shaping of Southern Culture* and *Southern Honor*; Ayers, *Vengeance and Justice*, 9–33; Greenberg, *Honor and Slavery*; Rosen, *Terror in the Heart of Freedom*, 222–41; and Farmer-Kaiser, *Freedwomen and the Freedmen's Bureau*, 88–95.

25. See Steinfeld, *Invention of Free Labor*, especially 147–84; Stanley, *From Bondage to Contract*, 1–97; and Vandervelde, "Labor Vision of the Thirteenth Amendment"; see also H. Richardson, *Death of Reconstruction*, 6–82; Forbath, *Law and the Shaping of the American Labor Movement*, 79–105; and Montgomery, *Citizen Worker*, 52–114.

Chapter 1

1. Recent scholarship has begun to focus on Woolson's southern work increasingly within the politics of Reconstruction. See Diffley, *Witness to Reconstruction*; Crosby, *Florida Facts*.

2. Benedict, *Constance Fenimore Woolson*, xvi; Rayburn Moore, *Constance Fenimore Woolson*, 26.

3. Sears, *Sacred Places*, 4. On nineteenth-century Florida tourism, see Rinhart and Rinhart, *Victorian Florida*, and Rowe, *Idea of Florida*. See also Foster and Foster, *Beechers, Stowes, and Yankee Strangers*, and Mendez, "From Adventure Travel."

4. Silber, *Romance of Reunion*, 78, 77.

5. Bill, *Winter in Florida*, 84; Noll, "Steamboats, Cypress, and Tourism," 22; Youngs, "Sporting Set," 57-67.

6. Rainey, *Creating Picturesque America*, 3-55.

7. Mott, *History of American Magazines*, 2:383-405.

8. Eacker, "Gender in Paradise," 502, 497; on the *Nation*, see Hedrick, *Harriet Beecher Stowe*, 348-49.

9. *Atlantic Monthly*, July 1880, 125; *Scribner's*, August 1880, 634; *Harper's New Monthly*, February 1887, 482.

10. Revels, *Grander in Her Daughters*, 83; Testimony of John W. Recks [n.d.], U.S. Congress, Joint Committee on Reconstruction, *Reports of the Committees*, "Part IV: Florida, Louisiana, Texas," 2:5; Williamson, *Florida Politics in the Gilded Age*, 190, 1-16. On Florida postwar politics, see Shofner, *Nor Is It Over Yet*; Canter Brown, *Ossian Bingley Hart*, 150-237; and Klingman, *Neither Dies Nor Surrenders*, 26-61.

11. Quoted in Solomon and Erhart, "Race and Civil War in South Florida," 336, 337; Coles, "'They Fought Like Devils,'" 41, and see 29-40 for further discussion. There was a nearly even breakdown of 96,057 white and 91,689 black citizens comprising Florida's 1870 population. In 1880, the populations increased to 142,605 and 126,690 respectively, making black Floridians 47.0 percent of the state's total population. "Florida—Race and Hispanic Origin: 1830-1990," in U.S. Bureau of the Census, Historical Census Statistics, Table 24, 42.

12. William Davis, *Civil War and Reconstruction*, 586; Ortiz, *Emancipation Betrayed*, 10; Shofner, *Nor Is It Over Yet*, 225-42; Newton, *Invisible Empire*, 11, 12-30, 183-216. For examples of vigilante violence and the poor response of civil authorities, see J. A. Remley to G. W. Gile, 30 November 1868, and to A. H. Jackson, 31 July 1867, Letters Sent and Received, ser. 617, and D. M. Hammond to A. H. Jackson, 7 October, 1867, Letters Sent, ser. 611, RG 105, BRFAL.

13. On the bureau's attitude toward freedpeople's enthusiastic political involvement, see, for example, [Name unclear] to E. Woodruff, 1 February 1867, and D. M. Hammond to A. H. Jackson, 10 September 1868, Letters Sent, ser. 611; John T. Sprague to O. O. Howard, 1 October 1867, Letters Sent, ser. 582; and S. W. Marlin to A. H. Jackson, 22 October 1868, Unregistered Letters and Narrative Reports Received from Subordinate Officers, ser. 591, RG 105, BRFAL. See also J. Richardson, "Evaluation," 232-34. On black Floridian political leadership, see Canter Brown, *Florida's Black Public Officials*; Klingman, *Josiah Walls*; Weinfeld, "'More Courage than Discretion'"; Darius Young, "Henry S. Harmon"; J. Richardson, *Negro in the Reconstruction of Florida*, 177-98; and for a firsthand account, Wallace, *Carpet Bag Rule*, although heavily edited by Democratic ex-governor William Bloxham. For more on military Reconstruction, see Richardson, *Negro in the Reconstruction of Florida*, 125-76.

14. Circular, Hd. Qtrs. District of Florida, 11 December 1866; see also Circular No. 9, Office of Assistant Commissioner, 15 November 1865, which defines the bureau's role as being "to give proper direction and permanency to a healthy system of labor," RG 105, BRFAL. On forced mobilization of workers, see Special Order No. 15, Office of Assistant Commissioner, 31 January 1866(?), Special Orders and Circulars Issued, ser. 588; see also Thomas Leddy to Thomas Osborn(?), 28 February 1866, Letters Sent, ser. 611, RG 105, BRFAL. For an example of planter cheating and other disputes, see J. A. Remley

to A. H. Jackson, 31 November 1866 and 31 July 1867, Letters Sent and Received, ser. 617, RG 105, BRFAL. See also Richardson, "Freedmen's Bureau and Negro Labor in Florida," and *Negro in the Reconstruction of Florida*, 40-70.

15. CFW, "Ancient City, Part I," 3; Urry, *Consuming Places*, 137-39; Pratt, *Imperial Eyes*, especially 111-227. Reconstruction writer Octave Thanet's "Six Visions of St. Augustine," for example, is an epistolary short story which jocularly demonstrates how gendered, classed, and malleable the construct of touristic vision is.

16. CFW, "Oklawaha," 179, 169, 170.

17. Barbour, *Florida for Tourists*, 225; 175; Solomon and Erhart, "Race and Civil War in South Florida," 320, 320-23. See also Mizrach, "North in the South."

18. CFW, "Oklawaha," 175.

19. CFW, "Ancient City, Part II," 166; Benedict, *Voices out of the Past*, 247; CFW, "Oklawaha," 163.

20. CFW, "South Devil," in *Rodman the Keeper*, 142; CFW, "Ancient City, Part I," 17. Woolson's work on Florida offers rich material for the New Southern Studies as set out by Smith and Cohn, *Look Away!*, 1-19. Her consistently transnational focus anticipates the call for a needed global approach to Florida scholarship, as urged by Cassanello and Murphree, "Epic of Greater Florida."

21. CFW, "Ancient City, Part II," 169; Stowe, *Letters from Florida*, 8.

22. CFW, "Up the Ashley and Cooper," 1; CFW, "Ancient City, Part I," 1; Canter Brown, *Florida's Black Public Officials*, 43-54.

23. Landers, "Gracia Real," and *Black Society in Spanish Florida*, 29-106 ; Rivers, *Slavery in Florida*, 65-84.

24. CFW, "French Broad," 631-32, 635.

25. CFW, "Ancient City, Part II," 169; CFW, "French Broad," 619. Oil magnate and developer Henry M. Flagler erected a swank hotel on the landfill, featuring an architecture which paid tribute to St. Augustine's eclectic heritage; see Waterbury, *Oldest City*, 192-96.

26. CFW, "French Broad," 630, 636, 627, 636.

27. Ibid., 630; Wyatt-Brown, *Shaping of Southern Culture*, 230-54; on Lost Cause commemoration, see Mills and Simpson, *Monuments to the Lost Cause*; Karen Cox, *Dixie's Daughters*, 49-72; and Neff, *Honoring the Civil War Dead*, 142-78.

28. *Florida Union* (Jacksonville), 6 February 1884. See also Williamson, *Florida Politics in the Gilded Age*, 96-143. For a case study, see Kenney, "LaVilla, Florida, 1866-1887." Not coincidentally, the Black Belt counties of Jackson, Madison, and Alachua were also the locations of the worst Klan violence in the state during Reconstruction. Newton, *Invisible Empire*, 16-21.

29. CFW, "Ancient City, Part I," 14; "Inaugural Address of the Hon. D. S. Walker, Governor-Elect, Delivered before the General Assembly of the State of Florida at Tallahassee, 20 December 1865," U.S. Congress, Joint Committee on Reconstruction, *Reports of the Committees*, "Part IV: Florida, Louisiana, Texas," 2:16.

30. CFW, "Ancient City, Part I," 14, and "Ancient City, Part II," 170.

31. CFW, "Ancient City, Part II," 178.

32. J. A. Remley to A. H. Jackson, 1867 Letter Book, p. 77, Letters Sent and Received, ser. 617, Subasst. Comr., RG 105, BRFAL; this definition was supplied by African

American boys when asked "what they understood freedom to mean." Quoted in Testimony of Governor William Marvin, 22 January 1866, *U.S. Congress, Joint Committee on Reconstruction, Reports of the Committees*, "Part IV: Florida, Louisiana, Texas," 2:10.

33. CFW, "Ancient City, Part I," 14; Hardy, *Oranges and Alligators*, 111; Crosby, *Florida Facts*, 1.

34. CFW, "Ancient City, Part I," 14, 13; Ortiz, *Emancipation Betrayed*, 87; Revels, *Grander in Her Daughters*, 92–109.

35. CFW, "Ancient City, Part I," 14, and "Ancient City, Part II," 176–77; CFW, "Black Point," 92.

36. CFW, "Florida Beach," 482–83; CFW, "Ancient City, Part II," 165, and "Ancient City, Part I," 1.

37. CFW, "Ancient City, Part II," 178; CFW, "Oklawaha," 163, 175, 170.

38. CFW, letter to *New York Times* reviewer [B. Phillips], 16 August, n.d., Lee Kohns Collection, Manuscripts and Archives Division, NYPL, Astor, Lenox, and Tilden Foundations.

39. Duncan, "Struggle to Be Temperate," 34. Duncan invoked the term in his work on the imperial literature about nineteenth-century Ceylonese coffee plantations; Ring, "Inventing the Tropical South," 620. On tropicality as a cultural form of environmentalism, see Arnold, *Problem of Nature*, 141–68.

40. CFW, "South Devil," in *Rodman the Keeper*, 139; Miller, *Dark Eden*, 72, 64.

41. CFW, "South Devil," in *Rodman the Keeper*, 154, 174, 177, 174, 175.

42. CFW, "Ancient City, Part I," 17; Rerick, *Memoirs of Florida*, 321.

43. CFW, "South Devil," in *Rodman the Keeper*, 142, 141, 176.

44. CFW, "Sister St. Luke," in *Rodman the Keeper*, 43, 51, 65, 74.

45. CFW, "Miss Elisabetha," in *Rodman the Keeper*, 75, 103, 83, 104; CFW, "South Devil," in *Rodman the Keeper*, 142.

46. Crosby, *Florida Facts*, 85. On Native American and African American interaction, see Rivers, *Slavery in Florida*, 189–209, and Klos, "Blacks and the Seminole Removal Debate, 1821–1835."

47. CFW, "Oklawaha," 168.

48. CFW, "Ancient City, Part I," 11–12.

49. See the letter book of Jacob Remley to A. H. Jackson, 31 October 1866, p. 42, 30 September 1867(?), p. 118, and 1 April 1868, p. 147, Letters Sent, ser. 611, RG 105, BRFAL.

50. Bill, *Winter in Florida*, 229–30; CFW, "Ancient City, Part II," 170; [S. W. Marlin] to A. H. Jackson, 22 October 1868, Unregistered Letters and Narrative Reports Received from Subordinate Officers, ser. 591, RG 105, BRFAL. On the difficulty of obtaining quality land for the freedpeople and their difficulty maintaining homesteads, see D. M. Hammond to A. H. Jackson, 19 February 1868 and 10 September 1868, Letters Sent, ser. 611, and J. A. Remley to A. H. Jackson, 30 January 1868, Letters Sent and Received, ser. 617, RG 105, BRFAL. See also J. Richardson, *Negro in the Reconstruction of Florida*, 71–82.

51. CFW, "Ancient City, Part II," 166–67, 174.

52. Michael Gannon, preface, ix.

53. Rerick, *Memoirs of Florida*, 325. See also Shofner, *Nor Is It Over Yet*, 258–74.

54. CFW, "Ancient City, Part II," 176, and "Ancient City, Part I," 7; CFW, "Oklawaha," 174.

55. CFW, "Ancient City, Part I," 7; CFW, "Voyage to the Unknown River," 616.

56. W. Bryant, *Letters of a Traveller*, 102, 111, 110.

57. CFW, "Dolores," 34; Bryant, *Letters of a Traveller*, 111; Sherry Johnson, "Marriage and Community," 2.

58. CFW, "Ancient City, Part II," 171.

59. CFW, "South Devil," in *Rodman the Keeper*, 141, 165; Landers, *Black Society in Spanish Florida*, 150-53. See also Sherry Johnson, "Marriage and Community," 1-13.

60. CFW, "Black Point," 85; CFW, "Voyage to the Unknown River," 616; CFW, "Ancient City, Part I," 7.

61. CFW, "Miss Elisabetha," in *Rodman the Keeper*, 79, 102, 104.

62. CFW, "Felipa," in *Rodman the Keeper*, 203, 199, 220.

63. Ibid., 210, 207, 197, 202, 204, 210, 199, 216; CFW, "Ancient City, Part II," 172.

64. CFW, "Felipa," in *Rodman the Keeper*, 203, 207, 203.

65. CFW, "Dolores," 34.

66. Ibid.

67. Rerick, *Memoirs of Florida*, 297.

68. CFW, "Ancient City, Part II," 172; J. Richardson, "Evaluation," 234. See also J. A. Remley to A. H. Jackson, 30 June 1868, Letters Sent and Received, ser. 617, RG 105, BRFAL; Rivers and Brown, "'Monument to the Progress of the Race'"; Wakefield, "Teachers of Freedmen"; and Heather Williams, *Self-Taught*, especially 30-95.

69. Trachtenberg, *Incorporation of America*, 79-80. For more on the persistence of unfree labor in informing contractual employment, see Steinfeld, *Invention of Free Labor*, 122-73, and Vandervelde, "Labor Vision of the Thirteenth Amendment."

70. Testimony of Rev. L. M. Hobbs, 28 February 1866, U.S. Congress, Joint Committee on Reconstruction, *Reports of the Committees*, Part IV, "Florida, Louisiana, Texas," 2:9; Stanley, *From Bondage to Contract*, 98-137. On newspaper reportage, see "From Florida," *New York Tribune*, 20 June 1865; "From Florida," *New York Times*, 1 August 1865; and "Negro Question," 27 May 1865; "[Bureau] Circular No. 11," 9 September 1865; "The Freedman as a Laborer," and "Gov. Marvin's Speech to the Freedmen," 30 September 1865; "Negro at the South," 21 October 1865; "What Will Become of Old Pompey?," 9 December 1865, all in *Florida Union* (Jacksonville).

71. Barbour, *Florida for Tourists*, 227, 238. See also Bill, *Winter in Florida*, 228-233; Crosby, *Florida Facts*, 125; and Ortiz, *Emancipation Betrayed*, 9-32.

72. CFW, "Dolores," 33; Stowe, *Letters from Florida*, 11.

73. Arnold, "'Illusory Riches,'" 7.

74. CFW, "Black Point," 84.

75. Vandervelde, "Labor Vision of the Thirteenth Amendment," 460; CFW, "Pine Barrens," 66; Hardy, *Oranges and Alligators*, 106.

76. Bill, *Winter in Florida*, 19; CFW, "Ancient City, Part II," 176; Steinfeld, *Invention of Free Labor*, 173-84.

77. CFW quoted in Rayburn Moore, *Constance Fenimore Woolson*, 27; CFW, "Black Point," 84.

78. Crosby, *Florida Facts*, 4; Landers, *Black Society in Spanish Florida*, 88.

79. Steinfeld, *Invention of Free Labor*, 139.

80. CFW, "Sister St. Luke," in *Rodman the Keeper*, 43, 52, 43, 45.

81. CFW, "Ancient City, Part I," 20, and "Ancient City, Part II," 170; Vandervelde, "Labor Vision of the Thirteenth Amendment," 459-60. On freedwomen's assertion of their rights, see Tera Hunter, *To 'Joy My Freedom*, 21-43; Edwards, *Gendered Strife*, 66-106; Jacqueline Jones, *Labor of Love*, 44-79; and Clinton, "Reconstructing Freedwomen," 306-19.

82. Schwalm, *Hard Fight*, 235; Holt, *Making Freedom Pay*, xviii. For more, see Schwalm, *Hard Fight*, 147-268; Farmer-Kaiser, *Freedwomen and the Freedmen's Bureau*, 64-95; Frankel, *Freedom's Women*, 56-78; O'Donovan, *Becoming Free in the Cotton South*, 162-207; and Saville, *Work of Reconstruction*, 102-41.

83. CFW, "A Voyage to the Unknown River," 616; Glymph, *Out of the House of Bondage*, especially 137-203; Tera Hunter, *To 'Joy My Freedom*, 74-97.

84. CFW, "Sister St. Luke," in *Rodman the Keeper*, 45; Bill, *Winter in Florida*, 90.

85. CFW, "Miss Elisabetha," in *Rodman the Keeper*, 80, 81.

86. Hatch, *Professions in American History*, 11; Kimball, *True "Professional Ideal" in America*, 12. See also Stanley, *From Bondage to Contract*, 60-97; Montgomery, *Citizen Worker*, 115-62; and Collins, "Changing Conceptions," 15-17.

87. Haber, *Quest for Authority*, 360-61, 3-14; JoAnne Brown, *Definition of a Profession*, 18-34.

88. CFW, "Ancient City, Part II," 172.

89. Ibid.

90. Ibid., 166.

91. CFW, "At the Smithy," 290.

92. Fernandina Petition to J. G. Foster, 9 February 1866, Unregistered Letters Received, ser. 587, RG 105, BRFAL.

93. CFW, *Jupiter Lights*, 62-63, 69, 120. For a fuller version of this discussion, see Kennedy-Nolle, "Merits of Transit."

94. Urry, *Consuming Places*, 165; Hale, "'For Colored' and 'For White,'" 162. While Hale dates this shift in consumption to the 1890s with black disfranchisement, Reconstruction writing suggests that this transformation began in the late 1870s with the formation of a black middle class.

95. Hardy, *Oranges and Alligators*, 102-3; Shofner, *Nor Is It Over Yet*, 236-37, 238-39.

96. Hardy, *Oranges and Alligators*, 101-2; Barbour, *Florida for Tourists*, 236.

97. CFW, "Ancient City, Part I," 4, 3; CFW, "South Devil," in *Rodman the Keeper*, 162.

98. U. S. Grant to Mississippi Attorney General Edwards Pierrepont, 13 September 1875, MS 400, Edwards Pierrepont Papers, Yale University Library.

99. Williamson, *Florida Politics in the Gilded Age*, 9; *Florida Sun* (Jacksonville), 4 January 1877. On Florida's role in the Compromise and its implications for freedpeople, see Shofner, *Nor Is It Over Yet*, 300-344; Williamson, *Florida Politics in the Gilded Age*, 17-45; and Klingman, *Neither Dies Nor Surrenders*, 65-79.

100. CFW, "Ancient City, Part I," 24.

Chapter 2

1. AWT, preface to *Toinette*, n.p.

2. AWT, *Royal Gentleman*, iii; AWT, preface to *Toinette*, n.p.

3. The *New York Arcadian* called it "a touching novel of very considerable merit," while the *Worcester Daily Spy* enthused, "It is a study of the principles of slavery, and its effects, and in its pages one may find many old problems solved." The *Atlanta Methodist Advocate* predicted, "This little volume is destined to exert a great influence both in the North and South, among the white and colored, and in pointing out past corruptions, it will do much to correct existing evils." See also other undated clippings in Scrapbooks, Tourgée Papers.

4. See Thomas, "'Plessy v. Ferguson' and the Literary Imagination," and *American Literary Realism*, 191–230. Although not focused on *Toinette*, Thomas explores how fictional "forms," including Tourgée's other work, and legal arguments inform each other.

5. West, *Narrative, Authority, and Law*, 181; Thadious Davis, *Games of Property*, 18.

6. "Just Out 'Toinette.' Thousands Selling," advertisement, n.d., Scrapbooks, Tourgée Papers.

7. Olsen, *Carpetbagger's Crusade*, 1–27.

8. Ibid., 28; Auman and Scarboro, "Heroes of America."

9. Olsen, *Carpetbagger's Crusade*, 26–67; Mark Elliott, *Color-Blind Justice*, 101–56.

10. Holden to Tourgée, 16 June 1865, Tourgée Papers. Tourgée later called the bungling governor "a more egregious ass than his bitterest enemy ever wished or thought him." Quoted in Gillette, *Retreat from Reconstruction*, 94. In 1860, 69 percent of North Carolina farms were fewer than 100 acres. Only 27.7 percent of families were slaveholders, about 71 percent of whom owned less than ten slaves. In Guilford County, slaves constituted less than 25 percent of the population. Alexander, *North Carolina Faces the Freedmen*, xiv–xvi.

11. See U.S. Congress, Joint Committee on Reconstruction, *Reports of the Committees*, "Part II: Virginia, North Carolina, and South Carolina," especially the testimony of Rev. James Sinclair, 29 January 1866, 2:166–75; Bureau Ass't Comr. of North Carolina, Col. E. Whittlesey, 3 February 1866, 2:181–85, 196; and Bureau Agent Dexter Clapp, 21 February 1866, 2:207–11. See also the Acting Asst. Comr. to O. O. Howard, 15 March 1867, Letters Sent, ser. 2446, RG 105, BRFAL; Brisson, "'Civil War Was Crumbling'"; Massengill, "Detectives of William W. Holden"; Raper, *William W. Holden*, 105–223; and Perman, *Struggle for Mastery*, 148–72.

12. Elias Halsey quoted in "Vindication of the Freedman's [*sic*] Bureau! By the Freedmen in a Public Meeting," Broadside E-224, May 1866, David M. Rubenstein Rare Book and Manuscript Library, Duke University, Durham, N.C. See also Escott, *Many Excellent People*, 85–135; Steven Nash, "Aiding the Southern Mountain Republicans"; Browning, "Removing the Mask of Nationality"; Starnes, "'Stirring Strains of Dixie.'" The Reports of Outrages, July 1867–October 1867, ser. 2656, and the "Police Court of the Freedmen's Bureau," in the Register of Rations Issued, ser. 2658, RG 105, BRFAL suggest that black-on-white crime was punished more severely than white-on-black crime, which was routinely transferred to dismissive civil authorities. General Nelson A. Miles pled for the bureau's continuation, which handled over 600 cases in four months. Nelson A. Miles to O. O. Howard, 4 December 1867, Letters Sent, ser. 2446, RG 105, BRFAL. On the prejudiced state judiciary, see "Report of Operations in the Seventh District" from 12 June 1867 to 25 September 1867 and from 28 July 1867 to 28 August 1867, ser. 2652, RG 105, BRFAL.

13. "The Southern Loyal Unionists," *Raleigh Daily Sentinel*, 31 August 1866; *North Carolina Progress*, as quoted in the *National Anti-Slavery Standard*, 12 October 1867; "Thoughts for the People," Tract One, "The Article on Education in the Proposed Constitution," *Greensboro Patriot*, 27 March 1868.

14. *Greensboro Patriot*, 10 September 1868.

15. Locke, *Second Treatise of Government*, 67, 4, 47.

16. Saks, "Representing Miscegenation Law," 47; see also Montgomery, *Citizen Worker*, 5–7.

17. Testimony of Colonel E. Whittlesey, 3 February 1866, U.S. Congress, Joint Committee on Reconstruction, *Reports of the Committees*, "Part II: Virginia, North Carolina, and South Carolina," 2:185; Kenzer, *Enterprising Southerners*, 9–34; Holt, *Making Freedom Pay*, 52–99.

18. Vandevelde, "New Property of the Nineteenth Century," 328, 330, 333–67.

19. Douglas, "'Most Valuable Sort of Property,'" 946.

20. Olsen, *Carpetbagger's Crusade*, 68–92.

21. AWT, *Royal Gentleman*, 117, 294, 74, 417, 74, 457, 455, 465, 442.

22. On black women's activism, see Waters and Conaway, *Black Women's Intellectual Traditions*; Maffly-Kipp and Lofton, *Women's Work*; Glymph, "'Liberty Dearly Bought'"; and Ann Gordon, *African-American Women and the Vote*. On postwar North Carolinians, Gilmore, *Gender and Jim Crow*, 1–91; Blanche Harris to Captain Hillebrandt, 24 December 1867, Letters Received, ser. 2650, RG 105, BRFAL; and Lofgren, *Plessy Case*, 25. For more on Harris, see "Mrs. Elias T. Jones (Blanche V. Harris)," Box 543, Folder, RG 28, Alumni Records, Oberlin College Archives, Oberlin, Ohio.

23. Welke, *Recasting Liberty*, 297, 280–322; Kenzer, *Enterprising Southerners*, 10, 13.

24. AWT, *Royal Gentleman*, iv, 121, 174.

25. Ibid., 262, 101, 261.

26. AWT, *Toinette*, 460, 461.

27. AWT, *Royal Gentleman*, 457, 238, 104.

28. Faust, *Mothers of Invention*, 53–80; Glymph, *Out of the House of Bondage*, 180–203, 209.

29. Andrews, *South since the War*, 177; AWT, *Royal Gentleman*, 101, 178, 104.

30. Trial transcript of Lyda Thompson and Letta Eckel, 9 July 1866, Records Relating to Court Cases, ser. 2660, RG 105, BRFAL; AWT, *Royal Gentleman*, 173.

31. See, for example, the inflammatory editorial "Work" in the *Daily North Carolina Standard*, 19 September 1868, and Josiah Turner's outraged rebuttal, "The Gross Assault of the *Standard* upon the Women of North Carolina," *Raleigh Daily Sentinel*, 22 September 1868.

32. See *"C" Letters as Published in "The North State"* (Greensboro, 1878); Draft of the 1868 Constitutional Convention Speech, Tourgée Papers; "Disgraceful Fight between Two North Carolina Judges," *Erie (Pa.) Gazette*, 14 April 1878. One interesting legacy of the emasculinized Confederate veterans is manifested in memorialization efforts. See Bishir, "'Strong Force of Ladies,'" and Crow, "'In Memory of the Confederate Dead.'"

33. AWT, *Royal Gentleman*, 314, 315, 313, 450, 449, 450, 446.

34. AWT, "To the Voters of Guilford," Broadsheet, 21 October 1867, Tourgée Papers. See also Escott, *Many Excellent People*, 136-95; Redding, *Making Race*, 58-111; and Zipf, "'WHITES Shall Rule the Land or Die,'" 529-32.

35. E. Whittlesey to O. O. Howard, Quarterly Report—Fall 1865, Letters Sent, ser. 2446, Raleigh Hdqrs., RG 105, BRFAL. Whittlesey included a copy of a 16 August 1865 letter showing what he termed "an interesting movement" on the part of organized freedmen to purchase homesteads with $10,000 worth of "joint stock." AWT, *Royal Gentleman*, 454; Siegel, "Home as Work," 1161-1205.

36. AWT, *Royal Gentleman*, 286, 455, 458; AWT, *Toinette*, 510.

37. On the history of marriage, see Cott, *Public Vows*, 24-104. In *American Literary Realism*, 208-15, Thomas disqualifies Tourgée as a realist because of his belief in right reason as evident in Tourgée's 1890 novel *Patroclus Prime*; overtly committed to Christian socialism, it reflects his increasing disillusionment with Reconstruction. However, I see in the complexity and tentative conclusions of *Royal Gentleman*, particularly in its rehearsal of a series of disappointments with the limits of contract law, more affinity for a realist aesthetic than Thomas allows.

38. Several Greensboro freedwomen appeared before the bureau to request child support. See Complaint of Isabella Holley, 28 June 1867, vol. 108, 17; Complaint of Matilda Bain, 23 June 1867; Complaint of Phoebe Slade, 18 July 1867; Complaint of Charlotte Wall, 6 August 1867, Registers of Complaints and Letters Sent Relating to Complaints, ser. 2659, and see H. Lomax to A. W. Bolenius, 9 August 1867, regarding Wall Complaint, Records Relating to Court Cases, ser. 2660; for examples of Greensboro freedwomen who pressed charges against white and black men for physical assault, see trial transcript of William L. Sherrod and Edmund Andrews, 10 April 1866, and trial transcript of freedman Nelson Gorrell for whipping his wife, 6 June 1866, ser. 2660, RG 105, BRFAL. On marriage, see Lebsock, "Radical Reconstruction"; Edwards, *Gendered Strife*, 37. See also Frankel, *Freedom's Women*, 79-122, and Farmer-Kaiser, *Freedwomen and the Freedmen's Bureau*, 14-63, 141-66.

39. A married woman was deemed to have no power to enter into an executory contract. She could only enter into a contract that could be enforced against property that had been "settled" to her own use. Even in that case, the contract, promissory note, or other agreement had to have her husband's express written permission combined with an express written description of the wife's separate property or the clear or necessary implication that the property be "charged." Moreover, courts of law would not enforce the contract against the married woman, but a court of equity would enforce the "charge" against her separate property. See *Pippen v. Wesson*. See also *Roun[d]tree v. Gay*. *Pippen* continued to be followed even in the early twentieth century. See *Mercantile Bank v. Benbow*.

40. AWT to Ellen Martin, Mayville, N.Y., 6 July 1886, Tourgée Papers; Article X, Sections 5 and 6, "To the People of North Carolina," Tract Pamphlet by William Rodman and George W. Gahagan, 16 March 1868, NYPL. On the 1868 convention debates on reforming married women's rights and their legacy, see Zipf, "No Longer under Cover(ture)." See also Bynum, "Reshaping the Bonds of Womanhood."

41. Van Tassel, "Only the Law Would Rule between Us," 874, 877; Zipf, "'WHITES Shall Rule the Land or Die,'" 522-26. For more on the southern shift to "violent

intolerance" of sex between black men and white women, see Hodes, *White Women, Black Men*, 147-208; Hodes, *Sex, Love, Race*, 237-330; Robinson, *Dangerous Liaisons*, 21-79; Sommerville, *Rape and Race in the Nineteenth-Century South*, 176-222; and Rosen, *Terror in the Heart of Freedom*, 133-75. On the bureau's response, see letter of L. V. Cazinc(?) to Nelson A. Miles, 10 November 1867, Letters Received, ser. 2452, RG 105, BRFAL. Only four antebellum slave states (Alabama, South Carolina, Georgia, and Mississippi) lacked these statutes, yet not all states punished miscegenation as sharply as North Carolina. *The Earliest Printed Laws of North Carolina* lists 1741 statute that made intermarriage between whites and "Indians, Negroes, Muskees, Mulattoes" a crime punishable by a fifty pound fine from both the offending white person and the minister (130). This fine was increased to $100 in 1837 (*Revised Statutes of North Carolina*, 387). In 1873, under Republican rule, this crime was made into a misdemeanor for ministers; the fine was dropped, and apparently the interracial couple was not punished (*Battle's Revisal*, 309). By 1883, however, North Carolina Democrats, like "Redemptive" legislators in nearly every southern state, had made miscegenation "an infamous crime," punishing the offending couple by imprisonment for "not less than four months, nor more than ten years," and making them also subject to a fine. The minister's crime remained a misdemeanor (*Code of North Carolina*, 437-38).

42. Saks, "Representing Miscegenation Law," 40.

43. AWT, *Royal Gentleman*, 442.

44. "Thoughts for the People," Tract No. 8, "To the White Men and Women of North Carolina," p. 3, NYPL; "To the People of North Carolina," Tract Pamphlet by William Rodman and George W. Gahagan, 16 March 1868, NYPL; *Greensboro Patriot*, 1 July 1874; "The Canby Constitution before and since Its Adoption: What Public Opinion Says of the Infamous Thing—'A League with Hell and Covenant with Death'" and "The Two Parties," *Raleigh Daily Sentinel*, 26 July 1875.

45. Washington, *Up from Slavery*, 69-71, 118-19.

46. *Raleigh Daily Sentinel*, 20 April 1869. Handwritten letter to "Ed. Standard," *Daily North Carolina Standard*, 12 November 1869, Tourgée Papers; *Baltimore Sun*, n.d.; Scrapbooks, Tourgée Papers; *Charlotte Observer*, 24 September 1874. For more on Patillo, see Mark Elliott, *Color-Blind Justice*, 136-51. Tourgée charged that Atkinson was a "cowardly braggart" because he "had been living in open adultery with a *colored woman* in that town ever since she was fourteen years old, and he declared that he always intended to do so, law or no law."

47. Scrapbooks, Tourgée Papers.

48. South Carolinian Sarah Grimke made the equation explicit: "Man seems to feel that Marriage gives him the control of a Woman's person just as the Law gives him the control of her property. . . . [Wives] have too soon discovered that they were unpaid housekeepers and nurses, and still worse, chattels personal to be used and abused at the will of a master." Cited in Lerner, *Female Experience*, 96. On antislavery feminist discourse in popular culture, see Yellin, *Women and Sisters*, 29-52; Sanchez-Eppler, *Touching Liberty*, 14-49; and Stanley, *From Bondage to Contract*, 175-217.

49. AWT, Brief for Plaintiff in Error at 19, *Plessy v. Ferguson* (No. 210); AWT, *Toinette*, 500.

50. AWT, *Toinette*, 509.

51. Quentin A. Alley to Asa Teal, 14 December 1865, Letters Received, ser. 2650, RG 105, BRFAL. Stanley, *From Bondage to Contract*, 139–48, 186–92, 215–17.

52. *New York Tribune*, 20 June 1865. Forbath, "Ambiguities of Free Labor," analyzes how courts broadened the Republican legacy of a person's right to own productive property to include the liberal notion that the worker's freedom meant ownership of his capacity to labor. Championing this "personal freedom," the courts struck down labor legislation as a violation of not only the capitalist's property rights but also the worker's right to dispose of the property of his labor. See also Forbath, *Law and the Shaping of the American Labor Movement*, 37–59. Vandervelde, "Labor Vision of the Thirteenth Amendment," 473–77; Vorenberg, *Final Freedom*, 185–250.

53. AWT, "To the Voters of Guilford," Broadsheet, 21 October 1867, Tourgée Papers, and "Speech on Elective Franchise," ms., 9, Tourgée Papers.

54. AWT, "A Lady Lawyer," *Current Thought*, February 1878; Kenzer, *Enterprising Southerners*, 56–57.

55. AWT, *Toinette*, 340, 469, 468.

56. Ibid, 470, 478; Santamarina, *Belabored Professions*, 103–69.

57. "Universal Suffrage," *Raleigh Weekly Sentinel*, 11 June 1867; *Greensboro North State*, 24 January 1878. With the Republican Party's decision to subordinate sexual to racial emancipation, the suffrage movement split in 1869. The Stanton-Anthony National Woman's Suffrage Association focused on women's enfranchisement by constitutional amendment and formed alliances with racist factions of the Democratic Party and then various elements of the labor movement. By contrast the Boston-based American Woman Suffrage Association remained loyal to the Republican Party's agenda. Both groups used the "deplorable" state of married women's property law to buttress their claims that women needed the vote. Ellen Du Bois, *Feminism and Suffrage*, 162–202; Flexner, *Century of Struggle*, 145–58.

58. AWT to M. B. Anderson, 11 May 1874; AWT to J. E. O'Hara, 4 August and 12 August 1876, Tourgée Papers.

59. AWT, *Royal Gentleman*, vii; Olsen, *Carpetbagger's Crusade*, 208.

60. Crèvecoeur, *Letters from an American Farmer*, 83; Locke, "An Essay," 17. See also Post, "Social Foundations of Defamation Law," 691–99. On self-ownership discourse as situated against evolving nineteenth-century feminist claims to joint property rights, see Siegel, "Home as Work," 1098–1108.

61. Douglas, "Most Valuable Sort of Property," 883.

62. Best, *Fugitive's Properties*, 270.

63. Rosen, *Terror in the Heart of Freedom*, 61–83.

64. Brief for Plaintiff in Error at 8, Plessy (No. 210).

65. AWT, *Royal Gentleman*, 115; Vogel, *Black Press*, 13–89; McHenry, *Forgotten Readers*, 24–140.

66. AWT, *Royal Gentleman*, 292, 293, 292, 294; Heather Williams, *Self-Taught*, 7–29; Davidson, *Revolution and the Word*, 110–51.

67. S. Hartman, *Scenes of Subjection*, 28; AWT, *Royal Gentleman*, 293. See also McHenry, "Reading and Race Pride," 499. Hartman answers the question of seduction's capacity to serve the seduced with a qualified "yes." Much like Tourgée, Hartman, *Scenes of Subjection*, stresses the "indebtedness of freedom to notions of property,

possession, and exchange" (112). Whereas Hartman argues for a perpetual "constancy of black subjection," I find a progressive intrigue in Tourgée's staging of seduction that permits more disruption and refiguring of master-slave relations than Hartman would allow. Tourgée's choice of *Mazeppa* as a liberating, subversive text would most likely resonate with contemporary readers familiar with Adah Mencken's wildly popular performance of the title character. In *Bodies of Dissent*, Daphne Brooks shows how Mencken performed a "politics of opacity," challenging conventional constructions of the racialized and gendered body (131–206). Her performance set the stage for Belle's own disruptive flight to freedom.

68. AWT, *Royal Gentleman*, 297, 129, 299.

69. Ibid., 213; Brooks, *Bodies in Dissent*, 49; AWT, Brief for Plaintiff in Error at 9, Plessy (No. 210).

70. AWT, *Royal Gentleman*, 300, 133, 132, 88–89.

71. Braxton, *Black Women Writing Autobiography*, 19. See also ibid., 18–38; Camp, *Closer to Freedom*, 35–39; and Farmer-Kaiser, *Freedwomen and the Freedmen's Bureau*, 97–140. For examples of North Carolinian "outrages," see "Charges against John Thomas and Dick Scales, etc.," 13 September 1865; specification and charge against Lucy Coltrain, 3 July 1865 and 21 August 1865; and the trial transcripts of Polly and Lucinda, 15 November 1865, Records Relating to Court Cases, ser. 2660, RG 105, BRFAL. For an example of a freedwomen's defiance of the bureau, see Major Eli Denny to A. W. Bolenius, 15 August 1867, Letters Received, ser. 2650, RG 105, BRFAL. For more on North Carolinian women's resistance, see Bynum, *Unruly Women*, 111–30; Edwards, "Reconstruction and North Carolina Women's Tangled History," and *Gendered Strife*, 145–84; Zipf, *Labor of Innocents*, 84–105. See also Regosin, *Freedom's Promise*, 79–147; and Frankel, *Freedom's Women*, 123–59.

72. John Robinson to O. O. Howard, Report for year ending 31 October 1866, Letters Sent, ser. 2446; Quentin A. Alley to Asa Teal, 23 December 1865, Letters Received, ser. 2650; for example, see Complaint of Elizabeth Tyre, 18 July 1867, Register of Complaints and Letters Sent Relating to Complaints, ser. 2659; for more, see other complaints in ser. 2659; 1867 Greensboro letters to Maj. A. W. Bolenius supporting women's requests for rations, Letters Received, ser. 2650; Freedpeople's Petition to Gen. Nelson A. Miles, 22 February 1868, Unregistered Letters Received, ser. 2453, RG 105, BRFAL. President Garfield incorporated much of Tourgée's analysis nearly verbatim into his inaugural address. Olsen, *Carpetbagger's Crusade*, 245–47.

73. See Foreman, *Activist Sentiments*, 2–17.

74. Higginbotham, *Righteous Discontent*, 14.

75. AWT, *Royal Gentleman*, 465. On emancipatory narratives, see Block, "Lines of Color, Sex, and Service"; Yellin, *Harriet Jacobs*, 117–53; and Haynes, *Radical Spiritual Motherhood*, 145–69.

76. AWT, *Royal Gentleman*, 440, 441, 463, 462; Frances D. Gage to Gerrit Smith, 24 December 1855, cited in Stanton and Anthony, *History of Woman Suffrage*, 842–43. On the free love movement and nineteenth-century women's rights advocacy, see Schroer, "State of 'The Union'"; Passet, *Sex Radicals and the Quest for Women's Equality*; and Hayden, *Evolutionary Rhetoric*.

77. AWT, *Royal Gentleman*, 466.

78. Post, "Social Foundations of Defamation Law," 721–27; Wyatt-Brown, *Shaping of Southern Culture*, 31–55, and *Southern Honor*, 362–401; Greenberg, *Honor and Slavery*, especially 3–23 and 51–86; and Forret, "Slave-Poor White Violence."

79. AWT, *Royal Gentleman*, 456, 466; Douglas, "Most Valuable Sort of Property," 912.

80. *New York Tribune*, 30 September 1876. See also Kaser, *Books and Libraries in Camp and Battle*, 77–124, and Kaestle and Radway, *Print in Motion*, 56–89, 170–89, 431–70.

81. A. Quinn, *Literature of the American People*, 591. Subscription publishers made enough of a dent in the market that an 1872 *New York Times* editorial predicted that the subscription trade would drive the regular trade to bankruptcy. Tebbel, *History of Book Publishing*, 515–18.

82. "Radical Misrule and Extravagance," *Raleigh Daily Sentinel*, 22 September 1868; *Greensboro Patriot*, 24 August 1866; "Judge Tourgée in Print Again," *Greensboro Patriot*, 18 May 1871. For more examples, see Tourgée to the editor of the *Greensboro Patriot*, 6 September 1866; Tourgée to W. H. Sweet, n.d.; and Tourgée to the "Ed. *Standard*," 12 November 1869, handwritten letter, Tourgée Papers.

83. AWT, letter to the editor and "An Important Question Settled," *Greensboro Patriot*, 14 September 1866.

84. AWT, *Greensboro North State*, 18 March 1878. The *Ladies Repository* speculated: "Henry Churton . . . is only a *nom de plume* to hide an author who tries hard to leave readers in doubt whether his pen is Northern or Southern, but who, while evidently thoroughly acquainted with the South by residence and intimate observation, nevertheless smacks strongly of the Yankee and Boston," n.d., Scrapbooks, Tourgée Papers.

85. AWT, *National Anti-Slavery Standard*, 9 November 1867; "C" letter to the editor, *Greensboro North State*, 26 March 1878. See also other clippings speculating on the identity of the "C" letters in Tourgée Papers.

86. *North Carolinian*, 1 February 1870; Tourgée quoted in Olsen, *Carpetbagger's Crusade*, 221, 56. See also Mark Elliott, *Color-Blind Justice*, 121–22.

87. AWT, *Royal Gentleman*, 312; AWT, letter to the editor, *Daily North Carolina Standard*, 10 April 1868.

88. AWT, *Royal Gentleman*, iv; Brief Plaintiff in Error at 3, Plessy (No. 210).

89. AWT, *Royal Gentleman*, 26, 173, 29; AWT, *Toinette*, 488, 487; Stanley, *From Bondage to Contract*, 138–74.

90. Vandevelde, "New Property of the Nineteenth Century," 344, 340–48; W. E. B. Du Bois, *Souls of Black Folk*, 78.

91. AWT, "Speech on Elective Franchise," p. 16 ms., Tourgée Papers; Best, *Fugitive's Properties*, 168.

92. AWT, *Royal Gentleman*, 163, 408, 43.

93. Ibid., 163, 458, 457–58, 422, 434. The narrator admits that while Certain was "glad" slavery had been abolished, she "had no love for the enslaved race either" and was "no more in favor of their farther advancement than the proudest aristocrat of the old slave *regime*" (ibid., 421).

94. Ibid., vi–vii.

95. AWT, *Royal Gentleman*, 240, 462; AWT, *Toinette*, 468; AWT, *Royal Gentleman*, 79, 446, 161.

96. AWT, *Royal Gentleman*, 370, 377, 378.

97. Ibid., 434.

98. Ibid., 448, 449, 448

99. AWT, *Toinette*, 510; AWT, *Royal Gentleman*, 467.

100. AWT, *Royal Gentleman*, viii; J. W. Smith to Tourgée, 18 February 1893, Tourgée Papers.

101. C. Vann Woodward, "Louisiana Traveler," 171; Olsen, *Carpetbagger's Crusade*, 261-67.

102. Tourgée to McKinley, 11 December 1900, McKinley Papers, Manuscript Division, Library of Congress, as quoted in Olsen, *Carpetbagger's Crusade*, 346. In 1979 a highway marker was erected in Tourgée's honor on Route 6 near an overpass, not far from where his beloved Carpet-Bag Lodge once stood. It reads, "Albion W. Tourgée: 1838-1905. Union army officer, author, judge. Member of 1868 Convention. Home was 2 blocks S." In the 2010 installation of a permanent exhibition, "Voices of a City," the Greensboro Historical Museum commemorated Tourgée as a controversial but "central figure in the history of North Carolina."

Chapter 3

1. From Clemmer Ames's weekly column, "Woman's Letter from Washington," *New York Independent*, 3 January 1867. It was reprinted in the local *Spirit of Jefferson* in a shortened form on 26 February 1867.

2. The "secret history" is a file of Brackett family letters about student John Clifford's 1899 accusations of discrimination and corruption against the college and its president, Nathan Brackett, and about the proceedings of the Niagara Movement, in SCD.

3. Because nearly all of my analysis concerns her work before she married, I refer to Coralie Franklin Cook by her maiden name throughout.

4. As Lewis and Hennen, *West Virginia History*, note, the state's political historiography and social history is lacking (v, vii). Consequently, I have had to rely on older secondary sources. For a general state history, see Otis Rice, *West Virginia*. On West Virginia's political history, see Link, *Roots of Secession*, 177-254; Zimring, "'Secession in Favor of the Constitution'"; Curry, "Virginia Background"; John Williams, *West Virginia*, 30-56; George Moore, *Banner in the Hills*, 195-207; and Phillips, "Transfer of Jefferson and Berkeley Counties," 42-64.

5. Phillips, "Transfer of Jefferson and Berkeley Counties," 9-41, 65-83; Bushong, *Historic Jefferson County*, 269-79; on slavery's import in state formation, see Link, "'This Bastard New Virginia'"; MacKenzie, "Slaveholders' War"; George Moore, "Slavery as a Factor"; Talbott, "Some Legislative and Legal Aspects"; and Posey, *Negro Citizen*, 5-16. West Virginia ranked first in the per capita rate of lynching between 1890 and 1900, when lynching peaked both nationally and within the state. Konhaus, "'I Thought Things Would Be Different There,'" 32.

6. Norris, *History of the Lower Shenandoah Valley*, 366-67; *SOJ*, 21 April 1914.

7. *VFP*, 11 March 1869; *Virginia v. West Virginia*; *SOJ*, 12 December 1865.

8. Joseph Harris, "Afro-American History Interpretation at Selected National Parks," 17–23, SCD. See also Geffert, "Annotated Narrative," 37–39, SCD, and Stealey, "Freedmen's Bureau," 104.

9. Burke, *American Phoenix*, 25–26; Stealey, "Freedmen's Bureau," 100–101, 105–7; "West Virginia Race and Hispanic Origin: 1790 to 1990," in U.S. Bureau of the Census, Historical Census Statistics, Table 63, 81; Posey, *Negro Citizen*, 32.

10. George Moore, *Banner in the Hills*, 13–22; Curry, *House Divided*, 13–27; Stealey, "Freedmen's Bureau," 103–4; Posey, *Negro Citizen*, 27–29. See also Otis Rice, *West Virginia*, 154–73.

11. Hearn, *Six Years of Hell*, 290–91; Trowbridge, *The South*, 62–68; Stealey, "Freedman's Bureau," 104.

12. Anne Dudley Bates to Henry McDonald, 8 November 1917, Box 1, A & M 1322, SCA; A. F. Higgs to J. M. Schofield, 28 February 1867, reprinted in Stealey, "Freedmen's Bureau Operations," 114–15.

13. A. F. Higgs to Francis Fessenden, 31 August 1866, reprinted in Stealey, "Freedmen's Bureau Operations," 107; see also Stealey, "Reports of Freedmen's Bureau District Officers," 148–55.

14. Anderson and Moss, *Dangerous Donations*, 7–9. Beginning with a grant of $374 in 1882, the state contributed modestly to Storer through scholarships and annual grants from $600 to $1,000. Pamphlet to the governor and legislature of West Virginia, 1902, Box 146, A & M 1322, SCA. While embracing mission schools, freedpeople rejected Congregationalists' religious dogma and worship rituals in favor of a more syncretic approach that incorporated African traditions. See Zipf, "'Among These American Heathens.'" See also Joe Richardson, *Christian Reconstruction*, 143–59, 237–55; DeBoer, *Be Jubilant My Feet* and *His Truth Is Marching On*. Despite its charter, Storer did not become a "degree-granting college" until 1938. Vivian Gordon, "History of Storer College," 448. For more, see Gozdzik, *Historic Resource Study for Storer College*.

15. Frederick Douglass to Nathan Brackett, 31 May 1889, Anacostia, D.C. SCD. Storer's bequest was printed in the 1869 College Catalog, p. 11, HFB-210, SCD. Exactly when it was discontinued is unclear, but it does not appear in the 1882–84 college catalog. Student enrollment rose from 96 in 1869 to 169 in 1870 to 223 in 1872 per Mongin, "College in Secessia," 9–10.

16. See Martha Stower, "Teacher's Monthly Report, February 1867," Reports Forwarded to Ass't. Comr. And Rec'd from Subordinates, ser. 4308, RG 105, BRFAL; Stealey, "Freedmen's Bureau," 118–26; Robertson quoted in McClain, "Storer College," 91–92; Heather Williams, *Self-Taught*, 67–173.

17. Anthony, "Storer College," 10–11; *VFP*, 3 January 1870, 21 January 1869, 14 October 1871; *SOJ*, 10 October 1871.

18. Wood Brackett, "Storer College: A Chapter of History," 2, typed ms., n.d., SCD; Brackett, *Biographical Sketch of the Rev. A. H. Morrell*, 10; Robertson, "Nathan Cook Brackett," n.p., black loose-leaf book, 1768, SCD; N. C. Brackett to Samuel Hunt, 28 February 1866, cited in Stealey, "Freedmen's Bureau," 110; Anthony, "Storer College," 10. See also Stealey, "Freedmen's Bureau," 107, 110–36, and Burke, *American Phoenix*, 34.

19. Brackett, "A Talk," 8–9, typed ms. 1906, SCD; "The Race Problem: A Dream by N. C. B. in Morning Star," *Lewiston (Me.) Daily Sun*, 29 December n.d. (likely from the 1890s), black loose-leaf book, 1737, SCD.

20. Brackett, letter to editor Haines, *SOJ*, 3 February 1891; Silas Curtis to N. C. Brackett, 28 November 1865, Box 1, A & M 2621, SCA; Anthony, "Storer College: A Brief Historical Sketch," 11, 15, HFB-50, SCD. The *Storer Record* was issued only occasionally until 1892, when it began as a bimonthly with the goal of becoming a monthly. There are no extant issues prior to 1892.

21. Handwritten paper by Lura Brackett Lightner read to [?] Women's Missionary Society, 188[?], n.p., black loose-leaf book, 1791, SCD; McDonald, "Thumb Nail Sketches," t.s., 3 May 1944, SCD; *SOJ*, 26 February 1867.

22. Mary Davis, *History of the Free Baptist Women's Missionary Society*, 29; Eulogy, "Dr. Nathan C. Brackett," 29 June 1911, *Morning Star*, Black Data Book, SCD; Anthony, "Storer College," 7. On northern women's activism in the freedmen's aid movement, see Faulkner, *Women's Radical Reconstruction*, especially 1–66.

23. Lyrics from "Colored School Exhibition, 27 March 1867," in SCD; McClain, "Storer College," 57–59.

24. "A Monstrous Roorback" [*sic*], *SOJ*, 29 April 1873.

25. Thomas E. Robertson, "Portrait of Dr. Nathan Cook Brackett," 2, Presentation Address, n.d., SCD; "Biographical Sketch of Miss Lue Brackett Lightner, 2, n.d., SCD; McClain, "Storer College," 57. Fox-Genovese, *Within the Plantation Household*, 31, defines a "plantation household" as "a basic social unit," which may or may not be "coterminous" with families, in which "people, whether voluntarily or under compulsion, pool their income and resources." See also Bardaglio, *Reconstructing the Household*, 121–213, and McCurry, *Masters of Small Worlds*, 208–76.

26. "The 'Freedmen,'" *SOJ*, 5 December 1865; "The Negro's Future," *Storer Record*, Spring 1893, p. 1, SCD; see also Morris, *Reading, 'Riting, and Reconstruction*, 149–212; Butchart, *Northern Schools, Southern Blacks, and Reconstruction*, 13–75; Anderson, *Education of Blacks in the South*, 33–109, 238–78; DeBoer, *His Truth is Marching On*, 151–71; Joe Richardson, *Christian Reconstruction*, 123–40.

27. Anthony, "Storer College," 17, 9; "Idleness," *Storer Record*, Spring 1893, p. 3, SCD; McClain, "Storer College," 61, 77–78.

28. "To the Class of '93," *Storer Record*, Spring 1893, p. 1, SCD; *Storer Record*, March 1897, p. 1, SCD; Anthony, "Storer College," 19, HFB-50, SCD; Best, *Fugitive's Properties*, 80–83.

29. Robertson cited in McClain, "Storer College," 77. See also Gilmore, *Gender and Jim Crow*, 138–39.

30. McClain, "Storer College," 77, 109; Burke, *American Phoenix*, 116. Although the number of women's jobs in manufacturing and mechanical industries doubled between 1880 and 1890, West Virginia's overall percentage of women in the workforce, 16 percent, lagged behind the national average of 26 percent. West Virginian female workers, typically white, were clustered in domestic industries well into the twentieth century. Hensley, "Women in the Industrial Work Force in West Virginia," 115. Racial segregation in employment persisted well into the 1950s, resulting in black women's lower pay. Pudup, "Women's Work in the West Virginia Economy," 18.

31. Mrs. H. Blackburn to Henry McDonald, 7 February 1900, in McDonald Diary, and McDonald Diary, 8 February, 1900, Box 8, A & M, 2621, SCA. For *Sentinel* examples of student disgruntlement, see "A Day at Storer," "The Little Bell" and "College Dictionary," on pp. 21-23 and 46 of the Storer *Sentinel* of 1909-10, one of the earliest extant student yearbooks, HFB-302, SCD; Vossler, "Women and Education in West Virginia," 283. On faculty-student conflict, see Faulkner, *Women's Radical Reconstruction*, 132-47.

32. Untitled tribute to the Bracketts by Nathan Brackett's niece, n.d., n.p. Storer College Data, black loose-leaf book, 4, SCD; "Valedictory," 1, SCD; Rev. M. Ford, Eulogy of Nathan Brackett on Commencement Day, 8 June 1911, Xerox of *Morning Star*, 28 June 1911, found in black loose-leaf book, 1030, 1035, SCD; Joe Richardson, *Christian Reconstruction*, 18. Obligations to the school were extensive; see, for example, "The Parent's Duty to the Free School," *Storer Record*, Fall 1894, p. 3, SCD.

33. *Storer Record*, Spring 1894, p. 2, and February 1897, p. 2, SCD; "Storer Spirit: The Contributions of My Family," 2, in black loose-leaf notebook, 1377, SCD; see also James Harrison Robinson, letter to the *Speaker*, clipping from late 1890s or early 1900s, incorrectly dated as 1880s, black loose-leaf book, 1743-44, SCD. By 1900 Jefferson County ranked second in the state for the greatest number of farms owned by black West Virginians. However, it also had the highest percentage of farms operated by African Americans under share tenant or cash tenant arrangements. Sheeler, "Negro Farmers in West Virginia in 1900," Table, 285.

34. Mary Davis, *History of the Free Baptist Women's Missionary Society*, 31; McClain, "Storer College," 81-82; Eagan, "'Woman's Work, Never Done.'"

35. *Storer Record*, March 1897, p. 2, and Winter 1892, p. 2, SCD.

36. Storer lacked both the benefits of an urban black infrastructure found at other AMA schools, such as Dillard or Fisk, and the insular self-sufficiency that buffered the rurally situated Hampton Institute. Unlike Tuskegee, Storer's buildings directly faced the community. Grandison, "Negotiated Space."

37. D. J. Young to A. B. Dyer, 20 March 1868, RG 156, OCO.

38. 1869 Storer College Catalog, 1869, pp. 10-11, 1882-84 Biennial Storer College Catalog, 1884, pp. 26, 28, HFB-210, SCD; "Excursions an Evil," *Storer Record*, Spring 1893, p. 3, SCD; *Storer Record*, January 1895, p. 1, SCD; 1897-98 Annual Storer College Catalog, 1898, pp. 24-25, 1898 Annual Storer College Catalog, 1898, p. 28, HFB-210.

39. *Storer Record*, March 1896, p. 2, Winter 1892, and H. W. Warner, letter to *Storer Record*, April 1898, p. 4, SCD; *Storer Record*, Winter 1894, as cited in McClain, "Storer College," 95. For expression of similar sentiments in another West Virginia community, see Fain, "Black Response to the Construction of Colored Huntington," 15-17.

40. 1869 College Catalog, p. 10, HFB-210, SCD; "Excursions an Evil," *Storer Record*, Spring 1893, p. 3, SCD; Jacqueline Jones, *Soldiers of Light and Love*, 14-48.

41. "Untitled Tribute," n.p., black loose-leaf book, 5-6, SCD; Celeste Brackett Newcomer, "Storer Spirit," p. 6, black loose-leaf book, 1381, SCD.

42. Newcomer, "Storer Spirit," pp. 2-3, black loose-leaf book, 1377-78, SCD.

43. 1882 College Catalog, pp. 30, 28, 30; 1889-1891 College Catalog, p. 24; 1905-6 Catalog, p. 35, all in HFB-210, SCD; *Storer Record*, May 1899, p. 2, SCD; Higginbotham, *Righteous Discontent*, 185-229.

44. *VFP*, 15 June 1872, and "Hard to Please," *VFP*, 13 June 1874.

45. Robertson, "Nathan Cook Brackett," n.p., black loose-leaf book, 1774, SCD.

46. Burke, *American Phoenix*, 28; Reilly, *Sarah Jane Foster*, 13. For more on northern white teachers' experiences, see Richardson, *Christian Reconstruction*, 163-86; Morris, *Reading, 'Riting, and Reconstruction*, 54-84; and Butchart, *Schooling the Freedpeople*, 78-119.

47. Brackett, letter to the editor, *Morning Star*, 6 December 1865. Foster letter to *Zion's Advocate*, 27 November 1865, as quoted in Reilly, *Sarah Jane Foster*, 33; McKenzie to W. Storer How, Martinsburg, WV, 31 January 1866, Registered Letters Rec'd, ser. 4306, RG 105, BRFAL. See also Butchart, *Schooling the Freed People*, 153-78.

48. See Diary, 19, 20, 21, 22, 25, 27, 28, and 29 January 1866, as quoted in Reilly, *Sarah Jane Foster*, 48-53; letter to *Zion's Advocate*, 1 February 1866, as quoted in ibid., 55.

49. Diary, 14, 15, and 28 February, 1866, 14 March 1866, as quoted in ibid., 61, 62, 68, 76; see also 13 February and 17 February 1866, as quoted in ibid., 61, 62; letters to *Zion's Advocate*, 28 February 1866 and 13 March 1866, as quoted in ibid., 68, 75.

50. Diary, 12 February 1866, 15 January 1866, 11 April 1866, and 25 May 1866, as quoted in ibid., 61, 47, 91, 119. See also the entry for 6 January 1866, ibid., 41. Whether Brown went to Bates is unclear. See note 16 in ibid., 136-37.

51. Diary, 14 March 1866, as quoted in ibid., 76, 22-23.

52. Hodes, *White Women, Black Men*, 147-75; Sheeler, "Negro in West Virginia," 207.

53. *Strauder v. West Virginia*, 100 U.S. 303, 308; 25 L. Ed. 664 (1879); Cresswell, "Case of Taylor Strauder."

54. *SOJ*, 26 February 1867.

55. Testimony of Samuel J. Gholson, 14 November 1871, U.S. Congress, Committee on Reconstruction, *Report of the Joint Select Committee to Inquire into the Condition of Affairs in the Late Insurrectionary States*, "Mississippi," 12:870. See also Weisenfeld, "'Who Is Sufficient for These Things?'" and Morris, *Reading, 'Riting, and Reconstruction*, 230-34, on relationships among black and white teachers and students.

56. Silas Curtis to Nathan Brackett, 8 February 1866, black loose-leaf book, 110, SCD.

57. Foster, letters to *Zion's Advocate*, 1 February 1866, 4 April 1866, and 4 August 1866, as quoted in Reilly, *Sarah Jane Foster*, 54, 85, 163; Sanchez-Eppler, *Touching Liberty*, 35.

58. Brackett to E. P. Smith, 29 December 1866, American Missionary Association Archives, Amistad Research Center, Tulane University, New Orleans.

59. Burke, *American Phoenix*, 93, 101.

60. *African American National Biography*, 132. See also Randy Langhenry, "Life and Times of John R. Clifford: A Pioneer Black Journalist," 180-81, manuscript courtesy of Rosemary Clifford McDaniel, author's collection.

61. Evans, *History of Berkeley County*, 271. For further context, see Pride and Wilson, *History of the Black Press*, 3-125, and Vogel, *Black Press*, 17-123.

62. Finkelman, "Not Only the Judges' Robes Were Black," 178; Connie Rice, "'Don't Flinch Nor Yield an Inch,'" 49.

63. *Martin v. Board of Education*; Connie Rice, "'Don't Flinch Nor Yield an Inch,'" 58–59.

64. Finkelman, "Not Only the Judges' Robes Were Black," 193; Connie Rice, "'Don't Flinch Nor Yield an Inch,'" 51–52.

65. Simmons, *Men of Mark*, 273; *African American National Biography*, 132–33. No full-length Clifford biography exists, but the J. R. Clifford Project (www.jrclifford .org) publicizes his life and civil rights contributions. Du Bois disbanded the Niagara group in 1911 because of internal divisions and declining attendance. See Lewis, *W. E. B. Du Bois*, 315–33 and 376–79.

66. "Among Former Pupils," *Storer Record*, Winter 1893, p. 1, SCD.

67. JRC, "A Reply," *PP*, August 1885; James H. Jones, "The Duty of the Hour," *PP*, March 1887.

68. Giggie, "'Disband Him from the Church,'" 252; *African American National Biography*, 132. See also Hahn, *Nation under Our Feet*, 384–89; Hugh Davis, *"We Will Be Satisfied with Nothing Less,"* 125–48.

69. JRC, "The W. V. Afro-American State Nomination," 28 September 1888; "Independent in Politics," *PP*, September 1886.

70. George T. Jones, "Republicanism vs. Communism," *PP*, July 1887; JRC, "A Moment If You Please," *PP*, 31 January 1888. For an example of an ex-slave's search to reunite with her sons, see "Are They in Eternity? Or on Earth? If So, Where?" *PP*, August 1888.

71. Pegues, "The Colored People of North Carolina," *PP*, 29 February 1888; George T. Jones, "Private Property in Land," *PP*, June 1887; "Stay on the Farm, *PP*, September 1884; Washington, *Up from Slavery*, 152.

72. JRC, untitled article, *PP*, June 1887; "Some Questions to Be Answered," December 1887, reprinted from the *Exchange*; Geffert, "Annotated Narrative," 96.

73. "An Educational Institution Needed in West Va," *PP*, October 1886; J. L. Champ, "Two Pictures," *PP*, 31 January 1888; "The Knights of Labor," *PP*, October 1886; Harlan, *Booker T. Washington*, 2:149; Norrell, *Up from History*, 98–99; Blair, *Cities of the Dead*, 144–70.

74. Francis Cardozo, "Industrial Education," *PP*, February 1887.

75. "Race Literature," *PP*, 30 April 1888; E. E. U., "Latent Powers of the Race," *PP*, December 1886.

76. See, for example, A. W. Pegues, "Live for a Purpose," *PP*, December 1886; A. W. Peguer [sic], "The True and the False," *PP*, February 1887; George T. Jones, "Are We Condemned to Servitude?" *PP*, 29 February 1888; Fon Gordon, *Caste and Class*, 85; Gaines, *Uplifting the Race*, 19–46.

77. JRC, untitled, *PP*, 31 January 1888, and "Independent in Politics," September 1886; Shaffer, *After the Glory*, 59–95; Barbara Gannon, *Won Cause*, 38–46, 188–95.

78. "Our Colored Policeman," *PP*, October 1886; "Buckwheat Faced Republicans," *PP*, September 1886; "The Thirty-Two," *PP*, October 1886.

79. A. W. Pegues, "Industrial Schools for Colored Youths," *PP*, November 1886.

80. Francis Cardozo, "Woman's Rights," *PP*, July 1887; "Young Housekeepers," *PP*, September 1884; Washington, *Up from Slavery*, 152.

81. JRC, *PP*, November 1886.

82. Simmons, *Men of Mark*, 274.

83. J. Nelson Wisner, "Thanks," *Martinsburg Independent*, 23 August 1884.

84. John Cromwell to the editor, *Journal of Negro Education* 8.3 (July 1923): 340; Connie Rice, "'Don't Flinch Nor Yield an Inch,'" 67 (n. 52) and 57; *PP*, 9 September 1911.

85. Anthony, "Storer College," 19. Anthony claims that for the most recent year, the profits exceeded $900 and showed no signs of declining; Brackett quoted in McClain, "Storer College," 63; Burke, *American Phoenix*, 108.

86. JRC, "Independence and Not Democracy," *PP*, November 1886; Storer College Record Books, 6 April 1897, Box 6, A & M 2621, SCA; Robertson to Mary Louise Moore, 21 March 1956, "Secret History" Files, SCD.

87. Robinson, letter, *Speaker*, clipping from late 1890s or early 1900s, incorrectly dated as 1880s, black loose-leaf book, 1744, SCD; *Storer Record*, April 1897, p. 2, SCD; Brackett, undated letter to the *New York Age*, "Secret History" Files, SCD.

88. Brackett, undated letter to the *New York Age*, "Secret History" Files, SCD.

89. Robertson to DeMeritte, 29 January 1900, "Secret History" Files, SCD.

90. DeMeritte to Robertson, 1 February 1900, "Secret History" Files, SCD; "Report of Investigation Committee Appointed by Storer College," broadside, 26 May 1900, HFD-672, SCD; Lightner to Louise Brackett, 6 August 1896, "Secret History" Files, SCD.

91. *Farmer's Advocate*, 15 July 1899; Brackett, undated letter to the *New York Age*, "Secret History" Files, SCD; see also "Editor J. R. Clifford of the Pioneer Press, Found Guilty," *Martinsburg Herald*, 21 September 1901; "Berkeley Circuit Court," *VFP*, 9 October 1901; *Farmer's Advocate*, 20 January 1906.

92. *Martinsburg Herald*, 15 July 1899; *Farmer's Advocate*, 28 October 1899; "Division News: Archives and History Section Posts Pioneer Press Editorials Online," West Virginia Division of Culture and History, www.wvculture.org (24 February 2009).

93. Wyatt-Brown, *Southern Honor*, 117–74.

94. Wells, *Women Writers and Journalists in the Nineteenth-Century South*, 134. See Franklin's entry in *African American National Biography* and in *Notable Black American Women*, although the latter's claim that Franklin helped found Storer is not substantiated by any archival records I have seen.

95. Jacqueline Moore, *Leading the Race*, 11. See Cook's entry in the *African American National Biography*; an untitled, anonymous, undated biography, SCD; and George William Cook Papers, Moorland-Spingarn Research Center, Howard University, Washington, D.C.

96. *Crisis*, July 1914, 117; Martha Jones, *All Bound Up Together*, 4.

97. "Storer College: An Appreciation," undated printed article, n.p., likely written for the Free Baptist Women's Missionary Society, SCD; officials' comments found in anonymous, post–World War II Founder's Day speech, "Building Roads for the Future," n.d., 9, SCD; Higginbotham, *Righteous Discontent*, 20, 19–46. For further context, see Wells, *Women Writers and Journalists in the Nineteenth-Century South*, 174–87.

98. Franklin, "Storer College: An Appreciation," SCD; on D.C. schools, see Jacqueline Moore, *Leading the Race*, 86–131.

99. Franklin, "Storer College: An Appreciation," SCD; Zackodnik, *Press, Platform, Pulpit*, especially 131–223.

100. Franklin, "The Girl Graduate," *PP*, June 1887; on "Republican Motherhood," see Kerber, *Women of the Republic*. See also Haynes, *Radical Spiritual Motherhood*, 10-88; Faulkner, *Women's Radical Reconstruction*, 67-82; Robbins, *Managing Literacy, Mothering America*, 157-93.

101. Franklin, letter to *Storer Record*, Storer Record, 14 February 1894, p. 3, SCD; on postwar black women's nonagricultural labors, see Santamarina, *Belabored Professions*, 139-69; Tera Hunter, *To 'Joy My Freedom*, 44-73; Jacqueline Jones, *Labor of Love*, 112-52; and Salem, *To Better Our World*, 12-21.

102. *PP*, June 1887, 31 January 1888, August 1888; Gilmore, *Gender and Jim Crow*, 147-202; Deborah White, *Too Heavy a Load*, 21-55.

103. "Society Greets a Negress," special to the *New York Times*, 12 December 1902, p. 2; Terborg-Penn, *African American Women and the Struggle for the Vote*, 70; Lue Brackett Lightner to Louise Brackett, 6 August 1896, "Secret History" Files, SCD.

104. The backwardness extends to historiography. See Howe, "Status of Women's History Research in West Virginia." The 1990 special issue of *West Virginia History* helped rectify the situation, and some more recent work includes Spindel, "Women's Legal Rights in West Virginia"; Fredette, "View from the Border"; and Effland, "Profile of Political Activists." Much work remains to be done.

105. Norrell, *Up from History*, 70; "Woman's Column," *PP*, July 1887. Although Clifford was skeptical about Prohibition and many *PP* articles explored the problem of temperance as a political issue, the paper recognized the value of women's leadership in the movement. See the *PP* editorials of September 1886 and 30 April 1888; George T. Jones, "Rum and Politics," *PP*, October and November 1886, and "The Prohibition Party," *PP*, September 1886. For the paper's support of women's involvement, see the untitled item on temperance in the *PP*, February 1887, and Jared Maurice Arter, "Why We Should Support Prohibition," *PP*, 30 June 1888; Mary L. Smith, "Intemperance," *PP*, August 1888.

106. *SOJ*, 3 December 1895. The *Storer Record* (November 1895, p. 2, SCD) also reprinted this highly favorable review of Franklin's 1895 address from the 10 October issue of the *Atlanta Constitution*; *PP*, 30 April 1888; Giddings, *When and Where I Enter*, 170.

107. McHenry, *Forgotten Readers*, 141-251; Jacqueline Moore, *Leading the Race*, 51-86, 161-86.

108. Handwritten, undated notebook, pp. 1, 8, Coralie Franklin Cook Papers, SCD; Franklin's short story, "A Slave for Life," appeared in *Opportunity* in June 1929. See also Roy L. Manker to CFC, 29 December 1925, Coralie Franklin Cook Papers, SCD; Hine, "Rape and the Inner Lives of Black Women in the Middle West," 915-17.

109. "You Can. Then Why Not Be a Good Reader?," *PP*, September 1886.

110. Prince, *Burnin' Down the House*, 2; Franklin, "Books for the Home," *PP*, December 1887; Gaines, *Uplifting the Race*, 78.

111. McDonald, letter to his mother, May 1900, Correspondence, Box 36, A & M 1322, Storer Records, SCA. In 1918 Storer students erected a tablet on the fort in tribute to Brown and his followers. Around 1900, in seeming counterpoint to Storer College's 1890s efforts, UDC members initiated a drive to erect a memorial to Heyward Shepherd, a free black man who was killed by Brown's men. The memorial was eventually completed and dedicated in 1931, amid bitter controversy. See Mary Johnson, "'Ever-Present Bone of Contention.'"

112. Lightner to Nathan and Louise Brackett, "Sunday, Very Confidential," 1906, "Secret History" Files, SCD. See also "Storer College," special issue of the *Free Will Morning Star* (30 May 1895), HFB-525, SCD. Faculty-written articles such as "An Old Teacher" are nostalgic for the humble ex-slaves, for whom "getting an education meant work and self-denial." They contrast with student articles such as E. V. Smith's "Emancipation Day" and Annie Avilla May Hatter's "Education," which posits schooling as "the passport to fame, and the road to greatness and honor." See also Anderson and Moss, *Dangerous Donations*, 13–39.

113. Vivian Gordon, "History of Storer College," 448.

Chapter 4

1. GWC, *Grandissimes*, 2; GWC, "My Politics," 15.

2. See Turner, "George W. Cable's Beginnings as a Reformer," and his biography, *George W. Cable*, 37–53. Cable's introduction to the House of Scribner coincided with the firm's bitter internal reorganization. *Scribner's Monthly* ran until 1881, when it was sold to outside investors and renamed the *Century Illustrated Monthly Magazine* (hereafter referred to its commonly known name as *Century Magazine* in the text) under Roswell Smith. Continuing to publish books, Charles Scribner's Sons launched *Scribner's Magazine* in 1886. Maintaining cordial relations with all the editors involved, Cable published in both magazines.

3. Quoted in Rankin, "Forgotten People," 73; Labbé and Lurie, *Slaughterhouse Cases*; Cable condemned a riot against an integrated girls' school in an open letter to the *New Orleans Bulletin* on 26 September 1875; it was his first public protest against the violation of African Americans' civil rights. Turner, *George W. Cable*, 75–77.

4. Hogue, *Uncivil War*, 4. See also Joe Taylor, *Louisiana Reconstructed*; Keith, *Colfax Massacre*; Lane, *Day Freedom Died*; and Tunnell, *Edge of the Sword*, 184–271. Goldman, *Reconstruction and Black Suffrage*, traces the Court's narrow interpretation of the Enforcement Acts and the Fourteenth and Fifteenth Amendments in *United States v. Cruikshank* and *United States v. Reese*.

5. Hogue, *Uncivil War*; Gillette, *Retreat From Reconstruction*, 104–35. See also Warmoth, *War, Politics and Reconstruction*, and Tunnell, *Crucible of Reconstruction*, 111–72; Rable, "Republican Albatross."

6. GWC's fellow columnist Daniel Dennett was a founder of the Knights of the White Camellia. Dauphine, "Knights of the White Camellia," 179. Cable dissented at least once with the newspaper in 1871 because of the stance of its editor, A. M. Holbrook, on segregation at a teacher's institute. Turner, *George W. Cable*, 45–51. See also Copeland, "New Orleans Press and Reconstruction."

7. Hollandsworth, *Absolute Massacre*, 3. Despite their attempts to surrender, 48 were killed and over 200 wounded. See also Vandal, "Origins of the New Orleans Riot of 1866, Revisited"; Hogue, *Uncivil War*, 5.

8. Hall, *Africans in Colonial Louisiana*, 157. In "Creoles and Americans," Tregle shows that white Creoles crystalized their mythic identity during Reconstruction. Contrary to their myth, in which Cable participates, colonial Creoles were poor and illiterate, and they would be overwhelmed between 1830 and 1860 by the influx of immigrants

eager to assimilate to American ways. While Tregle convincingly argues that Creole (native born) identity was first deployed to resist the onslaught of Americans from 1803 onward, he discounts prevailing racial tensions. The evident need for the imposition of the Code Noir, for example, suggests the relevance of race to conceptualizing the ethnic identity of the Crescent City's residents; Lachance, "Foreign French." See also Jerah Johnson, "Colonial New Orleans," and Hall, *Africans in Colonial Louisiana*, 120-55; if Dominguez, in *White by Definition*, focuses on the tensions inherent in the manipulation of Creole identity by individuals, Kein's edited essay collection, *Creole*, is skewed toward celebrating the expression of Creole identity as an unproblematic choice. For a more nuanced view, see Dormon, *Creoles of Color of the Gulf South*.

9. Hanger, *Bounded Lives*, 12, which remains central to understandings of the city's distinctive origins; Hanger, "Coping in a Complex World," 219, 228.

10. Gruesz, "Delta *Desterrados*," 55, 57. See also Ralph Woodward, "Spanish Commercial Policy in Louisiana." On the *libres*' population increase, see Rankin, "Forgotten People," 51. On the city's divisive politics, see Rousey, *Policing the Southern City*, 37-80, and G. Howard Hunter, "Politics of Resentment." On German settlement in New Orleans and other key areas, see Merrill, *Germans of Louisiana*, especially 19-118.

11. Schafer, "'*Voleur de Nègres*,'" 261. See also Rankin, "Origins of Black Leadership" and "Forgotten People," 107-35; Gehman, "Visible Means of Support"; Schweninger, "Antebellum Free Persons," 347-52, and for comparison to the prewar South, *Black Property Owners*, 97-141; Blassingame, *Black New Orleans*, 49-77. In the areas surrounding New Orleans, 98 percent of the black population was enslaved, but in New Orleans in 1860, 50 percent of black residents were free. Rankin, "Forgotten People," 56-57.

12. Walter Johnson, *Soul by Soul*, 19. For a transatlantic context, see Leglaunec, "Slave Migrations in Spanish and Early American Louisiana"; on black Creole dissent, see Bell, *Revolution, Romanticism, and the Afro-Creole Protest Tradition in Louisiana*; Logsdon and Bell, "Americanization of Black New Orleans"; on colonial 'libres'" organized activities against runaway slaves and on their wartime service, see Rankin, "Forgotten People," 58-61, 165-84.

13. Rankin, "Forgotten People," 264. See also Rankin, "Impact of the Civil War," 387-96; for examples of municipal abuse, see Thomas Conway to Mayor Kennedy, 10 July 1865, 17 July 1865. See also Conway's complaint to the justice of peace, 24 July 1865, and his letter to Governor James Madison Wells, 30 September 1865, all in Letters Sent, ser. 1297. See also A. Baird to O. O. Howard, 20 December 1865, Letters Sent, ser. 1297; Edward Hatch to O. O. Howard, September 1868 and October 1868, Ass't Comr. Monthly and Annual Reports, ser. 1309; and see Reports of Indigent Refugees and Freedmen from Subordinate Officers, ser. 1314. For the tax, see the October 1866 Annual Report to O. O. Howard and J. A. Mower to E. Whittlesey, 30 September 1867, ser. 1309, all in RG 105, BRFAL. See also Ripley, *Slaves and Freedmen in Civil War Louisiana*, 40-125; Crouch, "Black Education in Civil War and Reconstruction Louisiana"; for a firsthand account, see Willey, "Education of the Colored Population of Louisiana."

14. Using "peculiar" as a descriptor for slavery, Cable subtly implied the cross-racial nature of the term in an interview for the *Missouri Republican*, 11 January 1885. In *Creoles of Louisiana*, 41, Cable provided a footnote on the term's slippery etymology:

He cites the Louisiana linguist James A. Harrison, who paraphrases English philologist Walter William Skeat, who derived "creole" from the Spanish *criollo*, "a native of America or the West Indies; a corrupt word made by the negroes, said to be a contraction of *criadillo*, diminutive of *criado*—one educated, instructed or bred up, pp. of *criar*, lit. to create, also to nurse, instruct."

15. GWC, *Creoles of Louisiana*, 1, 41; GWC, interview, *Missouri Republican*, 11 January 1885.

16. GWC, *Creoles of Louisiana*, 23, 39; Cable's geographic approach was favored by a local literary rival who visited Cable's settings in *Old Creole Days* to understand his characters. Hearn, "The Scenes of Cable's Romances," 40–47.

17. GWC, *Creoles of Louisiana*, 210, 41–42; Ettinger, "John Fitzpatrick and the Limits of Working-Class Politics," 342–43.

18. "Speech of Major General O. O. Howard to the Colored People at the Orleans Theatre," 5 November 1865, Miscellaneous Records, ser. 1328, RG 105, BRFAL; GWC, *Creoles of Louisiana*, 150, 156.

19. Lathrop, quoted in Biklé, *George W. Cable*, 48; Kreyling, introduction to *The Grandissimes*, xiv–xv; GWC, "After-Thoughts of a Story-Teller," 18; on possible historical allusions in "Bibi," see Ladd, *Nationalism and the Color Line*, 66–70; Gavin Jones, *Strange Talk*, 130.

20. GWC, *Grandissimes*, 168, 117, 314; Turner, *George W. Cable*, 138; "Bras Coupé," 1886 *Century* advertisement, Cable papers.

21. GWC, *Grandissimes*, 105, 158, 80, 23, 15, 221.

22. Ibid., 323.

23. Ibid., 324, 326–27, 228, 19, 138, 84.

24. Ibid., 84, 22, 48, 228.

25. GWC, *Grandissimes*, 283, 302, 327, 156, 326; on the rhetoric of planter elites, see Hyde, "Feuding," and *Pistols and Politics*, 46–91, 139–99.

26. GWC, *Grandissimes*, 126, 32.

27. Ibid., 141, 46–47, 224, 39; Johnson quoted in Rubin, *George W. Cable*, 96; ibid., 95. To Howells, even Cable jokingly referred to "Poor Frowenfeld" as a "goody-goody," doomed to "die young." Biklé, *George W. Cable*, 72.

28. GWC, *Grandissimes*, 153, 152, 305.

29. Ibid., 103, 29, 81; for more on the household's centrality to the structuring of southern communities, see Edwards, especially *Gendered Strife*; Bercaw, *Gendered Freedoms*; McCurry, *Masters of Small Worlds*, and *Confederate Reckoning*, 85–217; Bardaglio, *Reconstructing the Household*, 3–115.

30. GWC, *Grandissimes*, 113, 114.

31. Ibid., 118.

32. Ibid., 286, 296.

33. Russell, "Intermarriage and Intermingling," 419–26. See also Hanger, "Coping in a Complex World," 220–21. This recognition was eroded in the eighteenth century by legislation aimed against intermarriage.

34. GWC, *Grandissimes*, 154, 221.

35. Ibid., 159, 158, 159, 221, 219.

36. Ibid., 38, 159, 161, 95; Russell, "Intermarriage and Intermingling," 408–9.

37. GWC, *Grandissimes*, 247, 223.

38. Ibid., 159, 38.

39. Ibid., 38, 191, 38.

40. Ibid., 220, 260, 246.

41. Ibid., 223, 154, 282.

42. Ibid., 215–16, 339. Haas, "Political Continuity in the Crescent City," 6–7; Nussbaum, "'Ring Is Smashed!'"

43. GWC, *Grandissimes*, 268, 294; Marler, "Merchants in the Transition to a New South," 182; Penningroth, *Claims of Kinfolk*, 111–30, 163–86.

44. GWC, *Grandissimes*, 156, 196, 156, 185, 279, 323.

45. Ibid., 195, 196.

46. Ibid., 299.

47. Ibid., 71; Washington, *Up from Slavery*, 63.

48. GWC, *Grandissimes*, 195, 196, 197, 196; G. Howard Hunter, "Politics of Resentment," 203–10.

49. See Rankin, "Origins of Black Leadership"; Tunnell, *Crucible of Reconstruction*, 66–91; Vincent, *Black Legislators in Louisiana*; Hennessey, "Race and Violence in Reconstruction New Orleans"; and, for firsthand accounts of freedpeople's political involvement, W. H. Wood to General Sewall, 3 July 1867; J. A. Mower to E. Whittlesey, 30 September 1867; Robert Buchanan to E. Whittlesey, January 1868, Ass't Comr. Reports, ser. 1309, RG 105, BRFAL.

50. GWC, *Grandissimes*, 330; Warner, *Studies in the South and West*, 50; Fabre, "New Orleans Creole Expatriates in France."

51. *Louisianian*, 18 May 1872; Rankin, "Forgotten People," 192. See also Rankin, "Impact of the Civil War," 396–416. Rankin found that only 11 percent of the 880 free African American heads of households in the third, fourth, and fifth wards of New Orleans in 1860 were still there ten years later ("Impact of the Civil War," 399). On the property loss of *libres*, see Schweninger, "Antebellum Free Persons," 354–60, and *Black Property Owners*, 142–232.

52. On black Creole efforts to unite politically with ex-slaves, see Rankin, "Forgotten People," 226–44. On the police, see Rousey, *Policing the Southern City*, 102–58. For the impact of Bras Coupé on the force, see Wagner, *Disturbing the Peace*, 58–115; on *La Tribune*, see Connor, "Reconstruction Rebels"; Senter, "Creole Poets on the Verge of a Nation"; and Bell, *Revolution, Romanticism, and the Afro-Creole Protest Tradition in Louisiana*, 222–75.

53. GWC, *Grandissimes*, 174, 171, 174; on planters' fears of losing a workforce, see the October 1866 Report to O. O. Howard, Ass't Comr. Reports, ser. 1309; see also comments found in the Assistant Inspector General's Consolidated Reports on Conditions of Freedmen on the Plantations, Jan. 1866–Nov. 1868, ser. 1311, RG 105, BRFAL; see also Howard White, *Freedmen's Bureau in Louisiana*, 101–33; Joe Taylor, *Louisiana Reconstructed*, 321–37 and, more generally, 364–406; and Cohen, *At Freedom's Edge*, 23–43; on planters' postwar recruitment of immigrants, see E. Russell Williams, "Louisiana's Public and Private Immigration Endeavors"; Jung, *Coolies and Cane*, 107–220.

54. GWC, *Grandissimes*, 37.

55. GWC, *Creoles of Louisiana*, 39. Howard located freedom in a northern-nuanced meaning of manhood involving "industry, labor, and application," to encourage freedmen to support their families. "Speech of Major General O. O. Howard to the Colored People at the Orleans Theatre," 5 November 1865, Miscellaneous Records, ser. 1328, RG 105, BRFAL. On Bureau criticism of black idleness and spending, see Robert Buchanan to E. Whittlesey, January 1868, Ass't Comr. Reports, ser. 1309, RG 105, BRFAL.

56. Black Louisianians' ambitions and eagerness to work are described in Hepworth, *Whip, Hoe, and Sword*, 140-70; Trowbridge, *South*, 405-14. See also Rodrigue, *Reconstruction in the Cane Fields*, 58-103; Fitzgerald, *Union League Movement*, 113-76; O'Donovan, *Becoming Free in the Cotton South*, 208-63; and see the October 1866 Annual District Report to O. O. Howard and the 1867 Annual Reports in "Monthly and Annual Reports of Ass't Comm'r. of Operations," ser. 1309, RG 105, BRFAL; Oubre, *Forty Acres and a Mule*, 110-36.

57. GWC, *Grandissimes*, 120, 37, 141-42, 243.

58. Ibid., 135, 1, 3, 151, 59.

59. Ibid., 315.

60. Ibid., 121, 255.

61. Ibid., 259, 255; Elfenbein, *Women on the Color Line*, 28-29, and Duet, "'Do You Not Know That Women Can Make Money?,'" 49-54, acknowledge Cable's interest in the plight of women but argue that it is tempered by his sexist treatment of them and his acceptance of convention, respectively.

62. GWC, *Grandissimes*, 260, 262.

63. Vandal, *Rethinking Southern Violence*, 115, 130. See also Steedman, "Gender and the Politics of the Household in Reconstruction Louisiana."

64. GWC, *Grandissimes*, 135, 184, 291, 99, 101, 71; GWC, "Creole Slave Songs," *Century Illustrated Monthly Magazine*, 811. For how gender and race shaped slave women's lives, see Hall, *Africans in Colonial Louisiana*, 166-87; Stevenson, *Life in Black and White*, 206-57; Schwalm, *Hard Fight*, 47-72; Glymph, *Out of the House of Bondage*, 32-62; and Edwards, *Scarlett Doesn't Live Here Anymore*, 48-64. On inheritance, see Rankin, "Forgotten People," 96-97.

65. GWC, *Grandissimes*, 71, 251, 175, 251, 135.

66. Ibid., 305, 306.

67. Ibid., 252, 250-51, 249; Dabel, "'My Ma Went to Work Early,'" 222; Long, "Marie Laveau"; Fandrich, "Birth of New Orleans' Voodoo Queen."

68. GWC, *Grandissimes*, 322.

69. Ibid., 315.

70. Twain to GWC, 12 October 1882, and GWC to Twain, 14 October 1882, in Cardwell, *Twins of Genius*, 85-86. After Twain sold the Hartford home in 1903, the whereabouts of this portrait became unknown. E-mail communication to author from Patti Philippon, Beatrice Fox Auerbach Chief Curator, Mark Twain House and Museum, 17 May 2013.

71. Lorch, "Cable and His Reading Tour with Mark Twain," 475; Turner, *George W. Cable*, 177.

72. Twain to Olivia Clemens, 13 February 1885 and 18 January 1885, in Wecter, *Love Letters of Mark Twain*, 237, 231; Railton, "Twain-Cable Combination," 180.

73. *Wisconsin State Journal* (Madison), 28 January 1885; *Quincy (Ill.) Daily Journal*, 13 January 1885.

74. "Two Noted American Authors in Montreal," Cable papers. See also their programs, especially (a) (Clemens). "Mark Twain"-Cable Readings. Program[m]e. [New York]: Chickering Hall, 18–19 Nov. 1884, with Mary W. B. Inness's signed ms. note on verso; Berg Catalog; (b) (Clemens). Program[me] [New York? 1884?]: broadside, 13 x 11 cm, with J. B. Pond's signed ms. note on verso; Berg Catalog; and (c) "Mark Twain"-Cable Readings. Holograph draft of program. Music Hall, Springfield Mass., 7 [8] Nov. 1884. Samuel Langhorne Clemens Collection of Papers, 1856–1938 [bulk 1870–1938]. The Henry W. and Albert A. Berg Collection of English and American Literature, NYPL, Astor, Lenox, and Tilden Foundations. Cable's influence on Twain has been well documented. Railton, "Twain-Cable Combination," 177–80; on "absorbed acting," see Knopfer, *Acting Naturally*, 74–80.

75. *Boston Herald Supplement*, 28 November 1883; *Boston Daily Advertiser*, 15 November 1884; Silber, *Romance of Reunion*, 39–65.

76. Lott, *Love and Theft*, 4–6; Berret, "Huckleberry Finn and the Minstrel Show," 40.

77. Gerteis, "Blackface Minstrelsy," 82; Wonham, "Mark Twain's Last Cakewalk," 268.

78. W. D. Howells to Cable, 2 October 1881, in Arms and Lohmann, *Selected Letters*, 297; *Daily Picayune* cited in Turner, *George W. Cable*, 85–86; *New Orleans Times-Democrat*, 1 June 1879.

79. Daniel Coit Gilman, "Mr. Cable's Lectures in Baltimore," *Critic* (New York), 24 March 1883, 131.

80. Garland is quoted in Nettels, *Language, Race, and Social Class*, 65; "Read what the Press says about Mr. Cable," undated advertisement, Cable papers; "George W. Cable," n.d., clipping, Scrapbook, Cable papers. See also "Mr. Cable's Recitations," *Scranton Truth*, 25 January 1890; "Mr. Cable's Readings," *Colorado Springs Gazette*, 26 November 1889; "Season 1889–90: George W. Cable: Compliments of the Press Where He Has Appeared This Season," advertisement, Cable papers, Lhamon, *Raising Cain*, 214.

81. GWC to Louise Cable, April 5–6, 1883, Cable papers; Warner, "On Mr. Cable's Readings," *Century Illustrated Monthly Magazine*, June 1883, 311, 312: GWC to Twain, 25 October 1884, in Cardwell, *Twins of Genius*, 105; Sotiropoulos, *Staging Race*, 242.

82. "Of Mr. George Cable's Readings for the Coming Season," n.d., Cable papers. GWC to Louise Cable, 1 January 1885, Cable papers.

83. GWC quoted in Turner, *George W. Cable*, 138.

84. GWC, *Dr. Sevier*, 467, 465.

85. Twain to Olivia Clemens, 10 February 1885, in Wecter, *Love Letters of Mark Twain*, 236.

86. Reviewer quoted in 1887 endorsement, "Creole Songs," Cable papers; Gavin Jones, *Strange Talk*, 115–33; Hall, *Africans in Colonial Louisiana*; Turner, *George W. Cable*, 177. For examples of songs in GWC's *Grandissimes*, see 168, 188, 306.

87. Bunner quoted in Jensen, *Life and Letters of Henry Cuyler Bunner*, 77; GWC to Louise Cable, 8 December 1884, Cable papers.

88. "Dance in Place Congo," *Century Illustrated Monthly Magazine*, February 1886, 522, 523, 525; "Creole Slave Songs," *Century Illustrated Monthly Magazine*, April 1886, 810, 820; Michelle Gordon, "'Midnight Scenes and Orgies,'" 782.

89. Brooks, *Bodies in Dissent*, 28.

90. Lhamon, *Raising Cain*, 149.

91. GWC quoted in Turner, *George W. Cable*, 182.

92. Roach, *Cities of the Dead*, 236; GWC quoted in Turner, *George W. Cable*, 182; Wonham, "Mark Twain's Last Cakewalk," 270; Cockrell, *Demons of Disorder*, 58; Bay, *White Image in the Black Mind*, 167.

93. "Bureau of Press Clippings," unnamed article in clippings file, month and day obscured, 1890, Cable papers.

94. Pennell, *Life and Letters of Joseph Pennell*, 57. This essay was adapted from his 11 September 1884 address before the American Social Science Association in Saratoga, New York; Kirt Wilson, *Reconstruction Desegregation Debate*, 61–120.

95. Grady, "In Plain Black and White," 911, 915–16, 917; GWC, "Silent South," 98; Butcher, "George W. Cable and Booker T. Washington," 463. Cable initiated a correspondence with Washington in November 1885 that lasted some nine years. Only Washington's responses to Cable's queries have survived, and they reveal a committed interest and appreciation for his work.

96. *Wisconsin State Journal* (Madison), 21 and 28 January 1885.

97. J. R. Clifford, *PP*, September 1888; *New Orleans Daily Picayune*, 15 February 1885, as cited in Turner, *George W. Cable*, 204.

98. See, for example, the *New Orleans Times-Democrat*, 29 June 1882, and *Memphis Daily Appeal*, 1 July 1882; Wonham, "'I Want a Real Coon,'" 118.

99. "Dr. Sevier," *New Orleans Daily Picayune*, 28 July 1884; Rouquette, *Critical Dialogue between Aboo and Caboo*, 20, 19; "Mr. Cable and the Creoles," 17 May 1884, *New Orleans Times-Democrat*; "The Lounger," *Critic* (New York), 5 July 1884, 6.

100. *New Orleans Times-Democrat*, 11 January 1885; Turner, *George W. Cable*, 203; Marion A. Baker to Cable, 25 May 1885, 5 February 1885, Cable papers. Marion's brother, Page Baker, was editor of the influential *New Orleans Times-Democrat* and the *Bulletin*.

101. "Invoking the Nation against the South," *New Orleans Daily Picayune*, 11 November 1888; "Cable and the Negroes," and "Cable Criticized," *New Orleans Times-Democrat*, 22 January 1885 and 2 February 1885, respectively; Jack Brown, letter to the editor, *Selma Times*, 13 January 1885; Dabney, "George W. Cable in the Century Magazine," 152, which was reprinted in the esteemed *Southern Historical Society Papers*; *Nashville Daily American*, 22 December 1889.

102. *New York Tribune*, 12 June 1887; "Mr. Cable and the South," *New York Star*, 13 June 1887. For more, see George Parsons Lathrop, "Mr. Cable's History of the Creoles," *Book Buyer*, December 1884, 277–79; W. S. Kennedy, "The New Orleans of George Cable," *Boston Literary World*, 24 January 1885, 29–31; Edward E. Hale, "Mr. Cable and the Creoles," *Critic*, 12 September 1885, 122.

103. [Pond (J. B.) Lyceum Bureau]. "Major Pond's Announcements" (New York: De Vinne Press, 1887), Berg Collection, NYPL, Astor, Lenox, and Tilden Foundations; "Read what the Press says About Mr. Cable" and "Advertisement of Mr. George W. Cable's Readings ... Testimonials from all Parts of the Union," Cable papers.

104. Edmund Wilson, *Patriotic Gore*, 579; GWC, "After-Thoughts of a Story-Teller," 16–17; Johnson quoted in Turner, *George W. Cable*, 95, and see also 66–69, 95–99. For examples of recent criticism, see Rubin, *George W. Cable*, 62–65,

144-49; Ladd, *Nationalism and the Color Line*, 44-46, 83-84; and Cleman, *George Washington Cable Revisited*, 185.

105. GWC to Louise Cable, 5 April 1883, Cable papers. See also Cardwell, *Twins of Genius*, 90-94, and Turner, *George W. Cable*, 135-41. Gilder, later editor in chief of *Century Illustrated Monthly Magazine*, had accompanied Cable in his initial visit to Johns Hopkins University, which resulted in his lecture debut, while Smith saw to it that Charles Dudley Warner's influential review of Cable's Hartford performance was published in *Century Illustrated Monthly Magazine*.

106. GWC to editor, *Boston Literary World*, 31 May 1875; GWC to Louise Cable, 24 November 1883, Cable papers; Twain to Olivia Clemens, 13 February 1885, in Wecter, *Love Letters of Mark Twain*, 237.

107. The entire *Century* staff attended Cable's performance in New York on 23 April 1883, which they critiqued (Turner, *George W. Cable*, 142).

108. University of Mississippi Commencement Address, 1882, "Literature in the Southern States," reprinted in Turner, "Cable's Revolt," 21; see also Greeson, *Our South*, 261-68.

109. King, *Memories of a Southern Woman*, 60.

Chapter 5

1. Because of her pen name's importance to French's relished celebrity, it is retained throughout this chapter.

2. OT, *Expiation*, 2, 214; Grady, "New South," in *New South*, 3-13.

3. McMichael, *Journey to Obscurity*, 3-53.

4. Carnegie's interest was caught by Thanet's essays such as "The Tramp in Four Centuries" (*Lippincott's Magazine* 23 [May 1879]: 565-74) per McMichael, *Journey to Obscurity*, 69. Their friendship was further cemented with a grand tour to Scotland; see June and July 1881 entries, "Diary of Alice French's coaching trip through Scotland as the guest of Andrew Carnegie," French Papers, Newberry Library, Chicago.

5. Ripley Hitchcock to Octave Thanet, 24 October 1894, French Papers; McMichael, *Journey to Obscurity*, 54-80.

6. Bentzon [Blanc], "In Arkansas," 41. On the Knights, see Forbath, *Law and the Shaping of the American Labor Movement*, 12-25. On Cooper, see Gaines, *Uplifting the Race*, 145-48.

7. Sewell, "Clover Bend Plantation," 313; McMichael, *Journey to Obscurity*, 181; Dougan and Dougan, *By the Cypress Swamp*, 4-9. Although little is known about Thanet's lifelong relationship with Crawford, a recent widow, Dougan and Dougan dismiss the possibility of lesbianism (ibid., 4). Throughout *An Adventure in Photography*, Thanet offers the most detailed glimpse of "that gentle spirit," Crawford, as patient, persevering, and creative (*Adventure in Photography*, 37). On contemporary attitudes toward Boston marriages, see Diggs, "Romantic Friends or a Different Race of Creatures"; Vicinus, *Intimate Friends*; and Behling, *Masculine Woman in America*.

8. McMichael, *Journey to Obscurity*, 93.

9. *Chicago Daily Journal*, 22 September 1914, as cited in Alice French obituary, *Davenport (Iowa) Democrat and Leader*, 9 January 1934. The Clover Bend population rose

from 75 to 90 in 1892 and to 100 in 1898, only to decline to 40 in 1912, three years after Thanet and Crawford sold Thanford. Dougan and Dougan, *By the Cypress Swamp*, 8.

10. Higginson, "Local Short Story," 5; Buck, *Road to Reunion*, 207-9.

11. Reid, "Four Women Writers of the West," 144; MacKethan, "Thomas Nelson Page," 317.

12. Garland, *Roadside Meetings*, 253-55; *Atlantic Monthly*, February 1892, 265; Payne, "Recent Books of Fiction," *Dial* (June 1891): 51.

13. Jung, *Coolies and Cane*, 175; Moneyhon, *Arkansas*, 23-40; Moneyhon, "Creators of the New South in Arkansas," 387-92. Of the first twelve teachers to come to Arkansas, the majority were from the Midwest; two hailed from Iowa. See Pearce, "American Missionary Association and the Freedmen in Arkansas."

14. W. E. B. Du Bois, *Souls of Black Folk*, 165.

15. Schaeffer, "American Authoresses of the Hour," *Harper's Bazaar*, 13 January 1900, 31; McMichael, *Journey to Obscurity*, 154. See also Foner and Lewis, *Black Worker*, 37-108, and Cronon, *Nature's Metropolis*, 57-93.

16. "Gossip from Octave Thanet," n.d., newspaper clipping, French Papers; Clara Barton to Alice French, 29 [no month] 1892, French Papers; Shinn, "Miss Alice French," 350.

17. *Book Buyer*, February 1893, 11. McMichael, *Journey to Obscurity*, 64. For her negotiating tactics with publishers, see Alice French to Charles Scribner's Sons, 22 April 1890, French Papers; Alice French to William Carey, 18 May and 22 October 1887, and Alice French to Richard Watson Gilder, 15 July and 13 August 1888, General correspondence, Century Company records, Manuscripts and Archives Division, Century, NYPL, Astor, Lenox, and Tilden Foundations. See also Mott, *History of American Magazines*, 4:35-42; Tebbel, *History of Book Publishing*, 130-49; Coultrap-McQuin, *Doing Literary Business*, 1-49, 193-200; and Christopher Wilson, *Labor of Words*, 40-86.

18. McMichael, *Journey to Obscurity*, 145; *Nation* 53, no. 1370 (1 October 1891): 264. Of all the Reconstruction writers considered herein, Thanet has received the least scholarly attention. Besides McMichael's biography, Michael Dougan has published several articles and coauthored, with Carol Dougan, a collection of Thanet's Arkansas stories, *By the Cypress Swamp*. More recently Csicsila, "'Been Reading the Horrors in the Newspapers?,'" and Berkove, "Octave Thanet's Rebuttal," have explored her short fiction. The French Papers contain many moving fan letters. On the request for an Arkansas history, see R. I. Holcombe to Alice French, 8 June 1892, French Papers.

19. Quoted in Sutherland, "Guerrillas," 275; OT to E. L. Burlingame, February 1889, French Papers. On Civil War Arkansas, see Moneyhon, *Impact of the Civil War and Reconstruction*, 101-74; Christ, *Rugged and Sublime*; and Bailey and Sutherland, *Civil War Arkansas*. Comprehensive book-length revisionist scholarship focused on Arkansas is lagging. On Rector's threat, see Mackey, "Bushwackers, Provosts, and Tories," 172. On guerrilla violence, see also Sutherland, *Savage Conflict*.

20. See testimonies by Jonas M. Tebbetts, 19 March 1866, 2:154-55, and Charles A. Harper, 17 February 1866, 2:75, in U.S. Congress, Joint Committee on Reconstruction, *Reports of the Committees*, "Part III: Georgia, Alabama, Mississippi, Arkansas"; Moneyhon, *Impact of the Civil War and Reconstruction*, 190-221. On the ongoing terrorism in Fulton County leading to an agent's murder, see letters of Simpson Mason

to C. H. Smith for 6, 25, and 31 January 1868, 30 April 1868, 30 June 1868, and to Governor Isaac Murphy, 26 January 1868, Letters Sent and Received, ser. 430; Joseph Martin to C. H. Smith, 11 and 31 October, 1868, 31 December 1868, Letters Sent, ser. 432, RG 105, BRFAL.

21. E. W. Gantt to John Sprague, 27 May 1866, Monthly Reports of Subordinate Officers, ser. 242; 2 August 1865 Inspection Report, included in letter of Jason Barnes to John Levering, 9 August 1865, Retained Copies of Reports, ser. 379, RG 105, BRFAL; Finley, *From Slavery to Uncertain Freedom*, 151, 141–70. See also Lovett, "African-Americans, Civil War, and Aftermath in Arkansas," 318–58; Nichols, "Changing Role of Blacks in the Civil War," 66–71; Urwin, "Poison Spring and Jenkins' Ferry," 124–29; and DeBlack, *With Fire and Sword*, 187, 146–73.

22. Clayton, *Aftermath of the Civil War*, 71; John R. Montgomery to "Major," 27 September 1865, Narrative Reports of Operations from Subordinate Officers, ser. 242; see also William Brian to J. Watson, 10 December 1866, and [Name Unclear] to J. Watson, 28 February 1867, Letters Sent, ser. 291; "Extract," George E. Dayton, 30 September 1866, Letters Received, ser. 292, RG 105, BRFAL; Moneyhon, *Impact of the Civil War and Reconstruction*, 242–63; Thompson, *Arkansas and Reconstruction*, 59–169; Gillette, *Retreat from Reconstruction*, 136–50; DeBlack, *With Fire and Sword*, 174–233.

23. Nichols, "Changing Role of Blacks in the Civil War," 61. See also Lovett, "African-Americans, Civil War, and Aftermath in Arkansas," 307; Lancaster, "'They Are Not Wanted.'"

24. Turner, *Indianapolis Freeman*, 5 January 1889; Niswonger, *Arkansas Democratic Politics*, 10. Demographic statistic per DeBlack, *With Fire and Sword*, 209. For an overview of postwar conditions for black Arkansans, see Horace Nash, "Blacks in Arkansas during Reconstruction." On black Arkansan political activism, see Wintory, "African-American Legislators"; Wintory, "William Hines Furbush"; Moneyhon, "Black Politics in Arkansas during the Gilded Age"; and Rosen, *Terror in the Heart of Freedom*, 87–175; and more generally, see Graves, *Town and Country*, 14–69, and Fon Gordon, *Caste and Class*, 8–22. Of the forty-seven black Arkansans who served in the General Assembly and the two in the Senate between 1876 and 1900, none represented Lawrence County (Moneyhon, "Black Politics in the Gilded Age," 232).

25. On the Knights' representation in Thanet's region, see the map "Knights of Labor and Farmer-Labor Parties in Arkansas" in Hild, *Greenbackers, Knights of Labor, and Populists*. For more on Arkansas's third-party politics, see Hild, "Labor, Third-Party Politics, and New South Democracy in Arkansas"; McCollom, "Agricultural Wheel, the Union Labor Party, and the 1889 Arkansas Legislature"; and Moneyhon, *Arkansas*, 77–93. To situate these Arkansas organizations within the greater southern Populist movement, see Hild, *Greenbackers, Knights of Labor, and Populists*, 45–200. See also Graves, *Town and Country*, 134–49; and Recken, "Rags to Respectability," 54–57.

26. Barnes, "Who Killed John M. Clayton"; Monks, *History of Southern Missouri and Northern Arkansas*, 207–44. On the Populist Movement's defeat and "Redemption," see Hild, *Greenbackers, Knights of Labor, and Populists*, 159–221; and Niswonger, *Arkansas Democratic Politics*, 1–104. On its effects on black Arkansans, see Fon Gordon, *Caste and Class*, 23–120; and Graves, *Town and Country*, 164–214.

Although black Arkansans constituted just 4 percent of the nation's black population in 1890, they comprised more than 50 percent of the emigrants in the 1890s. See Barnes, *Journey of Hope*, 195 (n. 3), 33–106, and "On the Shore beyond the Sea," 329; see also Cohen, *At Freedom's Edge*, 138–67.

27. Whites, *Civil War as a Crisis in Gender*, 13. On Confederate veterans, see Marten, *Sing Not War*.

28. OT, *Expiation*, 32–33, 115, 138, 139, 115. Thanet identified with the Colonel's viewpoint. She listed Montaigne (along with Sir Walter Scott) as her favorite "author of prose" for *Book Buyer*, February 1893, 11.

29. OT, *Expiation*, 99, 127, 100.

30. Ibid., 31, 134.

31. Ibid., 30, 153, 199.

32. Crouch and Brice, *Cullen Montgomery Baker*, 6; Sutherland, "Guerrillas," 265; see also Barnes, "Williams Clan"; Richter, "'Oh God, Let Us Have Revenge'"; and Hartman and Ingenthron, *Bald Knobbers*.

33. OT, "Plantation Life," 34; OT, "Ma Bowlin'," in *Knitters in the Sun*, 251; OT, "Loaf of Peace," in *Otto the Knight*, 172–73; OT, "Whitsun Harp, Regulator," in *Knitters in the Sun*, 303; OT, *Expiation*, 134. Thanet predicted the environmental disaster that would result from draining the Arkansas delta swamps and destroying virgin forests of cypress. See Dougan, "When Fiction Is Reality," 30–31.

34. Lawrence, *Studies in Classic American Literature*, 5; OT, *Expiation*, 103, 55, 153, 114.

35. OT, *Expiation*, 70, 71, 93.

36. Ibid., 147, 181; see Cardyn, "Sexualized Racism/Gendered Violence," 813–34, and Rosen, *Terror in the Heart of Freedom*, 179–221.

37. OT, *Expiation*, 119, 105.

38. OT, "Whitsun Harp, Regulator," in *Knitters in the Sun*, 301, 314; OT, "Ma Bowlin'," in *Knitters in the Sun*, 257.

39. OT, *Expiation*, 96, 97, 95, 96, 123.

40. Ibid., 103, 164, 168–73.

41. Ibid., 142, 143, 19–20, 29.

42. OT quoted in Tucker, "'Octave Thanet,'" 36; McMichael, *Journey to Obscurity*, 45–47; 26–28.

43. McMichael, *Journey to Obscurity*, 92; OT, "Plantation Life," 40.

44. McCurry, *Confederate Reckoning*, 38–84; Moneyhon, "Disloyalty"; Kantrowitz, *Ben Tillman*, 40–79; Bercaw, *Gendered Freedoms*, 75–93, 117–34.

45. OT, *Expiation*, 8.

46. OT, "Plantation Life," 36, For more examples, see OT, "Town Life in Arkansas," 335–36; "Folk-Lore in Arkansas," 122–24; and diary entries for 7 and 12 March 1908, French Papers. On the overwhelmingly large numbers of destitute white people, see John Sprague to O. O. Howard, 17 July 1865, Monthly and Quarterly Reports of Operations, ser. 241; on white resentment, see Edward Ord to O. O. Howard, 27 February 1867, Letters Sent to Commissioner Howard, ser. 225, RG 105, BRFAL; and Pierce, "Mechanics of Little Rock."

47. OT, *Expiation*, 171, 193.

48. *Harper's Bazaar*, 4 March 1882, 130. See also the typed fragments "Why We Are Obliged to Be Anti-Suffragists" and "Extracts From Address at Iowa City Federation of Women's Clubs," French Papers, and French, *Stories from a Long Journey*, 46; Dougan, "Arkansas Married Woman's Property Law," especially 13-22; and Bercaw, *Gendered Freedoms*, 51-74.

49. OT, *Expiation*, 127-28.

50. Ibid., 41, 71, 58.

51. Morrison, *Playing in the Dark*, 76, 80. The scholarship devoted to the activist writings of African American women, particularly journalists and preachers, is vast and growing. A few recent examples: Cooper, *Word, Like Fire*; Broussard, *Giving a Voice to the Voiceless*; Schechter, *Ida B. Wells-Barnett and American Reform, 1880-1930*; Logan, *"We Are Coming"*; May, *Anna Julia Cooper*; and Zackodnik, *Press, Platform, Pulpit*.

52. OT, *Expiation*, 155. "Half a Curse" can be found in *Knitters in the Sun*.

53. Ibid., 27, 149-50, 28; "Recent Southern Fiction," *Nation*, 51, no. 1311 (14 August 1890): 135.

54. OT, *Expiation*, 27-28, 109, 201, 161.

55. [Name unclear] Main to [name unclear] Mills, 30 September 1868, Letters and Endorsements Sent, ser. 387, RG 105, BRFAL; OT, *Expiation*, 10, 77, 76, 112.

56. OT, *Expiation*, 122, 109; Glymph, *Out of the House of Bondage*, 91-96, 152-53. See also Myers, "'Sisters in Arms,'" 147-48; Edwards, "Enslaved Women," 313-15; and Camp, *Closer to Freedom*.

57. Tera Hunter, *To 'Joy My Freedom*, 5; OT, *Expiation*, 52, 111, 140.

58. Hahn, *Nation Under Our Feet*, 328; David Casey to William Colby, 29 June 1867, Monthly Narrative and Statistical School Reports, ser. 272, RG 105, BRFAL; OT, *Expiation*, 208. On black "sauciness," see E. W. Gantt to John Sprague, 27 May 1866, Monthly Reports of Subordinate Officers, ser. 242, RG 105, BRFAL. On exploitative behavior, see a freedwoman's complaint of her master's physical abuse, anonymous letter written to William Brian, 24 December 1866, and a freedwoman seeking support from her former master for their child, affidavit of Amanda Grigsby against John Speddon, 30 April 1868, Letters Received, ser. 292, RG 105, BRFAL. Regarding a woman's complaint against the impressment of her daughter, see letter from E. A. Messick, 6 November 1866, also found in Letters Received, ser. 292, RG 105, BRFAL; for more examples of increasing defiance shown by Georgian slaves during wartime, see also O'Donovan, *Becoming Free in the Cotton South*, 59-110.

59. OT, *Expiation*, 166, 164, 165, 190, 129.

60. Elizabeth Young, *Disarming the Nation*, 47; OT, *Expiation*, 97, 98.

61. OT, "Folk-Lore in Arkansas," 121. See Palmer, "Miscegenation as an Issue," and Robinson, "'Most Shamefully Common.'"

62. OT, *Expiation*, 50; Alice French to William Carey, 19 April 1886, General correspondence, Century, NYPL.

63. OT, "Conjured Kitchen," in *Otto the Knight*, 74; OT, *Expiation*, 111, 166; Williams to OT, 2 September 1893, French Papers.

64. OT, *Expiation*, 3, 202; OT, "Plantation Life," 32.

65. Bentzon [Blanc], "In Arkansas," 136; John Sprague to O. O. Howard, 17 July 1865, Monthly and Quarterly Narrative Reports, ser. 241, RG 105, BRFAL. See also

Simpson Mason to Colonel C. H. Smith, 31, 30 April 1867, 31 May 1867, 30 November 1867, and Simpson Mason to E. O. C. Ord[?], Letters Sent, ser. 430; on the testimony surrounding the murder of Robin Kimbrough, a freedman, by his overseer, see ser. 434, Letters and Orders Received, Fulton County, RG 105, BRFAL. Thanet's workers, like others in Lawrence County, sharecropped one-fourth cotton and one-third corn and were charged an additional one-sixth for grinding corn at the mill per McMichael, *Journey to Obscurity*, 92. See also Penningroth, *Claims of Kinfolk*, 146–51, and Battershell, "Socioeconomic Role of Slavery."

66. Schaeffer, "American Authoresses of the Hour," 31; William Allen White, *Autobiography*, 311–12. Thanet recorded her frustration with defiant employers on 1 February 1908, 4 February 1908, 7 March 1908, and 12 March 1908, French Papers.

67. OT, "Plantation Life," 42–43, 47; Bentzon [Blanc], "In Arkansas," 136, 137.

68. Finley, *From Slavery to Uncertain Freedom*, 84, 124; OT, "Plantation Life," 48.

69. OT, *Adventure in Photography*, 24, 145, 25.

70. Ibid., 146.

71. OT, *Expiation*, 102; Moneyhon, *Impact of the Civil War and Reconstruction*, 176. Within Lawrence County alone, average real estate property assessments per acre declined from $4.31 in 1860 to $1.47 in 1866, and by 1870, they had risen to only $2.55, per Moneyhon, ibid., 255.

72. Freedman quoted in testimony of George R. Weeks, 29 February 1866, U.S. Congress, Joint Committee on Reconstruction, *Reports of the Committees*, "Part III: Georgia, Alabama, Mississippi, Arkansas," 2:77; statistics per Moneyhon, "From Slave to Free Labor," 142; DeBlack, *With Fire and Sword*, 154; and Finley, *From Slavery to Uncertain Freedom*, 101, 103. For more on Arkansas freedpeople's farming arrangements and efforts, including those on government-supervised plantations, see Moneyhon, "From Slave to Free Labor."

73. Battershell, "Socioeconomic Role of Slavery," 48; Moneyhon, *Arkansas*, 67, 70; see also Woodman, *New South—New Law*, 67–94. *Ponder v. Rhea*, initiated in Lawrence County, helped erode the laborers' rights to the crop. By 1900 several states allowed landlords to prosecute sharecroppers under criminal law if they attempted to seize or sell any portion of the crop promised the landlord. Landlords, however, could be sued for breach of contract only if they kept the entire crop and refused to pay their workers.

74. Penningroth, *Claims of Kinfolk*, 131–61; Edwards, *People and Their Peace*, 133–68; for Thanet on socialism and private property, see "Why We Are Obliged to Be Anti-Suffragists," n.d., typed ms., French Papers; on property's expanded meaning, see Ginnow, *Corpus Juris Secondum*, Section 4b, 165–69. To emphasize both the chattel goods status and the mobility of this type of property, I refer to it as "portable property."

75. OT, *Expiation*, 9, 62–63, 148.

76. Ibid., 129; William Taylor, *Cavalier and Yankee*, 203–59.

77. OT, *Expiation*, 29, 205, 99.

78. OT, "Plantation Life," 44–45; OT, *Expiation*, 66–67. On freedpeople and postwar consumer culture, see Glymph, *Out of the House of Bondage*, 204–26.

79. Hale, "'For Colored' and 'For White,'" 163; Lu Ann Jones, "Gender, Race, and Itinerant Commerce," 320; Forbath, *Law and the Shaping of the American Labor Movement*, 59–97. See also McGovern, *Sold American*, 23–134; Schlereth, "Country

Stores, Country Fairs, and Mail Order Catalogues," 364–75; and Bryant, *How Curious a Land*, 145–83.

80. W. E. B. Du Bois, *Souls of Black Folk*, 140; Woodman, *New South—New Law*, 28–66; Butcher, "George Washington Cable and Booker T. Washington," 464.

81. OT, "Loaf of Peace," in *Otto the Knight*, 170–71; OT, "Conjured Kitchen," in *Otto the Knight*, 60; Washington, *Up from Slavery*, 79.

82. OT, "Sist' Chaney," in *Otto the Knight*, 143; Glymph, *Out of the House of Bondage*, 208, 209; *Arkansas*, 155.

83. "Cripple," letter to the editor, *Daily Arkansas Gazette* (Little Rock), 12 July 1867; White and White, *Stylin'*, 138. See also Barnes, "'On the Shore beyond the Sea,'" 334–37, and Giggie, "'Disband Him from the Church,'" 259–63; on emancipation day commemoration, see Kachun, *Festivals of Freedom*; Clark, *Defining Moments*; and Blair, *Cities of the Dead*, 23–48.

84. "Cripple," letter to the editor, *Daily Arkansas Gazette* (Little Rock), 12 July 1867; Davies, *Black Women, Writing, and Identity*, 4; Thadious Davis, *Games of Property*, 2–3. The blurring of things with slaves as examples of corporeal property still prevailed in Thanet's day, and contemporary legal texts cite precedents involving slaves to clarify this definition of corporeal property. See *Schouler's Personal Property*, 6, and Lawson, *Selected Cases in the Law of Personal Property*, 35–37. See also Walter Johnson, *Soul by Soul*, 26, and Haynes, *Radical Spiritual Motherhood*, 115–44.

85. OT, "Ma Bowlin'," in *Knitters in the Sun*, 239; OT, "Mortgage on Jeffy," in *Otto the Knight*, 314, 313.

86. OT, "Sist' Chaney," in *Otto the Knight*, 144.

87. Williams to Samuel Mills, 3 August 1868, ser. 380; Isaac Adair to John Sprague, 30 June 1866, Narrative Reports of Operations from Subordinate Officers, ser. 242, RG 105, BRFAL. On the effects of black consumer's adornment, see Hale, *Making Whiteness*, 122–97; Jacqueline Jones, *Labor of Love*, 44–79; Hunt, "Struggle to Achieve Individual Expression through Clothing and Adornment," 232–37; and White and White, *Stylin'*, 125–52.

88. OT, "Ma Bowlin'," in *Knitters in the Sun*, 254; Dougan and Dougan, *By the Cypress Swamp*, 7. On the plantation store and the credit system, see Ayers, *Promise of the New South*, 81–103; Wiener, *Social Origins of the New South*, 77–133; Ransom and Sutch, *One Kind of Freedom*, 126–70; and Finley, *From Slavery to Uncertain Freedom*, 94–95.

89. Hale, *Making Whiteness*, 9, 188; OT, "Plantation Life," 35–37.

90. Sewell, "Clover Bend Plantation," 313.

91. OT, *Expiation*, 127.

92. Ibid., 120, 130.

93. Ibid., 69, 136, 58, 136, 204.

94. Ibid., 137–38, 202, 204; see also Wyatt-Brown, *Shaping of Southern Culture*, 255–69.

95. OT, *Expiation*, 203, 211–12, 153, 213, 214, 129.

96. Sewell, "Clover Bend Plantation," 318; "Clover Bend Poke Root," 25 May 1905, French Papers. See also the programs for "The Golden Story Book," 13 January 1896 and 20 April 1896, French Papers.

97. OT, "Town Life in Arkansas," 338, 333. On Arkansas stereotypes, see Shea, "Semi-Savage State."

98. OT, "Plantation Life," 49, 48; on white attitudes to black Arkansan emigration, see Barnes, *Journey of Hope*, 91–96; on the bureau's involvement with interstate reallocation of black labor, see Cohen, *At Freedom's Edge*, 44–108. On black immigration to Arkansas, see DeBlack, *With Fire and Sword*, 207–8; Graves, *Town and Country*, 90–96; Horace Nash, "Blacks in Arkansas during Reconstruction," 247–50; and Finley, *From Slavery to Uncertain Freedom*, 98–101. On postwar Arkansas farming conditions, see Moneyhon, *Arkansas*, 61–76.

99. Rosen, *Terror in the Heart of Freedom*, 183, 205, 181; Bieze, *Booker T. Washington and the Art of Self-Representation*, 2; see also Kantrowitz, *Ben Tillman*, 110–55; Parsons, "Midnight Rangers"; and Cardyn, "Sexualized Racism/Gendered Violence," 676–813.

100. OT, *Expiation*, 194.

101. Lovett, "African Americans, Civil War, and Aftermath in Arkansas," 338. Trotti, "What Counts," shows the problems associated with attempts at quantifying lynching, including the unmeasurable effects of inciting terror, on which Thanet's graybacks capitalized. See also Waldrep, *Many Faces of Judge Lynch*, 67–126, and Pfeifer, *Roots of Rough Justice*, 32–87.

102. Finley, *From Slavery to Uncertain Freedom*, 64–65, 160–61; Bentzon [Blanc], "In Arkansas," 136, 144, 136; see also Hahn, *Nation under Our Feet*, 265–313.

103. Psalm 45:4 found in OT, *Expiation*, 193; Wyatt-Brown, *Shaping of Southern Culture*, 283–94; see also Richter, "'Oh God, Let Us Have Revenge," 277–86.

104. OT, *Expiation*, 167, 159.

105. Ibid., 181.

106. J. Martin to C. H. Smith, 30 November 1868, Letters Sent, ser. 432; F. Thibant to J. Bennett, 1 October 1867, Letters Sent, ser. 435; [name unclear] Main to [name unclear] Mills, 30 September 1868, and 31 October 1868, Letters and Endorsements Sent, ser. 387, RG 105, BRFAL; OT, "Town Life in Arkansas," 336; Bentzon [Blanc], "In Arkansas," 141, 143; Finley, *From Slavery to Uncertain Freedom*, 145.

107. OT, "Whitsun Harp, Regulator," in *Knitters in the Sun*, 303, 329; OT quoted in McMichael, *Journey to Obscurity*, 108; Bentzon [Blanc], "In Arkansas," 141.

108. *Athenaeum*, 9 August 1890, 189; *Dial* (May 1890): 13; Fahs, *Imagined Civil War*, 314; R. I. Holcombe to Octave Thanet, 8 June 1892, French Papers. Although *Expiation* did not sell well, it enabled Thanet to raise her price to "$200 or $200 and something dollars" for her next *Century* contribution. Alice French to Richard Watson Gilder, 13 February 1891, General correspondence, Century, NYPL.

109. Reid, "Theories of Octave Thanet and Other Western Realists," 100, 101; Theodore Roosevelt to Alice French, 23 April 1904, Reel Number 334, Theodore Roosevelt Papers, Ser. 2, volume 47, 9, Library of Congress, Washington, D.C.; see also McMichael, *Journey to Obscurity*, 160, 172–73.

110. For more on the Lost Cause, see Brundage, *Southern Past*, 12–54; Karen Cox, *Dixie's Daughters*; Whites, *Civil War as a Crisis in Gender*, 160–98; Janney, *Burying the Dead*; Blair, *Cities of the Dead*, 77–105; and Mills and Simpson, *Monuments to the Lost Cause*.

Conclusion

1. Grady, "Race Problem in the South," in *New South*, 97-98.

2. The *New York Ledger* series appeared on 16, 23, and 30 November 7, 14, and 21 December 1889, thereby bracketing Grady's 12 December "Race Problem" speech.

3. Grady, "Sixth Article" of "New South," in *New South*, 107; Gaston, *New South Creed*, 18-42. In his Grady-inflected *Origins of the New South*, C. Vann Woodward classically characterized the New South movement as the triumph of largely middle-class, urban industrialists over established agrarian interests, an emergent elite then defeated by exploitative northern capitalists. Scholars have since amended Woodward's influential thesis in many ways, while others have expanded its scope through the lens of gender, ethnicity, and public memory. For recent examples, see Whites, *Gender Matters*; Boles and Johnson, *Origins of the New South Fifty Years Later*; and J. William Harris, *New South*.

4. Cable, excerpt from untitled poem for "The Progress of the Negro Race" speech, reprinted in the *Hartford Courant*, 12 and 13 January 1887.

5. Grady, "Race Problem in the South," in *New South*, 89. On his advertising acumen and his experiences during Reconstruction, see Nixon, *Henry B. Grady*, 257-58 and 41-141, respectively; on his vision of the New South, see Bryan, *Henry Grady or Tom Watson?*, 39-62, and Harold Davis, *Henry Grady's New South*, 111-32; on his helping to develop postwar Atlanta, see ibid., 164-90.

6. Maffly-Kipp and Lofton, *Women's Work*, 9. On black women's suffrage activism, for example, see Terborg-Penn, *African American Women and the Struggle for the Vote*, 36-106. See also Glass, *Courting Communities*, 37-101; Martha Jones, *All Bound Up Together*, 151-204; Parker, *Articulating Rights*, 97-138, 177-211; and Deborah White, *Too Heavy a Load*, 21-110.

7. Peterson, "Commemorative Ceremonies and Invented Traditions." Scholarship is extensive and expanding as the postwar "nadir" period is being reconceived, but for a good overview, see the essays in McCaskill and Gebhard, *Post-Bellum, Pre-Harlem*.

8. Foster, *Written by Herself*, 154-90; May, *Anna Julia Cooper*, 13-43.

9. Zackodnik, *Press, Platform, Pulpit*, 204-23; Kaestle and Radway, *Print in Motion*, 78-139, 431-70; Royster, *Traces of a Stream*, 108-238.

10. Gardner, *Unexpected Places*, 92-172; Foster, "Narrative"; Vogel, *Black Press*, 98-120; Danky, "Reading, Writing, and Resisting"; McHenry, "Reading and Race Pride"; Radway, "Learned and Literary Print Cultures," 224-33.

11. "In Memoriam. Tribute of Respect by Colored Citizens of Chicago to the Memory of Judge Albion W. Tourgée. Presented on the occasion of the funeral obsequies at Mayville, New York, November 14 A.D. 1905, by Mrs. Ida B. Wells Barnett," Pamphlet, No. 9838, Tourgée Papers; Lewis, *W. E. B. Du Bois*, 330.

12. Vandevelde, "New Property of the Nineteenth Century," 330, 362.

13. Ibid., 338, 333-57; Ohmann, *Selling Culture*, 81-117.

14. Margaret Mitchell's twentieth-century classic *Gone with the Wind* attests to land ownership's enduring value; however, following Reconstruction narratives' precedent, the novel radicalizes that vision: Mitchell's narrator, as well as Scarlett O'Hara and the

novel's chief patriarchal characters, repeatedly emphasize the importance and landed value (the "red earth") of Tara Plantation, as particularly *hers* to retain.

15. Grady, "Sixth Article" of "New South," in *New South*, 146.

16. Forbath, *Law and the Shaping of the American Labor Movement*, 85.

17. Foner, *Reconstruction*, 392–411. See also the classic work of Woodman, *New South—New Law*. For two case studies, see Reidy, *From Slavery to Agrarian Capitalism*, 136–60, 215–41, and Rodrigue, *Reconstruction in the Cane Fields*, 120–82.

18. Grady, "Race Problem in the South," in *New South*, 102.

19. Grady, "First Article" of "New South," in *New South*, 108.

20. Grady, "Race Problem in the South," in *New South*, 90; Blight, *Beyond the Battlefield*, 127.

21. W. E. B. Du Bois, *Black Reconstruction*, 726.

22. Williamson, *Florida Politics in the Gilded Age*, 96–194; Canter Brown, *Florida's Black Public Officials*, 43–69; Ortiz, *Emancipation Betrayed*, 33–127.

23. Beeby, "Red Shirt Violence, Election Fraud," 4. See also Beeby, *Revolt of the Tar Heels*, 85–214, and Cecelski and Tyson, *Democracy Betrayed*.

24. In "Votes for Women: A Symposium by Leading Thinkers of Colored America," *Crisis*, August 1915, 185; "Bullet in His Head: He Is Killed by a Clifford," *Martinsburg Herald*, 15 April 1905, and "Murder Trial Ends," *Martinsburg Herald*, 5 May 1905.

25. "Archives and History Section Posts Pioneer Press Editorials Online," West Virginia Division of Culture and History, http://www.wvculture.org/news.aspx?-Agency=Division&Id=1045 (accessed 2 November 2014); "Harpers Ferry Park Pays Tribute to Graduates of Black College," *Black Issues in Higher Education* 18, no. 26 (14 February 2002): 18.

26. Konhaus, "'I Thought Things Would Be Different There," 26–32; Bushong, *Historic Jefferson County*, 267–69; Transcript of Harpers Ferry Oral History Interview with Dr. Richard McKinney, 30 November 1988, Tape 1, SCD, 11.

27. Hogue, *Uncivil War*, 8, 185–94; Ettinger, "John Fitzpatrick and the Limits of Working-Class Politics," 345–47; Joe Taylor, *Louisiana Reconstructed*, 507–8.

28. OT, "Plantation Life," 36; Moneyhon, "Creators of the New South in Arkansas"; McCollom, "Agricultural Wheel, the Union Labor Party, and the 1889 Arkansas Legislature."

29. Moneyhon, *Impact of the Civil War and Reconstruction*, 240; Branam, "Another Look at Disfranchisement"; Fon Gordon, *Caste and Class*, 105–40; Graves, *Town and Country*, 150–200, 215–25; and Moneyhon, *Arkansas*, 95–150. For a history of the state's troubled race relations, see Stockley, *Ruled by Race*.

30. Mitchell, *Disturbing and Alien Memory*, 20.

31. On Simms's finances, see Rubin, "Simms, Charleston, and the Profession of Letters," 227.

BIBLIOGRAPHY

Primary Sources

Manuscript Collections

Chicago, Illinois
    Newberry Library
        Alice French Papers
Durham, North Carolina
    David M. Rubenstein Rare Book and Manuscript Library,
        Duke University
Harpers Ferry, West Virginia
    Harpers Ferry National Historical Park
        Storer College Documents
Morgantown, West Virginia
    West Virginia and Regional History Collection, West Virginia University
        Storer College Archives
New Haven, Connecticut
    Manuscripts and Archives, Yale University Library
        Edwards Pierrepont Papers, MS 400
New Orleans, Louisiana
    Amistad Research Center, Tulane University
        American Missionary Association Archives
    Louisiana Research Collection, Tulane University
        George Washington Cable papers
New York, New York
    The New York Public Library, Astor, Lenox, and Tilden Foundations
        Samuel Langhorne Clemens Collection of Papers. The Henry W. and Albert A. Berg Collection of English and American Literature.
        Alice French, General Correspondence, Century Company records. Manuscripts and Archives Division.
        Constance Fenimore Woolson letter to *New York Times* reviewer, Lee Kohns Collection. Manuscripts and Archives Division.
Oberlin, Ohio
    Oberlin College Archives
Washington, D.C.
    Library of Congress, Manuscript Division
        Reel Number 334, Theodore Roosevelt Papers

Howard University, Moorland-Spingarn Research Center, Manuscript Division
    George William Cook Papers
National Archives Building
    Records of the U.S. Bureau of Refugees, Freedmen, and Abandoned Lands,
        Record Group 105
    Records of the Office of the Chief of Ordnance, Record Group 156
Westfield, New York
    Chautauqua County Historical Society, McClurg Museum
        Albion W. Tourgée Papers

Newspapers

Boston Daily Advertiser
Boston Herald Supplement
Boston Literary World
Boston Morning Star
Charles Town (W.Va.) Farmer's Advocate
Colorado Springs Gazette
Daily Arkansas Gazette (Little Rock)
Daily Charlotte Observer
Daily North Carolina Standard (Raleigh)
Davenport (Iowa) Democrat and Leader
Erie (Pa.) Gazette
Florida Sun (Jacksonville)
Florida Union (Jacksonville)
Greensboro (N.C.) North State
Greensboro (N.C.) Patriot
Hartford Daily Courant/Hartford Courant
Indianapolis Freeman
Lewiston (Maine) Daily Evening Journal
Lewiston (Maine) Daily Sun
Martinsburg (W.Va.) Herald
Martinsburg (W.Va.) Independent
Martinsburg (W.Va.) Pioneer Press
Missouri Republican (St. Louis)
Nashville Daily American
National Anti-Slavery Standard
New Orleans Picayune
New Orleans Times-Democrat
New York Age
New York Independent
New York Ledger
New York Star/Daily Star
New York Times
New York Tribune
North Carolinian
Portland (Maine) Zion's Advocate
Quincy (Ill.) Daily Journal
Raleigh Daily Sentinel/Weekly Sentinel
San Antonio Express/Daily Express
Scranton (Pa.) Truth
Selma Times/Selma Morning Times
Spirit of Jefferson (Charles Town, W.Va.)
Tacoma Ledger
Virginia Free Press (Charles Town, W.Va.)
Weekly Louisianian (New Orleans)
Wisconsin State Journal (Madison)

Published Works

Ames, Mary Clemmer. "Yankee Teachers in the Valley of Virginia." *New York Independent*, 3 January 1867.

Andrews, Sidney. *The South since the War*. 1866. New York: Arno, 1969.

Anthony, Kate. "Storer College: A Brief Historical Sketch." 1891. Storer College Documents, Harpers Ferry National Historical Park, Harpers Ferry, West Virginia.

Barbour, George. *Florida for Tourists, Invalids, and Settlers*. New York: Appleton, 1882.

Battle's Revisal of the Public Statutes of North Carolina. Raleigh: Edwards, Broughton, 1873.

Bentzon, Thomas [Marie Thérèse Blanc]. "In Arkansas: Apropos of Octave Thanet's Romances." *Midland Monthly* 6 (July 1896): 37–47, and *Midland Monthly* 6 (August 1896): 136–45.

Bill, Ledyard. *A Winter in Florida, or Observations on the Soil, Climate, and Products of Our Semi-Tropical State*. New York: Wood and Holbrook, 1870.

Brackett, N. C. *Biographical Sketch of the Rev. A. H. Morrell*. Boston: F. B. Printing Establishment, 1886.

Brief for Plaintiff Homer Plessy in Error, *Plessy v. Ferguson*, 163 U.S. 537 (1895).

Brown v. Board of Education. 347 U.S. 483 (1954).

Bryant, William Cullen. *Letters of a Traveller; or, Notes of Things Seen in Europe and America*. New York: Putnam, 1850.

Cable, George Washington. "After-Thoughts of a Story-Teller." *North American Review* 158 (January 1894): 16–23.

———. "Creole Slave Songs." *Century Illustrated Monthly Magazine* 31 (April 1886): 807–28.

———. *The Creoles of Louisiana*. New York: Charles Scribner's Sons, 1884.

———. "The Dance in Place Congo." *Century Illustrated Monthly Magazine* 31 (February 1886): 517–32.

———. *Dr. Sevier*. 1884. New York: Charles Scribner's Sons, 1904.

———. "The Freedman's Case in Equity." 1885. In *The Negro Question*, edited by Arlin Turner, 54–82. New York: Doubleday, 1958.

———. *The Grandissimes*. 1880. Introduction by Michael Kreyling. New York: Penguin, 1988.

———. "My Politics." 1889. In *The Negro Question*, edited by Arlin Turner, 1–27. New York: Doubleday, 1958.

———. "The Progress of the Negro Race." *Hartford Courant*, 12 and 13 January 1887.

———. "The Silent South." In *The Negro Question*, edited by Arlin Turner, 83–131. New York: Doubleday, 1958.

Clayton, Powell. *The Aftermath of the Civil War in Arkansas*. New York: Neale Publishing, 1915.

The Code of North Carolina. New York: Banks and Bros., 1883.

Crosby, Oliver Marvin. *Florida Facts Both Bright and Blue: A Guide Book to Intending Settlers, Tourists, and Investors from a Northerner's Standpoint*. New York, 1887.

Dabney, R. L. "George W. Cable in the *Century Magazine*." *Southern Historical Society Papers* 13 (January 1885–December 1885): 148–53.

Davis, Mary A. *History of the Free Baptist Women's Missionary Society*. Boston: Morning Star, 1900.

Davis, William Watson. *Civil War and Reconstruction*. 1913. Gainesville: University Press of Florida, 1964.

Du Bois, W. E. B. *The Souls of Black Folk*. 1903; New York: Simon and Schuster, 2005.

Franklin [Cook], Coralie. "Votes for Mothers." In "Votes for Women: A Symposium by Leading Thinkers of Colored America." *Crisis* 10, no. 1 (August 1915): 178–92.

Grady, Henry Woodfin. "In Plain Black and White." *Century Illustrated Monthly Magazine* 24 (April 1885): 909–17.

———. "The New South: Articles from the New York *Ledger*." 1889. In *The New South: Writings and Speeches of Henry Grady*, 106–50. Savannah, Ga.: Beehive, 1971.

———. "The Race Problem in the South." 1889. In *The New South: Writings and Speeches of Henry Grady*, 87–105. Savannah, Ga.: Beehive, 1971.

Hardy, Iza Duffus. *Oranges and Alligators: Sketches of South Florida Life*. London: Ward and Downey, 1886.

Hearn, Lafcadio. "The Scenes of Cable's Romances." *Century Illustrated Monthly Magazine* 27 (November 1883): 40–47.

Hepworth, George H. *The Whip, Hoe and Sword: Or, The Gulf-Department in '63*. Boston, 1864.

Higginson, Thomas Wentworth. "The Local Short Story." *Independent*, 3 November 1892, 4–5.

King, Grace. *Memories of a Southern Woman of Letters*. New York: Macmillan, 1932.

Lawson, John D. *Selected Cases in the Law of Personal Property*. N.p.: E. W. Stephens, 1896.

Martin v. Board of Education, 42 W. Va. 514, 26 S.E. 348 (1896).

Mercantile Bank v. Benbow. 150 N.C. 781, 64 S.E. 891 (1909).

Norris, J. F., ed. *History of the Lower Shenandoah Valley*. Chicago: A. Warner, 1890.

Pace v. Alabama, 106 U.S. 583; 1 S. Ct. 637; 27 L. Ed. 207 (1882).

Pippen v. Wesson. 74 N.C. 437 (1876).

Plessy v. Ferguson. 163 U.S. 537 (1896).

Ponder v. Rhea, 32 Ark. 435 (1877).

Reid, Mary J. "Four Women Writers of the West." *Overland Monthly* 24 (August 1894): 138–44.

———. "The Theories of Octave Thanet and Other Western Realists." *Midland Monthly* 9 (February 1898): 99–108.

Rerick, Rowland H. *Memoirs of Florida*. Edited by Francis P. Fleming. Atlanta, Ga., 1902.

Revised Statutes of North Carolina. Raleigh: Turner and Hughes, 1837.

Roun[d]tree v. Gay. 74 N.C. 447 (1876).

Rouquette, Adrien. *Critical Dialogue between Aboo and Caboo*. Edited by E. Junius. [New Orleans], 1880.

Schaeffer, Evelyn Schuyler. "American Authoresses of the Hour: Octave Thanet." *Harper's Bazaar* (13 January 1900): 31–32.

Schouler's Personal Property: A Treatise on Law of Personal Property. Boston: Little, Brown, 1884.

Shinn, Josiah H. "Miss Alice French of Clover Bend." *Publications of the Arkansas Historical Association* 2 (1906): 344–51.

Simmons, Reverend William J. *Men of Mark*. Cleveland: George M. Rewell, 1887.

Simms, William Gilmore. *War Poetry of the South*. New York: Richardson, 1866.

Stanton, Elizabeth C., and Susan B. Anthony, eds. *History of Woman Suffrage*. Rochester, 1881.

Stowe, Harriet Beecher. *Letters from Florida*. New York: Appleton, 1879.

Strauder v. West Virginia, 100 U.S. 303; 25 L. Ed. 664 (1879).

Thanet, Octave [Alice French]. *An Adventure in Photography*. New York: Charles Scribner's Sons, 1893.

———. "Communists and Capitalists: A Sketch from Life." *Lippincott's Magazine* 25 (October 1878): 485–93.

———. *Expiation*. New York: Charles Scribner's Sons, 1890.

———. "Folk-Lore in Arkansas." *Journal of American Folk-Lore* 5 (April–June 1892): 121–25.

———. *Knitters in the Sun*. New York: Houghton Mifflin, 1887.

———. "A Neglected Career for Unmarried Women." *Harper's Bazaar* 15, no. 9 (4 March 1882): 130.

———. *Otto the Knight and Other Trans-Mississippi Stories*. New York: Houghton Mifflin, 1891.

———. "Plantation Life in Arkansas." *Atlantic Monthly* 68 (July 1891): 32–49.

———. "Six Visions of St. Augustine." *Atlantic Monthly* 58 (August 1886): 187–95.

———. "Town Life in Arkansas." *Atlantic Monthly* 68 (September 1891): 332–40.

Tourgée, Albion Winegar. *The "C" Letters*. Greensboro: North State Book and Job Printing Office, 1878.

———. *A Royal Gentleman*. 1881. Boston: Gregg Press, 1967.

———. *Toinette*. New York: J. B. Ford, 1874.

Trowbridge, John T. *The South: A Tour of Its Battle-Fields and Ruined Cities*. Hartford, Conn., 1866.

United States Congress Joint Committee on Reconstruction. *Report of the Joint Select Committee to Inquire into the Condition of Affairs in the Late Insurrectionary States: So Far As Regards the Execution of the Laws and the Safety of the Lives and Property of the Citizens of the United States and Testimony Taken*. 42nd Cong., 2nd sess., vol. 12. Washington, D.C.: Government Printing Office, 1872.

———. *Reports of the Committees of the House of Representatives*. Vol. 2. 39th. Cong., 1st sess., no. 30. Washington, D.C.: Government Printing Office, 1865–66.

United States v. Cruikshank. 92 U.S. 542 (1876).

United States v. Reese. 92 U.S. 214 (1876).

Virginia v. West Virginia, 78 U.S. 39 (1871).

Wallace, John. *Carpet Bag Rule in Florida: The Inside Workings of the Reconstruction of Civil Government in Florida after the Close of the Civil War*. 1888. Gainesville: University Press of Florida, 1964.

Warmoth, Henry Clay. *War, Politics, and Reconstruction: Stormy Days in Louisiana*. New York: MacMillan, 1930.

Warner, Charles Dudley. "On Mr. Cable's Readings." *Century Illustrated Monthly Magazine* 26 (June 1883): 311–12.

———. *Studies in the South and West with Comments on Canada*. New York: Harper and Brother, 1889.

Washington, Booker T. *Up from Slavery*. 1901. New York: Signet, 2000.

Willey, Nathan. "Education of the Colored Population of Louisiana." *Harper's New Monthly Magazine* 43 (1866): 244–50.

Williams v. Board of Education of Fairfax District. 45 W. Va. 199, 31 S.E. 985 (1898).

Woolson, Constance Fenimore. "The Ancient City, Part I." *Harper's New Monthly Magazine* 50 (December 1874): 1–24.
——. "The Ancient City, Part II." *Harper's New Monthly Magazine* 50 (January 1875): 165–86.
——. "At the Smithy: Pickens County, South Carolina, 1874." *Appletons' Journal* 12 (5 September 1874): 289–90.
——. "Black Point." *Harper's New Monthly Magazine* 59 (June 1879): 84–97.
——. "Crowder's Cove: A Story of the War." *Appletons' Journal* 15 (18 March 1876): 357–62.
——. "Dolores." *Appletons' Journal* 12 (11 July 1874): 33–34.
——. "The Florida Beach." *Galaxy* 18 (October 1874): 482–83.
——. "The French Broad." *Harper's New Monthly Magazine* 50 (April 1875): 617–36.
——. *Jupiter Lights*. 1889. New York: AMS Press, 1971.
——. "Matanzas River." *Harper's New Monthly Magazine* 50 (December 1874): 24.
——. "The Oklawaha." *Harper's New Monthly Magazine* 52 (January 1876): 161–79.
——. "Pine Barrens." *Harper's New Monthly Magazine* 50 (December 1874): 66.
——. *Rodman the Keeper: Southern Sketches*. New York: D. Appleton, 1880.
——. "Up the Ashley and Cooper." *Harper's New Monthly Magazine* 52 (December 1875): 1–24.
——. "A Voyage to the Unknown River." *Appletons' Journal* 11 (16 May 1874): 614–16.

Secondary Sources

Aaron, Daniel. *The Unwritten War: American Writers and the Civil War*. Madison: University of Wisconsin Press, 1987.
African American National Biography. Vol. 4. Edited by Henry Louis Gates Jr. and Evelyn Brooks Higginbotham. New York: Oxford University Press, 2013.
Alexander, Roberta Sue. *North Carolina Faces the Freedmen: Race Relations during Presidential Reconstruction, 1865–67*. Durham, N.C.: Duke University Press, 1985.
Anderson, Eric, and Alfred A. Moss Jr. *Dangerous Donations: Northern Philanthropy and Southern Black Education, 1902–1930*. Columbia: University of Missouri Press, 1999.
Anderson, James. *The Education of Blacks in the South, 1860–1935*. Chapel Hill: University of North Carolina Press, 1988.
Arkansas: A Guide to the State. Writers' Program of the Work Projects Administration in the State of Arkansas. American Guide Series. New York: Hastings House, 1941.
Arms, George, and Christoph K. Lohmann, eds. *Selected Letters of William Dean Howells*. Vol. 1. Boston: Twayne, 1979.
Arnold, David. "'Illusory Riches': Representations of the Tropical World, 1840–1950." *Singapore Journal of Tropical Geography* 21 (2000): 6–18.
——. *The Problem of Nature: Environment, Culture, and European Expansion*. Cambridge, Mass.: Blackwell, 1996.
Ash, Stephen V. *When the Yankees Came: Conflict and Chaos in the Occupied South, 1861–1865*. Chapel Hill: University of North Carolina Press, 1995.

Auman, William T., and David D. Scarboro. "The Heroes of America in Civil War North Carolina." *North Carolina Historical Review* 58 (1981): 327–63.

Ayers, Edward L. *The Promise of the New South: Life after Reconstruction.* New York: Oxford University Press, 1992.

———. *Vengeance and Justice: Crime and Punishment in the Nineteenth-Century South.* New York: Oxford University Press, 1984.

Bailey, Anne J., and Daniel E. Sutherland, eds. *Civil War Arkansas: Beyond Battles and Leaders.* Fayetteville: University of Arkansas Press, 2000.

Bardaglio, Peter W. *Reconstructing the Household.* Chapel Hill: University of North Carolina Press, 1995.

Barnes, Kenneth C. *Journey of Hope: The Back-to-Africa Movement in Arkansas in the Late 1800s.* Chapel Hill: University of North Carolina Press, 2004.

———. "'On the Shore beyond the Sea': Black Missionaries from Arkansas in Africa during the 1890s." *Arkansas Historical Quarterly* 61 (2002): 329–56.

———. "Who Killed John M. Clayton? Political Violence in Conway County, Arkansas, in the 1880s." *Arkansas Historical Quarterly* 52 (1993): 372–404.

———. "The Williams Clan: Mountain Farmers and Union Fighters in North Central Arkansas." *Arkansas Historical Quarterly* 52 (1993): 286–317.

Battershell, Gary. "The Socioeconomic Role of Slavery in the Arkansas Upcountry." *Arkansas Historical Quarterly* 58 (1999): 45–60.

Bay, Mia. *The White Image in the Black Mind.* New York: Oxford University Press, 2000.

Beale, Howard K. "On Rewriting Reconstruction History." *American Historical Review* 45 (1940): 807–27.

Becker, Lawrence. *Property Rights—Philosophic Foundations.* Boston: Routledge and K. Paul, 1977.

Beeby, James M. "Red Shirt Violence, Election Fraud, and the Demise of the Populist Party in North Carolina's Third Congressional District, 1900." *North Carolina Historical Review* 85 (2008): 1–28.

———. *Revolt of the Tar Heels: The North Carolina Populist Movement, 1890–1901.* Jackson: University Press of Mississippi, 2008.

Behling, Laura L. *The Masculine Woman in America, 1890–1935.* Urbana: University of Illinois Press, 2001.

Bell, Caryn Cossé. *Revolution, Romanticism, and the Afro-Creole Protest Tradition in Louisiana.* Baton Rouge: Louisiana State University Press, 1997.

Benedict, Clare. *Constance Fenimore Woolson.* Vol. 2. London: G. White, 1932.

———. *Voices out of the Past.* Vol. 1. London: G. White, 1930.

Bercaw, Nancy. *Gendered Freedoms: Race, Rights, and the Politics of Household in the Delta, 1861–1875.* Gainesville: University Press of Florida, 2003.

Berkove, Larry I. "Octave Thanet's Rebuttal of the Issue of Infallibility." *Eureka Studies in Teaching Short Fiction* 8 (2007): 81–88.

Berret, Anthony J. "Huckleberry Finn and the Minstrel Show." *American Studies* 27 (1986): 37–49.

Best, Stephen M. *The Fugitive's Properties: Law and the Poetics of Possession.* Chicago: University of Chicago Press, 2004.

Bieze, Michael. *Booker T. Washington and the Art of Self-Representation*. New York: Peter Lang, 2008.

Biklé, Lucy Leffingwell Cable. *George W. Cable: His Life and Letters*. New York: Scribner's, 1928.

Bishir, Catherine W. "'A Strong Force of Ladies': Women, Politics, and Confederate Memorial Associations in Nineteenth-Century Raleigh." *North Carolina Historical Review* 77 (2000): 455–91.

Blair, William. *Cities of the Dead: Contesting the Memory of the Civil War in the South, 1865–1914*. Chapel Hill: University of North Carolina Press, 2004.

Blassingame, John. *Black New Orleans, 1860–1880*. Chicago: University of Chicago Press, 1976.

Blight, David W. *Beyond the Battlefield: Race, Memory and the American Civil War*. Amherst: University of Massachusetts Press, 2002.

Blight, David W., and Brooks D. Simpson, eds. *Union and Emancipation: Essays on Politics and Race in the Civil War Era*. Kent, Ohio: Kent State University Press, 1997.

Block, Sharon. "Lines of Color, Sex, and Service: Comparative Sexual Coercion in Early America." In *Sex, Love, Race: Crossing Boundaries in North American History*, edited by Martha Hodes, 141–63. New York: New York University Press, 1999.

Boles, John B., and Bethany L. Johnson. *Origins of the New South Fifty Years Later: The Continuing Influence of a Historical Classic*. Baton Rouge: Louisiana State University Press, 2003.

Branam, Chris. "Another Look at Disfranchisement in Arkansas, 1888–1894." *Arkansas Historical Quarterly* 69, no. 3 (2010): 245–56.

Brandwein, Pamela. *Reconstructing Reconstruction*. Durham, N.C.: Duke University Press, 1999.

Braxton, Joanne M. *Black Women Writing Autobiography: A Tradition within a Tradition*. Philadelphia: Temple University Press, 1989.

Brisson, Jim D. "'Civil Government Was Crumbling around Me': The Kirk-Holden War of 1870." *North Carolina Historical Review* 88, no. 2 (2011): 123–63.

Bronner, Simon J. *Consuming Visions: Accumulation and Display of Goods in America, 1880–1920*. New York: Norton, 1989.

Brooks, Daphne A. *Bodies in Dissent*. Durham, N.C.: Duke University Press, 2006.

Broussard, Jinx Coleman. *Giving a Voice to the Voiceless: Four Pioneering Black Women Journalists*. New York: Routledge, 2004.

Brown, Canter, Jr. *Florida's Black Public Officials, 1867–1924*. Tuscaloosa: University of Alabama Press, 1998.

———. *Ossian Bingley Hart: Florida's Loyalist Reconstruction Governor*. Baton Rouge: Louisiana State University Press, 1997.

Brown, Elsa Barkley. "Negotiating and Transforming the Public Sphere: African American Political Involvement in the Transition from Slavery to Freedom." In *Jumpin' Jim Crow: Southern Politics from Civil War to Civil Rights*, edited by Jane Dailey, Glenda Gilmore and Bryant Simon, 28–66. Princeton: Princeton University Press, 2000.

Brown, JoAnne. *The Definition of a Profession: The Authority of Metaphor in the History of Intelligence Testing, 1890–1930*. Princeton: Princeton University Press, 1992.

Browning, Judkin. "Removing the Mask of Nationality: Unionism, Racism, and Federal Military Occupation in North Carolina, 1862–1865." *Journal of Southern History* 71 (2005): 589–620.

Brundage, W. Fitzhugh. *The Southern Past: A Clash of Race and Memory*. Cambridge, Mass.: Belknap Press of Harvard University Press, 2005.

Bryan, Ferald J. *Henry Grady or Tom Watson? The Rhetorical Struggle for the New South, 1880–1890*. Macon, Ga.: Mercer University Press, 1994.

Bryant, Jonathan M. *How Curious a Land: Conflict and Change in Greene County, Georgia, 1850–1885*. Chapel Hill: University of North Carolina Press, 1996.

Buck, Paul. *The Road to Reunion*. Boston: Little, Brown, 1937.

Burke, Dawn Raines. *An American Phoenix: A History of Storer College from Slavery to Desegregation, 1865–1955*. Pittsburgh: Geyer, 2006.

Bushong, Millard K. *Historic Jefferson County*. Boyce, Va.: Carr, 1972.

Busick, Sean R. *A Sober Desire for History: William Gilmore Simms as Historian*. Columbia: University of South Carolina Press, 2005.

Butchart, Ronald E. *Northern Schools, Southern Blacks, and Reconstruction: Freedmen's Education, 1862–1875*. Westport, Conn.: Greenwood, 1980.

———. *Schooling the Freed People: Teaching, Learning, and the Struggles for Black Freedom, 1861–1876*. Chapel Hill: University of North Carolina Press, 2010.

Butcher, Philip. "George Washington Cable and Booker T. Washington." *Journal of Negro Education* 17 (1948): 462–68.

Bynum, Victoria. "Reshaping the Bonds of Womanhood: Divorce in Reconstruction North Carolina." In *Divided Houses: Gender and the Civil War*, edited by Catherine Clinton and Nina Silber, 320–35. New York: Oxford University Press, 1992.

———. *Unruly Women: The Politics of Social and Sexual Control in the Old South*. Chapel Hill: University of North Carolina Press, 1992.

Camp, Stephanie. *Closer to Freedom: Enslaved Women and Everyday Resistance in the Plantation South*. Chapel Hill: University of North Carolina Press, 2004.

Cardwell, Guy. *Twins of Genius*. London: Neville Spearman, 1962.

Cardyn, Lisa. "Sexualized Racism/Gendered Violence: Outraging the Body Politic in the Reconstruction South." *Michigan Law Review* 100 (2002): 675–867.

Cassanello, Robert, and Daniel S. Murphree. "The Epic of Greater Florida: Florida's Global Past." *Florida Historical Quarterly* 84, no. 1 (2005): 1–9.

Cecelski, David S., and Timothy B. Tyson. *Democracy Betrayed: The Wilmington Race Riot of 1898 and Its Legacy*. Chapel Hill: University of North Carolina Press, 1998.

Christ, Mark K., ed. *"All Cut to Pieces and Gone to Hell": The Civil War, Race Relations, and the Battle of Poison Spring*. Little Rock, Ark.: August House, 2003.

———. *Rugged and Sublime: The Civil War in Arkansas*. Fayetteville: University of Arkansas Press, 1994.

Cimbala, Paul A. *The Freedmen's Bureau: Reconstructing the American South after the Civil War*. Malabar, Fla.: Krieger Publishing, 2005.

Cimbala, Paul A., and Randall M. Miller. *The Freedmen's Bureau and Reconstruction: Reconsiderations*. New York: Fordham University Press, 1999.

Clark, Kathleen Ann. *Defining Moments: African American Commemoration and Political Culture in the South, 1863–1913*. Chapel Hill: University of North Carolina Press, 2005.

Cleman, John. *George Washington Cable Revisited*. New York: Twayne, 1996.

Clinton, Catherine. "Reconstructing Freedwomen." In *Divided Houses: Gender and the Civil War*, edited by Catherine Clinton and Nina Silber, 306–19. New York: Oxford University Press, 1992.

Clinton, Catherine, and Nina Silber, eds. *Divided Houses: Gender and the Civil War*. New York: Oxford University Press, 1992.

Cockrell, Dale. *Demons of Disorder: Early Blackface Minstrels and Their World*. Cambridge: Cambridge University Press, 1997.

Cohen, William. *At Freedom's Edge: Black Mobility and the Southern White Quest for Racial Control, 1861–1915*. Baton Rouge: Louisiana State University Press, 1991.

Colburn, David R., and Jane L. Landers, eds. *African-American Heritage of Florida*. Gainesville: University Press of Florida, 1995.

Coles, David. "'They Fought Like Devils': Black Troops in Florida during the Civil War." In *Florida's Heritage of Diversity: Essays in Honor of Samuel Proctor*, edited by Mark L. Greenberg, William Warren Rogers, and Canter Brown Jr., 29–41. Tallahassee: Sentry, 1997.

Collins, Randolph. "Changing Conceptions in the Sociology of Professions." In *The Formation of the Professions: Knowledge, State and Strategy*, edited by Rolf Torstendahl and Michael Burrage, 11–23. London: Sage, 1990.

Connor, William P. "Reconstruction Rebels: The *New Orleans Tribune* in Postwar Louisiana." *Louisiana History* 21 (1980): 159–81.

Copeland, Fayette. "The New Orleans Press and Reconstruction." *Louisiana Historical Quarterly* 30 (1947): 149–337.

Cooper, Valerie C. *Word, Like Fire: Maria Stewart and the Rights of African Americans*. Charlottesville: University of Virginia Press, 2011.

Cott, Nancy. *Public Vows: A History of Marriage and the Nation*. Cambridge, Mass.: Harvard University Press, 2000.

Coultrap-McQuin, Susan. *Doing Literary Business: American Women Writers in the Nineteenth-Century*. Chapel Hill: University of North Carolina Press, 1990.

Cox, James. "Regionalism: A Diminished Thing." In *Columbia Literary History of the United States*, edited by Emory Elliott, 761–84. New York: Columbia University Press, 1988.

Cox, Karen. *Dixie's Daughters: The United Daughters of the Confederacy and the Preservation of Confederate Culture*. Gainesville: University Press of Florida, 2003.

Cresswell, Stephen. "The Case of Taylor Strauder." *West Virginia History* 44 (1983): 193–211.

Crèvecoeur, J. Hector St. John de. *Letters from an American Farmer and Sketches of Eighteenth-Century America*. Introduction and edited by Albert E. Stone. 1782. London: Penguin, 1987.

Cronon, William. *Nature's Metropolis: Chicago and the Great West*. New York: Norton, 1991.

Crouch, Barry A. "Black Education in Civil War and Reconstruction Louisiana: George T. Ruby, the Army, and the Freedmen's Bureau." *Louisiana History* 38 (1997): 287–308.

Crouch, Barry A., and Donaly E. Brice. *Cullen Montgomery Baker: Reconstruction Desperado*. Baton Rouge: Louisiana State University Press, 1997.

Crow, Amy. "'In Memory of the Confederate Dead': Masculinity and the Politics of Memorial Work in Goldsboro, North Carolina, 1894–1895." *North Carolina Historical Review* 83, no. 1 (2006): 31–60.

Csicsila, Joseph. "'Been Reading the Horrors in the Newspapers?': Octave Thanet's Trusty, No. 49 and the Arkansas Convict Lease System." *Essays in Arts and Sciences* 34 (2005): 65–68.

Cummings, Denise K., Anne Goodwyn Jones, and Jeff Rice, eds. "Souths: Global and Local." Special issue, *Southern Quarterly* 42, no. 1 (2003): 1–154.

Curry, Richard O. *A House Divided: A Study of Statehood Politics and the Copperhead Movement in West Virginia*. Pittsburgh: University of Pittsburgh Press, 1964.

———. "The Virginia Background for the History of the Civil War and Reconstruction Era in West Virginia: An Analytical Commentary." *West Virginia History* 20 (1959): 215–46.

Dabel, Jane E. "'My Ma Went to Work Early Every Mornin': Color, Gender, and Occupation in New Orleans, 1840–1860." *Louisiana History* 41 (2000): 217–29.

Dailey, Jane. *Before Jim Crow: The Politics of Race in Postemancipation Virginia*. Chapel Hill: University of North Carolina Press, 2000.

Dailey, Jane, Glenda Elizabeth Gilmore, and Bryant Simon. *Jumpin' Jim Crow: Southern Politics from Civil War to Civil Rights*. Princeton: Princeton University Press, 2000.

Danky, James P. "Reading, Writing, and Resisting: African American Print Culture." In *Print in Motion: The Expansion of Publishing and Reading in the United States*, edited by Carl F. Kaestle and Janice A. Radway, 339–58. Chapel Hill: University of North Carolina Press, 2009.

Dauphine, James G. "The Knights of the White Camellia and the Election of 1868: Louisiana's White Terrorists, a Benighting Legacy." *Louisiana History* 30 (1989): 173–90.

Davidson, Cathy N. *Revolution and the Word: The Rise of the Novel in America*. New York: Oxford University Press, 1986.

Davies, Carole Boyce. *Black Women, Writing, and Identity*. London: Routledge, 1994.

Davis, Harold E. *Henry Grady's New South: Atlanta, a Brave and Beautiful City*. Tuscaloosa: University of Alabama Press, 1990.

Davis, Hugh. *"We Will Be Satisfied with Nothing Less": The African American Struggle for Equal Rights in the North during Reconstruction*. Ithaca, N.Y.: Cornell University Press, 2011.

Davis, Thadious M. *Games of Property: Law, Race, Gender, and Faulkner's "Go Down, Moses."* Durham, N.C.: Duke University Press, 2003.

DeBlack, Thomas A. *With Fire and Sword, Arkansas, 1861–1874*. Fayetteville: University of Arkansas Press, 2003.

DeBoer, Clara Merritt. *Be Jubilant My Feet: African American Abolitionists in the American Missionary Association, 1839–1861*. New York: Garland, 1994.

———. *His Truth Is Marching On: African Americans Who Taught the Freedmen for the American Missionary Association*. New York: Garland, 1995.

Delfino, Susanna, and Michele Gillespie. *Neither Lady nor Slave: Working Women of the Old South*. Chapel Hill: University of North Carolina Press, 2002.

Diffley, Kathleen, ed. *Witness to Reconstruction: Constance Fenimore Woolson and the Postbellum South, 1873–1894*. Jackson: University Press of Mississippi, 2011.

Diggs, Marylynne. "Romantic Friends or a Different Race of Creatures: The Representation of Lesbian Pathology in Nineteenth-Century America." *Feminist Studies* 21 (1995): 317–40.

Disheroon-Green, Suzanne, and Lisa Abney, eds. *Songs of the Reconstructing South: Building Literary Louisiana, 1865–1945*. Westport, Conn.: Greenwood, 2002.

Dominguez, Virginia R. *White by Definition: Social Classification in Creole Louisiana*. New Brunswick, N.J.: Rutgers University Press, 1986.

Dormon, James H., ed. *Creoles of Color of the Gulf South*. Knoxville: University of Tennessee Press, 1996.

Dougan, Michael B. "The Arkansas Married Woman's Property Law." *Arkansas Historical Quarterly* 46 (1987): 4–26.

———. "When Fiction Is Reality: Arkansas Fiction of Octave Thanet." *Publications of the Arkansas Philological Association* 2 (1976): 29–36.

Dougan, Michael B., and Carol Dougan. *By the Cypress Swamp: The Arkansas Stories of Octave Thanet*. Little Rock: Rose Publishing, 1980.

Douglas, J. Allen. "'The Most Valuable Sort of Property': Constructing White Identity in American Law, 1880–1940." *San Diego Law Review* 40 (2003): 881–946.

Du Bois, Ellen Carol. *Feminism and Suffrage: The Emergence of an Independent Women's Movement in America*. Ithaca, N.Y.: Cornell University Press, 1978.

Du Bois, W. E. B. *Black Reconstruction*. New York: Harcourt Brace, 1935.

Duet, Tiffany. "'Do You Not Know That Women Can Make Money?': Women and Labor in Louisiana Literature." In *Songs of the Reconstructing South: Building Literary Louisiana, 1865–1945*, edited by Suzanne Disheroon-Green and Lisa Abney, 49–64. Westport, Conn.: Greenwood, 2002.

Duncan, James S. "The Struggle to Be Temperate: Climate and 'Moral Masculinity' in Mid-Nineteenth-Century Ceylon." *Singapore Journal of Tropical Geography* 21, no. 1 (2000): 34–47.

Eacker, Susan A. "Gender in Paradise: Harriet Beecher Stowe and Postbellum Prose in Florida." *Journal of Southern History* 64, no. 3 (1998): 495–512.

Eagan, Shirley C. "'Women's Work, Never Done': West Virginia Farm Women, 1880s–1920s." *West Virginia History* 49 (1990): 21–36.

The Earliest Printed Laws of North Carolina, 1669–1751. Vol. 1 of the Colonial Laws of North America Series. Edited by John D. Cushing. Wilmington, Del.: Michael Glazier, 1977.

Edwards, Laura F. "Enslaved Women and the Law: Paradoxes of Subordination in the Post-Revolutionary Carolinas." *Slavery and Abolition* 26, no. 2 (2005): 305-23.

———. *Gendered Strife and Confusion: The Political Culture of Reconstruction.* Urbana: University of Illinois Press, 1997.

———. *The People and Their Peace: Legal Culture and the Transformation of Inequality in the Post-Revolutionary South.* Chapel Hill: University of North Carolina Press, 2009.

———. "Reconstruction and North Carolina Women's Tangled History with Law and Governance." In *North Carolinians in the Era of the Civil War and Reconstruction,* edited by Paul D. Escott, 155-92. Chapel Hill: University of North Carolina Press, 2008.

———. *Scarlet Doesn't Live Here Anymore.* Urbana: University of Illinois Press, 2000.

Effland, Anne Wallace. "A Profile of Political Activists: Women of the West Virginia Woman Suffrage Movement." *West Virginia History* 49 (1990): 103-14.

Elfenbein, Anna Shannon. *Women on the Color Line: Evolving Stereotypes and the Writings of George Washington Cable, Grace King, and Kate Chopin.* Charlottesville: University of Virginia Press, 1989.

Elliott, Emory, ed. *Columbia Literary History of the United States.* New York: Columbia University Press, 1988.

Elliott, Mark. *Color-Blind Justice: Albion Tourgée and the Quest for Racial Equality from the Civil War to* Plessy v. Ferguson. New York: Oxford University Press, 2006.

Escott, Paul D. *Many Excellent People: Power and Privilege in North Carolina, 1850-1900.* Chapel Hill: University of North Carolina Press, 1985.

———, ed. *North Carolinians in the Era of the Civil War and Reconstruction.* Chapel Hill: University of North Carolina Press, 2008.

Ettinger, Brian Gary. "John Fitzpatrick and the Limits of Working-Class Politics in New Orleans, 1892-1896." *Louisiana History* 26 (1985): 341-67.

Evans, Willis F. *History of Berkeley County.* Wheeling: Evans, 1928.

Fabre, Michel. "New Orleans Creole Expatriates in France: Romance and Reality." In *Creole: The History and Legacy of Louisiana's Free People of Color,* edited by Sybil Kein, 179-207. Baton Rouge: Louisiana State University Press, 2000.

Fahs, Alice. *The Imagined Civil War: Popular Literature of the North and South.* Chapel Hill: University of North Carolina Press, 2001.

Fain, Cicero M. "Black Response to the Construction of Colored Huntington, West Virginia, during the Jim Crow Era." *West Virginia History,* n.s., 1, no. 2 (2007): 1-24.

Fandrich, Ina J. "The Birth of New Orleans' Voodoo Queen: A Long-Held Mystery Resolved." *Louisiana History* 46 (2005): 293-310.

Farmer-Kaiser, Mary. *Freedwomen and the Freedmen's Bureau.* New York: Fordham University Press, 2010.

Faulkner, Carol. *Women's Radical Reconstruction: The Freedmen's Aid Movement.* Philadelphia: University of Pennsylvania Press, 2004.

Faust, Drew Gilpin. *Mothers of Invention: Women of the Slaveholding South in the American Civil War.* Chapel Hill: University of North Carolina Press, 1996.

Finkelman, Paul. "Not Only the Judges' Robes Were Black: African-American Lawyers as Social Engineers." *Stanford Law Review* 47 (1994): 161–209.

Finley, Randy. *From Slavery to Uncertain Freedom: The Freedmen's Bureau in Arkansas, 1865–1869.* Fayetteville: University of Arkansas Press, 1996.

Fitzgerald, Michael W. *The Union League Movement in the Deep South: Politics and Agricultural Change during Reconstruction.* Baton Rouge: Louisiana State University Press, 1989.

Flexner, Eleanor. *Century of Struggle: The Woman's Rights Movement in the United States.* Cambridge, Mass.: Harvard University Press, 1975.

Foner, Eric. *Reconstruction: America's Unfinished Revolution, 1863–1877.* New York: Harper and Row, 1988.

Foner, Philip S., and Ronald L. Lewis, eds. *The Black Worker during the Era of the National Labor Union.* Philadelphia: Temple University Press, 1978.

Forbath, William. "The Ambiguities of Free Labor and Law in the Gilded Age." *Wisconsin Law Review* 1985 (1985): 767–817.

———. *Law and the Shaping of the American Labor Movement.* Cambridge, Mass.: Harvard University Press, 1991.

Foreman, P. Gabrielle. *Activist Sentiments: Reading Black Women in the Nineteenth Century.* Urbana: University of Illinois Press, 2009.

Forret, Jeff. "Slave–Poor White Violence in the Antebellum Carolinas." *North Carolina Historical Review* 81, no. 2 (2004): 140–67.

Foster, Frances Smith. "A Narrative of the Interesting Origins and (Somewhat) Surprising Developments of African-American Print Culture." *American Literary History* 17, no. 4 (2005): 714–40.

———. *Written by Herself: Literary Production by African American Women, 1746–1892.* Bloomington: Indiana University Press, 1993.

Foster, John T., and Sarah Whitmer Foster. *Beechers, Stowes, and Yankee Strangers: The Transformation of Florida.* Gainesville: University Press of Florida, 1999.

Fox-Genovese, Elizabeth. *Within the Plantation Household: Women in the Old South.* Chapel Hill: University of North Carolina Press, 1988.

Frankel, Noralee. *Freedom's Women: Black Women and Families in Civil War Era Mississippi.* Bloomington: Indiana University Press, 1999.

Fredette, Allison. "The View from the Border: West Virginia Republicans and Women's Rights in the Age of Emancipation." *West Virginia History,* n.s., 3, no. 1 (2009): 57–80.

French, George T. *Stories from a Long Journey.* Tucson, Ariz.: Sundance Press, 1996.

Gaines, Kevin K. *Uplifting the Race: Black Leadership, Politics, and Culture in the Twentieth Century.* Chapel Hill: University of North Carolina Press, 1996.

Gannon, Barbara A. *The Won Cause: Black and White Comradeship in the Grand Army of the Republic.* Chapel Hill: University of North Carolina Press, 2011.

Gannon, Michael V. Preface to *Minorcans in Florida: Their History and Heritage,* by Jane Quinn, i–xiii. St. Augustine, Fla.: Mission, 1975.

Gardner, Eric. *Unexpected Places: Relocating African American Literature.* Jackson: University Press of Mississippi, 2009.

Garland, Hamlin. *Roadside Meetings.* New York: Macmillan, 1930.

Gaston, Paul M. *The New South Creed: A Study in Southern Mythmaking*. New York: Knopf, 1970.

Geffert, Hannah N. "An Annotated Narrative of the African-American Community in Jefferson County, West Virginia." Unpublished NAACP project, 1992. Storer College Documents, Harpers Ferry National Historical Park, Harpers Ferry, West Virginia.

Gehman, Mary. "Visible Means of Support: Business, Professions, and Trades of Free People of Color." In *Creole: The History and Legacy of Louisiana's Free People of Color*, edited by Sybil Kein, 208–22. Baton Rouge: Louisiana State University Press, 2000.

Gerteis, Louis. "Blackface Minstrelsy and the Construction of Race in Nineteenth-Century America." In *Union and Emancipation: Essays on Politics and Race in the Civil War Era*, edited by David W. Blight and Brooks D. Simpson, 79–104. Kent, Ohio: Kent State University Press, 1997.

Giddings, Paula. *When and Where I Enter: The Impact of Black Women on Race and Sex in America*. New York: Bantam, 1984.

Giggie, John M. "'Disband Him from the Church': African Americans and the Spiritual Politics of Disfranchisement in Post-Reconstruction Arkansas." *Arkansas Historical Quarterly* 60 (2000): 245–64.

Gillette, William. *Retreat from Reconstruction*. Baton Rouge: Louisiana State University Press, 1979.

Gilmore, Glenda E. *Gender and Jim Crow: Women and the Politics of White Supremacy in North Carolina, 1896–1920*. Chapel Hill: University of North Carolina Press, 1996.

Ginnow, Arnold O., ed. *Corpus Juris Secundum*. Vol. 73. St. Paul, Minn.: West Publishing, 1983.

Glass, Kathy L. *Courting Communities: Black Female Nationalism and "Syncre-Nationalism" in the Nineteenth-Century North*. New York: Routledge, 2006.

Glymph, Thavolia. "'Liberty Dearly Bought': The Making of Civil War Memory in Afro-American Communities in the South." In *Time Longer Than Rope: A Century of African-American Activism, 1850–1950*, edited by Charles M. Payne and Adam Green, 111–39. New York: New York University Press, 2003.

———. *Out of the House of Bondage: The Transformation of the Plantation Household*. New York: Cambridge University Press, 2008.

Golay, Michael. *A Ruined Land: The End of the Civil War*. New York: Wiley, 1999.

Goldman, Robert M. *"A Free Ballot and a Fair Count": The Department of Justice and the Enforcement of Voting Rights in the South, 1877–1893*. New York: Fordham University Press, 2001.

———. *Reconstruction and Black Suffrage: Losing the Vote in* Reese *and* Cruikshank. Lawrence: University Press of Kansas, 2001.

Gordon, Ann D., ed. *African-American Women and the Vote, 1837–1965*. Amherst: University of Massachusetts Press, 1997.

Gordon, Fon Louise. *Caste and Class: The Black Experience in Arkansas, 1880–1920*. Athens: University of Georgia Press, 1995.

Gordon, Michelle Y. "'Midnight Scenes and Orgies': Public Narratives of Voodoo in New Orleans and Nineteenth-Century Discourses of White Supremacy." *American Quarterly* 64, no. 4 (2012): 767–86.

Gordon, Vivian Verdell. "History of Storer College." *Journal of Negro Education* 30 (1961): 445–49.

Gozdzik, Gloria, Principal Investigator for Horizon Research Consultants, Inc. *A Historic Resource Study for Storer College, Harpers Ferry, West Virginia.* BiblioGov Project. Harpers Ferry, W.Va.: [Harpers Ferry National Historical Park], 2002.

Grady, Henry Woodfin. *The New South: Writings and Speeches of Henry Grady.* Savannah, Ga.: Beehive, 1971.

Grandison, Kendrick Ian. "Negotiated Space: The Black College Campus as a Cultural Record of Postbellum America." *American Quarterly* 51 (1999): 529–79.

Graves, John William. *Town and Country.* Fayetteville: University of Arkansas Press, 1990.

Greenberg, Kenneth. *Honor and Slavery.* Princeton: Princeton University Press, 1996.

Greenberg, Mark I., William Warren Rogers, and Canter Brown Jr., eds. *Florida's Heritage of Diversity: Essays in Honor of Samuel Proctor.* Tallahassee: Sentry, 1997.

Greeson, Jennifer Rae. *Our South: Geographic Fantasy and the Rise of National Literature.* Cambridge, Mass.: Harvard University Press, 2010.

Gruesz, Kristen Silva. "Delta *Desterrados*: Antebellum New Orleans and New World Print Culture." In *Look Away! The U.S. South in New World Studies*, edited by Jon Smith and Deborah Cohn, 52–79. Durham, N.C.: Duke University Press, 2004.

Guilds, John Caldwell. *Simms: A Literary Life.* Fayetteville: University of Arkansas Press, 1992.

———, ed. *Long Years of Neglect: The Work and Reputation of William Gilmore Simms.* Fayetteville: University of Arkansas Press, 1988.

Guilds, John Caldwell, and Caroline Collins. *William Gilmore Simms and the American Frontier.* Athens: University of Georgia Press, 1999.

Haas, Edward F. "Political Continuity in the Crescent City: Toward an Interpretation of New Orleans Politics, 1874–1986." *Louisiana History* 39 (1998): 5–18.

Haber, Samuel. *The Quest for Authority and Honor in the American Professions, 1750–1900.* Chicago: University of Chicago Press, 1991.

Hahn, Steven. *A Nation under Our Feet: Black Political Struggles in the Rural South from Slavery to the Great Migration.* Cambridge, Mass.: Harvard University Press, 2003.

Hale, Grace Elizabeth. "'For Colored' and 'For White': Segregating Consumption in the South." In *Jumpin' Jim Crow: Southern Politics from Civil War to Civil Rights*, edited by Jane Dailey, Glenda Gilmore, and Bryant Simon, 162–83. Princeton: Princeton University Press, 2000.

———. *Making Whiteness: The Culture of Segregation in the South, 1890–1940.* New York: Vintage, 1999.

Hall, Gwendolyn Midlo. *Africans in Colonial Louisiana: The Development of Afro-Creole Culture in the Eighteenth Century.* Baton Rouge: Louisiana State University Press, 1992.

Hanger, Kimberly S. *Bounded Lives, Bounded Places: Free Black Society in Colonial New Orleans, 1769–1803.* Durham, N.C.: Duke University Press, 1997.

———. "Coping in a Complex World: Free Black Women in Colonial New Orleans." In *The Devil's Lane: Sex and Race in the Early South*, edited by Catherine Clinton and Michelle Gillespie, 218–31. New York: Oxford University Press, 1997.

Harlan, Louis R. *Booker T. Washington: Volume 2: The Wizard of Tuskegee, 1901–1915*. New York: Oxford University Press, 1983.

Harris, Joseph E. "Afro-American History Interpretation at Selected National Parks." Unpublished report, 1978. Storer College Documents, Harpers Ferry National Historical Park, Harpers Ferry, West Virginia.

Harris, J. William, ed. *The New South: New Histories*. New York: Routledge, 2008.

Hartman, Mary, and Elmo Ingenthron. *Bald Knobbers: Vigilantes on the Ozark Frontier*. Gretna, La.: Pelican, 1992.

Hartman, Saidiya V. *Scenes of Subjection: Terror, Slavery, and Self-Making in Nineteenth-Century America*. New York: Oxford University Press, 1997.

Hatch, Nathan O., ed. *The Professions in American History*. Notre Dame: University of Notre Dame Press, 1988.

Hayden, Wendy. *Evolutionary Rhetoric: Sex, Science, and Free Love in Nineteenth-Century Feminism*. Carbondale: Southern Illinois University Press, 2013.

Haynes, Rosetta R. *Radical Spiritual Motherhood: Autobiography and Empowerment in Nineteenth-Century African American Women*. Baton Rouge: Louisiana State University Press, 2011.

Hearn, Chester G. *Six Years of Hell: Harpers Ferry during the Civil War*. Baton Rouge: Louisiana State University Press, 1996.

Hedrick, Joan D. *Harriet Beecher Stowe: A Life*. New York: Oxford University Press, 1994.

Hennessey, Melinda Meek. "Race and Violence in Reconstruction New Orleans: The 1868 Riot." *Louisiana History* 20, no. 1 (1979): 77–91.

Hensley, Frances S. "Women in the Industrial Work Force in West Virginia, 1880–1945." *West Virginia History* 49 (1990): 115–24.

Higginbotham, Evelyn Brooks. *Righteous Discontent: The Woman's Movement in the Black Baptist Church, 1880–1920*. Cambridge, Mass.: Harvard University Press, 1993.

Hild, Matthew. *Greenbackers, Knights of Labor, and Populists: Farmer-Labor Insurgency in the Late-Nineteenth-Century South*. Athens: University of Georgia Press, 2007.

———. "Labor, Third-Party Politics, and New South Democracy in Arkansas, 1884–1896." *Arkansas Historical Quarterly* 63 (2004): 24–43.

Hine, Darlene Clark. "Rape and the Inner Lives of Black Women in the Middle West: Preliminary Thoughts on the Culture of Dissemblance." *Signs* 14 (1989): 912–20.

Hirsch, Arnold R., and Joseph Logsdon. *Creole New Orleans*. Baton Rouge: Louisiana State University Press, 1992.

Hodes, Martha, ed. *Sex, Love, Race: Crossing Boundaries in North American History*. New York: New York University Press, 1999.

———. *White Women, Black Men: Illicit Sex in the Nineteenth-Century South*. New Haven: Yale University Press, 1997.

Hogue, James. *Uncivil War: Five New Orleans Street Battles and the Rise and Fall of Radical Reconstruction*. Baton Rouge: Louisiana State University Press, 2006.

Hollandsworth, James G., Jr. *An Absolute Massacre: The New Orleans Race Riot of July 30, 1866*. Baton Rouge: Louisiana State University Press, 2001.

Holt, Sharon Ann. *Making Freedom Pay: North Carolina Freedpeople Working for Themselves, 1865–1900*. Athens: University of Georgia Press, 2000.

Homestead, Melissa J. *American Women Authors and Literary Property*. New York: Cambridge University Press, 2003.

Howe, Barbara J. "The Status of Women's History Research in West Virginia." In *West Virginia History: Critical Essays on the Literature*, edited by Ronald L. Lewis and John C. Hennen Jr., 149–87. Dubuque, Iowa: Kendall/Hunt, 1993.

Hunt, Patricia K. "The Struggle to Achieve Individual Expression through Clothing and Adornment: African American Women under and after Slavery." In *Discovering the Women in Slavery: Emancipating Perspectives on the American Past*, edited by Patricia Morton, 227–40. Athens: University of Georgia Press, 1996.

Hunter, G. Howard. "The Politics of Resentment: Unionist Regiments and the New Orleans Immigrant Community, 1862–1864." *Louisiana History* 44 (2003): 185–210.

Hunter, Tera W. *To 'Joy My Freedom*. Cambridge, Mass.: Harvard University Press, 1997.

Hyde, Samuel C., Jr. "Feuding Is Our Means of Societal Regulation: Elusive Stability in Southeastern Louisiana's Piney Woods, 1877–1910." *Louisiana History* 48 (2007): 133–55.

———. *Pistols and Politics: The Dilemma of Democracy in Louisiana's Florida Parishes, 1810–1899*. Baton Rouge: Louisiana State University Press, 1996.

Janney, Caroline E. *Burying the Dead but Not the Past: Ladies' Memorial Associations and the Lost Cause*. Chapel Hill: University of North Carolina Press, 2008.

Jensen, Gerard Edward, ed. *The Life and Letters of Henry Cuyler Bunner*. Durham, N.C.: Duke University Press, 1939.

Johnson, Jerah. "Colonial New Orleans: A Fragment of the Eighteenth-Century French Ethos." In *Creole New Orleans*, edited by Arnold R. Hirsch and Joseph Logsdon, 12–57. Baton Rouge: Louisiana State University Press, 1992.

Johnson, Mary. "An 'Ever-Present Bone of Contention': The Heyward Shepherd Memorial." *West Virginia History* 56 (1997): 1–26.

Johnson, Sherry. "Marriage and Community Construction in St. Augustine, 1784–1804." In *Florida's Heritage of Diversity: Essays in Honor of Samuel Proctor*, edited by Mark L. Greenberg, William Warren Rogers, and Canter Brown Jr., 1–13. Tallahassee: Sentry, 1997.

Johnson, Walter. *Soul by Soul: Life Inside the Antebellum Slave Market*. Cambridge, Mass.: Harvard University Press, 1999.

Jones, Gavin. *Strange Talk: The Politics of Dialect Literature in Gilded Age America*. Berkeley: University of California Press, 1999.

Jones, Jacqueline. *Labor of Love, Labor of Sorrow*. New York: Vintage, 1985.

———. *Soldiers of Light and Love: Northern Teachers and Georgia Blacks, 1865–1873*. Athens: University of Georgia Press, 1992.

Jones, Lu Ann. "Gender, Race, and Itinerant Commerce in the Rural New South." *Journal of Southern History* 66 (2000): 297–320.

Jones, Martha S. *All Bound Up Together: The Woman Question in African American Public Culture, 1830–1900*. Chapel Hill: University of North Carolina Press, 2007.

Jones, Suzanne W., and Sharon Monteith. *South to a New Place*. Baton Rouge: Louisiana State University Press, 2002.

Jung, Moon-Ho. *Coolies and Cane: Race, Labor, and Sugar in the Age of Emancipation*. Baltimore: Johns Hopkins University Press, 2006.

Kachun, Mitch. *Festivals of Freedom: Memory and Meaning in African American Emancipation Celebrations, 1808–1915*. Amherst: University of Massachusetts Press, 2003.

Kaestle, Carl F., and Janice A. Radway, eds. *Print in Motion: The Expansion of Publishing and Reading in the United States*. Vol. 4 of *A History of the Book in America*. Chapel Hill: University of North Carolina Press, 2009.

Kantrowitz, Stephen. *Ben Tillman and the Reconstruction of White Supremacy*. Chapel Hill: University of North Carolina Press, 2000.

Kaplan, Amy. "Nation, Region, and Empire." In *Columbia Literary History of the United States*, edited by Emory Elliott, 240–66. New York: Columbia University Press, 1988.

Kaser, David. *Books and Libraries in Camp and Battle: The Civil War Experience*. Westport, Conn.: Greenwood, 1984.

Kein, Sybil, ed. *Creole: The History and Legacy of Louisiana's Free People of Color*. Baton Rouge: Louisiana State University Press, 2000.

Keith, Leeanna. *The Colfax Massacre*. New York: Oxford University Press, 2008.

Kelly, Alfred H., Winfred A. Harbison, and Herman Belz. *The American Constitution: Its Origins and Development*. 7th ed. New York: Norton, 1991.

Kennedy-Nolle, Sharon. "The Merits of Transit: Woolson's Return to Reconstruction in *Jupiter Lights*." In *Witness to Reconstruction: Constance Fenimore Woolson and the Postbellum South, 1873–1894*, edited by Kathleen Diffley, 249–65. Jackson: University Press of Mississippi, 2011.

Kenney, Patricia L. "LaVilla, Florida, 1866–1887: Reconstruction Dreams and the Formation of a Black Community." In *African-American Heritage of Florida*, edited by David R. Colburn and Jane L. Landers, 185–206. Gainesville: University Press of Florida, 1995.

Kenzer, Robert C. *Enterprising Southerners: Black Economic Success in North Carolina, 1865–1915*. Charlottesville: University of Virginia Press, 1997.

Kerber, Linda K. *No Constitutional Right to Be Ladies: Women and the Obligations of Citizenship*. New York: Hill and Wang, 1998.

———. *Women of the Republic: Intellect and Ideology in Revolutionary America*. New York: Norton, 1986.

Kimball, Bruce. *The True "Professional Ideal" in America: A History*. Cambridge, Mass.: Blackwell, 1992.

Klingman, Peter D. *Josiah Walls, Florida's Black Congressman of Reconstruction.* Gainesville: University Press of Florida, 1976.

———. *Neither Dies nor Surrenders: A History of the Republican Party in Florida, 1867–1970.* Gainesville: University Press of Florida, 1984.

Klos, George. "Blacks and the Seminole Removal Debate, 1821–1835." In *African-American Heritage of Florida*, edited by David R. Colburn and Jane L. Landers, 128–56. Gainesville: University Press of Florida, 1995.

Knopfer, Randall. *Acting Naturally.* Berkeley: University of California Press, 1995.

Konhaus, Tim. "'I Thought Things Would Be Different There': Lynching and the Black Community in Southern West Virginia, 1880–1933." *West Virginia History*, n.s., 1, no. 2 (2007): 25–44.

Kreyling, Michael. Introduction to *The Grandissimes*, by George Washington Cable, vii–xx. New York: Penguin, 1988.

Labbé, Ronald M., and Jonathan Lurie. *The Slaughterhouse Cases: Regulation, Reconstruction, and the Fourteenth Amendment.* Lawrence: University Press of Kansas, 2005.

Lachance, Paul. "The Foreign French." In *Creole New Orleans*, edited by Arnold R. Hirsch and Joseph Logsdon, 101–30. Baton Rouge: Louisiana State University Press, 1992.

Ladd, Barbara. *Nationalism and the Color Line in George W. Cable, Mark Twain, and William Faulkner.* Baton Rouge: Louisiana State University Press, 1996.

Lancaster, Guy. "'They Are Not Wanted': The Extirpation of African Americans from Baxter County, Arkansas." *Arkansas Historical Quarterly* 69 (2010): 28–43.

Landers, Jane L. *Black Society in Spanish Florida.* Urbana: University of Illinois Press, 1999.

———. "Gracia Real de Santa Teresa de Mose: A Free Black Town in Spanish Colonial Florida." *American Historical Review* 95 (2001): 9–30.

Lane, Charles. *The Day Freedom Died: The Colfax Massacre, the Supreme Court, and the Betrayal of Reconstruction.* New York: Henry Holt, 2008.

Lawrence, D. H. *Studies in Classic American Literature.* New York: Viking, 1923.

Lebsock, Suzanne D. "Radical Reconstruction and the Property Rights of Southern Women." *Journal of Southern History* 43 (1977): 195–216.

Leglaunec, Jean-Pierre. "Slave Migrations in Spanish and Early American Louisiana: New Sources and New Estimates." *Louisiana History* 46 (2005): 185–209.

Lerner, Gerda, ed. *The Female Experience: An American Documentary.* Indianapolis: Bobbs-Merrill, 1977.

Lewis, David Levering. *W. E. B. Du Bois: Biography of a Race, 1868–1919.* New York: Holt, 1993.

Lewis, Ronald L., and John C. Hennen Jr., eds. *West Virginia History: Critical Essays on the Literature.* Dubuque, Iowa: Kendall/Hunt, 1993.

Lhamon, W. T. *Raising Cain: Blackface Performance from Jim Crow to Hip Hop.* Cambridge, Mass.: Harvard University Press, 1998.

Link, William A. *Roots of Secession: Slavery and Politics in Antebellum Virginia.* Chapel Hill: University of North Carolina Press, 2003.

———. "'This Bastard New Virginia': Slavery, West Virginia Exceptionalism, and the Secession Crisis." *West Virginia History*, n.s., 3, no. 1 (2009): 37–57.

Lively, Robert A. *Fiction Fights the Civil War*. Chapel Hill: University of North Carolina Press, 1957.

Locke, John. "An Essay concerning the True Original, Extent and End of Civil Government." In *Social Contract: Essays by Locke, Hume, and Rousseau*, 1–144. With an introduction and edited by Sir Ernest Barker. 1689. New York: Oxford University Press, 1947.

———. *The Second Treatise of Government*. Edited by Thomas P. Peardon. 1690. New York: Macmillan, 1952.

Lofgren, Charles A. *The Plessy Case: A Legal-Historical Interpretation*. New York: Oxford University Press, 1987.

Logan, Shirley. *"We Are Coming": The Persuasive Discourse of Nineteenth-Century Black Women*. Carbondale: Southern Illinois University Press, 1999.

Logsdon, Joseph, and Caryn Cossé Bell, "The Americanization of Black New Orleans." In *Creole New Orleans*, edited by Arnold R. Hirsch and Joseph Logsdon, 201–61. Baton Rouge: Louisiana State University Press, 1992.

Long, Carolyn Morrow. "Marie Laveau: A Nineteenth-Century Voudou Priestess." *Louisiana History* 46 (2005): 263–92.

Lorch, Fred W. "Cable and His Reading Tour with Mark Twain." *American Literature* 23 (1952): 471–86.

Lott, Eric. *Love and Theft: Blackface Minstrelsy and the American Working Class*. New York: Oxford University Press, 1995.

Lovett, Bobby L. "African Americans, Civil War, and Aftermath in Arkansas." *Arkansas Historical Quarterly* 54 (1995): 304–58.

MacKenzie, Scott A. "The Slaveholders' War: The Secession Crisis in Kanawha County, Western Virginia, 1860–1861." *West Virginia History* 44, no. 1 (2010): 33–57.

MacKethan, Lucinda H. "Thomas Nelson Page: The Plantation as Arcady." *Virginia Quarterly Review* 54 (1978): 314–32.

Mackey, Robert R. "Bushwackers, Provosts, and Tories: The Guerrilla War in Arkansas." In *Guerrillas, Unionists, and Violence on the Confederate Home Front*, edited by Daniel E. Sutherland, 171–85. Fayetteville: University of Arkansas Press, 1999.

Macpherson, C. B. "The Meaning of Property." In *Property: Mainstream and Critical Positions*, edited by C. B. Macpherson, 1–13. Toronto: University of Toronto Press, 1978.

Maffly-Kipp, Laurie F., and Kathyrn Lofton, eds. *Women's Work: An Anthology of African-American Women's Historical Writings from Antebellum America to the Harlem Renaissance*. Cambridge: Oxford University Press, 2010.

Majeske, Penelope. "Virginia after Appomattox: The United States Army and the Formation of Presidential Reconstruction Policy." *West Virginia History* 43 (1982): 95–117.

Marler, Scott. "Merchants in the Transition to a New South: Central Louisiana, 1840–1880." *Louisiana History* 42 (2001): 165–92.

Marten, James Allen. *Sing Not War: The Lives of Union and Confederate Veterans in Gilded Age America*. Chapel Hill: University of North Carolina Press, 2011.

Massengill, Stephen. "The Detectives of William W. Holden, 1869–1870." *North Carolina Historical Review* 62, no. 4 (1985): 448–87.

May, Vivian M. *Anna Julia Cooper: Visionary Black Feminist*. New York: Routledge, 2007.

McCaskill, Barbara, and Caroline Gebhard. *Post-Bellum, Pre-Harlem: African American Literature and Culture, 1877–1919*. New York: New York University Press, 2006.

McClain, Mary Ellen. "Storer College: Harpers Ferry, West Virginia." Honors thesis, Linfield College, 1974.

McCollom, Jason. "The Agricultural Wheel, the Union Labor Party, and the 1889 Arkansas Legislature." *Arkansas Historical Quarterly* 68 (2009): 157–75.

McCurry, Stephanie. *Confederate Reckoning: Power and Politics in the Civil War South*. Cambridge, Mass.: Harvard University Press, 2010.

———. *Masters of Small Worlds*. New York: Oxford University Press, 1995.

McGovern, Charles F. *Sold American: Consumption and Citizenship, 1890–1945*. Chapel Hill: University of North Carolina Press, 2006.

McHenry, Elizabeth. *Forgotten Readers: Recovering the Lost History of African American Literary Societies*. Durham, N.C.: Duke University Press, 2002.

———. "Reading and Race Pride: The Literary Activism of Black Clubwomen." In *Print in Motion: The Expansion of Publishing and Reading in the United States*, edited by Carl F. Kaestle and Janice A. Radway, 491–510. Chapel Hill: University of North Carolina Press, 2009.

McKee, Kathryn, and Annette Trefzer. "Global Contexts, Local Literatures: The New Southern Studies." Special issue, *American Literature* 78, no. 4 (2006): 677–924.

McMichael, George. *Journey to Obscurity*. Lincoln: University of Nebraska Press, 1965.

McWhirter, David, ed. "'Southern Literature'/Southern Cultures: Rethinking Southern Literary Studies." Special issue, *South Central Review* 22, no. 1 (2005): 1–149.

Mendez, Jesus. "From Adventure Travel to Leisure Tourism: The Florida Letters of William Drysdale in the *New York Times*, 1884–1893." *Florida Historical Quarterly* 89, no. 3 (Spring 2011): 437–68.

Merrill, Ellen C. *Germans of Louisiana*. Gretna, La.: Pelican, 2005.

Miller, David. *Dark Eden*. Cambridge, Mass.: Harvard University Press, 1989.

Mills, Cynthia, and Pamela Simpson, eds. *Monuments to the Lost Cause*. Knoxville: University of Tennessee Press, 2003.

Mitchell, Douglas L. *A Disturbing and Alien Memory: Southern Novelists Writing History*. Baton Rouge: Louisiana State University Press, 2008.

Mizrach, Steven. "The North in the South: Southern Florida as a Northern Colony." *Southern Quarterly* 42, no. 1 (2003): 11–21.

Moneyhon, Carl H. *Arkansas and the New South, 1874–1929*. Fayetteville: University of Arkansas, 1997.

———. "Black Politics in the Gilded Age, 1876–1900." *Arkansas Historical Quarterly* 44 (1985): 222–45.

———. "The Creators of the New South in Arkansas: Industrial Boosterism, 1875–1885." *Arkansas Historical Quarterly* 55 (1996): 383–409.

———. "Disloyalty and Class Consciousness in Southwestern Arkansas, 1862–1865." *Arkansas Historical Quarterly* 52 (1993): 223–43.

———. "From Slave to Free Labor: The Federal Plantation Experiment in Arkansas." *Arkansas Historical Quarterly* 53 (1994): 137–60.

———. *The Impact of the Civil War and Reconstruction on Arkansas: Persistence in the Midst of Ruin*. Baton Rouge: Louisiana State University Press, 1994.

Mongin, Alfred. "A College in Secessia: The Early Years of Storer College." Park Historian Research Report, 15 June 1960, Storer College Documents, Harpers Ferry National Historical Park, Harpers Ferry, West Virginia.

Monks, William. *A History of Southern Missouri and Northern Arkansas*. West Plains, Mo.: West Plains Journal, 1907.

Montgomery, David. *Citizen Worker*. Cambridge: Cambridge University Press, 1993.

Moore, George Ellis. *A Banner in the Hills: West Virginia's Statehood*. New York: Appleton-Century-Crofts, 1963.

———. "Slavery as a Factor in the Formation of West Virginia." Master's thesis, West Virginia University, 1939.

Moore, Jacqueline M. *Leading the Race: The Transformation of the Black Elite in the Nation's Capital, 1880–1920*. Charlottesville: University of Virginia Press, 1999.

Moore, Rayburn S. *Constance Fenimore Woolson*. New Haven: Twayne, 1963.

Morris, Robert C. *Reading, 'Riting, and Reconstruction: The Education of Freedmen in the South, 1861–1870*. Chicago: University of Chicago Press, 1981.

Morrison, Toni. *Playing in the Dark: Whiteness and the Literary Imagination*. New York: Vintage, 1992.

Morton, Patricia, ed. *Discovering the Women in Slavery: Emancipating Perspectives on the American Past*. Athens: University of Georgia Press, 1996.

Mott, Frank Luther. *A History of American Magazines*. Vols. 2, 3, and 4. Cambridge, Mass.: Harvard University Press, 1938.

Myers, Amrita Chakrabarti. "'Sisters in Arms': Slave Women's Resistance to Slavery in the United States." *Past Imperfect* 5 (1996): 141–74.

Nakamura, Masahiro. *Visions of Order in William Gilmore Simms*. Columbia: University of South Carolina Press, 2009.

Nash, Horace D. "Blacks in Arkansas during Reconstruction: The Ex-Slave Narratives." *Arkansas Historical Quarterly* 48 (1989): 243–59.

Nash, Steven E. "Aiding the Southern Mountain Republicans: The Freedmen's Bureau in Buncombe County." *North Carolina Historical Review* 83, no. 1 (2006): 1–30.

Neff, John R. *Honoring the Civil War Dead: Commemoration and the Problem of Reconciliation*. Lawrence: University Press of Kansas, 2005.

Nettels, Elsa. *Language, Race, and Social Class in Howell's America*. Lexington: University Press of Kentucky, 1988.

Newton, Michael. *The Invisible Empire: The Ku Klux Klan in Florida*. Gainesville: University Press of Florida, 2001.

Nichols, Ronnie A. "The Changing Role of Blacks in the Civil War." In *"All Cut to Pieces and Gone to Hell": The Civil War, Race Relations, and the Battle of Poison Spring*, edited by Mark K. Christ, 59–78. Little Rock, Ark.: August House, 2003.

Niswonger, Richard L. *Arkansas Democratic Politics*. Fayetteville: University of Arkansas Press, 1990.

Nixon, Raymond B. *Henry W. Grady: Spokesman of the New South*. New York: Knopf, 1943.

Noll, Steven. "Steamboats, Cypress, and Tourism: An Ecological History of the Ocklawaha Valley in the Late Nineteenth Century." *Florida Historical Quarterly* 83, no. 1 (2004): 6–24.

Norrell, Robert J. *Up from History*. Cambridge, Mass.: Harvard University Press, 2009.

Notable Black American Women. Book 1. Edited by Jessie Carney Smith, Detroit: Gale Research, 1992.

Nussbaum, Raymond O. "'The Ring Is Smashed!' The New Orleans Municipal Election of 1896." *Louisiana History* 17 (1976): 283–97.

O'Donovan, Susan Eva. *Becoming Free in the Cotton South*. Cambridge, Mass.: Harvard University Press, 2007.

Ohmann, Richard. *Selling Culture*. New York: Verso, 1996.

Olsen, Otto H. *Carpetbagger's Crusade: The Life of Albion Winegar Tourgée*. Baltimore: Johns Hopkins University Press, 1965.

Ortiz, Paul. *Emancipation Betrayed: The Hidden History of Black Organizing and White Violence in Florida from Reconstruction to the Bloody Election of 1920*. Berkeley: University of California Press, 2005.

Oubre, Claude F. *Forty Acres and a Mule: The Freedmen's Bureau and Black Landownership*. Baton Rouge: Louisiana State University Press, 1978.

Palmer, Paul C. "Miscegenation as an Issue in the Arkansas Constitutional Convention of 1868." *Arkansas Historical Quarterly* 24 (1965): 99–119.

Parker, Alison M. *Articulating Rights: Nineteenth-Century American Women on Race, Reform, and the State*. Dekalb: Northern Illinois University Press, 2010.

Parsons, Elaine Frantz. "Midnight Rangers: Costume and Performance in the Reconstruction-Era Ku Klux Klan." *Journal of American History* 92, no. 3 (2005): 811–36.

Passet, Joanne E. *Sex Radicals and the Quest for Women's Equality*. Urbana: University of Illinois Press, 2003.

Payne, Charles M., and Adam Green, eds. *Time Longer than Rope: A Century of African American Activism, 1850–1950*. New York: New York University Press, 2003.

Pearce, Larry Wesley. "The American Missionary Association and the Freedmen in Arkansas, 1863–1878." *Arkansas Historical Quarterly* 30 (1971): 123–44.

Pennell, Elizabeth Robins, *The Life and Letters of Joseph Pennell*. Vol. 1. Boston: Little, Brown, 1929.

Penningroth, Dylan C. *The Claims of Kinfolk: African American Property and Community in the Nineteenth-Century South*. Chapel Hill: University of North Carolina Press, 2003.

Perman, Michael. *Struggle for Mastery: Disfranchisement in the South, 1888–1908*. Chapel Hill: University of North Carolina Press, 2001.

Peterson, Carla L. "Commemorative Ceremonies and Invented Traditions: History, Memory, and Modernity in the 'New Negro' Novel of the Nadir." In *Post-Bellum, Pre-Harlem: African American Literature and Culture, 1877–1919*, edited by Barbara McCaskill and Caroline Gebhard, 35–58. New York: New York University Press, 2006.

Pfeifer, Michael J. *Roots of Rough Justice: Origins of American Lynching*. Urbana: University of Illinois Press, 2011.

Philbrick, Francis. "Changing Conceptions of Property in Law." *University of Pennsylvania Law Review* 86 (1938): 691–732.

Phillips, Edward Hamilton. "The Transfer of Jefferson and Berkeley Counties from Virginia to West Virginia." Master's thesis, University of North Carolina, 1949.

Pierce, Michael. "The Mechanics of Little Rock: Free Labor Ideas in Antebellum Arkansas, 1845–1861." *Arkansas Historical Quarterly* 67 (2008): 221–44.

Posey, Thomas E. *The Negro Citizen of West Virginia*. Institute, W.Va.: West Virginia State College Press, 1935.

Post, Robert. "The Social Foundations of Defamation Law: Reputation and the Constitution." *California Law Review* 74 (1974): 691–732.

Pratt, Mary Louise. *Imperial Eyes: Travel Writing and Transculturation*. New York: Routledge, 1992.

Pride, Armistead S., and Clint C. Wilson. *A History of the Black Press*. Washington, D.C.: Howard University Press, 1997.

Prince, Valerie Sweeney. *Burnin' Down the House: Home in African-American Literature*. New York: Columbia University Press, 2005.

Pryse, Marjorie. "'Distilling Essences': Regionalism and 'Women's Culture.'" *American Literary Realism* 25 (1993): 1–15.

Pudup, Mary Beth. "Women's Work in the West Virginia Economy." *West Virginia History* 49 (1990): 7–20.

Quigley, David. *Second Founding: New York City, Reconstruction, and the Making of American Democracy*. New York: Hill and Wang, 2004.

Quinn, Arthur Hobson. *The Literature of the American People*. New York: Appleton-Century-Crofts, 1951.

Quinn, Jane. *Minorcans in Florida: Their History and Heritage*. St. Augustine, Fla.: Mission, 1975.

Rable, George. "Republican Albatross: The Louisiana Question, National Politics, and the Failure of Reconstruction." *Louisiana History* 23 (1982): 109–30.

Radin, Margaret J. "Property and Personhood." *Stanford Law Review* 34 (1982): 957–1015.

Radway, Janice A. "Learned and Literary Print Cultures in an Age of Professionalization and Diversification." In *Print in Motion: The Expansion of Publishing and Reading in the United States*, edited by Carl F. Kaestle and Janice A. Radway, 197–233. Chapel Hill: University of North Carolina Press, 2009.

Railton, Stephen. "The Twain-Cable Combination." In *A Companion to Mark Twain*, edited by Peter Messent and Louis J. Budd, 172–85. Malden, Mass.: Blackwell Publishing, 2005.

Rainey, Sue. *Creating Picturesque America: Monument to the Natural and Cultural Landscape.* Nashville: Vanderbilt University Press, 1994.

Rankin, David C. "The Forgotten People: Free People of Color in New Orleans, 1850–1870." Ph.D. diss., Johns Hopkins University, 1976.

———. "The Impact of the Civil War on the Free Colored Community of New Orleans." *Perspectives in American History* 11 (1977–78): 379–416.

———. "The Origins of Black Leadership in New Orleans during Reconstruction." *Journal of Southern History* 40 (August 1974): 417–40.

Ransom, Roger, and Richard Sutch. *One Kind of Freedom: The Economic Consequences of Emancipation.* Cambridge: Cambridge University Press, 1977.

Raper, Horace W. *William W. Holden: North Carolina's Political Enigma.* Chapel Hill: University of North Carolina Press, 1985.

Recken, Stephen L. "Rags to Respectability: Arkansas and Booker T. Washington." *Arkansas Historical Quarterly* 67 (2008): 54–72.

Redding, Kent. *Making Race, Making Power: North Carolina's Road to Disfranchisement.* Urbana: University of Illinois Press, 2003.

Regosin, Elizabeth. *Freedom's Promise: Ex-Slave Families and Citizenship in the Age of Emancipation.* Charlottesville: University of Virginia Press, 2002.

Reich, Charles. "The New Property." *Yale Law Journal* 73 (1964): 733–87.

Reidy, Joseph D. *From Slavery to Agrarian Capitalism in the Cotton Plantation South.* Chapel Hill: University of North Carolina Press, 1992.

Reilly, Wayne E. *Sarah Jane Foster: Teacher of the Freedmen.* Charlottesville: University of Virginia Press, 1990.

Revels, Tracy J. *Grander in Her Daughters: Florida's Women during the Civil War.* Columbia: University of South Carolina Press, 2004.

Rice, Connie Park. "'Don't Flinch Nor Yield an Inch': J. R. Clifford and the Struggle for Equal Rights in West Virginia." *West Virginia History*, n.s., 1, no. 2 (2007): 45–68.

Rice, Otis. *West Virginia: A History.* Lexington: University of Kentucky Press, 1985.

Richardson, Heather. *The Death of Reconstruction.* Cambridge, Mass.: Harvard University Press, 2001.

Richardson, Joe M. *Christian Reconstruction.* Athens: University of Georgia Press, 1986.

———. "An Evaluation of the Freedmen's Bureau in Florida." *Florida Historical Quarterly* 41 (1963): 223–38.

———. "The Freedmen's Bureau and Negro Labor in Florida." *Florida Historical Quarterly* 39 (1960): 167–74.

———. *The Negro in the Reconstruction of Florida, 1865–1877.* Tallahassee: Florida State University Press, 1965.

Richter, William L. "'Oh God, Let Us Have Revenge': Ben Griffith and His Family during the Civil War and Reconstruction." *Arkansas Historical Quarterly* 57 (1998): 255–86.

Ring, Natalie J. "Inventing the Tropical South: Race, Region, and the Colonial Model." *Mississippi Quarterly* 56, no. 4 (2003): 619-31.

Rinhart, Floyd, and Marion Rinhart. *Victorian Florida: America's Last Frontier*. Athens: Peachtree, 1986.

Ripley, C. Peter. *Slaves and Freedmen in Civil War Louisiana*. Baton Rouge: Louisiana State University Press, 1976.

Rivers, Larry Eugene. *Slavery in Florida: Territorial Days to Emancipation*. Gainesville: University Press of Florida, 2000.

Rivers, Larry Eugene, and Canter Brown Jr. "'A Monument to the Progress of the Race': The Intellectual and Political Origins of the Florida Agricultural and Mechanical University, 1865-1887." *Florida Historical Quarterly* 85, no. 1 (2006): 1-41.

Roach, Joseph. *Cities of the Dead*. New York: Columbia University Press, 1996.

Robbins, Sarah. *Managing Literacy, Mothering America: Women's Narratives on Reading and Writing in the Nineteenth Century*. Pittsburgh: University of Pittsburgh Press, 2004.

Robinson, Charles F. *Dangerous Liaisons: Sex and Love in the Segregated South*. Fayetteville: University of Arkansas Press, 2003.

———. "'Most Shamefully Common': Arkansas and Miscegenation." *Arkansas Historical Quarterly* 40 (2001): 265-83.

Rodrigue, John C. *Reconstruction in the Cane Fields: From Slavery to Free Labor in Louisiana's Sugar Parishes, 1862-1880*. Baton Rouge: Louisiana State University Press, 2001.

Rosen, Hannah. *Terror in the Heart of Freedom: Citizenship, Sexual Violence, and the Meaning of Race in the Postemancipation South*. Chapel Hill: University of North Carolina Press, 2009.

Rousey, Dennis C. *Policing the Southern City: New Orleans, 1805-1889*. Baton Rouge: Louisiana State University Press, 1996.

Rowe, Anne E. *The Idea of Florida in the American Literary Imagination*. Gainesville: University Press of Florida, 1992.

Royster, Jacqueline Jones. *Traces of a Stream: Literacy and Social Change among African-American Women*. Pittsburgh: University of Pittsburgh Press, 2000.

Rubin, Louis D. *George W. Cable: The Life and Times of a Southern Heretic*. New York: Pegasus, 1969.

———. "Simms, Charleston, and the Profession of Letters." In *Long Years of Neglect: The Work and Reputation of William Gilmore Simms*, edited by John Caldwell Guilds, 217-36. Fayetteville: University of Arkansas Press, 1988.

Russell, Sarah. "Intermarriage and Intermingling: Constructing the Planter Class in Louisiana's Sugar Parishes, 1803-1850." *Louisiana History* 46 (2005): 407-34.

Saks, Eva. "Representing Miscegenation Law." *Raritan* 8, no. 2 (1988): 39-69.

Salem, Dorothy. *To Better Our World: Black Women in Organized Reform, 1890-1920*. Brooklyn, N.Y.: Carlson, 1990.

Sanchez-Eppler, Karen. *Touching Liberty*. Berkeley: University of California Press, 1993.

Santamarina, Xiomara. *Belabored Professions: Narratives of African-American Working Women*. Chapel Hill: University of North Carolina Press, 2005.

Saville, Julie. *The Work of Reconstruction: From Slave to Wage Laborer in South Carolina, 1860-1870*. Cambridge, Mass.: Harvard University Press, 1994.

Schafer, Judith Kelleher. "'*Voleur de Nègres*': The Strange Career of Jean Charles David, Attorney at Law." *Louisiana History* 44 (2003): 261-73.

Schechter, Patricia A. *Ida B. Wells-Barnett and American Reform, 1880-1930*. Chapel Hill: University of North Carolina Press, 2001.

Schlereth, Thomas J. "Country Stores, Country Fairs, and Mail Order Catalogues: Consumption in Rural America." In *Consuming Visions: Accumulation and Display of Goods in America, 1880-1920*, edited by Simon J. Bronner, 339-75. New York: Norton, 1989.

Schroer, Sandra Ellen. *State of 'The Union': Marriage and Free Love in the Late 1800s*. New York: Routledge, 2005.

Schwalm, Leslie A. *Emancipation's Diaspora: Race and Reconstruction in the Upper Midwest*. Chapel Hill: University of North Carolina Press, 2009.

———. *A Hard Fight for We: Women's Transition from Slavery to Freedom in South Carolina*. Urbana: University of Illinois Press, 1997.

Schweninger, Loren. "Antebellum Free Persons of Color in Postbellum Louisiana." *Louisiana History* 30 (1989): 345-62.

———. *Black Property Owners in the South, 1790-1915*. Urbana: University of Illinois Press, 1997.

Scully, Pamela, and Diana Paton, eds. *Gender and Slave Emancipation in the Atlantic World*. Durham, N.C.: Duke University Press, 2005.

Sears, John. *Sacred Places: American Tourist Attractions in the Nineteenth Century*. New York: Oxford University Press, 1989.

Sefton, James E. *The United States Army and Reconstruction, 1865-1877*. Baton Rouge: Louisiana State University Press, 1967.

Senter, Caroline. "Creole Poets on the Verge of a Nation." In *Creole: The History and Legacy of Louisiana's Free People of Color*, edited by Sybil Kein, 276-94. Baton Rouge: Louisiana State University Press, 2000.

Sewell, Rebecca. "Clover Bend Plantation." *Southwest Review* 21 (1936): 312-18.

Shaffer, Donald R. *After the Glory: The Struggles of Black Civil War Veterans*. Lawrence: University Press of Kansas, 2004.

Shea, William L. "A Semi-Savage State: The Image of Arkansas in the Civil War." In *Civil War Arkansas: Beyond Battles and Leaders*, edited by Anne J. Bailey and Daniel E. Sutherland, 85-100. Fayetteville: University of Arkansas Press, 2000.

Sheeler, John R. "The Negro in West Virginia before 1900." Ph.D. diss., West Virginia University, Morgantown, 1954.

Shofner, Jerrell H. *Nor Is It Over Yet: Florida in the Era of Reconstruction, 1863-1877*. Gainesville: University Press of Florida, 1974.

Siegel, Reva B. "Home as Work: The First Woman's Rights Claims concerning Wives' Household Labor, 1850-1880." *Yale Law Journal* 103 (1994): 1075-1217.

Silber, Nina. *The Romance of Reunion: Northerners and the South, 1865-1900.* Chapel Hill: University of North Carolina Press, 1993.
Smith, Jon, and Deborah Cohn, eds. *Look Away! The U.S. South in New World Studies.* Durham, N.C.: Duke University Press, 2004.
Smith, Jon, Kathryn McKee, and Scott Romine, eds. "Postcolonial Theory, the U.S. South, and New World Studies." Special issues of *Mississippi Quarterly* 56, no. 4 (2003): 491-693; and *Mississippi Quarterly* 57, no. 1 (2003-4): 1-194.
Smith, Rogers M. *Civic Ideals: Conflicting Visions of Citizenship in U.S. History.* New Haven: Yale University Press, 1997.
Solomon, Irvin D., and Grace Erhart. "Race and Civil War in South Florida." *Florida in the Civil War.* Special issue, *Florida Historical Quarterly* (1999): 320-41.
Sommerville, Diane Miller. *Rape and Race in the Nineteenth-Century South.* Chapel Hill: University of North Carolina Press, 2004.
Sotiropoulos, Karen. *Staging Race: Black Performers in Turn of the Century America.* Cambridge, Mass.: Harvard University Press, 2006.
Spindel, Donna J. "Women's Legal Rights in West Virginia, 1863-1984." *West Virginia History* 51 (1992): 29-44.
Spoo, Robert. *Without Copyrights: Piracy, Publishing, and the Public Domain.* New York: Oxford University Press, 2013.
Stanley, Amy Dru. *From Bondage to Contract.* New York: Cambridge University Press, 1998.
Starnes, Richard D. "'The Stirring Strains of Dixie': The Civil War and Southern Identity in Haywood County, North Carolina." *North Carolina Historical Review* 74 (1997): 237-59.
Stealey, John Edmund, III. "The Freedmen's Bureau in West Virginia." *West Virginia History* 39 (1978): 99-142.
———. "Report of Freedmen's Bureau Operations in West Virginia: Agents in the Eastern Panhandle." *West Virginia History* 42 (1981): 94-129.
———. "Reports of Freedmen's Bureau District Officers on Tours and Surveys in West Virginia." *West Virginia History* 43 (1982): 145-55.
Steedman, Marek. "Gender and the Politics of the Household in Reconstruction Louisiana, 1865-1878." In *Gender and Slave Emancipation in the Atlantic World,* edited by Pamela Scully and Diana Paton, 310-22. Durham, N.C.: Duke University Press, 2005.
Steinfeld, Robert J. *The Invention of Free Labor: The Employment Relation in English and American Law and Culture, 1350-1870.* Chapel Hill: University of North Carolina Press, 1991.
Stevenson, Brenda E. *Life in Black and White: Family and Community in the Slave South.* New York: Oxford University Press, 1996.
Stockley, Grif. *Ruled by Race: Black/White Relations in Arkansas from Slavery to the Present.* Fayetteville: University of Arkansas Press, 2009.
Sundquist, Eric. "Realism and Regionalism." In *Columbia Literary History of the United States,* edited by Emory Elliott, 502-24. New York: Columbia University Press, 1988.

Sutherland, Daniel E. "Guerrillas: The Real War in Arkansas." *Arkansas Historical Quarterly* 52 (1993): 257–85.

———. *A Savage Conflict: The Decisive Role of Guerrillas in the American Civil War*. Chapel Hill: University of North Carolina Press, 2009.

———, ed. *Guerrillas, Unionists, and Violence on the Confederate Home Front*. Fayetteville: University of Arkansas Press, 1999.

Talbott, Forrest. "Some Legislative and Legal Aspects of the Negro Question in West Virginia during the Civil War and Reconstruction." *West Virginia History* 24 (October 1962): 1–133.

Taylor, Joe Gray. *Louisiana Reconstructed, 1863–1877*. Baton Rouge: Louisiana State University Press, 1974.

Taylor, William R. *Cavalier and Yankee*. New York: George Braziller, 1961.

Tebbel, John, ed. *A History of Book Publishing in the United States*. Vol. 2. New York: R. R. Bowker, 1975.

Terborg-Penn, Rosalyn. *African American Women and the Struggle for the Vote, 1850–1920*. Bloomington: Indiana University Press, 1998.

Thomas, Brook. *American Literary Realism and the Failed Promise of Contract*. Berkeley: University of California Press, 1997.

———. "'Plessy v. Ferguson' and the Literary Imagination." *Cardozo Studies in Law and Literature* 9, no. 1 (1997): 45–65.

Thompson, George H. *Arkansas and Reconstruction*. New York: Kennikat Press, 1976.

Torstendahl, Rolf, and Michael Burrage, eds. *The Formation of the Professions: Knowledge, State, and Strategy*. London: Sage, 1990.

Trachtenberg, Alan. *The Incorporation of America: Culture and Society in the Gilded Age*. New York: Hill and Wang, 1982.

Tregle, Joseph G., Jr. "Creoles and Americans." In *Creole New Orleans*, edited by Arnold R. Hirsch and Joseph Logsdon, 131–88. Baton Rouge: Louisiana State University Press, 1992.

Trotti, Michael Ayers. "What Counts: Trends in Racial Violence in the Postbellum South." *Journal of American History* 100 (2013): 375–400.

Tucker, Ruth. "'Octave Thanet': A Biography of Alice French." 1934. Manuscript, Newberry Library, Chicago.

Tunnell, Ted. *Crucible of Reconstruction: War, Radicalism, and Race in Louisiana, 1862–1877*. Baton Rouge: Louisiana State University Press, 1984.

———. *Edge of the Sword: The Ordeal of Carpetbagger Marshall H. Twitchell in the Civil War and Reconstruction*. Baton Rouge: Louisiana State University Press, 2001.

Turner, Arlin. *George W. Cable*. Durham, N.C.: Duke University Press, 1956.

———. "George W. Cable's Beginnings as a Reformer." *Journal of Southern History* 17 (1951): 135–61.

———. "George W. Cable's Revolt against Literary Sectionalism." *Tulane Studies in English* 5 (1955): 5–27.

———, ed. *The Negro Question*. New York: Doubleday, 1958.

Urry, John. *Consuming Places*. New York: Routledge, 1995.

Urwin, Gregory J. W. "Poison Spring and Jenkins' Ferry: Racial Atrocities during the Camden Expedition." In *"All Cut to Pieces and Gone to Hell": The Civil War, Race Relations, and the Battle of Poison Spring*, edited by Mark K. Christ, 107–37. Little Rock, Ark.: August House, 2003.

U.S. Bureau of the Census. *Historical Census Statistics on Population Totals by Race, 1790 to 1990, and by Hispanic Origin, 1970 to 1990, for the United States, Regions, Divisions, and States*. Prepared by Campbell Gibson and Kay Jung, Population Division, Bureau of the Census, Washington, D.C., 2002.

Vandal, Gilles. "The Origins of the New Orleans Riot of 1866, Revisited." *Louisiana History* 22 (1981): 135–65.

———. *Rethinking Southern Violence: Homicides in Post–Civil War Louisiana, 1866–1884*. Columbus: Ohio State University Press, 2000.

Vandervelde, Lea S. "The Labor Vision of the Thirteenth Amendment." *University of Pennsylvania Law Review* 138 (1989): 437–504.

Vandevelde, Kenneth J. "The New Property of the Nineteenth Century: The Development of the Modern Concept of Property." *Buffalo Law Review* 29 (1980): 325–67.

Van Tassel, Emily. "Only the Law Would Rule between Us." *Chicago-Kent Law Review* 70 (1995): 873–926.

Vicinus, Martha. *Intimate Friends: Women Who Loved Women, 1778–1928*. Chicago: University of Chicago Press, 2004.

Vincent, Charles. *Black Legislators in Louisiana*. Baton Rouge: Louisiana State University Press, 1976.

Vogel, Todd. *The Black Press: New Literary and Historical Essays*. New Brunswick, N.J.: Rutgers University Press, 2001.

Vorenberg, Michael. *Final Freedom: The Civil War, the Abolition of Slavery, and the Thirteenth Amendment*. New York: Cambridge University Press, 2001.

Vossler, Kathryn Babb. "Women and Education in West Virginia, 1810–1909." *West Virginia History* 36 (1975): 271–90.

Wagner, Bryan. *Disturbing the Peace: Black Culture and the Police Power after Slavery*. Cambridge, Mass.: Harvard University Press, 2009.

Wakefield, Laura Wallis. "'Set a Light in a Dark Place': Teachers of Freedmen in Florida, 1864–1874." *Florida Historical Quarterly* 81, no. 4 (2003): 401–17.

Waldrep, Christopher. *The Many Faces of Judge Lynch: Extralegal Violence and Punishment in America*. New York: Palgrave, 2002.

Wang, Xi. *The Trial of Democracy: Black Suffrage and Northern Republicans, 1860–1910*. Athens: University of Georgia Press, 1997.

Waterbury, Jean Parker, ed. *The Oldest City: St. Augustine, Saga of Survival*. St. Augustine, Fla.: Historical Society, 1983.

Waters, Kristin, and Carol B. Conaway. *Black Women's Intellectual Traditions: Speaking Their Minds*. Burlington: University of Vermont Press, 2007.

Wecter, Dixon, ed. *The Love Letters of Mark Twain*. New York: Harper, 1949.

Weinfeld, Daniel R. "'More Courage than Discretion': Charles M. Hamilton in Reconstruction-Era Florida." *Florida Historical Quarterly* 84, no. 4 (2006): 479–517.

Weisenfeld, Judith. "'Who Is Sufficient for These Things?': Sara G. Stanley and the American Missionary Association." *American Society of Church History* 60, no. 4 (1991): 493–507.

Welke, Barbara Young. *Recasting American Liberty: Gender, Race, Law, and the Railroad Revolution, 1865–1920*. New York: Cambridge University Press, 2001.

Wells, Jonathan Daniel. *Women Writers and Journalists in the Nineteenth-Century South*. New York: Cambridge University Press, 2011.

West, Robin. *Narrative, Authority, and Law*. Ann Arbor: University of Michigan Press, 1993.

White, Deborah Gray. *Too Heavy a Load: Black Women in Defense of Themselves, 1894–1994*. New York: Norton, 1999.

White, Howard A. *The Freedmen's Bureau in Louisiana*. Baton Rouge: Louisiana State University Press, 1970.

White, Shane, and Graham White. *Stylin': African American Expressive Culture from Its Beginnings to the Zoot Suit*. Ithaca, N.Y.: Cornell University Press, 1998.

White, William Allen. *The Autobiography of William Allen White*. New York: Macmillan, 1946.

Whites, LeeAnn. *The Civil War as a Crisis in Gender*. Athens: University of Georgia Press, 1995.

———. *Gender Matters: Civil War, Reconstruction and the Making of the New South*. New York: Palgrave, 2005.

Whites, LeeAnn, and Alecia P. Long, eds. *Occupied Women: Gender, Military Occupation, and the American Civil War*. Baton Rouge: Louisiana State University Press, 2009.

Wiener, Jonathan M. *Social Origins of the New South: Alabama, 1860–1885*. Baton Rouge: Louisiana State University Press, 1978.

Williams, E. Russell, Jr. "Louisiana's Public and Private Immigration Endeavors: 1866–1893." *Louisiana History* 15 (1974): 153–73.

Williams, Heather Andrea. *Self-Taught: African American Education in Slavery and Freedom*. Chapel Hill: University of North Carolina Press, 2005.

Williams, John Alexander. *West Virginia*. New York: Norton, 1984.

Williamson, Edward C. *Florida Politics in the Gilded Age, 1877–1893*. Gainesville: University of Florida Press, 1976.

Wilson, Christopher. *The Labor of Words*. Athens: University of Georgia Press, 1985.

Wilson, Edmund. *Patriotic Gore*. 1962. New York: Norton, 1994.

Wilson, Kirt H. *The Reconstruction Desegregation Debate: The Politics of Equality and the Rhetoric of Place, 1870–1875*. East Lansing: Michigan State University Press, 2002.

Wintory, Blake. "African-American Legislators in the Arkansas General Assembly, 1868–1893." *Arkansas Historical Quarterly* 65 (2006): 385–434.

———. "William Hines Furbush: African-American Carpetbagger, Republican, Fusionist, and Democrat." *Arkansas Historical Quarterly* 63 (2004): 107–261.

Wonham, Henry B. "'I Want a Real Coon': Mark Twain and Late Nineteenth-Century Ethnic Caricature." *American Literature* 72.1 (March 2000): 117–52.

———. "Mark Twain's Last Cakewalk: Racialized Performance in *No. 44, The Mysterious Stranger*." *American Literary Realism* 40, no. 3 (Spring 2008): 262-71.

Woodman, Harold D. *New South–New Law: The Legal Foundations of Credit and Labor Relations in the Postbellum Agricultural South*. Baton Rouge: Louisiana State University Press, 1995.

Woodward, C. Vann. "The Case of the Louisiana Traveler." In *Quarrels That Have Shaped the Constitution*, edited by John A. Garraty, 157-74. New York: Harper and Row, 1987.

———. *Origins of the New South, 1877-1913*. Baton Rouge: Louisiana State University Press, 1951.

———. *The Strange Career of Jim Crow*. 1955. New York: Oxford University Press, 1974.

Woodward, Ralph Lee, Jr. "Spanish Commercial Policy in Louisiana, 1763-1803." *Louisiana History* 44 (2003): 133-64.

Wyatt-Brown, Bertram. *The Shaping of Southern Culture: Honor, Grace, and War, 1760s-1880s*. Chapel Hill: University of North Carolina Press, 2002.

———. *Southern Honor: Ethics and Behavior in the Old South*. New York: Oxford University Press, 1982.

Yellin, Jean Fagan. *Harriet Jacobs: A Life*. New York: Basic Civitas, 2004.

———. *Women and Sisters: The Antislavery Feminists in American Culture*. New Haven: Yale University Press, 1989.

Young, Darius J. "Henry S. Harmon: Pioneer African American Attorney in Reconstruction-Era Florida." *Florida Historical Quarterly* 85, no. 2 (2006): 177-96.

Young, Elizabeth. *Disarming the Nation: Women's Writing and the American Civil War*. Chicago: University of Chicago Press, 1999.

Youngs, Larry R. "The Sporting Set Winters in Florida: Fertile Ground for the Leisure Revolution, 1870-1930." *Florida Historical Quarterly* 84, no. 1 (2005): 57-79.

Zackodnik, Teresa. *Press, Platform, Pulpit: Black Feminist Publics in the Era of Reform*. Knoxville: University of Tennessee Press, 2011.

Zimring, David. "'Secession in Favor of the Constitution': How West Virginia Justified Separate Statehood during the Civil War." *West Virginia History*, n.s., 3, no. 2 (2009): 23-53.

Zipf, Karin L. "'Among These American Heathens': Congregationalist Missionaries and African American Evangelicals during Reconstruction, 1865-1878." *North Carolina Historical Review* 74 (1997): 111-34.

———. *Labor of Innocents: Forced Apprenticeship in North Carolina, 1715-1919*. Baton Rouge: Louisiana State University Press, 2005.

———. "No Longer under Cover(ture): Marriage, Divorce, and Gender in the 1868 Constitutional Convention." In *North Carolinians in the Era of the Civil War and Reconstruction*, edited by Paul D. Escott, 193-220. Chapel Hill: University of North Carolina Press, 2008.

———. "'The WHITES Shall Rule the Land or Die': Gender, Race, and Class in North Carolina Reconstruction Politics." *Journal of Southern History* 64 (1999): 499-534.

INDEX

Aaron, Daniel, 2
Abolitionism, 3, 67, 285
Acculturation, 24, 26, 30, 36, 57, 64, 74
Advertising, 289
Africa, in Woolson's Florida travel sketches, 44–45
African American men: voting rights of, 12, 13, 20; disfranchisement of, 20, 28, 41, 75, 170, 229, 286, 288, 290, 295, 296, 297, 298, 310 (n. 94); access to white women, 146, 148, 149, 152, 176
African American regiments: in Florida, 32; in New Orleans, 183, 186
African Americans: print culture of, 11, 12, 107, 123–24, 223, 287; literacy rates of, 12; activists influencing national Reconstruction policy, 19; in Florida, 32, 73, 296; stereotypes of, 42, 44, 68, 210, 219, 253, 280; Woolson on cultural contributions of, 69–70, 71; skin color of, 88, 96, 104; suffrage of, 126, 127, 128; and jury service, 148, 162–63; businesses of, 157–59; elite African Americans, 170, 172, 287–88; Reconstruction vision of, 174; of New Orleans, 185; as performers, 215; reactions to Cable's dramatization of characters, 219–21, 222; Cable's correspondence with, 222–23, 265, 332 (n. 95); labor demands of, 238; in Arkansas, 242, 243, 251, 274–75, 298–99, 335 (n. 24), 335–36 (n. 26); voting rights of, 281; postwar activism of, 294, 296. *See also* Free African Americans; Free people of color
African American veterans: John Clifford on intraracial economic cooperation, 3, 125, 159, 160, 169; postwar gender roles of, 86; reputation of, 289; Grady's postwar forgetting of, 294
African American women: citizenship lessons for, 3, 13; literary activism of, 11, 13, 285–87, 301; and consumer culture, 13, 23, 173, 264–67, 279; as agents of social change, 14, 20, 229, 285; subversive strategies within southern plantation households, 14, 253–54; political agency of, 20, 78; stereotype of "old auntie," 42, 44, 280; property ownership of, 78; as entrepreneurial business owners, 102; and trope of outraged mother, 108; emancipatory narratives of, 110; and club movement, 125, 172, 173, 285; limited employment opportunities of, 137, 320 (n. 30); and gender stereotypes, 160–61, 173; and literary societies, 172, 287; in Cable's *The Grandissimes*, 192, 206–10, 229, 330 (n. 61); stereotype of "Mammy," 210; resistance of, 229, 254; back talk of, 231, 253–58, 268, 280; and black protofeminist thought, 285; and dialectic of oppression and activism, 285; as journalists, 287; and reputation, 293. *See also* Freedwomen; Slave women

African American writers: literary activism of, 11–12; and regionalism, 18; and sentimental fiction, 173; African American women as, 285–86. *See also specific writers*
African Methodist Episcopal church, 242
Age of Contract, 94, 116, 122
Agrarian movement, 242–43
Agricultural Wheel, 242, 298
Aiken, South Carolina, 235
Alabama, in Military District Three, 7, 26
Albert, Octavia Victoria Rogers, 13, 208, 255, 286
Alcott, Bronson, 250
Alden, Henry Mills, 30
Ambivalence: in Reconstruction narrative, 17; and Woolson, 27, 35, 45, 56, 57, 61, 75; in Tourgée's *Toinette*, 90; and Storer College, 135, 152; and Cable, 210, 218, 227; in Cable's *The Grandissimes*, 191, 228; and Thanet, 231, 232, 236, 240, 252, 257, 268, 280; in work of Hopkins and Chesnutt, 286
American Bar Association, 68
American exceptionalism, 294
American Library Association, 112, 287
American literature, and regionalism, 24, 236
American Medical Association, 68
American Missionary Association (AMA), 87, 129, 130, 135, 138, 145, 147, 148, 151, 321 (n. 36)
American Negro Academy, 154
American Woman Suffrage Association, 315 (n. 57)
Ames, Mary Clemmer, 123, 133, 149, 155, 273
"Ancient City, Part I and Part II, The" (Woolson): publishing of, 31; northern tourists in, 33–36, 43–45, 52, 53, 54, 58, 59, 62, 65, 69–70; female tourists in, 34, 36, 43–45, 59; and Floridian landscape, 38, 45; and Confederate veterans, 39–40, 70; ex-slaves in, 41, 65, 73; freedwomen in, 41–44, 56; Native Americans in, 49, 50, 51–52; and cultural erasure, 49–52; and land acquisition, 50–51; race in, 53; and Minorcans, 53, 54, 62–63; racial identity in, 57; and freedpeople's labor, 59, 62–63, 65, 69–70, 73
Antebellum nostalgia: and Storer College, 134, 326 (n. 112); Thanet on, 231, 237, 259–60; for Civil War, 293, 294
Anthony, Kate, 131, 163, 324 (n. 85)
Anthony, Susan B., 171
Anti-Peonage Act (1867), 63
Appalachia, 81
Appletons' Journal, 29, 30, 31, 70, 182, 234
Apprenticeship laws, 291
Arkansas: Thanet's residence in, 4, 232, 235, 236, 240, 241; transplanted northerners and midwesterners in, 4, 237; in Military District Four, 7, 240–43, 250; guerrillas in, 230, 240, 241, 243, 246, 247–48, 250, 264, 275; labor struggles in, 231, 273; violence in, 235, 241–42, 274–76; Lawrence County, 235, 255, 258, 262, 276, 335 (n. 24), 338 (n. 65), 338 (n. 71), 338 (n. 73); Battle of Poison Spring, 241; emancipation in, 241; fusion party in, 241, 242; Democratic Party in, 241, 242–43, 257, 298–99; Freedmen's Bureau in, 241, 254, 255, 259–60, 262, 268, 273, 276; Constitutional Convention of 1868, 242; frontier aspects of, 242; African Americans in, 242, 243, 251, 274–75, 298–99, 335 (n. 24), 335–36 (n. 26); political coalition of industrial and farm workers, 242, 298; dialect in, 257; Home Farms, 262; real estate values in, 262, 338 (n. 71); absentee landlordism in, 274; and Agricultural Wheel, 298; midwestern teachers in, 334 (n. 13)

378   INDEX

Arkansas Historical Association, 238–39
Arnold, David, 61–62
Association for the Study of Negro Life and History, 154
Athenaeum, 277
Atkinson, Gus, 97, 314 (n. 46)
Atlanta, Georgia, 300
Atlanta Constitution, 222, 281, 284
Atlanta Exposition of 1895, 172
Atlanta University, 135
Atlantic Monthly, 11, 30, 31, 190, 235, 237, 273

"Badge of servitude," 3, 79, 108, 114, 115, 118, 119
Baha'i, 169
Baker, Cullen, 246
Baker, Marion, 224
Balearic Islands, 27
Baltimore and Ohio Railroad, 126, 127
Baltimore Methodist Protestant, 133–34
Baltimore Sun, 97–98
Banks, Nathaniel P., 186
Barbour, George, 35, 61, 72
Barton, Clara, 238
Bates College, 147
Beale, Howard, 16
Bell, William Henry, 151–52
Bennett College, 80
Bercaw, Nancy, 252
Best, Stephen M., 17, 104, 136
Bill, Ledyard, 51, 62, 67
Black Codes, 60, 186
Black Creoles: in Cable's *The Grandissimes* 179, 201, 204; 295 in New Orleans, 184–86, 189, 199, 202–3; and Cable's "Mammy portrait," 210; Cable's performances of, 217–19Blackface, 213, 219
"Black Four Hundred," 167
Blackstone, William, 20, 85, 289
Blanc, Marie Thérèse, 259, 275, 276–77
Blight, David, 294
Board of Public Welfare, 168
Bobbs-Merrill, 239

Bolivar Heights, West Virginia, 127
Book Lovers Club, 173
Booth, John Wilkes, 274
Boston Evening Transcript, 218
Bourbons, and Democratic Party, 41, 161, 181, 296
Bourgeois individualism, 124, 132, 133, 134, 176
Boycotts, 137, 264, 290–91, 296
Brackett, Louise Wood, 131
Brackett, Nathan: and freedpeople's education, 129, 130, 131; and regionalism, 131–33; eulogy of, 138; and freedpeople's property ownership, 139; on citizenship, 143; and Sarah Jane Foster, 145, 146–47, 150, 151; as officiant at Clifford's wedding, 155; John Clifford's discrimination charges against, 163–65, 166, 318 (n. 2)
Brackett family, 134, 318 (n. 2)
Bradstreet, Anne, 233
Braxton, Joanne, 108
Brooks, Daphne, 219, 316 (n. 67)
Brothers of Freedom, 242
Brown, Anna E., 170
Brown, Elsa Barkley, 14
Brown, John, 123, 125, 128, 129–30, 174–75
Brown, John (Sarah Jane Foster's assistant), 146, 147, 148, 150
Browning, Robert, 211
Brown v. Board of Education (1954), 3, 153, 177
Bruce, Blanche K., 167
Bryant, William Cullen, 54, 55
Buck, Paul, 236
Bunner, H. C., 218
Bureau of Refugees, Freedmen, and Abandoned Lands. *See* Freedmen's Bureau
Byron, Lord, 106, 107, 316 (n. 67)

Cable, George Washington: as southern reformer, 2; stage appearances with Twain, 4, 181, 210–13, 214, 215, 216, 217, 223, 224, 226, 331 (n. 74);

journalism of, 11; and editorial intervention, 15-16, 225-27, 228; Reconstruction vision of, 23, 64, 177, 178, 179, 180, 182, 187, 189, 202-6, 214, 216, 226, 228, 279; on mixed racial and ethnic identity, 55, 179; sales records of, 112; as spokesman for Creoles, 115; and compromise, 132; criticism of wealthy black Creoles, 170; and performative nature of identity, 178, 179, 210-13, 214, 215-16, 232, 269; dramatization of Creole characters, 178, 190, 214-17, 221, 222, 223-24, 225, 226-27, 228; and national identity, 178, 284; and doubling characterizations, 180, 181, 184, 191, 228, 256; postwar employment of, 181, 183, 187; civic work of, 181-82, 223, 224, 225, 228, 326 (n. 3); death of, 182; short stories of, 182; "Sieur George," 182; Old Creole Days, 182, 187; The Creoles of Louisiana, 187, 189, 191; on Creole identity, 187, 189, 327-28 (n. 14); "Bibi," 189-90; critics' response to, 194, 211, 214-16, 218-19, 221, 223-25, 227; on lecture circuit, 210, 333 (n. 105); Dr. Sevier, 211, 215, 216, 217; "Richling's Visit to Kate Riley," 211; dialects used by, 214, 215, 223, 224, 226, 227, 256, 257, 270; performance of Creole songs, 217-19, 221; "Pov' Piti Momzel Zizi," 218; "Creole Slave Songs," 219; "Dance in Place Congo," 219; African Americans' responses to performances, 219, 220-21, 222; racialized ventriloquism of, 220-21; dramatization of African American characters, 220-21, 223, 227; "The Freedman's Case in Equity," 221-22, 224, 297; Grady's response to "The Freedmen's Case in Equity," 222; "The Silent South," 222, 297; self-promotion of, 225; and marketplace pressures, 225-27; John March, Southerner, 227; Thanet compared to, 236; literary celebrity of, 239, 293; correspondence with Washington, 265, 332 (n. 95); on Grady, 282; Grady compared to, 283; and political activism, 287; and Du Bois, 288; on property, 289; on labor, 291; on duty, 292; press criticism of, 297-98; Bonaventure, 298; Home Culture and Garden Clubs, 298; Strange True Stories of Louisiana, 298. See also The Grandissimes (Cable)

Camp, Stephanie, 108

Capitalism: and New South, 23; Tourgée on, 79, 115, 116, 122, 291; and Storer College, 134; and freedpeople's labor, 136; and strikes, 237; Thanet on, 279, 291; and relations of workers and capitalists, 291; and reputation, 293; and property, 301. *See also* Market economy

Cardozo, Francis L., 148, 158, 161, 170, 174

Carnegie, Andrew, 234, 281, 333 (n. 4)

Carpetbaggers: Tourgée as carpetbag jurist, 2, 76, 80, 114, 115, 121, 149; in Florida, 32, 48, 73, 75; in North Carolina, 80; in Tourgée's *Toinette*, 94

Casey, David, 255

Cassanello, Robert, 307 (n. 20)

Central Methodist, 161

Century Magazine, 187-88, 221, 222, 235, 257, 326 (n. 2), 333 (n. 105), 340 (n. 108)

Cession, 179, 193

Champ, J. L., 158

Charles Scribner's Sons, 225, 326 (n. 2)

Charleston, South Carolina, 37, 300

Charles Town, West Virginia, 126, 131

Charlotte Observer, 98

Chautauqua, New York, Tourgée's writing *A Royal Gentleman* in, 78

Chesnutt, Charles, 286, 288

Chicago Daily Inter Ocean, 296

Chivalric code. *See* Honor

Churton, Henry. *See* Tourgée, Albion

Citizenship: constitutional guarantees of, 1; and immigrants, 2, 7; Woolson on freedpeople's citizenship, 2, 25, 26, 27, 38, 41-43, 49; in Tourgée's *Toinette*, 2-3, 77, 78-79, 83, 84, 106, 120, 207; and Emancipation Proclamation, 6; gendered conceptions of, 7, 13, 20, 160; and Reconstruction writers, 13, 20, 285, 286, 294; framing as racialized construct, 20; and property ownership, 20, 21, 28, 79, 83-84, 104, 121, 266, 279, 284, 288, 289-90, 301; definitions of, 20, 22-23, 25, 241, 284, 286, 288, 300; and tourism, 71-72; consumer citizenship, 72, 73, 268; in Tourgée's *A Royal Gentleman*, 78, 79, 84; freedpeople's entitlement to, 80-82, 220, 221; and literacy, 106, 172, 176; freedwomen's claiming of, 108, 120, 266; Storer College's hierarchical model of, 134; and African American men's access to white women, 148; and Niagara Movement, 154; and John Clifford's civil rights activism, 160; and *Slaughterhouse Cases*, 182; in Cable's *The Grandissimes*, 197, 216; in Thanet's *Expiation*, 230, 231, 232; and market economy, 231, 301; and Reconstruction literature, 281, 300, 301; Grady's renegotiation of, 282, 284, 293; and intermarriage, 286; and second civil rights movement, 301

Civil rights activism: and second civil rights movement, 3, 301; and Reconstruction writers, 14-15, 295; of Tourgée, 121; of Storer College students, 123, 145; of John Clifford, 153-59, 160, 164, 166, 176, 201, 221, 292, 297; and Cable's public addresses, 181; and Cable's civic work, 181-82, 223, 224, 225, 228, 326 (n. 3); and Cable's "The Freedman's Case in Equity," 221-22, 224; and Cable's "The Silent South," 222; of Du Bois, 287; of Washington, 287; of Franklin, 297

Civil War: sectional novels on, 18; Woolson's predictions concerning, 25; in Florida, 32; and publishing industry, 112; in Arkansas, 240; antebellum nostalgia for, 293, 294; Grady on, 293-94

Claiborne, William C. C., 197

Class distinctions: and Creole identity, 184; in Cable's *The Grandissimes*, 203; and Cable's representations of Creoles, 214; and African Americans in Arkansas, 243; in Thanet's *Expiation*, 248-49. *See also* Elite African Americans; Middle class; Planters; Poor whites; Yeoman class

Class relations: and Woolson's portrayals of freedpeople, 72; in Tourgée's *Toinette*, 78, 86-88; in Tourgée's *A Royal Gentleman*, 86; and race relations, 125, 176; and racial uplift, 158-59; in Cable's *The Grandissimes*, 200; in Cable's "The Freedman's Case in Equity," 221; and touristic vision, 307 (n. 15). *See also* Cross-class alliances

Clay, Henry, 69-70

Clayton, Powell, 241, 275

Clemens, Samuel. *See* Twain, Mark

Cleveland, Grover, 212-13, 281

Clifford, John Robert: and rhetoric of reputation, 3, 152, 161-67, 171, 176, 198, 289, 293, 297; literary activism of, 11, 12, 125, 126, 174; Reconstruction vision of, 23, 125; on African American veterans' war service as dues of citizenship, 91; "C" letters to *Greensboro North State*, 91-92; and *Strauder v. West Virginia*, 149; education of, 152; as attorney, 152-54, 162-63, 297; civil rights activism of, 153-59, 160, 164, 166, 176, 201, 221, 292, 297; and Niagara Movement, 154,

INDEX   381

288; as Storer College student, 154–55; press criticism of, 155, 162; and land-ownership, 156–57, 169; gendered rhetoric of, 159–61, 176, 292, 294; "Don't Whine," 160; "Hard Heads," 160; discrimination accusations, 163–65, 166, 318 (n. 2); and race relations, 167, 168; and reform organizations, 168; Franklin compared to, 170, 172; and reading, 173; endorsement of Cable, 223; ambition of, 283; on property, 289; literary reputation of, 293; and women's leadership in temperance movement, 325 (n. 105). *See also* *Pioneer Press*
Clifford, Mary Franklin, 155
Clover Bend plantation, Arkansas, 235, 238, 245, 250, 251, 333–34 (n. 9)
Code Noir, 327 (n. 8)
Cohn, Deborah, 307 (n. 20)
Colfax Massacre of Easter 1873, 182–83
Colored Farmers' National Alliance, 296
Colored National Labor Union, 238
Color line, Cable's representations acknowledging transgression of, 220, 221
Columbia Literary History of the United States, 18
Commemorative acts, 18, 39, 44
Compromise of 1850, 70
Compromise of 1877, 10, 11, 73–74
Comstock Law, 166
Confederacy: transcendence of state allegiances to, 4; and southern identity, 15; money of, 84
Confederate veterans: demands for property restitution, 22; in Woolson's Florida travel sketches, 39, 40, 41, 48, 70, 99, 266; in Tourgée's *Toinette*, 91, 92; of West Virginia, 126, 128; in Thanet's *Expiation*, 244; Grady's manipulation of reputation of, 293, 294, 295; and memorialization efforts, 312 (n. 32)

Consumer culture: in Thanet's *Expiation*, 4, 230, 231, 263, 264, 265–66; and African American women, 13, 23, 173, 264–67, 279; and Reconstruction writers, 15, 28; and Woolson's travel sketches of Florida, 25–26, 35, 73; and freedpeople, 28, 72–73, 75, 263, 264–67, 268; in Woolson's "The Ancient City," 35–36, 73; and Woolson's short stories, 47, 49, 71, 72; and politics of consumption, 71–72, 310 (n. 94); and Franklin, 173; and acts of reading, 173–74; Thanet on, 237; and Simms, 300
Cook, Coralie Franklin, 125, 318 (n. 3). *See also* Franklin, Coralie
Cook, George William, 167
Cooper, Anna Julia, 13, 168, 234–35, 253, 286–87
Copyright reform, 15–16, 239, 287
Coushatta Massacre of August 1874, 183
Cox, James, 19
Crane, Gregg D., 17
Crane, Stephen, 270
Crawford, Jane, 235, 250, 251, 258–60, 268, 333 (n. 7), 334 (n. 9)
Creole identity: in Cable's *The Grandissimes*, 4, 179, 180, 187, 189, 190–91, 193, 194–95, 203, 205–6, 218; malleability of, 178, 179, 187; composite nature of, 179; contested meaning of, 184–87, 215, 228, 326–27 (n. 8), 327–28 (n. 14); and chattel principle, 186; Cable's geographic boundaries of, 187–88, 191; in Cable's stage appearances with Twain, 210–11, 212, 213; and Cable's dramatization of Creole characters, 217–19 224. *See also* Black Creoles
Crèvecoeur, J. Hector St. Jean de, 104, 105, 139
Crisis, 168
Critic, 224
Critical race theory, 297

Crosby, Oliver Martin: *Florida Facts Both Bright and Blue*, 25, 27, 42, 43, 64; on Native Americans, 50

Cross-class alliances: mutual benefit of, 3; in Tourgée's *Toinette*, 4, 90, 92–93, 250; in Cable's *The Grandissimes*, 203; in Thanet's *Expiation*, 251, 256. *See also* Class relations

Cross-race alliances: mutual benefit of, 3; Franklin's appeals on, 3, 125, 171; in Thanet's *Expiation*, 4, 232, 256; in Tourgée's *Toinette*, 78, 88–89, 92–93, 250; in Tourgée's *A Royal Gentleman*, 78, 89, 93; and Republican Party, 86, 92–93. *See also* Race relations

Cuba, 185

Culture: commodification of, 3; testimonial culture, 44; Woolson's cross-cultural strategies, 67, 250; Chesapeake culture in Thanet's *Expiation*, 244–45. *See also* Consumer culture; Print culture

Curtis, Silas, 132, 145, 150

Dabney, R. L., 224
Daily Evening Journal, 131
Davies, Carole Boyce, 267
Davis, Jefferson, 232
Davis, Thadious, 77, 267
Davis, William Watson, 32
Declaration of Independence, 20
Defamation law: and reputation as property, 22, 104, 111; and whiteness as object of property, 85, 111
Delaney, Lucy, 13, 286
Delta Sigma Theta Sorority, 168
DeMeritte, Laura A., 165
Democratic Party: and conservative backlash, 16; in Florida, 32, 41, 73, 75, 296; and Bourbons, 41, 161, 181, 296; in North Carolina, 81, 92–93, 96, 103, 120, 296, 314 (n. 41); and white supremacy, 92–93, 126, 296; and miscegenation, 96, 314 (n. 41); and southern whites, 103; and Tourgée's "C" letters, 114; in West Virginia, 126, 128, 130, 149, 156; in New Orleans, 183; and distinctions in types of equality, 221; in Arkansas, 241, 242–43, 257, 298–99; and agrarian movement, 242–43; political control of, 281; and Grady, 284, 300

Dennett, Daniel, 326 (n. 6)
Dent, Marmaduke, 153
Dewey Classification System, 112
Dial, 237, 277
Dialect: and regionalism, 18; Tourgée's use of, 88; Cable's use of, 214, 215, 223, 224, 226, 227, 256, 257, 270; Thanet's use of, 256–58, 269, 270, 280; of yeoman class, 256, 270
Dickens, Charles, 214, 263
Diffley, Kathleen, 17
Dillard University, 135, 321 (n. 36)
Disability: represented in Woolson's "The French Broad," 39; in Woolson's "The Ancient City," 69, 70; in Tourgée's *Toinette*, 98, 99; in Cable's *The Grandissimes*, 208; in Woolson's short stories, 48–49, 59
Discipline, institutionalized forms of, 23
Disfranchisement: of African Americans, 20, 28, 41, 75, 170, 229, 243, 286, 288, 290, 295, 296, 297, 298, 310 (n. 94); of ex-Confederates, 86, 126, 127–28, 148, 289; and *Pioneer Press*, 152, 155, 170
Disguise: Reconstruction heroines' use of, 14; in Cable's *The Grandissimes*, 179, 187, 209; in Thanet's *Expiation*, 232, 270, 271, 272, 274, 277, 280, 293
"Dixie" (song), 31
Domestic obligations: and gendered rights of citizenship, 7; and gender relations, 13, 244; and freedwomen, 23; and gendered concepts of labor, 23; and Tourgée's *Toinette*, 99, 245; and Franklin, 173, 286, 289; in Cable's *The Grandissimes*, 206, 207,

217; in Cable's *Dr. Sevier*, 217; Cooper on, 286–87
Dominguez, Virginia R., 327 (n. 8)
Dougan, Carol, 333 (n. 7), 334 (n. 18)
Dougan, Michael, 333 (n. 7), 334 (n. 18)
Douglas, J. Allen, 111
Douglass, Frederick, 91, 129, 159, 167, 172
Dred Scott decision (1857), 242
Drew, George, 74
Du Bois, W. E. B.: *Black Reconstruction in America*, 1, 295; as model of racial progress, 14; Talented Tenth, 102, 201; and "Gospel of Pay," 116; and Niagara Movement, 154, 175, 288, 323 (n. 65); program of political activism, 158; and education, 170, 288; *Dusk of Dawn*, 172; John Clifford's friendship with, 175; on labor question, 237–38; *The Souls of Black Folk*, 265; Thanet compared to, 279; ideals of educational elite, 287–88
Dudley, Anne S., 128, 133–34, 138, 147, 160
Duet, Tiffany, 330 (n. 61)
Duncan, James S., 308 (n. 39)
Duty: and Reconstruction literature, 20, 21, 22, 23, 292, 299; as alternative form of property, 21; freedpeople's concept of, 22–23; and labor, 23, 122; and citizenship, 83–84, 294, 301; in Tourgée's *Toinette*, 93, 99, 106, 292; and Storer College students, 124, 125, 134, 152, 169, 170, 173, 176, 270, 292, 295; and Franklin's belief in, 142, 170, 173; and John Clifford's civil rights activism, 155; in Cable's *The Grandissimes*, 180, 191, 197, 198, 228; in Thanet's *Expiation*, 232, 269, 270, 271–72, 280, 292; Cable on, 292; and Reconstruction writers, 292; Woolson on, 292; and Grady, 295, 299; and paternalism, 295

Eacker, Susan, 30
East Gulf Blockading Squadron, 32
Eckel, Letta, 90
Economic self-sufficiency, 14
Education: of freedpeople, 29, 58–60, 69, 75, 79, 85, 87, 108, 109, 129, 130, 131, 132, 133, 135, 136, 145, 146–48, 149, 151, 157–58, 259, 276, 319 (n. 14); in Tourgée's *Toinette*, 87, 106, 108, 133, 173; establishment of public education, 96; Du Bois on, 170, 288; in New Orleans, 186; Reconstruction's legacy of, 287. *See also* Storer College
Eggleston, Joseph, 236
Elfenbein, Anna Shannon, 330 (n. 61)
Elite African Americans, 170, 172, 287–88
Emancipation: and Confederates' loss of property, 21; in Woolson's Florida travel sketches, 41–44; of Minorcans, 52; in Woolson's "Felipa," 58; and vagrancy laws, 60–61; in Tourgée's *Toinette*, 76, 83, 92; and plantation household, 89; as question of race, 98; Tourgée on, 101; gradual emancipation, 126; in West Virginia, 126; egalitarian tradition of, 159; in Arkansas, 241; in Thanet's *Expiation*, 255–56, 263; celebrations of, 279; and person as property, 290; and wage labor, 301; and Republican Party's subordination of sexual to racial emancipation, 315 (n. 57)
Emancipation Proclamation, 6, 92
Emerson College, 167
Empowerment: and labor, 23, 78–79, 291; sharecropping as self-empowerment strategy, 67; and consumer culture, 75; in Tourgée's *Toinette*, 78–79, 121, 122; in Tourgée's *A Royal Gentleman*, 121, 122; and Storer College, 125; John Clifford's strategy for, 152, 158, 159–60, 208, 288; and Cable's *The Grandissimes*,

179, 181, 192; in Thanet's *Expiation*, 231, 232, 279; of southern white women, 232; and Du Bois, 288; and meaning of property, 289; Franklin's empowerment of women, 297

Enforcement Acts of 1870-72, 183

Equity: and nonphysical forms of property, 85, 291; and Cable's "The Freedman's Case in Equity," 221-22, 224, 297

Erhart, Grace, 35

Ethnic boundaries: in Cable's *The Grandissimes*, 178, 191, 195, 197, 203; and Creole identity, 184, 186, 326-27 (n. 8)

Ethnicity: and Cable's dramatization of Creole characters, 22, 214, 216, 223; Woolson's focus on, 25, 52, 53; and American literature, 24; and Cable's stage appearances with Twain, 210, 213; and hybridity of Cable's Creole performances, 217-18, 219

Evans, George, 156

Ex-Confederates, 22-23, 183. *See also* Confederate veterans; Southern white men

Exoticism: Woolson's use of, 15, 24, 30, 31, 38, 47, 49, 53-54, 67, 273; Cable's use of, 212, 213, 219

Expiation (Thanet): consumer culture in, 4, 230, 231, 263, 264, 265-66; cross-race alliances in, 4, 232, 256; gender roles in, 230, 231, 232, 244, 245, 246, 247, 248-50, 253-54, 256, 257, 258, 265-66, 280; landscape in, 230, 231, 236, 246; swamp landscapes in, 230, 231, 240, 245, 246, 247-48, 249, 250, 252, 263; property in, 230, 232, 243, 262, 263-66, 269, 279, 280; violence in, 230, 233, 243, 244, 245, 247, 248, 249, 269-70, 274-76, 277, 278, 279; library in, 231, 245-46, 249, 250, 251-52, 263-64; masculinity in, 232, 247, 248, 256, 272, 277, 278, 279; duty in, 232, 269, 270, 271-72, 280, 292; disguise in, 232, 270, 271, 272, 274, 277, 280, 293; and code of chivalry, 233, 246, 247, 252, 278, 279, 293; and Thanet's revision of plantation fiction, 236; reviews of, 237, 277, 278; Chesapeake culture in, 244-45; servants in, 251, 253-56, 257, 258, 260, 280; cross-class alliances in, 251, 256; and rumor, 255, 256; dialect in, 256-58, 269, 270, 280; and Reconstruction vision, 258, 278-79, 280; publishing of, 284, 298; sales of, 340 (n. 108)

Ex-slaves: Woolson on citizenship claims of, 2, 27, 41-42, 58, 67-68, 74; alternative political identities of, 17; aspirations of, 21; and Freedmen's Bureau's agents, 33; in Woolson's "The Ancient City," 41, 65, 73; and property ownership, 51, 289; reaction to emancipation, 60-61; in Cable's *The Grandissimes*, 200; in Thanet's *Expiation*, 231. *See also* Freedpeople

Fahs, Alice, 17
Fairmont Convention, 160
Farmer-Kailser, Mary, 16, 108
Femme covert, 94-95
Fetterley, Judith, 19
Field, Stephen J., 23, 100-101
Fifteenth Amendment, 12, 81, 92, 103, 130, 183, 326 (n. 4)
Fifth Amendment, 84
Finkelman, Paul, 153
Fisk University, 135, 321 (n. 36)
Flagler, Henry M., 307 (n. 25)
Florida: Woolson's travel sketches of, 2, 25-31, 33-46, 47, 48, 50, 51, 52, 53, 59-60, 67, 73, 75; Woolson's relocating national origin myths to, 2, 26, 36, 38; in Military District Three, 7, 26, 29; tourist literature of, 25, 29-31; work ethic suitable to climate and landscape, 27, 61, 62;

and convalescents, 28; Woolson on property ownership of freedpeople in, 28; Reconstruction in, 29, 31, 73–74, 75; freedpeople's status in, 31–33; as lawless frontier, 32; Freedmen's Bureau in, 32–33, 51, 71, 73; ideology of slavery in, 35; reputation for leisure, 35, 63, 135; northerners in, 35–36; Woolson on cultural identities in, 36–38, 41, 49, 51–60, 67, 74, 75; Black Belt counties of, 41, 74, 307 (n. 28); Woolson on disillusionment of residents, 46–47; Woolson's short stories of, 46–52; Constitution of 1868, 60; smuggling between Florida and Cuba, 72; and freedpeople's education, 135; population statistics on, 306 (n. 11). *See also* St. Augustine, Florida

Ford, John B., 112–13

Forten, Charlotte, 12

Foster, Frances Smith, 18

Foster, Sarah Jane, 125, 145–48, 149, 150, 151, 152, 159, 176

Fourteenth Amendment: ratification of, 10; and *Slaughterhouse Cases*, 20, 182, 305 (n. 20); due process clause of, 85, 105; equal protection clause of, 100, 148, 153; enforcement of, 183, 288

Fowle, Daniel G., 91–92

Fox-Genovese, Elizabeth, 320 (n. 25)

Frankel, Noralee, 16, 167

Franklin, Coralie: and reputation, 3, 171, 174, 176, 289, 293, 297; literary activism of, 11, 12, 125, 172–73, 297; Reconstruction vision of, 23, 125; and racial uplift, 125, 142, 143, 167, 168–69, 170, 171, 172, 173, 201, 292; and gendered rhetoric, 125, 167, 168, 169–70, 176, 289, 292; on discourse of appearance, 143–44; Storer College faculty appointment of, 151–52; and *Pioneer Press*, 160, 167, 168, 169–70, 172, 173, 174; "Woman's Column," 160, 167, 168, 285, 286; education of, 167, 257; and reform organizations, 168, 170, 171–72, 174; "Cleanliness is Next to Godliness," 169; "The Girl Graduate," 170; "Here and There in Woman's World," 170; "Moral Education," 170; "The True End of Female Education," 170; on reading, 173–74; and print culture, 287; on duty, 292; "Votes for Mothers" appeal, 297

Free African Americans: in West Virginia, 127; in Arkansas, 242. *See also* Free people of color

Freedmen's Bureau: and military districts, 10; and refugees, 10, 100, 127; commitment of agents, 15, 33; and battles of Reconstruction, 17; and freedwomen's reputations, 22; in Florida, 32–33, 51, 71, 73; and labor disputes, 33, 306 (n. 14); and freedpeople's conceptions of freedom, 43, 204; and freedpeople's property ownership, 51, 84, 262; and freedpeople's education, 59–60, 131, 145, 146, 259; and labor contracts, 60, 61; in North Carolina, 81, 87, 90, 311 (n. 12); and freedpeople's civil rights, 87, 241, 268; and race relations, 90, 129; and freedwomen's marital status, 94; freedwomen's child support requests, 94, 108, 313 (n. 38); freedwomen's complaints against men for physical assault, 94, 313 (n. 38); and freedwomen's literacy, 109; in West Virginia, 124, 127, 128–29, 131; and Storer College, 141; in New Orleans, 186; and reconciliation between master and slave, 199; in Arkansas, 241, 254, 255, 259–60, 262, 268, 273, 276; freedwomen's pursuit of redress, 255

Freedmen's Bureau agents: importance of, 10; commitment of, 15, 33; treatment of freedwomen, 22;

in Florida, 33, 43, 51, 59, 61; in North Carolina, 87, 94, 95, 100, 108; in West Virginia, 128–29, 130, 146; in Arkansas, 241, 254, 255, 259, 268, 276, 334 (n. 20)

Freedom: and citizenship, 1, 2, 77; and freedwomen's activist role, 16–17; meaning of, 25, 27, 41–43, 46, 63, 135, 291; Woolson on freedpeople's sense of, 27, 41–43, 46, 65; and gender roles, 30; in Florida, 37, 52; and Freedmen's Bureau, 43, 204; freedpeople's conceptions of, 43, 266, 291, 307–8 (n. 32); in Woolson's "The Ancient City," 43–44; Woolson on freedpeople's transition to, 52, 58, 59, 73; of Minorcans, 52–53, 54, 64, 101; in Woolson's "Felipa," 58; in Tourgée's *Toinette*, 76, 82, 87, 89, 98–101, 107, 108–9, 110, 118, 122; in Tourgée's *A Royal Gentleman*, 88, 89, 118; and Storer College, 135, 137, 157, 176; and John Clifford's civil rights activism, 156, 159, 164; in Louisiana, 185, 186; in Cable's *The Grandissimes*, 200, 204, 206, 208–9; Howard on, 204, 330 (n. 55); in Arkansas, 231, 241; in Thanet's *Expiation*, 231, 245, 258, 266, 274, 276; Tourgée on, 288; and labor, 290

Freedpeople: constitutional guarantees of citizenship for, 1; aspirations of, 1, 2; literary activism on behalf of, 4; civil rights in New South, 5; as political agents, 16, 21, 24; and property ownership, 21, 22, 28, 50–51, 80, 82, 84–85, 92–93, 138–39, 203, 262, 263, 290, 291, 305 (n. 22); as labor force, 25; Woolson's travel sketches focusing on, 26–27, 28, 37, 38, 39–43, 50–51, 52, 53, 57, 59–60, 67, 69–70, 74; Woolson's portrayal of stereotypes of, 27, 41, 64, 68; Woolson's magazine articles damaging hopes of, 28; education of, 28, 29, 58–60, 69, 75, 79, 85, 87, 108, 109, 129, 130, 131, 132, 133, 135, 136, 145, 146–48, 149, 151, 157–58, 259, 276, 319 (n. 14); as consumers, 28, 72–73, 75, 263, 264–67, 268; reformers' mission work with, 29; in tourist literature, 29; status in Florida, 31–33; civil rights in Florida, 33; Woolson's poetry on, 58–59, 70–71; household production of, 66; and professional status, 68–69, 71, 72, 74; changing citizenship status of, 79; entitlement to citizenship, 80–82, 220, 221; and race relations, 90; and cross-race alliances, 93; Reconstruction vision of, 125; Cable on representation of, 178, 179; Cable's empowerment of, 181; in Cable's *The Grandissimes*, 189, 190, 196, 202, 203–4; Cable's dramatization of, 214, 215, 220; in Thanet's *Expiation*, 230, 242, 263, 275; civil rights in Arkansas, 241, 243; exploitation of, 265; Grady on, 290. *See also* Ex-slaves; Freedwomen

Freedwomen: in Tourgée's *Toinette*, 3, 77, 78–79, 83, 86, 87, 105, 120; resistance of, 13, 108; role in reorganizing communities, 16–17; exercise of rights, 20, 21, 22; and alternative forms of property, 21; sexual violence against, 22, 105; empowerment as workers, 23; Woolson's view as political agents, 25, 41–42, 74; in Woolson's travel sketches, 40–44, 54, 60; Woolson on labor of, 43, 61, 64, 65–66, 73, 74, 75; "female loaferism," 65; in Woolson's short stories, 65; Tourgée's *A Royal Gentleman* on land-ownership for, 86, 105; marriage as civil rights, 94; Tourgée's defense of labor rights of, 101–2; and reputation as property, 104, 105; education of, 105; womanhood claims of, 105; and parental rights, 108; and Storer

College, 137–38; in Cable's *The Grandissimes*, 179, 180, 207; Thanet's ambivalence regarding, 231, 232, 236, 240, 252, 257, 268, 280; in Thanet's *Expiation*, 231, 232, 252–60, 279; adornment, use of by freedwomen, 266, 268, 339 (n. 87); and property ownership, 266, 279; portrayals of, 285

Free labor: in Arkansas, 273; meaning of, 23, 60, 290; ideology of, 25, 33, 63, 64, 65, 67, 74, 89, 101, 204, 206, 231, 233, 234, 258; freedpeople's transition to, 27, 64; and Woolson's travel sketches, 33, 63, 74, 75; and gender roles, 66; in North Carolina, 81; and Storer College, 135; in Thanet's *Expiation*, 231, 233, 258; transition to, 237

"Free-labor ideology": and Woolson's contribution to, 25, 33, 75; and Freedmen's Bureau, 33; as part of postwar debates, 65; in Tourgée's *Toinette*, 89; in Cable's *The Grandissimes*, 204, 206; and Thanet's use of, 231, 233, 234, 258

Free love movement, 3, 79, 110

Free people of color: in Cable's *The Grandissimes*, 179–80, 190, 191, 198, 199, 200–202, 203, 204, 206, 207–8, 209; in New Orleans, 180, 184–86, 327 (n. 11), 329 (n. 51)

Free Will Baptists, and Storer College, 125, 129, 132–34, 135, 139, 145, 155, 156, 175, 176

Frelinghuysen College, 287

French, Alice. *See* Thanet, Octave

Froebel, Friedrich, 169–70

Frost, A. B., 270

Gage, Francis Dana, 110

Gaines, Kevin, 159

Galaxy, 30, 45, 182

Gallaher, H. N., 126, 127

Gardner, Eric, 12

Garfield, James A., 109

Garland, Hamlin, 214, 237

Gayarré, Charles, 224

Gaze: Woolson's use of, 25, 41, 42, 46, 67; bourgeois romantic gaze, 34; Thanet's use of, 246

Gender: and conceptions of citizenship, 7, 13, 20, 160; and regionalism, 19, 149; and reputation, 22, 105, 145–46; and labor, 23; in Woolson's Reconstruction vision, 25; and national identity, 26; and work ethic, 27; and tourist literature, 34, 35, 36, 307 (n. 15); in Woolson's feminized Florida landscape, 38–39; and legacy of slavery, 41, 78; stereotypes of, 53–55, 57, 160–61, 173; boundaries of, 57, 95, 178, 180; alliances of, 86, 92, 203, 208, 256

Gender differences: in Woolson's "Sister St. Luke," 66–67; and reputation, 105; in Cable's *The Grandissimes*, 178, 179

Gendered characterization: in Woolson's "The Ancient City," 34; in Cable's stage appearances with Twain, 210, 211, 213; and Cable's representations of Creole characters, 214

Gendered rhetoric: of Franklin, 125, 167, 168, 169–70, 176, 289, 292; of John Clifford, 159–61, 288, 292, 294

Gender oppression: in Tourgée's *Toinette*, 78; Cooper on, 286–87

Gender relations: and women writers, 12; in Reconstruction literature, 13; race relations interconnected with, 13, 14, 86–87, 90, 125; in Tourgée's *Toinette*, 86, 87, 89–90, 99, 100, 120; in Tourgée's *A Royal Gentleman*, 86, 120; in Thanet's works, 90; and Storer College, 124; in Cable's *The Grandissimes*, 189, 191, 193, 195, 199, 207, 210

Gender roles: in Woolson's "Felipa," 57, 58; in Woolson's "Dolores," 65–66; in Tourgée's *Toinette*, 86, 88, 90, 133,

248; and Storer College faculty, 134, 142–43; and Storer College students, 142–43, 255; and Sarah Jane Foster, 147, 149; and Cable's representations of Creole characters, 216–17; in Thanet's *Expiation*, 230, 231, 232, 244, 245, 246, 247, 248–50, 253–54, 256, 257, 258, 265–66, 280; and Niagara Movement, 288; and duty, 292

Georgia, 7, 26, 291

Giggie, John M., 156

Gilded Age: and regionalist writing, 18; economic conditions of, 63; rhetoric as tactic in, 288–94; definition of property in, 290; Arkansas in, 298

Gilder, Richard Watson, 182, 226, 257, 333 (n. 105)

Giles, Paul, 19

Gilman, Daniel Coit, 214

Glymph, Thavolia, 89, 266

Goldman, Robert M., 326 (n. 4)

Gordon, Michelle, 219

Gordon, W. H., 142

Gracia Real de Santa Teresa de Mose, 37

Grady, Henry W.: on New South, 5, 6, 23, 24, 231, 237, 266, 281, 282–84, 292, 294, 295, 298, 299; "The Race Problem of the South," 5, 281–82, 294, 299–300; and Lost Cause, 5, 294; response to Cable's "The Freedman's Case in Equity," 222; "The New South" series, 282; on property ownership, 290, 295; manipulation of reputation, 293–94; on sectional reconciliation, 294–95, 299–300; and Reconstructionist ideals, 299; Simms compared to, 300

Grand Army of the Republic, 277

Grandison, Kendrick, 140

Grandissimes, The (Cable): and Creole identity, 4, 179, 180, 187, 189, 190–91, 193, 194–95, 203, 205–6; and representation, 178; political vision of, 178, 181, 199, 201–2; and disguise, 179, 187, 209; free people of color in, 179–80, 190, 191, 198, 199, 200–202, 203, 204, 206, 207–8, 209; doubling characterizations in, 180, 181, 184, 191; Reconstruction vision of, 180, 191, 193, 194, 195, 196, 198, 199, 205, 212, 228–29, 230; duty in, 180, 191, 197, 198, 228; indeterminate narrator in, 180, 205, 206, 228; and sectional reconciliation, 180, 191, 197, 199, 206, 295; publishing of, 182, 225–26; and immigrants, 185, 202; and swamp landscape, 188, 189, 201, 204, 207, 247, 257; voodoo in, 189–90, 192, 201, 203, 208–9; male characters of, 191–94; African American women in, 192, 206–10, 229, 330 (n. 61); and New South, 193, 199, 205, 206, 228; and Cable's stage appearances with Twain, 211; Creole dialect in, 214, 223; and Cable's dramatization of Creole characters, 215–17, 220; French and African songs in, 217–18; Creole songs in, 218; and marketplace demands, 225–26

Grant, Ulysses S., 73, 183, 196, 216

Graybacks: featured in Thanet's *Expiation*: 248–49, 252, 254–56, 263, 275, 276

Greensboro, North Carolina: Tourgée writing *Toinette* in, 76, 78; Tourgée's choice of living in, 80; Ku Klux Klan in, 81

Greensboro North State, 91, 103, 285

Greensboro Patriot, 82, 91, 97, 113

Greeson, Jennifer, 19

Grimké, Archibald, 167

Grimke, Sarah, 314 (n. 48)

Hahn, Steven, 16, 255

Haines, George, 126, 127

Hale, Grace Elizabeth, 264, 269, 310 (n. 94)

Hall, Gwendolyn Midlo, 184

Hall, Lyman, 290

Halsey, Elias, 311 (n. 12)
Hampton Institute, 321 (n. 36)
Hancock, Ripley, 234
Hanger, Kim, 185
Hardy, Iza, 62, 72
Harper, Frances Ellen Watkins, 12, 159, 285
Harper's Bazaar, 266
Harpers Ferry, West Virginia: and Franklin, 3, 11; industrialism in, 15, 134, 157; U.S. Armory and Arsenal in, 124, 127, 128; and Storer College's relation to white residents, 124, 132, 133, 139–41, 143, 145, 174–76, 321 (n. 36); Haines's defense of, 126; postwar condition of, 128–29, 176; black neighborhoods of, 139; economic decline in, 297
Harpers Ferry National Historical Park, 297
Harpers Ferry Singers, 133, 134
Harper's Magazine, 182
Harper's Monthly, 11
Harper's New Monthly Magazine, 30, 31, 38, 235
Harris, Blanche V., 87
Harris, Joel Chandler, 211, 236
Harrison, James A., 328 (n. 14)
Harte, Bret, 236
Hartford Daily Courant, 216
Hartford Sumner League, 282
Hartgrove, Louisa, 137–38, 165, 255
Hartman, S., 315–16 (n. 67)
Hatter, Annie Avilla May, 326 (n. 112)
Hatter, Hamilton, 136
Hawthorne, Nathaniel, 181, 214
Hayes, Rutherford, 183
Henderson, William, 91
Higginbotham, Evelyn Brooks, 144, 168
Higginson, Thomas Wentworth, 236
Hine, Darlene Clark, 172–73
Historical romance, 286, 295
Hobbes, Thomas, 20
Hoke, Joseph, 146
Holbrook, A. M., 326 (n. 6)

Holden, William H., 81, 101, 311 (n. 10)
Holt, Sharon Ann, 66
Holton, Tabitha, 101, 103
Home Missionary Society, 145
Homestead Act (1862), 305 (n. 22)
Honor: and reputation, 22, 79, 111, 113, 115, 121, 145, 176, 198, 199, 232, 243, 292, 293; and meanings of masculinity, 90; in Tourgée's *Toinette*, 92, 107, 113, 115; discourse of honorable womanhood, 101–2, 105; in Cable's *The Grandissimes*, 192, 196; in Thanet's *Expiation*, 233, 243, 244, 245, 246, 247, 252, 256, 270, 275, 278, 279, 293; violence as means of restoring, 276
Hopkins, Pauline, 13, 172, 229, 255, 286
Hot Springs, Arkansas, 265–68
Houghton Mifflin, 235
Howard, O. O., 10, 189, 204, 330 (n. 55)
Howard University, 148, 167, 168, 169
Howells, William Dean, 31, 112, 214, 277
Humor: used in Cable-Twain performances, 4, 211–13, 215, 216; in Woolson's "The Oklawaha," 34; in Woolson's "Ancient City," 50; used by Storer students, 137; and African American spectatorship, 221; and Thanet, 250; in Thanet's *Expiation*, 255, 256, 258, 272; and Grady, 283
Hunter, Tera, 254

Identity: performative nature of, 57–58, 178, 179, 210–13, 214, 215–16, 232, 269, 272, 273, 274; in Woolson's "Felipa," 57–58, 274; reconstructed identities, 301. *See also* Creole identity; National identity; Racial identity
Immigrant Aid Society, 273
Immigrants and immigration: Woolson on citizenship claims of, 2, 7; and military districts, 19; in Woolson's Florida travel sketches, 37, 52–60; Tourgée on reputation of, 104; in West Virginia, 127; and *Pioneer Press*,

156; Creole identity distinguished from French immigrants, 184, 326–27 (n. 8); in Cable's *The Grandissimes*, 185, 202; Thanet's view of, 234–35

Imperialism: in Woolson's Florida travel sketches, 34, 46, 75; and literary marketplace, 227; in Thanet's *Expiation*, 233, 278; and American expansionism, 294; and Ceylonese coffee plantations, 308 (n. 39)

Independent Party: in Florida, 41, 296; in West Virginia, 223

Individualism: possessive individualism, 63, 67; and Storer College, 124, 132, 133, 134, 176; and Arkansas, 240

Industrial education: in West Virginia, 132; at Storer College, 137; as topic in *Pioneer Press*, 157, 160–61; in Clifford's vision, 166; Franklin's views of, 170

Inheritance laws, 3

Integration, and miscegenation, 95, 97

Intermarriage: Woolson's catering to fears of, 28, 56; in Woolson's short stories, 56, 64–65; in Tourgée's *Toinette*, 78, 94, 95, 97–99, 206, 207, 286, 292–93; in Tourgée's *A Royal Gentleman*, 119, 293; in Cable's *The Grandissimes*, 195–96. *See also* Marriage; Miscegenation

International Copyright Act (1891), 15–16, 287

International Council of Women, 172

Iowa: Thanet's residence in, 4, 233–34, 235, 236, 240, 249; labor struggles in, 231; and migration to Arkansas, 237, 334 (n. 13); settlement of immigrants in, 273

Irving, Washington, 46

Jackson, George S., 17
Jacobs, Harriet, 208
James, Henry, 18, 112
Jefferson, Thomas, 84, 125
Jim Crow segregation: and Storer College faculty, 3, 139–40; in Thanet's *Expiation*, 4; realities of, 7; freedwomen as agents of resistance to, 13; and testimonial culture, 44; and *Plessy v. Ferguson*, 77, 115, 121, 153, 202, 233, 296–97; separate-but-equal doctrine, 77, 121, 153; Washington on, 97; and miscegenation statutes, 100; and badge of servitude, 115; and labor, 137, 320 (n. 30); John Clifford's legal battles against, 153; Cable's public protests against, 182; in New Orleans, 185, 186; black performers' challenging, 215; in Arkansas, 243, 298; and defeat of Lodge Federal Elections Bill, 281; effects of, 284, 290, 295; African American women writers on, 286; in West Virginia, 297; Cable's dissent with *New Orleans Picayune*, 326 (n. 6)

Johns Hopkins University, 190, 214, 216, 333 (n. 105)

Johnson, Andrew, 7, 85, 183, 204, 295
Johnson, Joseph E., 76
Johnson, Robert Underwood, 182, 194, 226
Johnson, Walter, 186
Joint Committee on Reconstruction (1865), 32, 61
Jones, Gavin, 217–18
Jones, George T., 156, 157
Jones, James H., 155
Jones, Martha, 168
Joseph, Philip, 19
Judge magazine, 299
Jung, Moon-Ho, 237
Jury service, African Americans' exclusion from, 148, 162–63
Juvenile Protection Association, 168

Kansas, 273
Kaplan, Amy, 18
Keckley, Elizabeth, 12
Kein, Sybil, 327 (n. 8)
Kellogg, William Pitt, 183
King, Edward, 182

King, Grace, 228
Kinship claims, 21
Knights of Labor, 158, 234, 242, 296
Knights of the White Camellia, 183, 326 (n. 6)
Knights of the Wise Men, 154
Know-Nothing Party, 185
Ku Klux Klan: in Florida, 32, 41, 74, 307 (n. 28); in North Carolina, 81; in West Virginia, 149-50; in Arkansas, 246, 262, 275

Labor: Woolson's reconstructing meaning of, 2, 61, 62, 63-64, 66, 67-70, 135, 204, 291; and Reconstruction literature, 15, 20, 21, 299; as alternative form of property, 21; freedpeople's concept of, 22-23, 61, 65; as gendered concept, 23; "labor question," 23, 61, 67, 233, 234, 237-38, 258; and leisure, 27, 63, 65, 66, 69, 74, 133, 135, 137, 173, 204, 291; Woolson's focus of freedwomen's labor, 43, 61, 64, 65-66, 73, 74, 75; southern whites' fears of labor shortage, 51; compulsory labor, 60, 63, 64, 291; meanings of, 60-61, 291; workers' rights to "fruits of their labor," 62, 78-79, 85, 100-101, 315 (n. 52); and indentures, 64, 88; "female loaferism," 65; and work practices transformed into professional status, 67-69, 71, 72, 74; and self-regulation, 68-69, 74; in Tourgée's *Toinette*, 78-79, 102; person's right to labor, 85, 290; and Thirteenth Amendment, 101, 305 (n. 20); and Storer College students, 124, 125, 133, 152; and Democratic Party, 126; and free African Americans, 127; and Storer College curriculum, 134-35; in Cable's *The Grandissimes*, 180, 191, 201, 203-4, 205, 228; and *Slaughterhouse Cases*, 182; and white midwestern workforce, 205; in Thanet's *Expiation*, 231, 233, 269, 280; midwestern attitudes toward, 232, 258, 275; Thanet's theories of, 234, 235, 237, 240, 242-43, 259, 263, 277, 278, 284, 291, 295, 298; and market economy, 238; political coalition of industrial and farm workers, 242-43; and boycotts, 264; and citizenship, 301. *See also* Free labor; Unions; Wage labor
Ladies Repository, 317 (n. 84)
Lagby, Jedu. *See* Tourgée, Albion
Land acquisition: in Woolson's "The Ancient City," 50-51; and property ownership of freedpeople, 50-51, 84-85, 86, 88, 138-39, 204, 262, 268, 289, 290; in Tourgée's *Toinette*, 85, 86, 88-89, 121; in Tourgée's *A Royal Gentleman*, 85, 86, 121; and Storer College students, 125, 138-39; and *Pioneer Press*, 156-57, 158; in Cable's *The Grandissimes*, 180, 191, 192, 195-96; and restoration of plantations to white landowners, 289; and labor, 292; Mitchell's view of land ownership, 341-42 (n. 14)
Land of Opportunity. *See* Arkansas
Land redistribution policy, 85, 89, 103
Landscape: Woolson on Floridian landscape, 26, 27, 31, 34, 36, 37, 38-39, 45-46, 47, 48, 49, 55, 57, 62, 63, 188, 204, 246, 296; in Thanet's *Expiation*, 230, 231, 236, 246. *See also* Swamp landscapes
Land values, 84, 262, 338 (n. 71)
Lathrop, George Parsons, 190
La Tribune, 203
Laveau, Marie, 208
Lawrence, D. H., 247
Lee, Arthur, 222, 223
Lee, Jarena, 253
Lee, Robert E., 131
Lee Memorial Association, 126
Legal history: interconnections with literary history, 17; of property rights, 20; and Tourgée's writings, 77; antebellum legal precedence, 136

392   INDEX

Legal system: and paradigm of unfree labor, 60; and professionalism of work, 68; and Tourgée's *Toinette*, 77, 78; and property as legal relations among persons, 85

Leisure: and labor, 27, 63, 65, 66, 69, 74, 133, 135, 137, 173, 204, 291; Florida's reputation for, 35, 63, 135; and acts of reading, 173; racialized southern white leisure, 204; in Cable's *The Grandissimes*, 206

Lewiston Daily Evening Journal, 131

Lhamon, W. T., 215, 220

Liberia, 243

Liberty of contract doctrine, 291

Libraries: public, 79, 112, 122; in Tourgée's *Toinette*, 82, 105, 106, 107, 245; in Tourgée's *A Royal Gentleman*, 88, 105; and Franklin, 173; in Cable's *The Grandissimes*, 194; and gender relations, 231; in Thanet's *Expiation*, 231, 245–46, 249, 250, 251–52, 263–64; and education, 287

Libres: *See* Free people of color

Lightner, Lue Brackett, 132, 134, 138, 142–43, 163, 165, 175

Lily-white movement, 156

Lincoln, Abraham, 6, 92, 183, 206

Lippincott's, 31, 234, 235

Literacy: and establishment of black colleges, 12; and Woolson's "Dolores," 59; in Tourgée's *Toinette*, 79, 105–6; and citizenship, 106, 172, 176; of freedwomen, 108–9; postwar interest in, 122; and Tourgée, 122; and students of Storer College, 123; and Franklin, 172–74; in Thanet's *Expiation*, 245; Reconstruction's legacy of, 287. *See also* Reading, acts of

Literary canon, traditional periodization of, 5, 17–18

Literary marketplace: pressures of, 2, 7, 15–16, 225–26, 227, 239, 285; and Reconstruction writers, 15–16, 22; and editorial intervention, 15–16, 225–27, 228; and reputation, 22; Woolson's responsiveness to changes in, 27, 45, 74; and literacy, 122; Thanet's response to, 239–40; and magazine industry, 287, 289. *See also* Publishing industry

Little Rock Colored Citizens Convention (1865), 242

Lively, Robert, 18

Local color, 4, 18, 179, 212, 213, 227, 233

Locke, John, 20, 84, 104

Lodge, Henry Cabot, 281

Lodge Federal Elections Bill (1890), 5, 11, 281

Lost Cause: in Thanet's *Expiation*, 4, 232, 243, 278; in Simms's *War Poetry of the South*, 5; and Grady, 5, 294; as alternative form of property, 21; and monuments, 39; Haines's support for, 126; and plantation fiction, 236, 294; in Cable's performances, 247; and Reconstruction writers, 294–95; hierarchical structures of, 300

Lott, Eric, 213

Louisiana: in Military District Five, 7, 179, 182; violence toward African Americans in, 182–83; and Creole identity, 184; slaves suing for freedom in, 185; freedpeople's political activism in, 204; dual governments of, 216; sugar region of, 237. *See also* New Orleans, Louisiana

Louisiana Historical Society, 214

Louisiana National Guard, 298

Louisiana Purchase of 1803, 179, 180, 184, 185, 327 (n. 8)

Loyal Reconstruction League, 11, 80

Lutz, Tom, 19

Lynch, John R., 167

Lynchburg Virginian, 134

Lynching: Tourgée on, 120; in West Virginia, 126, 155–56, 297; and John Clifford's civil rights activism, 155–56; in Arkansas, 275, 277; quantification of, 340 (n. 101). *See also* Violence

Macaulay, Thomas, 264
McDonald, Henry, 132, 137, 138, 175
McKenzie, J. H., 146
Mackethan, Lucinda, 236
McKinley, William, 121
McKinney, Richard, 152
McMichael, George, 239, 334 (n. 18)
Madison, James, 84
Manhood: false pretensions of southern white manhood, 4; in Tourgée's *Toinette*, 92; Tourgée on, 92, 160; and prohibitions on interracial marriage, 95; universal manhood suffrage, 95; and John Clifford's strategy of empowerment, 152, 158, 159–60, 288; and Confederate defeat, 244; and Lost Cause cultural authority, 278; Howard on, 330 (n. 55). *See also* Masculinity
Manumission laws, 186
Maria Sanchez Creek, Florida, 38–39, 43, 55
Market economy: property bound up in, 22; and free market principles, 23; and property claims, 23; in Tourgée's *A Royal Gentleman*, 117–18; in Tourgée's *Toinette*, 117–18; in Cable's *The Grandissimes*, 196–200; in Thanet's *Expiation*, 231, 280; and citizenship, 231, 301; and labor, 238; and portable property, 264–65; and African American economic gain, 287. *See also* Capitalism
Marketplace: women's place in, 13; and wage labor, 60, 301; and panic of 1873, 64, 231, 234, 295; and professionalism, 68; and definition of property, 85; and reputation as property, 104; and real estate market, 108; and John Clifford's civil rights activism, 157–58, 166; and Cable's *The Grandissimes*, 225–26; and Cable's dramatization of characters, 226–27. *See also* Consumer culture; Literary marketplace

Marriage: and property relations, 94, 95, 99–100, 122, 196, 313 (n. 39), 314 (n. 48); and wage slavery, 100; in Cable's *The Grandissimes*, 180, 190, 192, 193, 195, 196, 197, 199, 206–7; in Thanet's *Expiation*, 250–51. *See also* Intermarriage
Martha's Vineyard Summer Institute, 167
Martin, Thomas, 153
Martinsburg, West Virginia, 127, 145–48, 151, 152, 155–56
Martinsburg Herald, 162
Martinsburg Independent, 162
Martin v. Board of Education (1896), 153, 162
Masculinity: and studies of New South, 13; in Woolson's "The Ancient City," 34; "Southron" as masculinized term, 39, 40; meanings of, 90, 92, 312 (n. 32); in Tourgée's *Toinette*, 92, 133; privileges of, 148; in Thanet's *Expiation*, 232, 247, 248, 256, 272, 277, 278, 279; Thanet's anticipation of Rough Riders' brashness, 233, 278; of Thanet's pseudonym, 239. *See also* Manhood
Masons, 154
Melville, Herman, 24
Memory: collective memory, 5, 23; and Woolson's travel sketches, 35, 36; creating social memory, 293
Men. *See* African American men; Northern white men; Southern white men
Mencken, Adah, 316 (n. 67)
Men of Mark, 162
Methodist Episcopal Church, 80
Middle class: African American middle class, 4, 87, 136, 141, 142, 170–72, 298, 310 (n. 94); white middle class, 11; and professionalization of work, 68
Midwest: and Thanet's background, 231, 232, 233, 238, 249–50, 284; attitudes toward labor in, 232, 258, 275; violent strikes in, 234; migrant work force from, 237

Miles, Nelson A., 311 (n. 12)
Military District One: and Storer College, 3, 124; Virginia in, 7
Military District Two: and Tourgée's *Toinette*, 3; North and South Carolina in, 7; and Tourgée's Reconstruction vision, 75, 76; freedpeople's citizenship in, 80–82; property ownership in, 84; and freedwomen's assertion of citizenship, 105
Military District Three: and tourism, 2; Alabama, Georgia, and Florida in, 7; Grady living in, 283
Military District Four: white labor force in, 4; Arkansas in, 7, 240–43, 250; Mississippi in, 7, 241; displaced property in, 230; violence in, 241
Military District Five: Cable on postwar development of, 4; Louisiana and Texas in, 7; and New Orleans, 177
Military districts: and Reconstruction literature, 2, 13, 15, 18, 284–85; southern attitudes toward, 4; duties of brigadier general supervising, 7; impact of, 7, 14–15; and Freedmen's Bureau, 10; officers of, 10; backlash to occupation, 10–11; and evolving experience of occupation, 18–19, 284–85; and regionalism, 19; and unpopular federal occupation, 50; and Woolson's "Dolores," 58–59; benefits of occupation, 59; and protracted occupation, 179; polarizing effects of, 219; resistance to imposition of, 236; ending of occupation, 282, 285; and alienability of property, 290
Military Reconstruction Act (1867), 7, 10
Miller, David C., 47
Miller, Joaquin, 47
Milton, John, 31, 264
Minorcans: Woolson's description of, 27, 51, 52–60, 61, 62–67, 69, 75, 102, 187, 228, 296; Woolson's highlighting self-determination of Minorcan women, 27, 53, 55–56, 58, 60, 61, 62, 65–66, 67, 69, 75, 102; Woolson's on Minorcan women as role model for freedpeople, 27, 64, 65, 66; Woolson's portrayals of Minorcan men, 28, 66–67, 75; as servants, 64, 88; as models of assimilation, 296
Minstrelsy, 144, 213, 214–15, 218–19, 220, 221
Minturn, Arkansas, 235
Miscegenation: punitive statutes on, 3, 78, 95, 96, 148, 314 (n. 41), 328 (n. 33); and Woolson's portrayal of Minorca women, 54–55; and whiteness as object of property, 85; mule as symbol of, 91; in Tourgée's *Toinette*, 93, 96; and integration, 95, 97; press on, 96–98; in Cable's *The Grandissimes*, 207; in Thanet's *Expiation*, 256–57. *See also* Intermarriage
Misrecognition, and proof of white identity, 85
Mississippi: in Military District Four, 7, 241; terrorism in, 73
Missouri Republican, 327 (n. 14)
Mitchell, Margaret, *Gone with the Wind*, 341–42 (n. 14)
Montaigne, Michel, 245, 246, 336 (n. 28)
Morning Star, 132
Morrison, Toni, 253
Morton, Oliver P., 266
Motherhood, Republican motherhood rhetoric, 169, 289, 297
Mountain State. *See* West Virginia
Murphree, Daniel S., 307 (n. 20)

Nabers, Deak, 17
Nashville Daily American, 224
Nation, 30–31, 240, 253
National Anti-Slavery Standard, 114
National Association for the Advancement of Colored People (NAACP), 155, 168, 175
National Association of Colored Women's Clubs (NACWC), 125, 174

National District Social Hygiene Association, 168
National Home for Destitute Colored Women and Children, 168, 170
National identity: and regionalism, 19, 26, 284; and tourism, 29; and property ownership, 79, 122, 268; in Cable's *The Grandissimes*, 178, 179, 180–81
National Negro Political League, 154–55
National origin myths, Woolson's relocating to Florida, 2, 26, 36, 38
National Society of Colonial Dames, 238
National Woman Suffrage Association (NWSA), 103, 171, 172, 174, 315 (n. 57)
Native Americans: Woolson on citizenship claims of, 2; Woolson's portrayals of, 28, 34, 52, 75; in Woolson's short stories, 49–50; in Woolson's travel sketches, 50–51, 75; in Cable's *The Grandissimes*, 192
Nativism, 234–35
Nebraska, 273
Newcomer, Celeste Brackett, 139, 143
New Deal, 296
New England: and national origin myths, 2, 24, 26; and Thanet's background, 231, 232, 233, 238, 239, 250, 253, 264, 269, 275
New England Society, 282
Newman (black pastor), 166
New Negro modernity, 286
New Orleans, Louisiana: Cable's *The Grandissimes* on virtues of Creole identity, 4; and Military District Five, 177; and Cable on hybridized nature of national identity, 178; postwar realities of, 179, 183; free people of color in, 180, 184–86, 327 (n. 11), 329 (n. 51); Cable's postwar employment in, 181, 183; strategic position of, 183, 185; political factions in, 183, 185, 199, 298; federal occupation of, 183, 186, 203; riot of 1866, 183, 326 (n. 7); racial identity in, 184; contested meaning of Creole in, 184–87; Spanish legacy in, 184, 185; dual governments of, 184, 228; Anglo-Americans in, 185; German immigrants of, 185; slave market of, 186; binary racial order of, 186, 202, 203; Cotton Exchange, 189; Reconstruction in, 189; Place Congo, 218; Mardi Gras, 291; African American population of, 298; Cable's rejection in, 298
New Orleans Bulletin, 326 (n. 3)
New Orleans Daily Picayune, 183, 214, 223, 224, 326 (n. 6)
New Orleans Times-Democrat, 214, 224
New Smyrna plantation, 52
New South: Thanet's vision of, 4, 237, 263, 266, 268, 273–74, 275, 280, 298; Grady on, 5, 6, 23, 24, 231, 237, 266, 281, 282–84, 292, 294, 295, 298, 299; Woolson's vision of, 70–71, 296; Tourgée's vision of, 80, 199; and Storer College, 134; in Cable's *The Grandissimes*, 193, 199, 205, 206, 228; in Thanet's *Expiation*, 231, 258; Du Bois on, 237–38; as malleable subject, 282; scholarly studies of, 282, 341 (n. 3); origins of, 294–95
New Southern Studies, 19, 307 (n. 20); masculinist focus of, 13
New York Age, 165
New York Herald, 283
New York Ledger, 282, 293
New York Star, 225
New York Times, 317 (n. 81)
New York Tribune, 112, 225
Niagara Movement for Civil Rights, 154, 288, 318 (n. 2), 323 (n. 65)
Nicholls, Francis T., 184
Niswonger, Richard, 242
Norrell, Robert, 171
Northampton, Massachusetts, 182
North Carolina: in Military District Two, 7; in Woolson's short stories, 38; Tourgée's years in, 76; Tourgée

on reform in, 79–80; Piedmont antislavery tradition in, 80; Freedmen's Bureau in, 81, 87, 90, 311 (n. 12); Democratic Party in, 81, 92–93, 96, 103, 120, 296, 314 (n. 41); Constitutional Convention of 1868, 86, 93, 96–97, 101; frontier traditions of justice in, 90; and married women's property rights, 95; Reconstruction Constitution of 1868, 95, 96, 97; Reconstruction policy in, 103; and elections of 1876, 103–4; black labor recruited from, 273; Fusionists of, 296; slave population of, 311 (n. 10); miscegenation statutes in, 314 (n. 41)

North Carolina Progress, 82

North Carolina Statesville American, 97

Northerners: as writers, 2, 25; and regional identities, 4; reputation as alternative form of property, 22; and Woolson's travel sketches, 26, 27, 29, 30, 31, 34, 38, 41–46, 50, 51–52, 53, 55, 69–70, 73, 75; ambivalence over freedpeople as citizens, 27; and Woolson's short stories, 47–49, 56, 57, 61, 63, 66–67; and Woolson's poetry, 58, 74; as teachers in South, 123; Cable's reconstruction of, 180; Reconstruction support of, 183; in Cable's *The Grandissimes*, 197; and Cable's dramatization of Creole characters, 215; and Cable's performance of Creole songs, 218; and Lost Cause, 294

Northern white men, 84

Northern white women: careerist ambitions of, 34, 145; as faculty at Storer College, 123, 125, 130, 131, 132, 133–34, 138, 142–43, 145–52; activism of, 132–33, 149

Ocala Demands (1890), 296
Occupation. *See* Military districts
O'Donovan, Susan, 16
O'Hara, James E., 103
Ohio, Western Reserve of, 80
Oliver, E. H., 133
Ortiz, Paul, 32
Our Continent, 121

Pace v. Alabama (1883), 100
Page, Thomas Nelson, *In Ole Virginia*, 236
Panic of 1873, 64, 231, 234, 295
Paramilitary clubs, 67
Paris Treaty of 1763, 36
Passing: and proof of white identity, 85; in Tourgée's *Toinette*, 87, 96, 102, 114; and Tourgée's use of pseudonyms, 114; in Tourgée's *A Royal Gentleman*, 118
Paternalism: and Grady's "The Race Problem of the South," 5; and Storer College, 124, 134, 135, 138, 174, 175, 176, 259, 292; and protection of white women, 184–85; and Cable's stage appearances with Twain, 213; of publishing industry, 239; in Arkansas, 240; of Thanet as plantation owner, 259, 260; of labor legislation, 290; and duty, 295
Patillo, Adaline, 97
Patriotism, 294
Payne, William Morton, 237
Pearce, Charles, 33
Pegues, Albert W., 157, 160–61
Pelican State. *See* Louisiana
Pennell, Joseph, 187–88
Performance: used in Reconstruction writing, 13, 14, 17, 292, 301; and southern black women's subversive strategies, 14; and identity, 57–58, 178, 179, 210–13, 214, 215–16, 232, 269, 272, 273, 274; and Cable's *The Grandissimes*, 178, 179, 181, 209; and Cable's stage appearances with Twain, 210–14; and Cable's dramatization of Creole characters, 214–16, 219; of Cable's Creole songs, 217–18; of vigilante violence, 269, 274, 276;

reputation as, 293; of Grady as New Southerner, 295, 300. *See also* Identity

Pete's Rock, North Carolina, 38, 39

Phelps, Elizabeth Stuart, 233

Phillips, Wendell, 103

Picturesque America series, 29

Pioneer Press: John Clifford's founding of, 12, 152, 297; and genres of African American literature, 123; and mission of Storer College, 125, 155; recasting moral duty of freedpeople, 155; African American activists writing for, 156, 157-58; and racial uplift, 156-61; and petty entrepreneurship, 157-59; and African American cultural contributions, 158; and African American veterans, 159; Franklin's contributions to, 160, 167, 168, 169-70, 172, 173, 174; and reputation, 161-62; and John Clifford's accusations against Storer College, 164-66; federal government's closing of, 166

Pippen v. Wesson (1876), 95

Pitzer, U. S. G., 162-63

Plantation fiction: and republicanism, 134; misperceptions of, 205; Thanet's revision of, 232, 236; Thanet's place in, 233, 236; and regionalism, 236; and Lost Cause, 236, 294; Reconstruction writers' challenge to, 286

Plantation household: African American women's subversive strategies within, 14, 252-54; patriarchal hierarchy in, 86, 95, 99, 117, 124, 134, 176, 191-92, 196, 251-52; and gender relations, 89-90, 122; and Storer College, 134, 137, 176; in Thanet's *Expiation*, 230, 231, 252-55, 260, 275, 279; Fox-Genovese on, 320 (n. 25)

Plantations: credit system of plantation store, 4, 265, 268, 269, 272, 274, 291; and labor of freedpeople, 33; Woolson's rejection of plantation hierarchy, 47; in Woolson's short stories, 48; in Woolson's travel sketches, 48, 52; in Tourgée's *Toinette*, 78, 82-83, 260; in Tourgée's *A Royal Gentleman*, 78, 83; paternalism of, 124; in Cable's *The Grandissimes*, 204; in Thanet's *Expiation*, 232, 265; restoration to white landowners, 289, 290; monopoly on land, 305 (n. 22); and imperialism, 308 (n. 39). *See also* Slaveholders

Planters (as a class): 33, 37, 41, 58, 93, 197, 203, 232, 237, 250, 258, 259, 262, 270, 273, 274, 275, 276, 280, 293, 295, 298, 329 (n. 53). *See also* Class

Plessy, Homer: Tourgée as defense counsel for, 3, 99, 115, 120, 121, 153, 221, 293, 296-97; Tourgée's brief on behalf of, 77, 79, 101, 105, 148; violation of civil rights, 88; and racial identity, 112, 221; and New Orleans, 182; role in postwar politics, 202

Plessy v. Ferguson (1896): Tourgée as defense counsel, 3, 79, 104, 115, 120, 121, 153, 221, 293, 296-97; Tourgée's brief on behalf of Plessy, 77, 79, 101, 105, 148; and Jim Crow segregation, 77, 115, 121, 153, 202, 233, 296-97; Tourgée's "badges of servitude," 79; and white selfhood as object of property, 85; Tourgée on racial identity, 104, 105, 108, 293, 296-97; New Orleans as setting for, 182

Pond, James Burton, 211, 225

Ponder v. Rhea (1877), 338 (n. 72)

Poor whites: Tourgée on class position of, 88; in Tourgée's *Toinette*, 88-89, 93, 117; and race relations, 90, 129; in West Virginia, 129; in Cable's *The Grandissimes*, 179; in Arkansas, 242, 262; in Thanet's *Expiation*, 251, 256; and property ownership, 262; and Creole identity, 326-27 (n. 8)

Popular literature, cultural work of, 17–18
Populism, 296
Possessive individualism, 63, 67
Pratt, Mary Louise, 34
Press: and Reconstruction literature, 11–12; in North Carolina, 81–82; on gender roles, 90; on Tourgée, 90–91, 97–98, 113–15, 122, 149, 155, 314 (n. 46); on miscegenation, 96–98; and Storer College, 125, 130, 131, 132, 133–34, 144, 149; in West Virginia, 126–27; on John Clifford, 155, 162; and Cable's civil rights activism, 223, 224–25, 228; and Cable's dramatization of Creole characters, 223–24, 227, 228. *See also specific newspapers and magazines*
Prince, Valerie Sweeney, 173
Print culture: of African Americans, 11, 12, 107, 123–24, 223, 287; and Reconstruction writers, 11, 15, 21; and regionalism, 18; and reputation, 176, 294; of New Orleans, 185; reputation of South in, 227; and property, 289
Progressivism, 23, 286, 297
Property: and trademarks, 3, 85, 115, 116, 289; and copyright reform, 15–16, 239; definitions of, 20–21, 51, 78–79, 85, 100–101, 116, 121, 122, 182, 262, 263, 264, 267, 288–92, 301; and Reconstruction literature, 20, 284, 289, 299, 301; person as property, 20–21, 22, 81, 104, 107, 115–16, 118, 122, 267, 280, 289–90, 339 (n. 84); and professional status, 68–69; and Tourgée's *Toinette*, 77, 78–79, 85, 100, 115–16; and Tourgée's *A Royal Gentleman*, 77, 79, 85, 100, 115–16; and goodwill, 85; as legal relations among persons, 85; and trade secrets, 85; white selfhood as object of, 85, 96; and rights of accession, 85, 189; "joint tenancy" reforms in, 86, 93, 95, 122, 313 (n. 35); and Storer College, 124–25, 176; and Cable's *The Grandissimes*, 180, 191, 198, 228; Thanet's exploration of forms of, 229; in Thanet's *Expiation*, 230, 232, 243, 262, 263–66, 269, 279, 280; and Reconstruction writers, 289–91; alienability of, 290. *See also* Reputation
Property ownership: Tourgée's traditional preference for, 3; Republican ideal of, 16; and Reconstruction writers, 16, 21, 288, 290, 301; and citizenship, 20, 21, 28, 79, 83–84, 104, 105, 121, 266, 279, 284, 288, 301; of freedpeople, 21, 22, 28, 50–51, 80, 82, 84–85, 92–93, 138–39, 203, 262, 263, 290, 291, 305 (n. 22); alternative forms of, 21, 79, 289; in Woolson's feminized Florida landscape, 39; in Woolson's short stories, 46–47, 50–51; and bodily ownership, 77, 78, 104, 105; of African American women, 78; and marriage, 78, 94–95, 196; and Tourgée's *A Royal Gentleman*, 78, 99, 115–17, 120; and Tourgée's *Toinette*, 78–79, 82–83, 86, 93, 94, 99, 115–17, 120; North Carolina press on, 81–82; franchise connected to, 84, 93; and racial uplift, 125; and Storer College students, 125, 152; and Storer College, 138–39; advocated by the *Pioneer Press*, 156–57; and Cable's *The Grandissimes*, 195–96, 197
Property, portable, 230, 232, 260, 262–69, 270, 271, 272, 279, 280, 284
Pryse, Marjorie, 19
Public spheres, women's roles within, 12, 13, 22, 244
Publishing industry: and postwar reading boom, 112, 122; and subscription market, 112–13, 317 (n. 81); changes in, 239; commercialization of, 285. *See also* Literary marketplace
Pullman Strike, 234
Putnam's, 30

Quantrill, William, 250

Race: as servitude, 3; interconnected to gender, 18, 39, 111, 146, 175, 207, 210, 274; and reputation, 22, 145–46; in Woolson's "The South Devil," 47, 55; in Woolson's "The Ancient City," 53; in Woolson's descriptions of Minorcan women, 54–55, 56, 57; and occupational status, 70; Cable's views on, 194, 222, 223

Race literature, 287

Race relations: gender relations interconnected with, 13, 14, 86–87, 90, 125; in Florida, 35; in Tourgée's *Toinette*, 78, 86, 90, 100, 103; Washington on interracial cooperation, 97; and Franklin, 125, 168, 169, 170, 171, 172, 176, 292; and class relations, 125, 176; and Storer College, 139, 155, 175–76, 287, 297; and African American middle class, 141; *Strauder v. West Virginia*, 149; and John Clifford, 167, 168, 172; and Cable's performances with Twain, 181, 211, 213; in Cable's *The Grandissimes*, 191, 193, 200, 202, 207; and Cable's performance of Creole songs, 217–19; and Cable's dramatization of characters, 220; in Thanet's *Expiation*, 231, 251, 253–54, 275; Thanet's response to, 240; in Arkansas, 240, 241, 251, 274–75; African American women's writings on, 286. *See also* Cross-race alliances

Racial amalgamation, 217–19, 223

Racial boundaries: and passing, 85, 87, 96, 102, 114, 118; in Tourgée's *Toinette*, 87; in Cable's *The Grandissimes*, 178, 209–10; and Cable's representations of Creoles, 214, 216;and Cable's performance of Creole songs, 217–19; and differences in types of equality, 221; and "Coon" era, 223

Racial identity: in Woolson's "The Ancient City," 57; in Woolson's "Felipa," 58; in Woolson's "Sister St. Luke," 65; in Tourgée's *A Royal Gentleman*, 79, 105; in Tourgée's *Toinette*, 79, 92, 102, 105, 107; as form of property, 85, 267; and miscegenation statues, 96; Washington on, 97; and Tourgée's defense of Plessy, 104, 105, 108, 293, 296–97; and reputation, 104, 293; in New Orleans, 184; and Creole identity, 185, 186, 326–27 (n. 8); and Cable's stage appearances with Twain, 210, 211; and binary racial categories, 221; elasticity of, 221; and Cable's stage appearances, 227

Racial indeterminacy, 286

Racial oppression, 286–87

Racial stereotypes: in Woolson's portrayals of freedpeople, 27, 41, 64, 68; African American women as "auntie," 42, 44, 280; in tourist literature, 72–73, 75; of Cable's dramatization of Creole characters, 181, 222; African American women as "Mammy," 210; and African Americans' servitude, 253

Racial uplift: and Reconstruction literature, 14; and reputation, 125; and Franklin, 125, 142, 143, 167, 168–69, 170, 171, 172, 173, 201, 292; and freedpeople's education, 136; and *Pioneer Press*, 156–61; and Storer College, 176, 197, 259; and bourgeois domesticity, 286; and Niagara Movement, 288

Racism: among North Carolina Democrats, 9; in Woolson's portrayals of Minorcans, 56, 75; scientific, 57; in travel writing about Florida, 72–73; and Storer College, 124, 145, 287; in Clifford's view of racial uplift, 159, 160; and Franklin's view of suffrage movement, 172, 315 (n. 57); in Cable's

The Grandissimes, 192; and Thanet, 232; in Arkansas, 298; and Grady, 300
Radical Reconstruction, 23-24, 32, 97, 155, 183, 184
Railton, Stephen, 211
Raleigh Daily Sentinel, 81-82, 96, 97, 103, 113
Rankin, David C., 329 (n. 51)
Reading, acts of: in Tourgée's *Toinette*, 106, 107, 108, 109, 110, 122, 173, 194, 245; in Tourgée's *A Royal Gentleman*, 109, 110; and consumer culture, 173-74; in Cable's *The Grandissimes*, 194; in Thanet's *Expiation*, 245
Realism: and African American writers, 18; regional literature as detour from, 18; preoccupation with manifestations of centralized power, 19; and Tourgée's Reconstruction vision, 94, 313 (n. 37); and Cable's dramatization of Creole characters, 214, 215; and Thanet's *Expiation*, 278
Recks, John, 32Reconstruction Acts of 1867, 183
Reconstruction Amendments, 4, 7, 23, 59, 84
Reconstruction Debates, 278
Reconstruction era: Americans' perceptions of, 1, 16-17; free-labor issues of, 7; impact of military districting, 7; and supervision of military districts, 7; conservative backlash to, 7, 16; intertextual collision of, 17; legal issues of, 17; African Americans' influence on policy, 19; Radical Reconstruction, 23-24, 32, 97, 155, 183, 184; ending of, 73; and "Redemptionism," 100, 184, 282, 290, 295, 297; performative complexities of, 181; political corruption in Louisiana, 182; and Creole identity, 184, 326-27 (n. 8)
Reconstruction literature: idealism of, 1, 5-6, 7, 16, 18, 281, 284; defining of, 2, 5; and geography, 2, 12, 13; and military districts, 2, 13, 15, 18, 284-85; role in reconstructing South, 4, 5-6, 11, 17; and literary periods, 5, 17-18; influential roles for female heroines, 7, 20, 22; and regionalism, 10-11, 18-19; gender relations in, 13; and labor, 15, 20, 21, 299; and duty, 20, 21, 292; and reputation, 20, 21, 299; and citizenship, 281, 301; cultural contribution of, 282
Reconstruction writers: and meaning of regionalism, 10-11, 18-19, 24, 284; and print culture, 11, 15, 21; literary activism of, 11, 285-87; African American authors as, 11-12; and gender relations, 13; and civil rights activism, 14-15, 295; on consumer culture, 15, 28; and literary marketplace, 15-16, 22; and reputation, 22; and labor, 23, 291-92; competing views of, 161; and New South, 281; experiences of military occupation, 284-85; legacy of, 284-88, 295; and citizenship, 285, 286; African American women's production and dissemination of writing, 285-86; challenges to Jim Crow segregation, 286; challenge to plantation fiction, 286; vision of, 287; conflicted vision of, 288, 292, 294, 295; and meaning of property, 289, 290; on meaning of work, 291; and duty, 292; and Lost Cause, 294-95. *See also specific writers*
Rector, Henry M., 240
Red Cross, 168
"Redemptionism": and Reconstruction, 100, 184, 282, 290, 295, 297
Red Shirts, 296
Refugee populations: and Freedmen's Bureau, 10, 15, 100, 127; influx into military districts, 15; in St. Augustine, 37; in Harpers Ferry, 127, 129; in New Orleans, 185, 189, 203; in Arkansas, 262

Regionalism: northerners imposing of regional identities, 4; Reconstruction writers interpreting, 10-11, 18-19, 24, 284; and African American writers, 18; Twain as regionalist writer, 18; and national identity, 19, 26, 284; and meaning of reputation, 22-23, 79, 110, 111, 113, 145, 176, 196, 292-93; and American literature, 24, 236; and work ethic, 27, 61, 62, 63, 75, 135; in Woolson's "The Ancient City," 34, 63; in Tourgée's *Toinette*, 77; and Tourgée, 114-15, 120-21; and Storer College, 125, 131-34, 145; and Cable's *The Grandissimes*, 179, 193, 196; in Thanet's *Expiation*, 233, 279; and Thanet's short stories, 236, 239; and Thanet's geographic counterpoint, 240; and self-determination, 284

Regosin, Elizabeth, 16

Regular Democratic Organization ("The Ring"/"Old Regulars"), 199

Regulators: in North Carolina, 81; in Arkansas, 275, 277

Reid, Mary, 236, 278

Reilly, John, 162

Remley, Jacob, 43

Representation: and Cable's *The Grandissimes*, 178; Cable's representations of Creoles, 214-17, 227

Republican, 113

Republican Party: and Lodge Bill, 11; in Florida, 32, 48, 73-74; divisions within, 73; and Tourgée's work on freedmen's equal rights, 80; in North Carolina, 81-82, 86, 90-91, 92, 101, 296; and cross-race alliances, 86, 92-93; in West Virginia, 155-56; and John Clifford's civil rights activism, 155-56, 166; lily-white movement in, 156; in New Orleans, 183; and distinctions in types of equality, 221; in Arkansas, 241; subordination of sexual to racial emancipation, 315 (n. 57)

Reputation: as protected form of property, 3, 103, 104, 105, 110, 121, 122, 125, 289, 292, 293; and Franklin, 3, 171, 174, 176, 289, 293, 297; John Clifford on, 3, 152, 161-67, 171, 176, 198, 289, 293, 297; and Reconstruction literature, 20, 21, 299; as alternative form of property, 21, 22, 79, 85, 176; as honor, 22, 79, 111, 113, 115, 121, 145, 176, 198, 199, 232, 243, 292, 293; and freedwomen's credibility, 22, 100; and property ownership of freedpeople, 22; regional definitions of, 22-23, 34, 121, 124, 145, 176, 196, 292-93; and Florida, 35, 39; and professional status, 68; in Tourgée's *A Royal Gentleman*, 79, 85, 100, 103, 105, 110-12, 293; in Tourgée's *Toinette*, 85, 102, 105-6, 107, 108, 109, 118, 163, 292-93; Tourgée on, 104, 108, 113-15, 121, 122, 144, 161, 162, 270, 289, 296-97; and possession of real estate, 105-6, 108; and Storer College students, 124, 125, 144-45, 152; and self-effacement, 124, 142, 169; and Storer College faculty, 125, 149; and Sarah Jane Foster, 145-46, 149, 150, 151, 152; in Cable's *The Grandissimes*, 180, 191, 192, 195, 196, 198-99, 228; and Cable's civil rights activism, 225; and Cable's relationship with marketplace, 227; in Thanet's *Expiation*, 232, 233, 243, 245, 247, 269, 272, 280; and Grady, 284, 293, 299; Thanet's use of, 269 270; Cable on, 293; as performance, 293; Woolson on, 293; and citizenship, 294, 301

Rerick, Rowland, 48

Resistance: of freedwomen, 13, 108; of whites to freedpeople's education, 132; as verbal strategies (gossip, rumor, and back talk) employed by African American women and female

characters, 208–9, 231, 252–58, 280; of African American women, 229, 254; to military districts, 236
Respectability, politics of, 144, 168, 174, 293
Reunion and reconciliation (postwar sentiment for national reunification): 4, 75, 286, 294, 299; and Woolson, 26, 31, 70; magazine promotion of, 29–30; in Tourgée's *Toinette*, 102; in Cable's *The Grandissimes*, 178, 180, 199, 206, 293; Cable's performances with Twain, 212–13; and Cable, 225; and Thanet, 233, 235, 238; in Thanet's *Expiation*, 263, 278; and Grady's New South, 281, 299
Richardson, Joe M., 59–60
Roach, Joseph, 220
Robertson, Mary Brackett, 130, 136–37, 138, 145, 164, 165
Robinson, James, 164
Romantic tradition, of Simms's *War Poetry of the South*, 5, 39
Roosevelt, Theodore, 278
Rosen, Hannah, 16, 105, 274
Rouquette, Adrien, 223
Royal Gentleman, A (Tourgée): as revision of *Toinette*, 2–3, 76, 83; and property, 77, 79, 85, 115–16; and citizenship, 78, 79, 84; and property ownership, 78, 115–17, 120; and reputation, 79, 85, 100, 103, 105, 110–12, 293; and land acquisition, 85, 86, 121; and inheritance claims, 86; Reconstruction vision in, 86, 120, 313 (n. 37); and acts of reading, 109, 110; publishing of, 112, 115; and slavery, 115, 117, 118–19, 120, 317 (n. 93); and servitude, 115–20; gendered market economy in, 117–18; and empowerment of freedpeople, 121, 122
Rubin, Louis, 194
Runaway slaves, 37, 64
Rural-urban interdependence, 238

St. Augustine, Florida: Unionist sentiment in, 31; Woolson's travel sketches on, 33–34, 37, 43–44, 307 (n. 25); tourist literature on, 38; Africa district of, 38, 43, 44, 55, 266; Minorca Town, 43, 55, 56; Confederate Monument, 44; social caste in, 55; Thanet's *Six Visions of St. Augustine*, 307 (n. 15). *See also* "The Ancient City, Part I and Part II" (Woolson)
Saint-Domingue, 185, 189
St. Nicholas, 265
Saks, Eva, 84, 96
San Antonio Express, 221
Sanborn, John B., 262
Sanchez-Eppler, Karen, 151
Schaeffer, Evelyn Schuyler, 238, 258–59
Schenck, David, 91
Schwalm, Leslie, 16, 65
Scott, Walter, 336 (n. 28)
Scribner's Magazine, 326 (n. 2)
Scribner's Monthly, 30, 31, 182, 190, 225–26, 326 (n. 2)
Sears, John, 29
Secession, 126, 192, 227, 240
Second Seminole War, 34, 49
2nd United States Colored Troops, 32
Secrets and secret places: Reconstruction heroines' use of, 14; in Tourgée's *Toinette*, 82, 83, 105, 106, 107, 109, 110, 163; trade secrets, 85; "secret history" of Storer College, 124, 163, 165, 175, 318 (n. 2). *See also* Disguise
Sectional reconciliation: slavery as basis of, 4; Woolson's alternative to, 26, 31, 75; and print culture, 30; in Tourgée's *Toinette*, 102; and Cable's *The Grandissimes*, 180, 191, 197, 199, 206, 295; and Cable's performance of scenes from *The Grandissimes*, 181; and Cable's stage appearances with Twain, 212, 213; and Cable's civil rights activism, 225; and Thanet's residences, 231, 235,

238; in Thanet's *Expiation*, 233, 278–79; and intermarriage, 286; Cable's arguments for, 293; Grady on, 294–95, 299–300
Segregation: school segregation, 85, 153. *See also* Jim Crow segregation
Self-improvement. *See* Racial uplift
Self-ownership (discourse of), 43, 67, 79, 104, 105, 109, 117, 122, 315 (n. 60)
Selma Times, 224
Separate spheres, bourgeois ideology of, 99–100
Sewell, Rebecca, 269
Sexuality: and African American men's access to white women, 146, 148, 149, 152, 176; and gender stereotypes of African American women, 173
Shakespeare, William, 211, 214, 264
Sharecropping: as self-empowerment strategy, 67; in Arkansas, 232, 258, 259, 260, 262, 273, 338 (n. 54), 338 (n. 73); and Thanet, 237, 259, 260, 263, 265, 267, 269, 273, 338 (n. 54); Washington on, 265; and "Redemptive" endings, 290; as transitional system of labor, 291; in West Virginia, 321 (n. 33)
Shenandoah Mission, 145
Shepherd, Heyward, 325 (n. 111)
Sherman's March, 300
Shoemaker School of Oratory, 167
Short stories: and Reconstruction literature, 2; and regionalism, 18, 236, 239; Woolson's short stories, 30–31, 38, 44, 45, 46–52, 61, 63, 64–67, 71, 72; Cable's short stories, 182; Thanet's short stories, 234, 235–36, 239, 253, 257, 267, 277
Silber, Nina, 29, 213
Simms, William Gilmore: *War Poetry of the South*, 5, 15, 22, 39, 299; and New South, 6; on southern nationalism, 15, 23, 24, 233, 279, 284; *The Yemasee*, 50; and national audience, 227; and southern presence in political and cultural affairs, 282; and Old South, 299, 300; Grady compared to, 300
Sizer, Lyde Cullen, 17
Skeat, Walter William, 328 (n. 14)
Slaughterhouse Cases (1873): and Fourteenth Amendment, 20, 182, 305 (n. 20); and Thirteenth Amendment, 23, 305 (n. 20); and definition of property, 100–101; and social equality, 153; New Orleans as setting of, 182
Slaveholders: demands for restitution, 21; and property in land, 84, 89, 289, 290; and gender relations, 86; temporary disfranchisement of, 86, 126, 127–28, 148, 289; sexual abuse of slave women, 94, 110; and property ownership, 117–18; indolence of, 133, 135; in New Orleans, 186; in Arkansas, 241; imagined punishment of, 285
Slave narratives, 11–12
Slavery: as basis of sectional reconciliation, 4; abolition of, 6–7, 23, 60, 78, 127; and person as property, 20–21, 104, 107, 115–16, 118, 122, 267, 280, 289–90, 339 (n. 84); Florida's ideology of, 35; Woolson on gendered differences in legacy of, 41; Woolson on Minorcans compared to, 52, 64; gradual abolition legislation, 64; Tourgée on gender's impact on legacy of, 78; postwar loss of slaves as property, 84, 89, 127, 129, 203; and Tourgée's *A Royal Gentleman*, 115, 117, 118–19, 120, 317 (n. 93); and market of romantic love, 118, 120; in West Virginia, 126, 127; slaves as debtors, 136; and debt due African Americans, 138; Storer College's approach to legacy of, 176; in New Orleans, 185; and Creole identity, 186; in Cable's *The Grandissimes*, 190, 192, 193, 204, 205, 207, 208, 216; and Cable's relationship with

Twain, 210, 213; in Arkansas, 242; in Thanet's *Expiation*, 254; Grady on, 300; Simms's defense of, 300; North Carolina population of, 311 (n. 10). *See also* Ex-slaves; Freedpeople; Runaway slaves; Slave women; Wage slavery

Slave women: and Tourgée's *Toinette*, 87, 106; slaveholders' sexual abuse of, 94, 110; and acts of reading, 106, 107; compared to libre women, 184; freedom suits of, 185; Thanet's strategy for empowerment, 231; in Thanet's *Expiation*, 254

Smallwood Farm, 139

Smith, E. V., 326 (n. 112)

Smith, Jon, 307 (n. 20)

Smith, Kirby, 250

Smith, Roswell, 226, 326 (n. 2), 333 (n. 105)

Social equality: Tourgée on, 77, 95, 97, 103, 111; and Republican Party, 97; in Tourgée's *Toinette*, 99; Dent on, 153; and *Slaughterhouse Cases*, 153; in Cable's *The Grandissimes*, 180, 192; and Cable's public addresses, 181; in Cable's "The Freedman's Case in Equity," 221

Social justice, 76

Society of Friends, 87

Solomon, Irvin, 35

Sotiropoulos, Karen, 215

South: cultural identity of, 10, 18, 19, 26, 284; assimilationist culture of, 15; lack of unified culture, 15, 19; postwar economy of, 71; reputation in print culture, 227. *See also* New South; *and specific states*

South Carolina: in Military District Two, 7; Forten teaching in, 12; in Simms's *War Poetry of the South*, 15

Southerners: as writers, 2, 299; attitudes toward military districts, 4; in Cable's *The Grandissimes*, 4, 191–92, 193, 196, 205; reputation as status of inequality, 22; Woolson's definition of, 74. *See also* Southern white men; Southern whites; Southern white women

Southern Homestead Act (1866), 21, 204, 262, 305 (n. 22)

Southern white men: false pretensions of manhood, 4; and sexual violence against freedwomen, 22, 105; fears of extinction of race and gender, 39; authority of, 99, 221, 231, 232, 233, 250, 255, 270, 289; identity of, 219, 220, 221, 274; in Thanet's *Expiation*, 243–44, 246, 247–48, 250, 251

Southern whites: on freedpeople's labor output, 25; violence toward African Americans in Florida, 32, 73; on freedpeople's property ownership, 51; in Woolson's "At the Smithy," 70, 71; violence toward African American in North Carolina, 81; hostility to freedpeople's assertions, 87; and marriage, 94; and moral economy of dependency, 95; and Democratic Party, 103; reaction to Cable's dramatization of characters, 223, 224; in Thanet's *Expiation*, 230, 243; Grady on, 281

Southern white women: poems in Simms's *War Poetry of the South*, 5; and miscegenation fears, 97; leisured womanhood of, 133; and Cable's dramatization of characters, 217; in Thanet's *Expiation*, 232, 245–46, 248, 249, 252, 256, 264, 272, 278

"Southron": as masculinized term, 39, 40; in Cable's *The Grandissimes*, 179; in Thanet's *Expiation*, 245; portrayals of, 285

Spencerian philosophy, 234

Spirit of Jefferson, 126, 130, 133, 144, 149

Sprague, John, 33

Stewart, Maria, 253

Storer, John, 129–30, 151, 319 (n. 15)

Storer College: closing of, 3, 177; and literary activism, 11, 12, 128; students as agents of social change, 14, 42, 123, 125–26; and professional status, 69; faculty of, 123, 124, 125, 128–29, 130, 131–34, 138, 142–43, 145–52, 155; students' shaping of education, 123, 124–25, 175; northern women as faculty, 123, 125, 130, 131, 132, 133–34, 138, 142–43, 145–52; and freedpeople's civil rights, 123, 145; mission of, 124, 125, 132, 134, 151, 166, 167, 176–77, 288, 319 (n. 14); and students' labor, 124, 130, 133, 135, 136–38, 139, 155, 169, 170, 206, 291; and citizenship preparation, 124, 143–45; "secret history" of, 124, 163, 165, 175, 318 (n. 2); faculty's contradictory advice, 124–25, 135, 137, 174; and press, 125, 130, 131, 132, 133–34, 144, 149; and administrators' writings, 125, 131–32, 176; and regionalism, 125, 131–34, 145; and faculty writings, 125, 132, 135, 139–40, 326 (n. 112); and student writings, 125, 137–38, 287–88, 298, 326 (n. 12); as normal school, 128; and northern philanthropy, 129, 132, 133, 135; Board of Trustees, 129, 163, 165; establishment of, 129–31; student enrollment in, 130, 319 (n. 15); and student harassment, 131; and students' servitude, 134, 136–38, 155, 158, 161, 175; curriculum's contradictions, 134–45, 151; *Labor Omnia Vincit* motto, 135; finances of, 135, 139, 163–64, 324 (n. 85); and students' moral indebtedness, 136, 138, 139, 155, 176, 197; and freedpeople's property ownership, 138–39; campus setting of, 140; and students' behavior prohibitions, 141, 142–43, 176; and students' self-reliance, 142; and students' appearance, 143–45, 169; and students' careers, 151, 255; African American faculty of, 151–52; and Niagara Movement, 154, 174–75; Reconstruction vision of, 157, 165, 175–76, 177; Franklin as student at, 167, 168; and John Brown's fort, 174–75, 325 (n. 111); Du Bois's address at, 288; and Harpers Ferry National Historical Park, 297; state contributions to, 319 (n. 14)

Storer Record, 123, 132, 135, 138–39, 142, 143, 164, 170, 285, 320 (n. 20)

Stowe, Harriet Beecher: *Uncle Tom's Cabin*, 17, 78, 107, 117, 253, 256; as writer-in-residence in Florida, 37; "Letter from Florida," 61; and freedpeople's education, 133; New England background of, 233

Strauder, Annie, 149

Strauder, Taylor, 148–49

Strauder v. West Virginia (1881), 148, 162

Strikes, 234, 237, 275, 290–91

Strong, William, 148

Sumner, Charles, 103

Sumner School, 152

Sundquist, Eric, 19

Supreme Court: and citizenship definitions, 20, 77; and Fourteenth Amendment, 20, 148, 153, 182; and married women's property rights, 95; on intermarriage, 100; and West Virginia, 127; and Enforcement Acts, 183, 326 (n. 4). *See also specific cases*

Swamp landscapes: in Woolson's travel sketches, 37, 47, 48, 55, 73, 188, 246; in Woolson's short stories, 47, 48; in Cable's *The Creoles of Louisiana*, 187, 188; Thanet's meaning of, 188; in Cable's *The Grandissimes*, 188, 189, 201, 204, 207, 247, 257; in Cable's work, 228; in Thanet's *Expiation*, 230, 231, 240, 245, 246, 247–48, 249, 250, 252, 263

Tacoma Ledger, 215
Talented Tenth, 102, 157, 168, 201
Tallifero, John, 155
Tar Heel State. *See* North Carolina
Tenant farming: in Arkansas, 262, 299; Thanet's fears of, 273; in West Virginia, 321 (n. 33)
Terrell, Mary Church, 171
Testimonial culture, 44
Texas: in Military District Five, 7, 182; black labor recruited from, 273
Thackeray, William Makepeace, 264
Thanet, Octave: as plantation co-owner, 2, 235, 236, 238, 250, 258–60, 268, 269, 272, 280, 285, 298; Reconstruction vision of, 4, 23, 232, 233, 238, 284; in mainstream press, 11; political conservatism of, 12; female characters of, 13, 88, 90, 229; and southern identity, 15; and editorial intervention, 15–16; northern workers in South, 48; on performative identity, 58, 232, 269, 272, 273; redefining property, 63; and politics of consumption, 71, 72, 75; Tourgée compared to, 76; and reputation, 150, 293; Cable's *The Grandissimes* compared to, 190, 205; and property ownership, 195; and misperceptions of plantation fiction, 205; and white midwestern workforce, 205; as pseudonym, 230, 239, 333 (n. 1); New England background of, 231, 232, 233, 238, 239, 250, 253, 264, 269, 275; midwestern upbringing of, 231, 232, 233, 238, 249–50, 284; and midwestern laboring attitudes, 232; local color sketches of, 233; "Communists and Capitalists," 234; "The Contented Masses," 234; "Otto the Knight," 234; "The Strike at Glascock's," 234; "We All," 234; labor theories of, 234, 235, 237, 240, 242–43, 259, 263, 277, 278, 284, 291, 295, 298; short stories of, 234, 235–36, 239, 253, 257, 267, 277; essays of, 234, 246–47, 251–52; and Carnegie, 234, 333 (n. 4); "The Bishop's Vagabond," 235; *Knitters in the Sun*, 235; critics' response to, 236, 237, 238–40, 253, 277–78; "Otto the Knight and Other Trans-Mississippi Tales," 236; literary celebrity of, 238–39; "Plantation Life in Arkansas," 246–47; "Whitsun Harp, Regulator," 247, 248, 277; "The Loaf of Peace," 247, 265; "Ma Bowlin," 248, 267; as antisuffragist, 251; "A Neglected Career for Unmarried Women," 251–52; "Half a Curse," 253; "Folk-Lore in Arkansas," 257; "The Conjured Kitchen," 257–58, 265; *An Adventure in Photography*, 260; "The Great Southern Problem," 260; on property, 262–63; "Sist' Chaney's Black Silk," 266, 267–68; "The Mortgage on Jeffy," 267; "Clover Bend Poke Root," 272; Grady compared to, 283–84; and African American economic gain, 287; and gradualist program for advancement, 288; on portable property, 289; "Six Visions of St. Augustine," 307 (n. 15); "The Tramp in Four Centuries," 333 (n. 4); *By the Cypress Swamp*, 334 (n. 18); on environmental disaster in Arkansas, 336 (n. 33). *See also Expiation* (Thanet)
Thanford plantation, Arkansas, 235, 238, 247, 251, 258–60, 268, 272, 277, 298, 333–34 (n. 9)
Thirteenth Amendment, 23, 78, 101, 305 (n. 20)
Thomas, Brook, 17, 311 (n. 4), 313 (n. 37)
Thompson, Lyda, 90
Tillman, Ben, 274
Tillman, Katherine Davis Chapman, 172
Toinette (Tourgée): and citizenship, 2–3, 77, 78–79, 83, 84, 105, 106, 120,

207; and freedom, 76, 82, 87, 89, 98–101, 107, 108–9, 110, 118, 122; Reconstruction vision of, 76–77, 86, 93–94, 95, 100, 120; and definition of property, 77, 78–79, 85; and intermarriage, 78, 94, 95, 97–99, 206, 207, 286, 292–93; and property ownership, 78–79, 82–83, 86, 93, 99, 115–17, 120; and empowerment of freedpeople, 78–79, 121, 122; and labor, 78–79, 102; secret room in, 82, 83, 105, 106, 107, 109, 110, 163; and land acquisition, 85, 86, 88–89, 121; and reputation, 85, 102, 105–6, 107, 108, 163, 292–93; and inheritance claims, 86, 93, 95, 102; and education, 87, 106, 108, 133, 173; Confederate veteran as character in, 91, 92; black soldiers as characters in, 92; reviews of, 97–98, 114, 311 (n. 3), 317 (n. 84); and servitude, 98–99, 108, 115–16; as commercial failure, 103; and acts of reading, 106, 107, 108, 109, 110, 173, 194, 245; and seduction, 106, 107, 316 (n. 67); and political change, 115; and capitalism, 116; and intertwining of moral and financial responsibilities, 116; gendered market economy in, 117–18; gender alliance in, 208; epistolary declarations of independence, 285

Tompkins, Jane, 17

Tourgée, Albion: as carpetbagger, 2, 76, 80, 114, 115, 121, 149; Reconstruction vision of, 3, 23, 75, 77, 82–83, 86, 94, 115, 120–22, 135, 199, 202, 296, 313 (n. 37); as defense counsel for Plessy, 3, 99, 115, 120, 121, 153, 221, 293, 296–97; and *Union Register*, 11; female characters of, 13, 82–83, 89–90, 206; and southern identity, 15; on mixed racial and ethnic identity, 55, 198; redefining property, 63, 85; and professional status, 68; *Bricks Without Straw*, 77; *A Fool's Errand*, 77; reviews of works, 77, 78, 311 (n. 3); literary celebrity of, 77, 79, 122, 225; on social equality, 77, 95, 97, 103, 111; pseudonyms of, 77, 97, 114, 162, 283, 317 (n. 84); critics' response to, 78, 311 (n. 3); as Superior Court judge, 80; political career of, 80, 103, 287; on freedpeople's thievery, 82; as Radical Republican, 82; male characters of, 82–83, 90; as attorney, 83–84, 103, 120, 121, 148, 152, 153, 293, 296–97, 298; and property ownership, 83–84, 195, 263, 267, 268, 295; contrary impulses to reform and retrench, 84; and Constitutional Convention of 1868, 86, 93, 96–97, 101; press criticism of, 90–91, 97–98, 113–15, 122, 149, 155, 314 (n. 46); on Confederate veterans, 91; congressional bids of, 91; on manhood, 92, 160; and women's rights, 95, 101–3; on labor rights, 101, 291; as federal pension agent, 103; finances of, 103, 121; modulated rhetoric of, 104; on reputation, 104, 108, 115, 121, 122, 144, 161, 162, 270, 289, 296–97; on education of freedpeople, 109; sales records of, 112, 114, 294, 296; and Reconstruction as literary theme, 112–13; literary reputation of, 113–14, 293; "C" letters of, 114, 285; on voting rights, 116; as U.S. consul to Bordeaux, 121; Cable compared to, 189; on servitude, 200, 276; and national identity, 284; and intermarriage, 286; and Du Bois, 288; eulogies for, 288; and literary marketplace, 289; "A Bystander's Notes," 296; *Murvale Eastman*, 296; *Patroclus Prime*, 313 (n. 37); highway marker in honor of, 318 (n. 102). *See also A Royal Gentleman* (Tourgée); *Toinette* (Tourgée)

Tourgée, Emma Kilbourne, 80, 97, 101

Tourism: and Military District Three, 2; regionalist literature as, 18; and

national identity, 29; and citizenship, 71–72; in Florida, 296
Tourist literature: of Florida, 25; Woolson's writings on Florida, 25–28, 33–46, 235, 243, 285, 293; and gender, 34, 35, 36, 307 (n. 15); racial stereotypes in, 72–73, 75
Trademarks, as protected form of property, 3, 85, 115, 116, 289
Trans-Mississippi West, 241
Travel sketches: and Reconstruction literature, 2; Woolson's travel sketches, 2, 25–31, 33–46, 47, 48, 50, 51, 52, 53, 59–60, 67, 73, 75, 273, 283; and regionalism, 18; and Native Americans, 50
Tregle, Joseph, 184, 326–27 (n. 8)
Trollope, Anthony, 264
Tropes, of national reunion, 4, 75, 213, 233
Trotter, William Monroe, 288
Trotti, Michael Ayers, 340 (n. 101)
Tucker, Frank W., 235, 259
Turnbull, Andrew, 52
Turner, Henry McNeal, 242
Turner, Josiah, 113
Tuskegee Institute, 135, 158, 288, 321 (n. 36)
Twain, Mark: Cable's stage appearances with, 4, 181, 210–13, 214, 215, 216, 217, 223, 224, 226, 331 (n. 74); as regionalist writer, 18; *Huckleberry Finn*, 210, 212, 213, 221; portrait purchased from Cable, 210, 213, 330 (n. 70); "The Jumping Frog," 211; "The Stammerer," 211; "Why I Lost the Editorship," 211; "King Sollermun," 211, 213, 221; "How Come a Frenchman Doan' Talk like a Man," 213, 215; Cable's dramatization of Creole characters compared to, 214; "Tragic Tale of a Fishwife," 214; "Jim's Investments," 221; racialized buffoonery of, 221; and ethnic comedy, 223

Underground Railroad, 285
Unionist sentiment: Tourgée's reliance on, 3; in Florida, 31; in North Carolina, 84; in West Virginia, 146; in New Orleans, 185; in Arkansas, 241
Union Labor Party, 298
Union Leagues, 103, 266
Union Register, Tourgée's founding of, 11, 80
Unions: and labor unrest, 231; and strikes, 234, 237, 275, 290–91; Thanet on, 234–35, 259, 262–63; formation of, 238; on wage slavery, 290. *See also* Labor
United Daughters of the Confederacy, 175, 325 (n. 111)
U.S. Armory and Arsenal, Harpers Ferry, West Virginia, 127
U.S. Christian Commission, 129
U.S. Postal Service, 297
United States v. Cruikshank (1876), 183, 326 (n. 4)
United States v. Reese (1876), 326 (n. 4)
Universal manhood suffrage, 95
University of Rochester, 80
Urry, John, 34, 71–72

Vagrancy legislation, and compulsory labor, 60, 63, 291
Vandevelde, Kenneth, 289
Van Tassel, Emily, 95
Vernacular: cult of, 214–15; African American vernacular, 218
Veterans. *See* African American veterans; Confederate veterans
Violence: toward African Americans in Florida, 32, 73; in North Carolina, 81, 296, 311 (n. 12); and freedpeople's education, 146–48, 149, 151; of "Southrons," 179; Cable's public addresses protesting violence against African Americans, 181; toward African Americans in Louisiana, 182–83; of Democratic Party in New Orleans, 183; in Cable's *The Grandissimes*, 192, 193,

207, 209–10; in Thanet's *Expiation*, 230, 233, 243, 244, 245, 247, 248, 249, 269–70, 274–76, 277, 278, 279; in Arkansas, 235, 241–42, 274–76; in West Virginia, 297. *See also* Lynching

Virginia: in Military District One, 7; and establishment of West Virginia, 126, 127; and sharecropping, 291

Virginia Free Press, 126, 127, 130, 144

Virginia Military Institute, 131

Virginius Island, 127, 128

Voodoo: in Cable's *The Grandissimes*, 189–90, 192, 201, 203, 208–9; narratives of, 219

Wage contracts, 99–100

Wage labor: congressional debates over Thirteenth Amendment, 23; and marketplace, 60, 301; as petty entrepreneurs, 101; and artisan-entrepreneurs, 102

Wage slavery, 100, 290, 291

Wahl, Frank, 238

Walker, D. S., 41

Wallace, John, 33

Walls, Josiah, 33

War Department: and Freedmen's Bureau, 10, 141; and Free Will Baptists, 129

Warner, Charles Dudley, 202, 215, 333 (n. 105)

Washington, Booker T.: as model of racial progress, 14; *Up from Slavery*, 97; and self-sufficiency, 135; accommodationist policies of, 154; and education, 157; materialist strategy of, 158, 161, 171, 288; and Franklin, 172; on labor, 201; and Cable's "The Silent South," 222; influence of, 243; Cable's correspondence with, 265, 332 (n. 95); public personae of, 274; Thanet compared to, 279; and Reconstruction writing, 287; and Storer College students, 287

Washington School of Expression, 168

Waterbury American, 215

Weekly Louisianian, 203

Wells, Jonathan Daniel, 167

Wells-Barnett, Ida B., 13, 172, 210, 253, 286, 288

Wenckar. *See* Tourgée, Albion

West, Robin, 77

Western Reserve of Ohio, 80

West Virginia: and literacy as social change, 122, 123; establishment as state, 123, 126, 127; African American literature of, 123–24; Freedmen's Bureau in, 124, 127, 128–29, 131; Reconstruction in, 125, 128, 145, 152, 166, 177; industrialism in, 127, 137, 139, 157; miscegenation laws of, 148; school segregation in, 153; progressivism in, 171; African Americans' emigration to, 297; African Americans owning farms in, 321 (n. 33). *See also* Harpers Ferry, West Virginia

West Virginia Civic League, 155

West Virginia Colored Institute, 131

Wheeling Conventions of May and June 1861, 126

White, Graham, 266

White, Shane, 266

White, William Allen, 259

White ancestral authority, 286

Whiteface: in Tourgée's *Toinette*, 87, 107–8; in Cable's performances with Twain, 181; and contrived nature of Cable's dramatizations, 220

White home rule, 5

White identity, 85, 219

White Leagues, 183, 298

Whites. *See* Poor whites; Southern whites

Whites, LeeAnn, 244

White supremacy: and Grady, 5, 294; Washington's capitulation to, 28; and Woolson's short stories, 56; and Democratic Party, 92–93, 126, 296; in Cable's *The Grandissimes*, 180, 192, 193; and Cable's writing for *New*

Orleans Daily Picayune, 183; and citizenship of African Americans, 219; in Thanet's *Expiation*, 233, 248, 252; and plantation fiction, 236; and freedpeople's consumerism, 268; ideology of, 279

White women: and citizenship definitions, 84; African American men's access to, 146, 148, 149, 152, 176; paternal protection of, 184–85. *See also* Northern white women; Southern white women

Whitman, Walt, 24

Whittier, John Greenleaf, 213

Whittlesey, E., 313 (n. 35)

William C. Black and Company, 183

Williams, Carrie M., 153

Williams, Martha M., 258

Williamson, John H., 97

Williams v. Board of Education of Fairfax District (1898), 153

Wilmington race riot of 1898, 121

Wilson, Christopher, 15

Wilson, Edmund, 225

Wilson, Harriet, 229

Wisner, J. Nelson, 156, 162

Woman's Christian Temperance Union (WCTU), 168, 171–72

"Woman's Era, The," 286

Woman's League, 172

Woman's Party Convention, 172

Woman's suffrage movement, 3, 161, 171, 172, 174, 286, 315 (n. 57)

Women: roles within public sphere, 12, 13, 22, 244; as writers, 12–13, 17; cross-race alliances of, 78; and state-enforced subordination and dispossession as wives, 94, 95, 313 (n. 39). *See also* African American women; Freedwomen; Intermarriage; Marriage; Northern white women; Slave women; Southern white women; White women

Women's Missionary Society, 132–33, 135, 168

Women's rights: and suffrage movement, 3, 161, 171, 172, 174, 286, 315 (n. 57); and Reconstruction writers, 15; and Tourgée's *Toinette*, 78, 79; and joint property ownership, 93; Tourgée's work on, 95, 101–3; and Tourgée's *A Royal Gentleman*, 110

Wonham, Henry, 214, 223

Woodson, Carter G., 154

Woodward, C. Vann, 11, 121, 341 (n. 3)

Woolson, Constance Fenimore: Reconstruction vision of, 2, 23, 25, 27, 28, 29, 31, 36, 45, 46, 56, 64, 74–75, 76, 135, 233, 296; on freedpeople's citizenship, 2, 25, 26, 27, 38, 41–43, 49; as northern writer, 2, 25, 28; Florida travel sketches of, 2, 25–31, 33–46, 47, 48, 50, 51, 52, 53, 59–60, 67, 73, 75, 273, 283; on meaning of labor, 2, 61, 62, 63–64, 66, 67–70, 135, 204, 291; in mainstream press, 11; female characters of, 13, 34, 35, 36, 38, 39, 40–45, 47, 48–49, 53–54; and southern identity, 15; and journey toward national origins, 24; and tourist literature, 25–28, 33–46, 235, 243, 285, 293; on Floridian landscape, 26, 27, 31, 34, 36, 37, 38–39, 45–46, 47, 48, 49, 55, 57, 62, 63, 188, 204, 246, 296; strategies of, 26–27; freedpeople in travel sketches of, 26–27, 28, 37, 38, 40–44, 46, 50–51, 52, 53, 59–60, 67, 73; literary devices deployed by, 27; on Minorcans, 27, 51, 52–60, 61, 62–67, 69, 75, 102, 187, 228; black characters of, 27, 102, 258, 266; critics' response to, 30, 31; "The South Devil," 30, 31, 38, 47–48, 55, 57, 73; poetry of, 30, 31, 44, 45, 49, 51, 55, 58, 61, 70, 73, 75; "Black Point," 30, 44–45, 55, 62; "The Florida Beach," 30, 45; *Rodman the Keeper*, 30, 46; "Miss Elisabetha," 30, 47, 49, 56–57, 65, 67; "Felipa," 30, 47, 57–58, 65, 209, 274; "Sister St.

Luke," 30, 48–49, 64–67; "Dolores," 30, 54, 58–59, 60, 61, 62, 65–66, 67; "At the Smithy," 30, 70–71; "The Legend of Maria Sanchez Creek," 30, 55; "Matanzas River," 30, 74; short stories of, 30–31, 38, 44, 45, 46–52, 56–57, 61, 63, 64–67, 71, 72; "The Oklawaha," 31, 34, 35, 36, 45–46, 50, 53; "A Voyage to the Unknown River," 31, 54, 56, 66; male characters of, 34, 35, 36, 38, 39, 46–48, 49, 53, 55, 57, 61, 63, 64–65; transnational focus of, 36, 307 (n. 20); "The French Broad," 38, 39, 243; Confederate veteran characters of, 39, 40, 41, 48, 70, 99, 266; "Crowder's Cove," 45; sectional impartiality of, 45; imaginary geography constructed by, 46; *Jupiter Lights*, 71, 295; moving South for health reasons, 79; tact of, 132; and professional status, 156; on African American professionals and artists, 156, 289, 292, 293; on leisure, 173, 204, 291, 296; Thanet compared to, 236; and hybrid social alliances, 250; and national identity, 284; and African American economic gain, 287; and gradualist program for advancement, 288; on duty, 292; in Italy, 295–96, 298. *See also* "The Ancient City, Part I and Part II" (Woolson)

Work ethic: and regionalism, 27, 61, 62, 63, 75, 135; Thanet's endorsement of Protestant work ethic, 239

World War I, 166

Wright, Fannie, 168

Writs of mandamus, 85

Wyatt-Brown, Bertram, 275–76

Yeoman class: and property ownership, 92–93; and cross-race alliances, 93; in Thanet's *Expiation*, 230, 245, 256, 262; dialect of, 256, 270; renting of slaves, 258; in Arkansas, 273

Young, Elizabeth, 17, 256

Young Men's Democratic Clubs, 32

Youth's Companion, 173

Zion's Advocate, 147, 150